PEANUTS®

The HOME COLLECTION

A Collector's Guide
To Identification And Value

By Freddi Karin Margolin

ANTIQUE TRADER BOOKS

A Division of Krause Publications
Iola, Wisconsin

Dedication

This book is dedicated to Lisa Margolin.

I really thought that when it came to knowledge of PEANUTS® collectibles, I was close to untouchable—until my daughter Lisa joined me midway in the production of this book. Lisa literally tore the whole thing apart; caught many errors of both omission and commission; did the final typing for every description (thousands of them); and assisted me in a dozen other ways to bring to you a work of superior quality. She gave up six months of her life for this project. Nothing I can say or do would be enough to show my everlasting gratitude—except to buy her a new computer, which I did. I love you, Lisa!

Allan W. Miller
Antique Trader Books/Krause Publications
P.O. Box 2686
Chesapeake, VA 23327-2686

ISBN: 0-930625-82-X

Library of Congress Catalog Card Number: 99-61592

Editor: Allan W. Miller
Assistant Editor: Wendy Chia-Klesch
Designers: Heather Ealey and Kevin Gilbert
Copy Editor: Sandra Holcombe
Production Assistants: Marshall McClure and Barbara Woerner

cover design concept courtesy of United Feature Syndicate, Inc.

Printed in the United States of America

To order additional copies of this book,
or to obtain a free catalog, please contact:

Antique Trader Books
P.O. Box 1050
Dubuque, IA 52004

or call:
1-800-334-7165

Contents

Acknowledgments

What sets this book apart from all others in the field is that it was produced and published with both the blessings and close cooperation of United Media, the syndicators of the PEANUTS® comic strip. Without them, this work would be little more than scraps of paper with words and pictures. Therefore, my BIGGEST thanks must go to Liz Conyngham, Worldwide Vice President for Licensing at United Media, who placed her trust in me and convinced "Sparky" Schulz to do the same. I am also grateful for the guidance and encouragement she gave me every step of the way.

Many others at United Media were also helpful to the cause. These include Liz' assistant, Heidi Inglese, and also Mike Posner, who came on the scene after Heidi left to have a baby—each of whom fielded questions and became my resource people on almost a daily basis. Also, a big hug to licensing manager Carmen Hartigan, who added so much to my knowledge of the Snoopy web site.

I have worked with many publishers and editors before. They were all good. But none of them could hold a candle to Allan Miller, Managing Editor at Antique Trader Books. Allan's positive attitude and cheerful demeanor were as refreshing as a summer breeze. His knowledge and skill in publishing books on collectibles is awesome, and his ability to hold my hand from hundreds of miles away will never be forgotten, nor will it go unappreciated.

I can't give enough credit to my photographer, Franc Tabaranza. Franc remained stoic and cheerful through what was sometimes a nerve-racking ordeal of taking over fifteen hundred pictures in a short-period of time. His talent is reflected on the pages of this book.

For information on the production and pricing of cels and lithographs, and for helping me with some excellent pictures, I was fortunate to be able to turn to two of the most knowledgeable people in the business. For cels, I had Nina Skahan, and for lithographs there was Sandy Thome—both affiliated with the Melendez studio (Sandy also did some additional research for me, for which I am very much indebted).They helped make two difficult but important subjects much easier to digest.

In the same vein, I would like to thank Richele Matsil, Manager of American Royal Arts Gallery in Westbury, Long Island, for allowing me to take pictures in her gallery and for being very patient in answering all of my questions.

In the course of my research I turned to many other people and vendors for their expertise, each of whom deserve special recognition.

Thank you to Donna Peterson, from Mall of America's Camp Snoopy, in Bloomington, Minnesota, and also to Dana Hammontree, from Camp Snoopy at Knott's Berry Farm, in Buena Park, California.

Thank you to Lee Stephenson, who was my resource person for Hallmark cookie cutters.

Thanks, also, to:
Audrey Basso, at Playskool (Hasbro).
Jim Doe, Manager of the Snoopy Gallery and Gift Shop in Santa Rosa.
Marge Morse, a real sweetheart at Colorforms.
Doug Markoff, my Canadian expert on PEANUTS® books.
The people at Hallmark for their efforts.
Rose Mazzuka, who helped me with much of the physical work involved in moving thousands of items before and after the photo sessions.
Karen Simon, a veritable font of knowledge when it comes to PEANUTS® collectibles.
Sandra Cramer made an extraordinary contribution to this book.
A special thank you to my lawyer, Paul Levenson, who guided me through uncharted waters and helped make this book possible.
Thanks, also, to Rich Hughes, my computer expert and pinch-hit photographer. Rich saved me more times than a St. Bernard on a ski slope.
Thanks to my soul sister, Delores Smith, who came up with the name for that catch-all category: "PEANUTS!® Perfect Throughout the House."

Although most of the items pictured in this book are from my personal collection, there are several which are not. Therefore, I am indebted to many of my fellow collectors who unselfishly shared some of their pieces (or pictures) for the benefit of this book. They include: Janet Tuccillo, Patty DeVoe, George Guzikowski, Anuk and Rahul Mullick, Joyce Orgera (who also was a great source of encouragement during some of the rougher times), Rose Elkins, Tom Bednarek, Sue Park, Jill Persch, Maureen McCarty, Pauline Graeber, Janice Hayes, Warren Chamberlin, and Kelly Tarigo.

A book of this nature requires thousands of hours of toil. When I most needed encouragement to forge ahead, many of my friends, literally from all over the United States, lent their spiritual support. These included Agnes Lau, Mark Cox, Tom Bernagozzi, Margaret Braun, Sue and Bob Harris, Diane Dovjak, Laurel Sherry, Patti Palfi, Jennifer Kiplinger, Jean Navikas, Diane VanWeelie, Arlene Cintron, Tami Aker, Anna Lee Campbell, Marian Wolff, and Margaret Kunitsky.

Thank you all, from the bottom of my heart!

Special Thanks
To my husband, Bob, my soul mate and my pillar of strength, who was always there to support and advise. With all my heart, I love you, Bob!

—**Freddi Karin Margolin**

Introduction

I set out to create a book that will both inform and entertain you—a book that will overwhelm you in its scope and beauty, yet make you feel as though it was written just for you.

I have included over 1,400 pictures and more than 4,000 items to present you with the most enchanting array of PEANUTS® collectibles ever assembled in one volume. The research was extensive, time consuming, and exhausting.

I kept in mind the beginning collector, who needs to be assured that there are still plenty of affordable PEANUTS® treasures out there. I also kept in mind the veteran collector, who delights in the "discovery" of rare and sometimes magnificent or exotic pieces. There is a third party—the dealer—who is also very important, and I will elaborate on this individual later in this work. Suffice it to say at this point that dealers, too, should derive much pleasure and benefit from this book.

Collecting is just one portion—albeit an important one—of the whole PEANUTS® feast. Thanks mainly to the creative genius of Charles "Sparky" Schulz, there are myriad other ways, both passive and interactive, in which you will find joy and excitement in this wonderful, whimsical world of Snoopy and the entire PEANUTS® gang. Much of this will unfold in the chapters that follow.

I sincerely hope that you have as much fun perusing this book as I did in creating it.

The Author Speaks

It has been almost ten years since the last major work on PEANUTS® collecting was first published.

Could anyone have even dared to imagine how different the world—and our lives—would become in ten short years? In 1990, the country was in the midst of a major recession, still reeling from the damage wrought by the stock market crash of 1987. E-mail was almost unheard of. A web site could only be a place where spiders hung out. Money was scarce. Jobs were in jeopardy, and ostentation was out.

Yet only six years later, in 1996, a businessman would bid $500,000 for a cigar box. Five hundred thousand dollars for a simple humidor that just happened to be a gift from comedian Milton Berle to President John F. Kennedy! The aura of prosperity had returned to America. And the Internet, seemingly overnight, began to have an effect on the lives of each and every one of us. Change was in the air.

So, too, have there been changes and additions in the world of PEANUTS®. These include more PEANUTS®-related events and attractions, more products, new licensed manufacturers, and, of course, changes in the marketplace itself. In fact, as we approach the 50th anniversary of the strip in the year 2000, it seems the only thing that has remained constant is the enjoyment of PEANUTS® collecting, which is still as much fun as ever.

During the past few years, I have been besieged with requests from collectors to publish a new up-to-date price guide. I accepted the challenge, but I decided to do much more. That is why, in addition to current pricing, you will find many more pictures, more color, and more variety, including a delightful chapter spotlighting some real collectors.

I trust you will find this book informative and useful in your collecting hobby. And, if it brings a bit of whimsy into your life, well that's okay, too!

Charles M. Schulz

The following is intended as a sincere tribute to the man who made all of this possible.

We honor a man whose adolescent struggles with rejection and insecurities, many of which linger to this day, provided the inspiration for what eventually became the world's most celebrated comic strip. He surely took unto himself the dictum, "If God gives you lemons, then make lemonade."

If ever there was a Charlie Brown in real life—and don't we all have a little of Charlie Brown in ourselves?—it was Schulz. Paul Aurandt, in his book *Destiny*, subtitled *More of Paul Harvey's The Rest of the Story*, tells us how it really was:

•   •   •

When he was a little boy, the other children called him Sparky—after a comic-strip horse named Sparkplug. Sparky never did shake that nickname.

School was all but impossible for Sparky. He failed every subject in the eighth grade. Every subject!

He flunked physics in high school. Receiving a flat zero in the course, he distinguished himself as the worst physics student in his school's history.

He also flunked Latin. And algebra. And English.

He didn't do much better in sports. Although he managed to make the school golf team, he promptly lost the only important match of the year.

There was a consolation match. Sparky lost that too.

And throughout his youth, Sparky was awkward socially. He was not actually disliked by the other youngsters. No one cared that much. He was astonished if a classmate ever said hello to him outside school hours. No way to tell how he might have done at dating. In high school, Sparky never once asked a girl out. He was too afraid of being turned down.

Sparky . . . rolled with it. Sparky made up his mind early in life that if things were meant to work out, they would.

Otherwise, he would content himself with what appeared to be inevitable mediocrity. But this is the rest of the story.

One something was important to Sparky: drawing. He was proud of his own artwork. Of course, no one else appreciated it. In his senior year of high school he submitted some cartoons to the editors of his class yearbook. Almost predictably, Sparky's drawings were rejected.

While the young man had rationalized virtually all of his failures, he was rather hurt by the general ignorance of what he believed was his one natural talent. In fact, he was so convinced of his artistic ability that he had decided to become a professional artist.

Upon graduating high school, he wrote a letter to Walt Disney Studios, a letter indicating his qualifications to become a cartoonist for Disney.

Shortly, he received an answer—a form letter requesting that he send some examples of his artwork. Subject matter was suggested: For instance, a Disney character "repairing" a clock by shoveling the springs and gears back inside.

Sparky drew the proposed cartoon scene. He spent a great deal of time on that and the other drawings. A job with Disney would be impressive, and there were many doubters to impress.

Sparky mailed the form and his drawings to Disney Studios.

And Sparky waited.

And one day the reply came. . . .

It was another form letter, very politely composed. It said that Disney Studios hired only the very finest artists, even for their routine background work. It had been determined from the drawings which Sparky submitted—that he was not one of the very finest artists.

In other words, he didn't get the job!

So you know what Sparky did? He wrote his autobiography in cartoons. He described his childhood self, the chronic underachiever, in a cartoon character the whole world now knows.

For the boy who failed the entire eighth grade; the young artist whose work was rejected by not only Walt Disney Studios but his own yearbook—that young man was "Sparky" Charles Monroe Schulz.

He created the "PEANUTS" comic strip and the little cartoon boy whose kite would never fly—Charlie Brown.

. . . And now you know the rest of the story.

•   •   •

       The PEANUTS Home Collection

Yes, it is true that Sparky's grades in junior high were less than exemplary, but by the time he finished high school he was earning all As and Bs. And, yes, it is true that he suffered from rejection, both professionally and personally, in his earlier years. It is also true that he still has insecurities and bouts of mild depression. But, give him credit! From the depths, despair, and disappointments that it seems every struggling young artist must endure, he drew his way into a new life—one of respect, comfort, and recognition. Compared to the accomplishments, awards, and honors of his life after 1950, his early failures fade into an insignificant footnote.

The following list, courtesy of United Media, highlights Sparky's life and the life of the PEANUTS® cartoon, neither of which can be easily separated from the other.

Milestones in PEANUTS® History

1950   First PEANUTS comic strip appears on October 2 in seven U.S. daily newspapers.

1952   First PEANUTS book published.

1955   National Cartoonists Society honors Charles M. Schulz with Reuben Award.

Kodak features PEANUTS characters in camera handbook.

1957   Ford Falcon campaign features first PEANUTS animation.

1958   Yale University names Schulz Cartoonist of the Year.

Snoopy stands on two legs for the first time in the comic strip.

First Snoopy plastic figure merchandised.

1960   Hallmark introduces series of PEANUTS greeting cards.

1962   PEANUTS named Best Humor Strip of the Year by National Cartoonists Society.

1964   National Cartoonists Society awards Schulz a second Reuben.

1965   First animated PEANUTS television special, "A Charlie Brown Christmas," airs on CBS-TV; wins Emmy and Peabody awards.

1967   "You're a Good Man, Charlie Brown" brings the PEANUTS characters to life in the form of a musical.

1968   NASA names Snoopy mascot for Manned Flight Space Awareness Program.

First Snoopy plush doll merchandised.

1969   Snoopy and Charlie Brown accompany astronauts into space aboard Apollo X.

1973   PEANUTS animated special, "A Charlie Brown Thanksgiving," airs on CBS-TV; wins Emmy award.

1976   PEANUTS 25th anniversary special, "Happy Anniversary, Charlie Brown," wins Emmy award.

1978   International Pavilion of Humor, Montreal, names Schulz Cartoonist of the Year.

1980   Women's Sports Foundation, led by Billie Jean King, appoints Schulz, the only male member, to the board of directors.

PEANUTS animated special, "Life Is a Circus, Charlie Brown," wins fifth Emmy award.

1981   National Hockey League awards Schulz the Lester Patrick Award for his outstanding contributions to hockey.

1983   Opening of Camp Snoopy at Knott's Berry Farm, Beuna Park, California.

The television special, "What Have We Learned, Charlie Brown?" wins a Peabody Award for "distinguished and meritorious public service in broadcasting."

1984   PEANUTS comic strip sold to 2,000th newspaper; Guinness Book of World Records recognizes milestone.

New York's Museum of Broadcasting opens retrospective of PEANUTS television specials, "Charlie Brown—A Boy For All Seasons: 20 Years on Television."

1985   Orange Bowl pays tribute to PEANUTS in national televised half-time show, "It's About Time, Charlie Brown."

Oakland Museum unveils PEANUTS exhibit, "The Graphic Art of Charles Schulz," on May 19; tours nine American cities.

A Very Brief Biography

The details of Sparky's early life seem straightforward enough. He was born on November 26, 1922 in St. Paul, Minnesota, where his father worked as a barber. A few years later, the family set out for a new life in Needles, California, which is where Sparky spent his seventh birthday. This experiment lasted about a year, and, in 1930, the family returned to St. Paul, where the elder Schulz reestablished himself as a popular barber in the neighborhood. For many years, the family lived in an apartment over the barber shop. (A plaque in a room in O'Gara's Bar, on the corner of Snelling and Selby, marks the exact location of the barber shop.)

As a boy, he developed an intense love for sports—a romance he pursues to this day. He is an avid golfer, and, at the age of 76, he still plays ice hockey at least once a week. His love for sports was exceeded only by his love for drawing, especially cartoons. He had a dog named Spike, and he submitted a drawing of Spike to *Ripley's Believe It or Not* in 1937, with the claim that Spike "eats pins, tacks, and razor blades." It was his first published work.

Following high school graduation, Sparky continued his studies of cartooning through an art school correspondence course. A stint in France and Germany during World War II briefly interrupted his career. When it resumed, he signed on as an instructor at that same art school, which just happened to have been located in nearby Minneapolis. For two years, beginning in 1947, he also drew a cartoon series for the Sunday *St. Paul Pioneer Express*. The name of the cartoon was "Li'l Folks" and many of the characters, including a dog, were the forerunners to the current PEANUTS gang.

During the late 1940s, Sparky had several cartoons published in the *Saturday Evening Post*, a popular general interest magazine of that era. These mild achievements gave him the courage to submit his work to a number of syndicates. Finally, in the spring of 1950, he was given an invitation to visit United Feature Syndicate in New York. The trip was obviously successful as seven newspapers ran his first syndicated cartoon on October 2, 1950.

Schulz believes that to be a good cartoonist you can't just make up stories. It has to come from within yourself. Which explains why so much of his PEANUTS strip is a reflection of his own experiences. Recalling memories of the antics of his own childhood, he is still able to interpret life through the eyes of a child. It didn't hurt, either, that he had five children (and eighteen grandchildren) of his own, all of whose experiences he mined for material for his strip. Little wonder that his own involvement in sports from an early age led to those marvelous works on hockey, baseball, football, tennis, and golf. Even his happy times at the art school did not go unrecognized. He named three of his characters after some of his fellow teachers: Frieda, Linus, and Charlie Brown. And is it more than coincidence that Snoopy's brother Spike lives with the cactus in the desert outside of Needles? Schulz is also a deeply religious man (he was a Sunday-school teacher through much of his adult life,) which explains why some of his cartoons contain insightful theological observations.

If there is one theme that runs throughout Sparky's life—a theme that must give inspiration to anyone who can relate to his fears, doubts, and insecurities—it is that, despite an occasional blue period, he basically approaches life with a strong belief in his own abilities. It is this belief, coupled with his strong sense of ethics and love for drawing, that sets him apart from almost every successful cartoonist who ever lived. The custom in the industry is that once an artist becomes successful, he hires a stable of writers and artists to produce the lion's share of the work. Schulz, alone, refuses to employ an assistant to do so much as the routine work in his studio. Every line, every stroke, every idea is his alone. And his family stands behind him, with the promise that when he is no longer able to draw the strip, they will not seek a replacement.

1986   The PEANUTS Saturday morning cartoon series, *The Charlie Brown and Snoopy Show*, wins the Youth in Film Award for best animated series.

The Charlie Brown and Snoopy Show wins daytime Emmy award.

1987   National Cartoonists Society presents Schulz with the prestigious Golden Brick Award as he is inducted into the Cartoonists Hall of Fame in Rye, New York.

1988   Premiere of the first-ever animated television mini-series, *This Is America, Charlie Brown*, in eight prime-time episodes.

1989   Snoopy shares the stage with renowned jazz trumpeter Wynton Marsalis in "Coolin It With Snoopy," part of the JVC Jazz Festival and the Berlin Jazz festival.

The first and only authorized biography of Charles M. Schulz, *Good Grief!* by award-winning journalist Rheta Grimsley Johnson.

1990   PEANUTS' 40th anniversary kicks off at the Super Bowl XXIV half-time show in New Orleans.

The Louvre Museum in Paris, France, presents the "Snoopy In Fashion" exhibit. Charles M. Schulz receives the Ordre des Arts et des Lettres from French Ministry of Culture.

"You Don't Look 40, Charlie Brown," debuts on CBS.

The Smithsonian Institution's National Museum of American History in Washington, D.C., presents "This Is Your Childhood, Charlie Brown—Children in American Culture, 1945-1970."

1991   The National Child Labor Committee presents the Lifetime Television Lewis Hine Award for the Advancement of Children to Charles M. Schulz in recognition of his efforts, through the PEANUTS comic strip, to further the understanding of children.

The PEANUTS gang celebrates the 75th anniversary of the National Park Foundation and helps promote the use and enjoyment of the National Parks among America's youth.

1992   The Montreal Museum of Fine Arts premieres "Snoopy, The Masterpiece," including a retrospective of PEANUTS.

Mall of America, largest mall in the U.S., opens in Bloomington, Minnesota, featuring Knott's Camp Snoopy, the largest indoor theme park in the nation.

"Il Mondo Di Snoopy," the art exhibit, debuts in Rome, Italy.

1993   Charlie Brown hits a game-winning home run on March 30, his first in 43 years.

1994   Charles Schulz is inducted into the Licensing Industry Merchandisers' Association's Hall of Fame, in recognition of his contributions to the licensing industry.

1995   "Around the Moon and Home Again: A Tribute to the Art of Charles M. Schulz," a summer-long exhibit at Space Center Houston, marks the strip's 45th anniversary.

In celebration of 45 years, "The Dog House," the official PEANUTS web site, is launched on the World Wide Web at http://www.unitedmedia.com.

1996   Charles Schulz is honored with a star on the legendary Hollywood Walk of Fame. His star lies next to that of the late Walt Disney.

1997   World premiere of, "Peanuts Gallery," a Carnegie Hall-commissioned orchestral work by composer Ellen Zwilich, based on the PEANUTS characters.

1999   A revised version of "You're a Good Man, Charlie Brown," featuring a multi-racial cast, opens on Broadway Thursday, February 4, at the Ambassador Theatre.

The International Museum of Cartoon Art, in Boca Raton, Florida, opens a four-month exhibit on October 2, celebrating "50 Years of PEANUTS: The Art of Charles M. Schulz."

The PEANUTS Home Collection

Price Guide Section

The House Concept:
Rooms for The Home Collection

Price guides can be boring. Even the best of them. The typical format of placing—or sometimes misplacing—an item in a given category can be both boring and a bit too arbitrary.

Fortunately, the very essence of PEANUTS® collectibles allowed me to pursue a better direction. Because PEANUTS® is a wholesome, family-oriented strip, and because most collectibles in some manner enhance the warm ambiance of any home—hence the title The Home Collection—it became easy to add a little "spice" to the format by taking a different approach.

I decided to create a collector's "dream house." It would have as many rooms as were needed to provide a special room that was just right for each piece in his or her collection. The house would have thirteen rooms (Snoopy isn't superstitious). That's more than will be found in most houses, you will agree, but it's just the right number for the collector. A hobby room for trophies, premiums, and other "promotional" items; a playroom for toys; a cabana for pool items; and so forth and so on. There are, however, some collectibles that fit easily in just about every room in the house. These items may be found in their own separate section called "PEANUTS!® Perfect Throughout the House."

The house concept allows us to group the collectibles in the room where you would most likely keep them yourself—if you had a house that big. Even if there is a difference of opinion as to what room you would place an item in, you won't have any trouble finding it in this book. There is a comprehensive index in the closing pages for easy reference.

One can't help but speculate that if Snoopy were a collector, he might have a house something like ours. His fans have never seen the inside of his house, but through the years we have learned from the comic strip that his house contains a diverse accumulation of many things—some practical, some not so practical. For instance, he has a pool table, a Van Gogh, and even a mural on his ceiling.

So what if . . . just what if . . . Snoopy were a collector? Hmmm!

What's In This book, and What's Not

When you consider the large number of different PEANUTS®-related licensed items and PEANUTS®-related ephemera produced worldwide over the past five decades—easily counted in the tens of thousands—it becomes a formidable task to decide which collectibles belong in the pricing section of this book.

It makes sense, of course, to include those items that are likely to be of the most interest to the largest number of readers.

Also to be taken into consideration are collectibility and age. With only a few important exceptions, this book is limited to those items which first appeared before the decade of the 1990s. Most of the products of the 1990s are too available to have shown any significant increase in value. Many, in fact, are still on the retail shelves today.

Items that are included from the 1990s are seasonal items such as ornaments, plates, and ceramic pieces, along with some of the watches, clocks, and advertising memorabilia of the early 1990s. In addition, you will find some important

pieces from companies such as Willitts and Silver Deer, which are not currently PEANUTS® licensees.

As for the older and/or more rare collectibles: I pictured most of the musicals that were ever made because they seem to be first on everyone's want list—and they are so very pleasing to look at. I included ornaments and plates for the same reasons. I have featured toys, ceramics, crystal pieces, ephemera, and so many other important collectibles from the 1960s, 1970s, and 1980s. Also included are examples of more expensive jewelry and works of art (see The Gallery, on page 97). Although these pieces may be out of reach for many collectors, they are still a very important part of the whole PEANUTS® collectible picture.

In addition, a large number of items that are priced under ten dollars are also represented. This demonstrates the idea that there are a lot of affordable objects out there, and that it is possible to begin to build a collection on a limited budget. Later, through judicious trading, buying, and selling, the collection can continue to grow without overly straining the family treasury.

I did not include much from two major categories—foreign items and wearable clothing.

Foreign items are considered to be items that are licensed to be sold outside of the United States only. As such, they are rare in this country and it would be difficult to establish value based on prior transactions. It stands to reason, however, that because of their limited availability, foreign objects will generally command a premium. I have not ignored foreign items here. Many are featured in the large display pictures which are used to introduce each "room" chapter of the pricing section. For purposes of filling out the pictures, a few domestic items are included, but in each case they are duly noted. An example of this is the sheet, pillow case, and bedspread cover ensemble in the bedroom picture, which was sold by Sears.

A final word about collectibles manufactured overseas. If the item is made specifically for consumption in the United States, PEANUTS® collectors look upon it as domestic, not "foreign."

Wearable clothing is just that. People like to wear clothing adorned with PEANUTS® characters, but the garments themselves are bought mainly for utilitarian purposes, not so much for collecting. They are sold in such large quantities that hardly anyone is interested in making them a part of their collection. Hence, the secondary market on these items is of little importance. The few exceptions to this generality are some of those magnificent sweaters and outer jackets that most people, whether or not they are collectors, would not be so quick to throw away.

Copyright and Dating

Identifying the age of a PEANUTS® collectible by using the copyright date as a guide is an exercise in futility. Don't even attempt it—it doesn't work. Here's why:

As a general rule, the copyright date refers only to the year the character itself first appeared in a publication, i.e. the comic strip. Notice that in all likelihood, this has no relationship to the release date of your collectible. That explains why two different collectibles, each featuring the same character, may differ in age by as many as twenty years and still carry the same copyright date. Since 1994, a manufacturer has the option of either showing the copyright date or not, as he sees fit. So, we now have a situation where if a copyright date is shown, the items may have been produced at any time, before or after 1994. However, if there is no copyright date, and it is otherwise a legal (licensed) PEANUTS® item, then the item definitely was manufactured after 1994, and it is not very old.

Of course, there were, over the years, even more rules referring to copyright date, thereby muddying the picture. All of these measures were rightly designed to help Mr. Schulz and United Features Syndicate protect their valuable property. None of them, maddening as they may seem, are of particularly great importance to the collector. But they are nevertheless interesting.

For instance, if the pose of a character, or its persona, changed drastically, it merited an additional copyright date. Snoopy is a classic example. His original copyright date was quite obviously 1950. But, shortly after he started walking on two legs instead of four, he earned another copyright date: 1958. His dancing pose and his appearances as the Flying Ace and Joe Cool were also different enough to warrant additional copyright dates.

All of the above referred to two-dimensional poses. When a character was first produced as a three dimensional figure, as in a plush, in came yet another copyright year. So, almost every character wound up with at least two copyright year-dates: One for its two-dimensional pose and another for its full-figure representation.

One more thing: New comic strips bear the copyright date of the year they are first printed. This is because an entirely new strip—or other creative work, for that matter—is considered original work and that takes precedence.

Times have a way of changing and, mercifully, so did some of the laws and procedures pertaining to copyright dates. As previously noted, beginning sometime in 1994, it became permissible for non-published items to omit the copyright dates. Most manufacturers went along with this option. However, they are still required to include the line "PEANUTS® United Features Syndicate, Inc." on every piece.

Now we can understand that, with the exception of a published work, copyright dating does not provide a good guideline to the age of a PEANUTS® collectible. There are other clues that will definitely be more helpful. As a starter, remember that except for the first books of cartoons published in the 1950s, including the PEANUTS® book collection by Rinehart Publishing Co. in 1952, the Saalfield coloring books (1959), and the Hungerford Dolls (1959), nothing was licensed and released before 1960.

It is helpful to learn the dates that the individual characters first appeared in the strip. Quite obviously, since the yellow bird, "Woodstock," received his name in 1970 (following the famous rock concert of 1969), any collectible including Woodstock must have made its debut in 1970 or later. Conversely, since Snoopy rarely appears without Woodstock, then the chances are good that a "solo" Snoopy item might well be older (earlier) than 1970.

It is true that many of the featured characters first appeared between 1950 and 1960. These include Snoopy, Charlie Brown, Shermy, and Patty (1950); Schroeder (1951); Lucy and Linus (1952); Pigpen (1954); and Sally (1959). However, an equal number of important characters did arrive later, and they can be a big help in estimating the age of certain collectibles. Among the later introductions are Frieda (1961), Snoopy, as the Flying Ace (1965), Peppermint Patty (1966), Franklin (1968), Marcie (1971), and Rerun (1972).

Some collectors enjoy becoming detectives of a sort. They peruse manufacturer and store catalogs (which have become hot collectibles in their own right) in order to determine when an item was being offered. These catalogs are extremely helpful in establishing the approximate time that most items were on the market, but they can be misleading if the piece had a long run. What immediately comes to mind is the SnoCone machine, by Hasbro, which has been in continuous production since 1960. Another thing collectors do is attempt to learn when certain manufacturers held their licenses—for example, Willitts music boxes came out only between the years 1987 and 1992, since that is the period covered by the licensing agreement.

In the future, of course, collectors will come to know that any legitimate item lacking a copyright date could not have been produced prior to 1994.

The Art of Pricing

THERE IS NO SUCH PERSON AS AN EXPERT ON PRICING!

No mortal can predict, with absolute certainty, the future behavior of a buyer and seller.

At best, a so called "expert" on prices is only a historian—a recorder of what has happened in the past, an observer of the trends in supply and demand. The psychology and the dynamics constantly change. How badly does the next buyer want or need an item? How willing is the seller to part with the object, and what price will be commensurate with his own interests? As in so much of life, what makes the future interesting is the mystery of the unknown.

The task of the author, therefore, is not to instruct the readers on how much to pay or to ask for a particular collectible. Rather, it is to report on sale prices in the recent past. With this information at hand, the collector has one more tool with which to make a decision: to buy, to negotiate a better price, or to pass-up the purchase with the expectation that a more favorable opportunity will present itself in another place and at another time. It must be noted, however, that every collector, at one time or another, has knowingly paid more for an item than the "experts" have reported. This is a part of the fluid dynamics and psychology of the situation—when the buyer's need (perhaps to fill in a set, or maybe just for the sheer joy of possession) becomes an overriding factor. "I want it! I can afford it! I'm getting it!" is the cry of many an impatient collector. And, this is why there is no such person as an "expert."

The prices reported in this section are the results of attending swap meets, collectible shows, and flea markets, in addition to literally thousands of contacts with hundreds of collectors and dealers throughout the year by telephone, e-mail, paper mail, and on-line auctions and chat rooms. To fairly represent the marketplace, isolated cases of unusually high or low prices were disregarded.

Where we report a range of prices, the lower price applies to items in "good" condition (some signs of wear, but nothing of great consequence; no parts missing, and all parts work) while the higher price is reserved for items that are in "mint" condition (no sign of wear and tear), or "mint in the box," as we shall explain below.

There is more to this mint condition business than first meets the eye. For one thing, it is not written in stone that a collectible has a great deal of value just because it is in perfect condition, or even because it is old. Take, as an example, the rubber pocket dolls by Boucher & Co. that came out in 1968. The company, later known as Determined Productions, was founded by the late Connie Boucher, who was on everyone's list as one of the most successful female entrepreneurs in the United States. Ms. Boucher was one of the first licensees of PEANUTS® characters, so the dolls have a lot of history behind them. Nevertheless, these dolls are still so plentiful that there has been relatively little increase in value over the past thirty-one years, no matter how well preserved they are. (See page 263 in the "Playroom.")

The above illustration is an excellent example of the supply-and-demand equation. If the supply (availability) is greater than the demand, then an orderly market will tend to put a brake on price escalation. Conversely, when demand outruns the supply, prices may escalate quickly. An example of this will be seen in the section on cels and lithographs. By limiting the number of cels or lithographs of each work he produces (known as a limited edition), the artist is deliberately keeping the supply low so as to enhance its value to the purchaser. It works!

Another example is "Snoopy the Critic," by Aviva. For some reason, Aviva chose to produce only 1,000 pieces of this well-made, animated toy. This rarity, combined with its desirability, enables the toy to command a relatively high value. (See page 282 in the "Playroom")

One variable to consider in pricing is the geographical area in which the item is sold. Yes, it's true: Find a collectible in an area where few collectors live or pass through, and the price is bound to be lower. After all, unless the seller is sophisticated enough to find a larger market through electronic auctions or some other advertising medium, how many interested buyers is he or she apt to see?

Believe it or not, the venue—or site—also plays a role. Garage sales and flea markets, where some sellers may tend to be less sophisticated, will generally provide more bargains than found at antique, toy, or collectible shows. These latter events will tend to attract more knowledgeable sellers and a greater number of interested buyers to the same location. Although the prices will be fair and more in line with the prices we are reporting in this book, the chances of finding a "bargain" will be slimmer.

Probably the worst place to find a bargain is at an Internet auction. People tend to get carried away and view it as a competition rather than a rational purchase. They get caught up in the moment. They don't want to lose the item to someone else. It becomes a very personal battle. Victory at all costs! Not surprisingly, the psychology of this type of auction will frequently boost the final price well above rational value. I must admit, it has even happened to me.

Very important is the question of the original container. If the box or other packaging has graphics—pictures of a PEANUTS® character or characters—and is itself in excellent condition (preferably unopened), then the item is known as "mint in the box." Examples of "other" packaging include blister-pack and window, or "see-through" boxes; that is, boxes with see-through plastic (see "Tub Time Snoopy" on page 49 in the Bathroom section.) Corrugated boxes, or other similar types of packaging without the graphics, are more for protection of the item and have no impact on the value.

Collectibles that are missing the important graphic packaging, even though they may be in excellent condition, are not considered mint in the box, and their value is greatly diminished. Exceptions to this rule are musicals, and items that are so rare they are in great demand with or without their original packaging. (For purposes of this discussion please consider the words "box" and "packaging" as interchangeable.)

You will notice that many of the prices in the price guide section will be followed by either one or two asterisks. One asterisk (*) indicates that the collectible was originally sold in a box. If only one range of prices precedes the asterisk, it means that the box is not a factor in the price. This will include musicals, some ornaments, rare items, and items so low in value—usually under twelve dollars—that the box doesn't add that much.

However, if the original box serves to enhance the value, then two ranges of prices will be shown. The first, and lower, range will designate the values if the box is missing. The second, higher range, will show the values if the packaging is included.

In a few cases you will see two asterisks (**). This tells you that not only did the collectible originally come in a box, but you should avoid buying it if the box is missing. This advice especially holds true for items like board games and jigsaw puzzles, where the condition could not possibly be very good, and more than likely pieces have been lost.

To review:

A. **No asterisk:** The collectible did not originally come in a box. Example:

      Planter.........................$40-50.

B. **One asterisk* and one price range:** The collectible originally came in a box, but the box is not important to the price (mostly musicals, some ornaments, rare items, and low priced items). Example:

      Musicals...................$70-90*
      Switch plates.............$3-5*

C. **One asterisk* and two ranges of price:** The box is important, but there is still some value even without it. Example:

      Hockey game: $35-50 $110-125*

D. **Two asterisks**:** The box or packaging is essential. Do not buy without it. Example:

      Board game: ....$ 40-50**

The foreign items in the attic, with just the few exceptions noted, are all from Japan. At the top is a square red pillow cover and a small artificial tree with fabric from the United States draped over the side, plus a wooden Charlie Brown ornament and a cloth gift bag in the front. Next to the fabric is a round decorative pillow cover.

Starting from the front left-hand corner of the chest are three cloth Christmas gift bags; two small Snoopy ornamental plushes with suction cups for hanging; a decorative tin containing sweet candies (England); and a plastic mini-tree with a plastic Snoopy on the top and Christmas decorations hanging from it. Behind the cloth gift bags in the front are a small cardboard puzzle and a Halloween mug featuring Snoopy on the handle. Three traveling cases occupy the back row. The black one on the left is plastic (New Zealand); the other two are cloth (USA).

Two small suitcases (England) are on the floor in front of the chest. Next to them is Snoopy in his Santa outfit (USA).

The PEANUTS Home Collection

The Attic

Alas, there are so many beautiful objects that only see the light of day on rare occasions. It's a pity we have little choice but to keep them hidden from view in our attic for months and months at a time. Most important are the seasonal treasures, such as Christmas ornaments, stockings, nativity scenes, etc. Halloween costumes, masks, and other accouterments also reside in the attic for most of the year, as do storage boxes and luggage when they aren't taken out of the house for a vacation.

SEASONAL ITEMS

1. Ball Ornaments

Satin. Hallmark.

• Snoopy, Woodstock, and his friends are in Santa's workshop. Printed: "1978." Reverse side: Snoopy hangs a stocking on the fireplace, as Woodstock looks at the Christmas tree. #QX206-3. 1978. $30-35 $45-50*

• Linus holds a wreath printed "1978." Reverse side: The gang sings "Joy To The World." #QX205-8. 1978. $25-30 $40-50*

• Snoopy, tangled in a string of lights, and Woodstock, dressed as Santa and standing on a present, look at a Christmas tree. Printed: "1977." Reverse side: Linus carries gifts and Charlie Brown and Lucy are pictured with a snowman. #QX135-5. 1977. $30-35 $45-50*

• Snoopy, wearing a Santa hat and decorating his doghouse, thinks, "Have a delightful Christmas!" Reverse side: Charlie Brown, tangled in a string of lights, says, "Sigh." #QX203-6. 1978. $30-35 #40-50*

• Snoopy and Woodstock each decorate a Christmas tree. Printed: "1978." Reverse side: Snoopy and Woodstock each pull a tree on a sled. 2-5/8" diam. #QX204-3. 1978. $25-30 $40-50*

2. Ball Ornaments

Dated. Satin. Hallmark.

• Snoopy, wearing a Santa hat, gives candy canes to Woodstock and his friends, who are wearing green stocking caps. Printed: "Merry Christmas 1979." Reverse side: Woodstock and his friends decorate a Christmas tree with candy canes. Printed: "Merry Christmas 1979." #QX202-7. 1979. $15-20 $30-35*

• Snoopy and Woodstock, wearing stocking caps, ride a sled down a hill. Printed: "A grandson…A special someone whose merry ways bring extra joy to the holidays" and "Christmas 1979." Reverse side: Snoopy is on a sled being pulled by Woodstock and his friends. #QX210-7. 1979. $12-15 $20-25*

• Snoopy sings as Woodstock and his friends act out lines from "The Twelve Days of Christmas" around the ornament. Printed: "Christmas 1980." Part of the chorus is printed around the ornament. #QX216-1. 1980. $12-15 $20-25*

• Snoopy, wearing a Santa hat and holding leaves of holly, dances and thinks, "Deck the halls with boughs of holly…" as Woodstock, wearing Santa hat, pushes a wheelbarrow full of holly. Printed: "Christmas 1981." Reverse side: Woodstock and his friends sing, "Fa la la la la." QX803-5. 1981. $12-15 $20-25*

3. Ball Ornaments

Dated. Hallmark.

• Snoopy, wearing a Santa hat and carrying a bag of gifts, and Woodstock and his friends, wearing antlers on their heads, ride a tandem bicycle around the ornament. Printed on a sign in the snow: "Christmas 1982." Satin. #QX200-6. $15-20 $20-25*

• Snoopy, wearing a Santa hat, walks away from a fireplace hung with stockings as Woodstock sits in his nest in front of the fire. Reverse side: Snoopy takes Woodstock and his nest out of the tree. Printed: "Christmas 1983" and "May the joy of the season warm every heart." Satin. #QX212-7. 1983. $10-12 $15-20*

4

5

6

•Woodstock is singing in the falling snow. Printed: "Sing a song of Christmas joy! 1985." Reverse side: Woodstock and his friends form a pyramid-shaped choir being directed by Snoopy. The bottom of the ornament comes to a rounded point. Glass. #QX266-5. 1985. $10-12 $15-20*

•Snoopy holds a banner printed "Merry Christmas" above a row of tiny snowmen. "1984" is printed below. Reverse side: Snoopy and Woodstock make snowballs. Satin. #QX252-1. 1984. $12-15 $20-25*

4. Ball Ornaments

•Snoopy hangs a stocking on the fireplace as Sally watches and Charlie Brown says, "A watched stocking never fills." Reverse side: Lucy gives Schroeder, sitting at his piano, a present and says, "Merry Christmas." Glass. #250QX162-2, Hallmark. 1977. $20-25 $40-45*

•Sold in sets of two. The first ornament features a continuous scene of Woodstock and his friends pulling a sled carrying Snoopy, wearing a Santa hat, and a bag of Christmas gifts. The second ornament features Charlie Brown and Woodstock with a snowman. Reverse side: Peppermint Patty, Snoopy, and Linus are ice-skating. Woodstock's nest has an igloo inside. Glass. #400QX163-5, Hallmark. 1977. As a set: $30-40 $55-65*

•Snoopy, wearing a stocking cap, is ice-skating. He etches "1980" into the ice. Woodstock is in the arms of a snowman in the background. Reverse side: Peppermint Patty etches "Merry Christmas" into the ice as Linus, Sally, Lucy, and Charlie Brown watch. Satin. Determined Productions. 1980. $12-15 $20-30*

•Snoopy leads a choir comprised of Woodstock and many of his friends. "1981" is printed underneath Snoopy. Printed above: "We Wish You A Merry Christmas..." Reverse side: Woodstock carries a star to a Christmas tree. Pigpen, Peppermint Patty, Lucy, Charlie Brown, Linus, and Sally sing "And A Happy New Year!" Satin. Determined Productions. 1981. $12-15 $20-28*

•Snoopy, Woodstock and his friends, and Lucy sing Christmas carols. Printed: "Merry Christmas 1982." Reverse side: Charlie Brown, Sally, Linus, and Peppermint Patty are singing. Satin. Determined Productions. 1982. $12-15 $20-25*

•Woodstock and his friends sit at a table set with food and a box of bird seed. Printed: "Happy Holidays." Satin. Determined Productions. Mid-1970s. $10-12 $15-20*

•Woodstock and his friends, wearing red and green Santa hats, prepare toys for Snoopy, dressed as Santa, on the reverse side. Printed: "Season's Greetings." Satin. Determined Productions. Late 1970s. $10-12 $15-20*

5. Ball Ornaments

Dated. Glass. Hallmark.

•Woodstock and his friends ice-skate around a sign printed "1986." Reverse side: Snoopy etches "Merry Christmas" into the ice as he skates. The bottom of the ornament comes to a rounded point. #QX276-6. 1986. $12-15 $20-25*

•Snoopy, Woodstock, and his friends sled down a hill in Snoopy's supper dish. Printed "1987." Reverse side: Woodstock's friends are all around playing, skiing, and sledding in the snow. Printed: "Everyone's Cool At Christmas Time!" The bottom of the ornament comes to a rounded point. #QX281-9. 1987. $10-12 $20-25*

•Woodstock, wearing a Santa hat, stands in the falling snow. Printed: "Where Friendship Goes, Happiness Follows! Christmas 1988." Reverse side: Snoopy, dressed as Santa, rides in a sleigh filled with gifts, and led by Woodstock and his friends, wearing antlers. The bottom of the ornament comes to a rounded point. #QX280-1. 1988. $12-15 $20-25*

•Charlie Brown looks at his scrawny Christmas tree pulled down by the weight of its single ornament. Printed: "A Charlie Brown Christmas Television Special. Happy 25th Anniversary 1965-1989." Reverse side: The gang is gathered around a Christmas tree singing. Printed: "Christmas... Season Of Love." #QX276-5. 1989. $10-15 $30-35*

6. Ball Ornaments

Dated. Hallmark.

•Schroeder plays his piano in front of a fireplace decorated with stockings, as Peppermint Patty, Marcie, Sally, Lucy, Charlie Brown, Linus, Pigpen, and Snoopy dance around the ornament. "1990" is printed on a present's gift tag. Printed: "Christmas is the merriest, lightest, jolliest time of the year." The 40th Anniversary logo and the words "40 Years of Happiness" appear on the ornament box. Chrome. #QX223-3. 1990. $10-12 $15-20*

•Snoopy sits beside his decorated doghouse with a sign on it printed "1991." The characters are pictured around the ornament. Printed: "It's the time of year for sharing good cheer!" Chrome. #QX225-7. 1991. $8-10 $15-20*

•The PEANUTS characters, dressed as shepherds, bring gifts to the manger. Printed: "Christmas 1992" and "Behold, I bring you good tidings of great joy, which shall be to all people." Glass. #QX224-4. 1992. $8-10 $15-20*

•Snoopy and Woodstock are dressed as Santas. Printed: "Merry Christmas 1993." Around the ornament the characters say "Merry Christmas" in German, French, Italian, and Spanish. Glass. #QX207-2. 1993. $5-7 $12-15*

7. Panorama Ornament

•Woodstock and his friends pull Snoopy on a sled past a snowman that looks like Snoopy. Third in the "Snoopy and Friends" series. #QX436-2, Hallmark. 1981. $60-65 $85-100*

8. Panorama Ornaments

• "Santa Snoopy." Snoopy, dressed as Santa, stands next to a bag of toys. Woodstock flies overhead, holding a banner printed "1983." Fifth (and final) in the "Snoopy and Friends" series. #QX416-9, Hallmark. 1983. $55-60 $75-85*

• "Ice Hockey Holiday." Snoopy skates with a hockey stick in his paw, and Woodstock sits on the hockey puck. "1979" is printed on a sign in the snow. First in the "Snoopy and Friends" series. #QX141-9, Hallmark. 1979. $80-90 $110-120*

9. Panorama Ornaments

• "Ski Holiday." Snoopy, wearing a stocking cap, skis as Woodstock goes by in Snoopy's supper dish, holding a pennant printed "1980." Second in the "Snoopy and Friends" series. #QX154-1, Hallmark. 1980. $80-90 $90-100*

• Snoopy rides in a sleigh pulled by Woodstock and his friends over rooftops. Fourth in the "Snoopy and Friends" series. #QX480-3, Hallmark. 1982. $75-80 $100-110*

10. Ball Ornaments

Glass (fragile). Series #30502, Silvestri. 1990. $45-55 ea.

• Lucy sits on top of the ornament with a red bow behind her back.

• Charlie Brown, holding an ornament, sits on top of the ornament with a red bow behind him. (Not pictured)

• Snoopy, wearing a green and red hat, lies on top of the ornament with a red bow behind him. (Not pictured)

Bell Ornaments

Printed in gold: "Baby's 1st Christmas." Glass. 4"H. #30021, Silvestri. 1990. $30-35 ea.

• Lucy, wearing red pajamas, stands on top of the bell.

• Linus, wearing green pajamas and holding a red blanket, sits on top of the bell.

Bell Ornaments with Holly

Glass. 4-1/4"H. Series #30503, Silvestri. 1990. $50-55 ea.

• Woodstock sits on a candy cane inside the bell.

• Snoopy wears a Santa hat inside the bell.

11. Micro-Mini Bell Ornaments

Ceramic. 1"H. Series #1945, Determined Productions. Mid-1970s. $12-18 ea.

• Snoopy is sitting in front of wrapped Christmas gifts.

• Snoopy and Woodstock each carry a Christmas tree.

• Snoopy lies on top of his decorated doghouse.

• Charlie Brown eats a candy cane as Snoopy, wearing a stocking cap, approaches.

• Snoopy is sitting, holding Woodstock, who is in his nest with a Christmas tree.

• Snoopy, dressed as Santa, gives a gift to Lucy.

12. Mini Bell Ornaments

Ceramic. 1-1/2"H. Series #1345, Determined Productions. Mid-1970s. $15-20 ea.

• Snoopy and Woodstock, wearing Santa hats, sit inside a stocking.

• Snoopy, with wings and a halo, is on a yellow cloud.

• Schroeder plays his piano, with Snoopy sitting next to it and a Christmas tree in the background.

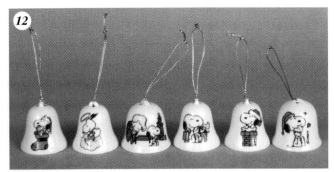

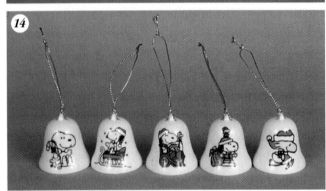

• Snoopy, sitting among presents, gives a candy cane to Woodstock, who is sitting on top of a gift.

• Snoopy, wearing a Santa hat, emerges from a chimney.

• Snoopy, wearing a red stocking cap, is hugging Woodstock.

13. Mini Bell Ornaments

Ceramic. 1-1/2"H. Series #1345, Determined Productions. Mid-1970s. $15-20 ea.

• Snoopy gives a candy cane to Linus, who sits with his thumb in his mouth, holding his blanket.

• Snoopy stands under the mistletoe, next to Lucy.

• Peppermint Patty walks with Snoopy, who holds a sign printed "Joy."

• Charlie Brown and Snoopy are dancing and singing. Printed: "Jingle Bells, Jingle Bells."

• Snoopy and Woodstock build snowmen.

• Woodstock, wearing a Santa hat, stands on a stool and looks into an open present.

14. Bell Ornaments

Ceramic. 1-1/2"H. Series #1345, Determined Productions. Mid-1970s. $15-20 ea.

• Snoopy sits, and holds a very tall candy cane, which Woodstock leans against.

• Snoopy, wearing a Santa hat, and Woodstock share a sleigh.

• Snoopy and Woodstock, wearing Santa hats, ride in a green and red locomotive.

• Snoopy, dressed as Santa, stands with a bag of gifts. Woodstock is on Snoopy's head.

• Woodstock is dressed as Santa.

15. Bell Ornaments

Ceramic with red trim. 3"H. Determined Productions. Mid-1970s. $20-25 ea.

• Snoopy and Woodstock sleep under a blanket atop Snoopy's doghouse. Printed on the reverse side: "Peace On Earth."

• Snoopy lies on top of his doghouse, which is decorated with stockings, as Woodstock looks at the house. Printed on the reverse side: "I Never Take Any Chances!"

• Snoopy and Woodstock drink eggnog. Charlie Brown, sitting, clearly does not like the eggnog. Printed on the reverse side: "Woodstock Makes Great Root Beer Eggnog."

• Snoopy, Sally, and Woodstock are surrounded by Christmas presents. Printed on the reverse side: "This Is A Happy Time Of Year!"

• Lucy, Linus, Charlie Brown, Peppermint Patty, Sally, and Snoopy stand together. Printed on the reverse side: "Christmas Is Together Time!"

16. Bell Ornaments

Ceramic with red trim. 3"H. Determined Productions. Mid-1970s. $20-25 ea.

• Woodstock entangles Snoopy in Christmas lights as he flies them around the doghouse while Charlie Brown watches. Printed on the reverse side: "OK! Who's The Decorator?"

• Snoopy and Woodstock, who is typing a letter, sit on top of Snoopy's doghouse. Printed on the reverse side: "Dear Santa Claus is Rather Stuffy... How About Dear Fatty?"

• Snoopy and Woodstock, standing on top of the doghouse, each with a Christmas gift behind his back. Printed on the reverse side: "It's Better To Give And Receive!"

• Snoopy, sitting among gifts, listens to a visibly singed Woodstock. Printed on the reverse side: "Someone Thought Woodstock Was A Christmas Goose!"

• Schroeder is playing his piano; Snoopy is dancing; and Lucy, Linus, and Peppermint Patty are around the Christmas tree. Printed on the reverse side: "O Christmas Tree..."

- Snoopy, wearing a large red bow and a tag printed "From Santa," gives himself to Woodstock. Printed on the reverse side: "Merry Christmas 1976."

- Woodstock leans on Snoopy, and Snoopy leans on Charlie Brown, who sits next to Lucy, who is holding a candle. Printed on the reverse side: "Merry Christmas 1977."

- Lucy, Charlie Brown, Snoopy, and Woodstock sing, as Schroeder plays the piano. Printed on the reverse side: "Merry Christmas 1978."

19. Ornaments

- Snoopy is sitting, and has a red ribbon around his neck. Crocheted yarn. 4"H. #817, Determined Productions. 1977. $8-10

- Woodstock is standing. Crocheted yarn. 4"H. #817, Determined Productions. 1977. $8-10

20. Ornaments

"PEANUTS Christmas Doll Ornaments." 12 styles. Packaging has the character's name on the back. Stuffed cotton. Assortment #4225, Determined Productions. Late 1970s. $3-4 ea. $6-10* ea.

- Snoopy in multicolored ski outfit and goggles. 4-1/8"H.

- Woodstock sits in a Christmas stocking, printed "Noel." 3-7/8"H.

- Lucy is wearing a red dress with candles around the bottom, and has holly in her hair. 4-1/2"H.

- Linus, wearing a green hat, plays a blue drum. 5"H.

- Woodstock is dressed as Santa. 3-1/2"H.

- Charlie Brown is dressed as a toy soldier. 5"H.

- Snoopy, wearing a red visor, has toys in his yellow pockets. 4"H.

- Sally wears a pink and white dress with angel wings on the back. 4-1/2"H.

- Snoopy wears a red and white striped nightshirt and a stocking cap. 3-7/8"H.

- Snoopy wears a tyrolean outfit and a green stocking cap. 3-7/8"H. (Not pictured)

- Peppermint Patty wears a red striped shirt, a pink dress, and an apron. 5"H. (Not pictured)

- Snoopy is dressed as Santa. 3-7/8"H. (Not pictured)

21. Ornaments

Flannel-type fabric. Union Wadding. 1989. $6-8 ea.

- Snoopy, wearing a red scarf, holds a gold star.

- Snoopy wears a Santa hat, and has a bell and a red ribbon around his neck.

- Snoopy, wearing antlers, holds a gold ornament with red ribbon in his lap.

- While standing under the mistletoe, Snoopy gives Woodstock a kiss. Printed on reverse side: "Merry Christmas Little Friend of Friends."

17. Bell Ornaments

Ceramic with green trim. 2-1/2"H. Determined Productions for Dupont Collection. 1977. $15-22 ea.

- Snoopy, looking through binoculars, and Woodstock stand on top of the decorated doghouse. A silhouette of Santa and his reindeer pass by a crescent moon. Printed on the reverse side: "Merry Christmas 1977."

- Charlie Brown, Lucy, Linus, and Sally stand with gifts around them. Snoopy and Woodstock, with a candle between them, are in the foreground. Printed on the reverse side: "Happy Holidays 1977."

- Snoopy is dressed as Santa and sitting in a big chair with Woodstock on the arm. Charlie Brown and Marcie wait in line to see Santa. Printed on the reverse side: "Merry Christmas 1977."

- Snoopy, wearing a Santa hat and a napkin around his neck, sits at a table eating dessert, as Woodstock flies overhead. Printed on the reverse side: "Happy Holidays 1977."

18. Bell Ornaments

Dated. Ceramic with patterned green trim. 2-7/8"H. Determined Productions. $20-25 ea.

- Snoopy and Woodstock sleep on top of Snoopy's doghouse, which is hung with two stockings. Printed on the reverse side: "Merry Christmas 1975."

• Snoopy wears a top hat, has a green ribbon around his neck, and holds a candy cane.

• Snoopy wears a Santa hat, and has a bell and a red scarf around his neck.

• Snoopy wears a plaid scarf around his neck, and holds a wreath.

22. Flat Ornaments (top two rows)

Satin. Union Wadding. 1989. $2-3* ea.

• Snoopy lies on top of his decorated doghouse.

• Snoopy is wearing a red bow tie.

• Snoopy, sitting face-front and wearing a Santa hat, holds a candy cane.

• Snoopy, sitting sideways, wears a Santa hat and striped scarf, and holds a candy cane.

• Snoopy, wearing a Santa hat, is coming out of a green chimney.

• Snoopy, wearing a red collar around his neck, holds his supper dish. (Not pictured)

Plush Ornaments (bottom two rows)

Assortment #9755, Union Wadding. 1986. $6-8 ea.

• Snoopy, wearing a patterned red scarf, holds a multicolored ring-shaped ornament. 5"H.

• Snoopy, lying on his tummy, wears a Santa hat and a red scarf with green fringes. 6"L.

• Snoopy is dressed as a reindeer, with green antlers and a red harness. 5-1/2"H.

• Snoopy, sitting, holds a candy cane and a green gift sack. 4"H.

• Woodstock is wearing a Santa hat. 5-1/2"H.

• Snoopy, sitting, wears a green ribbon and has a tiny red stocking around his neck. 4"H.

23. Ornaments

Plaster-of-Paris type material. Series #455, Determined Productions. Sold by Snoopy's Gallery and Gift Shop, Santa Rosa, CA. Early 1980s. $15-22 ea.

• Snoopy, dressed as Santa, carries a green gift sack. 3"H.

• Snoopy, in a green and red striped Christmas stocking. 3"H.

• Snoopy sits in front of a green and red wrapped gift. 2-1/2"H.

• Woodstock sits on a red bow, inside a wreath. 2-1/2"H.

• Snoopy hugs an oversized candy cane. 3"H.

• Snoopy lies on his doghouse, which is decorated with a wreath and green and white striped stockings. 3"H.

24. Ornaments

Ceramic. Series #1720, Determined Productions. 1978. $22-28 ea.

• Snoopy carries a gift box with Woodstock on top. #1721.

• Snoopy, wearing a multicolored striped stocking cap, holds Woodstock. #1725.

• Snoopy is sitting, holding Woodstock, who is in his nest with a Christmas tree. #1722.

• Snoopy is dressed as Santa, and has his arms outstretched. #1723.

• Snoopy, holding a candy cane (visible on the other side of the ornament), appears to be leaping. #1724.

• Woodstock is sitting on a red and green gift box. #1726.

25. Disk Ornaments

"Christmas Signature Collection." Part of a collection of dated musicals, plates, and bells, issued annually at holiday time. Porcelain. 2-3/4" diam. Willitts Designs.

• Snoopy, Woodstock, and his friend, standing under a lamppost, sing Christmas carols. Printed: "Christmas 1988." Ornament is trimmed in gold. #8430. 1988. $15-18 $18-20*

• Snoopy carries a Christmas tree over his shoulder, and pulls Woodstock on a sled. Printed: "Christmas 1989." #9353. 1989. $15-18 $18-20*

• Snoopy, wearing a Santa hat, is on top of his decorated doghouse being pulled through the air by Woodstock. Printed: "Christmas 1990." #44004. 1990. $12-15 $15-18*

•Woodstock, Snoopy, and Charlie Brown share a toboggan ride. Printed: "Christmas 1991." #44031. 1991. $18-10 $12-15*

26. Disk Ornament

•Snoopy, Woodstock, and Charlie Brown wear red bow ties. Printed above and below the characters: "40 Years Of Happiness." This is the 40th anniversary logo. Porcelain. 2-3/4" diam. #19002, Willitts Designs. 1990. $12-15 $15-18*

27. Ornament

•Snoopy is sitting. Hollow sterling silver. 1-3/4"H. #4512, Determined Productions. 1972. $75-90

Flat Ornaments

•Snoopy lies on top of a heart. Silver-plated. 3"H. #4515, Determined Productions. 1972. $6-8*

•Snoopy is walking. Silver-plated. 3"H. #4511, Determined Productions. 1972. $15-20*

28. Flat Ornaments

Round and heart-shaped ornaments. Available in gold tone or silver tone. Leonard Silver. 1979. $4-6 ea.

•Snoopy, holding a candy cane, and Woodstock, lie on top of Snoopy's decorated doghouse, surrounded by holly. Silver: #7103.

•Snoopy, dressed as Santa, and Woodstock are surrounded by little snowmen. Silver: #7181. Gold: #7182.

•Charlie Brown is dressed as Santa, with holly around the ornament.

•Snoopy, sitting, holds Woodstock, who is in his nest with a Christmas tree. Ornament contains a space under Snoopy for personalizing. Silver: #7109. Gold: #7110.

•Snoopy is sitting and playing a drum, as Woodstock flies overhead. Ornament contains a space above Snoopy for personalizing. Silver: #7101. Gold: #7102.

•Linus, dressed as Santa, carries a small red sack over his shoulder. Holly is around the ornament.

•Peppermint Patty is dressed as Mrs. Claus, surrounded by snowflakes.

•Sally, dressed as Mrs. Claus, holds a star and is surrounded by snowflakes.

•Snoopy, dressed as Santa, and Woodstock, flying, are surrounded by snowflakes.

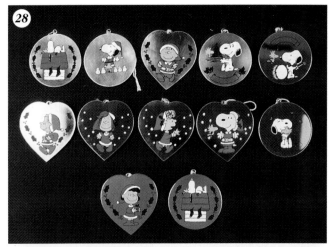

•Snoopy is sitting and hugging Woodstock. Ornament contains a space under Snoopy for personalizing. Silver: #7105. Gold: #7106.

•Lucy, dressed as Mrs. Claus, holds a Christmas gift. Holly is around the ornament.

•Snoopy, holding a candy cane, and Woodstock, lie on top of Snoopy's decorated doghouse, surrounded by holly. Gold: #7104.

29. Ornaments

"PEANUTS Mascot Dolls." Although not called ornaments, these dolls with jointed arms and legs came with a string for hanging. Hard cardboard. Determined Productions. Late 1970s. $5-8 $10-12* ea.

•Charlie Brown wears a baseball cap and glove. 4"H.

•Snoopy wears a red chef's hat and apron, and holds a spoon. 4"H.

•Snoopy, wearing a band uniform, plays a green and yellow drum. 4-5/8"H.

•Snoopy, wearing a striped stocking cap and coat, holds a candy cane and a stocking. 3-7/8"H.

•Sally wears a pink dress and red shoes. 4"H.

•Snoopy is holding sheet music and singing. He wears a green and yellow striped scarf and a yellow and red hat and coat. 3-1/2"H.

30. Frame Ornaments

Plastic. 3" diam. Came in non-descript packaging. Series #4369, Silvestri. 1990. $12-15 ea.

•Snoopy, as Joe Cool, stands on the side; a red bow and ribbon are on top of the frame.

•Charlie Brown stands next to a snowman, whose body comprises the frame.

•Snoopy and Woodstock, wearing top hats, sit on each side of the frame, which has a red bow and ribbon on top.

•Charlie Brown sits next to the frame, which has a red bow and ribbon on top.

31. Ornaments (top two rows)

The design appears on each side. Plastic. Came in non-descript packaging. Determined Productions. Late 1970s. $3-5 ea.

•Snoopy and Woodstock, wearing green hats and scarves, sing in the falling snow, against a red background. 3"H.

•Snoopy, wearing a Santa hat, and Woodstock, wearing an Eskimo hat, are ice fishing. Woodstock's nest with an igloo in it appears in the background, against the sun. 3-1/8"H.

•Snoopy and Woodstock sit in front of gifts and a Christmas tree. 4"H.

•Snoopy, wearing a Santa hat, lies on top of a locomotive while Woodstock, also wearing a Santa hat, stands on Snoopy's feet. 3-1/2"H.

•Snoopy and Woodstock, with wings and halos, walk on a cloud. 3-1/8"H.

Ornaments (bottom row)

Blue background. Wood. Came in non-descript packaging. Willitts Designs. 1990. $6-8 ea.

•Snoopy, wearing a red and white cap, sits on a bow set inside a wreath. 4" x 4-1/2". #8438.

•Snoopy, as Joe Cool, and wearing a Santa hat, leans against Christmas gifts. Woodstock, wearing sunglasses, sits on the tallest gift. 4-1/2" x 4-1/8". #8439.

•Snoopy, wearing a Santa hat, holds a red and green gift box. 2" x 3". $8440.

32. Flat Ornaments

Dated. Painted on each side. Wood. Came in non-descript packaging. Determined Productions 1977. $6-8 ea.

•Snoopy, wearing a red stocking cap and carrying a green sack of gifts, stands in a chimney. Printed: "Merry Christmas 1977." 4"H.

•Snoopy sits inside a Christmas wreath. Printed: "Merry Christmas 1977." 4"H.

•Snoopy leans on a red and yellow oversized candy cane. Printed: "Noel 1977." 3-1/8"H.

•Snoopy, wearing a green and red stocking cap, stands next to an oversized snowflake. Printed: "Noel 1977." 3"H.

•Snoopy, grinning, has his arms around a big present. Printed: "Noel 1977." 3"H.

•Snoopy dances in front of a red bell. Printed: "Happy Holidays 1977." 3-3/4"H.

33. Flat Ornaments

Dated. Painted on each side. Wood. Came in non-descript packaging. Determined Productions. 1977. $6-8 ea.

•Snoopy hugs Woodstock on a red heart-shaped ornament. Printed: "Merry Christmas 1977." 3-1/8"H.

•Snoopy sits in front of a green ornament, with a gift at his feet. Printed: "Happy Holidays 1977." 3-1/2"H.

•Snoopy lies on top of his red and yellow doghouse, which is hung with Christmas stockings. Printed: "Merry Christmas 1977." 4"H.

•Snoopy sits with gifts in front of a yellow star-shaped ornament. Printed: "Noel 1977." 3-1/2"H.

•Snoopy stands in front of a red and yellow ball ornament. Printed: "Happy Holidays 1977." 3-1/2"H.

•Snoopy stands in front of a Christmas tree. Printed: "Happy Holidays 1977." 4"H.

34. Ornaments

The design appears on each side. Wood. Came in non-descript packaging. Determined Productions. Late 1970s. $6-8 ea.

•Charlie Brown is carrying presents. 3-1/8"H. #8616.

•Snoopy sits next to several red and green gifts. 2-1/2"H. #8611.

•Lucy, wearing a green dress, holds a present. 3-1/2"H. #8617.

•Sally carries a gift. 3"H. #8621.

•Snoopy wears a Santa hat and has holly around his neck. 2-7/8"H. #8609.

•Woodstock holds a present. 3-1/8"H. #8615.

•Woodstock is inside a green and red striped stocking. 3"H. #8614.

•Peppermint Patty is tying a bow on the gift in her lap. 3-1/8"H. #6819.

•Snoopy, wearing a green stocking cap, lies on top of his decorated doghouse. 3-7/8"H. #8613.

•Linus holds a present. 3-1/2"H. #8618.

•Snoopy is inside a green and red striped stocking, with holly trim. 3-1/8"H. #8612.

•Snoopy sits with a present at his feet. 2-1/2"H. #8610. (Not pictured)

35. Ornaments

"PEANUTS String Toy Ornament." The design is on one side. The characters have jointed arms and legs that move when the wooden ball on the end of the string is pulled. Wood. Determined Productions. Mid-1970s. $7-10 ea.

•Woodstock wears a stocking cap, coat, scarf, and ice skates. 5"H.

•Snoopy, as the Flying Ace. 3-1/8"H.

•Snoopy wears a cowboy hat, vest, and a sheriff's badge. 4-1/8"H.

•Snoopy, as Joe Cool. 3-1/2"H. (Not pictured)

36. Flat Ornaments

Ceramic. 3"H. #1322, Determined Productions. 1980. $22-28 ea.

•Snoopy, wearing a Santa hat and carrying a sack of gifts, is in a chimney.

•Woodstock, holding a candy cane, sits on top of the word "Noel."

•Snoopy lies on his back across the top of a Christmas wreath.

•Snoopy wears a red robe, with a halo and wings.

•Woodstock, wearing a red robe, a halo, and wings, carries a present.

•Snoopy carries a decorated Christmas tree over his shoulder.

37. Ornaments

"Snoopy Personalized Ornaments." The design appears on each side. Wood. 3-1/2"W x 5-1/2"H. Series #4364, Silvestri. 1990. $7-10 ea.

•Schroeder plays his piano, while Lucy leans on it. A bar of music strung with lights is over their heads.

•Charlie Brown and Snoopy, each holding shovels, look at each other standing in the snow.

• Snoopy, wearing a red scarf, stands next to a snowman, while Woodstock sits on the snowman's green hat.

38. Ornaments

"Snoopy Doghouse Ornaments." The design appears on each side. Wood. 4-1/2"H. Series #4363, Silvestri. 1990. $7-10 ea.

• Snoopy lies on his yellow doghouse, which is decorated with a wreath, with Woodstock lying on his tummy. They both wear green and red striped stocking hats.

• Snoopy, hugging Woodstock, sits on his green doghouse, which is strung with Christmas lights.

• Snoopy lies on his green doghouse. He wears a red and white striped scarf that is wrapped around Woodstock and friends, who are on his tummy.

"PEANUTS Outdoor Fun Ornaments." The design appears on each side. Wood. Series #86474, Silvestri. 1990.

• Snoopy, as the Flying Ace, is on his green doghouse, which is decorated with a red bow. 2-1/2" x 4-1/8". $7-9

• Charlie Brown stands next to his "Charlie Brown" Christmas tree. 2-1/2" x 3". $8-10

• Charlie Brown stands by a snow mound where Snoopy, Woodstock, and his friends are buried in the snow showing only their faces. 4" x 3". $8-10

"PEANUTS In Wreath Ornaments." The design appears on each side. Characters are presented inside a green wreath with a red bow. Wood. 3-7/8" x 4". Series #86475, Silvestri. 1990. $7-10 ea.

• Linus is sucking his thumb and holding his blanket.

• Snoopy is giving Woodstock a big hug.

• Charlie Brown, with his arms outstretched in a welcoming-type of greeting.

39. Ornaments

"Snoopy Mistletoe Ornament." Each ornament is printed "Mistletoe." The design appears on each side. Wood. 4-1/2"H. Series # 4362, Silvestri. 1990. $8-12 ea.

• Snoopy hugs Charlie Brown under the mistletoe.

• Snoopy, wearing a stocking cap, kisses

Lucy on the nose under the mistletoe. Printed: "Smack!"

• Snoopy, sitting and wearing a Santa hat, hugs Woodstock under the mistletoe. Cookies, milk, and a note printed "for Santa" are on the mantel.

40. Ornaments

Ornaments flicker when plugged into a set of lights. Series of five. Resin, Hallmark.

• Snoopy and Woodstock are inside a Christmas stocking hung on a fireplace. Cookies, milk, and a note printed "For Santa," are on the mantel, "91" is printed on the stocking. Printed on the back of the fireplace: "The stockings were hung by the chimney with care…" Fire in the fireplace flickers. First in a series. 3"H. #QLX722-9. 1991. $35-40 $55-65*

• Snoopy and Woodstock sit atop Snoopy's snow-covered and decorated doghouse, wrapped in a blue blanket. "1992" is printed over the doorway; "Happy Holidays" is printed on the opposite side. Lights on the wreath blink. Second in a series. 3-15/16"H. #QLX721-4. 1992. $22-28 $45-50*

• Snoopy and Woodstock, wearing stocking caps, look at a Christmas tree decorated with Woodstock's friends and lights that blink. Presents are underneath the tree. The star on top of the tree is printed "93." Third in a series. 3-1/2"H. #QLX715-5. 1993. $20-25 $30-35*

41. Ornaments

• Snoopy, ringing a bell, and Woodstock, holding a book, stand under a blue lamppost. "94" is printed in the snow next to Woodstock. The light in the lamppost flickers. Fourth in a series. Resin. 4-1/8"H. #QLX715-5, Hallmark. 1994. $10-12 $30-40*

• Snoopy is ice-skating, and has etched "95 Merry Christmas" into the ice. Woodstock and his friend lie in the snow, and sit on top of a snowman. Snoopy spins when the ornament is turned on. Fifth and final in a series. Resin and plastic. 4-1/8"H. #QLX727-7, Hallmark. 1995. $15-20 $25-30*

• "Schroeder and Lucy," sculpted by Robert Chad. Schroeder, in formal attire, plays a white piano. Lucy, in a red dress, leans on the piano. Printed "1996" on the back of the base. Plays "Linus and Lucy," written by Vince Guaraldi. Resin. 4"L x 2-1/2"H. #QLX7394, Hallmark. 1996. $15-20 $25-30*

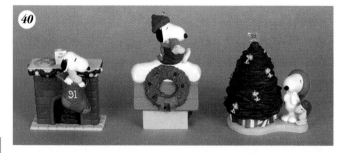

42. Ornament

•Charlie Brown, Snoopy, Linus, and Lucy ride carousel horses on a merry-go-round. Twist the base, and the ornament revolves, and the characters move up and down on the horses. Plastic. 3-1/2"H. #8518, Willitts Designs. 1988. $15-18 $20-25*

43. Ornaments

PVC. Assortment #21793, Applause. 1990. $15-18 ea.

•Snoopy, wearing a Santa hat, holds Woodstock inside a red stocking with a yellow bow. 2"H.

•Charlie Brown, wearing a Santa hat, rides on a shooting star. 2-3/4"H.

•Linus, wearing a Santa hat and sucking his thumb, holds his blanket, which points up in the air as if it were frozen. 3"H.

44. Ornaments

"Snoopy Miniature Enchantments." Approximately 1"H. Applause. 1989. $16-24 ea.

Series 53052

•Snoopy, dressed as the Easter Beagle, holds Woodstock.

•Woodstock hatches from an Easter egg.

•Snoopy sits in a basket with Easter eggs.

•Snoopy holds an Easter egg.

Series 660627

•Snoopy, dressed as Santa, carries a white gift sack over his shoulder.

•Snoopy sits in a red shoe decorated with holly.

•Snoopy sits with a blue and red gift box.

•Snoopy holds a wreath.

Series 510088

•Snoopy, wearing a yellow and green cap and green scarf, holds a yellow song book.

•Snoopy rides on a sled, his ears pointed straight back from the wind.

•Snoopy, dressed as Santa with a gift sack, goes down a decorated chimney.

•Woodstock stands on Snoopy's head, holding mistletoe. Snoopy has a lip print on his cheek.

45. Ornaments

"Charlie Brown & The PEANUTS Gang Christmas Ornaments." Set of twelve sold at a rate of one per month. At one point, the box was sent to the purchaser. Resin. Danbury Mint. 1993. $32-40* ea.

•Peppermint Patty is asleep at her desk, with "The Story of Christmas" on her head. A gift with an apple on top is at her feet. 3-1/2"H.

•Snoopy, as Joe Cool, and wearing a Santa hat, stands next to his decorated doghouse. Woodstock, wearing sunglasses, sits on top. 3"H.

•Schroeder plays his piano, which has a Christmas tree on top. 3" x 2-1/2".

•Sally sits on the floor, writing a note to Santa. Milk and cookies are at her side. 2-3/4"H.

•Woodstock, wearing a cap, holds a large ball ornament. 2"H.

•Lucy, wearing a Santa hat and a purple dress, is holding mistletoe. 2-3/4"H.

•Linus, dressed as Santa, holds a small green present and his blanket. 3"H.

•Charlie Brown gets tangled up in ribbon as he wraps a present. 3"H.

•Spike sits in a cactus that is decorated like a Christmas tree, with a star on top. 3-1/2"H.

•Snoopy comes out of a wrapped present with a tag that says "Don't Open Until Christmas." 3-1/2"H.

•Pigpen is tangled in a string of Christmas lights. 2-3/4"H.

•Marcie, with a box of ornaments at her feet, holds a banner printed "Merry Christmas." 3"H.

46. Ornaments

Adventure series. Ceramic. Series #1140, Determined Productions. 1975.

•Snoopy is dressed as an American Indian. #1144. $55-65

•Snoopy, is dressed as an outlaw. #1143. $55-65

•Snoopy is dressed as Davy Crockett in a coonskin cap. #1146. $55-65

•Snoopy is dressed as Robin Hood. #1142. $30-35

•Snoopy is dressed as Sherlock Holmes, and holds a magnifying glass. #1145. $30-35

•Snoopy, is dressed as a circus clown with a red nose. #1141. $70-80

47. Ornaments

Bicentennial series. Ceramic. Series #1099, Determined Productions. 1975-76. $50-55 ea.

•Snoopy waves a paper American flag. #1097.

•Snoopy plays a red, white, and blue drum. #1096.

•Snoopy wears a red, white, and blue Uncle Sam hat. #1098.

48. Ornaments

Cable Car series. Ceramic. Series #1330, Determined Productions. Early 1980s. $55-65 ea.

•Snoopy, wearing a Santa hat, sits on top of a green cable car. #1336.

•Woodstock sits on top of a red cable car. #1337.

•Snoopy lies on top of a red cable car, with his feet in the air. #1335.

•Woodstock, wearing a Santa hat, sits on top of a green cable car. #1338.

49. Ornaments

Dated and boxed. Each ornament is printed "Merry Christmas 1977." Ceramic. Made by Determined Productions exclusively for the Dupont Collection, Ltd., Chicago, IL. 1977. $20-25* ea.

•Snoopy lies on top of his doghouse, which has a wreath on the roof.

•Snoopy, wearing a Santa hat, holds Woodstock, who wears a green stocking cap.

•Snoopy, wearing a Santa hat, holds a poinsettia in his lap.

•Snoopy, wearing a Santa hat, holds a candy cane.

50. Ornaments

Dated. Ceramic. Determined Productions. 1978. $60-65 ea.

•Snoopy, dressed as Santa, goes down a chimney carrying a green sack. Printed on the chimney: "Merry Christmas 1978."

•Snoopy wears a red robe with angel wings on his back. Printed on the wings: "Merry Christmas 1978."

•Woodstock sits, with a green and red present at his feet. Printed on the present: "Merry Christmas 1978."

•Snoopy lies on top of a wreath. Printed: "Merry Christmas 1978."

•Snoopy stands on a green and red drum. Printed on the drum: "Merry Christmas 1978."

•Snoopy holds a red and white pole, with a sign printed "The North Pole" on the front and "Merry Christmas 1978" on the back.

•Snoopy, wearing a Santa hat, sits in a sleigh. Printed on the sleigh: "Merry Christmas 1978."

•Snoopy lies on top of the word "Noel." Printed: "1978."

51. Ornaments

Dated. Ceramic. Series #1370, Determined Productions. 1979. $60-65 ea.

•Snoopy, dressed as Santa, goes down a chimney carrying a green sack. Printed on the chimney: "Merry Christmas 1979."

•Snoopy, wearing a Santa hat, is sitting and holding a candy cane. Printed on his hat: "Merry Christmas 1979."

•Snoopy is lying on his decorated doghouse. Printed on the back of the doghouse: "Merry Christmas 1979."

•Snoopy lies on top of a wreath printed: "Happy Holidays 1979."

•Snoopy, wearing a Santa hat, is sitting and holding Woodstock. Printed on his hat: "Merry Christmas 1979." (Not pictured)

•Woodstock sits with a present at his feet. Printed on the present: "Merry Christmas 1979." (Not pictured)

52. Ornaments

Dated. Each ornament is printed "Merry Christmas 1980." Ceramic. Series #1998, Determined Productions. 1980. $60-65 ea.

•Woodstock sits inside of a red stocking with green trim.

•Snoopy, wearing angel's wings, lies in a crescent moon.

•Woodstock sits on a white star.

•Snoopy, dressed as Santa, carries a green stocking.

•Snoopy, wearing a red cap and a green coat, holds a song book while Woodstock sits on his hat.

•Snoopy, holding a candy cane and hugging Woodstock, sits inside a green stocking with red trim.

53. Ornaments

Dated. Ceramic. Determined Productions. 1981. $50-55 ea.

•Woodstock, wearing a Santa hat, sits in sleigh printed "Noel" on one side and "1981" on the other.

•Woodstock, wearing a Santa hat, holds a candy cane. Printed: "Joy 1981."

•Snoopy, wearing a Santa hat, sits on a green and red gift printed "Happy Holidays 1981."

•Snoopy, wearing a Santa hat, holds a green ball ornament printed "Merry Christmas 1981." Woodstock lies on Snoopy's nose.

•Snoopy holds a gift sack full of gifts and Woodstock. Printed on the sack: "Merry Christmas 1981."

•Snoopy leans against a candy cane printed "1981" on one side and "Noel" on the other.

54. Ornaments

Dated. Ceramic. Determined Productions. 1982.

•Snoopy, wearing a Santa hat, rides a reindeer. Printed on the reverse side: "Merry Christmas 1982." $40-45

•Charlie Brown, dressed as Santa, holds a yellow gift. Printed on the back: "Season's Greetings 1982." $40-45

•Spike is dressed as an elf in green, with red shoes. Printed on the reverse side: "Merry Christmas 1982." $60-65

•Peppermint Patty holds a gingerbread man. Printed on the back of her scarf: "Noel 1982." $45-50

•Woodstock stands next to a snowman. Printed on the snowman's hat: "Season's Greetings 1982." $45-55

•Belle, wearing a red dress, holds a green song book printed "Noel 1982." $40-45

55. Ornaments

Ceramic. Series #1028. Determined Productions. 1975. $30-35 ea.

•Linus holds a miniature Christmas tree.

•Charlie Brown holds a white present with a red bow.

•Snoopy holds a red Christmas stocking.

•Snoopy, wearing a Santa cap, carries a red sack over his shoulder.

•Lucy, wearing a red dress, holds an ornament.

•Woodstock wears a Santa cap trimmed with holly.

56. Ornaments

Ceramic. Series #1029. Determined Productions. 1975. $25-30 ea.

•Snoopy lies on a white present with a red bow.

•Woodstock sits on a red present with a green bow.

•Snoopy holds an oversized candy cane.

•Snoopy, dressed as Santa, holds a pair of yellow bells.

•Snoopy carries a Christmas tree over his shoulder.

•Snoopy holds a wreath with a red bow.

57. Ornaments

"Santa Hat Series." Ceramic. Series #1896. Determined Productions. 1981. $30-35 ea.

•Snoopy rides a hobby horse.

•Snoopy leans on two presents.

•Snoopy decorates a small Christmas tree.

•Snoopy, singing, holds a Christmas carol song book.

•Woodstock sits on a red bow inside a wreath.

•Snoopy rides on a red sled.

58. Ornaments

"General Series." Ceramic. Series #1897. Determined Productions. 1979.

•Snoopy lies inside a rainbow. $15-20

•Woodstock sits in his nest. $15-20

•Belle, wearing a pink dress, holds flowers. $18-20

•Snoopy, wearing a visor and red shirt, is roller-skating. $15-20

•Snoopy, sitting, as the Flying Ace. $15-20

•Spike wears blue overalls and a brown hat. $25-35

59. Ornaments

"International Series." Ceramic. Series #8860. Determined Productions. 1977. $55-65 ea.

•Transylvania. Snoopy wears a top hat and cape. #8879.

•Scandinavia. Snoopy, dressed as a Viking, wears a helmet and shield. #8878.

•England. Snoopy is dressed as a Royal Guard at Buckingham Palace. #8864.

•Mexico. Snoopy wears a sombrero and a serape. #8862.

•Germany. Snoopy is dressed in a Tyrolean outfit and holds a beer stein. #8863.

•India. Snoopy wears a turban. #8873.

•Italy. Snoopy is dressed as a Venetian gondolier. #8867.

•France. Snoopy, dressed as an artist, wears a beret and holds a painter's palette. #8865.

•Spain. Snoopy is dressed as a bullfighter. #8861

•England. Snoopy wears a bowler hat and carries a bumbershoot. #8880.

•Scotland. Snoopy wears a kilt and plays the bagpipes. #8866.

•Japan. Snoopy wears a kimono. #8868.

60. Ornaments

"Junk Food Series." Ceramic. Series #1905. Determined Productions. 1982. $75-85 ea.

•Snoopy stands in back of a cup of soda printed "Root Beer."

•Snoopy sits with his back to a chocolate ice cream cone.

•Snoopy lies on his tummy on top of a hamburger with "the works."

•Snoopy lies on top of a slice of cherry pie.

•Snoopy sits in a red and white bag of french fries printed "Fries."

•Snoopy lies on top of a hot dog, with mustard on it.

61. Ornaments

•"Charlie Brown Mascot Ornament." Charlie Brown wears a white baseball cap and an orange shirt with a black zigzag. Ceramic. 3"H. Determined Productions. Mid-1970s. $100-135

•"Snoopy Mascot Ornament." Snoopy is sitting on his haunches. Ceramic. 2-1/2"H. Determined Productions. Mid-1970s. $100-135

62. Ornaments

"Musician Series." Ceramic. Series #1700, Determined Productions. 1976.

- Linus plays the saxophone. #1704. $30-35
- Charlie Brown plays a red and yellow drum. #1701. $40-45
- Lucy plays the trumpet. #1703. $35-40
- Schroeder sits at his piano. #1705. $42-45
- Peppermint Patty plays the guitar. #1702. $40-45
- Snoopy plays the bass. #1706. $30-35

63. Ornament

- Snoopy is dressed as Santa. Snoopy's joints are articulated so he can stand or sit. This piece was also available as a figurine, without the ornament attachment. Ceramic. 3"H. Determined Productions. 1980. $175-250

64. Ornaments

"Sports Series." Ceramic. Series #1080, Determined Productions. 1975. Please note: Snoopy with the surfboard is not part of the Sports series, but is a stand alone ornament that also came out in 1975.

- Snoopy wears a visor and holds a tennis racket. #1086. $25-30
- Snoopy wears a red cap and holds a golf club. #1081. $40-45
- Snoopy wears pants and a white shirt printed "1976." #1085. $20-25
- Snoopy wears a red helmet and holds a football. #1083. $35-40
- Snoopy wears a green baseball cap and glove. #1084. $35-40
- Snoopy, wearing bathing trunks, flippers, and mask, stands next to a surfboard. #1152. $30-35

- Snoopy wears a green and white cap and holds a pair of skis. #1082. $25-30

65. Ornaments

"Transportation Series." Ceramic. Series #1315, Determined Productions. 1979. $30-40 ea.

- Snoopy powers a red, white, and blue boat with a Christmas tree behind him.
- Snoopy, wearing a Santa hat, sits in a locomotive.
- Snoopy, wearing a Santa hat, drives a blue convertible with a wreath on the hood.
- Woodstock, wearing a Santa hat, drives a decorated fire engine.
- Snoopy, as the Flying Ace with a gift bag, pilots a red airplane.
- Woodstock rides a red motorcycle, with presents behind him.

66. Ornaments

"Western Series." Ceramic. Series #1901, Determined Productions. 1982. $55-65 ea.

- Woodstock, wearing a white cowboy hat, sits on top of a blue and red boot.

•Snoopy, wearing a red cowboy hat, sits on a rock, playing a guitar.

•Snoopy, wearing a green neckerchief and blue shirt, rides a hobby horse.

•Snoopy, dressed as a sheriff, wears a cowboy hat, holster, badge, and red bandanna.

•Belle wears a red cowboy hat and a pink and red outfit.

•Spike wears jeans, a tall cowboy hat, and boots with spurs.

67. Ornament

•Snoopy, wearing a Santa hat, sits on top of a wreath with a red bow, hugging Woodstock. Ceramic. 4-1/8"H. Determined Productions. Late 1970s. $55-60

68. Ornaments

•Snoopy, wearing a red scarf, green boots, and a green and blue stocking cap, skis without poles, with Woodstock on the tip of the red skis. Resin. 4-1/4"L. #QX439-1, Hallmark. 1984. $40-45 $65-75*

•Snoopy, wearing a stocking cap and holding a hockey stick, tries to hit the puck, but Woodstock is sitting on it. Resin. 1-3/4"H. #QX491-5, Hallmark. 1985. $30-35 $45-50*

•Snoopy and Woodstock share a snow saucer printed "Beagle Express." Resin. 1-3/4"H. #QX438-3, Hallmark. 1986. $20-30 $30-40*

•Snoopy stands next to a Christmas tree with Woodstock sitting on top and "Snoopy" printed on the base. Resin. 2"H. #QX472-9, Hallmark. 1987. $15-18 $30-35*

•Snoopy and Woodstock are inside a red and white striped knit stocking, with a bone tied with a green bow. Resin. 2-3/8"H. #QX474-1, Hallmark. 1988. $12-15 $22-30*

•Snoopy is dressed in a top hat, bow tie, and cane, with Woodstock, dressed the same way, standing on Snoopy's hat. Resin. 3"H. #QX433-2, Hallmark. 1989. $10-12 $20-25*

69. Ornaments

•Snoopy, wearing a red and green stocking cap, is hugging Woodstock, who wears a red stocking cap. "40 Years of Happiness" is printed on the box. Resin. 2-1/4"H. #QX472-3, Hallmark. $10-12 $15-20*

•Snoopy holds a mug and a pizza on his lap. Woodstock holds a mug, and sits on the edge of the pizza. The pepperoni spells out "1991" on the pizza. Resin. 2-1/8"H. #QX519-7, Hallmark. 1991. $10-12 $18-22*

•Woodstock holds on to Snoopy's red stocking cap as Snoopy ice-skates. "92" is printed on the stocking cap's pom-pom. Resin. 2-3/4"H. #QX595-4, Hallmark. 1992. $10-12 $18-22*

•"A Tree For Snoopy." Snoopy, wearing a red and white stocking cap, pulls a Christmas tree on a sled. Resin. #QX5507, Hallmark. 1996. $10-12 $15-18*

•Miniature Ornament. "A Tree For Woodstock." Woodstock, wearing a green stocking cap, pulls a Christmas tree on a sled. Resin. #QXM4767, Hallmark. 1996. $7-10 $12-15*

70. Ornaments

"PEANUTS Gang Series." Dated. Resin. Hallmark.

•Charlie Brown is standing next to a snowman that looks like him. "93" is printed on the scarf on the snowman's back. First in the series. 2-3/8"H. #QX531-5. 1993. $12-18 $30-40*

•Lucy kneels next to a football, tied with a red ribbon. The gift tag reads, "For Charlie Brown." "94" is imprinted in the back of the football. Second in the series. 2-7/16"H. #QX520-3. 1994. $8-10 $15-20*

•Linus sits on a sled, with "95" printed on the sled behind him. Third in the series. 2-7/8"H. #QX505-9. 1995. $7-9 $12-15*

•Sally holds a pencil and a pad printed "Dear Santa." "96" is printed on the back of the pad. Fourth and final ornament in the series. #QX538-1. 1996. $6-8 $10-12*

71. Ornament Set

"A Charlie Brown Christmas." The five-piece set commemorates the 30th anniversary of the first telecast of "A Charlie Brown Christmas." Each piece in the set was boxed and sold

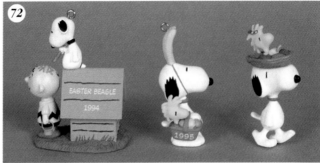

separately—one per week during the Christmas season—and required an additional Hallmark purchase. Resin. Hallmark. 1995. Set: $65-75*

•Snow-covered Base and Tree. Woodstock, wearing a Santa hat, sits in a "Charlie Brown" tree with a blue skirt and one dangling ornament. The base has fitted sections for each additional character. The underside of the base is printed "PEANUTS A Charlie Brown Christmas Television Special Happy 30th Anniversary 1965-1995 Christmas Season Of Joy." 6-7/8"L.

•Charlie Brown, arms outstretched and holding a bell, wears a yellow jacket, red scarf, green mittens, and a red and green cap. 3"H.

•Lucy, wearing a Santa hat and a purple dress, holds a candy cane. 2-1/2"H.

•Linus wears a blue jacket, with his hands in the pockets, and a yellow and green cap. 2-1/2"H.

•Snoopy wears a top hat trimmed with holly, a red shirt, and a green scarf. 2"H.

72. Ornaments

"Easter Collection." Dated. Resin. Hallmark.

•Charlie Brown stands with his back to Snoopy's lavender doghouse, printed "Easter Beagle 1994," as Snoopy paints the top of Charlie Brown's head like an Easter egg. 2-1/4"H. #QE0817-6. 1994. $10-15 $22-30*

•Snoopy, wearing bunny ears, holds onto a basket, printed "1995," filled with Easter eggs and Woodstock. 2-1/8"H. #QE0825-7. 1995. $8-10 $15-20*

•"Parade Pals." Woodstock sits on Easter eggs in his nest, which is on top of Snoopy's head. "1996" is imprinted in the side of the nest. 2-1/4"H. #QE0815-1. 1996. $8-9 $10-12*

73. Light Covers

•"PEANUTS Light Cover." Set of two light covers. Snoopy, in a green and red cap, sits with his back to a present. Snoopy and Woodstock, wearing red top hats, sit back to back. Plastic. 3-1/2"H. #30014, Silvestri. 1990. $10-12 $12-15*

Ornaments

"PEANUTS On Star." Set of three ornaments features the head of the featured characters in the center of a clear star. Resin. 4" square. #30012, Silvestri. 1990. Set: $25-35* If separate, not in package: $10-12 ea.

•Charlie Brown wears a red cap and bow tie.

•Snoopy wears red and green earmuffs and a scarf.

•Lucy wears a red beanie and muffler.

74. Ornaments

"Nightgown PEANUTS." Resin. 2-1/2"H. #30017, Silvestri. 1990. $20-25 ea.

•Sally wears a red nightgown and holds a star.

•Lucy, wearing a white nightgown and red beanie, holds a teddy bear.

•Snoopy, wearing a red nightshirt and red and green nightcap, holds a candle.

•Charlie Brown, wearing a green and red bathrobe and a red nightcap, holds a white mug.

75. Ornament Set

"PEANUTS In Santa Hat." Set of three ornaments. Resin. #30010, Silvestri. 1990. Set: $35-40* If separate, not in package: $12-15 ea.

•Lucy, dressed as Mrs. Claus, holds a gift.

•Snoopy, dressed as Santa, carries a green gift bag filled with dog bones.

•Charlie Brown wears a Santa outfit; his Santa hat is decorated with stars.

Ornament

•"Palm Tree Snoopy." Snoopy, as Joe Cool, stands under a palm tree strung with Christmas lights. Woodstock, wearing sunglasses, is sitting in the tree. Resin. 3-1/2"H. #4365, Silvestri. 1990. $20-25*

76. Ornaments

"PEANUTS Skaters." Resin. 2-1/2"H. #4366, Silvestri. 1990. $18-25* ea.

•Charlie Brown, wearing a Santa hat, red shirt, green pants, and ice skates, is sitting.

•Linus wears a Santa hat, green shirt, red pants, red and white striped scarf and ice skates.

•Lucy wears a Santa hat, red shirt trimmed in white, green skirt and red ice skates.

•Snoopy wears a top hat trimmed with holly, a green and red striped scarf and ice skates.

77. Ornaments

"PEANUTS In Stockings Ornaments." Resin. 3-1/4"H. #30015, Silvestri. 1990. $18-25* ea.

•Lucy, inside a red and green stocking with stars on it, holds a candy cane.

•Linus, wearing a red hat, is inside a red and green stocking decorated with strings of lights.

•Snoopy and Woodstock are inside a plaid red, green, and white stocking.

•Sally, holding a list for Santa, is inside a red and green stocking with snow flakes on it.

78. Ornaments

"PEANUTS Transportation." Resin. 3"H. #4367, Silvestri. 1990. $18-25* ea.

•Snoopy, dressed as Santa, rides a green skateboard with red wheels.

•Snoopy and Woodstock, wearing stocking caps, share a ride in Snoopy's supper dish.

"Snoopy/Linus Toboggan." Linus and Snoopy, wearing Santa hats, and Woodstock, share a ride on a red toboggan. Resin. 2-3/4". #4373, Silvestri. 1990. $20-25*

79. Ornaments

"Winter PEANUTS." Resin. #30013, Silvestri. 1990. $18-25* ea.

•Linus holds a snow shovel. (Good Grief! Linus is starting to look like Charlie Brown. While Silvestri identifies this ornament as Linus, it is clear that the face, although not the pose, belongs to Charlie Brown.)

•Snoopy wears a Christmas wreath with a red bow on his nose.

•Snoopy, wearing a red bow tie, is hugging Charlie Brown, who wears red earmuffs trimmed with holly, green pants, red jacket and a green scarf.

80. Ornaments

Papier-mâché. 2-1/2"H. Assortment #9752, Union Wadding. 1986. $15-20* ea.

• Snoopy lies on top of a Christmas wreath with a red bow.

• Snoopy lies on top of his doghouse, printed "Snoopy" over the doorway, and decorated with a wreath.

• Snoopy, wearing a Santa hat, carries a bag of gifts down the chimney.

• Woodstock sits with a red and green Christmas present.

• Snoopy, sitting and wearing a Santa hat, hugs Woodstock, who is wearing a green stocking cap.

• Snoopy, wearing a Santa hat, sits on top of a green cable car, trimmed with red.

81. Ornaments

Papier-mâché. Assortment #9700, Union Wadding. 1989. $15-20* ea.

• Snoopy, dressed as Santa, and Woodstock share a sleigh. 2-1/8"H.

• Sally sits in the snow. 2"H.

• Linus, holding a song book, sings Christmas carols. 3"H.

• Lucy holds a Christmas present. 2-1/2"H.

• Peppermint Patty holds a tiny present in her hand. 2-1/2"H.

• Charlie Brown carries a Christmas tree over his shoulder. 3"H.

82. Ornaments

Resin. Willitts Designs. 1992. 20-25* ea.

• Snoopy, sitting and wearing a lavender and blue stocking cap, holds a red Christmas gift. 2-1/4"H. #44043.

• Snoopy decorates the roof of his doghouse, while Woodstock decorates a Christmas tree on top of the doghouse. Printed under the base: "1992 Christmas Signature Series Sixth Limited Edition." Part of a collection of dated musicals, plates, and bells issued annually at holiday time. 2-1/2"H. #44040.

• Snoopy wears red antlers and gold sleigh bells around his neck. 2-1/2"H. #44044.

• Sally wears a pink dress and lavender angel wings on her back. 2-1/2"H. #44042.

83. Ornaments

"Miniature Snowfall Ornaments." Resin base decorated with holly. 2-3/4"H. Willitts Designs. 1991. $50-55 ea.

• Snoopy, dressed as Santa, carries a green sack over his shoulder. #44034.

• Snoopy holds a present, and Woodstock sits on his head. #44033.

Ornaments

"Christmas Pageant Ornaments." Porcelain. Willitts Designs. 1990. $20-25* ea.

• Snoopy, dressed as a shepherd, holds a staff. 1-3/4"H. #44014.

• Charlie Brown, dressed as a shepherd, clasps his hands under his chin. 2-1/4"H. #44015.

84. Ornaments

"Baseball!" Porcelain. 2"H. Willitts Designs. 1988. $30-35* ea.

• Lucy wears a blue dress, red baseball cap, and glove. #8519.

• Linus wears a red baseball cap, sucks his thumb, and holds his blanket. #8524.

• Charlie Brown wears a red baseball cap, and holds a baseball in his glove. #8520.

• Peppermint Patty wears a red baseball cap and glove. #8523.

• Schroeder wears a catcher's mask over his red baseball cap, a chest protector, and glove. #8522.

• Snoopy, wearing a red baseball cap with Woodstock sitting on top, holds a baseball bat. #8521.

85. Ornaments

Ceramic. 3"H. Willitts Designs. 1987. $20-25* ea.

• "Skating Snoopy." Snoopy, wearing a yellow and blue stocking cap and red scarf, is ice-skating. #7856.

• "Lucy." Lucy, wearing a green and red cap, holds a sign between her hands printed "Noel." #7857.

• "Sledding Snoopy." Snoopy, wearing a red, green, and white cap, and a green and yellow scarf, sits on a red and yellow sled. #7905.

86. Ornaments

• Snoopy, wearing a baby's bonnet and a diaper, lies on his tummy on top of his doghouse, printed "Baby's First Christmas" and trimmed with lace and a blue bow. Porcelain. 3"H. #9358, Willitts Designs. 1989. $15-20*

• Snoopy, wrapped in a pink blanket, is being delivered by Woodstock. The cloud above is printed "Baby's First Christmas." Resin. 3-3/4"H. #44026, Willitts Designs. 1992. $15-20*

• Snoopy and Woodstock share a swing printed "Our First Christmas." Resin. 3-3/8"H. #44025, Willitts Designs. 1992. $15-20*

87. Ornaments

Dated. Ceramic. Part of a collection of dated musicals, plates, and bells issued annually at holiday time. Willitts Designs.

• Snoopy, lying on his tummy and wearing a red, white, and green stocking cap, leans over the roof of his decorated doghouse. Woodstock sits on Snoopy's back. Printed on the back of the doghouse: "Christmas 1987." 3"H. #7707. 1987. $25-30*

• Snoopy, wearing a red and yellow top hat, red jacket and green scarf, sings Christmas carols. "1988" is printed on the yellow band on his hat. 3"H. #8929. 1988. $22-25*

• Snoopy, wearing a pink and blue stocking cap, carries a Christmas tree over his shoulder. "1989" is printed on the blue band on his cap. 3"H. #9353. 1989. $25-30*

• Snoopy, wearing a Santa cap, sits on his snow-covered decorated doghouse. "Christmas 1990" is printed over the doorway. 3-3/4"H. #44003. 1990. $20-25*

• Snoopy, wearing a green and white cap, and Woodstock share a red toboggan. Printed underneath the toboggan: "1991 Christmas Signature Series Fifth Limited Edition." 2-3/8"H. #44032. 1991. $18-22*

88. Ornaments

"PEANUTS Players Ornaments." Also sold as figurines. Porcelain. 2"H. Willitts Designs. 1988.

• Snoopy wears a visor, and holds a tennis racket. #9470. $15-20*

• Snoopy, wearing a yellow cap and green jacket, holds a golf club, ready to hit a golf ball. #9471. $15-20*

• Snoopy wearing a red, white, and blue uniform, holds a hockey stick. #9468. $18-25*

• Lucy, wearing a red dress, kneels beside a football. #9467. $15-20*

• Snoopy, wearing blue shorts and shirt, holds a basketball. #9469. $15-20*

• Snoopy, wearing a red and white uniform printed "2", kicks a soccer ball. #9476. $18-25*

89. Ornaments

Each character rides a carousel horse. Porcelain. 3"H. Willitts Designs. 1988. $22-30* ea.

• Snoopy. #8514.

•Linus. #8517.

•Charlie Brown. #8516.

•Lucy. #8515.

90. Ornaments

Ceramic. 3"H. Willitts Designs. 1987. $15-25* ea.

•Charlie Brown, wearing a yellow cap and green coat, holds a red Christmas stocking. #7854.

•Snoopy, as the Flying Ace, sits on top of a green present with a red bow. #7853.

•Woodstock, wearing a blue and green stocking cap, sits on a white bell trimmed in red. #7855.

•Snoopy, as Joe Cool, wears a Santa hat, sunglasses, and holds a yellow star. #7852.

91. Ornaments

"The Skaters." Ceramic. 3"H. Willitts Designs. 1988. $15-25* ea.

•Charlie Brown, arms outstretched and heels together, wears a red cap, green jacket, and ice skates. #8432.

•Lucy, arms outstretched and heels together, wears a red dress and white ice skates. #8431.

•Snoopy, arms outstretched and heels together, wears a red and white striped stocking cap and ice skates. #8433.

92. Ornaments

"PEANUTS Waterglobe Ornaments." Green and red holly design on top of each ornament. 2-1/4"H. Series #30019, Silvestri. 1990. $45-55* ea.

•Lucy holds a candy cane.

•Charlie Brown holds a Christmas wreath.

•Snoopy wears a Santa hat.

•Woodstock sits in the curve of a candy cane.

93. Glass Screen Candle Holder

•Snoopy, wearing a red and green stocking cap, rides in a sleigh being pulled by Woodstock. The candle, which is included, sits on the pine base behind the glass screen. 4"W x 4-1/2"H. #8513, Willitts Designs. 1988. $25-30*

Candle Holder

•Snoopy, Lucy, and Charlie Brown, wearing ice skates, stand on a snow-covered base with their arms outstretched and their backs to the candle holder. Candle is included. Ceramic and glass. 3"H x 4-1/2" diam. #8447, Willitts Designs. 1988. $25-30*

Pillar Candle Holder

•Snoopy, wearing a red and green stocking cap, rides in a sleigh being pulled by Woodstock. Candle not included. Ceramic. 4-1/4"H x 3-3/4" diam. #8621, Willitts Designs. 1988. $15-20

Tin With Candle

•Snoopy, wearing a red scarf, and Woodstock, wearing a Santa hat, are dancing in the snow on the lid, surrounded by holly. Woodstock and his friends, wearing Santa hats, are pictured flying around the candle tin. The tin has a holly berry scented candle. 2-1/2"H. #7862, Willitts Designs. 1987. $10-12

95

Candle Holder
•Snoopy, in a top hat and green scarf, holds a candy cane. The candle is placed beneath Snoopy. His hat is open at the top to allow the candle to breathe. Ceramic. 4-1/2"H. #7864, Willitts Designs. 1987. $25-35*

94. Candle
•"Snoopy Pumpkin Candle." Snoopy lies on his tummy atop a jack-o'-lantern. 3"H. #7908, Willitts Designs. 1987. $12-15

Candle Holder
•Snoopy, wearing a purple cape, sits with his back to a jack-o'-lantern and a "Trick or Treat" bag at his feet. Candle is included. Ceramic. 4"W x 2"H. #7907, Willitts Designs. 1987. $35-40*

Tin With Candle
•Woodstock and his friend, wearing masks, fly under a crescent moon on the lid. Snoopy, wearing a cape and eating treats, and Woodstock, sitting on a jack-o'-lantern, are in a pumpkin patch. The tin has a lemon-scented candle. 2-1/2"H. #7904, Willitts Designs. 1987. $10-12

95. Halloween Lighted Snowfall
•Snoopy wears a mask and cape inside the snowfall. Some snowfalls had a blinking light. Non-blinking snowfalls had a weak light. Warning: Water in snowfalls may become cloudy, figures inside may become moldy. Battery-operated. Ceramic figure, wood base. 5"H. #7906, Willitts Designs. 1987. Flashing: #40-55* Non-Flashing: $25-30*

96. Nativity Set
"Christmas Pageant Collection." Seven porcelain figurines and cardboard pop-up crèche backdrop. #9912, Willitts Designs. 1989. $200-250*

•"Christmas Pageant Collection With Musical Wooden Crèche." Seven porcelain figurines. The star on the crèche revolves as it plays "O Little Town Of Bethlehem." #44029, Willitts Designs. 1990. $300-400*

Note: The musical wooden crèche and the figurines could also be purchased individually. Like the Hungerford Schroeder and his piano, where the piano has no features tying it to the PEANUTS characters, the baby Jesus in the cradle has no features tying it to the PEANUTS characters, and may require some hunting.

•Musical wooden crèche. #44039. $135-140*

•Charlie Brown. 2-1/4"H. #9692. $45-50*

•Linus. 2-1/4"H. #9693. $45-50*

•Schroeder at his piano, with Woodstock on top. 2-1/2"W x 2"H. $45-50*

•Snoopy. 1-3/4"H. #9690. $45-50*

•Lucy. 2"H. #9691. $45-50*

•Baby Jesus in a cradle. 1-1/2" x 1"H. #9689. $45-50*

•Sally. 2-1/4"H. #9694. $45-50*

97. Package Toppers
Stuffed fabric dolls. 4"H. Assortment #21791, Applause. 1990. $4-6 ea.

Woodstock wears a red cap and a green apron with painted items in the pocket.

Snoopy wears a green cap and a red apron with painted items in the pocket.

Snoopy is dressed as Santa.

Package Toppers
Stuffed fabric dolls. 4-1/8"H. Assortment #21581, Applause. 1989. $5-8 ea.

•Snoopy, with a red body, wears a red and white striped stocking cap and holds a candy cane.

•Snoopy, with a red body, wears a red and white striped stocking cap and holds a green stocking.

•Snoopy, with a red body, wears a red and white striped stocking cap and holds a teddy bear.

•Woodstock wears a red scarf, and red and white striped booties.

96

97

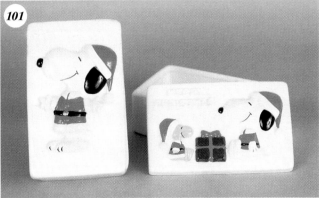

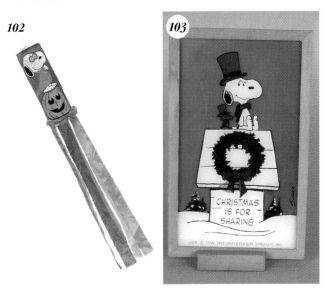

98. Figurines

"PEANUTS Pumpkin Patch Miniatures." Came as a set of five. Resin. #QFM813-1, Hallmark. 1996. $50-55*

• Snoopy, as the Flying Ace, is atop his doghouse. Printed "Welcome Great Pumpkin."

• Sally, wearing a blue dress, leans on two pumpkins.

• Linus, wearing a red shirt and black pants, rests his elbows on a pumpkin.

• Lucy, wearing a purple and black witch's outfit, holds a green mask.

• Charlie Brown, wearing a white sheet, carries a purple bag with a jack-o'-lantern on it.

99. Card/Gift Holders

"PEANUTS Plumpies." Plush faux fur fabric. Each plumpie has a pocket in the front and back to hold small gifts or holiday cards. Series #45-043, Holiday Products, Inc. 1986. $15-20 ea.

• Woodstock, dressed as Santa, has a green stocking around his neck. 20"H.

• Snoopy, dressed as Santa, has a small fabric Woodstock mascot in his front pocket. 21"H.

100. Christmas Stockings

Felt with felt appliqués. Simon Simple. 1971.

• Lucy, Charlie Brown, and Linus are featured, with holly leaves under their chins, and Snoopy, wearing a yellow scarf, is seen ice-skating on a white stocking with red trim. $12-15

• Snoopy, as the Flying Ace, stands inside a green wreath on a red stocking with red and white trim. 12"H. $8-12

101. Christmas Boxes

Lift-off lids. Ceramic. 4-1/2" x 2-3/4" x 2". Determined Productions. Late 1970s.

• Snoopy, dressed as Santa, is featured in a raised design. $42-46

• Snoopy and Woodstock, both dressed as Santa, sit with a gift between them in a raised design. Printed in raised lettering: "Merry Christmas." $45-50

102. Windsock

• Snoopy, dressed in a cape and mask, stands on top of a jack-o'-lantern, against a purple background. The windsock's tail pieces are purple, orange, and white. Nylon. 5'H x 6-1/2" diam. #8446, Willitts Designs. 1988. $15-25

103. Plaque

• "Little Gallery Iridescent Plaque." Snoopy and Woodstock, wearing top hats and scarves, sit on top of Snoopy's doghouse, which is decorated with a wreath. Printed on the doghouse: "Christmas Is For Sharing." The plaque has a mirrored backing to reflect light, thereby giving the design a stained glass look. The frame and stand are hand-finished wood. 3-3/8" x 5-3/8". #NLG151-3, Hallmark. 1979. $25-35

104

107

105

106

Ceramic. Determined Productions. Early 1980s.

•Large wreath. 12" diam. $175-225

•Small wreath. 5" diam. $55-65

106. Inflatables

Vinyl. Intex Recreation. 1989.

•Snoopy, dressed as Santa, rides in a sleigh pulled by Woodstock and his friends. 7'L. #48307. $15-20 $25-35*

•Snoopy, dressed as Santa, holds a gift printed "Happy Holidays." 36"H. #48305. $12-15 $18-25*

107. Stocking Hangers

•"Snoopy Christmas Stocking Hanger." Snoopy, wearing a Santa cap and sitting with a gift at his feet, holds a candy cane upside down to hang a stocking on. Plastic. 5"H. #450-60, Holiday Products, Inc. 1986. $4-6 $10-12*

•Snoopy, wearing a green and red cap and hugging Woodstock, sits on top of his doghouse, which is decorated with a wreath adorned with lights that blink. A brass hook for hanging a stocking is attached to the snow-covered base. Battery-operated. Plastic, 7"H. #XSH311-7, Hallmark. 1995. $4-6 $10-12*

•Snoopy and Woodstock share a red toboggan. Snoopy's green scarf hangs down to form the hook to hang the stocking. Plastic. 2-1/2" x 3". #QHD816-3, Hallmark. 1984. $5-7 $15-18*

108. Christmas Tray

•Snoopy, wearing a red scarf, and Woodstock, wearing a Santa hat, are dancing in the snow, surrounded by holly. Metal. 12" diam. #7859, Willitts Designs. 1987. $10-15

Christmas Stationery

•Snoopy, wearing a red scarf, and Woodstock, wearing a Santa hat, are dancing in the snow on the lift-off lid. Plain white paper is inside the blue tin. 5"W x 3-1/2"H x 1-1/2" diam. #7860, Willitts Designs. 1987. $7-9

104. Decorative Tile

•"PEANUTS Collector Tile." Woodstock and his friends wrap presents and put them in the sleigh, as Snoopy checks a list. Printed: "Merry Christmas 1978." Ceramic. 5-3/4" x 5-3/4". Determined Productions. 1978. $25-35*

Coasters

•Tin with lid, comes with six coasters featuring Snoopy wearing a red scarf, and Woodstock, wearing a Santa hat, dancing in the snow. 3-1/2" diam. #7861, Willitts Designs. 1987. $20-25

105. Christmas Wreaths

Snoopy, wearing a Santa hat and hugging Woodstock, sits on top of a dark green wreath with a red bow and holly berries.

109. Ornament Books

Hard cover mini-books, with gold string for hanging. Also available without the gold string. See page 185 in Library chapter. 2-1/8" x 2-3/4". Assortment #1048, Determined Productions. 1981. $7-10 ea.

•"Love Is ... Walking Hand-In-Hand." Charlie Brown and Peppermint Patty hold hands on a pink background.

•"Christmas Is Together Time." Snoopy lies on top of his doghouse, while Woodstock, dressed as Santa, and his friends stand on Snoopy's nose, tummy, and feet against a green background.

•"I Need All The Friends I Can Get." Snoopy lies on top of his doghouse, while Woodstock and his friends stand on Snoopy's nose, tummy, and feet against a blue background.

•"Happiness Is ... A Warm Puppy." Snoopy sits against a red background.

110. Christmas Decoration

•"Snoopy Sleigh—House Home Decoration." Snoopy, wearing a Santa hat and red scarf, sits on his doghouse holding green yarn reins which are attached to Woodstock and his friend, both of whom have real feathers. Cardboard. 20"H. Hallmark. 1972. $7-9 $15-20*

111. Bowl

•Woodstock and his friends, wearing ice skates, pull the letters of the word "Noel." A wreath stands in for the letter "O." Snoopy, sitting with small hearts around him, watches. Milk glass. 2-3/8"H x 4" diam. Anchor Hocking. Late 1970s. $10-12

Mug

•Snoopy holds a wreath with a red ribbon on it. Woodstock is flying, with one end of the ribbon in his beak. "Noel" is printed on the mug. The wreath stands in for the letter "O." Milk glass. 10 oz. Anchor Hocking. Late 1970s. $8-10

STORAGE

112. Skate Cases

•Snoopy and Woodstock sit together on a bench, wrapped in a blanket and hold pennants printed "Rah." The inside of the case is lined with white paper, featuring Snoopy in different poses. Metal. 16" x 6-1/2" x 12". Armored Luggage. Mid-1970s. $70-85

•Schroeder plays his piano; Snoopy sits on top of it; Sally, Charlie Brown, Violet, Peppermint Patty, Lucy, and Linus are all around the piano; and Woodstock flies upside down overhead. The case was available in different colors. It is pictured in full color on a green background and in black and white. The inside of the case is lined with white paper, featuring Snoopy in different poses. Metal. 17-1/2" x 5-1/4" x 10". Armored Luggage. Mid-1970s. Black & white: $75-100 Green: $65-75

113. Skate Case

•Snoopy is featured in different poses and outfits, such as the Flying Ace, a golfer, lying on his doghouse, and Joe Cool. The inside of the case is lined with white paper, featuring Snoopy in different poses. Metal. 16" x 6-1/2" x 12". Armored Luggage. Mid-1970s. $70-85

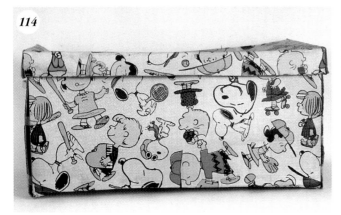

114

Suitcase

•Snoopy is featured in different poses and outfits such as the Flying Ace, a golfer, lying on his doghouse, a skier, and Joe Cool. Canvas-like fabric with red vinyl piping and red plastic handle. 19" x 4" x 12". Armored Luggage. Mid-1970s. $25-30

114. Storage Box

•Snoopy, Charlie Brown, Lucy, Schroeder, Sally, Linus, and Peppermint Patty appear in different poses on the chest and cover. Corrugated fiberboard, with plastic handles. 28" x 16-1/2" x 12-1/2". Sold through Sears. 1974. $25-35

115. Storage Box

•Snoopy, Charlie Brown, Lucy, Sally, and Linus appear in different poses on the chest and cover. Corrugated fiberboard, with divider in center. 13-1/2" x 13-1/2". Sold through Sears. 1974. $25-35

116. Steamer Trunk

•Schroeder plays his piano; Snoopy sits on top of it; Sally, Charlie Brown, Violet, Peppermint Patty, Lucy, and Linus are gathered all around the piano; and Woodstock flies upside down overhead. Printed around the characters: "Happiness Is..." The sides feature Snoopy and Woodstock dancing; Snoopy and Woodstock wrapped in a blanket and holding pennants printed "Rah"; and Snoopy lying on Charlie Brown's head. Metal. 30" x 16" x 12". Armored Luggage. Mid-1970s. $250-350

117. Trunk

•Snoopy is featured in different poses and outfits such as the Flying Ace, a golfer, lying on his doghouse, and Joe Cool.

116

The inside of the case is lined with white paper, featuring Snoopy in different poses. Metal with vinyl handles. 17-1/2" x 17-1/2" x 16-1/2". Armored Luggage. Mid-1970s. $170-190

118. Storage Chest

•Snoopy, as Joe Cool, appears on each side and on the removable cover. Printed: "Joe Cool." Fiberboard with metal trim. 15-1/2" x 16-1/2". #000090-05, Trojan Luggage Co. 1988. $65-80

119. Storage Chest

•Snoopy is surrounded by skis, a soccer ball, basketball, hockey stick, baseball and glove, and a football, on each side and on the removable cover. Printed: "A Beagle For All Seasons." Fiberboard with metal trim. 15-1/2" x 16-1/2". #000090-03, Trojan Luggage Co. 1988. $65-80

•Snoopy and Charlie Brown ride in a pink convertible, with Woodstock sitting on the hood on each side and on the removable cover. Printed: "SNOOPY & CO.!" Fiberboard with metal trim. 15-1/2" x 16-1/2". #000090-02, Trojan Luggage Co. 1988. $65-85

120. Storage Chest

•Snoopy is lying on top of his doghouse, with Woodstock lying on his tummy on each side and on the removable cover. Printed: "Best Of Friends." Fiberboard with metal trim. 15-1/2"W x 16-1/2"H. #000090-04, Trojan Luggage Co. 1988. $65-85

•Snoopy, as the Flying Ace, and Woodstock, dressed in aviator gear, sit on top of the doghouse, surrounded by WWI airplanes on each side and on the removable cover. Printed:

"Flying Ace." Fiberboard with metal trim. 15-1/2"W x 16-1/2"H. #000090-01, Trojan Luggage Co. 1988. $65-85

121. Storage Chest

•Woodstock, wearing pale pink sunglasses, is pictured on each side and on the removable cover. Printed: "Joe Cool." Fiberboard with metal trim. 15-1/2"W x 16-1/2"H. #000090-06, Trojan Luggage Co. 1988. $70-90

The mini garbage pail on the floor; the quilted Snoopy's head on the wall; and the luxurious yellow Joe Cool towel set are all from Japan. On the shelf is a whimsical tissue box cover in the shape of Snoopy's dog house (Japan), and several containers of toiletry items (shampoo, talcum powder, etc.) from England. On the right of the shelf is a ceramic cup with toothbrush (Japan), and on the shelf is a pink hairbrush, also from Japan. The ceramic cup on the sink is from Japan, as is the pink and white soap dish next to it. The sign on the wall, which reads "toilet," was purchased in Singapore.

The PEANUTS Home Collection

The Bathroom

Needless to say, the items in the bathroom are devoted mostly to cleanliness and cosmetics. Bathtub toys are very popular both with mothers and with collectors. It is interesting to note that although most of the PEANUTS characters are represented in the bathroom, Pigpen is conspicuously absent—except on the laundry bag!

AVON PRODUCTS

PEANUTS Avon products can be found incomplete, either in or out of the box. An asterisk (*) after the second range of prices means, for example, that the shampoo is still in the container, the soaps are there, etc., and that the box is present. Know what you should be getting, and pay accordingly.

1. Snoopy's Surprise Package

•Snoopy is wearing a blue baseball cap. His body holds men's cologne. Packaged in a cardboard box resembling a crate, with a red ribbon. The cologne was available in three scents: Wild Country After Shave, Sports Rally Lotion, and Excalibur. Milk glass container with vinyl ears and plastic baseball cap. 5 oz. Avon Products. 1969. $7-9*

Snoopy & Doghouse Non-Tear Shampoo

•Snoopy stands against his doghouse, which holds the shampoo. Plastic. 3"H. 8 oz. Avon Products. 1969. $4-6 $10-12*

PEANUTS Pals

•Snoopy hugs Charlie Brown, who wears a yellow baseball cap. Their bodies hold non-tear shampoo. Plastic. 6 oz. Avon Products. 1971. $4-7 $10-12*

2. Charlie Brown Bath Mitt and Soap

•Charlie Brown, wearing a red shirt with a black zigzag, is the sponge bath mitt. A wrapped bar of soap is included. The bath mitt will dry out and deteriorate over time. 10"H. 3 oz. Avon Products. 1969. $15-22**

3. Toiletry Mugs

Milk glass, with color-coordinated metal lids. The lid is often missing when item is found out of the box. 5"H. 5 oz. Avon Products. 1969. $4-10 ea. $15-20* ea.

•"Charlie Brown Bubble Bath." Charlie Brown wears a baseball cap and glove, and holds a baseball against a blue background. Printed: "Charlie Brown."

•"Lucy Non-Tear Shampoo." Lucy, wearing a red dress, holds a balloon against a yellow background. Printed: "Lucy."

•"Snoopy Liquid Soap." Snoopy, as the Flying Ace, is standing against a red background. Printed: "Snoopy."

4. Children's Sun Protection Products

"Avon Sun Seekers." Avon Products. 1989. $1-2 ea.

•"Sunblocking Stick SPF 19." Snoopy and Woodstock, wearing sunglasses, sun themselves on a beach blanket against a green and orange background. The sunblock contains aloe and Vitamin E. Plastic tube. 0.5 oz.

•"Sunblock Lotion SPF 15." Snoopy lies on top of his doghouse, under an umbrella. A sign printed "Made In The Shade" hangs on the roof. Woodstock, under an umbrella, sits in a beach chair next to the doghouse. Plastic tube. 3 oz.

•"Protective Lip Sunscreen SPF 15." Snoopy and Woodstock are windsurfing on a blue and green background. Plastic tube. 0.15 oz.

•"Ultra Sunsafe Superblocking Lotion SPF 23." Snoopy as Joe Cool, wearing sunglasses, leans against a palm tree while Woodstock, also wearing sunglasses, sits in the top of the tree against a yellow and orange background. The lotion contains aloe and Vitamin E. Plastic tube. 3 oz.

5. Snoopy and Woodstock Soap Set

•Snoopy stands next to a half of an Easter egg, and Woodstock sits with a smaller Easter egg. The graphic box features Snoopy on top of his doghouse, and Woodstock and his friends painting Easter eggs. A sign printed "Break Time" hangs on the roof of the doghouse. The box is perforated to "pop up" Snoopy on the doghouse. 3 oz. Avon Products. 1990. $3-7*

Schroeder Bubble Bath

•Schroeder, sitting, contains the bubble bath. The graphic box is shaped like a piano. It comes with a bust of Beethoven and a sheet of music that both fit onto the box. Printed: "Happiness Is . . . A Whole Tub Full Of Bubbles." Plastic. 6 oz. Avon Products. 1970. $4-6 $15-20*

Snoopy's Pal Soap Dish and Soaps

•Snoopy's red supper dish, printed "Snoopy" in raised lettering, comes with two dog bone-shaped soaps. Woodstock sits on the edge of the bowl. The dog-bone soaps are often missing when found out of the box. Plastic. Soap dish: 4-1/2" diam. Soap: 2 oz. each. Avon Products. 1973. $5-7 $12-18*

6. Soap Dish

•"Snoopy Soap Dish." A green turtle, on its back, is the soap dish that floats in water. Snoopy, hugging Woodstock, sits on the turtle's tail. Rubber. 5"L. Danara. Early 1980s. $6-9*

7. Avon Products. Plastic

4 oz. $4-10 ea. $12-20* ea.

•"Charlie Brown Non-Tear Shampoo." Charlie Brown wears a red baseball cap and a white glove. 1968.

•"Linus Non-Tear Shampoo." Linus, wearing a white sailor hat, holds his blanket and sucks his thumb. 1970.

•"Lucy Bubble Bath." Lucy wears a red dress and a red beanie. 1969.

8. Snoopy's Ski Team Bubble Bath

•Snoopy, dressed in a white turtleneck sweater, is on a pair of red skis, with Woodstock sitting on one ski. Plastic. 8 oz. Avon Products. 1974. $4-10 $12-18*

•"Snoopy Snow Flyer Bubble Bath." Snoopy, wearing a red scarf, sits on a red sled. Plastic. 10 oz. Avon Products. 1972. $4-10 $12-15*

9. PEANUTS Gang Soaps

•Set of three full-figured character soaps: Lucy in pink, Snoopy in white, and Charlie Brown in yellow. 1.75 oz. each. Avon Products. 1970. $3-5 ea. $14-20*

Snoopy Dish and Soap

•Snoopy lies on his back and holds the soap on his tummy. Comes with an oval-shaped bar of soap. Plastic. Avon Products. 1968. $3-5 $8-10*

10. Snoopy Come Home Soap Dish and Soap

•The soap dish resembles a wooden raft, with a sail featuring Woodstock sitting on Snoopy's head. Soap comes in a graphic box that matches the larger box. Plastic. 9-1/2"H. Avon Products. 1973. $4-10 $15-22*

Snoopy the Flying Ace Bubble Bath

•Snoopy, as the Flying Ace, is sitting and wearing a blue helmet and green goggles. Plastic. 6"H. 4 oz. Avon Products. 1969. $7-9*

11. Snoopy's Bubble Bath Tub

•Snoopy is in a bathtub up to his neck in light green bubbles. Plastic. 5"L. 12 oz. Avon Products. 1971. $3-8 $10-12*

12. Great Catch, Charlie Brown Soap Holder and Soap

•Charlie Brown wears a red baseball cap and a removable baseball glove palm-side-up to hold the soap. The soap holder can be mounted on a wall. Plastic. Avon Products. 1974. $4-8 $12-20*

Linus Bubble Bath Holder with Snoopy Gel Bubble Bath

•Linus holds the tube of bubble bath. Includes a suction cup for wall-mounting. Rubber. 6-1/2"H. 4 oz. Avon Products. 1968. No gel: $3-8 Complete: $20-25*

13. Brush and Comb Sets

Head of each character has the brush on the reverse side, while their bodies are the handle. Combs have no PEANUTS graphics. Plastic. Avon Products. $3-5 ea. $10-15 ea.*

• Charlie Brown wears a white cowboy hat. 1971.

• Snoopy is sitting. Brush: 5-1/2"L. 1970.

• Woodstock. 1975.

COSMETICS AND TOILETRIES

14. Toiletries and Cosmetics

Creative Specialties. 1985.

• "Snoopy Bath Bubbles." Snoopy is pictured sitting on the front of the bottle, with Woodstock sitting on top of the cap. Plastic. 16 oz. #01916. 1985. $4-6*

• "Snoopy Dresser Set." Snoopy is featured in a different pose on the comb, brush, and mirror. Each piece is printed "Hi, Sweetie!" Plastic. #01910. 1985. $3 ea. piece $10-12*

• "Snoopy & Belle Puff & Talc." Snoopy is featured on the handle of the puff, which is printed "Hi, Sweetie!" The talc comes in red canister which pictures Belle and Snoopy. Plastic. #01903. 1985. $2-3 ea. piece $8-10*

15. Soaps and Perfumes

• Snoopy Solid Perfume Pin. Snoopy is sitting. His feet slide down to reveal the solid perfume. Metal pin on back. Plastic. 0.05 oz. #01914. $3-5 $8-10*

• "Snoopy Soap." Snoopy is standing. 3.5 oz. #01911. $5-6*

• "Woodstock Soap." Woodstock. 3.5 oz. #01912. $5-6*

• "Charlie Brown Soap." Charlie Brown is wearing a baseball cap and glove. 3.5 oz. #01913. $5-6*

• "Snoopy Bath Time Gift Set." The three-piece set includes bubble bath and shampoo in bottles, with Snoopy's picture on the front, and a bar of soap shaped like Woodstock. A ribbon is wrapped around the inside of the box along the bottom. The outer cardboard box features Snoopy and Woodstock in bubbles. #01918. $2-3 ea. piece $8-12*

• "Belle Lip Glow, Blush & Roll-On Cologne Set." Belle is featured on the lip glow container, and is shown surrounded by butterflies on the blush container. "Belle" is printed on all three pieces. #01917. $6-8*

• "Snoopy Cologne." Snoopy is wearing a black top hat. Glass. 2 oz. #01906. $4-6 $8-10*

• "Belle Cologne." Belle is wearing a pink hat. Glass. 2 oz. #01902. $4-6 $8-10*

• "Snoopy and Belle Gift Set." Three-piece set includes talc, featuring Snoopy and Belle dancing on the red canister; bubble bath, in a bottle with Snoopy's picture on the front; and hand cream featuring Snoopy and Belle in tennis outfits on the tube. A ribbon is wrapped around the inside of the box along the bottom. The outer cardboard box features Snoopy and Woodstock in bubbles. #01915. $2-3 ea. piece $8-10*

16. Mirror, Brush and Comb Set

"Snoopy Bath Boutique Dresser Set." The back of the hand-held mirror features Snoopy and Woodstock dancing on a pink paper decal background printed "It's Been A Good Day!" The mirror is available with different designs. The brush and comb have no PEANUTS graphics. Plastic. #7900, Determined Productions. 1980. $8-10*

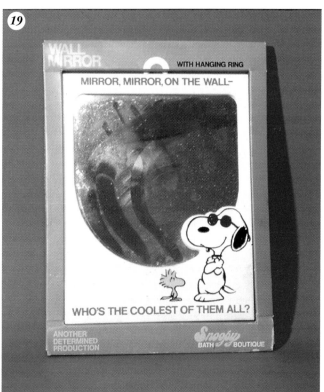

17. Bath Mitt

"Snoopy Scrubbin' Mitten." Snoopy, taking a shower, is lathering himself up with soap as Woodstock flies nearby. Terry cloth with elastic wrist band. 6" x 6". #8088, Determined Productions. 1980. $6-8*

•Powder Mitt. "Snoopy Beauty Boutique Powder Puff Mitten." Snoopy, sitting, is dusting Woodstock with a powder puff. The mitten is filled with rose-scented talcum powder. Cotton. 2.5 oz. 4-1/2" x 6". #7949, Determined Productions. 1980. $6-8*

DECORATIVE ITEMS

18. Decorative Boxes

Ceramic. Determined Productions. 1979. $45-50 ea.

•"Snoopy Bubble Tub." The lid of the green and white striped bath tub-shaped box features Snoopy up to his neck in pastel-colored bubbles. 4-1/2" x 3". #8458.

•"Snoopy Bubble Bucket." The lid of the yellow bucket-shaped box features Snoopy, up to his neck in pastel-colored bubbles. "Bubble Bath" is printed in raised lettering on the bucket. 5- 1/2" x 3-1/2". #8453.

19. Mirror

•"Snoopy Bath Boutique Wall Mirror." Snoopy, as Joe Cool, and Woodstock are pictured in the lower right corner. Printed: "Mirror, Mirror On The Wall—Who's The Coolest Of Them All?" Polystyrene. 6 1/2" x 8-1/4". #7851, Determined Productions. 1979. $8-10*

HEALTH-RELATED ITEMS

20. Vaporizer/Humidifier and Hot Water Bottle

•"Snoopy Cool Mist Vaporizer/Humidifier." Snoopy lies on top of his doghouse. Mist is released though an opening in the roof of the doghouse. Plastic. 11" x 12" x 16". #0105, AMSCO, a Milton Bradley company. 1975. $20-30 $40-45*

•Hot Water Bottle. "Snoopy Happiness Is A Warm Puppy Water Bottle." The water bottle, which holds cool, warm, or hot water, pictures a sitting Snoopy. The water bottle comes with a red plastic screw-in safety plug, and is washable and non-toxic. Vinyl. 7-1/8" x 9-1/2". #F3009, AMSCO, a Milton Bradley company. 1975. $10-15 $20-25*

LAUNDRY BAGS

21. Laundry Bags

•Snoopy carries a hobo pack over his shoulder, and wears his supper dish on his head, as Woodstock follows against an orange background with felt appliqués. Drawstring closure. Plastic lined. 18"W x 21"L. Simon Simple. 1972-1973. $15-25

•Woodstock carries three flowers on very long stems against a yellow background with felt appliqués. A hanger comes with the laundry bag. 17-1/2"W x 21"H. Simon Simple. 1974. $12-15

22. Laundry Bag

•Pigpen, wearing overalls and a baseball glove, stands in a cloud of dust on a white background. Cotton, with a drawstring closure. 22"W x 28"L. #F670, Import Specialties. 1988. $10-15

23. Laundry Bag

•Linus and Snoopy battle for Linus's blanket against a blue background around a crescent moon. Woodstock, looking dazed, spins in the air above the blanket. Cotton, with a drawstring closure. 22"W x 28"L. #F668, Import Specialties. 1988. $8-10

24. Laundry Bag

•"PEANUTS Security Bag." Schroeder, Snoopy, and Sally are featured on the front of the bag and Linus, Lucy, and Charlie Brown are featured on the reverse side. Available in orange, yellow, and red. Cotton, with a drawstring closure. 24"W x 30"L. #586, Determined Productions. 1970. $25-35

MISCELLANEOUS BATHROOM ITEMS

25. Electric Comb and Brush Set

• "Snoopy 'Lectric Comb & Brush." Snoopy holds the brush and comb, which are included, in his head. When not in use, Snoopy rests on a blue raft with a white sail printed "Snoopy." The raft stores the brush and comb. Includes instructions with PEANUTS graphics. Battery-operated. Plastic. #30900, Kenner. 1975. $12-15 $30-40*

Hair Dryer

•"Snoopy's Hair Dryer." Snoopy's nose blows the air, his body is the base, and his bow tie is the on-off switch. Plastic. #HD5061, Salton. 1990. $15-20 $25-35*

Soap Dispenser

•"Snoopy Soaper." Snoopy sits behind a booth printed "Snoopy Clean Hands Inspector." Pressing a button behind Snoopy releases soap beads. A suction cup under the base secures the dispenser to a counter top. Includes a 5-oz. box of Ivory Soap Beads and instructions with PEANUTS graphics. Plastic. #30700, Kenner. 1975. $8-10 $15-25*

Soap Refill

•"Snoopy Soaper Soap Refill." 5 oz. box of Ivory Soap Beads. The refill could be purchased where the toy was sold, or by ordering directly from the manufacturer. #30750, Kenner. 1975. $4-6*

26. Step Stool

•Snoopy's head and body form the back of the stool, and his hands surround the base, which has a non-skid rubber top. Snoopy's eyes, ear, nose, and mouth are decals. A decal printed "Snoopy Step Stool" is on the front of the base. Molded plastic. #2661 9098, Knickerbocker. 1980. $8-12 $15-22*

27. Toilet Trainer

•"Snoopy Toilet Trainer." Snoopy's head and body form the back, and his hands surround the seat. Snoopy's eyes, ear, nose, and mouth are decals. Fits any standard toilet seat. Plastic. #1560, Knickerbocker. 1980. $8-10 $15-20*

PAPER ACCESSORIES

28. Guest Towels

Paper. Hallmark. $8-10 ea.**

•Snoopy, as the Flying Ace, thinks, "Notice this is not a guest towel! It's a genuine WWI RAF flight scarf!" Woodstock, standing nearby, says, "!" 12"x17". #75GT97-2. Mid-1970s.

•Snoopy, as Joe Cool, stands in front of his doghouse thinking, "Gimme ten!" 11-3/4" x 17". #GT1087. Late 1970s.

•Pigpen, standing in a cloud of dust, says, "Cleanliness is next to impossible." 11-3/4" x 17". #75GT36-7. Mid-1970s.

•Woodstock sits in a swing under his nest, which has a rainbow in it. 11-3/4" x 17". #75GT116-2. Late 1970s.

29. Paper Cups and Dispenser

Dixie Products Group of the James River Corporation. 1986. $7-10 ea.**

•"Snoopy's Many Faces Dixie Cups." On the front of the box, Snoopy, as the Flying Ace, sits on top of his doghouse. Charlie Brown stands in front, looking at Woodstock, who wears a WWI helmet. One side of the box has a mail-in offer for a PEANUTS Dixie cup dispenser, and the reverse side of the box features puzzles and games with the PEANUTS characters. 200 3-oz. cups. UPC#42000 43900.

•"Snoopy Pop-Up Bathroom Cup Dispenser." Snoopy is hugging Woodstock against a blue background. Includes 25 3-oz. paper cups. Came in two sizes to hold either the 3-oz. or 5-oz. cups. Plastic. UPC#42000 40306.

•"Snoopy's Sports." Woodstock sits in a tennis referee's chair under an umbrella printed "New," while Snoopy plays tennis on the front of the box. One side of the box has a mail-in offer for a PEANUTS Dixie cup dispenser. The reverse side has an offer for a non-PEANUTS ice pop set. 200 3-oz. cups. UPC#42000 43900.

SOAP AND SOAP DISHES

30. Soaps

Full-figure characters. 3-1/2"H. 3.5 oz. Determined Productions. 1979. $6-10** ea.

•Charlie Brown. #8060.

•Snoopy. #8061.

•Woodstock (Not pictured). #8062.

31. Soap Dishes

•Snoopy lies on his tummy on top of the two-piece soap dish. The soap dish came trimmed in black, yellow, red, pink, or blue. Ceramic. #8422, Determined Productions. 1979. $45-50

•The old-fashioned tub-shaped soap dish features Linus; Schroeder giving a flower to Lucy; Charlie Brown holding a "Have A Nice Day" sign; Snoopy holding a sign that reads "Everyone," with Woodstock sitting on top; Peppermint Patty, Sally, and Pigpen. The image appears on both sides of the tub. The soaps pictured are not included. Ceramic. 5"L x 2-1/2"H. Determined Productions. Late 1970s. $40-45

•Snoopy is sitting, with an oval soap dish at his feet. The soaps pictured are not included. Ceramic. 6-3/4"L x 3-3/4"H. #8459, Determined Productions. 1979. $35-40

TOOTHBRUSHES AND HOLDERS

32. Electric Toothbrush

•"Snoopy & Friends Toothbrush." Snoopy, standing on a red base, holds the toothbrush in his head. Charlie Brown, Woodstock, and Lucy, holding an open tube of toothpaste, sit on the base. Includes two toothbrushes. Battery-operated. Plastic. #330, Aviva/Hasbro. 1980. $12-20 $30-40*

•Electric Toothbrush. "Snoopy Toothbrush." Snoopy is the handle when the toothbrush is inserted in his head. Toothbrush is included. Battery-operated. Plastic. #332, Determined Productions. 1980. $6-10 $15-20*

•Electric Toothbrush. "Snoopy Brusha Brusha Toothbrush." Snoopy, standing on a red base, holds the toothbrush in his head. The base holds a cup featuring Snoopy, with Woodstock leaning against him and singing atop his dog-house, and two toothbrushes. Battery-operated. Plastic. #70330, Aviva/Hasbro. 1982. $8-12 $18-22*

33. Soap Dish and Toothbrush Holder Bath Set

•Woodstock, wearing an engineer's hat, sits on a flatbed rail car which is the soap dish. Snoopy is the engineer of the locomotive that holds four toothbrushes and 3-oz. paper cups. Ceramic. Soap dish: 5-3/4"L x 2-5/8"H. Toothbrush holder: 6"L x 5-1/4"H. #45032, Willitts Designs. 1991. The toothbrush holder was also sold separately under #45031. Soap dish: $10-12. Locomotive: $12-15. Set: $25-30*

34. Electric Toothbrushes

•"Snoopy Doghouse Toothbrush." Snoopy lies on one end of his elongated doghouse, while Woodstock is in his nest at the other end. Printed: "Snoopy." The toothbrush is inserted into the doorway of the doghouse beneath Woodstock.

Includes two toothbrushes. Battery-operated. Plastic. 7"L. #311, Aviva/Hasbro. 1980. $12-18 $22-32*

•"Snoopy Toothbrush." Snoopy holds the toothbrush in his head. He rests on his doghouse when not in use. The roof of the doghouse holds two toothbrushes, which are included, and a toothpaste tube. Also includes hardware for mounting on a wall, a dental care booklet, and two adapters for use with refill toothbrushes. The graphic box features four-panel comic strips on two of the sides. Battery-operated. Plastic. #30301, Kenner. 1972. $10-15 $30-35*

Toothbrushes

"Snoopy And The Gang." The graphic boxes depict the scene on the toothbrushes. Characters' names are printed on the toothbrush handles. Oral B Laboratories. 1985. $2-4** ea.

•"Woodstock." Woodstock and Snoopy roller-skate on a green toothbrush.

•"Charlie Brown." Snoopy and Charlie Brown are tangled in kite string on a blue toothbrush.

•"Lucy." Lucy and Snoopy are featured on a red toothbrush.

•"Snoopy." Snoopy and Woodstock dance on an orange toothbrush.

Toothbrush Holder

•"Snoopy Brush With Me." Snoopy, wearing pajamas and holding a toothbrush and cup, stands on a blue base in front

32

33

31

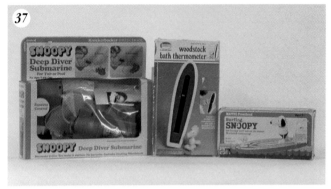

of a large red toothbrush and next to a yellow cup featuring Woodstock. Printed on the cup: "I Have A Super Smile!" Storage for toothbrushes is next to the red toothbrush. When the red toothbrush is pressed, Snoopy's eyes and the toothbrush in his hand move back and forth rapidly. No batteries required. Plastic. #5001, Determined Productions. 1985. $10-20 $30-35*

35. Toothbrush Holders

•"Snoopy Bath Boutique Toothbrush Holder." Snoopy is sitting on top of his doghouse, hugging Woodstock. They are surrounded by hearts. Plastic. 3-3/8"H. #7854, Determined Productions. 1979. $4-6*

•Snoopy lies on top of a toothbrush. Four holes extend from the handle to hold toothbrushes. There is a hole at each end for mounting the holder on the wall. Ceramic. 7-1/2"L x 4"H. #8454, Determined Productions. 1979. $30-38

•"Snoopy Bath Boutique Toothbrush Holder." Snoopy is down on one knee with his arms outstretched on top of the words "Super Smile" in front of a large red star. Plastic. 3"H. #7854, Determined Productions. 1979. $4-6*

TUB TOYS

36. Bath Tub Toys

•"Woodstock Swimmer." Woodstock swims in water after he is wound. Plastic. #743, Knickerbocker Preschool. 1982. $8-10*

•"Tub Time Snoopy." Snoopy is dressed in a removable red terry cloth robe, and has a yellow towel and brush. He is jointed, and safe to play with in water. Woodstock pilots a blue tugboat with a sponge on the bottom. #0539, Knickerbocker. Early 1980s. $15-25 $35-45*

•"Snoopy Swimmer." Snoopy swims in water after he is wound. Plastic. #742, Knickerbocker Preschool. 1982. $8-10*

37. Bath Tub Toy

•"Snoopy Deep Diver Submarine." Snoopy rides in a blue submarine. Squeeze the control device, and the submarine dives and resurfaces. Includes a floating Woodstock. Plastic. #0553, Knickerbocker. Early 1980s. $15-18 $40-50*

Bath Tub Thermometer

•"Snoopy's Pal Woodstock Bath Thermometer." The blue and white surfboard contains a liquid crystal thermometer with a range of 88-106 degrees to measure the temperature of bath water. Woodstock locks onto the surfboard, and can be removed from the surfboard with an easy twist. Wooden surfboard and plastic Woodstock. #F3006, AMSCO, a Milton Bradley company. 1975. $8-12 $15-22*

Bath Tub Toy

•"Surfing Snoopy." Snoopy and Woodstock ride a yellow and orange surfboard. Comes with a battery-pack rudder/propeller attachment which clips to the bottom of the surfboard. When turned on, Snoopy can surf to the left, the right, or straight ahead. Plastic. 9-1/2"L. #3477, Mattel Preschool. 1981. $15-20 $40-45*

In the master bedroom (above), the bedspread, sheets, and pillowcases are from the U.S.A. (see page 59, in this section.) The red, yellow, and blue pillow covers and pillows are from Japan. The three dolls—a large and small Snoopy and a small Spike—are from Mexico. Also on the bed are magazines (Japan) and, to the left of the larger Snoopy, a watch (Germany), and a card (Spain). On the wall behind the bed are three fans (Japan). The lamp on the night table is from Italy; the wooden jewelry box next to it is from Japan. In front of the jewelry box is a clock, shaped like a shoe (Hong Kong).

All of the following items are from Japan: A kimono hanging on the door; a doorknob caddie—where else?—on the doorknob; a ceramic plate high on the wall near the door; and a plastic wastebasket and green cloth magazine holder, both on the floor near the door.

On the bureau is a picture frame (Hong Kong), a wooden storage box with three drawers for little items (Japan), a bank (Hong Kong) featuring Snoopy lying on his supper dish, a small decorative Snoopy dressed in a Japanese costume (Japan), and a smaller two-drawer storage box (Japan) with a watch (Japan) on top of it. To its right is a small wooden stor-

age box with a carved Snoopy as the lid (Japan). The red diary in the front is from Italy. A large Woodstock, a product of the U.S.A., peeks through the door.

In the child's bedroom (below left), a red Joe Cool pillow cover (Japan) graces the top of the futon. On the futon itself is a yellow pillow cover complete with the PEANUTS gang (Japan), a Snoopy plush (Japan), a diary (Italy), and a cartoon book (Germany). On the stand next to the bed is a plastic Snoopy lamp (Japan) that is operated by manually opening Snoopy's mouth. Also on the stand is a glass case (Japan), and a musical jewelry box (Japan).

Above the stand is a bulletin board with stick pins (Japan), and a plastic Snoopy (Spain). A cloth zipper bag and a height-measuring device (both from Japan) hang nearby. Immediately to the right, hanging from a Snoopy-decorated doorknob (France), is a leather camera bag (Japan) with a Snoopy mask (Japan) on its strap. The tee-shirt was purchased at a Canine Companions for Independence dogfest in the USA.

In the corner, above the shelves, is a small mirror with a wooden frame (Japan). On the top shelf are two plastic banks (Japan), and a candle (The Netherlands). The middle shelf holds a clock (Germany) and two candle holders (Japan). A mailbox-shaped tissue holder (Japan) and a Peppermint Patty picture frame (Hong Kong) adorn the bottom shelf.

On the closet door, a shoe bag (Japan) hangs from another Snoopy-decorated knob-styled hanging fixture (France). A mini-kite (Japan) is in one of the pockets. A robe (Japan) hangs from the top of the door, while three cloth carry-all bags (Japan) hang from the doorknob. On the floor, in the foreground, is a backpack with school books (Japan) and a loose-leaf binder (Canada). Inside the red basket on the right (Japan) is a collection of books (Japan), and notebooks and pads (Canada and Norway). On the blue pillow (Japan) is a pair of slippers (USA). The tall basket in the rear (Japan) holds a ruler (Italy) and coloring books (Japan).

For the nursery (below), probably one of the most functional, best constructed, and visually appealing of any PEANUTS object ever produced is the baby's crib from Japan. The crib is made to rock, but a simple adjustment to bars under each end converts it to a stationary bed. Attached to the side of the crib is a large musical mobile, also from Japan—the delight of any baby. Japan also takes credit for the feeding chair/rocker to the right, and the bottle, plate and Peppermint Patty rubber doll resting on its table top. In front of the crib is a colorful diaper basket, while to the left is a wooden rocking horse, both from Japan.

The plastic, wiggly Snoopy on the front of the table to the left is from France. Next to it is a miniature car from Japan. Behind them is a white picture frame from Hong Kong, and a yellow jar, a Snoopy-on-his-house clock, a Snoopy plastic night-light, and a green-capped storage jar—all from Japan.

The Bedroom

In the real world, the nuclear family's house includes, at minimum, an adult bedroom for the parents; at least one child's room; and, if needed, an infant's bedroom (the nursery) for baby. Here in our ultimate house, since some of the collectibles can be found in more than one of the three different types of rooms, we took the liberty of grouping all of our bedroom objects into a single chapter.

A special word about the jewelry collection. Much of it is very affordable, fun to wear, and easily stored in a jewelry box. However, if you delve into the more elegant and pricey pins and charms, we highly recommend you install a wall safe in the Gallery... behind a picture of Snoopy, of course.

BABY ROOM ITEMS

1. Bibs

•Sally, Linus, Charlie Brown, Lucy, and Snoopy stand around the pitcher's mound dressed in baseball gear. Woodstock sits on Snoopy's head. Light blue and white striped terry cloth. 15" x 10-1/8". Danara. Early 1990s. $2-3*

•Woodstock flies, holding onto Snoopy wrapped in a pink blanket. Snoopy's nose squeaks when pressed. Terry cloth. 8" x 12-1/2". #3692, Determined Productions. Early 1980s. $4-6

Crib Toy

•"Snoopy Musical Crib Exerciser." Snoopy and Woodstock hang from each end, with rings on a bar in the middle. Wind the key on the back of Snoopy's doghouse to play "It's A Small World." Plastic with fabric straps. #99942, Danara. Early 1980s. $6-10 $12-16*

Blanket

•"Snoopy Security Blanket." Snoopy's head and hands are attached to a pink and blue plaid washable blanket. 13-1/2" x 13-1/2". #1430, Knickerbocker. Early 1980s. $8-10 $15-20*

Dish Set

•"Snoopy Dining-In For Toddlers." Three-piece set includes a plate, bowl, and cup. Snoopy, Woodstock, and his friends

are dressed as clowns with balloons and confetti all around. Plastic. #11113, Danara. Early 1980s. $1-3, ea. $10-15*

Teething Ring

•"Snoopy Gum Soother." Snoopy and Woodstock are pictured around the teething ring, which can be refrigerated. Vinyl. Danara. Early 1980s to the present. $2-3*

Plush Toy

•Snoopy is sitting in a baby blue and pink airplane. He is attached to the airplane, but can be removed from the seat of the plane. Plane: 9"L. Snoopy: 5"H. Determined Productions. Early 1980s. $5-8

2. Diaper Holder

•"Snoopy Doghouse Diaper Stacker." Snoopy lies on top of a light blue doghouse that opens in the front to stack diapers. Cotton diaper holder and felt Snoopy. 27"H. #S-41, Simon Simple. 1969-1970. $25-35

3. Baby Block

Snoopy is featured on each side with an object representing a letter of the alphabet—A, B, C, D, and E. A bell is inside the block. Terry cloth. 8" x 8". #8811, Determined Productions. 1978. $3-6

Toys

"Playpen Pals." The image appears on both sides. Terry cloth-covered foam. Machine washable. 8"H. Series # 8890, Determined Productions. 1978. $2-4 $8-10*

•Snoopy is dressed as a scout.

•Snoopy wears a striped jacket, bow tie, and straw hat.

•Peppermint Patty.

Not pictured:

•Snoopy is dressed as an engineer in overalls, cap, and neckerchief.

•Snoopy wears an orange cap and a yellow turtleneck sweater printed with an "S."

•Lucy is wearing a yellow dress.

•Charlie Brown.

•Linus.

4. Squeeze Toys

Each toy whistles when squeezed. Many of these squeeze toys are still available. Rubber. $4-7* ea.

•Snoopy is sitting and holding a yellow flower. 3-1/2"H. Danara. Late 1970s/Early 1980s.

•Snoopy is wearing blue overalls and a yellow hat. 6"H. Danara. Late 1970s/Early 1980s.

•Snoopy, with Woodstock sitting on his nose, and his supper dish on his head, carries a suitcase. 5-1/2"H. #55508, Danara. Late 1970s/Early 1980s.

•Snoopy is dressed as a fireman, with a yellow coat and red and yellow hat. 4-1/2"H. Danara. Late 1970s/Early 1980s.

•Snoopy is sitting and holding Woodstock. 5"H. #1566, Knickerbocker. 1980.

•Snoopy, wearing a Santa hat, holds a gift sack over his shoulder. 6"H. ConAgra. Late 1970s.

•Snoopy wears a visor and holds a tennis racket. 4-1/2"H. Danara. Late 1970s/Early 1980s.

•Snoopy wears a green and white striped hat and holds a pair of skis. 4-1/2"H. #55514, Danara. Late 1970s/Early 1980s.

•Snoopy wears a red cap and holds a golf club. 4"H. #55513, Danara. Late 1970s.

•Snoopy is standing. 5-1/8"H. Danara. Late 1970s/Early 1980s.

•Snoopy's head is above the bow of a Christmas wreath. 4-1/2"H. ConAgra. Late 1970s.

•Snoopy, dressed as a mailman, carries a sack of letters. 4-1/8"H. Danara. Late 1970s/Early 1980s.

•Snoopy is dressed as an Indian. 6"H. Danara. Late 1970s/Early 1980s.

•Snoopy, as the Flying Ace, pilots a plane. 6"L. Danara. Late 1970s/Early 1980s.

5. Baby Grooming Sets

Packaged in graphic boxes. Silver-plated. Godinger Silver Art Co., Ltd. 1990.

•"Snoopy Hairbrush/Comb Set." The oval-shaped brush features Charlie Brown in a barber shop chair, and the comb features Snoopy looking into a mirror held by Woodstock and his friends. Brush: 4-1/2". Comb: 5". #504. Brush $6-10; comb $4-8; set $15-25*

•"Snoopy 3-Pc. Child's Dresser Set." The hand-held mirror features Snoopy on his doghouse with Woodstock and his friends. The brush with a handle features Snoopy leaning over the edge of his doghouse to look at Woodstock holding a flower. The comb features Snoopy looking into a mirror held by Woodstock and his friends. Mirror: 7". Brush: 7". Comb: 5". #506. Mirror $8-12; brush $6-10; comb $4-8; set $25-35*

"Snoopy Hairbrush/Comb Set"

•"Snoopy Hairbrush/Comb Set." The brush with a handle features Lucy sitting at a vanity table brushing her hair, and the comb features Snoopy looking into a mirror held by Woodstock and his friends. Brush: 5-1/2". Comb: 5". #505. Brush $6-10; comb $4-8; set $15-25*

6. Baby Feeding Set

•"Snoopy 4-Pc. Feeding Set." The plate and cup feature Snoopy and Woodstock wearing party hats and holding root beer mugs. The fork features Snoopy wearing a party hat on the top of the handle, and the spoon features Woodstock sitting on a present on the top of the handle. Packaged in a graphic box. Silver-plated. Plate: 7" diam. Cup with plastic cover: 2-3/4" diam. Fork and spoon: 5"H ea. #503, Godinger Silver Art Co., Ltd. 1990. Plate $6-12; cup $4-8; spoon and fork $5-7 ea.; Set $32-38*

• "Baby's First Bank." Snoopy, sitting with his front paws between his back paws, wears a blue ribbon around his neck. Resin. 5"H. #3685, Justin Products, Inc. for Determined Productions. 1988. $35-45

• Snoopy and Woodstock are featured in various poses on each side of the toy block-shaped bank on a yellow and white checkered background. Objects in the scenes are accented in different colored gingham prints. Ceramic. 3" x 3". Assortment #1505, Determined Productions. Late 1970s. $25-30

11. Banks

"Baby Banks." Hard plastic. 6"H. Assortment #99999, Danara. 1985. $15-22 ea.

• Snoopy wears a green sleeper with a small Snoopy lying on his back on it.

• Snoopy, wearing a green and white hat and a red scarf, holds a pair of snow skis.

• Snoopy, wearing a red cap, holds a golf club.

• Snoopy, holding a diploma, wears a yellow graduation cap and gown.

• Snoopy wears a red diaper with a big safety pin.

• Snoopy wears a visor and holds a tennis racket.

Baby Cup

"Snoopy Baby Cup." Snoopy, wearing a party hat and holding a mug of root beer, is the handle. Comes with a plastic cover. Packaged in a graphic box. Silver-plated. 2-1/2" diam. #507, Godinger Silver Art Co., Ltd. 1990. $6-8 $10-12*

Rattle

"Snoopy Baby Rattle." Snoopy lifts weights on each side of the barbell-shaped rattle. Packaged in a graphic box. Silver-plated. 4-1/2"L. #507, Godinger Silver Art Co., Ltd. 1990. $5-7 $8-10*

7. Mobile

"PEANUTS Musical Mobile." Snoopy and Woodstock sitting on his doghouse; Linus, Lucy, Charlie Brown, and Sally hang from the mobile that plays "Brahm's Lullaby." Wood. #231-800, Nursery Originals. 1980. $20-30 $40-45*

8. Wall Hanging

"PEANUTS Wall Hanging." Snoopy is sitting, holding Woodstock and his friends and pink flowers (one of many designs). Quilted cotton. 24" x 24". Infantino. 1992. $15-25 $30-35*

BANKS

9. Banks

"Animal Series Banks." Papier-mâché. Determined Productions. Mid-1970s.

• Snoopy is sitting on a light blue chicken. #8441. $45-50

• Snoopy is sitting on a white swan. #8443. $50-55

• Snoopy lies on his back on top of a gray elephant. #8442. $55-60

10. Mini Bank

• Snoopy, wearing sunglasses, lies on top of his doghouse. "Cool Cash" is printed on the roof. Available in three colors. Ceramic. 3-1/4"H. #40019, Willitts Designs. 1989. $15-18

Banks

• Snoopy is featured on each side of the toy block-shaped bank with an object representing a letter of the alphabet—A, B, C, D, and E. Ceramic. 3" x 3". Assortment #1505, Determined Productions. Late 1970s. $25-35

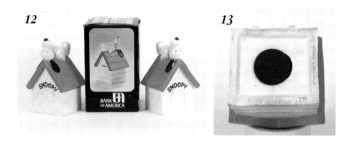

12　　　　*13*

14

12. Bank

•"Snoopy Doghouse Bank." Snoopy lies atop his doghouse. "Snoopy" is printed over the doorway. This bank was widely available for purchase in retail stores. Papier-mâché. 3-1/4" x 6". #0918, Determined Productions. 1969. $8-12

13. Bank

•"Snoopy 'Bank Of America' Doghouse Bank." This bank, while identical to the bank described above, was a premium given to customers who opened accounts with Bank of America in the early 1970s. "Bank Of America" is printed on the bottom of the bank. The bank came packaged in a box with the bank's name and logo on it. Papier-mâché. 3-1/4" x 6". Determined Productions for Bank of America. Early 1970s. Stamped BANK OF AMERICA　$25-35　$45-55*

14. Banks

"Baseball Series Banks." Papier-mâché. Approximately 7"H. Determined Productions. 1973.

•Peppermint Patty, wearing a red baseball cap to the side, leans on a bat. #0929. $50-60

•Schroeder wears a green baseball cap to the back, a face mask, chest protector, and a glove. #0924. $50-55

•Charlie Brown, wearing a blue baseball cap to the side, a red shirt with black zigzag, and a glove, holds a baseball. #0925. $45-50

•Linus, wearing a red baseball cap to the side, holds his blanket and glove. #0926. $50-55

•Lucy, wearing a green baseball cap and red dress, holds a baseball bat over her shoulder. #0927. $50-60

•Snoopy wears an orange baseball cap and glove. #0928. $40-45

15. Banks

•Egg-shaped bank features Snoopy lying on top of his doghouse, with Woodstock asleep in his nest on Snoopy's tummy. Printed: "This Has Been A Good Day!" Ceramic, 2" x 3", #1562, Determined Productions. 1976. $15-20

•Egg-shaped bank features Woodstock giving a bouquet of flowers to Snoopy. Printed: "How Nice!" Ceramic, 2" x 3", #1561, Determined Productions. 1976. $15-20

•Egg-shaped bank features Snoopy, as Joe Cool, leaning

against his doghouse. Printed: "Cool Cash." Ceramic. 3-3/4"H, #88071, Willitts Designs. 1988. $15-20

•Egg-shaped bank features Snoopy dancing with a basket of flowers in his hand. Printed: "I Feel Free." Ceramic, 2" x 3", #1563, Determined Productions. 1976. $15-20

•Egg-shaped bank features Snoopy sitting and hugging Woodstock. Printed: "Surprise A Friend With A Hug!" Ceramic. 2" x 3". #1564, Determined Productions. 1976. $18-22

•Snoopy is lying on top of the horizontal egg-shaped bank, which has a flower print on it. Ceramic, #1551, Determined Productions. 1977. $25-35

16. Banks

"Fruit Series Banks." Papier-mâché. Determined Productions. 1976.

•Snoopy lies on his tummy, on top of an orange. #1168. $60-65

•Snoopy lies on a slice of watermelon. #1169. $38-45

•Snoopy leans back on a strawberry. #1164. $38-45

•Snoopy lies on his tummy, on top of a lemon, with Woodstock lying on his head. #1167. $55-60

•Snoopy lies on top of a banana. #1165. $35-40

•Snoopy lies on his tummy, on top of an apple. #1166. $60-65

17. Bank

•"Snoopy Gumball Machine Coin Bank." Snoopy, as Joe Cool, and Woodstock, wearing "flip-up" sunglasses and standing on a red base, lean on the gumball machine/bank. Insert a

15

16

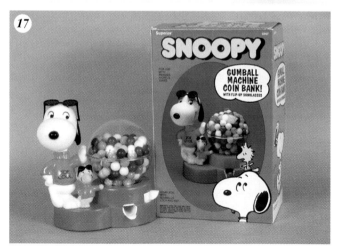

17

18

19

22

23

19. Banks

"Hat Series Banks." Ceramic. Determined Productions. 1979.

•Snoopy, sitting, wears a tuxedo, top hat, and holds a cane. #8549. $35-40

•Snoopy, sitting, wears a gray hard hat, blue pants, and a yellow and white checked shirt, and holds a red lunch box. #8547. $30-35

•Snoopy, sitting, wears a red baseball cap and a red and white striped uniform, and holds a bat and baseball. #8546. $40-45

•Snoopy, sitting, wears a gold football helmet and a blue and white uniform, and holds a football. #8544. $30-35

•Snoopy, sitting, wears a light blue visor, and holds a tennis ball and racket. #8545. $35-40

•Snoopy, sitting, wears a yellow raincoat and hat, and holds an umbrella. #8548. $35-40

20. Banks

Hand-painted ceramic, made in Italy—no two are exactly alike. 6"H. Determined Productions. 1969.

•Lucy standing. $175-200

•Charlie Brown standing. $150-175

•Linus standing. $150-175

•Snoopy sitting. $125-135

21. Banks

Hand-painted ceramic, made in Italy—no two are exactly alike. 8-1/2"H. Determined Productions. 1969.

•Charlie Brown standing. $225-250

•Linus standing. $250-275

•Lucy standing. $255-275

•Sally standing. $300-375

•Snoopy sitting. $135-140

22. Bank

•Snoopy is sitting. Hand-painted ceramic made in Italy—no two are exactly alike. 15"H. Determined Productions. 1969. $450-475

23. Bank

•Linus is sitting, sucking his thumb and holding his blanket. Hand-painted ceramic made in Italy—no two are exactly alike. 8-1/4"H. Determined Productions. 1969. $375-425

penny, nickel, or dime, and receive a gumball. Includes gumballs and a key lock. Plastic. 7-1/2"H. #3247, Superior Toy and Manufacturing Co., Inc. 1987. $15-20 $25-35*

18. Banks

"Happy Snoopy Banks." Ceramic. Determined Productions. Mid-1970s.

•Large sitting Snoopy. 16"H. #1558. $300-375

•Medium sitting Snoopy. 11"H. #1557. $195-225

•Small sitting Snoopy. 6"H. #1556. $22-28

24. Banks

"Junk Food Series Banks." Ceramic. Assortment #1535, Determined Productions. 1982.

•Snoopy, sitting, leans against a chocolate ice cream cone. $70-75

•Snoopy lies on his tummy across a hamburger with lettuce and tomato on it. $60-65

•Snoopy, surrounded by french fries, sits inside a red and white striped container printed "Fries." $75-85

•Snoopy lies on top of a hot dog with mustard. $60-65

25. Banks

•"Snoopy and Woodstock Doghouse Bank." Snoopy lies on top of his doghouse, with Woodstock sitting against his feet. Papier-mâché. #8555, Ideal Toy Corp. (Manufacturer's identification is found only on the box.) 1977. $45-50 $55-65*

•"Lucy's Advice Bank." Lucy sits behind a box-like wooden table with a sign on it that reads "Opinions—5¢ Thoughts For The Day—10¢ Sound Advice—25¢." Ceramic. 4" x 4". #8118, Willitts Designs. 1988. $20-30 $25-35*

•Woodstock, sitting on top of Snoopy's head, and Snoopy, also sitting, both wear red bow ties. Ceramic. 8"H. #19017, Willitts Designs. 1990. $30-35 $35-38*

26. Banks

•Snoopy, as Joe Cool, wears sunglasses and an orange shirt printed "Joe Cool." Papier-mâché. 6"H. Assortment #5255-5, Ideal Toy Corp. 1977. $35-42 $45-50*

•Snoopy, dressed as a fireman in a red and yellow coat and hat, holds an ax. Papier-mâché. 6"H. Assortment #5255-5, Ideal Toy Corp. 1978. $38-42 $45-50*

•Snoopy, as Joe Cool, wearing sunglasses and a blue turtleneck sweater, stands on a green base with his arms and feet crossed. Papier-mâché. 5-3/4"H. #1516, Determined Productions. 1982. $30-35

•Snoopy, wearing sneakers and a blue sweat suit, and Woodstock are jogging on a white base. Papier-mâché. 5-3/4"H. #1515, Determined Productions. 1982. $30-36

27. Banks

•Snoopy wears various sports uniforms around the top half of the globe-shaped bank. The flags of countries around the world appear on the bottom half of the bank. Metal. #187, Ohio Art. 1984. $38-44

•Snoopy, sitting, wears a red ribbon around his neck. Plush. Determined Productions. 1983. $18-25

•Snoopy, wearing an engineer's hat, sits on top of a yellow, red, blue, and white locomotive printed "No. 1." Ceramic. 7" x 7-1/4"H. #45033, Willitts Designs. 1991. $25-30

28. Banks

•Snoopy is sitting. The coin slot is on top of his head. There is no opening in the bank to retrieve deposited money. Early editions of this bank have "United Feature Syndicate, Inc." embossed on the bottom of the bank. Later issues had a paper sticker on the bottom with the UFS markings or the bank came packaged with the UFS markings on the box. Glass. 6"H. #39, Anchor Hocking. 1979. Embossed markings: $15-20 Paper sticker (1980): $5-8

•"Snoopy Rainbow Bank." Snoopy lies on top of a rainbow. Papier-mâché. #8533, Determined Productions. 1976. $8-12

•Belle, sitting, wears a pink dress with red polka dots and a red ribbon over her ear. Papier-mâché. #1500, Determined Productions. 1981. $15-20

29. Banks

•Snoopy lies on his tummy, propped up on his elbows, on top of a penny. Papier-mâché. #1617, Determined Productions. Early 1980s. $45-50

•Snoopy is dressed as Uncle Sam in a red, white, and blue top hat and tail coat. Ceramic. 10-1/2"H. #45007, Willitts Designs. 1990. $125-135*

Bank

Snoopy lies on top of a savings account passbook printed "Savings." Available in two colors. Papier-mâché. #8532, Determined Productions. 1976.

•Blue Passbook Bank. $35-38

•Gold Passbook Bank. $30-38

30. Musical Banks

•Charlie Brown, Woodstock, Peppermint Patty, Linus, Franklin, and Lucy ride a ferris wheel. The backdrop features Charlie Brown nose-to-nose with Snoopy inside a mailbox and Woodstock on top. The bank plays "Spinning Wheel," and the ferris wheel turns when money is dropped in the coin slot in the back of the bank. Wood. 8"H. #277-408, Schmid. 1972. $265-285

•Snoopy, in his dancing pose, is in front of his orange dog-house, and Woodstock sits on top. The bank plays "We've Only Just Begun," and Snoopy dances when money is put in the bank. Wood. 6-1/2"H. #277-353, Schmid. 1973. $135-150

•Snoopy lies on his tummy on top of his yellow doghouse and looks over the edge. When his tail is pushed down, the bank plays "Raindrops Keep Falling On My Head," and Woodstock appears in the doorway holding a tray to put coins on. Wood. 6-1/2"H. #276-761, Schmid. 1971. $140-150

31. Musical Banks

Ceramic. 5" x 4-1/2". Schmid. 1973. $85-95 ea.

•Charlie Brown's face is on an orange background. Plays "I'd Like To Teach The World To Sing." #278-041.

•Linus's face is on a yellow background. Plays "If I Were A Rich Man." #278-043.

•Lucy's face is on a pink background. Plays "Second Hand Rose." #278-042.

•Snoopy as the Flying Ace. Plays "Superstar." #278-040. (Not pictured)

32. Bank

•Snoopy is sitting and wearing a red shirt printed "$ Future Millionaire." Plush. 8-1/2"H. Applause. 1989. $12-16

33. Bank

•Snoopy, dressed as Santa, holds a green gift sack filled with toys and wrapped presents. Ceramic. 15"H. Determined Productions. Early 1980s. $400-500

34. Banks

Silver-plated. Leonard Silver. The first group of banks manufactured was much heavier than those that came after. In time may tarnish beyond repair. 1979.

• Snoopy is featured on each side of the toy block-shaped bank with an object representing a letter of the alphabet—A, B, C, D and E. 3" x 3". #9669 $15-25

• Snoopy lies on top of his doghouse. "Snoopy" is printed over the doorway in raised letters. 6"H. #9670. $18-22*

• Snoopy, standing, is dressed as a fireman. 6"H. #9684. $50-60

• Snoopy, standing, wears a baseball cap and glove. 6"H. #9683. $50-60

• Snoopy is sitting. 4-3/4"H. #9672. $18-22

Bank

• Snoopy is featured standing next to his supper dish on the clear plastic dime bank with a metal cover. Printed: "Snoopy Dime Bank." By-mail premium. 3"L tube-shaped bank. Rival Dog Food. Early 1970s. $10-15

35. Banks

• Snoopy, as the Flying Ace, sits on top of his doghouse. "Snoopy" is printed over the doorway in raised letters. The graphic box features the 40th Anniversary logo. Silver-plated. 5-1/2"H. #501, Godinger Silver Art Co., Ltd. 1990. $15-20 $25-30*

• Snoopy sits at his typewriter on top of his doghouse. "Snoopy" is printed over the doorway in raised letters. The graphic box features the 40th Anniversary logo. Silver-plated. 5-1/2"H. #500, Godinger Silver Art Co., Ltd. 1990. $15-20 $25-30*

36. Banks

"Sports Series Banks." Papier-mâché (which tends to crack and peel with weather changes). Determined Productions. 1976.

• Baseball. 5"H. #8531. $32-38

• Bowling Ball. 5"H. #8539. $35-40

• Football. 4-1/2"H. #8534. $35-42

• Basketball. 5"H. #8538. $32-38

• Soccer Ball. 5"H. #8535. $32-38

37. Banks

"Transportation Series Banks." Papier-mâché. Determined Productions. 1977.

• Snoopy drives a red car with "Racer" printed on the side. 4-3/4" x 4". #8473. $25-32

• Snoopy, as the Flying Ace, pilots an orange plane with "Flying Ace" printed on the side. 3-1/2" x 5". #8475. $25-30

• Snoopy drives a yellow delivery truck with "The Express" printed on the side. 5" x 3-1/4". #8476. $25-30

• Snoopy, wearing a yellow hat, drives a blue car. 4-1/2" x 4". #8472. $25-30

• Snoopy, wearing a sailor outfit, pilots a yellow, white, and green boat with "Sailor" printed on the side. 5-1/4" x 4". #8474. $25-30

• Snoopy drives a green delivery truck with "The Express" printed on the side. Somewhat rarer than the yellow delivery truck bank. 5" x 3-1/4". #8476. $30-35

38. Banks

• Woodstock. Gold-tone silver plate. 5-1/2"H. #9673, Leonard Silver. 1979. $35-45

• Woodstock. "Schulz" is printed on the side. Ceramic. 6"H. #1503. Made in Japan for Determined Productions. 1977. $30-35

35

36

37

38

BEDDING

(See room introduction picture.)

Bedding

Sheets and pillow cases feature Lucy, Linus, Charlie Brown, Snoopy, and Woodstock pictured on multicolored backdrops accompanied by sayings. Muslin. Shrink wrapped. Sold exclusively through Sears. 1974.

•Set of flat and fitted twin sheets. $5-15 $25-30*

•Set of two standard pillowcases. $4-7 $12-15*

Bedspread

•In the center, Snoopy, as the Flying Ace, is on top of his bullet-riddled doghouse with a red, white, and blue bull's-eye target on the side. Printed: "He's Our Hero" and "Snoopy." Snoopy, Lucy, and Linus are featured in scenes around the edges of the bedspread. Available with a white or pale yellow background. Coordinating curtains were sold separately. Twin-size. Cotton. Shrink wrapped. Sold exclusively through Sears. 1973. $12-16 $30-35*

CLOTHING ACCESSORIES

39. Earmuffs

•Shaped like Snoopy's head. Plush. R & R Accessories. Early 1990s. $4-7

Hand Muff

•Worn around the neck, Snoopy's body has openings on each side to insert hands for warmth. Plush. 5-1/2" x 12". #9698, Butterfly Originals. 1982. $15-22

Earmuffs

•Shaped like Woodstock's head. Plush. R & R Accessories. Early 1990s. $4-7

40. Hats

•This hat came with three PEANUTS pinback buttons. The color of the hat and the button designs varied. (See pinback buttons in the HOBBY Room for a listing of the Simon Simple 1-3/4" diameter buttons.) Cotton. Simon Simple. 1971-1972. $12-15

•Snoopy, as the Flying Ace, sits on top of the blue and white hat on a piece of red felt. Snoopy is stuffed and made of felt. The hat is cotton. Simon Simple. 1969-1970. $20-30

•The hat is Snoopy's body; his head, arms, and feet are on each side. Felt and cotton. 15"L. Simon Simple. 1970. $22-30

•Snoopy, wearing a "Snoopy For President" button, stands with his hand over his heart on a red and white hat with a red, white, and blue ribbon on top. Felt and cotton. Simon Simple. 1972. $15-30

41. Baseball Cap

•The embroidered patch on the cap features Charlie Brown carrying a glove on a baseball bat over his shoulder. Available in various colors. Wool and rayon. Determined Productions. Sold through the Sears catalog. 1970. $22-30

42. Straw Hat

•Decorated with a red, white, and blue ribbon and four presidential campaign-theme pinback buttons: Snoopy standing with his hand over his heart, printed "Snoopy For President." Lucy standing, printed "Vote For Lucy - Diplomatic Service." Linus standing, printed "I Believe In Statehood, Countryhood, Cityhood, and Neighborhood!" Charlie Brown standing, printed "You're A Good Man, Charlie Brown." Simon Simple. 1972. $50-60

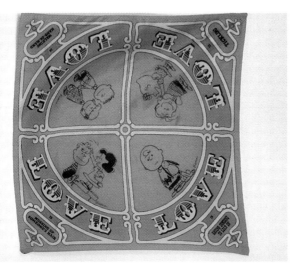

45. Ties

Wembley. Mid-1970s.

•Snoopy and Woodstock are fishing on a background of colors in the red and brown families. Polyester. 4"W. $15-20

•Snoopy, wearing skis, hat, and goggles, is at the top of a hill. Woodstock is at the bottom shoveling snow. The background is of colors in the red and brown families. Polyester. 4"W. $15-20

•Snoopy lies on top of his doghouse and Woodstock flies overhead on the bottom of a maroon tie. Polyester. 3"W. $8-12

•Charlie Brown is being counseled by Lucy at her psychiatrist booth on a navy blue background. Polyester and silk. 4"W. $15-20

•Lucy looks at large snowflakes on a background of colors in the green family. Polyester. 4"W. $15-20

DECORATIVE ITEMS

46. Pillows

"PEANUTS Pillowettes." Each mini pillow has a design on the front and a caption on the back. Stuffed cotton. Determined Productions. 1978. $4-6 ea.

•Snoopy kisses Charlie Brown on the cheek, against an orange and blue background. Printed: "We're Pals." Square-shaped pillow. 4" x 4". #5941.

•Sally and Linus walk hand-in-hand in front of a yellow heart on a green and yellow background. Printed: "Love One Another." Round pillow. #5945.

•Snoopy is sitting and hugging Woodstock, against an orange and yellow background. Printed: "Be A Friend." Square-shaped pillow. 4" x 4". #5943.

43. Scarf

•This scarf is made up of four sections with different characters and sayings in each section. Lucy stands on Schroeder's piano and musses his hair: "Love Is Mussing Up Someone's Hair." Shermy and Patty hold hands: "Love Is Walking Hand In Hand." Sally tickles Linus: "Love Is Tickling." Snoopy leans on Charlie Brown: "Love Is Having Someone To Lean On." 31" square. Determined Productions. Early 1970s. $30-35

44. Ties

•Snoopy is wearing a raccoon coat and carrying a banner printed "S" on a navy blue background. Polyester. 3-1/4"W. Western Neckwear. Early 1980s. $12-15

•Schroeder is playing his piano. Lucy is on top of it, nose to nose with Schroeder. Brown with diagonal white stripes. Polyester and silk. 4"W. Resilio. Mid-1970s. $18-22

•Snoopy, as the Flying Ace, appears over a comic strip background. Silver, black, and white. Polyester and silk. 3-1/2"W. Cervantes Neckwear. Early 1990s. $10-12

•Snoopy, wearing a visor and carrying a tennis racket, is embroidered on the bottom of the salmon-colored tie. Polyester, rayon and flax. Polyester. 4"W. Wembley. Mid-1970s. $8-10

•Snoopy lies on top of a Christmas wreath printed on a navy blue background. 3-1/4"W. Western Neckwear. Early 1980s. $12-15

47. Pillows

"PEANUTS Pillowettes." Each mini pillow has a design on the front and a caption on the back. Stuffed cotton. Determined Productions. 1978. $4-6 ea.

•Snoopy kisses Peppermint Patty on the cheek against an orange and green background. Printed: "I Like You." Heart-shaped pillow. #5942.

•Peppermint Patty kisses Charlie Brown on the cheek against a red and white background. Printed: "First Kiss." Round pillow. #5944.

•Snoopy kisses Lucy on the nose against a red and blue background. Printed: "Kiss And Tell." Heart-shaped pillow. #5946.

48. Mobile

"PEANUTS Mobile." Snoopy dancing on top of his doghouse, Lucy, Charlie Brown, Linus, and Schroeder hang from the sun and clouds. Glossy cardboard press-outs. Packaged in unmarked shrink wrap. Determined Productions. 1973.

•Small mobile. 8-3/4" x 12". $10-12 $15-20*

•Large mobile. 18" x 24". $12-20 $25-35*

DIARIES

49. Diaries

•Snoopy, laughing with his hands over his mouth, thinks "Happiness is having secrets!" on a multicolored polka-dot background. Diary has a key lock. 4" x 5". #RA3617, Hallmark. Early 1990s. $6-8

•Snoopy is sitting in a red club chair while Woodstock and his friends stand one on top of the other behind the chair trying to see what he is writing in his diary; depicted against a blue background. Printed: "No Snooping Allowed!" Diary has a key lock. 6-1/4" x 7 1/4". #RA3814, Hallmark. Early 1990s. $6-9

•Snoopy, grinning, has his arms and ears up in the air as he thinks "No snooping!" against a multicolored background. Diary has a key lock. 4" x 5". #RA3629, Hallmark. Early 1990s. $6-8

50. Diary

•Lucy, holding a diary and making a fist, says, "Keep out!" against a red background. Diary has a key lock. 6-1/4" x 7-1/4". Hallmark. Early 1990s. $6-8

Diaries

Diaries have a key lock. 4-1/2" x 6". Determined Productions. $8-10

•Snoopy and Woodstock are repeated walking across the diary. Printed: "Snoopy Diary." Red and blue with white stars. 1984.

•Snoopy is sitting and hugging Woodstock in front of a red heart against a yellow background. Printed: "Diary." 1980.

•Snoopy and Woodstock slide down a red, orange, and yellow rainbow on a blue background. Printed: "Diary." #8447-7. 1981.

JEWELRY AND ACCESSORIES

51. Earring Holders

Enameled metal on brass base. 5"H. Aviva. Mid-1970s. $5-8 ea.

•Snoopy lies on top of his doghouse with Woodstock lying on top of Snoopy's nose.

•Snoopy and Woodstock sit against the trunk of a tree.

52. 14 Karat Gold Jewelry

The value of the gold charms is determined by two factors: the value of gold and that the figure is licensed. Verilyte Gold pieces came in a graphic box.

•Charm. Snoopy is sitting and holding a "puffed" heart. 5/8"H. #3612P, Verilyte Gold. 1984. $30-40*

•Charm. Snoopy is standing. This charm is very fragile. 3/4"H. Michael Anthony. 1988. $18-22

•Charm. Snoopy is dancing. 5/8"H. #3602, Verilyte Gold. 1983. $25-30*

•Charm. Snoopy is standing. Decorative soldered bale. 5/8"H. Michael Anthony. 1988. $35-40

•Charm. Snoopy is sitting and holding a mug. Available in two sizes. Verilyte Gold. 1983. 5/8"H (pictured). #3610. $25-28*. 3/8"H (not pictured). #3618. $22-24*

•Charm. Snoopy, as Joe Cool, is standing. 5/8"H. #3603, Verilyte Gold. 1983. $25-28*

•Charm. Snoopy, as the Flying Ace, is sitting. Available in two sizes. Verilyte Gold. 1983. 5/8"H (pictured). #3608. $25-28*. 3/8"H (not pictured). #3617. $22-25*

•Charm. Snoopy is lying on top of his doghouse. 5/8"H. #3611, Verilyte Gold. 1983. $25-28*

•Charm Holder. Snoopy lies on his tummy on top of a rainbow. 1"H. #3600, Verilyte Gold. 1983. $40-45*

•Charm. Snoopy wears a baseball cap and carries a bat.

1/2"H. #5144, Michael Anthony. 1991. $15-18

•Charm. Snoopy is sitting with Woodstock. Available in two sizes. Verilyte Gold. 1983. 5/8"H (pictured). #3605. $25-28*. 3/8"H (not pictured). #3614. $22-25*

•Charm. Snoopy is sitting and holding the outline of a heart. Available in two sizes. Verilyte Gold. 1983. 5/8"H (pictured). #3612. $25-28*. 3/8"H (not pictured). #3615. $22-25*

•Charm. Snoopy is on a pair of skis. 3/8"H. #5145, Michael Anthony. 1991. $12-15

•Charm. Snoopy, as Joe Cool, is standing on the words "Joe Cool." 5/8"H. #5146, Michael Anthony. 1991. $12-15

•Charm. Woodstock is standing. This charm is very fragile. 7/16"H. #5380, Michael Anthony. 1988. $12-15

•Charm. Woodstock is standing. Decorative soldered bale. 11/16"H. Michael Anthony. 1988. $35-40

•Ring. Two bands with a twist design form the ring. #SWR, Michael Anthony. 1988. $40-45 ea. Woodstock (pictured) is positioned between the bands. Snoopy (not pictured) is positioned between the bands.

•Earrings. Post earrings. 1/8"H. Michael Anthony. 1988. $20-25 ea. Woodstock (pictured) is standing. Snoopy (not pictured) is standing.

CLOISONNÉ JEWELRY

In 1968, the Aviva Company secured the license for PEANUTS costume jewelry, 14K gold jewelry, and a few other types of items. The first piece of jewelry made was a gold-plated Snoopy as the Flying Ace pin. With its success, a tie tac, tie bar, and key chain followed. Cloisonné jewelry was made for the adult market, and enamel jewelry and hand-painted jewelry were made for children. The cloisonné jewelry that most of us are familiar with was available beginning in the early 1970s and continued to be produced through the mid-1980s. New designs were added and older designs were retired periodically.

Some jewelry was region-specific, such as those that identified ski resorts or colleges. I was at a University of Michigan football game in Ann Arbor and tried to persuade a young woman wearing a Snoopy "Go Blue" cloisonné pin on her jacket to sell it to me. She clutched it protectively telling me she had it for years, wears it to every Michigan game, and would never sell it. The picture below shows the steps taken to produce a piece of cloisonné jewelry.

53. Pins

"Quips & Quotes Pins." Cloisonné. Aviva. Mid-1970s. $4-7 ea.

•Snoopy, wearing a jogging suit, is running. Printed: "Run For Fun!"

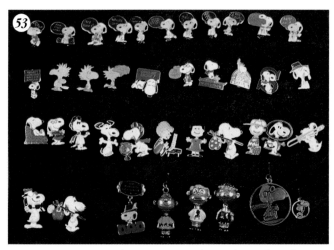

• Snoopy is sitting and eating. Printed: "Junk Food Junkie!"

• Snoopy is wearing a jacket with a red vest underneath. Printed: "Hey Babe!"

• Snoopy is sitting. Printed: "What's Up?"

• Snoopy is standing. Printed: "Hi Sweetie!"

• Snoopy is sitting. Printed: "Good Grief!"

• Snoopy, sitting, sticks out his tongue. Printed: "Bleh!"

• Snoopy is sitting and grinning. Printed: "Hee! Hee! Hee!"

• Snoopy is standing with his hands over his heart. Printed: "Ah! Love!"

• Snoopy is sitting and yawning. Printed: "Yawn."

• Snoopy is sitting with outstretched arms. Printed: "Why Me?"

Pins

Cloisonné. Aviva. Mid-1970s unless otherwise noted.

• Snoopy carries a sign printed "Project Concern's Walk for Mankind." 1"H. Early 1980s. $25-28

• Woodstock. Early 1970s. $6-8

• Woodstock is smiling. Late 1970s. $4-6

• Woodstock. Printed: "Chirp". 7/8"H. Late 1970s. $6-8

• Snoopy is lying on his tummy. Printed "Conserve Energy!" 1"H. Early 1980s. $18-22

• Snoopy is wearing a plaid jacket, bow tie, and glasses. Printed: "Joe Preppy." 3/4"H. Early 1980s. $6-8

• Snoopy is skiing with Woodstock sitting on one ski. Printed: "Mount Snow." The resort name on this design and other ski designs reflected the ski resort at which it was sold. After Aviva, Quantasia produced some of these pins. 1"H. $12-18

• Snoopy poses as the Statue of Liberty. Printed: "I (heart) N.Y." 1"H. Early 1980s. $15-20

• Snoopy leans against the letter "S." This pin came in variety of colors and in the more popular letters of the alphabet. 1"H. $4-6

• Spike, wearing a brown hat, is sitting. 7/8"H. Early 1980s. $6-9

• Snoopy sits on an orange club chair. 1"H. $6-8

• Belle is wearing a red dress. Printed: "Belle." 1"H. Early 1980s. $4-6

Pins

Enamel. Aviva. 1972.

• Snoopy, as the Flying Ace, is standing. 1-1/8"H. $15-20

• Snoopy is dancing. 1-1/4"H. $15-18

• Snoopy as the Flying Ace is looking at a globe. $25-28

• Schroeder is playing his piano. 1"L x 1-1/8"H. $12-15

• Lucy, wearing a blue dress, stands with her arms outstretched. 1-1/8"H. $15-18

• Snoopy carries a hobo pack over his shoulder. 1-1/4"H. $15-18

• Charlie Brown wears a baseball cap and glove. 1-1/8"H. $15-18

• Snoopy is dressed as an astronaut. 1-1/8"H. $25-35

• Snoopy is playing a trombone. 1-1/2"L x 1"H. $22-25

Pins

• Snoopy, dressed as movie director, wears a beret, gold glasses, and holds a megaphone. Hand-painted on gold. 1-1/4"H. Aviva. 1969. $25-30

• Snoopy is carrying a red hobo pack over his shoulder. Hand-painted on gold. 1-1/8"H. Aviva. 1969. $25-30

• "The World's Greatest" is printed above Snoopy, who wears a hat on top of the word "Dad." 1-3/4"H. Aviva. Late 1970s-early 1980s. $7-9

Pins and Charms

Hand-painted and hollow, the characters were available as pins or charms. Aviva. 1969. $35-50 ea.

• Charlie Brown.

• Schroeder.

• Pigpen.

• Lucy (Not pictured).

Charms

Silver-tone. Aviva. 1975.

• Snoopy as the Flying Ace is sitting inside a circle. 1-1/4" diam. $5-7

• Snoopy wears a cowboy hat and plays the guitar in a circle. 1/2" diam. $4-6

54. Necklace

• "Snoopy On Parade Necklace." Snoopy, wearing a red bow tie with black polka dots, dances on a necklace with multicolored beads and two Woodstocks. Plastic. 12"L. Avon. 1990. $4-5*

Earrings

• "Snoopy On Parade Earrings." Snoopy's head is on a blue background circled in yellow. Post earrings. Plastic. 1/2" diam. Avon. 1990. $1-2*

• Snoopy, wearing a tri-cornered hat, carries an American flag with 13 stars. 1"H. $20-25

• Snoopy lies on his tummy on top of the Liberty Bell. Printed: "1776-1976." $15-20

• Snoopy lies on top of his doghouse decorated with red, white, and blue trimmings. Printed: "Happy Birthday, America 1776-1976." 7/8" diam. $15-20

• Snoopy, wearing a tri-cornered hat, carries an ax. Three cherries are pictured between "1776" and "1976." 3/4" diam. $15-20

• Snoopy is standing and holding an Uncle Sam hat. 1"H. $5-7

Pin

• Snoopy, as the Flying Ace, is sitting. This was the first pin made by Aviva and was also sold as a tie tac, key chain, and mini tie bar. 1969. $7-9

Pin and Earrings Set

• Snoopy is sitting and holding a dog bone. Cloisonné. Pin: 1"H. Earrings on wire hooks: 7/8"H. Aviva. Mid-1970s. $9-12

Charm Bracelet

• Comes with 5 charms: Schroeder at his piano, Linus with his blanket, Lucy wearing a blue dress, Charlie Brown with baseball cap and glove, and Snoopy as the Flying Ace. Cloisonné charms on a gold-tone bracelet. Aviva. 1969. $35-40

Money Clip

• Snoopy, as the Flying Ace, sits on his doghouse against a sky blue background with clouds. Cloisonné. 1-3/4"L. Aviva. 1969. $10-15

Charm Bracelet

• Comes with three charms: Lucy, Snoopy dancing, and Charlie Brown. Enameled charms on a gold-tone bracelet. Aviva. 1969. $25-30

Money Clip

• Snoopy, dressed as a prince, wears a crown and a cape and carries a scepter. Cloisonné. 1-3/4"L. Made by Aviva for distribution by Interstate Brands. Later for sale to the public by Aviva. 1973. $12-16

Initial Bracelet

• Snoopy lies on top of the letter "O." Made in the more popular letters. Aviva. Mid-1970s. $6-9

57. Pins

"Snoopy's Pin Pals." Plastic. Aviva. 1972. $7-9 ea. $10-12* ea.

• Snoopy, as the Flying Ace, is standing. 2-1/8"H.

• Charlie Brown, wearing a baseball cap and glove, holds a baseball. 2-1/2"H.

55. Cuff Link Set

• Snoopy, holding a football, wears a Washington Redskins uniform with "Go Skins" printed underneath. Standard cuff links. Cloisonné. 7/8"H. Aviva. Early 1970s. $20-25

Cuff Link and Tie Tac Sets

• Snoopy holds a red, white, and blue Uncle Sam hat. Standard cuff links. Cloisonné. 3/4"H. Aviva. Early 1970s. $15-20

• Snoopy, wearing a hat and goggles, is on a pair of skis. Standard cuff links. Cloisonné. Aviva. Early 1970s. $30-35

Cuff Link Set

• Snoopy, wearing a hat and goggles, is on a pair of skis. Wrap-around cuff links. Cloisonné. Aviva. Early 1970s. $20-25

Tie Bars

Cloisonné. Aviva. 1969.

• Snoopy, wearing bathing trunks, stands next to a surfboard. 3"L. $12-15

• Snoopy, dressed as an astronaut, wears a helmet, space suit, and a life support pack. 1-1/2"L. $25-30

Rings

Soldered on an adjustable gold-tone metal band. Cloisonné. Aviva. Mid-1970s. $4-6 ea.

• Snoopy and Woodstock are shaking hands.

• Snoopy, dressed as a fireman, carries a hose.

• Snoopy wears a stocking cap and holds a hockey stick.

56. Pins

"The Bicentennial Collection." Cloisonné. Aviva. 1976.

• Snoopy, dressed as an Indian, holds a package of tea. Printed: "1776-1976." $15-18

• Snoopy wears a cowboy hat and holds a guitar. 2-1/2"H.

• Snoopy, wearing a red shirt, is dancing. 2-1/8"H.

• Snoopy stands under a yellow umbrella. 2-1/8"H.

• Snoopy and Woodstock shake hands against a green background. 2"L x 2"H.

• Snoopy, as the Flying Ace, is sitting. 2"H.

• Snoopy, wearing a red fireman's hat, carries a bucket. 2-1/2"H.

• Linus sucks his thumb and holds a yellow blanket. 2-1/8"H.

• Snoopy, wearing a baseball cap and glove, holds an apple. 2-1/8"H.

PAJAMA BAGS
58. Clothes Hanger

• Snoopy's head is in the center of the hanger. A Woodstock appliqué is glued on the reverse side. Plush. 16"L. #8800, Butterfly Originals. 1983. $15-20

Pajama Bags

• Snoopy, with a plush body and arms, wears a yellow and orange striped nightshirt printed "ZZZ." A Woodstock appliqué is glued to the nightshirt. Although not shown, a matching nightcap is included. The nightshirt opens in the back with a zipper. 20"H. #7172-8, Butterfly Originals. 1983. $9-12

• The full-figured plush Snoopy has a Woodstock appliqué glued to his chest and opens in the back with a zipper. 18-1/2"H. #0170, Butterfly Originals. 1981. $9-12

59. Pajama Cases

• Snoopy, wearing a helmet and holding a football, stands with his hand over his heart surrounded by falling leaves. Felt appliqués on red felt trimmed in cotton with a zipper in the back. 12" diam. Simon Simple. 1971. $10-15

• Snoopy is dancing as Woodstock watches. Felt appliqués on red

felt trimmed in cotton with a zipper in the back. 12" diam. Simon Simple. 1973. $10-15

60. Pajama Bags

• Linus, wearing a red and white striped shirt and blue pants, holds his blanket. Comes with a hanger and a pinback button printed "Little brothers are the buck privates of life." Cotton and felt. #PJ-94, Simon Simple. 1969. $14-18

• Sally wears a white dress with red polka dots. Comes with a hanger. Cotton and felt. Simon Simple. 1970. $14-18

61. Pajama Bags

Each comes with a hanger and a pinback button. Cotton and felt. Simon Simple. 1969.

• "Snoopy Baseball." Snoopy is wearing a red baseball cap, a yellow glove and a button printed "Just what a manager likes... A player who isn't bothered by tension!" 25"H. #PJ-92. $14-20

• "Snoopy vs. The Red Baron." Snoopy, as the Flying Ace, is wearing a green helmet with yellow goggles and a button printed "Curse you, Red Baron." 22"H. #PJ-95. $14-20

• "Beau Snoopy." Snoopy wears a foreign legion hat and a button printed "Here's Beau Snoopy of the Foreign Legion marching across the desert." 24"H. #PJ-90. $14-22

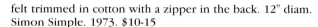

62. Pajama Bags

Each comes with a hanger. Cotton and felt. Simon Simple. $12-15 ea.

•Charlie Brown is wearing black shorts, a red shirt with a black zigzag, and a button printed "You're a good man, Charlie Brown." 26"H. #PJ-96. 1969.

•Charlie Brown is wearing black shorts, a yellow shirt with a black zigzag, a baseball cap and glove, and a button printed "All I need is one hit and I can raise my lifetime batting average to .001!" 1970-1971.

•"Lucy In Nightgown." Lucy is wearing a pink and white nightshirt with a button printed "I don't care if anybody likes me... Just so I'm popular!" 28"H. #PJ-93. 1969.

63. Pajama Bags

Each comes with a hanger. Cotton and felt. Simon Simple.

•Franklin, with yarn hair, wears a horizontal multicolored striped shirt, green shorts, and holds a lollipop. 1970-1971. $25-35

•Lucy wears a pink dress and holds a flower. 1970-1971. $10-14

•"Charlie Brown In Pajamas." Charlie Brown wears blue striped pajamas. Although not shown, this pajama bag did come with a pinback button. 28"H. #PJ-91. 1969. $10-14

64. Pajama Bags

•Snoopy is hugging Woodstock on a heart-shaped bag with yellow hearts in the background. They both are wearing blue and white striped nightcaps. Cotton lined with vinyl and a zipper in the back. 16"H. Butterfly Originals. Late 1970s. $8-10

•Snoopy, wearing a tri-cornered hat, sits with Woodstock. Printed: "1776-1976." Comes with a hanger and a pinback button printed "Happy Birthday America!!" Cotton and felt. 15"W x 21"H. Simon Simple. 1976. $10-15

65. Pajama Bag

Snoopy is lying on his back. His head is stuffed and his body holds the pajamas. Felt. 24"L. #PJ-72, Simon Simple. 1969. $15-20

PURSES AND TOTE BAGS

66. Child's Purses

•Shaped like Snoopy's doghouse. Charlie Brown, pictured with Snoopy's dinner, says "Suppertime!" The door opens to show Snoopy hugging Woodstock. The other sides of the house feature Snoopy, Woodstock, and his friends. Vinyl-covered cardboard with gold-colored shoulder chain. 3-1/2" x 5". Butterfly Originals. Late 1970s. $5-10

67

69

68

70

67. Adult Shoulder Bag

•Shaped like Snoopy's doghouse. A plush Snoopy wearing a cotton suede vest lies on top of the bag. "Snoopy" is printed over the doorway. Quilted cotton. Bag: 11" x 10". Snoopy: 11"L. Determined Productions. 1979. $30-40

68. Tote Bags

•The red bag features images of PEANUTS pinback buttons and includes two buttons attached to felt. Red cord handles. Rubber-backed cotton bag. 11" x 13-1/2". Simon Simple. 1971-1972. $25-30

•Snoopy, as the Flying Ace, stands in front of his doghouse thinking "Here's the pilot standing next to his Sopwith Camel chatting with his faithful mechanics. Even at this early hour, they admire his calm courage." Felt Snoopy with yellow ribbon scarf. Black plastic handles. Rubber-backed cotton bag. 12-1/2" x 15". Simon Simple. 1972. $30-35

•Snoopy, wearing a tri-cornered hat, and Woodstock sit with a birthday cake between them. Snoopy is thinking, "Happy Birthday America!!" Felt Woodstock. The bag and the handles are trimmed in red, white, and blue stripes. Rubber-backed cotton. 10-1/2" x 12-1/2" with the flap closed. Simon Simple. 1976. $20-30

69. Tote Bags

•Snoopy is lying on his back in the grass with Woodstock standing on his tummy against a lime green background. Felt Woodstock and Snoopy. Yarn grass. Cotton bag. 14" x 12". Simon Simple. 1971-1972. $15-25

•Snoopy dances with Lucy against an orange background and thinks, "Close dancing is coming back!" Rubber-backed cotton. 11" x 12". Simon Simple. 1974. $20-30

70. Tote Bag

•Woodstock appears on each side. Printed: "Topflight" and "n. 1: The highest level of achievement, excellence, or eminence. 2: Over a layer of clouds." Blue canvas with handles and a snap closure. 12-1/2" x 12-5/8". Butterfly Originals. Early 1980s. $6-10

•Shaped like a house. Charlie Brown and Lucy can be seen in the windows. The other sides feature Snoopy with a present at the front door, Peppermint Patty and Marcie at the back door, and Linus and Sally in the windows. A note pad with Woodstock and Snoopy on top is attached to the gold-colored shoulder chain. Vinyl-covered cardboard. 3-1/2" x 6". Butterfly Originals. 1978. $5-10

•"Snoopy Play Purse And Doll." The heart-shaped pocket featuring Woodstock on the front includes a cloth Snoopy doll. Printed on the pocket: "Happiness Is Taking A Friend Or Two Along!" and "Snoopy." Tan cotton purse with red vinyl trim, shoulder strap. 6" x 7". #1593, Knickerbocker. 1980. $8-10*

•Snoopy, holding a bunch of balloons behind his back, faces Woodstock who holds one balloon. The purse squeaks when squeezed. Orange vinyl. 4" x 4-1/2". #9730, Determined Productions. 1981. $2-3

•Snoopy lies on top of the quilted purse shaped like his doghouse. Cotton. 3-1/2" x 5". Determined Productions. 1979. $4-8

•Log-cabin design and shape. Charlie Brown, wearing a sailor hat, is in the doorway and Woodstock is in the window as Snoopy stands outside the clubhouse on the back and front. "Clubhouse" is printed on the back and front of the purse. Vinyl-covered cardboard. 5-1/2" x 5". Butterfly Originals. Late 1970s. $4-6

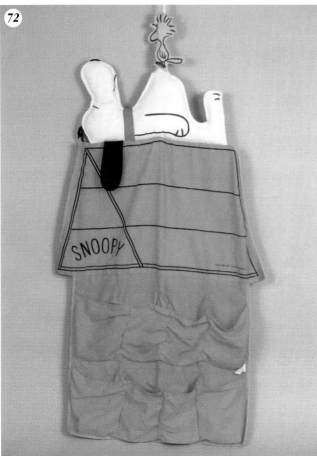

SHOE BAGS

72. Shoe Bag

•"Snoopy Doghouse Utility Shoe Bag." Snoopy lies on top of the red doghouse-shaped bag with Woodstock standing on his tummy. There is room for four pairs of shoes. Pajamas can be stored in the roof of the doghouse. Felt Snoopy and 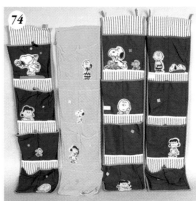 Woodstock, cotton bag with cord for hanging. 21" x 36". Simon Simple. 1971. $15-20

73. Shoe Bags

•"Snoopy Doghouse Utility Shoe Bag." Snoopy lies on top of the red doghouse-shaped bag. There is room for four pairs of shoes. Pajamas can be stored in the roof of the doghouse. Felt Snoopy and cotton bag with cord for hanging. 22" x 33". #US-1, Simon Simple. 1968. $15-20

•"Snoopy Doghouse Utility Shoe Bag." Snoopy sits at his typewriter on top of the red doghouse-shaped bag with Woodstock standing looking over his shoulder. There is room for four pairs of shoes. Pajamas can be stored in the roof of the doghouse. Felt Snoopy and Woodstock, cotton bag with cord for hanging. 22" x 33". Simon Simple. 1972. $15-20

74. Shoe Bags

"PEANUTS Slim Jim Shoe Bag." Room for four pairs of shoes. Felt appliqués on cotton. 36"H. Simon Simple. 1971. $8-10

•Snoopy, performing with his paw-pets, along with Lucy, Woodstock, and Charlie Brown, are featured on the blue pockets with red and white striped backgrounds.

•Charlie Brown talking on the telephone, Snoopy, Lucy talking on the telephone, and Woodstock are featured on the orange shoe bag.

•Snoopy, arms resting on a tree stump, and Woodstock, Charlie Brown, and Lucy are featured on the blue pockets with red and white striped backgrounds.

•Charlie Brown and Snoopy lying on his tummy, and Lucy are featured on the blue pockets with red and white striped backgrounds.

71. Tote Bags

"Snoopy Jumbo Travel Totes For Pets." "Snoopy" is printed on the handles and along the top of each tote bag. Canvas. 14-1/2" x 14". ConAgra. Sold exclusively through Sears. 1980. $6-10

•Snoopy, with a hobo pack over his shoulder, and Woodstock stand at a signpost with markers pointing toward "Antibes," "Nice," "Monaco," and "Cannes." Printed: "Dog Gone." #71-63339-6.

•Charlie Brown hands a postcard to Snoopy on top of his doghouse and says, "You got a card from the cat next door. He's traveling in the mountains!" Snoopy thinks, "The Catskills, no doubt." Printed: "Kitten Kaboodle." #71-63347-9.

WALLETS AND CHANGE PURSES

75. Wallet

•Snoopy is kissing Lucy on the nose. Three small hearts rise above them. Inside is a change purse, billfold, and room for photos. Vinyl with snap closure. 4-1/8" x 3-1/8". Butterfly Originals. Early 1980s. $10-12

Change Purses

Zippered vinyl. Hallmark. Mid-1970s. $5-8

•Snoopy lies on top of his doghouse with Woodstock sitting on his tummy. 3" x 5".

•Lucy, wearing a red dress, dances barefoot with her arms outstretched and says "I feel free!!" 3-7/8" x 4".

•Snoopy approaches Lucy with puckered lips. Red background. "MMMMM" is printed surrounded by hearts. 3-7/8" x 4".

•Lucy, standing under mistletoe, is approached by Snoopy with puckered lips. "MMMMM" is printed surrounded by hearts. 3" x 4-7/8".

Wallet

•Sally is carrying Snoopy under her arm. Printed: "Speak Softly And Carry A Beagle." The reverse side features Snoopy shaking hands with Woodstock. Printed: "Snoopy & Woodstock…One Of The Best Things In The Whole World Is A Friend." Vinyl with a snap closure. 8-7/8" x 3" when open. #300-2914, Butterfly Originals. Early 1980s. $6-10

Change Purses

Zippered vinyl. Hallmark. Mid-1970s. $5-8

•Woodstock sits in his nest with a decorated Christmas tree in it. 3" x 4".

•Lucy sits at her psychiatrist booth printed "Romantic Advice 5¢…The Doctor Is In." 3" x 4-1/2".

•Snoopy holds an umbrella over his head with Woodstock, with an umbrella over his head, sitting on top. 3-7/8" x 4".

•Snoopy, wearing a Santa hat, is pictured inside a Christmas wreath. 3-1/2" x 4".

Clutch Purse

•Linus holds balloons, and Sally holds cotton candy as Snoopy rides a unicycle and juggles balls with Woodstock sitting on his head. Vinyl with a snap closure. 6-7/8" x 4". #2813, Butterfly Originals. Late 1970s. $4-7

Change Purse

•Snoopy and Woodstock are dancing. Zippered vinyl. 3" x 5". Hallmark. Mid-1970s. $5-8

Wallet

•Charlie Brown is shouting at Lucy. They are both wearing baseball caps and gloves. Printed: "PEANUTS." The reverse side features Snoopy sleeping on top of his doghouse. Inside is a change purse, billfold, and room for photos. A Mattel logo is on the outside of the wallet. Vinyl with snap closure. 8-1/2" x 3-1/2" when open. #5057, Mattel, Inc. Late 1960s. $30-40

Change Purse

•Snoopy appears to be giving Woodstock a bouquet of balloons. Zippered vinyl. 3" x 4-1/8". Hallmark. Mid-1970s. $5-8

Wallet

•Snoopy sings into a microphone surrounded by musical notes. Printed: "Snoopy." The reverse side features Woodstock wearing two musical notes as headphones. Vinyl with a zipper closure. 4-1/8" x 3-1/8". #2905, Butterfly Originals. Early 1980s. $6-9

WATCHES

76. Quartz Watches

"Snoopy Armitron Collectibles Classic Characters." The watches came in a black metal box featuring Snoopy, as the Flying Ace, on top of his doghouse. As of the publication of this book, some of these watches may still be available in retail outlets. Armitron.

•Snoopy is standing on a red face. His hands tell the time. Watch has a second hand. The hours are numbered 1-12. Clear plastic strap and case. 1-1/4" diam. #900/93. 1993. $8-12 $15-20*

•Snoopy is standing on a black face. The hours 6, 9, and 12 are in Roman numerals. On the outside of the silver case are 12 raised gold tabs with the 1/4 hours numbered 15, 30, 45, and 60. Watch face has a numeral date. Black leather band. 1-1/4" diam. #900/92. 1993. $20-25 $40-55*

•The faces of Snoopy, Linus, Charlie Brown, and Lucy, wearing green or red Santa caps, are the hours 12, 3, 6, and 9 and snowmen represent the other hours on the blue face with snowflakes. Woodstock flies near Snoopy's face. Blue plastic strap and white plastic case. 1-1/4" diam. #900/98. 1993. $10-12 $20-30*

•Snoopy lies on top of his doghouse with Woodstock sitting on his tummy. The design is raised from the gold face. The

hours are represented by gold dots. Brown leather band. 1-1/4" diam. #900/95. 1993. $40-50 $50-55*

•Snoopy and Charlie Brown, sitting, are eating on the multi-colored face. A yellow knife and fork tell the time. Watch has a second hand. The hours are numbered 1-12. The minutes/seconds are numbered in increments of 5. Red plastic strap and white case. 1-1/4" diam. #900/90. 1993. $8-10. $15-20*

•Snoopy's face is featured on a green watch face. The number 12 is a Roman numeral. The other hours are represented by gold dots. Light brown leather strap and gold-tone case. 1-3/8" diam. #900/99. 1994. $20-25 $30-45*

•Snoopy is standing on the black face. The hours 6, 9, and 12 are in Roman numerals. On the outside of the silver case are 12 raised gold tabs with the 1/4 hours numbered 15, 30, 45, and 60. Watch face has the day abbreviated in Spanish and English and a numeral date. Black leather band. 1-1/2" diam. #900/91. 1993. $30-45 $50-65*

•Charlie Brown, Lucy, Linus, and Snoopy are lined up vertically on one side of the black and gold face. The hours are numbered 3, 6, 9, and 12. A gold Woodstock sits on the number 6. "PEANUTS" is printed in raised gold lettering. Black leather strap and gold-tone case. 1-1/2" diam. #900/96. 1993. $40-50 $65-70*

•Linus, Peppermint Patty, Woodstock, Sally, Charlie Brown, Snoopy, and Lucy are featured on a pink background circled in black on the face of the watch. The hours are represented by gold dots. Black leather strap and gold-tone case. 1-1/2" diam. #900/94. 1993. $40-50 $67-70

•Schroeder plays his piano as Snoopy leans against it. Push the button on the case and the watch plays "Ode To Joy." The number 12 is a Roman numeral. The other hours are represented by gold dots. Light brown leather strap and gold-tone case. 1-3/8" diam. #900/97. 1993. $25-35 $40-45*

77. Watches

•"Snoopy & Friends." Snoopy sits on top of his doghouse with Woodstock, who holds three balloons on the white face. The hours are numbered 1-12 in red. Battery-operated. Comes with three interchangeable plastic bands in red, white and blue. 1" diam. #900/59, Armitron. 1989. $10-15 $22-28*

•"Snoopy Quartz Digital Watch." Snoopy as the Flying Ace holds a package marked "Top Secret." Push the button on the box to display the time in hours, minutes, and seconds, and the month and date. "Psst!" is repeated in thought balloons on the striped light blue and navy blue band. #900/54, Armitron. 1989. $10-15 $22-28*

78. Quartz Watches

"PEANUTS Armitron Collectibles." The watches came in a white plastic box featuring Linus, Peppermint Patty, Woodstock, Sally, Charlie Brown, Snoopy, and Lucy on a pink background. Armitron. 1995.

•Snoopy, as the Flying Ace, sits on the white face. His red scarf tells the time. The hours are numbered 1-12. Woven brown leather band and gold-tone case. 1-1/2" diam. #900/201. $20-30 $50-60*

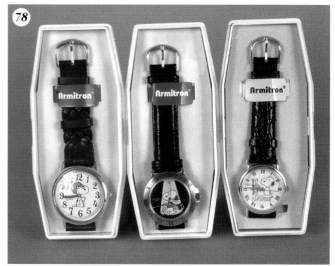

•Snoopy, wearing a red jacket, black bow tie, top hat, and cane, dances in a green spotlight with a star above his head. The spotlight area glows in the dark. The hours are numbered 1-12 in Roman numerals on the outside of the silver-tone case. Black leather band. #900/203. $22-30 $45-50*

•Snoopy stands next to the words "45th Anniversary" on the white face. The hours are numbered 1-12 in gold Roman numerals. Black leather band. #900/213. $20-30 $45-50

79. Quartz Watches

"Snoopy By Armitron." The watches were packaged in white vinyl cases which came in plain white cardboard boxes. Armitron.

•Snoopy is standing on the gold face. His hands tell the time. Watch has a second hand. Stars represent the hours 3, 6, 9, and 12. Dots represent the other hours. Black leather band and gold-tone case. Pictured in two sizes. 1989.

   1-1/4" diam. #900/52. $25-40 $55-60*

   1" diam. #900/53. $20-35 $50-55*

•Snoopy stands next to the word "Snoopy" printed vertically. The design is raised from the gold face. The hours are represented by gold dots. Brown leather band and gold-tone case. 1-1/4" diam. #900/58. 1989. $35-50 $60-70*

•Snoopy, as the Flying Ace, pilots his Sopwith Camel with Woodstock sitting on the wing on a sky blue background with clouds. The plane's red propeller is the second hand. The face has nothing on it to indicate the hours. On the outside of the silver-tone case are the numbers 13-24 representing the hours in military time. White leather band. 1-3/8" diam. #900/80. 1990. $30-45 $50-60*

80. Quartz Watches

"Snoopy By Armitron." The watches were packaged in three-piece white plastic boxes. Armitron.

• Snoopy, Woodstock, and his friends, dressed as scouts, paddle a red canoe printed "Camp Snoopy" on a white face. The hours are numbered 3, 6, 9, and 12. Red plastic band and white plastic case. 1-1/4" diam. #900/88. 1990. $15-18 $22-26*

• Snoopy sits on a red, white, and blue face printed "Before" and "After." The hours are numbered 1-12. The minutes/seconds are numbered in increments of 5 up to 30 on the right side and then back down to 5 on the left side. Yellow plastic case and red and blue plastic band. 1" diam. #900/51. 1989. $10-15 $22-28*

• Snoopy is standing on the gold face. His hands tell the time. Watch has a second hand. The hours are numbered 1-12. Black plastic case and band. 1-1/2" diam. #900/81. 1990. $12-15 $20-30*

• Snoopy is standing on the white face. His hands tell the time. Watch has a second hand. Stars represent the hours 3, 6, 9, and 12. Dots represent the other hours. Black plastic band and white plastic case. 1-1/4" diam. #900/82. 1990. $12-15 $20-30*

• Snoopy is standing on the white face. His hands tell the time. Watch has a second hand. The hours are numbered 1-12. Black plastic band and silver-tone case. 1-1/4" diam. #900/83. 1990. $12-15 $20-30*

• Snoopy, wearing a formal jacket, bow tie, and holding a top hat on a multicolored face, stands next to a screen printed "Starring" where the face of one of the characters appears. As the time changes, Lucy, Linus, Charlie Brown, and Woodstock, with their names printed underneath each face, appear one at a time. The face has nothing on it to indicate

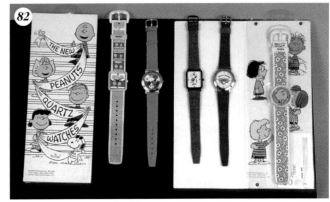

the hours. Blue plastic band and white plastic case. 1-1/4" diam. #900/57. 1990. $15-20 $30-35*

81. Watches

"PEANUTS Five Function Digital Watches" and "PEANUTS Quartz Analog Watches." Blister package features Charlie Brown, tangled in kite string, looking up at his kite stuck in a tree with Snoopy perched on a branch. Armitron. $10-12 $20-25

• Charlie Brown sits in a red bean bag chair with Snoopy behind him, leaning his head on top of Charlie Brown's head, on a blue and yellow face. "Snoopy" is printed on the face. The bean bag chair displays the time. White plastic case and blue plastic band. #900/49. 1988.

• Snoopy is dancing on the white and yellow face. "Snoopy" is printed on the face. His hands tell the time. Watch has a second hand. The hours are numbered 3 and 6. The other hours are represented by white dots. White plastic band and case. 1-1/4" diam. #900/46. 1988.

• Snoopy and Woodstock are sitting on top of the doghouse on a blue face. Snoopy's thought balloon displays the time. Yellow plastic case and blue plastic band. #900/50. 1988.

• Snoopy, as the Flying Ace, sits on top of his bullet hole-riddled doghouse on a sky blue face with clouds. The roof of Snoopy's doghouse displays the time. #900/48. 1988.

• Charlie Brown laughs and dances on the blue and white checkered face. His hands tell the time. Watch has a second hand. The hours are numbered 1-12. Blue plastic case and band. 1-1/4" diam. #900/47. 1988.

• Schroeder sits at his piano with a bar of music above it on the white face. The numbers 3, 6, 9, and 12 are represented by musical notes. The plastic band looks like the keys on a piano. Black plastic case. #900/56. 1990.

82. Quartz Watches

"The New PEANUTS Quartz Watches." The watches came in a cardboard folder with Woodstock, Charlie Brown, Sally, Linus, Lucy, and Snoopy as Joe Cool on the outside and Pigpen, Marcie, Peppermint Patty, and Schroeder on the inside. Sutton/Armitron. 1988.

• The red, white, and blue watch band features the first three panels of a comic strip. The last panel appears on the face. The strip features Charlie Brown and Linus leaning on a brick wall. The hours are numbered 3, 6, 9, and 12. White plastic case. #900/45. $12-15 $30-35*

• Snoopy, wearing a green scout hat and backpack, walks with a forest, clouds, and blue sky in the background. "Camp Snoopy" is printed on the gold-tone case. The face has nothing on it to indicate the hours. Tan fabric band. 1-1/4" diam. #900/41. $15-25 $35-40*

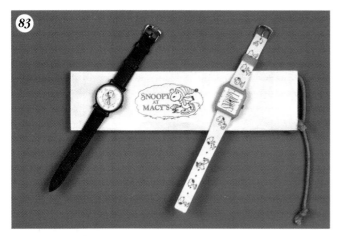

• Snoopy, as Joe Cool, wears sunglasses, a blue jacket, yellow shirt, and green tie on the white face. Printed: "Joe Cool." The hours are numbered 3, 6, 9, and 12 in red triangles. Black and white herringbone pattern band and black plastic case. #900/42. $15-22 $30-35*

• Snoopy, as the Flying Ace, appears inside a flight insignia design on a white face. Printed: "World Famous Superbeagle." The hours are numbered 3, 6, 9, and 12. On the outside of the silver-tone case are the numbers 1-24, representing the hours in military time. Brown pigskin band. 1-3/8" diam. #900/43. $25-40 $50-60*

• Charlie Brown's face appears over the hands of the watch. The hours are numbered 3, 6, 9, and 12 on the red face. "Good Grief!" in voice balloons is repeated on the red and white plastic band. White plastic case. 1-1/4" diam. #900/44. $12-22 $30-35*

83. Watches

• Snoopy is standing on the white face. His hands tell the time and his eyes blink as the watch ticks. The hours are numbered 1-12 in different colors. "Snoopy " is imprinted on the black leather band. Determined Productions. Sold exclusively through F.A.O. Schwarz. #364174. 1990. $85-95

• "Snoopy" is printed vertically in red on the white face. The hours are numbered 1-12. Snoopy appears in various poses on the white plastic band. The watch came packaged in a white gift bag featuring Snoopy and Woodstock wearing stocking caps and ice-skating. Printed: "Snoopy At Macy's." Only the packaging tells you it was a Macy's exclusive. Red plastic case. #900/40. Made by Sutton Time exclusively for Macy's. 1987. $30-40 $75-85*

84. Watch

• "Lucy's Wardrobe Watch." Lucy, wearing a pink dress, is standing on the white face. Her hands tell the time. The watch came with interchangeable plastic bands in white, pink, and blue. Silver-tone case. 7/8" diam. Determined Productions. 1974. $35-45 $90-100*

85. Watches

The watches came packaged in a two-piece box. A clear plastic cover fit over a green base with the roof of Snoopy's doghouse on top. Timex.

• Snoopy is dancing on the red face. His hands tell the time. The hours are numbered 1-12. Red plastic band and silver-tone case. 1" diam. #390121. 1976. $20-30 $65-70*

• Snoopy plays tennis on the yellow face. His hands, one of which holds a tennis racket, tell the time. A green tennis ball is the second hand. The hours are numbered 3, 6, 9, and 12. Vinyl yellow band. 1-1/4" diam. #390161. 1977. $20-35 $70-75*

• Snoopy is dancing on the red face. His hands tell the time. Woodstock is the second hand. The hours are numbered 3, 6, 9, and 12. Vinyl red band. 1-1/4" diam. #390151. 1977. $20-30 $65-70*

• "Snoopy Animated Soccer." Snoopy and a soccer goalie's net are featured on the face. The time, day, and date appear on the digital display. Soccer balls bounce across the display. Quartz LCD display. Blue plastic band. #77321. 1986. $8-10 $15-18*

• "Snoopy Red Baron." Snoopy, as the Flying Ace, sits on top of his doghouse on the black face. The Red Baron's plane is the second hand. The hours are numbered 1-12 in white on the outside of the black case. Black macramé and beaded band. #84111. 1979. $35-50 $70-75*

• "Snoopy Denim." Snoopy plays tennis on the blue denim face. His hands, one of which holds a tennis racket, tell the time. A yellow tennis ball is the second hand. The hours are numbered 1-12. Blue denim fabric band and gold-tone case. 1-1/4" diam. #390191. 1976. $20-40 $65-70*

• Lucy, wearing a yellow dress, is standing on the white face. Her hands tell the time. Watch has a second hand. White plastic band and silver-tone case. 1" diam. #390141. 1976. $20-30 $70-75*

• Snoopy is standing on the light blue face. His hands tell the time. Watch has a second hand. The hours are numbered 1-12. Light blue plastic band and silver-tone case. 1" diam. #390131. 1976. $20-30 $65-75*

• Snoopy lies on top of his doghouse with Woodstock sitting on his feet on a light blue face. The hours are numbered 1-12. This watch came packaged in a non-graphic gray plastic box with a black interior. Light blue plastic band and silver-tone case. 1" diam. #81771, Timex. 1988. $20-30 $65-70*

86. Quartz Watches

•"Snoopy Pop Up Watch." Snoopy and Woodstock sit back-to back on the black case printed "Woodstock & Snoopy." The digital display pops up when the paw print button on the case is pushed. Black nylon band. The watch and band also came in yellow and red. #95-3480, Determined Productions. 1985. $12-15 $35-40*

•"Snoopy Digital Watch." Snoopy, wearing a red bow tie, has his hands around the blue plastic case that houses the LCD display. The watch displays the time in hours, minutes, and seconds, and the month and day. Red and blue striped nylon band. #5000, Determined Productions. 1987. $12-15 $30-35*

Watch

•"Snoopy Hero-Time Watch." Snoopy is dancing on the red face. His hands tell the time. The hours are numbered 1-12. Red plastic band and silver-tone case. 1" diam. Includes an embroidered blue patch with red trim featuring Snoopy wearing a ribbon printed "Hero." Printed on the patch: "It's Hero Time." Determined Productions. 1973. $20-35 $75-80*

87. Watch

•Snoopy is dancing on the red face. His hands tell the time. Woodstock is the second hand. The hours are numbered 1-12. Black band. Lafayette Watch Company. Early 1970s. $95-150

88. Watch

•"Snoopy Time." Snoopy is dancing on the face. His hands tell the time. The hours are numbered 1-12. This watch was available in many different face and band color combinations. Wide vinyl band. 1-1/4" diam. Determined Productions. 1968. $35-45 $75-85*

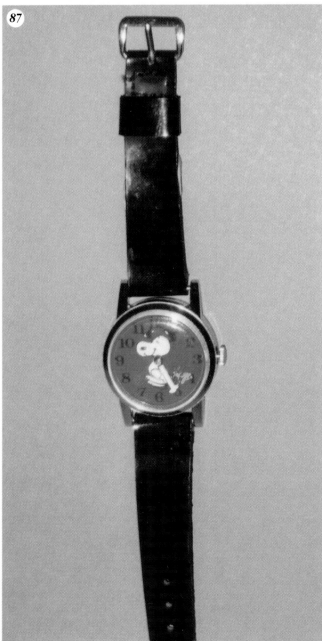

The white terry cover-up on the right is from Japan. Next to it is a towel from the United States. On the floor are a blue beach bag (second from the left) and three inflatables. They are all from Japan, except for the yellow life saving ring, which is from Portugal. Continuing clockwise from the left side are a blue cloth tote bag (Japan), another cloth beach bag (Japan) which is next to a red bathing suit (Italy), and another inflatable (Japan). In the top cubby holes, from left to right, are two beach bags followed by two inflatables—all from Japan. In the cubby hole over the terry cover-up is—surprise—another inflatable from Japan.

With the exception of two items noted below, everything shown in this picture is from Japan. I can't say enough for the rugged beauty, utility, and sturdiness of most of these Japanese objects.

A sleeping bag is on the left, and a large plastic floor mat is on the right. Resting near the bottom of the sleeping bag is a green rubber ball from Spain. Immediately below the sleeping bag is a small cook pot. To the right of the bag are a plastic water bottle, a yellow camper's coffee pot, an enamel serving dish, and a hibachi. Below these items are, left to right, a red enamel plate, a tray, a red enamel mug, a thermos, a blue plastic dog dish (from Italy), and a pink ceramic dog dish.

The PEANUTS Home Collection

Cabana/Outdoors

I f you like the joys of summer—swimming, bicycling, camping, and other outdoor games and sports—then cabana/outdoors is certain to become one of your favorite areas. Anything that is normally used or stored outside the house will be found here. The bird feeders, welcome mats, giant thermometers, wind chimes, and others will be a welcome addition to your home.

If you are addicted to summer and the great outdoors, then cabana/outdoors provides the prime setting for displaying your favorite collectibles.

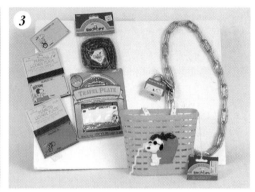

BICYCLE ACCESSORIES

1. Bicycle Accessory

•"Snoopy Pedal Blocks." Snoopy and Woodstock are shaking hands against a pink and red rainbow. Assembly required. All necessary parts are included. Plastic and rubber. #B3140, Butterfly/Hollywood Accessories. Early 1980s. $3-4 $8-10*

Bicycle Accessory

•"Snoopy Valve Caps." Snoopy, as the Flying Ace, screws onto most tire valve stems. Plastic. 1-3/8"H. #B3040, AC International. Early 1980s. $3-5*

Bicycle Accessories

"PEANUTS SnapOn Collector Reflector Bike Reflectors." Plastic. 3-5/8" diam. Butterfly Sports Inc. 1980. $5-7* ea.

•Snoopy, wearing a blue helmet, rides a bicycle against a red background. Printed: "Scrambler." #2006605.

•Snoopy, leaning back from a basket on the front of a bicycle, gives Lucy a kiss against a yellow background. Printed: "Smak!" #2006603.

•Snoopy, wearing a red helmet, rides a bicycle against a blue background. Printed: "Motocross Champ." #2006602.

•Snoopy rides a bicycle against a green background. Printed: "Pedal Power." #2006604.

2. Bicycle Accessories

•"Snoopy Handlebar Grips." The front of the red grip is shaped like Snoopy's head. "Snoopy" is printed in raised letters. Fits 7/8" handlebars. Molded plastic. 5-1/2"L. #B3010, Butterfly/Hollywood Accessories. Early 1980s. $3-4*

•"Snoopy Tape And Plugs." The handlebar plugs feature Snoopy's face. The screw-in plugs secure the tape to wrap the handlebars with. #B3080, Butterfly/Hollywood Accessories. Early 1980s. $3-4*

•"Snoopy Handlebar Grips." The white grips feature Snoopy and hearts. Fits 3/4" handlebars. Molded plastic. 3-1/8"L. #B3015, Butterfly/Hollywood Accessories. Late 1970s. $3-4*

•"Snoopy Streamers." Snoopy is riding a bicycle with Woodstock in the bike's basket. Multicolored streamers are attached. Plastic. #B3100, Butterfly/Hollywood Accessories. Early 1980s. $3-4*

•"Snoopy Handlebar Toy." Snoopy, as the Flying Ace, pilots a red and yellow biplane. The plane's propeller spins in the wind. Plastic. 4-1/2"L. #B3031, AC International. Late 1980s. $4-6 $7-10*

•"Snoopy Bicycle Mirror." Snoopy, lying on his tummy, looks over the edge of his doghouse, which is the mirror. Plastic. 7-1/2"H. #3110, Butterfly/Hollywood Accessories. Early 1980s. $5-7*

3. Bicycle Accessories

•"PEANUTS License Plate." Snoopy rides a unicycle with Woodstock on the back against a yellow background. Printed: "Property Of." Includes self-stick letters. Metal. 3-3/4" x 2-1/8". Hallmark. Late 1970s. $4-6*

•"Snoopy Bicycle Combination Lock." Snoopy is riding a bicycle on the side of his doghouse, which is the lock. 36" metal chain covered with green vinyl. Metal lock, plastic doghouse cover. #B3061, Butterfly/Hollywood Accessories. Early 1980s. $7-10 $12-16*

•"PEANUTS License Plate." Snoopy, wearing a blue helmet, sits on top of his doghouse against a yellow background. Printed: "Varoom!" and "Property Of." Includes self-stick letters. Metal. 3-3/4" x 2-1/8". Hallmark. Late 1970s. $4-6*

•"Travel Plate." Snoopy, Woodstock, and his friend are dressed as scouts on a white background. Printed: "Camp Snoopy." Includes self-stick letters. Plastic. 3-3/4" x 2-1/8". Monotex. Early 1980s. $3-4*

Bicycle Key Lock and Chain

•Snoopy, lying on his tummy, is featured on the side of his doghouse, which is the lock. Printed: "Snoopy." The 36" metal chain covered in clear plastic featuring Snoopy, Woodstock, and his friends riding a bicycle. Two keys are included. Metal lock, plastic doghouse cover. AC International. Mid/Late 1980s. $6-8 $10-14

Bicycle Accessories

•"PEANUTS License Plate." Woodstock rides a bicycle against a red background. Printed: "Powered By." Includes self-stick letters. Metal. 3-3/4" x 2-1/8". Hallmark. Late 1970s. $4-6*

•"Snoopy Basket." Snoopy, as Joe Cool, wears sunglasses and leans against a strawberry on the pink basket. Plastic. 5-1/2"H. #B3070, Butterfly/Hollywood Accessories. Early 1980s. $3-5

4. Bicycle Accessories

•"Snoopy Bicycle Horn." Squeeze the head of Snoopy as the Flying Ace to sound the horn. Plastic and rubber. 7"L. #B3022, AC International. Late 1980s. $3-5*

•"Snoopy Siren." Snoopy, as the Flying Ace, pilots a red and yellow plane printed "Snoopy Siren" on each side. A button, connected to the plane by a wire, activates the siren when pushed. Battery-operated. Plastic. 4"L x 4-1/2"H. #B3005, Butterfly/Hollywood Accessories. Early 1980s. $8-12 $16-22*

•"Snoopy Bike Bell." Snoopy, as the Flying Ace, sits on top of the bell under a clear dome. A decal around the bell is printed "Snoopy....Starship." Plastic and metal. 2-1/2"H x 2-1/8" diam. #B3050, Butterfly/Hollywood Accessories. Early 1980s. $6-8*

•"Snoopy Bicycle Horn." Squeeze the head of Snoopy as the Flying Ace to sound the horn. Plastic and rubber. 3-1/2"H. #B3026, AC International. Late 1980s. $3-5*

•"Snoopy Bicycle Horn." Squeeze Snoopy's head to sound the horn. Plastic and rubber. 3-1/2"H. #B3025, AC International. Late 1980s. $3-5*

•"Snoopy Bike Horn." Squeeze Snoopy's head to sound the horn. Plastic and rubber. 7"L. #B3020, Butterfly/Hollywood Accessories. Early 1980s. $3-5*

CAMPING EQUIPMENT

5. Pillow

•Snoopy, dancing, is repeated across the red pillow. Cotton. 17" x 23". #6102, Determined Productions. 1972. $18-22

Sleeping Bags

Cotton. 68" x 80". Determined Productions. Early 1970s. $20-30 ea.

•Linus, Charlie Brown, and Snoopy are pictured in bed together under a blanket. Printed: "Happiness Is Having Some Friends Sleep Overnight!" Red and black with a blue lining. Style #652-2.

•Snoopy, lying on top of his doghouse apparently asleep in his sleeping bag. Printed: "There's Nothing Cosier Than A Sleeping Bag." Red and black with a red lining. (Not pictured)

•Snoopy, sleeping on top of his house, with Woodstock standing on his tummy. Printed: "One Of Us Has to Stay Awake In Case Of Vampires." Orange and black with a red lining. (Not pictured)

INFLATABLES, POOL/BEACH TOYS AND OTHER OUTDOOR TOYS

6. Pool

•"Snoopy & Friends Snapset Pool." The gang plays volleyball on a beach around the pool. Printed: "Snoopy & Friends." No assembly required. Vinyl. 12"H x 5" diam. Intex Recreation, 1989. $15-22**

Playtent

•"Snoopy Safari Playtent." One side of the yellow tent features Snoopy leading Woodstock and his friends on a safari. The other side features Sally, Marcie, Rerun, Charlie Brown, Lucy, Linus, and Peppermint Patty among tropical plants and palm trees. Each side printed "Snoopy Safari." There is a tie-back door and open windows. Includes a 28" x 30" airmat. 42"L x 34"H. Vinyl. #48638, Intex Recreation. 1989. $15-25**

Inflatable Pool Float

•"Snoopy & Friends Famous Fabric Surfer." Snoopy, wearing sunglasses, sits in a lifeguard chair while Woodstock and his friends are all around. One Woodstock sits on the life preserver, one dives into Snoopy's supper dish where another Woodstock is swimming and two are listening to a radio. Rayon. 45" x 30". #58132, Intex Recreation. 1989. $12-20**

7. Inflatable Pool Float

•"PEANUTS Surfer." Snoopy and Woodstock are pictured sitting with Charlie Brown on a doghouse-shaped float surrounded by hearts. Printed: "PEANUTS." Vinyl. 36"L #5675-4, Ideal Toy Company. 1976. $20-25**

8. Beach Ball

•Snoopy wears a whistle around his neck and a shirt printed "Life Guard." The Dolly Madison logo appears on the red panels. By-mail premium. Dolly Madison. Mid-1970s. $15-20

9. Beach Ball

•Snoopy is pictured with a pail and shovel, with a beach ball and sunbathing on alternate panels on the multicolored ball. 51" circumference. Ideal Toy Company. 1977. $8-10*

10. Pail

•Snoopy, Lucy, and Charlie Brown are pictured on each side of the pail among the faces of many different boys and girls. Metal. 8"H x 8" diam. Late 1960s. The pail has no United Features Syndicate markings although the manufacturer, Chein and Company, was a PEANUTS licensee in the late 1960s and early 1970s and given permission to use the characters on this pail. $65-75

11. Water Toy

•"Snoopy Splash 'N Play." Snoopy and Woodstock sit on a blue and red base with spray nozzles in their hands. Attach a hose to the base and Snoopy and Woodstock spin around and spray water. Plastic. #5350, Hasbro. Late 1980s. $8-12 $20-25*

12. Water Toys

Battery-operated. Plastic. Concept 2000. Late 1970s. $10-20 $30-40* ea.

•"Swimming Snoopy." Snoopy is wearing bathing trunks. He spouts water and swims and floats with the help of his battery-powered ears. #106.

•"Rowing Snoopy." Snoopy, wearing a striped blue and white shirt, rows a blue boat with red oars. Woodstock sits on the bow. #107.

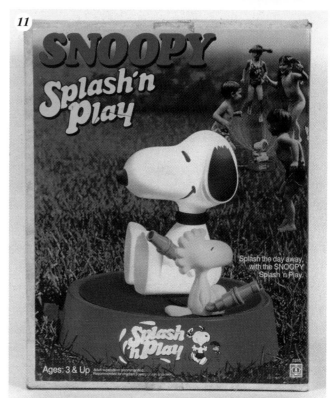

MATS

13. Mats

•Rear Car Floor Mat. Snoopy, as the Flying Ace, is sitting on top of his doghouse. Set of two mats. Rubber. #171, Plasticolor Designs. 1984. Set: $12-25

•Front Car Floor Mat. Snoopy, as the Flying Ace, sits on top of the words "King Of The Road." Comes as a set of two mats. Rubber. #11, Plasticolor Designs. 1984. Set: $15-25

14. Welcome Mats

Rubber. Plasticolor Designs. 1984. $8-15 ea.

•Snoopy is lying on top of his doghouse. Printed: "Home Sweet Home." 15" x 25". #884.

•Snoopy, dressed as Santa, holds a gift sack over his shoulder. Printed: "Happy Holidays." 15" x 25". #640.

•Snoopy sits on top of his doghouse surrounded by Woodstock and his friends. Printed: "Welcome To Our Home." 17" x 28". #886.

MISCELLANEOUS OUTDOOR ITEMS

15. Bird House

•"Woodstock Wild Bird Home." Snoopy is lying on top of his doghouse. A sign on the side of the house is printed "Vacancy (Birds Only)." A sign over the entrance is printed "Snoopy's Feathered Friends." Plastic. #71-63231-5, ConAgra. Early 1980s. $10-12 $18-22*

Bird Food

•"Woodstock's Wild Bird Food." Snoopy, lying on top of his doghouse, is thinking, "It's for the birds!" Woodstock is flying across the packaging. Net weight 4 lbs. #202516, ConAgra. 1978. $4-5*

Bird Feeder

•"Snoopy's Wild Bird Feeder." Snoopy lies on top of a doghouse-shaped feeder. Woodstock, pictured on each side of the feeder, holds signs printed "Take A Bird To Lunch!" and "I'm For The Birds!" Snoopy is removable, exposing an opening to pour in bird seed. Assembly required. The

Woodstock on the feeder's ledge is not included. Plastic. 9-1/2"H. #71-63444-4, ConAgra. Early 1980s. $12-14 $20-30*

16. Gardening Set

•Snoopy and Woodstock, sitting on top of the doghouse, water the flowers below using a garden hose and a watering can. A red, green, and blue rainbow is behind them on the yellow apron. The cotton apron comes with three plastic garden tools. Determined Productions. Mid-1970s. $8-12**

17. House Marker Kit

•"Snoopy House Number Marker Kit." Snoopy lies on top of his doghouse when assembled. The kit comes with paint, a paint brush, letter and number stencils, instructions, and all other parts necessary to complete. Wood. 14-3/4"H without ground stake. #GK1-1, Springbok Editions. 1970. $55-75*

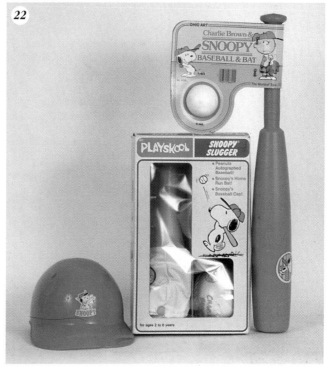

18. Lawn Decoration

•"Whirls Of Fun Lawn Decoration." Snoopy as the Flying Ace, wearing a blue ribbon scarf, and Woodstock sit on Snoopy's doghouse, which has a propeller in front. The propeller spins in the wind. Assembly required. Includes a 22" metal pole. Wood. Avon Products. 1990. $10-15

SPORTS EQUIPMENT

19. Footballs

•"Wilson Official Charlie Brown Football." Schroeder plays his piano as Snoopy kicks a football. Linus runs with his blanket to intercept the pass as Sally waits to catch it. On the reverse side of the football, Charlie Brown goes flying as Lucy pulls the football out from under him. Brown leather with lacing. 13"L. Wilson Sporting Goods. Early 1970s. $30-50

•"Snoopy Football." Snoopy appears in a football uniform on the shrink-wrap packaging. The orange and white football contains no PEANUTS graphics. Foam. Distributed by Sportcraft for Butterfly Sports, Inc. Early 1980s. $4-6**

Basketball

•"Snoopy Sportball." Snoopy is featured dribbling a basketball. Printed: "Snoopy Basketball." Distributed by Sportcraft for Butterfly Sports, Inc. Early 1980s. $8-10 $12-20*

20. Baseballs

"Official PEANUTS Baseballs." Each baseball is printed "Official PEANUTS League." The baseballs came packaged in a graphic multicolored cardboard box featuring the characters in baseball gear. Horsehide cover. Wilson Sporting Goods. 1969. $125-130 $135-150* ea.

•Lucy, Patty, Snoopy, Schroeder, Pigpen, Shermy, Charlie Brown, Violet, and Linus have autographed the baseball. Snoopy's signature is a paw print.

•Three scenes are depicted on the baseball: Snoopy sitting with Charlie Brown and Linus; Charlie Brown on the pitcher's mound as Schroeder walks away, and Snoopy stands with his supper dish in his mouth; and Charlie Brown and Lucy (apparently yelling), with Linus in the background.

21. Bowling Bag

•Snoopy, wearing a bowling shirt and shoes, is ready to release the ball. Available in different colors. Nylon. 14" x 10" x 10-1/2". Brunswick. Early 1990s. $20-35

Bowling Ball

•Snoopy, in a bowling shirt and shoes, is ready to release the ball. Available in different colors and weights. Comes undrilled. Brunswick. Early 1990s. Drilled: $20-30 Undrilled: $45-50*

22. Batter's Helmet

•Snoopy, wearing a baseball cap, swings a bat. Printed: "Snoopy." Hard plastic with adjustable band inside. E.S. Cap Co. Early 1980s. $8-15

Baseball, Bat, and Cap Set

•"Snoopy Slugger." The three-piece set includes a PEANUTS autographed baseball, a bat, and a baseball cap. The bat and cap each have a picture of Snoopy swinging a bat. Plastic bat and ball. Fabric cap. #411, Playskool. 1979. $25-35*

Bat and Ball Set

•"Charlie Brown & Snoopy Baseball And Bat." The decal on the red bat features Snoopy swinging a bat. The ball has no PEANUTS graphics. Plastic. #669B, Ohio Art. 1984. $4-6**

23. Fishing Equipment

Plastic. Zebco, a division of Brunswick Corp. Late 1980s.

•"Snoopy Catch 'Em Kit." The set includes a rod, reel, and fishing line, and a practice casting plug. Snoopy is featured on the reel holding a fishing rod and a fish he has caught. "Snoopy" is printed around the reel. Fiberglass rod. 34"H. #1281. $6-8 $12-15*

•"Snoopy Catch 'Em Bobber." When a fish bites, a floating Snoopy will "bob" up and down in the water. Plastic. 2-1/2"L. $4-5*

•"Snoopy Catch 'Em Box." Snoopy and Woodstock are featured on the orange tackle box carrying fishing poles. The boxes were sold empty or including a 101-piece fishing kit. Plastic. Without supplies: $4-6* With supplies: $8-12*

24. Golf Club Covers

"Country Clubbers." Plush. Carousel by Guy. 1989. $6-9 ea. $12-15* ea.

•Snoopy. 9"H. #3421B.

•Woodstock. 12"H. #3423B.

•Snoopy, with blue neck, wears plaid cap. 9"H. #3422B.

25. Jump Rope

•"Snoopy Jump Rope." Snoopy sits on the end of each handle. Plastic handles. #250PF118-9, Hallmark. Mid-1970s. $5-7 $15-20*

26. Roller Skates

Nash Manufacturing, Inc. 1990.

•"Snoopy Roller Skates." Snoopy's face is the toe piece of these skates. The skates are adjustable. Blue, white, and yellow plastic. $6-10 $12-20*

•"Snoopy and Woodstock Roller Skates." Woodstock and his friends are pictured skating in a row on the side of the yellow and white shoe skate. "Snoopy and Woodstock" is printed around Snoopy on the ankle portion of the skate. $6-8 $10-15*

27. Scooter

•"The Official Snoopy Scooter." The scooter features Snoopy, as Joe Cool, wearing a helmet and leather jacket, standing next to a scooter. Below him Woodstock and his friends, wearing leather jackets and caps, ride scooters. Printed: "Joe Cool" and "The Scooters." Assembly required. Scooter: 8"W x 29"L. Handle: 24"H. #700, Nash Manufacturing, Inc. 1986. $12-20 $30-40*

Skateboard

•The underside of the skateboard features Snoopy as Joe Cool skateboarding on top of his doghouse. Woodstock and his friends are all around

Snoopy. Printed: "Slammin' Joe Cool." The top side of the skateboard is printed "Joe Cool," which is cut from the non-skid surface. Other designs were available. 8"W x 28-1/2"L. Nash Manufacturing, Inc. 1986. $8-14 $20-25*

28. Tennis Racket Cover

•Snoopy is featured swinging his tennis racket on an orange background. Printed: "Ace." Fits an adult-size racket. Zippered vinyl. 10-1/4" x 14-1/2". Butterfly. 1979. $8-12

29. Toys

"Official Snoopy Tosserino." Plastic. 9" diam. Series #900, Aviva. 1977. $8-10* ea.

•Snoopy, as the Flying Ace, on a yellow disk printed "Official Snoopy Tosserino."

•Snoopy, as Joe Cool, on a white disk printed "Official Snoopy Tosserino."

30. Water Skis

•The front end of the water skis feature Snoopy piloting a motorboat while Woodstock and his friends water ski in formation. Printed: "Snoopy Ski School." The back end of the

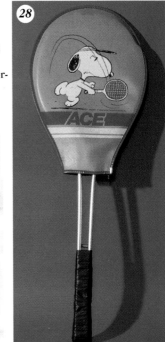

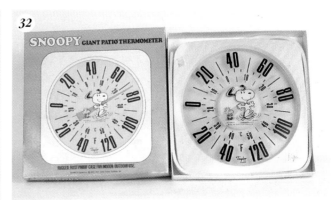

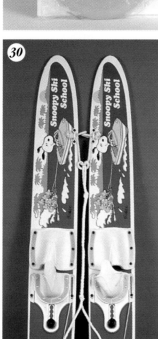

skis feature Snoopy water skiing. Adult-size skis. #N-68, Nash Manufacturing, Inc. 1989. $12-18 $25-45*

THERMOMETERS

31. Thermometers

Packaged in a non-graphic blister card. Plastic. 4-1/2" x 6". Assortment #5220, Sybron/Taylor. 1979. $5-8* ea.

•Snoopy puts Woodstock, in his nest, on top of the thermometer.

•Snoopy, dressed as a scout, looks up at Woodstock and his friends, also dressed as scouts, sitting in a tree.

•Charlie Brown is flying a green kite.

•Lucy sits behind her booth with a red stool in front. Printed on the booth: "Weather Forecast The Weather Person Is In."

Thermometer

•"Snoopy & Friends Wall Thermometer." Snoopy, dressed as an artist, is standing in front of an easel painting at the top of thermometer. Woodstock, also dressed as an artist, is at the bottom. Plastic. 8"H. #5194, Sybron/Taylor. 1979. $5-7*

32. Thermometer

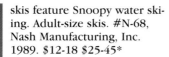

•"Snoopy Giant Patio Thermometer." Snoopy and Woodstock are dancing in the center of the thermometer. The indoor/outdoor thermometer measures the temperature in both Celsius and Fahrenheit. Plastic casing of the clock has a tendency to yellow from the sun. 11" x 12". #5374, Sybron/Taylor. 1979. $15-25 $35-40*

33. Thermometer

•"Snoopy Thermometer." Snoopy, Woodstock, Lucy, Sally, Linus, and Charlie Brown are featured at the top and bottom in scenes

that reflect summer and winter. The thermometer measures the temperature in both Celsius and Fahrenheit. Wood with a paper decal/22"H. #5192, Sybron/Taylor. 1979. $8-12 $18-22*

WIND CHIMES

34. Wind Chimes

•Snoopy, wearing headphones and roller skates, and Woodstock hang among musical notes. Available in other colors. Ceramic. #124001, Quantasia. 1984. $35-40

•Snoopy is standing. A clear plastic disk picturing Woodstock hangs beneath Snoopy. Ceramic. 8-1/2"H. #8115, Willitts Designs. 1988. $15-20

•Snoopy is lying on top of his doghouse. Metal chimes and Woodstock hang beneath the doghouse. Plastic. Aviva. 1973. $15-20

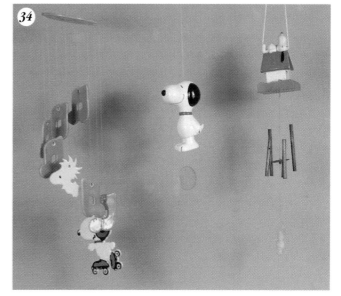

The honored guests (clockwise from the right), Peppermint Patty, Linus, Lucy, and Charlie Brown, were sold in America (see "Playroom" for details). The ceramic planter on the top left of the cabinet is from Hong Kong, and the glass on the table (holding the silverware and chopsticks) is from England. All of the other items are Japanese. These include:

On/In the Cabinet
Continuing on the top: A ceramic vase and a three-tier plastic container (for small items), pictured with its decorative cover standing vertically.

Top interior shelf: A variety of decorative glassware by Sasaki. Middle interior shelf: A decorative glass plate portraying Snoopy as ringmaster, along with cups, saucers, teapot, and salt and pepper shakers. Bottom interior shelf: Decorative glass plate, rice bowls, tea cups, salt and pepper shakers, and Snoopy on a spring, dressed in Japanese clothes.

On the Dining Room Table
Chopstick holder (in front of Peppermint Patty), cloth napkins, four sherbet glasses, teapots, rice bowls, cooking and serving pieces, salt and pepper shakers, place mats, a decorative plate by Sasaki (to the left of Charlie Brown), and various other plates.

The Dining Room

Plates and bells, which comprise most of the memorabilia in the dining room, are on almost everyone's list of all-time favorite PEANUTS collectibles. On the whole, they are decorative, tastefully done, and add a feeling of warmth to any home—one reason why many people prefer to keep the Christmas plates and bells on display year round.

BELLS

1. Annual Dated Bells

• "PEANUTS In Concert." Snoopy stands on Schroeder's piano conducting a band made up of Lucy, Linus, Sally, and Charlie Brown, all wearing uniforms and playing musical instruments. Woodstock sits above them in a bar of music. Printed on the rim of the bell: "PEANUTS In Concert 1983." A red ribbon is on top of the bell. First limited edition of 10,000 numbered pieces. Ceramic. 3-1/2"H. #279750, Schmid. 1983. $45-55*

• "Snoopy And The Beaglescouts." Snoopy, Woodstock, and his friends, dressed as scouts, are hiking. Printed on the rim of the bell: "Snoopy And The Beaglescouts 1984." A green ribbon is on top of the bell. Second limited edition of 10,000 numbered pieces. Ceramic. 3-1/2"H. #279751, Schmid. 1984. $45-50*

2. Annual Dated Bells

Limited editions of 10,000 numbered pieces. Ceramic. Schmid.

• "Clown Capers." Snoopy, standing with Woodstock sitting on his head, is the bell's handle. On the bell itself, the gang, dressed in clown costumes, piles into a circus car. First edition limited to 10,000 numbered pieces. Ceramic. #279752, Schmid. 1985. $55-60*

• "Flyin' Tamer Snoopy." Snoopy, dressed as a circus ringmaster, is the bell's handle. On the bell Snoopy, as a circus lion tamer, holds a whip in one hand and a chair in the other as Woodstock with a lion's mane "jumps" over a stand. Second limited edition. Ceramic. #279753, Schmid. 1986. $40-50*

• "Big Top Blast Off." Snoopy, wearing a tuxedo jacket, bow tie and top hat, is the bell's handle. On the bell Charlie Brown is inside a cannon; Woodstock, sitting on the back end, prepares to light it; and Snoopy, holding a cane, directs the action. This was to be the 1987 annual bell, but Schmid gave up its license and it was never mass-produced. The pieces that are in circulation were intended for proofs. 1987. $250-275

3. Bells

"Face Bells." 6"H. Ceramic. Schmid. 1974.

• Linus. #278-418. $130-140
• Schroeder. #278-419. $135-145
• Lucy. #278-417. $135-145
• Snoopy. #278-415. $130-140
• Charlie Brown. #278-416. $160-175

4. Bells

Dated Mother's Day bells. Ceramic. 6"H. Schmid. $40-50* ea.

• "Dear Mom." Snoopy is on top of his doghouse typing. He is thinking, "Dear Mom" with a heart. A chain of flowers surrounds the scene. Printed: "Mother's Day 1977."

• "Thoughts That Count." Snoopy and Woodstock, each sitting and holding a flower, are thinking of their mothers. Snoopy thinks, "Mom," and Woodstock chirps. A chain of flowers surrounds the scene. Printed: "Mother's Day 1978." Third limited edition. 1978. #279029

• "A Special Letter." Snoopy is on top of his doghouse typing. "Dear Mom" with a paw print for the "o" is printed above. A chain of flowers surrounds the scene. #279017. 1979.

• "Mission For Mom." Snoopy, as the Flying Ace, sits on top of his doghouse with heart-shaped clouds around him. Third edition limited to 10,000 numbered pieces. #279326. 1981.

5. Bell

• "40th Anniversary Bell." Snoopy, sitting and wearing a red bow tie, is the bell's handle. The bell features the 40th anniversary logo of Charlie Brown, Woodstock, and Snoopy wearing red bow ties with "40 Years of Happiness" printed above and below. Ceramic. 5-1/4"H. #19003, Willitts Designs. 1990. $30-35*

6. Bell

•"Bicentennial Bell." Snoopy lies on top of the Liberty Bell with white stars around him on a blue background. Printed: "1776-1976." Ceramic. Schmid. 1976. $25-30*

7. Bells

Dated Christmas bells. Ceramic. 6"H. Schmid.

•"Christmas Eve At The Doghouse." Snoopy, wearing a green and red stocking cap, lies on top of his doghouse decorated with Christmas stockings. Woodstock stands on a tree beside the doghouse. Printed on reverse side: "United Features Syndicate 1973." #279020. 1973. $40-45*

•"Woodstock, Santa Claus." Snoopy is lying on top of his doghouse with Woodstock, dressed as Santa, standing on his nose. Printed: "Christmas 1975." 1975. $40-45*

•"Woodstock's Christmas." Snoopy looks up at Woodstock with a decorated Christmas tree in his nest. Colored snowflakes surround the scene. Printed: "Christmas 1976." #279026. 1976. $35-42*

•"Filling The Stockings." Snoopy, dressed as Santa with a sack of gifts, stands in front of a fireplace decorated with stockings. Woodstock is in one of the stockings. Printed: "Christmas 1978." Fourth limited edition. #279030. 1978. $35-40*

•"Deck The Doghouse." Snoopy lies on top of his doghouse decorated with strings of Christmas lights. Printed: "Christmas 1977." Third limited edition. #279028. 1977. $35-38*

•"Waiting For Santa." Snoopy looks up at Woodstock in his nest in a tree decorated with Christmas stockings. Printed on the reverse side: "1980." Second limited edition of 10,000 numbered pieces. #279325. 1980. $45-48*

•"Perfect Performance." Snoopy, wearing a red scarf and a red and yellow stocking cap, is ice-skating. Printed on the reverse side: "1982." Fourth limited edition of 10,000 numbered pieces. #279327. 1982. $35-40*

8. Bells

"Christmas Signature Series Bells." Part of a collection of dated musicals, plates, and ornaments issued annually at holiday time. Ceramic. Willitts Designs.

•Snoopy, wearing a stocking cap and lying on his tummy, looks over the roof of his decorated doghouse. Woodstock, wearing a Santa hat, sits on Snoopy's back. Printed on the back of the doghouse: "Christmas 1987." The bell's ringer is shaped like a dog bone. 4-3/4"H. #7706. 1987. $25-35*

•Snoopy, wearing a red coat, top hat, and green scarf, is the bell's handle. On the bell Snoopy, Woodstock, and his friend sing Christmas carols in the snow beneath a lamppost. Another of Woodstock's friends flies overhead blowing a horn. Printed: "Christmas 1988." #8429. 1988. $25-35*

•Snoopy, wearing a pink hat and scarf and carrying a Christmas tree over his shoulder, is the bell's handle. On the bell Snoopy, carrying a Christmas tree over his shoulder, pulls Woodstock on a sled. Printed: "Christmas 1989." 5"H. #9356. 1989. $30-35*

•Snoopy, wearing a Santa hat, sits on top of his snow-covered doghouse decorated with lights and a wreath. "Christmas 1990" is printed over the doorway. 5"H. #44003. 1990. $25-30*

•Charlie Brown, Snoopy, and Woodstock share a toboggan in the snow. Printed: "Christmas 1991." 5"H. #44029. 1991. $25-30*

PLATES

9. Plates

Dated Valentine's Day plates. 7-1/2" diam. Ceramic. Schmid. $15-20 ea. $20-25* ea.

•"Home Is Where The Heart Is." Snoopy lies on top of a red, white, and pink gingham heart trimmed with lace. Printed: "Valentine's Day 1977." #279306. 1977.

•"Heavenly Bliss." Snoopy stands under a red umbrella as it rains red hearts all around him. Printed: "Valentine's Day 1978." #279307. 1978.

•"Love Match." Snoopy, wearing a visor and holding a tennis racket, stands ready to return a heart that has been served to him. The plate is trimmed around the edge with red hearts. Printed: "Valentine's Day 1979." Third edition. #279308. 1979.

10. Plates

Dated Valentine's Day plates. 7-1/2" diam. Ceramic. Schmid. $15-20 ea. 20-25* ea.

•"From Snoopy, With Love." Snoopy blows pink heart-shaped bubbles as Woodstock looks on. Printed: "Valentine's Day 1980." Fourth limited edition. #279309. 1980.

•"Hearts A-Flutter." Charlie Brown runs with a heart-shaped red kite as Snoopy watches. Printed: "Valentine's Day 1981." #279310. 1981.

•Snoopy, dressed as a scarecrow in a straw hat and burlap jacket, watches over hearts growing in a field. Printed: "Valentine's Day 1982." 1982.

11. Plates

Limited edition dated Mother's Day plates. 7-1/2" diam. Ceramic. Schmid. $15-20 ea. $20-25* ea.

•"Linus." Linus holds a single red rose. Printed: "Mother's Day 1972." #279000. 1972.

•"Mom?" Woodstock holds a sign that reads "Mom?" as Snoopy looks on. Printed: "Mother's Day 1973." #279002. 1973.

•"Snoopy And Woodstock On Parade." Snoopy carries a flag with a red heart on it, and Woodstock carries a flag printed: "Mom." The plate is trimmed around the edge with red hearts. Printed: "Mother's Day 1974." #279004. 1974.

12. Plates

Limited edition dated Mother's Day plates. 7-1/2" diam. Ceramic. Schmid. $15-20 ea. $22-25* ea.

•"A Kiss For Lucy." Snoopy kisses Lucy on the cheek. The plate is trimmed around the edge with red hearts and roses. Printed: "Mother's Day 1975." #279007. 1975.

•"Linus And Snoopy." Linus and Snoopy, sitting on the ground, and Woodstock, flying above, each hold a single flower. The plate is trimmed around the edge with flowers. Printed: "Mother's Day 1976." #279009. 1976.

•"Dear Mom." Snoopy is on top of his doghouse typing. He is thinking, "Dear Mom" with a heart. The plate is trimmed around the edge with flowers. Printed: "Mother's Day 1977." #279011. 1977.

13. Plates

Limited edition dated Mother's Day plates. 7-1/2" diam. Ceramic. Schmid. $18-20 ea. $22-28* ea.

•"Thoughts That Count." Snoopy and Woodstock, each sitting and holding a flower, are thinking of their mothers. Snoopy thinks, "Mom," and Woodstock chirps. The plate is trimmed around the edge with flowers. Printed: "Mother's Day 1978." #279013. 1978.

•"A Special Letter." Snoopy is on top of his doghouse typing. "Dear Mom" with a paw print for the "o" is printed above. The plate is trimmed around the edge with flowers. Printed: "Mother's Day 1979." Eighth edition limited to 10,000 numbered pieces. #279015. 1979.

•"A Tribute To Mom." Snoopy is inside the "O" in an over-sized wall-like depiction of the word "Mom." Woodstock stands in front holding flowers. The plate is trimmed around the edge with flowers. Printed: "Mother's Day 1980." #279017. 1980.

14. Plates

Limited edition dated Mother's Day plates. 7-1/2" diam. Ceramic. Schmid. $18-20 ea. $22-28* ea.

• "Mission For Mom." Snoopy as the Flying Ace is on top of his doghouse. The clouds above him spell out "Mom." Printed: "Mother's Day 1981." #279316. 1981.

• "Which Way To Mother?" Snoopy and Woodstock, holding a flower, stand in front of a directional signpost with "Mom" printed in several different languages. The plate is trimmed around the edge with flowers. Printed: "Mother's Day 1982." #279317. 1982.

Plates

• Snoopy, standing atop his doghouse, holds yellow, orange, and pink heart-shaped balloons that spell "Mother." X's and o's trim the edge pf the plate. Printed: "Mother's Day 1988." A poem is on the back of the plate. Ceramic. #8116, Willitts Designs. 1988. $22-25 $30-35*

15. Plates

"Signature Collection Mother's Day Plates." Porcelain. 7-1/2" diam. Willitts Designs. $20-24 ea. $25-32* ea.

• Snoopy, sitting on top of his doghouse at his typewriter, types, "Dear Mom, Thinking of you and your chocolate chip cookies." The plate is trimmed around the edge with flowers. Printed: "Mother's Day 1989." A poem appears on the back of the plate. #9361. 1989.

• Snoopy dances on a lavender background surrounded by pink, purple, and blue hearts, three of which spell out "Mom." The plate is trimmed around the edge with tiny multicolored hearts. Printed: "Mother's Day 1990." A poem appears on the back of the plate. #40009. 1990.

• Snoopy, dressed as a chef, holds a cake with a candle in it in front of a window full of flowers. Woodstock stands behind him holding a bouquet of flowers. The plate is trimmed around the edge with flowers. Printed: "Mother's Day 1992." Fourth limited edition. #40012. 1992.

16. Plates

Limited edition dated Christmas plates. 7-1/2" diam. Ceramic. Schmid.

• "Snoopy Guides The Sleigh." Snoopy, wearing a red and green stocking cap, rides in a red sleigh being pulled by Woodstock. The plate is trimmed around the edge with holly. Printed: "Christmas 1972." #279001. 1972. $20-24 $25-30*

• "Christmas Eve At The Doghouse." Snoopy, in a red and green stocking cap, lies atop his doghouse decorated with Christmas stockings. Woodstock stands on a tree beside the doghouse. The plate's edge is trimmed with evergreen trees. Printed: "Christmas 1973." #279003. 1973. $80-85 $90-125*

• "Christmas Eve At The Fireplace." Snoopy and Woodstock lean on wrapped presents against a fireplace trimmed with stockings, candles, and a wreath above the mantle. The plate is trimmed around the edge with presents. Printed: "Christmas 1974." #279005. 1974. $35-40 $45-50*

17. Plates

Limited edition dated Christmas plates. 7-1/2" diam. Ceramic. Schmid. $22-30 ea. $35-40* ea.

• "Woodstock, Santa Claus." Snoopy is lying on top of his doghouse with Woodstock, dressed as Santa, standing on his nose. Printed: "Christmas 1975." #279008. 1975.

• "Woodstock's Christmas." Snoopy looks up at the decorated Christmas tree in Woodstock's nest. Colored snowflakes surround the scene. Printed: "Christmas 1976." #279010. 1976.

• "Deck The Doghouse." Snoopy lies on top of his doghouse decorated with strings of Christmas lights. Printed: "Christmas 1977." #279012. 1977.

18. Plates

Limited edition dated Christmas plates. 7-1/2" diam. Ceramic. Schmid.

• "Filling The Stockings." Snoopy, dressed as Santa with a sack of gifts, stands in front of a fireplace decorated with stockings. Woodstock is in one of the stockings. Printed: "Christmas 1978." #279014. 1978. $25-30 $35-40*

• "Christmas At Hand." Snoopy, standing atop his doghouse decorated with presents and a wreath, plays with paw-pets of Santa Claus and a reindeer. Printed: "Christmas 1979." Eighth limited edition. #279016. 1979. $25-28 $30-35*

• "Waiting For Santa." Snoopy looks up at Woodstock in his nest, which is in a tree decorated with Christmas stockings. Printed: "1980." Ninth limited edition of 15,000 numbered pieces. #279320. 1980. $30-34 $35-40*

19. Plates

Limited edition dated Christmas plates. 7-1/2" diam. Ceramic. Schmid. $20-25* ea. $30-35* ea.

• "A Christmas Wish." Snoopy lies on top of his doghouse, which is completely covered with a collage of multicolored stockings. Printed: "Christmas 1981." #279232. 1981.

• "Perfect Performance." Snoopy, wearing a red scarf and a red and yellow stocking cap, ice-skates the word "Merry." Printed: "Christmas 1982." Eleventh limited edition of 15,000 numbered pieces. #279322. 1982.

Plate

• "Merry Christmas, Charlie Brown." Snoopy, dressed as Santa, rings a bell; Lucy and Linus sing carols; and Charlie Brown and Peppermint Patty dance. Woodstock and his friend, wear reindeer antlers, stand on a "Merry Christmas" banner strung across the plate. A wreath with a big red bow circles the plate. Design is based on an original drawing by Tom Everhart. Issue was limited to 45 firing days. Each plate is hand-numbered. Porcelain, trimmed in 24-karat gold. 8" diam. Franklin Mint. 1994. $65-75

20. Plates

"Christmas Signature Series Plates." Part of a series of dated musicals, bells, and ornaments issued annually. Porcelain. 7-1/2" diam. Willitts Designs. $22-24 ea. $25-30* ea.

• Snoopy, wearing a stocking cap and lying on his tummy, looks over the roof of his decorated doghouse. Woodstock, wearing a Santa hat, sits on Christmas tree. Printed: "Christmas 1987." #7705. 1987.

• Snoopy, Woodstock, and his friend sing Christmas carols in the snow beneath a lamppost. Another of Woodstock's friends flies overhead blowing a horn. Printed: "Christmas 1988." #8445. 1988.

• Snoopy, wearing a pink hat and sweater and carrying a Christmas tree over his shoulder, pulls Woodstock on a sled. Printed: "Christmas 1989." #9354. 1989.

21. Plates

"Christmas Signature Series Plates." Part of a series of dated musicals, bells, and ornaments issued annually. Porcelain. 7-1/2" diam. Willitts Designs. $18-20 ea. $25-30* ea.

• Snoopy, wearing a Santa hat, sits on top of his snow-covered doghouse—decorated with lights—which is being flown through the sky by Woodstock. Printed: "Christmas 1990." #44001. 1990.

• Charlie Brown, Snoopy, and Woodstock share a toboggan in the snow. Printed: "Christmas 1991." #44027. 1991.

• Woodstock decorates a tree on top of Snoopy's doghouse while Snoopy, standing on the ground, hangs Christmas stockings on the roof. Printed: "Christmas 1992." #44037. 1992.

22. Plates

• Snoopy, standing on a gift, plays with his paw-pets as Charlie Brown, Lucy, Linus, Peppermint Patty, and Schroeder—all wearing green or red stocking caps—hold toys, and Woodstock and his friends decorate the Christmas tree. The plate is trimmed around the edge with toys, bells, and candy canes. Printed: "Merry Christmas." Ceramic. 9" diam. Determined Productions. Mid-1970s. $55-60

• Schroeder plays the piano as Snoopy, Woodstock, and Charlie Brown dance. Linus and Peppermint Patty decorate the Christmas tree and Lucy carries a present. Musical notes appear all around and "O' Christmas Tree" is printed around the edge of the plate. Ceramic. 9" diam. Made by Determined Productions for Joy, Inc. Limited Editions in Chicago, Illinois. 1976. $75-80

23. Plates

"World's Greatest Athlete Collection." Limited to 10,000 pieces. Ceramic. 6-1/2" diam. Schmid. 1983. $30-32 ea. $35-40* ea.

• "The Crowd Went Wild." Snoopy, wearing a red baseball cap, swings a bat. Printed: "Pow." #279704.

• "The Way You Play The Game." Snoopy, wearing a visor and holding a tennis racket, is ready to swing at the tennis ball. #279703.

24. Plates

"World's Greatest Athlete Collection." Production limited to 10,000 pieces. Porcelain. 6-1/2" diam. Schmid. 1983. $30-32 $35-40* ea.

•"Go Deep." Snoopy, wearing a red helmet, throws the football to Woodstock who is running forward but looking back at the ball. #279701.

•"The Puck Stops Here." Snoopy and Woodstock are playing ice hockey. #279702.

25. Plates

Porcelain. 7-1/2" diam. Schmid. $30-35 ea. $38-42* ea.

•"PEANUTS In Concert." Snoopy stands on Schroeder's piano conducting a band made up of Lucy, Linus, Sally, and Charlie Brown, all wearing uniforms and playing musical instruments. Woodstock sits above them in a bar of music. First limited edition of 20,000 numbered pieces. 1983.

•"Snoopy And The Beaglescouts." Snoopy, Woodstock, and his friends, dressed as scouts, are hiking. Second limited edition of 20,000 numbered pieces. 1984.

•"Clown Capers." Dressed in clown costumes, Snoopy, Woodstock and the gang pile into a circus car. First edition limited to 20,000 numbered pieces. #279741. 1985.

26. Plates

Porcelain. 7-1/2" diam. Schmid.

•"Flyin' Tamer Snoopy." Snoopy, as a circus lion tamer, holds a whip in one hand and a chair in the other as Woodstock with a lion's mane "jumps" over a stand. Second limited edition. #279743. 1986. $20-22 $25-30*

•"Big Top Blast Off." Charlie Brown is inside a cannon; Woodstock, sitting on the back end, prepares to light it; and Snoopy, wearing a tuxedo jacket, bow tie, and top hat, while holding a cane, directs the action. This was to be the 1987 annual plate but Schmid gave up its license and it was never mass-produced. The pieces that are in circulation were intended for proof and sample purposes. 1987. $195-225.

27. Plate

•"40th Anniversary Plate." The plate features the 40th anniversary logo of Charlie Brown, Woodstock, and Snoopy wearing red bow ties with "40 Years of Happiness" printed above and below. Porcelain. 7-1/2" diam. #19001, Willitts Designs. 1990. $15-18 $20-25*

•"PEANUTS 30th Anniversary Commemorative Plate." The plate shows Snoopy, as the Flying Ace, sitting atop his doghouse and surrounded by Charlie Brown, Woodstock in his nest, Lucy leaning on Schroeder's piano as he plays, Franklin, Linus sucking his thumb and holding his blanket, Peppermint Patty, Marcie, Spike standing next to a cactus, and Sally reading a letter. Printed: "1950 Happy Anniversary 1980." Limited to 15,000 numbered pieces. Porcelain. 10-1/2" diam. #279330, Schmid. 1980. $20-22 $25-30*

•Snoopy, as the Flying Ace, is sitting on his doghouse as it flies through the sky past the earth and clouds. Printed: "Around The World And Home Again A Tribute To The Art Of Charles M. Schulz September 18 To October 2, 1994 Mall Of America Exhibition Center, Bloomington, Minnesota." Porcelain, trimmed in gold. 8" diam. 1994. $22-25

28. Plates

•"PEANUTS Bicentennial Plate." Snoopy lies on top of the Liberty Bell with white stars around him on a blue background. Printed: "1776-1976." 7-1/2" diam. Porcelain. Schmid. 1976. $12-14*

•"PEANUTS Birthday Plate." Snoopy and Woodstock, in the center of the plate, hold balloons printed "Happy Birthday." The plate is trimmed around the edge with locomotives and train cars with Snoopy as the engineer and Woodstock, Peppermint Patty, Sally, Lucy, Linus, Schroeder and Charlie Brown as the passengers. Linus, Schroeder and Charlie Brown hold balloons in an open car. Production limited to 5,000 pieces. See the matching mug on page 153 in Kitchen. Determined Productions for Dupont Collection Ltd. 1978. $55-60

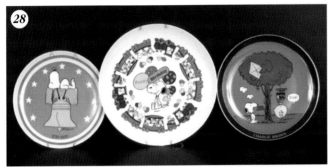

•"Snoopy And Charlie Brown." Snoopy, standing under a tree with his supper dish in his mouth, looks at Charlie Brown tangled in kite string and hanging upside down from the tree. Charlie Brown says, "Sigh!" "Snoopy And Friends" is printed on the top of the plate and "Charlie Brown" is printed on the bottom. The number of plates produced was limited to 25 firing days. Each plate is hand-numbered. Porcelain, trimmed in 24-karat gold. 8" diam. Danbury Mint. 1990. $65-75

STEINS

29. Steins

Dated Christmas steins. Ceramic. 3-3/4"H. Determined Productions. $30-40 ea.

•Snoopy, wearing a stocking cap, sits on his doghouse holding a pair of reins attached to Woodstock in the air as Charlie Brown, Lucy, and Linus walk by singing. Printed on the reverse side: "Merry Christmas 1975." 1975.

•Snoopy, wearing a stocking cap, sits in a red sleigh holding a pair of reins attached to Woodstock in the air. Printed on the reverse side: "Merry Christmas 1976." 1976.

•Snoopy and Charlie Brown watch as Woodstock flies a gold star to the top of the Christmas tree. Printed on the reverse side: "Merry Christmas 1977." 1977.

•Snoopy, dressed as Santa, stands in front of a decorated fireplace with a gift sack. Woodstock sits on the mantle, and Charlie Brown stands behind a small Christmas tree. Printed on the reverse side: "Merry Christmas 1978." 1978.

30. Steins

Dated Christmas steins. Ceramic. 3-3/4"H. Determined Productions. $25-35

•Snoopy is sitting inside a Christmas wreath with a red bow. Printed on the reverse side: "Merry Christmas 1979." #1984. 1979.

•Snoopy, wearing a Santa hat, sits on top of his decorated doghouse with a present. Woodstock flies above wearing earmuffs and holding mistletoe. Printed on the reverse side: "Merry Christmas 1980." #1943. 1980.

•The continuous scene pictures Woodstock on a sled with a large gift bag being pulled by Charlie Brown, Lucy, Linus, Sally, Marcie, Schroeder, Peppermint Patty, and Snoopy, who are all wearing reindeer antlers. Printed: "Merry Christmas 1981." #1303. 1981.

•Charlie Brown brings the turkey to the table as Lucy, Snoopy, and Woodstock look on. Printed vertically: "Merry Christmas 1982." #1765. 1982.

•The continuous scene pictures Snoopy, dressed as Santa, putting presents into his gift sack as Woodstock and his friends, dressed as elves, help out. Printed: "Merry Christmas 1983." #1309. 1983.

The story of cels

The evolution of animated cels as a desired collectible is a story perhaps unique in the annals of collecting.

Most collectible items were originally acquired to serve a purpose—either as a decoration or a work of art—or for a more functional use such as a music box or a toy. In contrast, animated cels were used in the actual production of something. When the production was over, the artists considered them to be valueless. Consequently, after the day's shooting of an animated film sequence was completed, most of the cels involved were discarded. Good Grief! It was like throwing away winning lottery tickets—not just one, but literally hundreds or thousands—every day of every week.

Today, for a variety of reasons, animated cels of all sorts are among the fastest growing—and one of the most expensive—areas in the world of collectibles. How did this happen? Let's first discuss animated films themselves.

The main ingredients of an animated cartoon are the clear sheets of celluloid or plastic (known as the "cel") on which artists sketch and paint the character, plus a painted background against which each cel is shot. This combination of cel and painted background is known as a "set-up." In some cases, more than one cel is projected over the background in what is known as a "multi-cel set-up."

For example, if the script calls for Snoopy to hit a tennis ball, there will be one background—the tennis court—and dozens of cels painted with Snoopy's body in various positions as he goes through the motion of hitting the ball. Each cel is photographed individually against the background (the set-up). It is the rapid projection of these individual pictures that gives the appearance of motion.

An animated film will require many more cels than backgrounds. Therefore, a "set-up" will be far more valuable than the cel itself. A half hour show may require 20,000 individually hand-painted cels, but as few as 200 backgrounds. It takes about six months to produce a half-hour TV film.

The majority of images on the cels are unattractive. In the example of Snoopy hitting the tennis ball, a single cel depicting his twisted arm really doesn't mean much to anybody. It was these cels, known in the trade as "in betweens" (as opposed to the "key poses"), that debased the value of cels in the eyes of the artists. In the 1950s and 1960s, some studios would occasionally celebrate the completion of production by holding "skating parties," which included the ritual of sliding on the cels. (The people in Bill Melendez's studio,

where the PEANUTS animated films were created, and are still created today, never participated in this kind of behavior.) Lost in the revelry were many of the "key poses," which today would hold great value. Also, back in the early 1940s (pre-PEANUTS), when celluloids were expensive, studios would remove the paint and recycle the cels, resulting in the loss of original artwork.

The fragile nature of the older cels, and the paints that were used at the time, made them susceptible to damage. Unless stored carefully, they became victims to the ravages of time. For instance, most of the cels that had been saved from "A Charlie Brown Christmas," "A Boy Named Charlie Brown," and "It's the Great Pumpkin, Charlie Brown," were destroyed by water damage. Fortunately, a number of "key pose" cels from these works were discovered unharmed when Nina Skahan, the Melendez studio voice casting director, was rummaging through a closet in the studio a few years ago.

Since the early 1980s, there has been a surge in interest in cels, to the amazement of animators and collectors alike. One expert theorizes that cels spark the interest of baby boomers who grew up with Saturday morning TV cartoons and have found them to be artistically non-threatening. This increased demand, coupled with the aforementioned scarcity, could explain any rise in value. But there is yet another reason: Computers. The increasing dependence on computer-generated images could eventually render the use of cels obsolete.

The production of animated art is labor intensive and, subsequently, very expensive. A great deal of today's animated work has shifted to Pacific rim countries where labor in the art field is relatively inexpensive. Much of what hasn't been relegated to foreign countries has been consigned to computers, which use a different process completely and bypass the use of cels. In fact, the Melendez studio is one of the few in the United States that is still using cels exclusively, relying on computers only for special effects.

Through the late 1980s and early 1990s, the demand for cels has become so great that most studios are now putting out limited editions of their character cels. These later-day cels may have been inspired by earlier films, but obviously they were not specifically created for use in the actual production of any film. While they are strictly issued to meet consumer demands, and they are selling like hot cakes, these limited editions can command almost as much money as the original art work.

The Gallery

Every home needs a gallery: A quiet place to contemplate rare and beautiful works of art. We are fortunate in our house to have a room full of masterpiece cels, lithographs, and original art by Charles Schulz, Bill Melendez, and Tom Everhart. Because of their delicacy, beauty, and high value, it also seems logical to display a few major pieces of PEANUTS jewelry and Cartier enameled boxes in the gallery.

Cels and lithographs are relative newcomers to the family of PEANUTS collectibles. Their rise in value has been so meteoric they transcend the scope of ordinary collecting to the point of being a financial investment.

As works of art, they have limited availability. Except for limited edition reproductions, cels are one-of-a-kind. PEANUTS lithographs are also very limited in number. Therefore, particularly in the case of cels, value becomes subjective in the purchaser's mind. There can be great swings in the market for these works.

Even more noteworthy than the value of the cels and lithographs is the fact that most of these works were created by the only two artists in the world—Bill Melendez and Tom Everhart—who are permitted by Mr. Schulz to affix their own signatures to PEANUTS illustrations.

All pieces of artwork are priced as unframed.

How can the collector tell if a cel is authentic? Frankly, it is difficult. The artists at Melendez's studio have no problem at all—they can even recognize which of their associates drew a particular cel—but most of us are not that fortunate. The best advice is to purchase your cel from a reputable source and, if possible, establish the provenance (history of owner-ship) of the cel.

There are some basic guidelines to keep in mind. The cels themselves are horizontal in shape, 10-1/2" by 12-1/2", to be exact. They must have three "peg holes" across the bottom, and they should each have at least two sets of numbers. The peg holes fit over pegs at the bottom of the work table and enable the photographer to perfectly align the cel with the background. One set of numbers corresponds to the identification number of the scene to which the cel belongs. The other number instructs the photographer as to the proper order in which the cels appear in the scene. There may also

HAPPINESS IS A WARM PUPPY

342/500

Charles Schulz

be a number specifying the year and production number of the job. Without these numbers, there would be chaos.

Will you ever see a cel without numbers? Very, very rarely. A single cel might have been produced for publicity or other special purpose, but in comparison to the thousands of cels required for an original film, the number of these cels is minuscule.

How does one establish value? One doesn't! Set-ups with cels from key scenes and poses from the earlier and more popular TV films command such high prices that they have taken this genre far beyond the area of collectibility for the average person, and into the realm of investment.

The first significant auction of PEANUTS animated art took place at Sotheby's, in New York, on June 18, 1991. One of the items auctioned was a multi-cel set-up from the 1965 "A Charlie Brown Christmas," that depicted a skating Charlie Brown, Snoopy pulling on Linus' blanket, and Linus falling through the ice. The Sotheby's catalog estimated its value at $4,000-6,000. It sold for $25,000. Another multi-cel set up from the same film, featuring three images of Charlie Brown carrying a tree down a snowy path, against a background of a starry night, went for $31,000.

Of course, there were examples of more earthly prices, particularly for cels from later films. Thus, a multi-cel set-up from the 1988 "Snoopy the Musical," showing Charlie Brown and Peppermint Patty sitting under a tree, was estimated to be worth $700-900, and was auctioned for "only" $3,750. And, a multi-cel set up from the 1974 "It's the Easter Beagle, Charlie Brown," depicting Snoopy, Linus, and Sally, sold for only $2,000—well within the estimate of $1,000 to $2,500.

Perhaps the one "stabilizing" influence on the prices of cels is that studios in the past two decades have become more conscientious about saving them, which in the long run increases availability. The primary reason for saving them is that they can be reused in subsequent productions (sometimes with minor alterations), thereby saving a great deal of labor. As for Bill Melendez, he never intentionally destroys his cels. Consequently, with the exception of those cels that were damaged, there remains extant a large body of PEANUTS cels and backgrounds from the more than fifty films and commercials that followed. Most of them still remain in Bill Melendez's possession.

Cel enthusiasts suggest the following criteria to consider when shopping for a cel:

The most important feature is the pose of the characters. They must be in a key pose from an important scene in the production. Unless there is a real craziness out there, in-betweens won't cut it.

Secondly, the more important characters—Snoopy, Lucy, Charlie Brown, Linus, Peppermint Patty, etc.—command the higher prices, and a cel with several characters will generally be of higher value than a cel with only a single character. For some strange reason, the male characters seem to be slightly

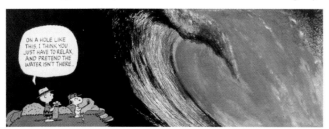

more popular than the female characters, with Snoopy being the most popular of all. Also, scenes or cels from major productions will command a far higher premium than those from the lesser known films.

Finally, there is the case of Pigpen. Although he doesn't necessarily command higher prices, he is of special interest to the aficionado because it takes the artists more time to draw all those specks of dirt that constantly surround him—a task they do not relish.

When you consider the tremendous interest in cartoon characters of all sorts generated by the proliferation of stores like Disney and Time-Warner, and then factor in the declining production of cels in this country, it may well be that cels have a rosy future as an expensive collectible.

If collecting cels becomes your bag, we can only wish you happy hunting.

Lithographs

It is safe to say that comic strip cartoonists as a group have never been considered "serious artists." Even Schulz himself, perhaps with characteristic modesty, has been known to downplay his own creative gifts.

It was the appearance of his lithographs in 1992 that helped to elevate the perception of Schulz as an artist. In lithography, Schulz found a departure from the pencil sketch and story line. The focus here is on imagery, and he acquits himself well.

Since the golfing series of four lithographs was released in 1992, Schulz has done a total of eighteen signed pieces. Except for the first one, "Hitting the Green," which had a limited edition of 250 pieces, subsequent editions had 500 copies each. Thus, there are only 8,750 in existence. Originally sold for $600, they are now going for $2,800 and more on the secondary market.

In addition to the signed, limited edition series, Schulz did lithographs of eight strips which are now selling for $170 at the galleries.

Contrasting with Schulz's straightforward styling and basic choice of colors, Tom Everhart paints his PEANUTS characters big and drenched with color. Everhart has also done the Met Life billboards, among other things, and his works have appeared with those of Schulz in the Louvre, and elsewhere around the world.

ART—ORIGINAL CELS BY BILL MELENDEZ

1. "Pigpen."

•Cel from the production of an unknown PEANUTS film. #1-39 PP33. Given to the American Embassy in New York by Bill Melendez Productions, in 1973. Purchased at an art gallery in 1996 for $500.

2. "Why Charlie Brown, Why?"

•Cel with original hand-painted background. From the TV Special of the same name. #88/490 BG 1A. 1990. Dedicated to the author; signed by Bill Melendez on 8/19/91. $2,200

3. "You're A Good Sport, Charlie Brown."

•Cel from the film, which first aired in 1975. $400

4. "Snoopy's Getting Married, Charlie Brown"

•The cel, and its original drawing from the film, which aired in 1985, are pictured. Value of cel without original drawing: $400. Value of cel with original drawing: $550.

ART—REPRODUCTIONS OF CELS BY BILL MELENDEZ

5. "Interesting Discussions."

•Limited edition of 500. Individually signed by Bill Melendez. 30"H x 12.5"L. 1994. #PL-09. $1,000

6. "Joe Cool."

•Limited edition of 250. Individually signed by Bill Melendez. 12"H x 10"L. 1995. #PL-13. $795

7. "Dress Rehearsal."

•Limited edition of 500. Individually signed by Bill Melendez. 12"H x 10"L. 1993. #PL-03. $895

A word about the team of Schulz and Melendez

The highly successful creative relationship between Charles Schulz and Bill Melendez can be traced to their first collaboration in 1957. Melendez was already a successful animator in his own right, having produced over 200 animated TV films and commercials. Schulz, who enjoyed driving Fords

in those days, agreed to do his first commercial for the introduction of the Ford Falcon. Melendez got the animating assignment and the rest, as they say, is history.

Their first full length TV show, "A Charlie Brown Christmas," was completed in 1965, with Lee Mendelson as producer, and Vince Guaraldi as musical composer and director. This program won both an Emmy and a Peabody award, and has already become an American Christmas institution almost on a par with the annual Macy's Thanksgiving Day parade. Over fifty films and commercials followed, many of them equally as popular.

The work of Melendez and his staff is so painstaking, time consuming, complex, and demanding that Schulz, who normally keeps his licensees on a very tight leash, exercises very little oversight over the Melendez studio. Melendez is so much in sync with Sparky that he has almost carte blanche permission to draw Snoopy and the PEANUTS characters almost any way he sees fit. It is rumored that Melendez draws Snoopy in his sleep.

ART—COMIC STRIP

8. Original Sunday Strip dated 2/8/81

•Dedicated to the author and her husband, and signed by Charles M. Schulz on 3/23/81. $7,000-$8,000

9. Original Weekly Strip dated 6/9/55

•Dedicated to E. E. Person, and signed by Charles M. Schulz. Valued at $3,000-$5,000

Lithographs

A lithograph is anything that is printed by the process known as lithography, as opposed to other printed reproduction techniques such as silk screening, letterpress, and so forth. Posters, calendars, and perhaps even your daily newspaper, may be lithographed products. There are two different methods of producing lithographs: Offset printing, which relies on photographic technology and is relatively new; and the more traditional "fine arts" method that has its roots in medieval times.

Briefly, offset printing employs photographic materials, known as separations, which are laid over metal plates. The image is then transferred from the plates onto the paper by means of a roller, with a different separation used for each color.

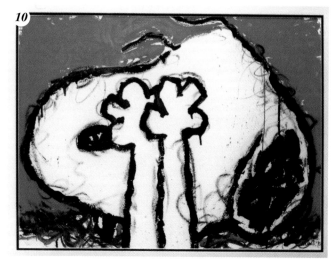

In works where the coloration is more complex, the "fine arts" method is employed. The work is engraved on a series of stones or metal plates—a separate plate for each different color. A skilled artisan called a "chromist" is responsible for the layering of the individual colors on separate stones. The process of running the paper through the press numerous times is difficult, time consuming (each sheet must be allowed to dry thoroughly before it is run through the press again), and expensive. There must be perfect color registration, as even the slightest overlap or blurring of colors can render a lithograph valueless. Lithographs of this fine quality will usually be reproduced on a better grade of paper, which will also contribute to a more satisfactory end result.

Like most of the lithography produced today, Schulz's work is done on offset presses. Everhart, on the other hand, because of the complexity of his textures, requires that the colors be hand-separated in the "fine arts" tradition. To capture Everhart's colorings exactly, the chromist needs to use as many as seventeen different stones or plates.

Besides the popularity of the artist himself, and the quality of the end product, a lithograph will become far more valuable if it is printed in limited editions and individually signed by the artist, as are most of the lithographs by Schulz and Everhart.

ART—LITHOGRAPHS BY TOM EVERHART

10. "I Can't Believe My Eyes."

•Hand pulled. Limited edition of 200. Individually signed by the artist, Tom Everhart. 32"W x 24"H. 1995. $1,000

11. "Lucy's Scream."

•Hand pulled. Limited edition of 200. Individually signed by the artist, Tom Everhart. 32"W x 24"H. 1995. $625

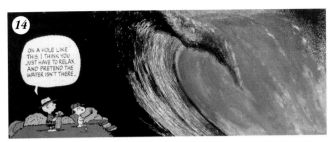

12. "To Every Dog There Is A Season: Winter."

•Limited edition of 250. Individually signed by the artist, Tom Everhart. 22-1/2"W x 30-1/2"H. 1996. $625

ART—LITHOGRAPHS BY CHARLES M. SCHULZ

13. "Wanted Man's Best Friend."

•Limited edition of 500. Individually signed by Charles M. Schulz. 10-1/2"W" x 9-1/2L". 1995. $800

14. "The Wave."

•Limited edition of 500. Individually signed by Charles M. Schulz. 23-1/2"W" x 9-1/4D". 1994. $2,100

15. "Five Cents Please."

•Limited edition of 500. Individually signed by Charles M. Schulz. 16"W x 13"H. 1993. $2,800

16. "Snoopy Sonata."

•Limited edition of 500. Individually signed by Charles M. Schulz. 18"W x 13"H. 1993. $2,800

17. "Circle The Zambonis."

•Limited edition of 500. Individually signed by Charles M. Schulz. 16"W x 7"H. 1995. $800

18. "Snoopy's Approach."

•Unsigned limited edition of 500. 19-1/2"W x 5-1/2"H. 1996. $175

19. "It's My Destiny."

•Unsigned limited edition of 500. 19-1/2"W x 5-1/2"H. 1996. $175

20. "In The Puddles."

•Unsigned limited edition of 500. 19-1/2"W x 5-1/2"H. 1996. $175

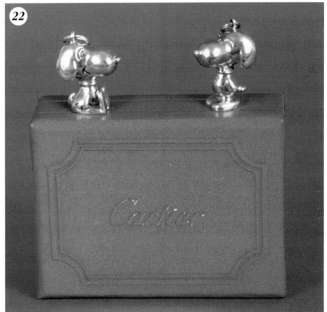

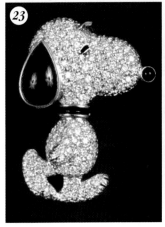

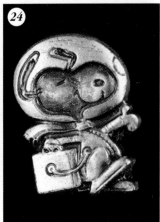

DECORATIVE ITEMS

21. Cartier Enameled Boxes, known as "Bilston & Battersea Enamels."

Handcrafted from copper shapes. The technique used to enamel the copper produces a soft creamy glaze which distinguishes these pieces. Certificate of Authenticity is included. UFS markings and "Cartier Made in England" are on the bottoms of the boxes. Halcyon Days Ltd., for Cartier. 1977.

•Woodstock carries an envelope adorned with a red heart in his mouth, against a green background trimmed in gold. "For You" is printed inside the removable cover. 1/2"H x 7/8" diam. Appraised by Cartier (1997) at $300-400.

•Snoopy is sitting and holding a red flower, against a blue background circled in pink and trimmed in gold. "Let's Be Friends" is printed on the hinged cover. "Always" is printed inside the cover. 1/2"H x 1-7/8" diam. Appraised by Cartier (1997) at $400-500.

JEWELRY

22. Charms

"Cartier Snoopy." Snoopy is sitting. Solid sterling silver. Cartier. 1977. $500-600

•"Cartier Snoopy." Snoopy is standing. Solid gold. Cartier. 1977. $5,000-6,000

23. Diamond Brooch

•Snoopy is encrusted with diamonds in pavé, 14K gold, and black onyx. Limited edition of 950 pieces. 1-1/4"H. #SNA-1, Circle Gallery. 1994. $3,000-4,000

24. Pin

•Snoopy, dressed as an astronaut, is wearing a helmet and space suit, and carrying a life support pack. This pin was issued to the Apollo 10 astronauts by NASA to commemorate the naming of Snoopy and Charlie Brown as mascots for their lunar and command modules. Sterling silver. 1/2"H. 1969. $400-500

The PVC fun figures positioned along the front of the desk on the left side are from Spain. Behind them, on the left, are two stamper sets purchased in Japan and Thailand. And, behind these objects are jigsaw puzzles from Japan. Also on the desk are several decks of playing cards (Japan, Belgium, and the Netherlands).

The telephone with lamp, and the puzzle next to the computer, are sold in America. On the wall to the right of the lamp is a cuckoo clock (Japan). To the left are two banners (England),

with pinback buttons (Japan). A beautiful wall hanging with a soccer motif (Italy) is above the banners.

To the left of the desk, on the upper shelf of the cabinet, are picture albums, camera, and film—all from Japan. The next shelf down features a sewing machine and fabric (Japan). Between the shelves is a "No Smoking" sign (Singapore). On the bottom shelf is the box for a puzzle from Italy. Many of the unfinished pieces of this puzzle rest on the low table in front of the cabinet.

The Hobby Room

The hobby room is a private place to unwind or to share a part of yourself with friends—a place especially great for rainy days. Ours is a unique hobby room inasmuch as everything in it is related to PEANUTS.

A hobby within a hobby. Perfect! PEANUTS collectors enjoying other pursuits, but always with PEANUTS characters nearby. In the hobby room, one can play cards, collect coins, do jigsaw puzzles, enjoy crafts such as needlepoint and crewel, or do so many other things. The hobby room is a great place to save ephemera and advertising display pieces. Also, to show off banners, NASA memorabilia, fun figures, MetLife items, trophies, and photo albums holding pictures taken with PEANUTS cameras.

ADVERTISING, DISPLAYS, AND PREMIUMS

Unless otherwise noted, plushes and other props have been added to the pictures of promotional items for esthetics. See Playroom for information on plushes.

1. A&W Pumpkin

•Snoopy, as the Flying Ace, and Linus are in a pumpkin patch. Printed: "Halloween Is A&W." The reverse side features a jack-o'-lantern. Printed "A&W" and "Great Pumpkin." Vinyl. 120" diam. x 44"H. A&W. 1991. $25-30

2. A&W Pumpkin

•Linus sits, holding a can of A&W root beer, on both sides of the pumpkin. Printed: "The Great Pumpkin" and "A&W." Vinyl. 120" diam. x 44"H. A&W. 1992. $20-25

3. A&W Doghouse

•Promotional display unit given to retailers. Assembly required. Cardboard. A&W. 1990. $35-40

4. A&W Joe Cool Cups

Cups come in four designs and include a lid and a straw with an attached cap. By-mail premium. Plastic. A&W. 1991. $4-6 ea.

•Snoopy, as Joe Cool, walks on the beach on an orange cup.

•Snoopy, as Joe Cool, dances on a pink cup.

•Snoopy, as Joe Cool, surfs on a blue cup.

•Snoopy, as Joe Cool, barbecues on a yellow cup.

5. A&W Clik! Case

•Promotional display unit given to retailers. Snoopy, as Joe Cool wearing an A&W T-shirt, holds a mug of A&W root beer and a glass of A&W cream soda. Snoopy thinks, "The necessities of life." Woodstock is sitting on Snoopy's head. The carrying case contains four cans of A&W root beer and cream soda, diet and non-diet. Each can depicts Snoopy in a different Joe Cool pose. Orange foam lines the inside of the plastic case. Inside the case is a cardboard piece that lays out the marketing strategy/promotion of the Joe Cool cans and the by-mail 32-ounce Joe Cool Cups premium. 10-1/2"W x 7"H x 3-1/4" deep. A&W. 1991. $95-125

6. A&W Float Making Kit

•"WWI Flying Ace Float Making Kit." Kit contains two root beer mugs featuring Snoopy wearing an orange shirt and holding a mug, two long-handled spoons, and an ice cream scoop. The scoop handle and the reverse side of the mugs are printed "A&W." The spoon handles have a floral design. A&W. 1990. $65-75**

7. A&W Mugs

•Snoopy, Charlie Brown, Lucy, Woodstock, Schroeder, Linus, and Sally circle the mug. All but Lucy hold mugs of root beer. The 40th Anniversary logo appears on the reverse side. Plastic. A&W. 1990. $6-8

•Snoopy, wearing an orange shirt, holds a mug of root beer. Printed on reverse side: "A&W." Glass. 6"H. A&W. 1990. $15-20

A&W Pen

•Retractable ball point pen features the repeated pattern of Snoopy and Woodstock sitting back to back. The top front of the pen features Snoopy wearing sunglasses. Plastic. 6"H. A&W. 1990. $6-10

8. Butternut Bread Premiums

Multicolored sew-on patches. Embroidered on fabric. 2-7/8"H. Interstate Brands. Early 1970s. $6-8 ea.

•Snoopy wears a cape and a crown. Printed: "The Prince."

•Linus. Printed: "Cheer Up!"

•Charlie Brown. Printed: "Good Grief!"

•Lucy. Printed: "Kiss Me!"

•Frieda. Printed: "I'm In Love!"

Butternut Bread Premiums

Clip-on emblem. Came on a card that advises kids to watch for the patches that will be coming out. Plastic. 1-3/8" oval-shaped. Interstate Brands. Early 1970s. $4-6* ea.

•Linus. Printed: "Cheer Up!"

•Lucy. Printed: "Kiss Me!"

•Snoopy wears a cape and a crown. Printed: "The Prince."

•Frieda. Printed: "I'm In Love!"

•Charlie Brown. Printed: "Good Grief!"

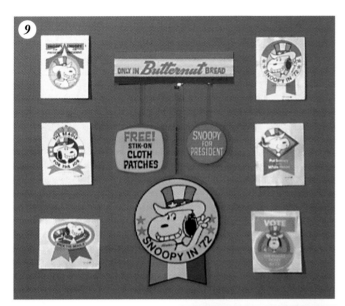

Chex Canteen

•The yellow canteen features a decal of Lucy, Charlie Brown, and Linus with a bowl of Chex party mix. Printed: "Chex Party Mix and PEANUTS." Canteen includes clip for attaching to a belt, a strap for carrying, and an attached blue cap. Plastic. 16 oz. C4 Marketing Ltd for Ralston Purina. 1990. $3-4

Chex Tin

•Charlie Brown and Snoopy, wearing red and white baseball caps, have a red bowl of Chex in front of them. Stars and stripes decorate green container and lid. Lid features Charlie Brown with baseball cap. Printed around the tin: "Chex Muddy Buddies The All-Star Chocolate Snack." By-mail premium. Metal. 6"H x 5-1/8" diam. Ralston Purina. 1994. $4-6

Chex Bank

•The red doghouse bank with Snoopy lying on top was attached to specially marked boxes of Chex cereal. It features a decal of Charlie Brown, Lucy, and Linus with a bowl of Chex party mix. Printed: "Chex Party Mix and PEANUTS 40 Years Of Tradition." The cereal box has an order form for the Chex Party Mix tin. Plastic. 7"H. Ralston Purina. 1990. Bank: $2-4
Cereal & Bank: $10-12*

Chex Tin

•Peppermint Patty, Lucy, Charlie Brown, Linus, and Sally wear party hats and hold balloons. Lucy, Charlie Brown, and Linus are featured with their hands in a bowl of Chex party mix on the lid. Printed around the top of the yellow tin: "Chex Party Mix Makes The Party." Printed on the lid: "Chex Party Mix and PEANUTS 40 Years Of Tradition." By-mail premium. Metal. 6"H x 5-1/8" diam. Ralston Purina. 1990. $4-6

Chex Seasoning Mix

Packets of seasoning for Chex Party Mix were available by mail or found in specially marked boxes of Chex cereal. 4"H x 3"W. Ralston Purina. 1991. 50¢-$1.00 ea.

•Linus' Pizza Party Mix.

•Lucy's Maple Nut Party Mix.

Chex Bowl

•Microwaveable bowl features the 40th Anniversary logo on each side, printed "40 Years Of Happiness." By-mail premium. Plastic. 4"H x 8"diam. Tara Product Corporation for Ralston Purina. 1990. $8-10

Chex Recipe Book

•Charlie Brown, wearing a chef's hat, holds a bowl of Chex party mix, and Lucy holds a plate of cupcakes. Printed: "I Can Make It With Chex!" and "12 Recipes For Kids And Parents To Make Together!" By-mail premium. Paper. 5-1/2" x 6". Ralston Purina. 1991. $2-3

Chex Seasoning Mix

•"Charlie Brown's Traditional Party Mix." Packets of seasoning for Chex Party Mix were available by mail or found in specially marked boxes of Chex cereal. 4"H x 3"W. Ralston Purina. 1991. 50¢-$1.00

11. Coca-Cola Premium

•"The Red Baron's Albatros." Snoopy, as the Flying Ace, is on his doghouse, which is printed "See 'He's Your Dog Charlie Brown' On CBS, June 5, 1973." A paper model of the Albatros was slipped over the necks of Coca-Cola bottles. The reverse side includes an order form for purchasing working models

9. Butternut Bread Display

•Snoopy wears an Uncle Sam hat in the center circle, with a red, white, and blue ribbon below, and printed "Snoopy in '72." To the left and the right of Snoopy are a circle and square printed "Free! Stick-on Cloth Patches" and "Snoopy for President." Across the top is printed "Only In Butternut Bread." Plastic. 9-1/2"H x 4-3/4"W. Interstate Brands. 1972. $10-12

Butternut Bread Premiums

Iron-on patches. Each patch features Snoopy, wearing an Uncle Sam hat, in a different pose campaigning for the 1972 presidential election. Each patch is printed with a campaign slogan. Fabric. 2-1/2" x 2". Interstate Brands. 1972. $2-4 ea.

•"Snoopy For President Snoopy For President."

•"Snoopy In '72."

•"The Beagle For The Job."

•"Put Snoopy In The White House."

•"Back The Beagle."

•"Vote The Beagle Ticket In '72."

10. Chex Shopping Cart Display

•Charlie Brown and Snoopy, wearing red and white baseball caps, have a red bowl of Chex in front of them. Three Chex cereal boxes are pictured. Printed: "Make Chex Muddy Buddies!" Cardboard. 8"H x 10"W. Actmedia, Inc. for Ralston Purina. 1991. $1-2

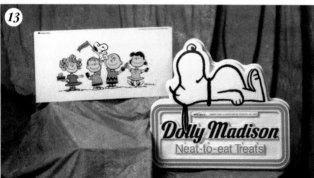

12. Dolly Madison Premium

•"Lucy's Lemonade Stand." Snoopy, Lucy, and Linus are featured on the front. Lucy holds a sign printed "Dolly Madison And Lemonade." The by-mail premium also included ten watercolor markers and a 96-oz. pitcher with a lid picturing Snoopy, Woodstock, Linus, Charlie Brown, and Lucy. Assembly required. Cardboard stand, plastic pitcher. Interstate Brands. 1986. $30-35

13. Dolly Madison Display

•Frieda, Linus, Charlie Brown, and Lucy hold Dolly Madison cakes. Snoopy, being held up by Charlie Brown and Linus, holds a pennant printed "Dolly Madison." Metal. 24"W x 12"H with a 2" wide lip on the bottom. Interstate Brands. Early 1970s. $65-75

•Snoopy lies on top of a sign printed "Dolly Madison Neat-To-Eat Treats." Molded plastic. 24" x 21" x 1-1/2". Interstate Brands. Early 1970s. $50-60

14. Dolly Madison Displays

Set of 4 two-sided display pieces featured the characters on one side and the Dolly Madison logo on the other side. A hole in the top of each was used to hang the pieces mobile-style. Cardboard. 12"H. Interstate Brands. 1976. $15-18 ea.

•Woodstock appears on a blue background.

•Snoopy, wearing an Uncle Sam hat, dances on a green background.

•Charlie Brown, wearing a baseball cap and carrying a bat, appears on a yellow background.

•Lucy, wearing a green dress with her arms outstretched, appears on an orange background.

15. Dolly Madison Premium

•Snoopy, in an Uncle Sam hat, appears at the top of a combination bookmark, ruler, and cartoon stencil. Printed: "Snoopy for President." Premium was pictured on the back and found inside specially marked boxes of Dolly Madison cakes. Plastic. Interstate Brands. 1972. Cake Box: $3-5 Premium: $10-12

16. Dolly Madison Premiums

Christmas tree ornaments. Ten different ornaments were available inside specially marked boxes of Dolly Madison cakes. The foil-coated ornaments require assembly and include instructions. Interstate Brands. 1976. $2-3 ea.

•Woodstock is pictured on top of a Christmas tree. 4-1/4"H assembled.

•Sally is pictured on top of a Christmas tree. 8-1/4"H unassembled.

•Lucy is pictured inside a spiral design. 4"H unassembled.

•Charlie Brown is dressed as Santa Claus. 8-1/4"H unassembled.

•Lucy is dressed as Santa Claus. 8-1/4"H unassembled.

(engine included, but not battery or fuel) of the Albatros and Snoopy's Sopwith Camel. Paper. Coca-Cola. 1973. $8-10

Coca-Cola and Sprite Premium Offer

•Order form for purchasing working models (engine included, but not battery or fuel) of the Red Baron's Albatros and Snoopy's Sopwith Camel. Snoopy, as the Flying Ace, is on his doghouse, which is printed "See 'He's Your Dog Charlie Brown' On CBS, June 5, 1973." A dogfight between the Albatros and the Red Baron is taking place in Snoopy's thought balloon. Printed: "Get The Red Baron's Albatros Or The Sopwith Camel From Bottlers Of Coca-Cola And Sprite." The reverse side of the order form features detailed descriptions of the model planes in Snoopy's thought balloon, and the Coca-Cola and Sprite logos. Paper. Coca-Cola. 1973. $6-8

Dolly Madison Newspaper Advertisement

•The ten assembled ornaments are pictured on a Christmas tree. Linus describes the ornaments, tells how they are available, and wishes the reader a Merry Christmas. Paper. 1976. $7-9

17. Dolly Madison Display

•Snoopy lies on his doghouse thinking, "I must be dreaming." Printed: "Dolly Madison Snacks." Particle board. 24"H x 20"W. Interstate Brands. Late 1970s. $40-45

18. Dolly Madison Newspaper Advertisement

•Linus and Snoopy hold the inflatables while Charlie Brown blows one up. An actual size inflatable of Snoopy, as the Flying Ace, is pictured in the ad. Printed: "Free Snoopy Inflatables." Paper. 1976. $7-9

Dolly Madison Premiums

Self-sealing inflatables. Six different designs were available inside specially marked boxes of Dolly Madison cakes. Plastic. Interstate Brands. 1976. $3-4 ea.

•Lucy wears a pink dress.

•Snoopy is dressed as Uncle Sam in a red, white, and blue outfit with hat.

•Charlie Brown wears a yellow shirt with a black zigzag.

•Snoopy dressed as a beagle scout. (Not pictured)

•Snoopy as Joe Cool. (Not pictured)

19. Dolly Madison Newspaper Advertisement

•Snoopy is dressed as a farmer wearing a hat and neckerchief. Pictures of vegetables are to his right. The ad includes an order form for a mini-garden kit. Printed: "Snoopy's Mini-Garden Kit Free!" Paper. 1973. $7-9

Dolly Madison Premium

•"Mini-Garden Kit." The kit was mailed in a folded-over card with three clear packets of seeds taped to the mailer. Directions for planting are on the card. The inside of the mailer features Snoopy lying on his doghouse thinking, "It doesn't matter how small the crop is . . . My hired hand still hates harvest time," as Woodstock pushes a wheelbarrow filled with vegetables through the garden. The outside of the mailer features Snoopy dressed as a farmer, and drawings and descriptions of tomatoes, corn, and melons. By-mail premium. Interstate Brands. 1973. $15-20

20. Dolly Madison Premiums

Inflatable characters available as a by-mail premium. Vinyl. Interstate Brands. 1975.

•Charlie Brown. 30"H. $30-40

•Snoopy. 30"H. $30-40

•Charlie Brown. 15"H. $8-12 (Not pictured)

•Snoopy. 14"H. $8-12 (Not pictured)

21. Dolly Madison Premium

Six baseball cards featuring the characters dressed in baseball gear with their names printed beneath their picture. Heavy paper. 2-1/4" x 3-1/2". Interstate Brands. 1983. $15-22 ea.

•Charlie Brown.

•Linus.

•Lucy.

•Peppermint Patty.

•Schroeder.

•Snoopy.

Ziploc Premium

Nine baseball cards featuring the characters dressed in baseball gear with their names printed beneath their picture. They were available one at a time in specially marked boxes of Ziploc sandwich bags or as a complete set though the mail. Each card lists player statistics on the reverse side as well as the player's favorite sandwich. Heavy paper. 2-1/2" x 3-1/2". 1993. $3-5 ea.

•Charlie Brown.

•Franklin.

•Linus.

•Lucy.

•Peppermint Patty.

•Sally.

•Schroeder.

•Snoopy.

•Woodstock.

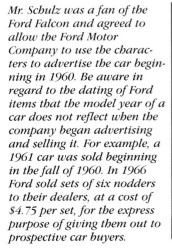

Mr. Schulz was a fan of the Ford Falcon and agreed to allow the Ford Motor Company to use the characters to advertise the car beginning in 1960. Be aware in regard to the dating of Ford items that the model year of a car does not reflect when the company began advertising and selling it. For example, a 1961 car was sold beginning in the fall of 1960. In 1966 Ford sold sets of six nodders to their dealers, at a cost of $4.75 per set, for the express purpose of giving them out to prospective car buyers.

22. Ford Falcon Advertising Brochure

•Tri-folded, two-sided brochure features Snoopy running through the brochure with a tape measure in his mouth. Color drawings of the characters appear to illustrate features of the car. Printed on the front: "Ford Falcon '61 The World's Most Successful New Car" and "New Measure Of Compact Car Value." Paper. 7"H x 10"W folded. Ford Motor Company. 1960. $15-20

Ford Falcon Matchbook

•Snoopy is shown running with a tape measure in his mouth printed "New Measure Of Compact Car Value." The matchbook cover is also printed "'61 Ford Falcon World's Most Successful New Car." The reverse side of the cover is printed with the name and location of a Ford auto dealer. 1-1/2" x 2". Lion Match Company for Ford. 1960. $8-12

Ford Falcon Booklet

•Lucy, Pigpen, Charlie Brown, Snoopy and Linus are featured throughout the 12-page booklet about the 1963 Falcon. Printed: "A Scrapbook About Your Falcon Prepared By Charlie Brown And His Friends." Paper. 7-3/4"H x 10-1/2"W. Ford Motor Company. 1962. $25-35

23. Hallmark Display

•Snoopy is dressed as a reporter with a brown trench coat, press card in his hat, and a pencil behind his ear. He holds a newspaper printed "Thinking of You Daily—The Peanuts Gang." Cardboard. 39"H x 17"W. Hallmark. 1983. $25-35

24. Hallmark Display

•Woodstock sits on top of Snoopy's doghouse. On the roof is a notice printed "Register To Win This Super Snoopy." The display was used to promote a contest to win the pictured Snoopy-hugging-Woodstock plush. Cardboard. 43"H. Hallmark. 1989. $20-30

25. Mrs. Karl's Bread Premium

•"Snoopy's World War I Airplane Album." The four-page booklet features a crossword puzzle, information on the metric system, and a page for stickers of World War I airplanes. The front cover features Snoopy, as the Flying Ace, on top of his doghouse with several different airplanes above him. Paper. 9"W x 11"H. Interstate Brands. 1975. $5-7

Mrs. Karl's Bread Premium

Set of eight stickers featuring Snoopy, as the Flying Ace, with different World War I airplanes. Stickers found in specially marked packages of Mrs. Karl's Bread. Interstate Brands. 1975.

•Fokker D VII, $6-8

•Fokker DR-1, $6-8

•Sopwith Camel, $6-10

•Albatros D.Va, $6-8

•Morane-Saulnier N, $6-8

•The Bristol F2-B, $6-8

•Spad XIII, $6-8

•Nieuport-Ni 17, $6-8

26. Mrs. Karl's Bread Premiums

"PEANUTS Reflector Stickers." Set of eight stickers featuring the characters on a silver reflective background. Stickers could be found in specially marked packages of Mrs. Karl's Bread. 1-1/2" x 1-7/8". Interstate Brands. 1974. $1-3 ea.

•Snoopy wears a Boy Scout hat and has his hand over his heart.

•Snoopy, as the Flying Ace, is sitting.

•Charlie Brown, standing next to his kite, is tangled in its string.

•Lucy is standing with her arms outstretched and her mouth wide open.

•Linus is sitting, sucking his thumb and holding his blanket.

•Lucy throws a punch. Printed: "Pow!"

•Linus is standing and holding an American flag.

•Charlie Brown, wearing a baseball cap, carries his bat over his shoulder.

Mrs. Karl's Bread Newspaper Advertisement

• The advertisement features a boy on a bicycle with stickers on his hat, his back and on his bicycle. Printed: "Free PEANUTS Reflector Stickers" and "Mrs. Karl's. The Great White Bread." Paper. 1974. $7-9

27. Mrs. Karl's Bread Premiums

"PEANUTS Iron-On Patches." Set of 12 patches featuring the characters. Available in specially marked packages of Mrs. Karl's bread as well as in other brands of bread, such as Millbrook, made by Interstate. 2" x 2". 1972. $2-4 ea.

• Peppermint Patty, surrounded by hearts, has her arms out-stretched. Printed: "I Love You!"

• Lucy sits behind her psychiatrist booth. Printed on booth: "Psychiatrist" and "1/2 Off Sale."

• Snoopy wears a beret, sunglasses, and leans on a cane. Printed: "Beagle Power."

• Woodstock sits on a football.

• Woodstock sleeps standing up. Printed: "Z."

• Lucy shakes her fist. Printed: "I've Got A Big What?"

• Pigpen is standing in a cloud of dust. Printed: "Keep America Clean."

• Charlie Brown stands with his kite which is in shreds.

• Schroeder sits at his piano. Printed: "Beethoven Lives."

• Linus, his hair standing up, sits in a pumpkin patch. Printed: "Here Comes The Great Pumpkin."

• Snoopy, as the Flying Ace, sits on his doghouse.

• Charlie Brown is upside down on a pitcher's mound with his clothes whirling around him. (Not pictured)

Mrs. Karl's Bread Newspaper Advertisement

• The advertisement features Linus with patches all over his blanket and his shirt. Printed: "Dress Up Your Favorite Things With These Free PEANUTS Iron-On Patches" and "Mrs. Karl's. The Great White Bread." Paper. 1972. $7-9

Mrs. Karl's Bread Wrapper

• Snoopy wears a crown and a red cape, and holds a sword. Plastic. Interstate Brands.

28. Mrs. Karl's Bread Premiums

"PEANUTS Bi-Centennial Name Stickers." Set of 10 stickers feature the characters in patriotic scenes with stars and stripes backgrounds. The stickers have a space to fill in your name. Available in specially marked packages of Mrs. Karl's bread as well as in other brands of bread, such as Millbrook, made by Interstate. 3" x 3". 1975. $1-3 ea.

• Woodstock is wearing a tri-cornered hat and carrying a rifle over his shoulder. Printed: "This Belongs To ———— And Woodstock Is Guarding It."

• Snoopy wears a colonial outfit and rides a horse. He is thinking "The British Are Coming! The British Are Coming! I'm Going To ———— Home For Milk And Cake."

• Snoopy lies on top of his doghouse which has a sign on it that reads "George Washington's Dog Slept Here." He is thinking "I Would Never Have Known, If ———— Weren't A History Nut."

• Sally is dressed as an Indian with a feather in her hair. She says, "I'm Inviting ———— To Boston For The Tea Party."

• Peppermint Patty, dressed in a colonial outfit, says, "Three Very Famous American Signatures." Printed: "John Hancock, Peppermint Patty and ————."

• Charlie Brown, wearing a tri-cornered hat and a drum, says, "Somehow, The Spirit Of '76 Isn't The Same Without ———— Here."

• Schroeder plays his piano. Lucy leans on it and says "———— Knows All The Words To The Star Spangled Banner."

• Linus, wearing a tri-cornered hat, stands next to a birthday cake printed "Happy 200th Birthday United States." He says "I Need ———— To Help Me Blow Out The Candles."

• Snoopy dressed as Uncle Sam is thinking, "My Friend ———— Knows All 13 Original Colonies. Do You?"

• Charlie Brown is dressed as George Washington, and stands in a boat. He says, "Crossing The Delaware Would Be A Lot Easier If ———— Were Here." (Not pictured)

Mrs. Karl's Bread Newspaper Advertisement

• All ten stickers are shown in the ad. A hand is shown holding a feather quill pen filling in a name on one of the stickers. Printed: "Write Your Name In History. Free PEANUTS Bi-Centennial Name Stickers. One Inside Every Loaf." 1975. $7-9

29. Mrs. Karl's Bread Newspaper Advertisement

• The advertisement shows each of the six seed packets on top of the corresponding vegetable. Printed: "Free PEANUTS Vegetable Seeds." Paper. 1975. $7-9

Mrs. Karl's Bread Premiums

"PEANUTS Vegetable Seeds." The characters are featured on the six different seed packets. Available in specially marked packages of Mrs. Karl's bread. 2" x 2-1/2". Interstate Brands. 1975. $5-8 ea.

• Frieda's Ravishing Radishes.

• Snoopy's Super Spinach.

• Woodstock's Farm Fresh Onions.

• Snoopy juggles "Ripe Red Tomatoes."

• Charlie Brown's Carrots.

• Lucy's Loudmouth Lettuce.

Mrs. Karl's Bread Premiums

"PEANUTS Vegetable And Flower Seeds." The characters are featured on the eight different seed packets. Available in specially marked packages of Mrs. Karl's bread. 2" x 2-1/2". Interstate Brands. 1976. $6-9 ea.

• Silly Sally's Summer Squash.

• Cry Baby Onions features Lucy knocking someone over.

• Woodstock's Salad Bowl Lettuce.

• Gentleman Farmer Tomatoes features Snoopy lying on his doghouse.

• Peppermint Patty Parsley.

• Patriotic Mix Petunias features Frieda holding an American flag and flowers.

• Charlie Brown holds a bunch of "Roundhead Radishes."

• Linus' Lunch Box Carrots.

Mrs. Karl's Bread Newspaper Advertisement

• The advertisement shows Snoopy pushing a wheelbarrow full of vegetable and seed packets with Woodstock at the top. "Free PEANUTS Vegetable And Flower Seeds." Paper. 1976. $7-9

30. McDonald's Premiums

"Camp Snoopy Collection" glasses. Given to customers with the purchase of a beverage, the five glasses promoted the opening of Knotts Berry Farm's Camp Snoopy in California. These glasses also came in white plastic in some parts of the country. 5-3/4"H. 1983. Glass: $3-5 ea. Plastic: $2-3 ea.

• Snoopy, dressed as a Beagle Scout, is dancing and thinking, "Civilization is overrated!" Marcie, Peppermint Patty, Charlie Brown, Sally, and Linus are pictured around the glass.

• Woodstock, in his nest tent in a tree, blows a bugle. Snoopy, in a sleeping bag on the ground below, thinks, "Morning people are hard to love." Woodstock's friends, Charlie Brown, and Linus are also awakened by Woodstock's bugle blast.

• Linus pulls his blanket out from beneath the picnic that Lucy, Charlie Brown, Snoopy, and Woodstock have set up on it. The food and the characters are up-ended. Linus says, "The struggle for security is no picnic!"

• Snoopy hooks Charlie Brown's raft with his fishing pole. Charlie Brown says "Rats! Why is having fun always such hard work?" Franklin, Linus, Sally, and Lucy are also pictured on the glass.

• Lucy, in a lounge chair, sips lemonade and listens to a radio next to her pitched tent while Sally, Charlie Brown, Linus, and Franklin struggle to put up their tent. Lucy says, "There's no excuse for not being properly prepared." Snoopy and Woodstock are also pictured on the glass.

31. McDonald's Displays

Each display matched a Camp Snoopy glass, announcing the character whose glass was available. Cardboard. 6-1/2"H. McDonald's. 1983. $12-15 ea.

• Lucy. "Get Your Lucy Glass This Week!"

• Snoopy. "Get Your Snoopy Glass This Week!"

• Woodstock. "Get Your Woodstock Glass This Week!"

• Linus. "Get Your Linus Glass This Week!"

• Charlie Brown. "Get Your Charlie Brown Glass This Week!"

32. McDonald's Premiums

Children's meals were served in "Happy Meals" containers. A different container was available each week. The characters are featured with games and pictures to color on the sides of the containers. Cardboard. 5" x 9". McDonald's. 1989. $2-4 ea.

• The front of the box features Charlie Brown feeding chickens. Printed: "PEANUTS E-I-E-I-O."

• The front of the box features Lucy, Linus, Sally, and Charlie Brown roasting marshmallows and hot dogs. Printed: "PEANUTS The Hoedown."

• The front of the box features Lucy sitting at a kissing booth. Printed: "PEANUTS The Country Fair."

• The front of the box features Charlie Brown in the field taking care of his crops. Printed: "PEANUTS Field Day."

McDonald's Premiums

"Happy Meals Collectible Toys." The characters are dressed as farmers and are using farm equipment. Each toy consists of three parts: the character, the farm implement, and its contents. The parts could be interchanged to create new scenarios. A different toy was available each week. In some parts of the country, two one-piece toys were available for children under the age of three. Plastic. McDonald's. 1989. $1-2 ea.

• Snoopy pushes a hay hauler with a pig in it. Woodstock sits on top of the pig. 2-7/8".

• Linus pushes a milk mover with a milk can and a cat inside. 2-1/8".

• Charlie Brown sits with an egg basket and a chick on top of the eggs. 2-1/2".

• Snoopy carries a sack of potatoes. 2-1/2".

•Charlie Brown carries a bag of seed and pushes a seed tiller. 3".

•Lucy pushes a basket of apples in a wheelbarrow. 2-7/8".

33. McDonald's Display

•This case displays Happy Meals Collectible Toys. The name of each toy is printed on the display: "Snoopy's Hay Hauler," "Charlie Brown's Seed Bag N Tiller," "Lucy's Apple Cart," and "Linus' Milk Mover." Also printed: "PEANUTS Collect All 4!" and "Switchable Parts For Heaps Of Fun Combinations." Cardboard and plastic. McDonald's. 1989. $75-85

Metropolitan Life Insurance Company ("MetLife") began to use PEANUTS to advertise its insurance products in 1985. The items shown below were not for sale to the public. They were sold to employees and used as promotional merchandise by Metropolitan's insurance agents. They were given to employees, for example, as a thank you for taking part in charitable events such as a blood donor drive. They were also given to fans at sporting events.

34. Display

•Franklin, Lucy, Linus, Peppermint Patty, and Sally carry Snoopy and Charlie Brown on their shoulders. Woodstock flies overhead. Printed: "Join Met. It Pays." Cardboard. 24"W x 36"H. $15-20

Note Pad

•Two sides of the cube picture Snoopy in different poses with pen and paper. The other two sides are printed: "Get Met. It Pays." Paper. 3" x 3". $3-5

Watch

•The watch face features Snoopy using his hands to tell the time on a gold background. There is a small attaché case with the MetLife logo on it. The watch face is 1-1/8" diam. and set in a gold-colored metal casing. Black leather band. $40-50

Duffel Bag

•Snoopy, wearing baseball gear and swinging a bat, is shown on each end of the bag. Printed: "Get Met. It Pays" and "MetLife." The sides of the bag depict Shea Stadium and the New York City skyline. Printed: "New York Mets." Blue canvas. 19" x 11-1/2". $12-15

Paper Holder/Clip

•Snoopy, wearing a cap with goggles, red scarf, and blue checked jacket, holds a MetLife attaché case and drives a red convertible. Plastic. 3" x 2-7/8". $2-3

Date Book

•Snoopy holds open a gate which Charlie Brown walks through. Linus and Lucy stand behind the picket fence on each side of the gate. Further in the background is Sally in a convertible, Woodstock flying overhead, and Snoopy's doghouse. Printed: "MetLife." The reverse side pictures Franklin, Peppermint Patty, and Marcie behind a picket fence. The MetLife blimp featuring Snoopy as the Flying Ace flies above them. The calendar inside, which has no PEANUTS graphics, can be replaced each year. Vinyl and paper. 3-1/2"W x 6-1/8"H. 1995. $3-4

Figure

•Snoopy, wearing a bow tie, carries an attachè case with the MetLife logo on it. Solid pewter. 3"H. $40-50

Date Book

•Snoopy, wearing a red bow tie, carries an attachè case with the MetLife logo on it. The calendar inside, which has no PEANUTS graphics, can be replaced each year. Vinyl and paper. 3-1/2"W x 6-1/8"H. 1991. $1-2

Key Chain

•Snoopy, wearing a red bow tie, carries an attaché case with the MetLife logo on it. Rubber with silver key ring. 3"H excluding key ring. $1-2

Mug with Lid

•Snoopy, with a mug in his hand, sits on top of his doghouse with Woodstock on each side. Printed on the red mug: "Get Met. It Pays." The MetLife logo is on the lid. Hard plastic. 3-1/2" diam. $5-7

Puzzle in a Canister

•The canister pictures Franklin, Lucy, Linus, Peppermint Patty, and Sally carrying Snoopy and Charlie Brown on their shoulders. Woodstock and his friends fly overhead carrying a banner printed "Get Met. It Pays." Cardboard with plastic cover. 4" diam. x 5-3/4"H. $8-12

License Plate Holder

•On the bottom of the plate holder, Snoopy's face appears on each side of the words "Get Met. It Pays." The top of the holder is printed with the MetLife logo and "MetLife." Plastic. 12-1/8"W x 6-1/6"H. $2-3

Display Stand

•Snoopy is pictured on scaffolding, painting a billboard sign. Printed: "Get Met. It Pays." Originally this item came with a Post-It pad. Plastic. 7"W x 6"H. $10-12

35. Oscar Mayer Premium

These cups feature the Peanuts characters playing baseball. Printed on the back of the cups was the Oscar Mayer logo or the names of the supermarkets or delis where the cups were available, for example Randall's and Stop 'N Shop. Plastic. 16 oz. Made by Sterling Products for Oscar Mayer. Early 1990s. $4-7 ea.

•Snoopy, wearing a baseball cap, leans on his bat and holds a baseball printed "Oscar Mayer." He is thinking, "Let's break for lunch."

38. Thom McAnn Displays

Snoopy and Woodstock were used by this shoe-store retailer to promote PEANUTS sneakers. Papier-mâchè. 1986.

•Woodstock. 12-1/2"H. $150-175

•Snoopy. 22-1/2"H. $125-135

39. Timex Displays

•Snoopy, wearing a watch, dances in front of a display that looks like a yellow picket fence. The display case holds six watches in their boxes. Printed: "Snoopy & Friends Timex." Used by retailers throughout the 1970s and early 1980s when Timex made PEANUTS watches. Plastic. $65-75

•Snoopy, wearing a watch, lies on top of a display that looks like his doghouse. He holds a sign over the side printed "Snoopy & Friends." The display case holds six watches in their boxes. Used by retailers throughout the 1970s and early 1980s when Timex made PEANUTS watches. Plastic. $55-65

40. Timex Display

•Snoopy appears inside the face of a large red watch with a band against a yellow case which holds six watches in their boxes. Printed: "Snoopy & Friends Timex." Used by retailers throughout the 1970s and early 1980s when Timex made PEANUTS watches. Plastic. $85-95.

41. Worlds of Wonder Display

•Snoopy and Woodstock are attached to a platform. The story tape is inserted into Snoopy's back. Plug the unit in, push the button, and Snoopy talks. His ears go up and down. Woodstock is not animated on this display. Printed: "A Friend For Life Has Come To Life." Some displays did not include Woodstock.

•Charlie Brown, dressed in baseball gear, stands on the pitcher's mound holding a baseball printed "Oscar Mayer." Woodstock stands at his feet chirping. Charlie Brown says, "I have a strange team."

•Lucy, dressed in baseball gear, shouts, "I Got It! I Got It!" as the baseball printed "Oscar Mayer" hits the ground behind her.

36. Pelham Puppets Display

•Woodstock, Snoopy, and Charlie Brown dance when the unit is plugged in. This display was used by retailers to promote the puppets. Printed: "Pelham Puppets Loved By Children All Over The World Marlborough-Wiltshire, England." Display—wood and fabric. Puppets - hard plastic composition. 22"H x 14"W x 10" diam. Made in England by Pelham. Distributed by Tiderider. 1979. $400-475

37. Rival Dog Food Label

•The label features Snoopy thinking, "Dressing for dinner is the least I can do." The label promotes a free patch offer. Snoopy also appears lying on his tummy on his doghouse, looking over the edge at the ingredients. He is thinking, "Can't be too careful about protecting the secret family recipe!" The order form for the patch is on the reverse side of the label. Paper. 1974. $3-5

Rival Premium

•"Snoopy Patch." Snoopy, wearing a baseball cap, stands ready to swing a bat as a baseball flies by him. Printed: "Strike Three!" By-mail premium. Cloth. 3" x 2" oval. Rival. 1974. $8-10

Rival Dog Food Six-Pack Carton

•The top of the carton features Charlie Brown bringing Snoopy his dinner. He says, "Did I hear a request for seconds?" Snoopy wears a dog dish on his head. Printed: "Rival Blue Ribbon Recipe." The two sides of the carton feature Snoopy carrying his supper dish in his mouth and saying, "Ahem!" Printed: "Rival Blue Ribbon Recipe for Dogs." Rival. 1974. $3-4

Charlie Brown is pictured on the backdrop but was never manufactured. Plastic and plush. 18" x 36" x 36". Worlds of Wonder. 1986. $300-350

AUTOGRAPH BOOKS, PHOTO ALBUMS & CAMERAS, AND SCRAPBOOKS

42. Autograph Books

•Linus, standing behind a movie camera, films Charlie Brown and Lucy, while Snoopy directs. The characters all wear red baseball caps and clothing on a white background. Printed: "Autographs" and "Stars Of The Movie A Boy Named Charlie Brown." Leather-like material. 4" x 6". #9336. A & M Leatherlines, distributed by Determined Productions. 1969-1970. $20-25

•Snoopy, holding a pencil against a polka-dot background, is thinking, "Sign in, please!" 5-1/2" x 4". #425RA2055, Hallmark. Early 1990s. $4-6

•Snoopy and Woodstock are holding autograph books and have pencils behind their ears. Printed: "Autographs." 4-3/4" x 6". #425RA201-7, Hallmark. Early 1980s. $4-6

•Snoopy, dressed in a cape, top hat and cane, walks in front of a theatre with "Autographs" on the awning. He is thinking,

"Here's Joe Movie Star making his grand entrance..." 4-1/2" x 6". #200-1712, Butterfly Originals. 1979. $4-6

43. Photo Album

•Snoopy and Woodstock, sitting on grass, are looking at photos of themselves. Printed: "Good Times Are For Sharing." 5-3/4" x 4-3/4". #PHA4010, Hallmark. Mid-1980s. $3-5

Autograph Book

•Snoopy hands Woodstock an autograph book for him to sign. Printed: "Autographs." 4-3/4" x 6". #250RA754-6, Hallmark. Mid-1970s. $5-10

Autograph Book

Snoopy rides a bicycle with Woodstock and his friend on the back. They are all wearing headphones. Printed: "School's Out! Summer's In!" and "Autographs." This autograph book came in two sizes. Hallmark. Late 1980s. $3-4 ea.

•4-1/2" x 6". #395RA2042.

•4" x 5-1/2". #395RA2046.

44. Camera

•"Snoopy-Matic Instant Load Camera." Snoopy lies on his tummy looking over the edge of his doghouse, which is the camera. Flash cubes and 110 film are used with this camera. Plastic. #975, Helm Toy Corp. 1976. $75-90 $175-200*

45. Album

•"The PEANUTS Thoughtfulness Album." Against a red background, Snoopy lies on top of a mailbox, while looking down at Woodstock, who holds a letter. The inside of the album has a lined page with the days of the month to write information such as birthdays, anniversaries, and any other special events or occasions. Each page displays a four-panel, vertical-format comic strip. In the back are two pages with decorated pockets on each side to keep cards in until you are ready to mail them. Cardboard and paper. 8" x 10". Hallmark. Early 1970s. $20-30

Photo Albums

•Snoopy is grinning with his arms outstretched on a multicolored background. The album has a fold-over flap with a velcro closure. Printed

on the flap: "Lookin' Good!" 3-1/2" x 4". #PHA1007, Hallmark. Early 1990s. $2-3

•On a polka-dot background, Snoopy holds a camera and thinks, "Look inside!" The album has a fold-over flap with a velcro closure. 3-1/2" x 4". #PHA1006, Hallmark. Early 1990s. $2-3

46. Photo Albums

•Snoopy is drinking from baby Sally's bottle. Printed on a white background: "Aren't Babies Wonderful!" #250PHA107-1, Hallmark. 1969. $20-25

•Snoopy is walking with a hobo pack over his shoulder on a red background. Printed: "It Was A Great Trip!" #250PHA108-1, Hallmark. 1972. $15-20

•Linus has a camera around his neck. Printed on a white background: "Want To See My Pictures?" #250PHA105-1, Hallmark. Early 1970s. $15-20

47. Scrapbook

•A decal of Snoopy, as the Flying Ace atop his doghouse, is on the cover, which looks like burlap. The first page inside

has a story and pictures the characters. Three-ring binder design. 12-1/2" x 10". #595BK500-1, Hallmark. 1968. $20-25

Photo Album

•On a yellow background, Snoopy stands next to a camera on a tripod, holding the control with one hand and Woodstock on a stick in the other. He is thinking, "Watch the birdie!" 7" x 10". Hallmark. Mid-1970s. $12-15

48. Scrapbooks

•Snoopy, wearing a blue shirt printed "Super" with a red star underneath, is frolicking on a multicolored polka-dot background. 12-1/2" x 11". #RA6034, Hallmark. Early 1990s. $6-8

•On a green background trimmed in blue, Snoopy and Woodstock sit on Snoopy's doghouse. Snoopy is looking at a book. Printed in blue on the cover: "Scraps." 10-3/4" x 9". #450PA605-5, Hallmark. Early 1970s. $12-15

49. Scrapbook

•Snoopy, as Joe Cool, holds a book while Woodstock and his friends carry school supplies such as glue, pencils, pictures, and scissors. Snoopy is thinking, "It's cool to keep it all together!" Spiral-bound design. 12" x 11". #RA600-6, Hallmark. Early 1980s. $4-6

50. Album

•Linus is kneeling in front of Lucy, who is lying on her tummy reading a newspaper. Printed: "Snaps Scraps & Souvenirs." The album has a burlap look to the cover. 10" x 8". Hallmark. 1969. $15-25

BANNERS AND PENNANTS

51. Banners

•Linus and Sally are walking, holding hands. Printed: "Love Is Walking Hand-In-Hand" and "Linus & Sally." Felt. 14"W x 33-1/2"H. Determined Productions. 1970. $8-12

•Snoopy is sitting in mailbox. Printed: "I've become allergic to people!" Felt. 14"W x 33-1/2"H. Determined Productions. Early 1970s. $8-12

52. Banners

•Snoopy is dancing. Printed: "I've got to start acting more sensible...tomorrow!" and "Snoopy." Felt. 14"W x 33-1/2"H. #571-1, Determined Productions. 1970. $10-15

•Snoopy, with his lips ready to give a kiss, holds a sign printed "Snoopy For President" and "Snoopy." Felt. 14"W x 33-1/2"H. Determined Productions. Early 1970s. $10-15

53. Banner

•Snoopy, wearing a space suit and helmet, is standing on the moon. Printed: "The Moon Is Made Of American Cheese!" and "Snoopy." Felt. 14"W x 33-1/2"H. Determined Productions. 1970. $20-30

54. Banner

•Snoopy, wearing a space suit and helmet, holds life-support gear. Printed: "All Systems Are Go!" and "Snoopy." Felt. 14"W x 33-1/2"H. Determined Productions. 1969. $25-35

55. Banners

•Linus, holding his blanket, sucks his thumb. Printed: "I love mankind...It's people I can't stand!" and "Linus." Felt. 14"W x 33-1/2"H. Determined Productions. Early 1970s. $8-10

•Snoopy, as the Flying Ace, drags his goggles beside him. Printed: "Curse this stupid war! Curse you, too, Red Baron!" Felt. 14"W x 33-1/2"H. Determined Productions. Early 1970s. $15-18

56. Banner

•Sally, Charlie Brown, Violet, Frieda, Lucy, and Linus surround Schroeder playing his piano with Snoopy sitting on it. Printed: "Merry Christmas From All Of Us" and "The PEANUTS Gang." Felt. Determined Productions. Early 1970s. $30-35

57. Banners

•Lucy is sitting. Printed: "It's amazing how stupid you can be when you're in love..." Felt. 14"W x 33-1/2"H. Determined Productions. Early 1970s. $15-20

lobby. Printed: "Happiness Is A Bustling Popcorn Concession. Happiness Is A Pre-Sold Film. Happiness Is SRO. Happiness Is 'A Boy Named Charlie Brown,' Cinema Center Films' Christmas Release For 1969." This banner was distributed as a promotional item for the film "A Boy Named Charlie Brown," and was not made available to the general public. Felt. 1969. $15-18

BUMPER STICKERS

62. Bumper Stickers

Set of two. Paper. #60KF1-1, Hallmark. 1972. $10-12*

•Charlie Brown stands with his kite broken over his head. Printed: "Win With Charlie Brown."

•Linus sits holding his blanket and sucking his thumb. Printed: "Elect Linus." (Not pictured)

Set of two. Paper. #60KF2-1, Hallmark. 1972. $10-12*

•Snoopy is pictured lying on the word "president." Printed: "Snoopy For President."

•Lucy is campaigning, and is seen standing, shaking her fist and shouting her slogan. Printed: "Lucy For First Lady." (Not pictured)

•Pigpen and Snoopy are walking together. Printed: "A Friend Is Someone Who Accepts You For What You Are!" and "Pigpen & Snoopy." Felt. 14"W x 33-1/2"H. Determined Productions. Early 1970s. $18-25

58. Banners

•Linus, wearing a hat and coat, sticks out his tongue to catch the falling snowflakes. Printed: "Polluted snowflakes!" and "Linus." Felt. 14"W x 33-1/2"H. #571-29, Determined Productions. 1970. $10-12

•Charlie Brown is standing and frowning. Printed: "I need all the friends I can get!" and "Charlie Brown." Felt. 14"W x 33-1/2"H. #571-3, Determined Productions. 1970. $10-12

59. Banners

•Linus, holding his blanket, makes the peace sign with his fingers. Printed: "Peace" and "Linus." Felt. 14"W x 33-1/2"H. Determined Productions. Early 1970s. $18-25

•Snoopy sits with two bunnies on his lap. Printed: "Happiness Is Loving Your Enemies" and "Snoopy." Felt. 14"W x 33-1/2"H. Determined Productions. Early 1970s. $18-25

60. Banner

•Snoopy, arms outstretched, holds an Uncle Sam hat. Printed: "America, You're Beautiful!" and "Snoopy." Felt. 14"W x 33-1/2"H. Determined Productions. 1972. $15-25

61. Banners

•Snoopy, Charlie Brown, Schroeder, Lucy, and Linus sit in directors' chairs. Printed: "Stars of the Movie 'A Boy Named Charlie Brown.'" Felt. 26"W. Determined Productions. 1970. $20-25

•Charlie Brown looks out from the projection room, as Lucy sits at a cash register, Peppermint Patty works behind the concession stand, and Snoopy, as the Flying Ace, sells tickets to an adult, who is holding a film reel. Schroeder, Linus, Pigpen, and others are seen milling around the theatre

The PEANUTS Home Collection

63.

HAPPY BIRTHDAY, AMERICA!

I Never Get A Break.

Honk If You're A C.B.'er.

Smokey Is Watching You.

Don't Be A Bumper Sticker.

GET IN THE SPIRIT OF '76

• Snoopy, wearing a top hat and walking, is pictured inside a star. Printed: "Snoopy For President!" Paper. #100HD124-6, Hallmark. 1976. $5-8

• Dolly Madison premium. Snoopy, inside a circle surrounded by stars, wears an Uncle Sam hat. Printed: "Dolly Madison Supports…Snoopy for President." Paper. 1972. $5-7

• Lucy is standing with her arms folded across her chest. Printed: "If You Don't Vote Don't Crab." Paper. #100HD124-1, Hallmark. 1976. $5-8

63. Bumper Stickers

Paper. Hallmark.

• Snoopy, wearing a tri-cornered hat, holds a flag with Woodstock perched on the top. Printed: "Happy Birthday America!" #75HD119-6. 1976. $4-6

• Charlie Brown sits, talking into the microphone of a CB radio. Printed: "I never get a break." #100HD123-6. Mid-1970s. $4-6

• Snoopy, standing, wears a cap printed "CB." Printed: "Honk If You're A C.B.'er." #100HD123-3. Mid-1970s. $4-6

• Snoopy, sitting on a motorcycle and wearing a ranger's hat, is hiding in the bushes. Printed: "Smokey Is Watching You." #100HD123-4. Mid-1970s. $5-8

• Snoopy, wearing roller skates, sits on the ground dazed with his hands on his nose. Printed: "Don't Be A Bumper Sticker." #100HD123-2. Mid-1970s. $4-6

• Snoopy, wearing a tri-cornered hat, stands grinning with his arms outstretched. Printed: "Get In The Spirit Of '76." #75HB119-7. 1976. $4-6

COINS AND COIN HOLDERS

64. Coin Collection Books

• Snoopy, as the Flying Ace, walks against a black background. Printed: "Snoopy's Penny Coin Collection Book." Slots inside the book hold pennies. Jerry Brisken Enterprises. 1976. $12-18

• Snoopy carries an American flag with Woodstock perched on top of the flagpole. Printed: "Coins Of The Presidents." Slots inside hold coins. Jerry Brisken Enterprises. 1976. $12-18

In today's market, there does not appear to be a demand for the coins described below at their original selling price. Prices fluctuate with the rise and fall of gold and silver. Some have been selling for less than the 1987-1988 wholesale price.

65. Coins

Rarities Mint produced gold and silver coins to commemorate Christmas 1987/New Year's 1988 and silver coins to commemorate Valentine's Day 1988. The coins were produced in limited quantities and came in three sizes. The largest coins came packaged in a red or burgundy velvet gift box with a sash inside printed "PEANUTS" for Valentine's Day and "PEANUTS Happy Holiday First Edition" for Christmas/New Year's. The two smaller coins came inside cardboard book-type folders protected by a hard plastic container that could be opened to remove the coin. A certificate of authenticity that includes the issue date, serial number, and weight of the coin comes with each coin.

• The Valentine Coin holder features Lucy handing Linus a red heart. Printed: "My Heart Is Yours." A four-panel comic strip featuring Snoopy and a mailbox is on the inside of the cover. The coin is surrounded by Woodstock and his friends holding a flower, sitting on and flying around Snoopy's doghouse. The back cover features Snoopy hugging Charlie Brown.

The Valentine Coin features Sally handing Linus a heart. Printed: "My Heart Is Yours 1998." The weight of the coin is printed along the edge of the coin. The reverse side of the coin features Snoopy hugging Charlie Brown.

5 Troy Oz. Fine Silver. 1 of 3,000. 2-1/2" diam. $95-120*

1 Troy Oz. Fine Silver. 1 of 30,000. 2" diam. $35-40*

1/10 Oz. Fine Silver. 1 of 30,000. 3/4" diam. $20-35*

• The Happy Holiday Coin holder features Snoopy decorating a Christmas tree with Woodstock on top, and Charlie Brown and Peppermint Patty watching. Printed: "We Wish You A Merry Christmas." A four-panel strip on the inside of

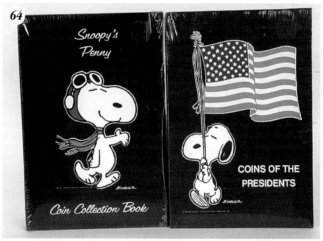

64
Snoopy's Penny
Coin Collection Book

COINS OF THE PRESIDENTS

65
MY HEART IS YOURS

"WE WISH YOU A MERRY CHRISTMAS"

the cover features Snoopy and a snowman. The coin sits on top of a picture of Linus lying across the huge body of a snowman in progress as Snoopy looks on. The back cover features Schroeder playing his piano, and Charlie Brown, Lucy, Woodstock, Sally, Linus, Peppermint Patty, and Snoopy dancing. They are all wearing party hats.

The Happy Holiday Coin features Snoopy decorating a Christmas tree with Woodstock on top. Printed: "Merry Christmas 1987." The reverse side of the coin features Schroeder playing his piano, Woodstock, and Lucy, Charlie Brown, and Snoopy dancing. Printed: "Happy New Year 1988." The weight of the coin is printed along the edge of the coin.

    5 Troy Oz. Fine Silver. 1 of 3,000. 2-1/2" diam. $95-120*

    1 Troy Oz. Fine Silver. 1 of 30,000. 2" diam. $35-40*

    1/10 Oz. Fine Silver. 1 of 30,000. 3/4" diam. $20-35*

    1 Troy Oz. Fine Gold. 1 of 500. 1-1/8" diam. $600-700*

    1/4 Troy Oz. Fine Gold. 1 of 2,500. 3/4" diam. $150-200*

66. Coin

•Snoopy wears a wreath of leaves on his head and wears a ribbon printed "Hero." The coin is printed: "E Pluribus Snoopy." The reverse side features Woodstock and is printed "Tails." This coin was a prize in a contest sponsored by Interstate brands. Came in a brown velvet pouch, with a red, white, and blue ribbon tied in a bow on the front. Bronze. 1-1/2" diam. Early 1980s. $35-45

67. Coin

•"Snoopy Astronaut Commemorative Coin." The coin features Snoopy wearing a space suit, a helmet, and carrying life support gear. Printed around the edge of the coin: "All Systems Go" and "Snoopy." The reverse side of the coin features Snoopy, as the Flying Ace, sitting on his doghouse wearing a space helmet. Printed: "First Landing On The Moon Commemorative 1969." The coin is packaged on a red, white, and blue card featuring Snoopy in a space suit and helmet. Silver plated. 1-1/2" diam. #311, Determined Productions. 1969. $12-20 $30-40*

CLOTHING BUTTONS AND RIBBONS

68. Clothing Buttons

Sold in sets of two. The character's name appears on the card. Some cards included a voice balloon. JHB. Set: $3-4 ea.

•Snoopy holds his dog dish. White plastic. 3/4" diam. #25142. 1991.

•Woodstock rides a bicycle. White plastic. 3/4" diam. #25139. 1991.

•Snoopy plays golf. White plastic. 5/8" diam. #25141. 1991.

•Sally's head. Printed on the card: "My sweet babboo says it's true." White plastic. 5/8" diam. #4277. 1987.

•Charlie Brown's head. Printed on the card: "Good Grief!" White plastic. 5/8" diam. #23260. 1987.

•Snoopy dances. Printed on the card: "Whoopee! Bring on the Beaglettes!" Red plastic. 3/4" diam. #4281. 1987.

•Snoopy as the Flying Ace. White plastic. 3/4" diam. #860. 1992.

•Snoopy has hearts around him. White plastic. 3/4" diam. #25140. 1991.

•Snoopy, wearing a helmet, runs with a football. Hand-painted enamel on metal. 7/8"H. #95055. 1990.

•Snoopy's head. Hand-painted enamel on metal. 7/8"H. #94992. 1988.

•Woodstock. Printed on the card: "?" White plastic. 5/8" diam. #23254. 1991.

•Snoopy is standing against a light blue background. Printed on the card: "I could have sworn I heard a chocolate chip cookie calling me." 5/8" diam. #858. 1987.

•Lucy's head. Printed on the card: "I'm surprised you didn't fall in love with me the very first time you saw me." White plastic. 5/8" diam. #23258. 1987.

•Linus' head. Printed on the card: "I'm just a kid." White plastic. 5/8" diam. #4278. 1987.

•Charlie Brown wears baseball gear. Printed on the card: "You mean you want me to pitch?" White plastic. 5/8" diam. #864. 1987.

•Snoopy eats an ice cream cone against a light blue background. 3/4" diam. #25235. 1989.

•Snoopy sits at the piano while Woodstock sits on top. White plastic. 3/4" diam. #25138. 1989.

•Woodstock. Hand-painted enamel on metal. 7/8"H. #863. 1987.

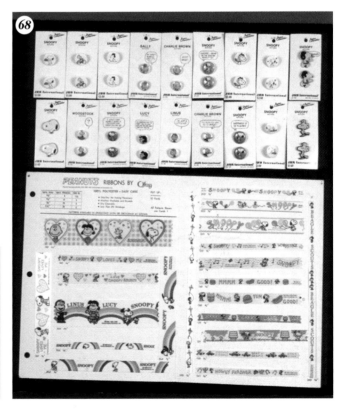

68. Clothing Ribbons

Offray. 1983. $1.50-2.00 per yard

Hearts Pattern. Satin. #1301.

•Charlie Brown, Lucy, Woodstock, and Snoopy are each inside a heart against a pink and white checkered background. 1-1/2"W.

•Snoopy and hearts are pictured between the words "Snoopy Loves Me." 3/8"W.

•Snoopy, Woodstock, and hearts are pictured between the words "I Love Snoopy." 5/8"W.

•Snoopy, Woodstock, and hearts are pictured between the words "Snoopy Loves Me." 7/8"W.

Rainbow Pattern. Grosgrain. #3541.

•Linus, Lucy, Snoopy appear between their names, which are printed above the rainbow. 1-1/2"W.

•Snoopy is at the end of the each rainbow. Printed between the rainbows: "Snoopy." 7/8"W.

•Snoopy sits under the rainbows in various poses. Printed between the rainbows: "Snoopy." 5/8"W.

•Snoopy's face appears under the rainbows. Printed between the rainbows: "Snoopy." 3/8"W.

Balloon Pattern. Grosgrain. #3521.

•Snoopy and Woodstock hold balloons between the word "Snoopy." 3/8"W.

•Snoopy and Woodstock lie on and hold balloons. "Snoopy" is spelled out in balloon-like print. 5/8"W.

•Snoopy holds balloons. "Snoopy" is spelled out in balloon-like print. 7/8"W.

Musical Notes Pattern. Satin. #1321.

•Snoopy and Woodstock appear between musical notes and their names. 3/8"W.

•Snoopy and Woodstock appear between musical notes and the word "Snoopy." 5/8"W.

Junk Food Pattern. Satin. #1361.

•Snoopy appears between hamburgers and hot dogs and the words "MMMM" and "Good!" 3/8"W.

•Snoopy and Woodstock appear between hamburgers, hot dogs, and French fries and the words "MMMM!" "Yum," and "Good!" 5/8"W.

Doghouse Pattern. Satin. #1311.

•Snoopy and his doghouse appear between the word "Snoopy." 3/8"W.

•Snoopy, Woodstock and his friends appear between the word "Snoopy" and his doghouse. 5/8"W.

Car Pattern. Satin. #1351.

•Snoopy and Woodstock drive cars between the words "Zoom!!" "Beep!!" and "Honk!!" 3/8"W.

Western Pattern. Satin. #1371.

•Snoopy and Woodstock, wearing cowboy hats, appear between horseshoes, cacti, and the words "Howdy Pardner." 3/8"W.

Kite Pattern. Satin. #1331.

•Snoopy, Charlie Brown, Linus, and Lucy fly kites. 3/8"W.

Scout Pattern. Grosgrain. #3681.

•Snoopy, Woodstock, and his friends, dressed as scouts, appear between the words "Beagle Scouts." 3/8"W.

You will note that many, if not all, of the crafts have a double star, which signifies that I recommend your buying it in the package. These items have so many pieces that, if found without the box, it's very likely that they will be missing some of the materials. If you choose to buy it out of the box at least know what pieces should be with the item.

CRAFTS

69. Craft

•"Charlie Brown Bisque Kit." Charlie Brown is sitting, wearing his baseball hat, and holding his bat. His glove is at his side. Includes the kiln-fired ceramic piece ready for painting, paint, paint brush, and instructions. The bisque kit came in other designs which are pictured on the back of the box. Craft House. 1981. $135-145**

70. Crafts

"Color Stitch Kits for Kids." Kits include all necessary materials. JCA, Inc. Early 1990s. $8-10** ea.

•Sally sits and tries to do her homework. Printed: "Homework Hurts." #07201.

•Snoopy, wearing a stocking cap, lies on his tummy across a pillow. Woodstock also lies on the pillow. Printed: "Do Not Disturb." #07208

"Weekenders Counted Cross Stitch Kits." Kits include all necessary materials. JCA, Inc. Early 1990s. $8-10** ea.

•Linus holds his blanket and sucks his thumb. Printed: "A thumb tastes best at room temperature." #02740.

•Snoopy sits at a typewriter, with Woodstock sitting on the return carriage, writing a poem about chocolate chip cookies. #02741.

71. Crafts

•"Counted Cross Stitch Baby Collection." The "PEANUTS Gang Birth Sampler" kit includes all necessary materials. The

72

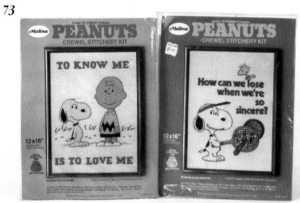

73

74

72. Crafts

"PEANUTS" crewel stitchery and needlepoint kits. All necessary materials are included. Malina. Late 1970s. $15-20** ea.

•Lucy sits behind her psychiatrist booth, Woodstock sits on top, and Snoopy stands next to the booth. Printed: "No One Understands My Generation." 12" x 16". #8110/018.

•Lucy sits with her feet up on her psychiatrist booth while Charlie Brown sits on a stool next to the booth. 8" x 10". #8110/014.

•Snoopy kisses a sitting Lucy on the cheek. Frame is included. Printed: "Smak!" 8" x 10". #8110/006.

•Snoopy, wearing a raccoon coat and a hat, walks carrying a pennant printed "State." Frame is included. 8" x 10". #8110/011.

•Snoopy, on the fourth hole of the golf course, has just hit the ball. Frame is included. 8" x 10". #8110/002.

•Snoopy, on the tennis court, is ready to serve the ball. Frame is included. 8" x 10". #8110/001.

73. Crafts

•"PEANUTS Crewel Stitchery Kit." Snoopy and Charlie Brown stand next to each other, smiling. Printed: "To Know Me Is To Love Me." All necessary materials and a frame are included. 12" x 16". #8110/016, Malina. Late 1970s. $15-20**

•"PEANUTS Crewel Stitchery Kit." Snoopy, wearing a visor, holds a tennis racket with another racket pushed through it. Woodstock sits on top of the caption "How Can We Lose When We're So Sincere?" All necessary materials and a frame are included. 12" x 16". #8110/019, Malina. Late 1970s. $15-20**

74. Crafts

"PEANUTS" crewel stitchery and needlepoint kits. All necessary materials are included. Frame is included. 8" x 10". Malina. Mid-1970s. $10-12** ea.

•Snoopy is sitting on his doghouse. Woodstock sits on a flag hanging from the doghouse. #8110/004.

•Snoopy, on his back, lies across a beach ball. Woodstock sits under an umbrella on Snoopy's tummy. Printed: "Beach Fun." #8110/007.

•Snoopy, wearing a stocking cap, carries a pair of skis over his shoulder. #8111/001.

•Sally stands holding a teddy bear. #8111/004.

75

75. Crafts

Jeweled needlepoint calendar kits. All necessary materials are included. 16" x 30". Bucilla. 1982. $10-12** ea.

•Snoopy lies on his doghouse with Woodstock on his tummy. The doghouse is repeated for each month in the year. #48974.

•Snoopy, dressed as a chef, is in a kitchen with pots and pans. A frying pan is repeated for each month in the year. #48970.

76. Crafts

•"PEANUTS Needlepoint Kit." Snoopy is dressed as Santa Claus. All necessary materials and a frame are included. 8" x 10". #8111/005, Malina. Mid-1970s. $12-15**

finished 10" x 10" sampler features Peppermint Patty, Snoopy, Linus, Sally, Marcie, Charlie Brown, Lucy, and Woodstock dancing, surrounded by flowers. #04401, JCA, Inc. Early 1990s. $18-25**

"Stamped Cross Stitch Baby Collection." Kits include all necessary materials. JCA, Inc. Early 1990s.

•"The PEANUTS Gang Bib Set." One bib features Snoopy dancing and Woodstock flying overhead. The other bib features an oval floral design with space for the baby's name inside. 9" x 11". #04205. $8-10**

•"The PEANUTS Gang Quilt." The quilt features Peppermint Patty, Snoopy, Linus, Sally, Marcie, Charlie Brown, Lucy, and Woodstock dancing, surrounded by flowers. 35" x 43". #04204. $25-35**

•"Snoopy's Dream Quilt." The quilt features Snoopy asleep on a pillow with Woodstock in a red stocking cap sitting on his feet. Each corner of the quilt features Snoopy driving a different vehicle—a boat, a fire truck, a rocket and a train. 35" x 43". #04206. $25-35**

•"Needlepoint Needle Treasures A Snoopy Christmas Stocking." Snoopy and Woodstock decorate a Christmas tree. A free ornament and all necessary materials are included. Stocking—10" x 16". Ornament—4" triangle. #06855, JCA, Inc. Early 1990s. $8-10**

•"Needlepoint Needle Treasures Ho Ho Ho Stocking." Snoopy and Woodstock, both dressed as Santa Claus, carry gift-filled sacks to put under a decorated Charlie Brown tree. A free ornament and all necessary materials are included. Stocking—10" x 16". Ornament—3-1/2" diam. #02856, JCA, Inc. Early 1990s. $8-10**

"PEANUTS Christmas Stocking Kits." All necessary materials are included. 18"H. Malina. Late 1970s. $15-20** ea.

•Snoopy, sitting in front of a Christmas tree, holds Woodstock in his nest. Needlepoint. #8500/003.

•Snoopy, wearing a stocking cap, and Woodstock, standing on top of a gift, are on top of Snoopy's decorated doghouse with a decorated tree branch overhead. Needlepoint. #8500/004.

•Snoopy sits at a typewriter on top of his decorated doghouse. Woodstock flies overhead. Jeweled. #8450/001.

77. Crafts

"PEANUTS Set of 4 Jeweled Hanging Ornaments Kit." All necessary materials are included in the kit. Felt. Malina. Late 1970s. $15-20** ea.

•#8400/002. Snoopy carries a wreath; Snoopy carries skis; Snoopy decorates a Christmas tree; and Woodstock sits on top of Snoopy's doghouse.

•#8400/001. Snoopy is walking; Snoopy lies on his decorated doghouse; Snoopy sits inside a wreath; and Snoopy sits inside a stocking.

78. Crafts

•"PEANUTS Jeweled Christmas Stocking Kit." Woodstock sits on top of a snowman as Snoopy puts on the finishing touches. All necessary materials are included. Felt. 18"H. #8450/003, Malina. Mid-1970s. Shown completed, the price represents the kit in the package. $15-20**

•"PEANUTS Jeweled Christmas Panel Kit." Woodstock and Snoopy stand on top of Snoopy's decorated doghouse ready to exchange Christmas gifts. All necessary materials are included. Felt. 16" x 20". #8350/001, Malina. Mid-1970s. Shown completed, the price represents the kit in the package. $35-40**

79. Crafts

•Needlepoint kit. Charlie Brown stands on the pitcher's mound surrounded by Snoopy, Peppermint Patty, Linus, Schroeder, and Lucy, all wearing baseball gear. All necessary materials are included. Finished size 15" x 15". #4102, Determined Productions. 1973. Shown completed, the price represents the kit in the package. $30-35**

•Needlepoint kit. Snoopy lies on his doghouse with Woodstock on his tummy. Peppermint Patty, Charlie Brown, Lucy, Linus, and Schroeder playing his piano are in the foreground. All necessary materials are included. Finished size 15" x 15". Designed by Dorothy Lambert Brightbill for Determined Productions. 1973. Shown completed, the price represents the kit in the package. $30-35**

78

76

77

79

80. Crafts

•Quickpoint kit. Snoopy and Woodstock are sitting and laughing. All necessary materials are included. 18" x 18". #4111, Determined Productions. 1972. $18-25**

81. Crafts

•"PEANUTS Latch Hook Kit." Snoopy lies on top of his doghouse. All necessary materials are included. 20" x 27". #26/8, Malina. Late 1970s. $30-35**

•"PEANUTS Latch Hook Kit." Snoopy rides a wave on a surfboard. All necessary materials are included. 20" x 27". #26/5, Malina. Late 1970s. $30-35**

82. Crafts

•"PEANUTS Latch Hook Kit." This kit features the head of Snoopy as the Flying Ace. All necessary materials are included. 15" x 15". #33/1, Malina. Late 1970s. $20-30**

•"PEANUTS Latch Hook Kit." Linus, sitting, sucks his thumb and holds his blanket. All necessary materials are included. 20" x 27". #26/6, Malina. Late 1970s. $20-30**

83. Crafts

•"PEANUTS Latch Hook Kit." Snoopy is hugging Woodstock. All necessary materials are included. 20" x 27". #26/13, Malina. 1980. $30-35**

•"PEANUTS Latch Hook Kit." Snoopy carries a hobo pack over his shoulder. All necessary materials are included. 20" x 27". #26/3, Malina. Late 1970s. $30-35**

84. Crafts

"Snoopy ...The Great Master! Acrylic Paint By Numbers Set." Snoopy appears on the box wearing a beret, holding a palette, and thinking, "Painting is such fun!" The set includes two 6" x 8" panels, paints, a brush, and instructions. Craft House, for Determined Productions. Mid-1970s. $15-18** ea.

•#3074. The two panels to paint feature golf scenes with Charlie Brown, and Snoopy and Woodstock.

•#3072. The two panels to paint feature Woodstock and Snoopy with his hobo pack.

82

83

84

80

81

85. Crafts

"Snoopy's Fast Dry Paint By Number On Black Velvet." Snoopy appears on the box wearing a beret, holding a palette, and thinking, "Painting black velvet is my thing!" The set includes one 8" x 10" velvet panel, paints, a brush, and instructions. Craft House. 1983. $15-20** ea.

•Snoopy, sitting, holds an umbrella while asleep. Woodstock sits on top of Snoopy's umbrella asleep under his own umbrella. Printed: "Z." #8572.

•Snoopy kisses Lucy on the cheek. They both wear baseball caps and gloves. Printed: "Smak!" #8574.

•Snoopy dances on top of Schroeder's piano while he plays. #8571.

•Sally sits on a bench with her lunch bag as Linus walks by. #8573.

86. Crafts

•"Snoopy Mosaic Crushed Stone Craft Kit." Kit contains one 8" x 10" panel featuring Snoopy and Woodstock wrapped together in a blanket and seated on a bench; crushed stone; non-toxic glue; and instructions. #9574, Craft House for Determined Productions. Late 1970s. $15-20**

87. Crafts

•"Snoopy Fast Dry Paint By Number." The packaging features the beach scene panel to paint and the gang carrying Snoopy and Charlie Brown on their shoulders. Printed: "Saturday Morning T.V." All necessary materials are included. 9" x 12". #04741, Craft House. Early 1980s. $15-18**

•"Snoopy Big 3 Fast Dry Paint By Number." The kit includes one 8" x 10" panel and two 6" x 8" panels. The panels feature Snoopy playing tennis, football, and jogging. All necessary materials are included. The packaging features the panels included in the kit and Snoopy wearing a beret painting a picture of himself. #2572, Craft House for Determined Productions. Late 1970s. $15-20**

•"Snoopy Fast Dry Paint By Number Set." The packaging features the panel to paint of Snoopy fishing on a sailboat and Snoopy wearing a beret and down on one knee, holding the painting. All necessary materials are included. 8" x 10". #13571, Craft House. Mid-1980s. $10-12**

88. Crafts

•"Snoopy's Wood Painting Christmas Ornaments. Acrylic Paint By Number Set." The set includes 20 wooden ornaments and all other necessary materials. The packaging features all 20 ornaments and Snoopy wearing a stocking cap sitting in front of a Christmas tree. Each ornament is approximately 3"H. Series #8070, Craft House. 1983. $30-35**

•"Snoopy Big Set Fast Dry Acrylic Paint By Number Set." The packaging features Snoopy wearing a beret and a collage of Snoopy in different scenes. All necessary materials are

included. 12" x 16". Craft House for Determined Productions. Late 1970s. $20-25**

89. Crafts

•"Snoopy Fun Figures You Paint." The set includes four plastic figures of Snoopy playing baseball, dressed as a sailor, roller-skating, dressed in scuba diving gear. All necessary materials are included. #04802, Craft House. 1984. $25-30**

•"Snoopy Snap 'n Paint Figure Painting." Snoopy, as the Flying Ace, is on his doghouse with Woodstock. All necessary materials are included. #19121, Craft House. Mid-1980s. $12-15**

•"Snoopy Snap 'n Paint Figure Painting." Lucy holds a football. All necessary materials are included. #19123, Craft House. Mid-1980s. $12-15**

90

93

91

94

92

90. Crafts

•"Snoopy Paint By Number Christmas Ornaments." The kit includes six plastic ornaments and all other necessary materials. #8125, Craft House. Mid-1980s. $10-12**

•"Snoopy Sun Charmers." This paint-by-number kit includes four plastic ornaments that can be used as key chains, shade pulls, or as window decorations. All necessary materials are included. Each ornament is approximately 3"H. #40075, Craft House. Mid-1980s. $10-12**

91. Crafts

•"Snoopy Color 'n Recolor Deluxe Playcloth Set." The set includes a 40" x 63" wipe-off playcloth, crayons, and ten stand-up play pieces. #943, Avalon. 1980. $15-20**

•"Snoopy Sign Mobile." An automobile holds the materials included to create signs: a roll of paper, a pencil, crayons and sharpener, and stencils. #262, Avalon. Late 1970s. $50-65**

•"Snoopy Color 'n Recolor Mug, Bowl, Place Mat Gift Set." All materials necessary to decorate a snap-together mug and bowl, and place mats are included in this set. #742, Avalon. 1980. $45-50**

92. Crafts

"Snoopy Sun Catcher Paint by Number." Each kit includes all materials necessary to paint translucent stained-glass type ornaments. Series #8090, Craft House. Mid-1980s. $10-12 ea.**

•Linus pats Woodstock on the head.

•Charlie Brown eats an ice cream cone.

•Snoopy, as Joe Cool, leans against his doghouse.

•Snoopy is wearing a party hat and carrying balloons.

93. Crafts

•"Snoopy Window Picture Paint By Number." Each kit includes all materials necessary to paint translucent stained-glass type pictures. Craft House. Mid-1980s. $15-22** ea.

•Snoopy and Woodstock sit on a bench, wrapped in a blanket and holding pennants. Printed: "Love Is Rooting Together For Your Team." #48061.

•Snoopy lies on his doghouse in the rain, while Woodstock and his friends stand on him from head to toe covering him with umbrellas. Printed: "Love Is Looking Out For Your Friends." #48063.

•Peppermint Patty kisses a beet-red Charlie Brown on the cheek. Printed: "Love Is Accepting A Person For What He Is." #48062.

94. Crafts

•"Snoopy Doodles Felt Pen Picture Set." The set includes all necessary materials to color a camping scene on cardboard and an amusement park scene on paper. 9-1/4" x 13-1/4". Series #7570, Craft House for Determined Productions. 1976. $15-18**

•"Snoopy Poster Pen Set." The set includes all necessary materials to color two posters that feature a collage of different scenes. 12" x 16". Series #63051, Craft House. Early 1980s. $10-15**

95

98. Crafts

Snap-tite model kits. Easy to assemble. No glue or paint required. The packages feature Snoopy, as the Flying Ace, driving the vehicles. Battery-operated. Plastic. Monogram/Mattel. 1971.

•"Snoopy And His Motorcycle." Woodstock rides in the side-car. #5902. $140-145**

•"Snoopy And His Bugatti Race Car." A display base is included. #6894. $125-135**

99. Crafts

Snap-tite model kits. Easy to assemble. No glue or paint required. Battery-operated. Plastic. Monogram/Mattel. 1971.

97

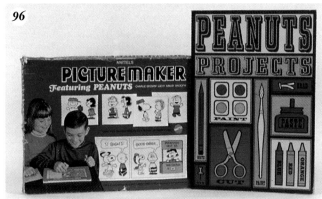

96

98

•"Snoopy Poster Pen Set." The set includes all necessary materials to color two posters that feature a collage of different scenes. The packaging is printed "Saturday Morning T.V." 14" x 20". #63071, Craft House. 1983. $12-15**

95. Crafts

•"Super Cartoon-Maker Featuring Snoopy And His PEANUTS Pals." Snoopy, Charlie Brown, Linus, Lucy, and a non-Woodstock bird can be made in 14 different poses using cast iron molds and Plastigoop. All necessary materials are included. #4696, Mattel. 1970. $175-250**

96. Crafts

•"Picture Maker Featuring PEANUTS Charlie Brown! Lucy! Linus! Snoopy!" The kit includes all necessary materials to draw each character in different poses. #4153, Mattel. 1970. $60-70**

•"PEANUTS Projects." This is an activity book with projects that feature the characters and which requires all the supplies shown on the cover. The cover has no PEANUTS graphics. 12" x 17". Determined Productions. 1968. $30-40

97. Crafts

"PEANUTS! Sculpt-Sure." A mold, clay and all other necessary materials are included to make sculptures of Snoopy and Charlie Brown. Mattel. 1972. $160-200** ea.

•Snoopy as the Flying Ace. 10-1/2"H. #8957.

•Charlie Brown wearing a baseball glove and cap. 12"H. #8956.

•"Snoopy And His Sopwith Camel." Snoopy's doghouse is the display base. Packaged in a 9-1/2" x 9-1/2" square box. #6779. $130-140**

•"Snoopy And His Sopwith Camel." Snoopy's doghouse is the display base. Same as the above kit, but packaged in a rectangular box. #6779. $120-135**

•"Red Baron Fokker Triplane." This is not a licensed PEANUTS item but it is associated with Snoopy as the Flying Ace. #5903. $85-110**

100. Crafts

Snap-tite model kits. Easy to assemble. No glue or paint required. Plastic. Monogram/Mattel.

•"Snoopy Ice Hockey." Snoopy and Woodstock play hockey in a birdbath. #5696. 1972. $160-185**

•"Snoopy's High Wire Act ." Snoopy rides across a wire with Woodstock sitting in a trapeze below attached to the unicycle. #6661. 1973. $95-100**

•"Snoopy Is Joe Cool." Snoopy, wearing shorts and sunglasses, rides a wave on a surfboard. Battery-operated. #7502. 1971. $95-100**

99

100

101

ENTERTAINMENT COLLECTIBLES

101. Play Programs

•"You're A Good Man, Charlie Brown." Cover sheet printed: "Spotlight" and "Theatre 80 St. Marks April." 1967. $10-15

•"Snoopy." Printed: "Showbill Lamb's Theatre." 1982. $10-15

Souvenir Books

•"A Boy Named Charlie Brown." Radio City Music Hall. 1969. $15-20

•"You're A Good Man, Charlie Brown." 1967. $15-20

102. Pressbooks

•"Snoopy Come Home." The cover features Snoopy, supper dish on his head, carrying a hobo pack with Woodstock walking behind him. The pressbook contains materials relating to the promotion of the movie—information, photos, scenes from the movie, advertising suggestions, and promotional items to be sold in conjunction with the movie. Printed: "Cinema Center Films Press book." Paper. 8-1/2"W x 14"H. National General Pictures. 1972. $12-15

•"A Boy Named Charlie Brown." The cover features Snoopy wearing a beret, sunglasses and holding a megaphone, Lucy, Charlie Brown, and Linus. The pressbook contains materials relating to the promotion of the movie—information, photos, scenes from the movie, advertising suggestions, and promotional items to be sold in conjunction with the movie. Printed: "Cinema Center Films Press book." Paper. 8-1/2"W x 14"H. National General Pictures. 1969. $12-15

Poster

•"A Boy Named Charlie Brown." This poster features Snoopy wearing a beret and sunglasses, and holding a megaphone, along with Lucy, Charlie Brown, and Linus. At the bottom of the poster Snoopy, Charlie Brown, Linus, Sally, Schroeder,

102

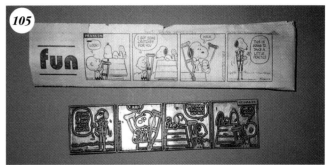

Lucy, Frieda, and Pigpen are depicted sitting in directors' chairs. Along with title information, the poster is printed: "Charlie Brown And The PEANUTS Gang In Their First Movie!" Paper. 13-1/2"W x 30"H. 1969. $10-15

103. Framed Poster

• "Macy's Thanksgiving Day Parade." Snoopy, as the Flying Ace, floats above Broadway in front of Macy's along with the cartoon characters Superman, Olive Oyl, Woody Woodpecker, and Yogi Bear. Printed on top: Melanie Taylor Kent. Printed on bottom: Edward Weston Graphics. 30"H x 24"W. 1983. $75-100

Plate

• "Macy's Thanksgiving Day Parade." Snoopy, as the Flying Ace, floats above Broadway in front of Macy's along with the cartoon characters Underdog, Bullwinkle, Olive Oyl, and Yogi Bear. Printed on plate: The World's Largest Store * Macy's. 10" diam. Ceramic trimmed in gold. From an original painting by Melanie Taylor Kent, licensed by Edward Weston Editions. Signed by Melanie Taylor Kent. Limited edition. Includes certificate of authenticity. The Carmel Collection, Briggsmore China. 1983. $90-125*

104. Photos

• Black-and-white publicity photo from "This Is America, Charlie Brown." Snoopy, standing in front of the White House, wears a tuxedo and top hat and holds a sign printed "Vote Snoopy." 1990. $6-8

• Photo. Black-and-white publicity photo from "Bon Voyage, Charlie Brown (and don't come back!)." Snoopy, sitting at a cafe table with a mug and a candle on it, cries while Woodstock, perched on the back of a chair, plays the violin. 1980. $6-8

• Photo. Black-and-white publicity photo from "You're In Love, Charlie Brown." Lucy, Violet, and Snoopy are laughing at Charlie Brown. 1967. $8-10

• Photo. Black-and-white publicity photo from the television production of "You're A Good Man, Charlie Brown." Sally, Linus, Lucy, Schroeder, and Snoopy, wearing baseball caps and carrying bats over their shoulders, walk past a scoreboard. 1988. $6-8

MISCELLANEOUS HOBBY ITEMS

105. Newspaper Printing Plate

• This particular plate was used by the Long Island, New York newspaper *Newsday*, to reproduce the PEANUTS comic strips in the late 1970s. Each strip's plate was discarded after it was used. Heavy metal. $30-35 with original cartoon.

106. Plaque

• In the center, Snoopy lies on his doghouse and Woodstock flies above him with "Snoopy 35th Anniversary Celebration" printed above them. A metal plate below is printed "1984 United Features Syndicate, Inc. Limited Edition Set #." Twelve multicolored enameled designs of Snoopy, Charlie Brown, Lucy, Linus, and Sally lie on black velvet inside a glass-covered six-sided wooden frame. Each design is set against a six-sided background. 12-3/4" x 10". #G-111900, Quantasia. 1985. $65-75

NASA MEMORABILIA

The decals, patches, and posters pictured below were not for sale to the public. The use of NASA insignia designs was authorized by NASA administration officials. The items were made available to the men and women who made the Apollo space flights possible, from aerospace manufacturing employees to the astronauts themselves.

107. Decal

•Snoopy as an astronaut dances next to a launched rocket. Printed: "Apollo Launch Team." Vitachrome, Inc. 1969. $20-25

Newspaper Article

•Charles Schulz drew the articles accompanying picture of Charlie Brown and Snoopy as returning astronauts from the Apollo 10 launch. The article's headline reads "Apollo Return Flawless Pickup Of Astronauts Is Fastest Yet." Chicago Tribune. May 27, 1969. $40-45

Decals

•Snoopy is dressed in full space flight gear against a blue background. Printed: "Eyes On The Stars" and "pS." Vitachrome, Inc. 1969. $25-35

•Snoopy as an astronaut sits on his doghouse, which floats in the ocean. Printed: "Project Apollo Recovery Team." Vitachrome, Inc. 1969. $25-35

Newspaper Article

•Contains text and a picture of a patch that features Snoopy and a Russian bear, joint mascots for the July 15, 1975, Apollo-Soyuz space flight. $4-6

Decals

•Snoopy and a Russian bear, wearing space gear, sit on rockets facing each other. Snoopy is thinking, "Right on!" while the bear is thinking, "Noexaan! (Let's go)." "Apollo-Soyuz" is printed in English and Russian around the decal along with the words "Space Teams." This decal was also available as a patch. 1975. $40-50

•Snoopy, wearing space gear and holding a valise and a wrench, sits on a space capsule printed "E.D. Mitchell." Under his helmet he wears a hard hat printed "Safety." Printed on the decal: "On Target for Safety." Vitachrome, Inc. 1971. $30-40

•Snoopy, wearing space gear, sits on his doghouse. Printed: "Apollo 11 Lunar Team." Vitachrome, Inc. 1969. $25-35

•Snoopy, wearing space gear and holding a valise and a wrench, sits on a space capsule printed "Steve Roasa." Under his helmet he wears a hard hat printed "Safety." Printed on the decal: "It Can Happen To You." Vitachrome, Inc. 1971. $25-35

•Snoopy, wearing space gear and holding a valise and a wrench, sits on a space capsule printed "Alan B. Shepard." Under his helmet he wears a hard hat printed "Safety." Printed on the decal: "Zero In On Safety." Vitachrome, Inc. 1971. $25-35

108. Posters

•Snoopy, as an astronaut, stands atop the launch tower as the rocket blasts off. Printed: "Up Up & Away", "Good Work...Is The Only Way!" and "Keep Apollo The Symbol Of Excellence." 11-1/4" x 14-1/2". NASA. 1969. $95-125

•Snoopy, as an astronaut, holds an umbrella over himself and a large carton with decals on it. Printed: "Kid Gloves Care Will Get Us There," "NASA Critical Space Item Special Care Moon Cargo" and "Manned Flight Awareness." 11-1/4" x 14-1/2". NASA. 1969. $95-125

109. Posters

•Snoopy, as an astronaut, holds a paint bucket in outer space. He paints "Skylab" on the space station and thinks, "Fantastic!!!" Printed: "Manned Flight Awareness." 16" x 21-1/2". NASA. 1969. $145-175

•Snoopy, as an astronaut, is on top of his doghouse holding a pointer to a blackboard. Three birds look at the blackboard from various vantage points. The blackboard is printed with tips for handling parts. Snoopy is thinking, "Take pride, think cleanliness." Also printed: "Manned Flight Awareness." 16" x 21-1/2". NASA. 1969. $145-175

110. Patch

•Snoopy, as the Flying Ace, has his fist raised and appears to be talking. Emblem was sewn on washcloths and towels used aboard the spaceship. The background color identified which astronaut the item belonged to: red for the commander, white for the scientist, and blue for the pilot. Embroidered on fabric. No UFS on it. 4-1/4" oval. NASA. 1969. $10-12

PATCHES

111. Patches

"Snoopy Stick On Patches." Plastic. Determined Productions. 1973. $5-8* ea.

•Snoopy, in yellow, is dancing. 4"H.

•Snoopy lies on his doghouse. Woodstock stands on Snoopy's tummy. 3-7/8"H.

•Snoopy, in orange, wears an award ribbon printed "Hero." 3-7/8"H.

•Snoopy, in blue, as Joe Cool. 3-7/8"H.

•Snoopy, in red, is walking. 4"H.

112. Patches

These sew-on patches commemorate the 1984 Los Angeles Summer Olympics. They feature Snoopy and Belle participating in different events. Printed: "Snoopy Patch L.A. 1984" and "Belle Patch L.A. 1984." Multicolored. Embroidered on fabric. 3-1/8" diam. Determined Productions. 1984. $6-8* ea.

•Belle poses in gymnastics clothing.

•Belle plays volleyball.

•Snoopy is a cyclist.

•Snoopy paddles a kayak.

•Snoopy is ready to throw a discus.

•Snoopy dives into a pool.

•Snoopy poses in fencing gear.

•Snoopy performs on the pommel horse.

•Snoopy performs on the rings.

•Snoopy is pole vaulting.

•Snoopy runs a foot race.

•Snoopy lifts weights.

113. Patches

"PEANUTS Patch." These patches inspired the patch pillows found on page 325-326. Multicolored sew-on patches. Embroidered on fabric. 2-1/2" diam. Determined Productions. 1972. $5-8* ea.

•Snoopy is dancing. Printed: "Come Dance With Me Baby." #721.

•Snoopy, as the Flying Ace, is on top of his doghouse. Printed: "Curse You, Red Baron." #726.

•Snoopy holds a hockey stick. Printed: "Hat Trick." #738.

•Snoopy, wearing a stocking cap, is ice-skating. Printed: "Ice Is Nice." #729.

•Snoopy is jogging. Printed: "Jogging Is My Thing." #737.

•Snoopy wears an award ribbon. Printed: "It's Hero Time." #723.

•Snoopy, wearing a helmet, is rollerskating. Printed: "Jamming." #731.

•Snoopy flexes his muscles. Printed: "Raw Strength & Courage." #722.

•Snoopy flashes a grin. Printed: "Smile." #740.

•Snoopy holds a tennis racket. Printed: "Tennis Anyone?" #732.

•Snoopy carries a pair of skis over his shoulder. Printed: "To The Bunny Slope." #739.

•Snoopy leans on a golf club. Printed: "You're Away." #730.

•Lucy is standing. Printed: "World's Crabbiest Female." #727.

•Charlie Brown carries his baseball bat and glove over his shoulder. Printed: "I Need All The Friends I Can Get." #724.

•Snoopy swings a baseball bat. Printed: "Home Run King." #734.

•Schroeder carries his piano. Printed: "I Love Beethoven." #725.

•Snoopy as Joe Cool. Printed: "Joe Cool."

•Snoopy kicks a football. Printed: "The Mad Punter." #733.

•Linus holds his blanket and sucks his thumb. Printed: "To Know Me Is To Love Me." #728.

•Snoopy is on skis. Printed: "World Famous Ski Champion." #735. (Not pictured)

•Snoopy is bowling. Printed: "Strike." #736. (Not pictured)

114. Patches Display

"PEANUTS Patches." Linus, Peppermint Patty, Charlie Brown, Snoopy as Joe Cool, and Woodstock are featured on a blue background. The display rack holds 12 sets of patches. Metal and cardboard. EZ International. 1981. $15-20

Patches

Plastic stick-on patches. #PP1000, EZ International. 1981. $4-6* ea.

• Snoopy as Joe Cool. 2-7/8"H.

• Charlie Brown wears a baseball cap and glove. 2-1/2"H.

• Linus, sitting, holds his blanket and sucks his thumb. 3"H.

• Peppermint Patty. 3"H.

• Woodstock. 2-7/8"H.

• Snoopy is dressed as a cowboy. 2-5/8"H.

"PEANUTS Patches." Multicolored sew-on patches. Embroidered on fabric. 3" x 3". #PP1000, EZ International. 1981. $5-8* ea.

• Snoopy and Woodstock are sitting and laughing together.

• Charlie Brown and Snoopy sit with their arms outstretched.

• Snoopy hands Charlie Brown his supper dish.

• Snoopy kisses Peppermint Patty on the nose. Printed: "SMAK."

• Snoopy is sitting and laughing at Woodstock, who wears a derby, smokes a pipe, and has a handlebar mustache.

• Snoopy performs a pawpet show for Lucy.

PINBACK BUTTONS

115. Pinback Buttons

Metal and celluloid. 1-3/4" diam. Simon Simple.

• Snoopy, wearing a tri-cornered hat, sits with a birthday cake thinking, "Happy Birthday America!" Printed: "1776-1976." 1976. $8-12

• Snoopy lies on top of his doghouse thinking, "Sleeping is an art." Early 1970s. $8-10

• Snoopy, dressed a legionnaire, crosses the desert thinking, "Here's Beau Snoopy of the Foreign Legion marching across the desert." Early 1970s. $10-12

• Snoopy is playing golf. Charlie Brown, standing nearby, says, "Good grief!" 1969-1970. $8-10

• Snoopy, dressed as an astronaut, stands on the moon and thinks, "I'm on the moon!" 1969-1970. $10-12

• Snoopy, as the Flying Ace, is on top of his doghouse thinking, "Here's the World War I pilot flying in his Sopwith Camel searching for the Red Baron." Early 1970s. $10-12

• Lucy and Charlie Brown lean against a brick wall. Lucy says, "I don't care if anybody likes me…just so I'm popular!" 1969-1970. $6-8

• Snoopy sleeps on Charlie Brown who says, "Just what a manager likes…a player who isn't bothered by tension!" Early 1970s. $8-10

• Lucy says to Charlie Brown, "All I need is one hit, and I can raise my lifetime batting average to .001!" Early 1970s. $8-10

• Linus hugs Snoopy and says, "Dogs accept people for what they are." 1969-1970. $8-10

• Snoopy, wearing a stocking cap, lies on his back on the ice thinking, "I think my feet need sharpening." Early 1970s. $8-10

• Snoopy standing thinks, "Big man on campus." Early 1970s. $8-10

• Snoopy dancing thinks "To those of us with real understanding, dancing is the only pure art form." 1969-70. $8-10

• Linus, standing and holding his blanket, says, "I believe in statehood, countryhood, cityhood and neighborhood." 1972. $6-8

• Snoopy, wearing a necklace of flowers and beads, thinks, "How do things like this happen to me?" 1969-1970. $8-12

• Snoopy, as the Flying Ace, is on top of his doghouse. Printed below: "Curse You, Red Baron." 1969-1970. $6-8

• Linus and Lucy walk in the rain. Lucy says, "It always rains on our generation!" Early 1970s. $8-10

• Snoopy carries a hobo pack over his shoulder and wears his supper dish on his head. Woodstock walks behind him. Printed below: "Snoopy, Come Home." 1972. $6-8

• Linus, standing, says, "Little brothers are the buck privates of life!" 1969-1970. $10-12

116. Pinback Buttons

Known as "movee" buttons, the image changes back and forth when the button is moved, giving the appearance of animated scenes. The back of the button features Snoopy standing on a director's chair with his name on it. Plastic and metal. 2-1/2" diam. Aviva. 1972-1973. $7-10 ea.

• Woodstock is buried in snow up to his neck as Snoopy looks on. Alter image: Snoopy looks up as Woodstock flies overhead and then toward the ground.

• Snoopy is dancing in three different poses among falling leaves.

• Snoopy, Woodstock and his friends walk together.

• Snoopy, baseball bat on his shoulder, sees the ball zoom by him. The caption changes from "Strike One!" to "Strike Three!"

• Snoopy, as the Flying Ace, tumbles off his bullet-riddled doghouse. Printed: "Aaugh!" Alter image: Snoopy, as the Flying Ace, is on top of his doghouse.

The PEANUTS Home Collection

•Snoopy, upside down, is surrounded by his tennis racket and visor. Alter image: Snoopy, wearing his visor and holding his tennis racket, thinks "I hate it when they serve hard!"

•Snoopy, wearing a cowboy hat, plays the guitar. He taps his foot and changes the position of his hands.

•Snoopy kisses Lucy on the nose. Printed: "SMAK." Alter image: Snoopy smiles at Lucy.

•A football bounces off Woodstock's head. Printed: "Bonk!" Alter image: Snoopy, wearing a helmet, throws a football.

•Charlie Brown is running. Alter image: Lucy pulls the football out from under him. He flies through the air yelling "Aaugh!"

•Snoopy is lying on his doghouse. Alter image: Woodstock flies onto Snoopy's nose just as he sneezes, causing Woodstock to land on Snoopy's feet. Printed: "Ahchoo!"

•Charlie Brown throws a pitch from the mound. Alter image: The baseball comes back across the mound turning him upside down and causing his clothes to fly off. Printed: "Pow!"

117. Pinback Buttons

Multicolored Valentine's and Easter designs. Cloth. 2-1/4" diam. Valentine's series #2505. Easter series #2506. Butterfly Originals. 1981. $4-8 ea.

•Snoopy hugs Woodstock against a heart background. Printed: "You're Sweet."

•Snoopy approaches Woodstock, who holds three flowers. Printed: "Hearts & Flowers."

•Snoopy holds a large Easter egg, while Woodstock paints it.

•Snoopy, sitting, hugs a bunny. Printed: "Happy Easter."

•Snoopy and Woodstock shake hands. Printed: "Snoopy and Woodstock One Of The Best Things In The Whole World Is A Friend."

•Snoopy lies on top of his doghouse. On the side of the roof is a heart made of Valentines. Printed: "Happy Valentine's Day."

•Sally and Lucy wear matching Easter bonnets.

•Snoopy is wearing a pair of bunny ears.

•Snoopy, sitting and grinning, is surrounded by hearts. Printed: "Love Me."

•Snoopy, dressed as a scout, holds a walking stick with a heart on top.

•Snoopy juggles Easter eggs while riding a unicycle with Woodstock sitting on his head.

•Snoopy is dancing with a basket of Easter eggs in his hand. Printed: "Happy Easter."

118. Pinback Buttons

Multicolored Halloween and Christmas designs. Cloth. 2-1/4" diam. Halloween series #2503. Christmas series #2504. Butterfly Originals. 1980. $4-8 ea.

•Snoopy and Woodstock read scary stories. Printed: "Happy Halloween."

•Lucy, dressed as a witch, carries a broom.

•Charlie Brown is tangled up in Christmas lights. Printed: "Happy Holidays."

•Woodstock stands on a bow which is attached to a wreath.

•Snoopy, as Joe Cool, leans against a pumpkin.

•Snoopy and Woodstock sit on top of the doghouse. Snoopy howls at the moon.

•Snoopy sits on a sleigh with a bag of gifts behind him. Woodstock sits on top of the bag. Printed: "Merry Christmas."

•Snoopy is dressed as Santa. Printed: "Ho Ho Ho."

•Snoopy grins and holds a trick or treat bag. Printed: "Trick Or Treat."

•Snoopy lies on top of a jack-o'-lantern.

•Woodstock leans against a sitting Snoopy. They both wear green stocking caps. Printed: "Happy Holidays."

•Snoopy, as Joe Cool, wears a green shirt and stocking cap and leans against his doghouse decorated with lights.

119. Pinback Buttons

Multicolored. Metal. 2-1/4" diam. Butterfly Originals. 1981. $3-5 ea.

•Snoopy, as Joe Cool, has his arms folded across his chest. Printed: "Hey Babe."

•Snoopy is sitting and blowing bubbles. Printed: "Sundays Beat School Days."

•Snoopy wears a helmet and rides a bicycle. Printed: "Go Ride A Bike."

•Snoopy sits with his arms outstretched. Printed: "I Love You."

•Snoopy has his eyes closed and his hands folded over his heart. "Foxy" is printed four times around the button.

•Snoopy sits with a large hero sandwich in his lap. Printed: "Homework Builds Appetites."

•Snoopy and Woodstock ride a skateboard. Printed: "Superstars."

•Snoopy holds a large trophy. Printed: "All American."

•Snoopy, as Joe Cool, lies against a pile of books. Printed: "Official Students."

•Snoopy eats food out of a bag. Printed: "Cheeseburger Tester."

•Snoopy wears a cap and a warmup suit as he roller-skates. Printed: "Hot Gear Hot Gear."

•Snoopy, wearing a bow tie, holds the ace of spades. Printed: "One Of A Kind." (Not pictured)

120. Pinback Buttons

Multicolored. Metal. 2-1/4" diam. Butterfly Originals. 1979.

•Charlie Brown is flying his kite. Printed: "Go Fly A Kite." $2-3

•Peppermint Patty shakes hands with Snoopy as the Flying Ace. Printed: "Good Luck." $2-3

•Lucy holds a pad and pencil. Printed: "Gal Friday." $2-3

•Snoopy and Woodstock play hockey. Printed: "Score!" $3-5

•Snoopy is dancing. Printed: "Enjoy, Enjoy!" $3-5

•Snoopy watches Woodstock as he flies upside down and chirps. Printed: "Try To Understand Me." $3-5

•Snoopy lies on top of his doghouse. Woodstock lies on Snoopy's tummy. Printed: "I'll Do It Tomorrow." $3-5

•Snoopy, sitting and wearing a cap, talks into a CB radio. Printed: "Ten-Four Good Buddy!" $2-3

•Woodstock sits in his nest which is in a tree branch. Printed: "Nests Are Best." $2-3

•Snoopy, sitting and grinning, is surrounded by hearts. Printed: "Love Me." $3-5

•Snoopy is walking. Printed: "Out To Lunch." $2-3

•Snoopy, wearing a sailor's hat, appears in the center of a life preserver. Printed: "I'd Rather Be Sailing." $2-3

121. Pinback Buttons

Multicolored. Metal. 2-1/4" diam. Butterfly Originals. Early 1980s.

•Snoopy is dressed as a scout with a backpack, hat, and walking stick. Printed: "Hike It." $2-3

•Snoopy is playing tennis. Printed: "Ace" and "Smash." $2-3

•Snoopy is playing the piano. The musical notes in the air are made from his paw prints. Printed: "Music Power." $3-5

•Snoopy, wearing a scout hat, stands with one hand over his heart. Printed: "Beagle Scout." $3-5

•Snoopy, as Joe Cool, wears shorts and drinks soda from a can. Printed: "Cool." $2-3

•Woodstock does a wheelie on a bicycle. Printed: "Bike It." $2-3

•Snoopy is hugging Woodstock. Printed: "Love." $3-5

•Snoopy, wearing a goalie glove, extends his hand. Printed: "Let's Be Friends." $2-3

•Snoopy lies on his back with one foot raised in the air toward his nose. Woodstock stands on the foot, looking down at Snoopy. Printed: "Let's See Eye To Eye." $2-3

•Snoopy, dressed as a director, wears a beret, sunglasses, and holds a megaphone. Printed: "Boss." $3-5

•Snoopy wears sunglasses, a baseball cap, and glove. Printed: "Left Fielder." $2-3

•Woodstock chirps as Snoopy translates in a thought balloon, "Woodstock says take a bird to lunch." $3-5

•Snoopy is sitting. He wears a button of Snoopy sitting. $2-3

122. Pinback Buttons

Multicolored. Metal. 2-1/4" diam. Butterfly Originals. 1983. $5-8 ea.

•Snoopy looks at Woodstock through a magnifying glass. He thinks, "Life is full of surprises."

•Snoopy kisses Peppermint Patty on the nose. He thinks, "Just call me sugar lips."

•Snoopy and Charlie Brown lean against a brick wall. Charlie Brown says, "I'm still hoping that yesterday will get better."

•Peppermint Patty has her arm around Snoopy. She says, "The cutest of the cute."

•Snoopy has his hand on his tummy which says, "Hi there!" Snoopy thinks, "When my stomach talks, I listen."

•Snoopy lies on top of his doghouse thinking, "Born to sleep."

•Snoopy leans against a rock with Woodstock on his foot thinking, "I'm afraid my brain has left for the day."

•Snoopy, leaning to the right, thinks, "Somewhere I can hear someone eating a chocolate chip cookie."

123. Pinback Buttons

These multicolored buttons have raised designs and captions. Molded plastic. 2-1/4" diam. Butterfly Originals. 1982. $5-7 ea.

•Snoopy and Woodstock are jogging. Printed: "Jog."

•Snoopy, wearing a jacket, is disco dancing. Printed: "Hustle."

•Snoopy is playing tennis. Printed: "Ace."

•Snoopy wears a bow tie and a top hat. Printed: "Suave."

•Snoopy is hugging Woodstock. Printed: "Love."

•Snoopy is lying on top of his doghouse. Printed: "Snoopy Fan."

•Snoopy as Joe Cool. Printed: "Cool."

•Snoopy, lying on his tummy, hangs his head over the roof of his doghouse. Printed: "T.G.I.F."

•Snoopy, dressed as a movie director, holds a megaphone. Printed: "Boss."

•Snoopy handstands on a skateboard. Printed: "High Roller."

124. Pinback Buttons

•Snoopy and Lucy stand beside Linus, who holds a sign reading: "Help Stamp Out Things That Need Stamping Out!" Metal and celluloid. 6" diam. Simon Simple. 1969-1970. $15-20

•Snoopy sits on his doghouse, surrounded by non-Woodstock birds chirping in one balloon. Printed: "My home is always open to those who enjoy discussion groups." Metal and celluloid. 6" diam. Simon Simple. 1969-1970. $15-20

125. Pinback Buttons

Metal and celluloid. 6" diam. Simon Simple. 1972. $15-20 ea.

•Linus is talking to Lucy and Snoopy who are on either side of him. Printed: "No Problem Is So Big Or So Complicated That It Can't Be Run Away From."

•Woodstock sits at a typewriter on top of Snoopy's doghouse. Snoopy pats him on the head as he types thinking, "That's very nice." Printed: "All Secretaries Need A Little Compliment Now And Then."

•Snoopy carries a hobo pack over his shoulder and wears his supper dish on his head. Woodstock walks behind him. Printed: "Snoopy, Come Home."

126. Pinback Buttons

•Charlie Brown and Linus lean against a brick wall. Charlie Brown says, "I've developed a new philosophy. . . I only dread one day at a time!" Metal and celluloid. 6" diam. Simon Simple. 1969-1970. $15-20

•Snoopy, as the Flying Ace, is on top of his doghouse. Printed: "Curse You, Red Baron." Metal and celluloid. 6" diam. Simon Simple. 1969-1970. $15-20

•Snoopy, wearing a crown, rides a toboggan with a snowman on board. Printed: "Celebrate 1990 Saint Paul Winter Carnival." Metal and celluloid. 6" diam. 1990. $15-20

127. Pinback Buttons

•Snoopy stands with one hand over his heart. Printed: "Snoopy For President." Metal and celluloid. 2-1/2" diam. 1972. $6-8

•The image changes back and forth when the button is moved. Snoopy is dancing surrounded by stars. Alter image: "Snoopy For President" is printed and surrounded by stars. Plastic. 3" diam. Hallmark. 1972. $8-10

128. Pinback Buttons

•There are no PEANUTS graphics on this red, white, and blue button with stars. Printed: "Snoopy For President" and "Abraham & Straus." Metal and celluloid. 1976. $8-12

•Charlie Brown's head is pictured wearing a baseball cap on a red background. Printed: "1950-1995 45 Years." Metal and celluloid. 1-3/4" diam. Distributed by United Media. 1995. $4-6

•Charlie Brown is pictured standing next to a snowman made in his image. Printed: "Hallmark Keepsake Ornament." Worn by employees of Hallmark stores. Metal and celluloid. Hallmark. 1993. $10-15

•Snoopy walks carrying books on his head. Woodstock flies behind him holding a book with his feet. Printed: "Take Snoopy Back To School." Promotional button for school supplies. Metal and celluloid. 2-1/2" diam. Butterfly Originals. 1981. $8-10

•A front-face Snoopy as Joe Cool wearing sunglasses is on a purple background. Printed: "Happy Anniversary, Charlie Brown!" Promotional button for the album of the same name. Metal and celluloid. 2-1/2" diam. GRP Records. 1990. $6-8

•Snoopy licks his lips inside a red and white striped circle. Printed underneath Snoopy: "Fisherman's Wharf, San Francisco." Printed around the button: "Snoopy For President" and "Snoopy's Ice Cream & Cookie Store." Metal and celluloid. 3-1/2" diam. 1984. $15-20

•Snoopy lies on top of a jack-o'-lantern. Printed: "Camp Spooky." Worn by employees of Camp Snoopy at the Mall of America. Metal and celluloid. 3" diam. 1995. $8-10

•Snoopy stands and talks on a telephone against a red background. Woodstock stands on top of the phone. Printed: "Snoopy's Good Grooming Gang Is Here!" Promotional button for Creative Specialties, Inc. line of children's grooming items. Metal and celluloid. 3" diam. 1985. $10-12

129. Pinback Buttons

•Snoopy, as the Flying Ace, stands on Schroeder's piano as he plays. They are surrounded by Frieda, Violet, Patty, Pigpen, Sally, Linus, Lucy, and Charlie Brown. Printed: "The In Crowd." Metal and celluloid. 3" diam. Manufacturer unknown. Mid-1960s. $35-45

•Snoopy wears a bow tie and tips his top hat in the air. Printed: "Snoopy's Gallery And Gift Shop Santa Rosa, CA." Metal and celluloid. 2" diam. Late 1980s. $3-4

•Snoopy stands with one hand over his heart. Printed: "Snoopy For President." Metal and celluloid. 1-3/4" diam. 1972. $6-8

•Snoopy stands with one hand over his heart. Printed: "Snoopy For President." Metal and celluloid. 1" diam. 1972. $8-10

•Snoopy wears a green cap and sweater and has his lips puckered ready to give a kiss. Printed: "I'm Irish." This button has a two-dimensional design and caption. Molded plastic. 2-1/2" diam. #20819, Applause. 1989. $6-8

•Charlie Brown, wearing a baseball cap and glove, stands on the pitcher's mound against a red background. Printed: "You're A Good Man, Charlie Brown." Metal. 1-3/8" diam. 1968. $4-6

•Charlie Brown is standing, and holds a piece of paper in his hand. Printed: "You're A Good Man, Charlie Brown." Metal and celluloid. 1-3/4" diam. Simon Simple. 1972. $5-7

•Snoopy wears a green derby and bow tie, with a shamrock on each side of him. Printed: "Blarney Beagle." This button has a two-dimensional design and caption. Molded plastic. 2-1/2" diam. #20819, Applause. 1989. $6-8

•Schroeder carries a sign with a message that changes when the button is moved. Printed: "Halloween's Here!" and "Only 40 Shopping Days 'Til Beethoven's Birthday!" Plastic. 3" diam. Hallmark. 1972. $15-20

•Linus is sitting in a pumpkin patch. His voice balloon changes when the button is moved. Printed: "The Great Pumpkin Is Watching You!" and "You'd Better Have A Happy Halloween!!!" Plastic. 3" diam. Hallmark. 1972. $25-35

• Snoopy holds a balloon, and he and Woodstock wear party hats. Printed: "125 Years MetLife." This button came in different colors. Metal and celluloid. 3" diam. 1993. $8-10

• Snoopy stands on ice holding a hockey stick and wearing a stocking cap. Printed: "Redwood Empire Arena Santa Rosa, Calif." Metal and celluloid. 2" diam. Late 1980s. $2-4

• Snoopy, as Joe Cool, is framed in red, white, and black. Promotional button for the J.G. Hook Snoopy Clothing Collection. Metal and celluloid. 2" x 2". 1987. $6-8

• Snoopy, dressed as a scout, is framed by chaffs of wheat. A red ribbon underneath Snoopy reads "10th Anniversary." Printed: "Camp Snoopy Knott's." Metal and celluloid. 2" diam. Knott's Berry Farm. 1993. $3-4

• Snoopy, grinning, wears sunglasses on his head against a red background. Printed: "Snoopy's In L.A. At The Natural History Museum." Metal and celluloid. 1-1/4" diam. Early 1990s. $5-7

• Snoopy, dressed as a scout, is dancing and thinking, "Happiness is..." He is inside a crest framed by chaffs of wheat. Red ribbons read, "Our First Birthday" and "Minnesota 1993." Also printed: "Camp Snoopy." Metal and celluloid. 3" diam. $3-5

130. Pinback Buttons

• Charlie Brown, wearing a red shirt with a black zigzag, stands on a white background. Printed: "Get Newsday For Peanuts." Button worn by employees of the Long Island, NY newspaper, *Newsday*. Metal and celluloid. 2-1/2" diam. Early 1960s. $35-40

• Snoopy, grinning, wears an Uncle Sam Hat against a red, white, and blue background. Printed: "Snoopy For President." Dolly Madison premium. Metal and celluloid. 3" diam. Interstate Brands. 1972. $15-18

• Snoopy wears a gold crown and a red cape against a yellow background. Printed: "The Prince of Sandwiches Weber's Bread." Weber's Bread premium. Metal and celluloid. 4" diam. Interstate Brands. 1975. $20-25

• Snoopy, as the Flying Ace, is on top of his doghouse. Printed: "Get Newsday For Peanuts." Button worn by employees of the Long Island, NY newspaper, *Newsday*. Metal and celluloid. 2-1/2" diam. Early 1960s. $35-40

• Snoopy, as the Flying Ace, lies on his back looking through binoculars in the center of a red, white, and blue ringed button. Printed: "Butternut Bread" and "Snoopy's Spotters Club." Butternut Bread premium. Metal and celluloid. 2" diam. Interstate Brands. 1975. $10-15

Tab Buttons

• Snoopy, smiling, has his arms outstretched. Printed: "Snoopy for President" and "Sweetheart Bread for Lunch." Sweetheart Bread premium. Metal. 2" diam. Interstate Brands. Mid-1970s. $6-8

• Snoopy wears a gold crown and a red neckerchief against a yellow background. Printed: "The Prince of Sandwiches." Metal. 1-7/8" diam. Interstate Brands. Mid-1970s. $6-8

Pinback Button

• Lucy holds a tennis racket, and Linus wears golf shoes and holds a golf club while it rains on Charlie Brown, who stands between them wearing a baseball cap and glove. Printed: "Southwest Spring Sports." Metal and celluloid. 3" diam. Manufactured by Wendell Northwestern, Inc. Minneapolis, MN. Mid-1960s. $40-50

Tab Button

Snoopy, as the Flying Ace, sits on the ground with his fist raised in the air against a red background. Printed: "Curse You Red Baron." Metal. 1-1/2" diam. Interstate Brands. Early 1970s. $4-6

Pinback Button

Snoopy, grinning, wears an Uncle Sam Hat on a red, white, and blue background. Printed: "Snoopy For President" and "Dolly Madison For Cakes." Dolly Madison premium. Metal and celluloid. 3" diam. Interstate Brands. 1972. $12-18

131. Pinback Buttons

• A plush Snoopy wears a knit scarf and a cap printed "Macy's." Printed on the button: "Snoopy At Macy's." A white ribbon with red print attached to the button reads "We're stocking Snoopy for Christmas! And he's yours for $10.95 with any $50 purchase." Worn by employees of Macy's department stores. Metal, fabric, and celluloid. 2-1/4" diam. 3" ribbon. 1987. $12-15

• Snoopy, wearing a red sweater, hugs Woodstock. The button is in the shape of Snoopy. Printed: "Macy's." A red ribbon with white print attached to the button reads "Do You Need A Best Friend?" Worn by employees of Macy's department stores. Plastic coated cardboard and fabric. 6-3/4"H with ribbon. 1988. $12-15

• Snoopy wears a McDonald's employee visor and shirt as he approaches the McDonald's logo on a white background. Printed: "McDonald's." Worn by employees of McDonald's. Metal and celluloid. 2-3/4" x 1-3/4". Late 1980s. $20-25

• Snoopy, as the Flying Ace, waves against a blue background. Printed: "Snoopy's In St. Louis At The Dog Museum." This button, sold in the Dog Museum gift shop, commemorated both an exhibit devoted to Snoopy and the opening of the museum's new wing. Metal and celluloid. 1-1/4" diam. 1990. $6-8

• Charlie Brown, Woodstock, and Snoopy wear bow ties against a white background. Printed around the button: "40 Years Of Happiness." This scene is the logo for the 40th anniversary of the PEANUTS comic strip. Metal and celluloid. 2-3/4" oval-shaped button. distributed by United Media. 1990. $4-6

• Snoopy, as Joe Cool, rides a skateboard. Printed: "Silver Deer." Worn by Silver Deer employees at trade shows. Metal and celluloid. 1-3/4" diam. Late 1980s. $10-15

• Snoopy is walking on green grass against a blue sky. Printed: "Snoopy Fan Club." This button was given to new members of the Snoopy Fan Club and later was sold to the general public. Metal and celluloid. 2-1/4" diam. Distributed by United Features Syndicate. 1983. $3-5

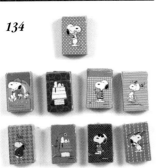

• Snoopy is dancing against a horizontal, rainbow-striped background. Printed vertically: "Snoopy Fan Club." Metal and celluloid. 1-1/4" x 1-1/4". United Features Syndicate. 1983. $3-5

132. Pinback Buttons

• Schroeder sits at a computer against a blue background. Printed: "National Small Business Week" and "MetLife Small Business Center." Metal and celluloid. 2-7/8" diam. Early 1990s. $10-15

• This red, white, and blue button has no PEANUTS graphics. Printed: "Ask Me About Free Snoopy Glasses." Promotional button for Interstate Brands. Metal and celluloid. 3" diam. 1980. $4-6

• Snoopy is sitting against a black background. Printed: "MetLife-United Way Day October 12, 1990 I Make A Difference!" Metal and celluloid. 3" diam. 1990. $10-15

• This button has no PEANUTS graphics. Printed: "I Saw Snoopy At Burdines." Metal and celluloid. 2" diam. Late 1980s. $3-5

PLAYING CARDS AND ACCESSORIES

133. Tally Cards

Set of twelve. Paper. Hallmark. $3-4* per set

• Woodstock and his friends are dressed in red bow ties and straw hats, and hold canes. 2-1/4" x 4-1/2". #125TC9814. Early 1980s.

• Snoopy, dressed as the Flying Ace, is thinking, "You mean we've been playing for money?" 2-3/4" x 4-1/2". #70TC975. Early 1970s.

• Woodstock holds four flowers on very long stems. Printed: "Tally." 2-3/4" x 4-1/2". #65TC974. Mid-1970s.

Playing Cards

Two decks of cards came in a plastic box with a clear cover. Each deck is sealed in plastic. There are no graphics on the packaging. Plastic coated paper. 4-3/4" x 3-1/2". Hallmark.

• Snoopy, dressed as a court jester, appears on a yellow background. Woodstock and his friends, on a green background, peek out from behind a card with the four suits on it. Late 1970s. $12-15*

• Snoopy as the Flying Ace stands with his hand over his heart on a blue background. Snoopy as the Flying Ace sits on top of his bullet-riddled doghouse. Early 1970s. $15-18*

• Snoopy lies on his tummy across a pink and orange balloon on a white background. Snoopy dances on a pink and orange background that matches the balloon on the other deck of cards. Mid-1970s. $15-18*

134. Miniature Playing Cards

Plastic coated paper cards, 2-1/2" x 1-3/4" in size, in sealed cardboard boxes. Hallmark. Mid-1970s. $7-12** ea.

• Snoopy hugs Woodstock on a red background with white polka dots. Printed on reverse side: "Snoopy Miniature Playing Cards." #89BC96-6.

• Snoopy, Woodstock and his friend, wearing scout hats, walk in front of a rainbow. Printed on reverse side: "PEANUTS Miniature Playing Cards." #100BC121-1.

• Snoopy lies on top of his doghouse, against a blue background with green polka dots. Printed on reverse side: "PEANUTS Playing Cards." The faces of Charlie Brown, Lucy, and Snoopy appear below. A gold seal featuring Snoopy lying on his doghouse is on the top of the box. #75BC98-7.

• Snoopy, dressed as a referee, holds a whistle against a red and white checked background. Printed on reverse side: "PEANUTS Playing Cards." The faces of Charlie Brown, Lucy, and Snoopy appear below. A gold seal featuring Snoopy lying on his doghouse is on the top of the box. #75BC103-5.

• Snoopy dances against a pink and orange striped background. Printed on reverse side: "PEANUTS Playing Cards." The faces of Charlie Brown, Lucy, and Snoopy appear below. A gold seal featuring Snoopy lying on his doghouse is on the top of the box. #75BC98-8.

• Snoopy is dressed in a raccoon coat and carries a pennant printed "Rah!" on a red and mustard background. Printed on reverse side: "PEANUTS Playing Cards." The faces of Charlie Brown, Lucy, and Snoopy appear below. A gold seal featuring Snoopy lying on his doghouse is on the top of the box. #75BC101-8.

• Snoopy lies on top of his doghouse. A flower on a very long stem hangs over him on a blue background. Printed on reverse side: "PEANUTS Playing Cards." The faces of Charlie Brown, Lucy, and Snoopy appear below. A gold seal featuring Snoopy lying on his doghouse is on the top of the box. #75BC102-8.

• Snoopy, as Joe Cool, stands against a two-toned blue background. Printed on reverse side: "PEANUTS Playing Cards." The faces of Charlie Brown, Lucy, and Snoopy appear below. A gold seal featuring Snoopy lying on his doghouse is on the top of the box. #75BC101-9.

• A baseball zooms past Snoopy, seen wearing a baseball cap with a bat over his shoulder against a green and yellow background. Printed on reverse side: "PEANUTS Playing Cards." The faces of Charlie Brown, Lucy, and Snoopy appear below. A gold seal featuring Snoopy lying on his doghouse is on the top of the box. #75BC103-1.

135. Miniature Playing Cards

Plastic coated paper cards, 2-1/2" x 1-3/4" in size, in sealed cardboard boxes. Mid-1970s. $7-12** ea.

• Snoopy carries a pair of skis over his shoulder, against a light blue background with white clouds. Printed on reverse side: "PEANUTS Playing Cards." The faces of Charlie Brown, Lucy, and Snoopy appear below. A gold seal featuring Snoopy lying on his doghouse is on the top of the box. #75BC104-2, Hallmark.

• Snoopy, as the Flying Ace, stands against an orange and yellow diagonally striped background. Printed on reverse side: "PEANUTS Playing Cards." The faces of Charlie Brown, Lucy, and Snoopy appear below. A gold seal featuring Snoopy lying on his doghouse is on the top of the box. #89BC760J, Ambassador.

• Snoopy sits with Woodstock reclining on his feet against a yellow and orange checkered background. Printed on reverse side: "PEANUTS Playing Cards." The faces of Charlie Brown, Lucy, and Snoopy appear below. A gold seal featuring Snoopy lying on his doghouse is on the top of the box. #75BC103-4, Hallmark.

• Snoopy wears a visor and carries a tennis racket against a blue background with green polka dots. Printed on reverse side: "PEANUTS Playing Cards." The faces of Charlie Brown, Lucy, and Snoopy appear below. A gold seal featuring Snoopy lying on his doghouse is on the top of the box. #75BC103-2, Hallmark.

• Snoopy, wearing a stocking cap, glides against a blue background with white polka dots as if he is skating. Printed on reverse side: "Snoopy Miniature Playing Cards." #89BC96-9, Hallmark.

• Snoopy, wearing a helmet, holds a football in his hands ready to kick it against a red background. Printed on reverse side: "PEANUTS Playing Cards." The faces of Charlie Brown, Lucy, and Snoopy appear below. A gold seal featuring Snoopy lying on his doghouse is on the top of the box. #75BC104-1, Hallmark.

• Snoopy carries a hobo pack over his shoulder against a yellow background. Printed on reverse side: "PEANUTS Playing Cards." The faces of Charlie Brown, Lucy, and Snoopy appear below. A gold seal featuring Snoopy lying on his doghouse is on the top of the box. #75BC102-7, Hallmark.

• Snoopy holds a bag of jelly beans against a multicolored background of jelly beans. Printed on reverse side: "Snoopy Miniature Playing Cards." #100BC118-7, Hallmark.

136. Miniature Playing Cards

Plastic coated paper cards, 2-1/2" x 1-3/4" in size, in sealed cardboard boxes. Mid-1970s. $7-12** ea.

• Lucy dressed as a cheerleader holds a pom pom against a yellow background. Printed in reverse side: "PEANUTS Miniature Playing Cards." #100BC121-2, Hallmark.

• Woodstock holds four flowers on very long stems against a green background with white polka dots. Printed: "Woodstock Miniature Playing Cards." #89BC96-8, Hallmark.

• Lucy, in an olive-colored dress, stands against a pink and orange background. Printed on reverse: "PEANUTS Playing Cards." The faces of Charlie Brown, Lucy, and Snoopy appear below. A gold seal featuring Snoopy lying on his doghouse is on the top of the box. #75BC97-1, Hallmark.

• Snoopy lies on his yellow doghouse blowing a bubble against a background of multicolored gum balls. Printed on reverse side: "Snoopy Miniature Playing Cards." #100BC118-8, Hallmark.

• Charlie Brown stands against a green and blue diamond checkered background. Printed on reverse side: "PEANUTS Playing Cards." The faces of Charlie Brown, Lucy, and Snoopy appear below. A gold seal featuring Snoopy lying on his doghouse is on the top of the box. #89BC780J, Ambassador.

• Charlie Brown hugs Snoopy against an orange and yellow striped background. Printed on reverse side: "PEANUTS Playing Cards." The faces of Charlie Brown, Lucy, and Snoopy appear below. A gold seal featuring Snoopy lying on his doghouse is on the top of the box. #75BC101-7, Hallmark.

• Charlie Brown runs with his kite in the air across a red background. Printed on reverse side: "PEANUTS Playing Cards." The faces of Charlie Brown, Lucy, and Snoopy appear below. A gold seal featuring Snoopy lying on his doghouse is on the top of the box. Hallmark.

• Linus holds his blanket and sucks his thumb against a yellow background with orange polka dots. Printed on reverse side: "PEANUTS Playing Cards." The faces of Charlie Brown, Lucy, and Snoopy appear below. A gold seal featuring Snoopy lying on his doghouse is on the top of the box. #75BC98-9, Hallmark.

137. Card Games

Each deck of cards is a different game. Instructions are printed on the reverse side of the box. Plastic coated paper cards in sealed cardboard boxes. 2-1/4" x 3-1/2". Hallmark. 1975. $8-15** ea.

•"Go Fly A Kite A PEANUTS Card Game." Charlie Brown attaches kite string to his kite against a green background. #125BC98-5.

•"Security A PEANUTS Card Game." Linus sits holding his blanket and sucking his thumb against a yellow background. #125BC98-1.

•"Rats! A PEANUTS Rummy Game." Snoopy, as the Flying Ace, sits on his bullet-riddled doghouse with smoke coming out thinking, "Rats!" #125BC99-3.

•"Fussbudget A PEANUTS 'Old Maid' Game." Lucy, wearing a yellow dress against a red background, holds her hand to her heart and appears to be shouting. #125BC98-2.

•"Snooping Around A PEANUTS Card Game." Snoopy wears a hunting cap, a handlebar mustache, and holds a magnifying glass against an orange background. #125BC98-3.

•"Born Loser A PEANUTS Card Game." Charlie Brown wears a red baseball cap and a blue shirt printed "Born Loser" against an orange background. #125BC98-7.

138. Playing Cards

Two decks of cards come in a plastic box with a clear cover. Each deck of cards is sealed in plastic. There are no graphics on the packaging. Plastic-coated paper. 4-3/4" x 3-1/2". Hallmark.

•Snoopy sits and Woodstock stands on top of Snoopy's doghouse against a yellow and orange striped background. Snoopy walks with Woodstock standing on his head against a pink and orange striped background. #295BC763-3. Mid-1970s. $10-15*

•Snoopy sits on his doghouse, ears standing up straight, as Woodstock flies upside down against a blue background.

137

Snoopy lies on top of his doghouse, with Woodstock standing on his tummy, against a red background. Mid-1970s. $10-15*

•Woodstock sits in a house of cards, set on a tree branch, against a red and white checkered background. Snoopy, wearing a bow tie, holds four aces and a king and winks against a red background with white polka dots. #400BC980-3. Late 1970s. $10-12*

•Snoopy, as the Flying Ace, sits on his doghouse against a blue background. Snoopy, as the Flying Ace, walks against a dark green background. Mid-1970s. $10-12*

139. Playing Cards

Two decks of cards came in a plastic box with a clear cover. Each deck is sealed in plastic. No graphics appear on the package. Plastic-coated paper. 4-3/4" x 3-1/2". Hallmark.

•Snoopy dances against a red patterned background. Snoopy cries, beating his fists on his chest, against a mustard-colored patterned background. 1974. $12-15*

•Snoopy roller-skates against a multicolored, vertically striped background. Woodstock, holding a multicolored striped balloon, roller-skates across a white background. Early 1980s. $7-10*

•Snoopy, as the Flying Ace, is on top of his doghouse against a blue background with red polka dots. Snoopy, as the Flying Ace, stands shaking his fist and shouting, against a red background with blue polka dots. Mid-1970s. $12-15*

•Snoopy, ears down, dances on a green and blue vertically striped background. Snoopy, ears up, dances on a green and blue vertically striped background. #295BC763-4. Mid-1970s. $12-15*

140. Playing Cards

Plastic-coated paper cards in sealed cardboard boxes. 2-1/4" x 3-1/2". Hallmark. Mid-1970s. $10-15** ea.

•Snoopy, dressed in a raccoon coat, is carrying a pennant printed "Rah!", against a red and orange checkered background. The reverse side features a miniature of the picture on the front and is printed "Snoopy Playing Cards." #125BC99-6.

•Charlie Brown hugs Snoopy against a pink background with red hearts. The reverse side features a miniature of the picture on the front and is printed "Snoopy Playing Cards." #125BC99-7.

•Snoopy, as Joe Cool, stands against a red and yellow woven background. The reverse side features a miniature of the pic-

138

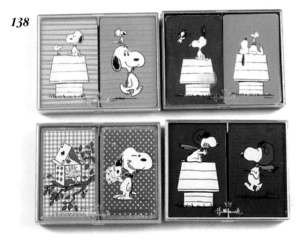

139

ture on the front and is printed "Snoopy Playing Cards." #125BC99-5.

•Snoopy and Woodstock play cards on top of Snoopy's doghouse, against an orange background. The reverse side features a miniature of the picture on the front and is printed "PEANUTS Playing Cards." #150BC96-6.

141. Playing Cards Set

•Includes two decks of cards and a score pad. Woodstock and his friends are dressed in red bow ties, straw hats, and hold canes. Snoopy, dressed in a suit, a red bow tie, a straw hat, and holding a cane thinks, "Want to see some fancy shuffling?" Snoopy appears on the score pad thinking, "Here's the score!" The set comes in a cardboard box with a clear cover. Each deck of cards is sealed in plastic. There are no graphics on the packaging. Plastic-coated paper. Hallmark. Early 1980s. $10-15*

Playing Cards Set

•Includes two decks of cards, a score pad, and a pencil. Snoopy, with Woodstock leaning on his side, sits, holding four long-stem flowers, against a red background. The second deck depicts Woodstock, sitting on Snoopy's head and holding four flowers, against a blue background. Score pad depicts Woodstock, sitting on Snoopy's head and holding four flowers, against a red background. The set comes in a cardboard box with a clear cover. Each deck of cards is sealed in plastic. There are no graphics on the packaging. Plastic-coated paper. Hallmark. 1976. $20-25*

Playing Cards Set

•Includes two decks of cards and a score pad. Woodstock roller-skates across a white background, holding a multicolored striped balloon. Snoopy roller-skates against a multicolored, vertically striped background. The score pad features Snoopy and Woodstock roller-skating against a multicolored, vertically striped background. The set comes in a cardboard box with a clear cover. Each deck of cards is sealed in plastic. There are no graphics on the packaging. Plastic-coated paper. Hallmark. Early 1980s. $10-15*

PUZZLES

142. Puzzle

•Snoopy and Woodstock ride in a hot air balloon. Plastic. 10" x 12". #88895, Danara. 1989. $8-10*

143. Puzzles

•"PEANUTS Floor Puzzle Tennis Anyone?" Giant sized pieces put together on a floor depict Linus, Rerun, Schroeder, Charlie Brown, Marcie, Lucy, Snoopy, Woodstock, and Peppermint Patty playing tennis. Finished puzzle measures 9 square feet. #325-2, Playskool. Early 1990s. $25-30**

•"Snoopy Giant Puzzle." Snoopy, dressed as a cowboy, rides a hobby horse through the desert, and swings a lasso. Woodstock sits on the lasso's loop. Cardboard. #514, Avalon. 1980. $12-18**

144. Puzzles

•"Snoopy And Friends A Little Golden Puzzle." Charlie Brown hugs Snoopy with hearts above them. Woodboard. 8" x 12". #4188A-1, Golden Books. Late 1980s. $3-5*

•"Snoopy And Friends A Little Golden Puzzle." Snoopy rides a unicycle and juggles Easter eggs, while Woodstock sits on his head. Woodboard. 8" x 12". #41888, Golden Books. Late 1980s. $3-5*

145. Puzzles

•"Schroeder & Snoopy." Schroeder plays his piano, while Snoopy dances on top of it. A bar of musical notes is in the background. 10 pieces. Wood. Shrink-wrap packaging. 9-1/2" x 11-1/2". #230-14, Playskool. 1979. $5-10*

•"Jumping Rope." Lucy jumps rope against a yellow background. 11 pieces. Wood. Shrink-wrap packaging. 9-1/2" x 11-1/2". #230-12, Playskool. 1974. $5-10*

146. Puzzles

Wood. Shrink-wrap packaging. 9-1/2" x 11-1/2". Playskool. 1974. $5-10* ea.

•"Giddy-Yap!" Snoopy rides a hobby horse against a yellow background. 9 pieces. #230-4.

•"Sigh!" Linus is hugging his blanket, against a yellow background. Printed: "Sigh." 10 pieces. #230-8.

•"Chasing The Red Baron." Snoopy, as the Flying Ace, is on top of his doghouse against a blue background. 8 pieces. #230-2.

147. Puzzles

Wood. Shrink-wrap packaging. 9-1/2" x 11-1/2". Playskool.

•"Roller Skate Champ." Snoopy roller-skates past Charlie Brown. 7 pieces. #230-20. 1980. $5-8*

•"Good Grief!" Woodstock lies on top of Snoopy's nose. 7 pieces. #230-5. 1974. $5-10*

•"Coffee Break." Snoopy, holding a doughnut and a mug, sits on his doghouse with Woodstock. 9 pieces. #230-22. 1983. $5-8*

148. Puzzles

•"Sigh!" Linus sits holding his blanket and sucking his thumb. 6 pieces. Wood. Shrink-wrap and cardboard packaging. 9-1/2" x 11-1/2". #230-8, Playskool. 1979. $5-10*

•"Be A Friend." Charlie Brown and Snoopy lean against each other with hearts around them. 7 pieces. Wood. Shrink-wrap and cardboard packaging. 9-1/2" x 11-1/2". #230-10, Playskool. 1980. $5-8*

149. Puzzles

•"Snoopy Superstar." Snoopy, wearing a baseball cap, leans against his bat. 6 pieces. Wood. Shrink-wrap packaging. 9-1/2" x 11-1/2". #230-17, Playskool. 1980. $5-8*

•"Snoopy Come Home." Snoopy, wearing his supper dish on his head, carries a hobo pack over his shoulder. Woodstock walks behind him. 7 pieces. Wood. Shrink-wrap packaging. 9-1/2" x 11-1/2". #230-19, Playskool. 1980. $5-8*

150. Puzzles

•"The Head Beagle." Snoopy, shaking Linus' hand, thinks, "Meet the head beagle!" 8 pieces. Wood. Shrink-wrap and

cardboard packaging. 9-1/2" x 11-1/2". #230-15, Playskool. 1979. $5-10*

•"Smak!" Snoopy kisses Lucy on the nose. Printed: "Smak!" 8 pieces. Wood. Shrink-wrap and cardboard packaging. 9-1/2" x 11-1/2". #230-7, Playskool. 1979. $5-10*

151. Puzzles

"PEANUTS Jigsaw Puzzle." Puzzles were sold separately or in packages of three. 5-1/4" x 7". Milton Bradley/Determined Productions. 1970-1971. $3-5** ea. Set of three: $10-15**

•Sally roller-skates against a red background. #4381-3.

•Snoopy walks against a pink background. #4381-5.

•Linus stands with his arms outstretched against a yellow background. #4381-6.

•Charlie Brown stands against a green background. #4381-12.

•Snoopy wears an award ribbon printed "Hero" against a blue background. #4381-11.

Packaged set of three pictured. #4381-A.

•Snoopy dances against a red background.

•Linus holds his blanket and sucks his thumb against a green background.

•Charlie Brown carries his baseball bat and glove over his shoulder against a blue background.

152. Mini Puzzles

Springbok. $4-6** ea.

•Snoopy sits next to a basket of Easter eggs, holding an egg and a paintbrush. 4-1/2" x 6-3/4". #PZL1208. 1988.

•Snoopy, as Joe Cool, wears braces. Printed: "Braces Make Beautiful Faces!" 7" x 10-1/2". #PZL4731. Mid-1980s.

•Charlie Brown hangs upside down from a tree, tangled in kite string with his kite. He says, "Why me?" 7" x 10-1/2". #PZL4722. 1984.

•Snoopy sits on his doghouse, surrounded by Woodstock and many of his friends. 7" x 10-1/2". #PZL4721. Mid-1980s.

154

155

156

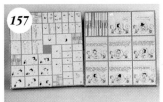

157

158

• Snoopy and Woodstock, dressed in pink, wear heart-shaped sunglasses. Printed: "Valentine, You're Cool." #PZL7301. Mid-1980s.

• Snoopy and Woodstock play soccer. Printed: "Sock It To Me!" #PZL7274. Mid-1980s.

• Lucy, reclining on a sofa, says, "Nobody's perfect but you come close! I come closer, of course, but that's only to be expected!" #PZL7335. 1989.

154. Puzzles

Springbok.

• The PEANUTS gang is all around a baseball diamond. It is raining over Charlie Brown, who is standing on the pitcher's mound. 12" x 17". #PZL1170. 1984. $5-8**

• Snoopy, Woodstock and his friends play soccer. Printed: "Pow!" 25 pieces. 10" x 14-3/16". #PZL1403. Mid-1980s. $4-6**

• Charlie Brown, Lucy, and Peppermint Patty prepare cookies at a table, Snoopy sits with Linus and Sally as they string beads, and Woodstock decorates the Christmas tree. 100 pieces. 13-1/2" x 17-7/8". #XZL1223. 1990. $4-8**

• The PEANUTS gang is outdoors in the snow, around a decorated Christmas tree. They appear to be singing. Printed: "Merry Christmas!" 100 pieces. 13-1/2" x 18-7/8". #XZL1215. Late 1980s. $4-8**

• Snoopy, Woodstock, and many of his friends sit in bleachers holding "Rah" pennants and wrapped in blankets. 48 pieces. 12" x 17". #PZL1305. 1985. $4-6**

155. Multi-Puzzle

• "It Takes All Kinds!" Four separate 7" x 7" puzzles make up a four-panel comic strip featuring Snoopy and Woodstock eating ice cream cones on top of Snoopy's doghouse. 70 pieces. #PZL3510, Springbok. 1988. $7-10**

Puzzle

• The PEANUTS gang involve themselves in winter activities such as ice-skating and sleigh-riding in this winter scene. 48 pieces. 12" x 17". XZL1310, Springbok. Early 1990s. $5-10**

Puzzle

• The PEANUTS gang is at an amusement park in this collage of scenes showing them on different rides. 13-1/2" x 18-7/8". #PZL1171, Springbok. Mid-1980s. $5-9**

156. Puzzles

• This puzzle is a ten-panel comic strip featuring Snoopy edging closer and closer to Linus in an attempt to snatch his blanket. 1000 pieces. 24" x 24". #711-1, Determined Productions. 1972. $10-15**

159

• This puzzle is made up of four sections, with different characters and sayings in each section. Lucy stands on Schroeder's piano and musses his hair: "Love Is Mussing Up Someone's Hair." Shermy and Patty hold hands: "Love Is Walking Hand In Hand." Sally tickles Linus: "Love Is Tickling." Snoopy leans on Charlie Brown: "Love Is Having Someone To Lean On." 1000 pieces. 24" x 24". #711-4, Determined Productions. 1971. $10-15**

157. Puzzles

• This puzzle is made up of four comic strips of eight to twelve panels each, featuring Charlie Brown, Lucy, Schroeder, Linus, and Snoopy. 1000 pieces. 24" x 24". #711-3, Determined Productions. 1971. $10-20**

• An eight-panel comic strip puzzle featuring Lucy jumping a rope held by Linus and Charlie Brown. 1000 pieces. 24" x 24". #711-2, Determined Productions. 1971. $10-20**

158. Puzzle

• "Dog Of 1000 Faces." Snoopy, Belle, and Woodstock plushes of all sizes are pictured in many of their outfits. Lucy and Peppermint Patty are also pictured. 1000 pieces. 24" x 30". #PZL5955, Springbok. 1984. $10-20**

159. Puzzle

• "Charles M. Schulz's PEANUTS." This puzzle features PEANUTS collectibles belonging to collector Pauline Graeber. The 45th anniversary logo—depicting Snoopy lying on his doghouse—appears on the puzzle box. 500 pieces. 20-1/2" x 26-3/4". #PZL7000, Springbok. 1995. $15-30**

160. Puzzles

• This puzzle features a photographed scene of a large Snoopy plush, dressed as Santa, surrounded by small Snoopy plushes dressed as elves. A Woodstock plush decorates a Christmas tree, and a Snoopy and Woodstock plush

153. Mini Puzzles

7" x 7". Springbok. $4-6** ea.

• Charlie Brown and Snoopy hug each other. Printed: "Thanks, I Needed That!" #PZL7271. Mid-1980s.

• Snoopy wears a painter's cap and holds a paintbrush and paint can, against a pastel rainbow background. #PZL7270. 1985.

• Snoopy and Woodstock, walking and grinning, wear their sunglasses on their heads. Printed: "Keep Smiling! It Makes People Wonder What You've Been Up To!" #PZL7315. Late 1980s.

are both asleep on a nearby bed. 20" x 20". #UZL1F, Ambassador. 1988. $7-20**

•"30th Anniversary A Charlie Brown Christmas." Commemorates the 30th anniversary of the TV show. The PEANUTS gang is outdoors in the snow around a decorated Christmas tree. They appear to be singing. Snoopy's decorated doghouse and Lucy's psychiatrist booth are in the background. 500 pieces. 20-1/2 x 26-3/4". #XZL4600, Springbok. 1995. $7-12**

161. Mini Puzzles

"Matchbox" size. Series #7130, Determined Productions. 1980. $2-3** ea.

•Linus sits on his knees with Woodstock and his friend. Printed: "Let's Be Friends."

•Peppermint Patty, Linus, Charlie Brown, Sally, Lucy, Woodstock, and Snoopy smile and have their arms outstretched. Printed: "Greetings."

•Snoopy looks at a map with Woodstock and his friends. All wear scout hats and backpacks. Printed: "Beagle Scout."

•Snoopy and Woodstock, holding a large trophy, sit on top of Snoopy's doghouse. Printed: "Congratulations."

•Snoopy and Peppermint Patty dance against a multicolored background. Printed: "Disco Dancer."

TROPHIES

Aviva began manufacturing trophies in 1969. They continued to be produced until the mid-1980s, when Aviva went out of business. It is difficult to tell which designs were produced in the earlier years, since the same designs were used over and over with different captions. The gold-tone plates with the captions on them were also interchangeable from one trophy to another.

My experience with trophies is that you either love them and collect every one you find, or you hate them but pick them up if the price is right—$1.00 or less. The trophies came in boxes suitable for mailing, but they have no PEANUTS graphics and do not affect the price.

162. Trophies

Plastic figures and bases. Aviva. 1969 through the mid-1980s. $4-7 ea.

•Snoopy wears a red baseball cap. Printed: "Superstar."

•Snoopy wears a stocking cap and holds a pair of skis. Printed: "Think Snow."

•Snoopy kicks a soccer ball. Printed: "World's Greatest Soccer Player."

•Snoopy, on skis with poles, wears a sweater, cap, and goggles. Printed: "World's Greatest Skier."

•Snoopy is poised to release a bowling ball. Printed: "World's Greatest Bowler."

•Snoopy, wearing a hat and raccoon coat, carries a pennant. Printed: "World's Greatest Fan."

•Snoopy, wearing a football uniform, kicks a football. Printed: "World's Greatest Football Player."

163. Trophies

Plastic figures and bases. Aviva. 1969 through the Mid-1980s.

•Snoopy, wearing his supper dish on his head, carries a globe. Printed: "I Think The World Of You!" $5-8

•Snoopy lies on a cloud with Woodstock lying on his tummy. A rainbow is behind them. Printed: "You've Got Me On Cloud Nine." $5-8

•Snoopy wears a backpack and checks a compass. Printed: "I'm Lost Without You." $5-8

•Snoopy has a tear rolling down his cheek. Printed: "I Miss You." $3-5

164. Trophies

Plastic figures and bases. Aviva. 1969 through the Mid-1980s.

•Snoopy, as Joe Cool, sits under a tree, while Woodstock pushes a cart. Printed: "Work Is For The Birds." $5-8

•Snoopy reclines in an easy chair. Printed: "Ahhh! Retirement." $5-8

•Snoopy is shaking nervously as he walks. Printed: "This Is A Difficult Time. I'm Going Through Life!" $5-8

•Lucy sits behind her psychiatrist booth advising Charlie Brown. Printed: "Keep The Corners Of Your Mouth Turned Up." $6-9

165. Trophies

Plastic figures and bases. Aviva. 1969 through the Mid-1980s.

•Snoopy, dressed as George Washington, carries an axe and a cherry tree. Printed: "Spirit of '76. 1776-1976." 1976. $5-8

•Snoopy as Joe Cool. Printed: "You're The Joe Coolest." $3-5

•Snoopy holds an Uncle Sam hat. Printed: "America, You're Beautiful!" $5-8

•Snoopy, dressed as a chef, wears an apron and holds a frying pan. Printed: "Joe Gourmet." $6-9

166. Trophies

Plastic figures and bases. Aviva. 1969 through the Mid-1980s. $4-6 ea.

•Snoopy, wearing a blue suit jacket, has his arms outstretched. Printed: "I Love You This Much."

•Snoopy, surrounded by red and pink hearts, puckers his lips. Printed: "Affection Needed Immediately."

•Snoopy, carrying a basket of flowers, is dancing. Printed: "Thinking About You Makes My Whole Day."

•Snoopy hugs Woodstock. Printed: "You're Close To My Heart!"

•Snoopy, grinning and eyes popping out, holds a bouquet of flowers. Printed: "I'm In The Mood For Love."

167. Trophies

Plastic figures and bases. Aviva. 1969 through the Mid-1980s.

•Snoopy as the Flying Ace. Printed: "World's Greatest." $3-5

•Snoopy, as Joe Cool, holds books and papers. Printed: "World's Greatest Teacher." $3-5

•Snoopy wears a red plaid jacket and bow tie. Printed: "World's Best Salesman." $3-5

•Snoopy, wearing a big orange wig and holding a blow dryer, combs Woodstock's feathers. Printed: "World's Greatest Hair Stylist." $6-9

•Snoopy wears a yellow plaid jacket and bow tie. Printed: "World's Best Friend." $3-5

168. Trophies

Plastic figures and bases. Aviva. 1969 through the Mid-1980s.

•Woodstock sits in front of a rainbow. Printed: "Have A Beautiful Day." $4-6

•Snoopy holds a heart over his chest. Printed: "Have A Beautiful Day." $3-5

•Snoopy plays the piano with Woodstock on top of it. Printed: "They're Playing Our Song." $5-8

• Woodstock sits on top of a duffel bag. Printed: "Wish You Were Here." $6-9

•Snoopy wears a cowboy hat and plays a guitar. Printed: "I Can't Stop Loving You." $3-5

•Snoopy dances in front of pink and red hearts. Printed: "Love Me Now And Beat The Crowd." $4-6

169. Trophies

Plastic figures and bases. Aviva. 1969 through mid-1980s. $5-8 ea.

•Snoopy and Woodstock wear caps and gowns. Printed: "World's Greatest Graduate."

•Snoopy, wearing a jacket, holds handfuls of money. Printed: "World's Greatest Boss."

•Snoopy wears a police officer's uniform. Printed: "World's Greatest Policeman."

•Snoopy sits at a school desk. Printed: "World's Best Student."

170. Trophies

Plastic figures and bases. Aviva. 1969 through the Mid-1980s.

•Peppermint Patty. Printed: "You Are A Rare Gem." $6-9

•Snoopy stands on a scale, weighing himself. Printed: "I Can't Believe I Ate The Whole Thing." $6-9

•Snoopy, wearing a red shirt, is dancing. Printed: "Feeling Groovy." $3-5

•Linus holds his blanket and sucks his thumb. Printed: "We All Have Our Hang-Ups." $6-9

•Snoopy wears a top hat, a yellow coat, and holds a cane. Printed: "There's No Greater Burden Than A Great Potential." $6-9

171. Trophies

Plastic figures and bases. Aviva. 1969 through the Mid-1980s. $6-9 ea.

•Snoopy, wearing his supper dish on his head, carries a hobo pack over his shoulder. Woodstock walks behind him. Printed: "Friendship Is For Sharing."

•Snoopy is draped over Charlie Brown's head as he reads a book. Printed: "Happiness Is Togetherness!"

•Snoopy hugs Charlie Brown. Printed: "I Need All The Friends I Can Get."

172. Trophies

Plastic figures and bases. Aviva. 1969 through the Mid-1980s.

•Snoopy sits, and holds a sign with a paw print on it. Printed: "Paw Power!" $15-20

•Snoopy, lying on his tummy and looking very tired, hangs his head over the roof of his doghouse. Printed: "Happy Monday!" $6-9

•Snoopy, wearing a pith helmet and a safari jacket, holds binoculars. Printed: "Be Kind To Nature." $6-9

•Snoopy sits on his doghouse with an antenna on it, talking on a CB radio. Printed: "What's Your Handle, Good Buddy?" $6-9

173. Trophies

Plastic figures and bases. Aviva. 1969 through the Mid-1980s.

•Snoopy, wearing a chef's hat, holds his supper dish with a candle in it. Printed: "Happy Birthday." $5-8

•Lucy wears a party hat and holds a party favor. Printed: "Have A Happy One." $5-8

•Snoopy sits with a large wrapped present. Printed: "Have A Happy One!" $3-5

•Snoopy, wearing a party hat, blows a party favor. Printed: "World's Greatest Party-Goer." $4-6

•Charlie Brown wears a jacket, bow tie, and party hat. Printed: "Happiness Is A Happy Birthday." $4-6

174. Trophies

Plastic figures and bases. Aviva. 1969 through the Mid-1980s.

•Woodstock. Printed: "Smile." $3-5

•Snoopy, wearing a red shirt, is dancing. Printed: "Thank You." $3-5

•Snoopy, lying on a pink blanket on top of the word "Baby," is surrounded by the moon and stars. Printed: "Congratulations." $5-8

•Snoopy lies on his doghouse. Woodstock stands on his tummy. Printed: "Peace." $6-9

•Woodstock sits in front of a four-leaf clover. Printed: "Good Luck." $4-6

•Belle is a cheerleader holding a megaphone and pom pom. Printed: "Cheers." $5-8

The PEANUTS Home Collection

•Linus, wearing a wizard's hat, sits with a crystal ball in his lap. Printed: "Good Luck." $7-10

175. Trophies

Plastic figures and bases. Aviva. 1969 through the Mid-1980s.

•Snoopy wears a knit cap and carries a pair of skis over his shoulder. Printed: "Ski Bum." $3-5

•Snoopy, on water skis, is holding on to a tow rope. Printed: "World's Greatest Water Skier." $3-5

•Snoopy holds a bowling ball. Printed: "World's Greatest Bowler." $3-5

•Snoopy runs after a soccer ball. Printed: "World's Greatest Soccer Player." $4-6

•Snoopy holds a tennis racket and grins. Printed: "Your Fault Or Mine?" $3-5

•Snoopy wears a baseball cap and glove. Printed: "World's Greatest Baseball Player." $3-5

176. Trophies

Plastic figures and bases. Aviva. 1969 through the Mid-1980s.

•Snoopy lies on top of a cable car. Printed: "Love From San Francisco." $7-10

•Snoopy, wears a space suit and carries a life support system. Printed: "Manned Spacecraft Center Houston, Texas." $15-20

•Snoopy, dressed as the Statue of Liberty, stands against a city skyline and a rainbow. Printed: "I (heart) New York." $10-15

177. Trophies

Plastic figures and bases. Aviva. 1969 through the Mid-1980s.

•Snoopy, wearing a purple bathrobe, sits with Woodstock, who holds a thermometer. Printed: "Get Well Soon!" $5-8

•Snoopy, standing, reads a book with a red cross on its cover. Woodstock sits at his feet. Printed: "Poor, Sweet Baby!" $6-8

•Snoopy is dressed as a doctor. Printed: "Get Well Soon!" $4-6

•Snoopy, dressed as a doctor, examines Woodstock in his nest. Printed: "Doctor Beagle." $6-9

178. Trophies

Plastic figures and bases. Aviva. 1969 through the Mid-1980s.

•Snoopy, dressed as Santa Claus, carries a sack with presents over his shoulder. Printed: "Merry Christmas." $6-8

•Snoopy lies on his tummy in a bed of pink and red hearts. Printed: "Happy Valentine's Day." $5-8

179. Trophies

Plastic figures and bases. Aviva. 1969 through the Mid-1980s. $5-8 ea.

•Snoopy wears a baseball cap, glasses, and smokes a pipe. Printed: "Top Grampa."

•Snoopy and Belle stand on each side of a pink heart. Printed: "Simply Super Sister."

•Snoopy leans his elbows on the word "Mom." Printed: "You're The World's Greatest."

180. Scenic Trophies

Plastic figures and bases. Packaged in a window box trimmed with hearts, and depicting Snoopy standing and Woodstock sitting. 4-1/2"W. Aviva. Early 1980s. $6-10* ea.

•Woodstock sits on a heart with the word "Love," as Snoopy aims a bow and arrow at it. Printed: "You've Captured My Heart."

•Snoopy, wearing skis, goggles, cap, and sweater, stands in front of a snow-covered mountain slope. Printed: "World's Greatest Skier."

•Snoopy is in his dancing pose, as Woodstock watches from atop Snoopy's doghouse. Printed: "Keep Smiling."

•Snoopy, arms outstretched and wearing a red jacket, looks at himself in a full-length mirror. Printed: "You're The Fairest One Of All."

181. Trophy Boxes

The characters are attached to the lids of boxes which can be used to store small items. Plastic. Approximately 6"H. Quantasia. 1986. $5-10 ea.

•Lucy shouts at Linus, who drops his pencil and papers. Printed: "The Pen May Be Mightier Than The Sword, But Not Louder." #G-121419.

•Snoopy, sitting, is surrounded by Woodstock and his friends. Printed: "It's Great To Have Friends." #G-121413.

•Lucy stands with her arms outstretched. Printed: "Don't Blame People Who Are Born With Crabby Genes." #G-121420.

•Lucy hugs Snoopy. Printed: "A Hug Is Better Than All The Theology In The World." #G-121417.

•Charlie Brown and Snoopy eat ice cream cones as they walk. Printed: "Life Is Like An Ice Cream Cone: You Have To Learn To Lick It." #G-121418.

•Charlie Brown unwraps a candy bar. Printed: "Candy Bars Are Like Years. We're Paying More But They're Getting Shorter." #G-121422.

182. Trophy Pins

The characters, with pinbacks, can be removed from the base and worn on clothing. Packaged on a blister card. Plastic. Aviva. Mid-1970s. $6-9* ea.

•Snoopy rolls his eyes as Woodstock sits in his supper dish. "Smile" is printed in the background. Printed on the base: "You Don't Know What You're Missing."

•Snoopy as the Flying Ace. Printed: "I Care Not For Fame And Glory."

•Snoopy, lying on his tummy, looks over the roof of his doghouse at Woodstock below. Printed: "Howdy."

183. Mini-Grams

"The Snoopy Mini-Gram." Plastic figures and bases with captions on decals. Packaged on a blister card. 3"H. Aviva. 1972. $7-9* ea.

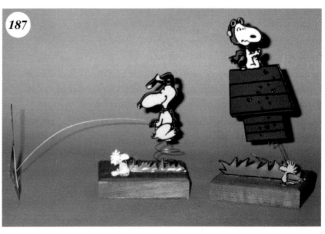

•Snoopy, grinning, holds his supper dish. Printed: "Thank You!"

•Snoopy puts his hand out ready to shake someone else's hand. Printed: "Congratulations."

•Snoopy grins as he walks along. Printed: "Smile."

•Snoopy, grinning, is sitting at a typewriter. Printed: "Hello!"

•Charlie Brown, wearing a yellow baseball cap, is frowning. Printed: "Nobody's Perfect."

•Snoopy is dancing. Printed: "Snoopy."

184. Mini Trophies

Ceramic figures and bases. 2"H. Aviva. 1974. $10-12* ea.

•Snoopy is lying on his doghouse. Printed: "Get Well."

•Snoopy holds a basket. Printed: "Have A Heart."

•Snoopy is sitting and holding a flower. Printed: "Sorry."

•Snoopy is walking and carries a suitcase. Printed: "Ordinary Beagle."

185. Trophies

Ceramic figures and bases. 4-1/4"H. Series #098, Aviva. 1980. $10-12 ea.

•Snoopy is holding flowers. Printed: "Thank You."

•Snoopy holds, in his mouth, his dog dish with a menu in it. Printed: "Suppertime."

•Snoopy holds a tennis racket. Printed: "World's Greatest Tennis Player."

•Woodstock. Printed: "World's Best Friend."

•Snoopy and Charlie Brown share a bean bag chair. Printed: "Friendship."

•Snoopy, sitting, wears a party hat. Printed: "Happy Birthday."

•Snoopy as the Flying Ace. Printed: "World's Greatest."

186. Trophies

Ceramic figures and bases. 4-1/4"H. Series #098, Aviva. 1980.

•Snoopy, wearing goggles, stands on skis. Printed: "Ski." $10-12

•Snoopy, wearing a cowboy hat, plays a guitar. Printed: "They're Playing Our Song." $10-12

•Snoopy stands on the word "Mom." Printed: "World's Greatest." $10-12

•Snoopy is dressed as the Statue of Liberty. Printed: "World's Greatest." $12-18

•Snoopy is holding flowers. Printed: "Thank You." $10-12

•Snoopy wears a medal with a "1" on it around his neck. Printed: "Snoopy." $10-12

187. Trophies

Known as "Sparkies" these plastic figures of Snoopy are attached to a teakwood base by a spring. Aviva. 1971-1972. $18-30 ea.

•Snoopy flies a kite while Woodstock watches. 8-1/2"H.

•Snoopy, as the Flying Ace, sits on his bullet-riddled doghouse while Woodstock watches. 7"H.

Most of the items that appear in the kitchen scene are from Japan. Exceptions are the pot holder mitts from England, the towel from Germany, and the ceramic container with the wood closure, which is from Hong Kong.

The Japanese items include the red coffee pot, red cup and saucer, casserole, a one-cup drip coffee maker, plastic pail with swing top cover, chocolate mold, cookie cutters, cake top decorations, and pots. All of these items are well made and totally usable.

A kitchen that is not only fun, but functional.

The Kitchen

Statistics tell us two things about American eating habits: First, more and more meals are being consumed outside the home each year. And, second, for those meals taken inside the home, there is a continuing trend towards spending less time in their preparation.

Does this mean Americans spend less time in the kitchen—in food preparation and eating? Yes! For other reasons? Maybe not. After all, the kitchen still remains the focal place for family life. Kids like to do their homework there. Friends and neighbors prefer the informality of the kitchen for brief social visits. There is a TV in many kitchens, and a computer in some. The kitchen table is still a great place for family discussions or family projects. Pets still eat there. And, yes, many moms still do more than their share of the cooking.

All of which makes the kitchen an important repository of PEANUTS objects. What makes the kitchen different is that, unlike items in some of the other rooms, a good many kitchen items do not remain idle. They are constantly being put to work as a part of our everyday lives. That's why, in addition to the expected dishes, mugs, cooking aids, utensils, cutting boards, glasses, cookie cutters, aprons, napkins, lunchboxes, and food storage containers, you will also find party goods, pet items, key chains, and sundry other items in this kitchen section.

CONDIMENT HOLDERS PLUS...

1. Salt and Pepper Shaker Set

•Woodstock, wearing a chef's hat, is sitting on top of the pepper shaker, which has an embossed "P" on the front. Snoopy, dressed as a chef, is the salt shaker, which has an embossed "S" on the front. Ceramic. Pepper shaker, 3-1/2"H. Salt shaker, 4-1/2"H. #8830, Determined Productions. 1977. Pepper shaker: $30-35 Salt shaker: $25-30 Set: $55-65

Mustard Jar

•Woodstock, wearing a chef's hat, is sitting on top of the lid. The jar has the word "Mustard" embossed on the front. A plastic spoon is included. Ceramic. 4"H. #1771, Determined Productions. 1977. $30-35

Egg Cup

•Snoopy, standing, is dressed as a chef wearing a yellow neckerchief. His chef's hat is indented to hold an egg. Ceramic. 4-1/2"H. #1567, Determined Productions. 1979. $50-55

Jam Jar

•Snoopy is sitting on top of the lid. The jar has the word "Jam" embossed on the front. A plastic spoon is included. Ceramic. 5-1/4"H. #8490, Determined Productions. 1977. $30-35

2. Creamer

•Linus, with his blanket, appears to be seated on a club chair whose back is the creamer. Light blue. Ceramic. 5"H. #45020, Willitts Designs. 1990. $18-22 $24-28*

Salt and Pepper Shaker Set

•A removable Charlie Brown, eating a sandwich, and Lucy, holding a mug, are seated on a light blue sofa. Ceramic. 5"W x 2-1/2"D x 5"H. #45021, Willitts Designs. 1990. $30-35 $40-45*

Sugar Bowl

•Snoopy sits atop a round ottoman, eating a cookie. Light blue. Ceramic. 3" diam. x 4-1/2"H. #45026, Willitts. 1990. $18-22 $24-28*

COOKBOOKS

3. "The Cartoonist Cookbook"

•Forty-five cartoonists are featured, with a sample of their work and favorite recipe. Charles Schulz is featured on pages 75 and 76. Hard cover. 5-1/2" x 7-1/2". Gramercy Publishing Co., 1966. $75-90

"The Cartoonist Cookbook"

•Same content as smaller version. Hard cover. 7-1/8" x 10-3/4". Edited by Theodora Illenberger and Avonne Eyre Keller of the Newspaper Comics Council, Inc. Hobbs, Dorman & Co., Inc. 1966. $110-130

4. "Snoopy's Gourmet Guide"

•Printed on cover "12 Great Thoughts of Food With Snoopy's Favorite Recipes by Charles M. Schulz." Snoopy is pictured sitting in front of his dog dish, wearing a chef's hat and bib napkin, preparing to eat dinner. Envelope included. 10" x 15". #200M400-5, Hallmark. Early 1970s. $15-20

5. "The Women's Sports Foundation Cookbook"

•Cover pictures Snoopy sitting at a table reading a cereal box. Below is a cereal recipe. Recipes donated by different women athletes. Spiral bound. Illustrations by Charles M. Schulz, 1983. $45-50

COOKIE CUTTERS

Are You Cookie-Cutter Curious?

The cookie cutters may look the same, but which came out first? And are they Hallmark or Ambassador?

Let's consider the red, heart-shaped Charlie Brown and Snoopy. The original Hallmark cookie cutters had "©United Features Syndicate, Inc." printed on the vertical handle in very small print. It was reissued at least three times. On the first reissue, "United Features Syndicate, Inc. © 1958" on Snoopy and "© 1950" on Charlie Brown was printed on the back, above the vertical handle, and there was no printing on the handle. For the second reissue, the color was red/orange and "© United Features Syndicate, Inc." was printed on the back above the vertical handles.

Also, on another set, there is printing on both sides of the front of the cutters close to the rim—"United Features Syndicate, Inc." and a copyright date. The last reissue that we know of was in red/orange. Printing was on the front of the cutter, but only on the left side. These could possibly have been made by Ambassador, not Hallmark, but the only proof would be in the packaging.

Then there were the elusive Hallmark Painted PEANUTS Cookie Cutters, two of which I have pictured and which belong to Pauline Graeber, a PEANUTS collector. It is believed that only three or four sets are in the hands of collectors. They were supposedly manufactured in 1981, but were they produced in quantity? Were they even sold in retail stores? These particular cookie cutters are even a mystery to Hallmark. They were manufactured by Monogram Products, Inc., but have Hallmark item numbers. Also, unlike any of the other PEANUTS cookie cutters, these have an eyelet, and they are the only cutters with Charles Schulz's signature on the front. "© United Features Syndicate, Inc." is on the back.

Another set of Hallmark cookie cutters features Snoopy sitting, Lucy, Linus, and Charlie Brown with hands outstretched. "© United Features Syndicate" is printed on the back of the cutters—on the left side of Charlie Brown, Lucy, and Linus, and on the right side of Snoopy. The handles are shaped differently than the handles on any other Hallmark cutters. They are a vertical, short, thick half-circle inside a circle that is embossed on the cutter. In 1976, these cutters were reissued individually with different numbers and might have been brighter colors than the original set of four. A set of these cutters has been found in translucent white.

Hallmark also put out a set of cookie cutters depicting Snoopy as an astronaut; dancing; as the Flying Ace; and on his doghouse. This set was possibly reissued because they have been found in two shades of blue. "© United Features Syndicate" is printed on the back above a vertical handle.

A set of four cookie cutters depicting the characters holding Christmas items was produced by Hallmark as item number 150XPF38-4. "© United Features Syndicate, Inc." is printed on the back. Reissued, it had the same printing, but colors varied. Later, the set was issued by Ambassador, as item number 150XPF9G. In the Ambassador set, the red is brighter, the blue is navy rather than marine, the green is brighter, and the white, whiter. The cutters are more transparent. "© United Features Syndicate, Inc." is printed below the vertical handles. And, each character has its own copyright date. Ambassador reissued these cookie cutters. In addition to the print on the back, the reissue has "© United Features Syndicate" printed on the front—backwards starting from right to left, with the letters facing left instead of right. It is in very small print and easily overlooked.

To learn more about the cookie cutters, consult A Guide To Hallmark Cookie Cutters, by Lee Stephenson and Byrna Fancher. For more information, see Suggested Reading.

6. Cookie Cutters

Various colors. Plastic. Hallmark.

•Snoopy, full figure with thought balloons. Set of two. One has him holding his dog dish and thinking, "What's Cookin'?" White. The other portrays him as Joe Cool, thinking, "Hi Sweetie!" Yellow. 4-1/2". #75PF96-6. 1974. $20-25 ea. Set: $50-55*

•Great Pumpkin. Snoopy lies on his back atop a large, smiling pumpkin. Orange. 5-1/2" x 6-1/2". #75HPF14-6. 1972. $85-95 $140-150*

•Heart-shaped. Set of two. Charlie Brown, surrounded by hearts. Snoopy sits with a heart inside his thought balloon. #75VPF 25-3. 1974. Red. Plastic. Set: $50-55

7. Cookie Cutters

Set of four. Charlie Brown holds an ornament. Snoopy wears a Santa hat. An ornament hangs from his collar. Linus holds a string of lights. Lucy, smiling, holds a gift package. Plastic. Various colors. Produced by Hallmark and Ambassador.

•#150XPF384, Hallmark. 1972. Set: $50-55*

•#150XPF9G, Ambassador. 1975. Set: $40-45*

Cookie Cutter

•Snoopy reclines on his doghouse. Plastic. Red. 8"H. #75PF102-3, Hallmark. 1973. $6-8 $10-15*

8. Cookie Cutters

Set of four, shrink-wrapped on a doghouse-shaped card. Various colors. Plastic. #150PF97-4, Hallmark. 1971. $10-15 ea. Set: $80-95*

•Snoopy sitting.

•Charlie Brown with his arms outstretched.

•Linus with his arms outstretched.

•Lucy with her arms outstretched.

Cookie Cutters

Set of four, shrink wrapped on a doghouse-shaped card. Various colors. Plastic. #150PF97-4, Hallmark. 1971. $10-15 ea. Set: $80-85*

•Snoopy, as the Flying Ace, with helmet and scarf.

•Snoopy, as an astronaut, wearing a spacesuit.

•Snoopy lying on his doghouse.

•Snoopy dancing.

9. Cookie Cutters

The painted outsides and the hooks at the top for hanging are unique features. Packaged individually. Plastic. 5"H. Hallmark. 1981. $200-250* ea.

•Lucy. Wears a red dress and laughs. #200KK295-1.

•Snoopy and Woodstock. Sitting back to back. #200KK297-1.

•Charlie Brown, in red shirt. #200KK294-1. (Not pictured)

•Woodstock. (Not pictured)

•Snoopy. Holding a sign. #200KK296-1. (Not pictured)

COOKIE JARS

10. Cookie Jar

•Snoopy is sitting and eating a chocolate chip cookie. Woodstock, eating a cookie, sits on top of Snoopy's light blue baseball cap. Ceramic. 14-1/2"H. #45018, Willitts Designs. 1990. $100-110 $140-150*

11. Doghouse "Pet Snax" Jar

•The lid has Snoopy lying on the roof. Printed on the side of the house in thought balloon, "One Of The Great Joys Of Life Is Scarfing Junk Food." Ceramic. 6" x 9" x 12-1/2". ConAgra (sold through Sears). 1981. $275-300

Doghouse Cookie Jar

•The lid has Snoopy lying on the roof. "Snoopy" is printed above the entrance (base of cookie jar turned for better viewing). Ceramic. 11"H. McCoy, for Determined Productions. 1973. $185-200

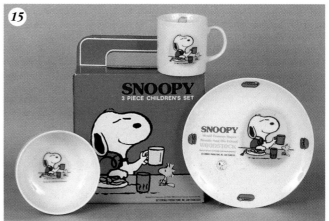

12. Chef Cookie Jars

Snoopy is sitting, and wearing a yellow bandanna around his neck. His chef's hat is the lid. Ceramic. Determined Productions.

• Small. 7-1/2"H. #0983. 1979. $80-90

• Large. 11"H. #8480. 1977. $255-300

13. Pet Goodies Jar

• Snoopy appears to be rising out of a paper bag. Printed: "Snoopy Brown Bag Pet Goodies." #71-63428-7, ConAgra Pet Products Co. Sold exclusively at Sears. 1980. $200-225 $250-300*

14. Cookie Jar and Glasses Set

• Cookie Jar depicts Snoopy sitting, and eating chocolate chip cookies. Printed: "Scarf....Mumph." Reverse side printed "I Love Cookies." Glass. One gallon Cookie Jar. Two 8-oz. glasses. #3100/346. #300/426 came boxed without glasses. Anchor Hocking. 1983. $55-65 $75-85*

DISH SETS

15. Dish Set

• Snoopy, sitting at the table, holds up a cup. Woodstock sits on the table. Design is on bowl, plate, and mug. The rim of the plate depicts hot dogs and hamburgers. Printed on plate: "Snoopy . . . World Famous Super Beagle And His Friend Woodstock." Ceramic. #SN 1800, Determined Productions. 1985. Mug: $10-15 Plate: $15-20 Bowl: $10-15 Set: $50-60*

16. Dish Set

• Pictured on the bowl, cup, and plate is Snoopy, Sally, Schroeder, Franklin, Peppermint Patty, Linus, and Charlie Brown, all holding kitchenware. Printed on all pieces is "Suppertime" and "Supper." Ceramic. Bowl, 12 oz. Plate, 7-3/4" diam. Taylor Smith and Taylor, division of Anchor Hocking. 1976. Cup: $18-22 Plate: $25-30 Bowl: $30-35 Set: $90-125*

17. Dish Set

• Pictured on the plate is Schroeder and his piano, Charlie Brown with bat and glove, Snoopy dancing, Linus with his blanket, and Lucy jumping rope. Snoopy is pictured inside the bowl. The names of the characters are printed around the rim of the cup. China. Plate, 7-3/4" diam.; Bowl, 6" diam. Iroquois China, for Determined Productions. Early 1970s. Cup: $14-16 Bowl: $20-25 Plate: $30-35 Set: $95-130*

18. Dish Set

• The cup pictures Lucy jumping rope, Charlie Brown flying his kite, Snoopy, and Woodstock. The bowl depicts Snoopy and Woodstock sitting on top of the doghouse. The plate incorporates the designs of the bowl and the cup along with Linus, Sally, and Peppermint Patty. Ceramic. Plate, 7-3/4" diam. Bowl, 6" diam. Johnson Brothers for Determined Productions. Late 1970s. Cup: $15-20 Bowl: $20-30 Plate: $35-40 Set: $90-120*

DRINKING GLASSES, PITCHERS, MUGS, AND STEINS

19. Drinking Glasses

12 oz. Anchor Hocking. Late 1970s. $6-8 ea.

• Baseball—Snoopy, wearing a baseball cap, is swinging a bat.

- Golf—Snoopy, wearing a golf cap, is holding a golf club.
- Tennis—Snoopy, wearing a sun visor, is hitting a tennis ball.

20. Drinking Glasses

16 oz. Anchor Hocking. Late 1970s. $5-7 ea.

- Snoopy is down on one knee with arms outstretched. Large stars encircle the glass. Woodstock sits on top of a star. Printed: "Superstar!"
- Snoopy hugs Woodstock, and Peppermint Patty holds hands with Charlie Brown. Large hearts encircle the glass. Printed: "Love!"
- Snoopy, as the Flying Ace, sits at a cafe table drinking root beer as Woodstock watches. Printed: "Cheers!"

21. Drinking Glasses

Premium. Manufactured for Interstate Brands at election time by Anchor Hocking. 1980. $4-6 ea.

- Snoopy, wearing a red, white, and blue bow tie, is sporting a big grin. Printed: "The People's Choice."
- Snoopy, wearing an Uncle Sam hat, sits on his doghouse. Printed: "Put Snoopy in the White House."
- Snoopy is wearing an Uncle Sam hat and his famous grin. Printed: "Vote for the American Beagle."

22. Stein

- Snoopy is walking as Woodstock flies upside down. Printed: "Too Much Root Beer." Glass. Anchor Hocking. 1978. $6-8

Glass

- Snoopy is walking as Woodstock flies upside down. Printed: "Too Much Root Beer." Glass. Anchor Hocking. 1978. $4-6

Pitcher

- Snoopy, Lucy, Peppermint Patty, Charlie Brown, and Woodstock sit in front of a row of trees and sip drinks. Glass. 72 oz. #3650H-7781, Anchor Hocking. 1978. $18-25

Chillers

- Snoopy, in different poses, is pictured above oranges encircling the chiller. Comes with a white plastic cover. Glass. 54 oz. #2147 Anchor Hocking. 1978. $15-20
- Snoopy and Woodstock are pictured dancing. Printed: "Life Is Too Short Not To Live It Up." (Note the different white plastic cover.) Glass. Anchor Hocking. 1978. $20-25

Juice Set

- The chiller pictures Snoopy dressed as a chef as he hits a triangle to announce dinner. Sally holds a plate, while Woodstock sits on top of a chair at the table. Printed: "Snoopy's Kitchen." Comes with four glasses picturing Charlie Brown and Lucy. Glasses—8 oz., Chiller—54 oz. #3100/345, Anchor Hocking. 1979. Glasses: $6-8 ea. Chiller: $15-20 Set: $30-35*

Glasses

- Lucy stands behind a lemonade stand. Linus, Snoopy, Woodstock, Charlie Brown, and Peppermint Patty appear around the glass. 13 oz. #3607G-7781, Anchor Hocking. 1978. $3-5
- Lucy stands behind a lemonade stand. Linus, Snoopy, Woodstock, Charlie Brown, and Peppermint Patty appear around the glass. 7 oz. #3607G-7782, Anchor Hocking. 1978. $3-4

Highball Glasses

- Snoopy is lying on his house. Printed on the reverse side: "This Has Been a Good Day." 3" diam. x 3-1/2"H. Anchor Hocking. 1978. $4-5

•Snoopy and Woodstock are dancing. Printed on the reverse side: "Life is Too Short Not to Live It Up." 2-1/2" diam. x 3-1/2"H. Anchor Hocking. 1978. $4-5

23. Juice Set

•Chiller (with white plastic cover) features Snoopy and Woodstock sitting and holding juice glasses. The word "Juice" and the characters are repeated. The four glasses have the same graphics. Chiller—54 oz., Glasses—6-3/4 oz. #2100/78, Anchor Hocking. Early 1980s. Chiller: $10-20 Glasses: $4-6 ea. Set: $30-35*

24. Soda Mugs

•Snoopy is pictured as a soda jerk standing behind a counter. Woodstock is sitting on the counter. Both are eating ice cream. Printed on the front of the counter is "Sodas." 5-1/4"H. Determined Productions. Mid-1970s. $30-35

•Snoopy, standing, holds a bouquet of balloons. Reverse side pictures Woodstock holding one balloon. 5"H. Determined Productions. Mid-1970s. $35-40

25. Root Beer Mugs

•Snoopy sits, while Woodstock sleeps on his paw. Printed on the reverse side: "It Never Fails...Three Root Beers and Woodstock Falls Sound Asleep!" Glass. 5-3/4"H. Anchor Hocking. Early 1980s. $8-10

•Snoopy, wearing a cowboy hat, stands in front of a bar. Woodstock stands on the bar. Both are drinking root beer. Glass. 7-3/4"H. #3031T-438, Anchor Hocking. 1981. $20-25

26. Stein

•Snoopy, as Joe Cool, and Woodstock lean against a wall. Printed: "Here's Joe Cool Hanging Around on a Saturday Afternoon...No Wheels, Man!" Ceramic. 4-1/2"H. Determined Productions. Mid-1970s. $35-40

Mug

•Woodstock and his buddies watch Snoopy as he poses in different sports gear. Ceramic. 3"H. Determined Productions. Mid-1970s. $25-30

27. Steins

Ceramic. Determined Productions. Mid-1970s.

•Snoopy, as the Flying Ace, sits at a table. In front of him are three empty bottles and a glass. Printed on reverse side: "Girls and Root Beer Are Not Always The Answer." 4-1/2"H. $35-40

•Snoopy, in a raccoon coat, carries a "RAH" banner as Woodstock walks behind him. 4-1/4"H. $30-35

•Snoopy is pictured in a variety of poses above each letter of the word "Snoopy." 5"H. Determined Productions. $25-30

28

30

29

31

32

28. Mugs

Ceramic. 10 oz. 3-1/2"H. Determined Productions. 1980. $8-10 ea.

•Snoopy and Woodstock, wearing cowboy hats, stand at the bar, toasting with their steins. Printed on the reverse side: "Pardners." #2170.

•Snoopy and Woodstock are surrounded by cacti in the desert. "Texas" is spelled out with Snoopy's lariat. Woodstock's lariat is in the shape of a star.

•Snoopy, in his cowboy outfit, twirls a lasso with Woodstock and his friends nearby. Printed: "Get Along Little Doggies."

29. Mugs

Created and decorated for specific geographical locations. Descriptions on the items include a continuing scene around each mug. The city or state is printed on the mug. Ceramic. 3-1/2"H. 10 oz. Determined Productions. Early 1980s. $15-20 ea.

•New Orleans. Woodstock and his friends, wearing costumes, carry a banner printed "New Orleans Mardi Gras." Snoopy appears in a devil's costume.

•Atlantic City. Snoopy holds a microphone and thinks, "And The Winner Of 'Ms. Atlantic City Boardwalk' Is....Miss New Jersey!" Lucy wears a gold crown, a cape and a New Jersey banner, and carries flowers. Peppermint Patty is wearing a Florida banner while Sally sports a California banner.

•Florida. Woodstock lounges on a beach chair under the sun, as does Snoopy.

•Chicago. Woodstock flips over in the wind. Snoopy's ears stand up straight as buildings sway and leaves fly.

30. Mugs

By geographical location. Descriptions include a continuing scene around each mug. The city or state is printed on the mug. Ceramic. 3-1/2"H. 10 oz. Determined Productions. Early 1980s. $15-20 ea.

•Los Angeles. Snoopy drives a red convertible. His passenger, Woodstock, sits next to a surfboard. Road signs point to Venice, Santa Monica, Orange County, and Hollywood.

•California. Woodstock wears diving gear, and Snoopy is carrying a surfboard.

•San Francisco. Skyscrapers appear over the caption as Snoopy, Woodstock, and friends ride a cable car.

31. Mugs

By geographical location. Descriptions include a continuing scene around each mug. The city or state is printed on the mug Ceramic. 3-1/2"H. 10 oz. Determined Productions. Early 1980s. $15-20 ea.

•New York. Snoopy and Woodstock, wearing top hats and canes, dance on a stage.

•New York. Snoopy hugs Woodstock as they sit in front of a big red apple.

•New York. Snoopy, holding a hot dog, poses as the Statue of Liberty. Snoopy, Woodstock and friends take pictures as they ride on the Staten Island Ferry.

32. Mugs

By geographical location. Descriptions include a continuing scene around each mug. The city or state is printed on the mug. Ceramic. 3-1/2"H. 10 oz. Determined Productions. Early 1980s. $15-20 ea.

•Washington D.C. The White House is viewed by Snoopy, Woodstock, and friends.

•Massachusetts. Woodstock, dressed as a chef, stands, as Snoopy prepares to eat a large red lobster.

•Philadelphia. In colonial garb, Charlie Brown, Lucy, and Snoopy surround an American flag in the making.

33. Mugs

Ceramic. 3-1/2"H. Determined Productions.

•Snoopy is sitting on top of his doghouse fishing into his dog dish on the ground below, thinking, "Find a Good Spot and Everyone Moves In." Shermy, Roy, and Linus are sitting around the dog dish. #1783. Mid-1970s. $6-9

•Sally is talking to Linus, who holds a soccer ball. She says, "How could soccer be your favorite sport? What about hugging and kissing?" Snoopy and Woodstock are watching. #1797. 1980. $6-9

•Snoopy, looking dejected and dragging his tennis racket behind him, thinks, "I'm seriously thinking about not taking tennis so seriously." Woodstock flies behind him. #1762. 1980. $6-8

34. Mugs

Continuing sports scenes. The name of the sports are repeated around the mugs. Ceramic. 10 oz. Determined Productions. 1979. $5-7 ea.

33

34

•Jogging. Snoopy is jogging with Woodstock, who is walking beside him at first, then flying. Snoopy collapses, and Woodstock starts walking again. #1975.

•Football. Snoopy is pictured wearing a helmet, running toward the ball on the ground, then kicking the ball and continuing to run, this time with Woodstock on the tip of his foot. #1973.

•All Star. Snoopy is dribbling a basketball, batting a baseball, and kicking a football. #1976.

35. Mugs

Ceramic. 10 oz. Determined Productions.

•Snoopy is holding a football, running toward Woodstock. Both are wearing helmets. Printed on the reverse side: "Touchdown!" #1254. Mid-1970s. $5-7

•Snoopy, Woodstock, and his friends are white-water rafting. The Woodstocks are paddling. Early 1980s. $5-7

•Woodstock, dressed in ski gear, is riding a chair lift up the mountain. Snoopy and Woodstock ride a chair lift going down. Early 1980s. $5-7

•Snoopy is serving a tennis ball, as Woodstock watches with racket in hand. Printed on the reverse side: "My Serve!" #1257. Mid-1970s. $5-7

•Snoopy is pictured in three different stages of lifting weights. #1771. Early 1980s. $6-8

•Snoopy and Lucy are pictured in baseball gear. Woodstock stands nearby. Lucy says, "Who Cares About Tomorrow...Let's Play Ball!" Early 1980s. $6-8

36. Mugs

Three-panel sports scenes. Ceramic. 10 oz. Determined Productions. Early 1980s. $5-7 ea.

•Snoopy is pitched a ball by Woodstock, he hits it and acts like a hero as he reaches home plate. Printed: "Snoopy" and "Home Run Hero."

•Snoopy is running through the panels after a soccer ball. Woodstock appears in the last panel. Printed: "Snoopy" and "Soccer King."

•Snoopy and Woodstock are jogging through the panels. Printed: "Snoopy" and "Jogging Hound."

35

36

37

40

38

39

birthday cake between them. Ceramic. #1982, Determined Productions. 1979. $5-8

• Snoopy is engineer of a locomotive. The next car in the train, with Woodstock flying overhead, holds gifts. The following two cars hold Peppermint Patty, Sally, Lucy, Charlie Brown, Schroeder, and Linus. The caption, "Happy Birthday," is inside a cloud of smoke from the engine. This mug matches the "Happy Birthday" plate on page 89. Ceramic. 3-1/2"H. Determined Productions for the Dupont Collection, Ltd. 1978. $8-10

• Spike, Lucy, and Charlie Brown, wearing party hats, sit at a cloth-covered table printed "Happy Birthday." Snoopy, Belle, and Woodstock sit on either side of the pictured characters. Ceramic. #1305, Determined Productions. 1981. $5-8

39. Mugs

• Snoopy, dressed as a vampire, walks beside Charlie Brown toward a "Great Pumpkin Country" sign. Waiting at the sign is Lucy, dressed as a witch, and Woodstock, dressed as a bat. Ceramic. Determined Productions. Early 1980s. $8-10

• Snoopy, wearing a nightshirt and cap, stands near a window with the moon and stars shining through. Woodstock, dressed as Santa and carrying a sack of gifts, sits on the window sill. On the reverse side, Snoopy sees from afar what appears to be Santa in his sleigh. Ceramic. #1304, Determined Productions. 1981. $6-8

• Snoopy sits in a pumpkin patch, dressed in a cape and mask, and eating treats from a bag. Woodstock sits nearby on a pumpkin. Stoneware. 11 oz. #7846, Willitts Designs. 1987. $7-9

• Snoopy sits on his doghouse. Woodstock and his friends form a heart made of flowers around him. On the reverse side, Snoopy is holding a bouquet of flowers. Printed: "I Love You." Stoneware. 11 oz. #8137, Willitts Designs. 1988. $5-8

40. Mugs

• Snoopy carries a gift, then sits and opens the gift to find Woodstock with a Christmas tree in his nest. Woodstock and his friends fly over head. Ceramic. 3-1/2"H. #1215, Determined Productions. Mid-1970s. $5-8

• Snoopy plays with his paw-pets; Lucy, Linus, Peppermint Patty, Schroeder, and Charlie Brown are readying gifts to put under the tree, while Woodstock and his friends drape garland around the tree. Printed: "Merry Christmas 1978." See matching plate on page 87. Ceramic. 3-1/2"H. Determined Productions. 1978. $8-10

• Sally is sitting with a teddy bear. Charlie Brown sits beside her with a candy cane. He says "1977." The scene continues, featuring Snoopy wearing a Santa hat and holding a present, Lucy with holly in her hair, and Woodstock singing in his nest with his Christmas tree. Printed: "Merry Christmas." Ceramic. 3-1/2"H. Determined Productions, for the Dupont Collection, Ltd. 1977. $8-10

37. Mugs on Pedestals

Sports scenes. Ceramic. 8 oz. Determined Productions. Mid-1970s. $6-8 ea.

• Snoopy swings a baseball bat as his cap flies off his head. On the reverse side, Woodstock is wearing a baseball hat. Printed: "Home Run King." #1258.

• Snoopy is getting ready to let go of a bowling ball. On the reverse side, Woodstock is flying above the bowling pins. Printed: "Strike."

• Snoopy, holding a golf club, stands behind Woodstock, who is carrying a golf bag. Printed on the reverse side: "You're Away." #1256.

38. Mugs

• Snoopy, wearing a party hat, is dancing amidst bows and confetti on the front, and stands holding a mug on the back. Caption continues from front to back: "This is Not the Same Ol' Song 'N Dance...It's Just Another Way to Say Happy Birthday!" Stoneware. 11 oz. #8133, Willitts Designs. 1989. $5-8

• Snoopy, dressed in a tuxedo and top hat, is presenting a bouquet of flowers to Woodstock. Ceramic. 4"H. #1183, Determined Productions. Mid-1970s. $7-10

• Woodstock sits on the words "Happy Birthday To You!" Reverse side shows Snoopy and Woodstock singing, with a

41

42

•Lucy holds a present, and Snoopy holds a candy cane. The scene continues, with Woodstock holding a wreath and Peppermint Patty holding a sign that reads, "Joy." Printed: "Merry Christmas 1976." Ceramic. 3-1/2"H. Determined Productions, for Joy's Inc. 1976. $8-9

41. Mugs

•Snoopy, dressed as Santa, flies an airplane with Woodstock dropping gifts into a chimney, as Charlie Brown looks out the window. Ceramic. Determined Productions. Early 1980s. $6-8*

•Charlie Brown has just opened a gift from Santa, finding Snoopy inside. The scene continues, with Lucy carrying gifts and a stocking, and Woodstock, with a star in his nest, on top of the Christmas tree. Garland decorated with ornaments and stockings adorn the mug above the characters. Ceramic. Determined Productions. Early 1980s. $5-7

•Snoopy is the handle. He is dressed as Joe Cool Santa, and appears to lean against the mug. Printed: "Have a Cool Yule." Above the words are holly leaves and a bow. The mugs came as a set of four identical mugs in a graphic box, but many retailers sold them individually. Porcelain. 10 oz. #7865, Willitts Designs. 1987. Individual mug: $6-9 ea. Set: $35-40*

42. Mug

•Snoopy and Woodstock sleep on presents in front of a fireplace, which is decorated with stockings, candles, and a wreath. A large wreath encircles the scene. Ceramic. 11 oz. Determined Productions. Mid-1970s. $12-16

43. Mugs

Ceramic. Determined Productions. 1981. $8-10 ea.

•Snoopy, wearing glasses, a bow tie, and holding a pointer, covers his eyes as Woodstock writes on a blackboard. Printed: "My Mug." The scene continues, showing a desk with textbooks and an apple on top and a globe in front.

•Snoopy, holding papers, sits at a rolltop desk. The sign above reads, "Attorney at Law." The scene continues, with Woodstock being weighed on the scales of justice, which sits on top of three big books. Printed: "My Mug."

•Snoopy, dressed as a doctor, uses a stethoscope to listen to Woodstock's nose. Bottles of lemonade sit on a shelf. The scene continues, with pictures of a microscope, bottles of medicine, and a diploma that reads, "Doctor of Medicine." Printed: "My Mug."

44. Mugs

Premium Collectors Series. Milk glass. 10 oz. Anchor Hocking for Interstate Brands. 1980. $4-6 ea.

•Snoopy, grinning and wearing an Uncle Sam hat, is encircled by the words "Vote for the American Beagle." Woodstock, posing as an eagle, sits on the edge of the circle above Snoopy. Printed on the reverse side: "1980 Collectors Series #2."

•Snoopy, wearing an Uncle Sam hat and with arms outstretched, sits on top of his doghouse. Printed on the roof of the house "Put Snoopy in the White House." Printed on the reverse side: "1980 Collectors Series #3."

•Snoopy, wearing a red, white, and blue bow tie, is grinning and has his arms outstretched. Printed: "The People's Choice." Printed on the reverse side: "1980 Collectors Series #4."

45. Mugs

Snoopy poses with different colored letters of the alphabet. The letters I, O, Q, U, V, X, and Y were not made. Ceramic. 8 oz. Determined Productions. $6-8 ea.

•Snoopy, holding a flower, is sitting next to a red letter "Z". #1752.

•Snoopy is walking past a mustard-yellow letter "N". #1743.

•Snoopy is sitting next to a lime-green letter "W". #1751.

46. Mugs

Ceramic. 8 oz. Determined Productions. Mid-1970s. $6-8 ea.

•Snoopy is dancing inside a yellow circle. Printed inside the circle "Come Dance With Me Baby."

•Snoopy is the Flying Ace on his doghouse inside a red circle. Printed inside the circle: "Curse You, Red Baron."

•Snoopy leans on a golf club inside a green circle. Printed inside the circle: "You're Away."

43

44

45

47. Mugs

Ceramic. Determined Productions. Early 1980s. $6-8 ea.

•Snoopy sits in a club chair with a cup on its arm. Woodstock sits above Snoopy on the back of the chair. Printed on the reverse side: "This Has Been a Good Day." #1912.

•Charlie Brown stands between Snoopy, who has his hand on his heart, and Woodstock, who holds a flower. Printed on the reverse side: "How Can We Lose When We're So Sincere."

•Snoopy stands between Spike and Belle, who are seated. Printed on the reverse side: "Beagles Are My Favorite People."

48. Mug on Pedestal

•Snoopy sits in the snow, in front of his supper dish. Printed on the reverse side: "I Hate It When It Snows on My French Toast." Ceramic. #1187, Determined Productions. Mid-1970s. $5-7

Mugs

Ceramic. Determined Productions. 1980.

•Snoopy stretches in front of his typewriter atop his doghouse and says, "Yawn." On the reverse side, Woodstock sits with his typewriter on top of the words "I'm Not Worth A Thing Before Coffee Break!" $5-7

•Snoopy sits in front of his doghouse, his tongue hanging out, and says "Bleh!" Printed on the reverse side: "I Think I'm Allergic to Morning." #1992. $5-7

•Snoopy is lying on top of his doghouse. Printed on the reverse side: "I'm Not Worth A Thing Before Coffee Break!" #1993. $4-5

49. Mugs

Ceramic. Determined Productions. $8-10 ea.

•Snoopy is pictured as Joe Cool, a cowboy, a pirate, and Joe Gourmet. Woodstock and his friends copy Snoopy's outfits. #1223. 1977.

•A Rolls Royce limousine encircles the mug. Snoopy, dressed as a chauffeur, holds the door open for Woodstock, who is dressed in formal attire. 3-1/2"H. #1928. Late 1970s.

•Lucy looks at herself in a hand-held mirror. Snoopy, covering his eyes, and Woodstock watch. Printed on the reverse side: "How Can You Explain A Summer Sky, Or A Winter Moon, Or A Pretty Face?" Ceramic. Early 1980s.

50. Mugs

•Snoopy, as Joe Cool, stands in front of a yellow star. Printed on the reverse side: "Superstar." Ceramic. 18 oz. #1227, Determined Productions. 1977. $15-18

•Snoopy, as Joe Cool, stands in front of a rainbow. Printed on the reverse side: "Actually, We Joe Cools Are Scared To Death Of Chicks." Ceramic. 16 oz. #1226. 1977. $22-25

51. Mugs

Ceramic. Determined Productions.

•Charlie Brown, Peppermint Patty, and Snoopy ride a bicycle built for three, while Woodstock rides along in a basket. #1930. Early 1980s. $6-9

•Snoopy lies on his doghouse, which is surrounded by tall sunflowers. The graphics on this mug are embossed. 3-3/4"H. #1104. Mid-1970s. $15-18

46

47

49

48

50

of Everything." Charlie Brown paints Snoopy's doghouse, and Lucy brings him cookies. Woodstock and his friends are all around.

•Snoopy, in his vulture pose, dives out from a tree, frightening Lucy and Woodstock. He is thinking, "I Need A Release From My Inner Tensions!"

54. Mugs

Milk glass. 10 oz. Anchor Hocking. $4-6 ea.

•Snoopy, on his tummy, lies on top of his doghouse. Printed on the reverse side: "I Think I'm Allergic To Morning." 1976.

•Snoopy, wearing a helmet, rides on a skateboard in front of a yellow circle. Printed on the reverse side: "It's Great To Be An Expert." 1980.

•Snoopy, wearing headphones, is roller skating in front of a rainbow and clouds. Printed on the reverse side: "How Nice... They're Playing 'The Skater's Waltz.'" 1980.

•Snoopy, as the Flying Ace, sits on top of his doghouse. Printed on the reverse side: "Curse You, Red Baron!" 1976.

55. Mugs

Milk glass. 10 oz. Anchor Hocking. $4-6 ea.

•Snoopy, wearing his supper dish on his head and carrying a hobo pack, walks in front of Woodstock. Printed on the reverse side: "Snoopy, Come Home." 1976.

•Charlie Brown dances as Snoopy looks on. Printed on the reverse side: "I Feel Strangely Confident Today." 1976.

•Snoopy jogs past a landscape scene. Printed on the reverse side: "Keeping Fit Is Hard Work." 1980.

56. Mugs

Milk glass. 10 oz. Anchor Hocking. $4-6 ea.

•Snoopy sits, looking tired, as Woodstock brings him a cup of coffee. Printed on the reverse side: "I'm Not Worth A Thing Before Coffee Break!" 1976.

•Snoopy and Woodstock dance. Printed on the reverse side: "At Times Life Is Pure Joy." 1976.

•Snoopy, wearing a stocking cap, sits in front of his supper dish in the snow. Printed on the reverse side: "I Hate It When It Snows on My French Toast!" 1976.

•Snoopy, sitting, is hugging Woodstock inside a large red heart. Printed around the bottom: "Gee Somebody Cares." #1219. 1977. $6-8

52. Mugs

Stoneware. 3-3/8"H. Taylor International, division of Anchor Hocking. Late 1970s. $6-8 ea.

•Snoopy sits with his back against a piece of chocolate cake.

•Snoopy sits in front of a slice of cherry pie.

•Snoopy sits in front of a mug of hot chocolate with marshmallows.

•Snoopy, as Joe Cool, leans on a chocolate-covered donut.

53. Mugs

Came with a flattened box that pictured various mugs in the series. Ceramic. Determined Productions. Early 1980s. $6-8* ea.

•Charlie Brown lies in bed and says, "Six Fifty-nine is the Worst Time of Day!" Snoopy is seen through a window asleep on his doghouse.

•Snoopy sits in a director's chair wearing a beret and sunglasses and holding a megaphone. He is thinking, "Director

57. Mug with Candy

•Snoopy, wearing ice skates, scarf, and a stocking cap that reads, "Macy's," is a Thanksgiving Day parade balloon being held aloft by handlers on the ground. Printed: "Macy's Parade 1987." Ceramic. 10 oz. Made exclusively for Macy's. 1987. With or without original candy. $15-18

Mug

•This mug takes on the appearance of a tree trunk. The heart carved into it is surrounded by pink and red flowers. Woodstock sits on the handle, which resembles the branch of a tree. Stoneware. 12 oz. Teleflora. 1990. $4-6

58. Soup Mugs (commonly called a chili bowl)

•Snoopy is posed around the mug in various international costumes. Ceramic. 2-3/4"H. Determined Productions. Late 1970s. $20-25

•Snoopy is pictured around the mug in various poses. Ceramic. 2-3/4"H. Determined Productions. Late 1970s. $18-20

Chili Mugs

•Charlie Brown cooks chili as Snoopy, Lucy, and Woodstock wait to be served. Printed: "Wanted: World's Greatest Mug of Chili!" Ceramic. 2-3/4"H. Determined Productions. Late 1970s. $25-30

•A continuous scene pictures Snoopy, Woodstock, and his friends heading toward a campfire where Spike is cooking chili. Printed: "Come And Get It." Ceramic. 2-3/4"H. Determined Productions. Late 1970s. $25-30

FOOD AND CANDY

Foreign food items are included for informational purposes only. American food products are described and priced.

56

57

59. Peanut Butter from Australia

•Sanitarium Health Food Co. 1992.

Lollipops from England

•Early 1990s.

Corn Snacks from Japan

•Late 1980s.

Jelly

•Each jar depicts a different scene: Snoopy surfing, Snoopy floating in an inner tube, Lucy on a swing, and Charlie Brown flying his kite. Printed: "Collectible PEANUTS Glass." 18 oz. Kraft, Inc. Late 1980s. Unopened $8-10

Cereal from Japan

•Early 1990s.

Cola from England

•A.G. Barr & Co., Ltd. Early 1980s.

A&W Root Beer

•Snoopy, as Joe Cool, is pictured in different poses on A&W cans and bottles. Shown: 67.6 fl. oz. bottle. 1990. Unopened: $2-3

Frozen Dinners

•Snoopy is pictured in different poses with a thought balloon announcing the name of the dinner inside the package.

58

59

Printed: "Snoopy's Choice." Woodstock carries a sign that reads, "New!" The dinner comes with a microwave-safe dish that depicts Snoopy dancing. ConAgra Healthy Foods. Early 1990s. Empty box with dish: $2-3

Ice Cream Cones

•Snoopy, wearing roller skates, licks his lips while looking at a cone filled with ice cream. Printed: "Snoopy's Crazy Cones." Sold at the "Snoopy Ice Cream & Cookie Store," San Francisco, no longer in business. 1989. Unopened: $3-4

Nuts

•A smiling Charlie Brown, with arms outstretched, is pictured inside a circle. Printed: "Good Ol' Charlie Brown's." Available varieties: Peanuts, Unsalted peanuts, Party peanuts, Mixed nuts, and Mix & Stix. Available in cans and jars. Snoopy appears to the side of Charlie Brown, with a different thought balloon for each variety of nuts. Reverse sides feature different scenes with various characters. Georgia Food. 1987. Unopened: $6-8

Chewing Gum from Singapore

•Early 1990s.

Apple Drink from Canada

•SunPac. 1987.

Marshmallows from Japan

•Early 1980s.

Bubble Gum

•The lid and the bucket picture Lucy, Snoopy, Charlie Brown, Linus, Peppermint Patty, and Schroeder dressed in Halloween costumes. The lid is printed "Charlie Brown & Friends Super Bubble Gum Treat Bucket." The bucket is printed "125 Pieces Super Bubble Gum Treat Bucket." Leaf, Inc. 1994. Unopened: $5-7

Candy from Japan

•Early 1980s.

Cookies

•Snoopy is shown sitting in front of his doghouse eating cookies from a bag. The doghouse is printed with the type of cookie in the package: Honey grahams, cinnamon grahams, or chocolate grahams. The cookies come in the four shapes pictured on the package: Snoopy as Joe Cool, Snoopy smiling, Snoopy as the Flying Ace, and Snoopy eating cookies. Printed: "Cookies With A Little Character." Sold in 2-oz. and 10-oz. bags. Famous Amos Corp. Late 1980s. 2 oz.—$1-3, 10 oz.—$3-5

60. Cookies

•Snoopy, wearing ice skates, scarf, and a stocking cap that reads, "Macy's," is a Thanksgiving Day parade balloon being held aloft by handlers on the ground. Printed: "Fancy Cookie Assortment." Cardboard. 7-1/2" x 5-7/8". Made exclusively for Macy's. 1987. Empty box: $2-3 Unopened box: $7-9

Candy

•The box is shaped like Snoopy's doghouse. Snoopy is seated in front, dialing a telephone. Printed: "Perugina Snoopy's Hard Candy Treats." The reverse side depicts Snoopy as Joe Cool. Cardboard. 5" x 6". Made by Perugina exclusively for Macy's. 1987. Empty box: $1-2 Unopened box: $6-8

Candy

•The top of the container depicts Snoopy, as the Flying Ace, and Woodstock, on his doghouse. Printed: "Snoopy Macy's."

The cylindrical container pictures Snoopy, Woodstock, and his friends in various poses. Cardboard. 4"H x 3-1/2" diam. Printed: "Snoopy Treats Chocolate Covered Bananas Perugina." Made by Perugina exclusively for Macy's. 1987. Empty box: $3-5 Unopened box: $7-9

61. Pez Dispensers

The heads of the characters dispense the candy contained in the narrow body. The blister package contains one dispenser and two packs of the Pez candy and is printed "Pez Candy & Dispenser" and "Snoopy and the PEANUTS Gang." The packaging depicts Woodstock, Charlie Brown, and Snoopy on his doghouse. Plastic. 4"H. Pez Candy, Inc. 1990. $5-7* ea.

•Snoopy with his eyes closed.

•Snoopy with his eyes open.

•Charlie Brown.

•Lucy.

•Woodstock

Gumball Dispenser

•The dispenser is in the form of Charlie Brown standing next to a mailbox, printed "U.S. Mail." The blister package contains ten gumballs. The packaging depicts Linus blowing a bubble while Lucy watches. Printed: "Charlie Brown Gumball Pocket Pack Dispenser." Plastic. 3"H. #5034, Superior Toy & Manufacturing Co., Inc. 1987. $4-8 $10-15*

62. Candy Boxes

Shaped as the various PEANUTS characters, who are pictured on top. The boxes come filled with different types of candy. Shrink-wrapped. Plastic. States Plastic. 1989. Without candy: $5-7 ea. Unopened: $10-15 ea.

62

63

•Lucy. #1920-001.

•Charlie Brown. #1910-001.

•Snoopy dancing. #1900-001.

•Snoopy, dressed in formal attire, dancing. #1900-002

63. Candy Boxes

Boxes, shaped as states or countries, came filled with different types of candy. Shrink-wrapped. Plastic. States Plastic. 1989-1990. Without candy: $5-7 ea. Unopened: $10-15 ea.

•Snoopy, wearing a beret, is seated at a cafe table with the Eiffel Tower behind him. The box, in the shape of France, is printed "Vive La France!" #1240-002.

•Snoopy and Charlie Brown are depicted in ski gear on a box shaped like California. Printed: "Ski Mammoth Mountain." #1110-009

•Sally and Charlie Brown, dressed in beach attire, and Snoopy, dressed in diving gear, are pictured on a box shaped like California. #1110-011.

•Snoopy, dressed in green and holding a green top hat, dances on a box shaped like Ireland. Printed: "Ireland." #1220-004.

•Snoopy, Woodstock, and his friends are dressed in scout gear on a box shaped like California. Printed on a flag: "Camp Snoopy." #1110-010.

64. Candy Boxes

Shaped as various Hawaiian islands. Printed: "Aloha." Boxes came filled with different types of candy. Shrink-wrapped. Plastic. States Plastic. 1989-1990. Without candy: $5-7 ea. Unopened: $10-15 ea.

•Hawaii. Snoopy, wearing sunglasses, reclines against a palm tree. Woodstock, also wearing sunglasses, sits in the palm tree. #1310-003.

•Maui. Snoopy, a lei around his neck, is dancing in front of tropical flowers as Woodstock, also wearing a lei, flies overhead. #1330-002.

•Oahu. Snoopy and Woodstock ride a wave on the same surfboard. #1340-007.

•Kauai. Snoopy stands amid tropical flowers as Woodstock flies overhead. #1320-004.

65. Candy Boxes

Heart-shaped. Boxes came filled with different types of candy. Plastic. States Plastic. 1989-1990. Without candy: $5-7 ea. Unopened: $10-15 ea.

•Snoopy sits on his doghouse, surrounded by Woodstock and many of his friends, who are holding flowers. Printed: "I Love You." #1340-001.

•Sally gives a red heart to Linus. Printed: "Be Mine." #1340-002.

•Sally gives a red heart to Linus. Printed: "Happy Valentine's Day." #1340-003.

66. Candy Boxes

Boxes came filled with different types of candy. Shrink-wrapped. Plastic. States Plastic. 1989-1990. Without candy: $5-7 ea. Unopened: $10-15 ea.

•Snoopy, Woodstock and—dressed in green—Linus, Lucy, Peppermint Patty, Marcie, Sally, and Charlie Brown all dance among the shamrocks on a box in the shape of Ireland. Printed: "Happy St. Patrick's Day." #1220-005.

•Snoopy is seated holding a pennant that reads, "PEANUTS" on a box shaped as a football helmet. #1110-012.

•Snoopy, Woodstock, and Charlie Brown, all wearing red bow ties, are inside a circle. Printed around the circle is "40 Years of Happiness." Printed underneath the circle is "PEANUTS." #1340-008. 1990.

ICE BUCKETS

67. Ice Bucket

Musical and non-musical. A continuous scene features Peppermint Patty, Snoopy, Charlie Brown, Lucy, Linus, Woodstock, and Schroeder playing baseball. Printed: "Pow!" and "Bonk!" Plays "Theme from Love Story." 7"H x 8" diam. Musical: #276935. Non-musical: #276934. Schmid. 1973.

64

65

66

Musical: $300-325 Non-musical: $165-185 (comes with a non-graphic box that does not affect the value)

68. Ice Buckets

•Snoopy and Woodstock appear in formal attire walking in front of a continuous scene of a city skyline. Black. Vinyl bucket and handle. 10"H x 7-1/2" diam. #9003, Shelton Ware. 1979. $150-160

•Snoopy, Woodstock, and his friends dance around the ice bucket which is encircled by the striped colors of a rainbow. Handle and cover—lucite. Bucket—plastic. 8"H x 9" diam. #9002, Shelton Ware. 1979. $135-145

Highball Glasses

•A seated Snoopy is pictured around the glass against a rainbow background. In one scene, Woodstock is standing in a pitcher, while Snoopy's ears stand on end. In another scene, he holds a cherry and licks his lips. In the last scene, Snoopy holds a glass adorned with a lemon slice. Packaged in a set of eight. 9 oz. Anchor Hocking. 1978. $6-8 ea. $35-40*

JARS AND CANISTERS

69. Goodie Jars

Glass. Three sizes to a set. Lids come with a plastic insert to create a tight seal. Anchor Hocking. 1978.

•Snoopy, dressed as a chef, holds utensils in front of a table with ingredients on it. Woodstock brings him a cup. The word "Goodies" is repeated around Snoopy and Woodstock. 7-1/2"H. #3283N-444. $12-15

•Snoopy, dressed as a chef, carries a birthday cake. Woodstock and a friend fly behind him. The word "Goodies" is repeated around them. 7"H. #3282V-443. $10-14

•Snoopy, dressed as a chef, sits reading a cookbook with bowls and canisters in front of him. Woodstock sits on a canister. The word "Goodies" is repeated around them. 5-1/2"H. #3281U-442. $8-12

•Snoopy sits in front of a rainbow eating popcorn from a bowl. Reverse: Snoopy opens a box of candy in front of a rainbow as Woodstock watches. The word "Goodies" is printed on each side under the rainbow. 5-1/2"H. #3282-N-7795. $6-8

•Snoopy, in front of a rainbow, offers nuts to Woodstock. Reverse side: Snoopy stands in front of a rainbow with his hands together over his heart. The word "Goodies" is printed on each side under the rainbow. 7"H. #DK3281-7795. $7-9

•Snoopy offers a cookie jar to Woodstock who appears to be sitting on a rainbow. Reverse side: Snoopy is in front of a rainbow with candy in his hands. The word "Goodies" is printed on each side under the rainbow. 7-1/2"H. #3283-DH-7795. $10-12

70. Canisters

Three sizes to a set. Graphics wrap around the container. Tin. #037, Determined Productions. 1979. Large: $20-25 Medium: $18-20 Small: $12-15 Set: $50-55

•Snoopy, sitting, holds a large hero sandwich. Woodstock sits on one end of the hero. 5-3/4" diam. x 4-3/8"H.

•Snoopy, dressed as a chef, stands in a kitchen filled with cookware. Woodstock sits in a frying pan held by Snoopy. 6-3/4" diam. x 5"H.

•Snoopy sits at a cafe table around the canister in various poses. The word "Snoopy's" is printed around the lid and the word "Cafe" is printed on the can. 6-1/2" diam. x 7-3/4"H.

71. Canisters

Tin. Confections. 1989.

•Snoopy and Charlie Brown, wearing party hats, sit in front of a birthday cake. Printed: "Happy Birthday." 4-1/8" diam. x 6-1/2"H (1 qt.) #421-08-00. $10-12

•Snoopy, wearing a party hat, is surrounded by falling confetti. Printed: "Congratulations." 4-1/8" diam. x 6-1/2"H (1 qt.) $10-12

•Snoopy, Woodstock, Sally, Peppermint Patty, Lucy, Marcie, Charlie Brown, and Linus are dancing. Printed: "You're Terrific!" 4-1/8" diam. x 6-1/2"H (1 qt.) #432-08-00. $10-15

•Snoopy is dressed as Joe Cool Santa. Printed: "Have A Cool Yule!" 7-1/2" diam. x 10"H (2 gallons). #434-20-00. $15-20

•Snoopy, dressed as Santa, flies his decorated doghouse like a sleigh, with Woodstock and his friends as the reindeer. 7-1/2" diam. x 10"H (2 gallons). #435-20-00. $15-20

The PEANUTS Home Collection

• Snoopy hugs a big red heart. 7-1/2" diam. x 10"H (2 gallons). #433-20-00. $15-20

• Snoopy, Woodstock, Sally, Peppermint Patty, Lucy, Marcie, Charlie Brown, and Linus are dancing. Printed: "You're Terrific!" 7-1/2" diam. x 10"H (2 gallons). #432-20-00. $18-20

KEY CHAINS

72. Key Chains

Known as "Classics." Two-sided. Plastic. 3" x 3-1/2". Aviva. Early 1970s. $4-6 ea. $8-10*

• Snoopy, as the Flying Ace on his doghouse, thinks, "It's The Red Baron! He Has Me In His Sights!!" Reverse: Snoopy thinking, "Give My Regards To Broadway."

• Snoopy is standing and thinking, "I Should Have Stayed Home..." Reverse: Snoopy is surrounded by snowmen and thinks, "I Hate These Parties Where You Just Stand Around And Nobody Says Anything!"

• Lucy and Patty walk barefoot in the grass. Lucy says, "Running Around In The Grass In Your Bare Feet Can Be Very Exciting...." Reverse: Snoopy lying on his house thinking, "After A Few Years, However, The Excitement Wears Off!"

• Lucy pinches Snoopy's nose. The word "Beep" is printed. Reverse: Lucy says, "It's Been Three Hundred and Sixty-Four Days Since I Last Beeped You."

• Linus and Lucy are watching TV. Lucy says, "On Your Seventy-Fifth Birthday, I'll Bake You A Cake." Reverse: Linus is walking and saying, "Life Is More Pleasant When You Have Something To Look Forward To…"

• Woodstock is fast asleep on Snoopy's dog dish. Reverse: Woodstock obviously fell into the dish. Snoopy thinks, "That's Just What I Need…Feathers In My Drinking Water!"

• Peppermint Patty says to her dance partner, Snoopy, "I'm Sort Of Self-Conscious About Dancing With A Boy..." Reverse: As they dance, Peppermint Patty says, "But There's So Many Kids Here I Doubt If Anyone Will Even Notice Us…"

• The heads of Charlie Brown, Lucy, and Schroeder are pictured, with Lucy, saying, "I Read Where One Doctor Said That Human Arms Are Not Made For Pitching Baseballs." Schroeder asks, "What Are They Made For?" Reverse: Charlie Brown and Schroeder watch Lucy as she says, "Hugging!"

• Linus says "Bleah!" as he stands in the snow catching snowflakes with his tongue. Reverse: Linus says "Polluted Snowflakes!"

• Charlie Brown, speaking to Snoopy sitting on his doghouse, says, "It's Your Responsibility to Guard This House, This Yard and This Neighborhood. Reverse: Charlie Brown is in bed looking at Snoopy, who is under the covers and thinking, "I Can't Stand All That Responsibility!"

• Schroeder plays the piano. Lucy leans against it and says, "It Says Here That Some Scholars Feel That Beethoven Was Black." Reverse: Schroeder responds "Do You Mean To Tell Me That All These Years I've Been Playing 'Soul' Music?"

73. Key Chains

Brass. Sold in individual blister packages or as a loose assortment (#553000). Series #554000, Aviva. 1979. $4-6 ea. $8-10* ea.

• Snoopy holds a heart. 1-7/8"H.

• Snoopy as the Flying Ace. 1-7/8"H.

• Woodstock. 2"H.

• Snoopy on roller skates. 2"H.

• Snoopy holding a tennis racket. 1-7/8"H.

• Snoopy carrying skis. 1-7/8"H.

Key Chains

Lucite. Sold in individual blister packages or as a loose assortment (#556000). 1-1/2" x 1-1/2". #555000, Aviva. 1979. $3-4* ea.

• Snoopy, lying on his tummy, leans over the side of his doghouse, looking at Woodstock below.

• Snoopy, on his tummy, lies on a rainbow and looks down at Woodstock.

• Snoopy, as the Flying Ace, is on top of his doghouse being followed by the Red Baron in his airplane.

• Snoopy, as a crossing guard, holds a "Stop" sign as Woodstock and his friends cross. Printed: "Drive Carefully."

Key Chains

• Snoopy, holding a box of tea, wears an Indian headdress. Printed: "1776 * 1976." Wood. 2" diam. Aviva. 1976. $2-3

• Snoopy, dressed in a blue sweat suit, jogs with Woodstock. Lucite. 3-7/8"H. Aviva. 1979. $3-4

• Snoopy is pictured on a green cola bottle. Printed: "Snoopy." Lucite. 4"H. #112005, Quantasia. Mid-1980s. $3-4

• Snoopy appears to kick a soccer ball which is pictured above his head. Lucite. 3-7/8"H. #112010, Quantasia. Mid-1980s. $3-4

• Snoopy, wearing a suit, is disco dancing. Lucite. 3-1/2"H. Aviva. 1979. $3-4

• Snoopy carries a flag with a red heart on it. Several red hearts appear behind him as part of an outline around Snoopy. Leather. 3-1/2"H. Aviva. Mid-1970s. $1-3

• Shaped like a tee-shirt on a hanger. Snoopy holds a tennis racket to his heart. Printed: "Snoopy." Blister package shows Woodstock and his friends on a clothesline with clothes pins. Printed: "Snoopy Keychains." Plastic/lucite. 3"H. #552000, Aviva. 1979. $3-4*

• Snoopy lies on his tummy on top of the word "Love." Leather. 4"H. Aviva. Mid-1970s. $1-3

LUNCHBOXES

Back in the late 1980s a lunchbox price guide was published, provoking dealers and anyone owning a lunchbox to price them at extraordinarily high prices. Dealers even bought them up at higher prices than they would customarily pay. Collectors like myself bought them at higher prices. Then the bottom fell out. There might be some PEANUTS lunchboxes that command high prices, but surely not impossible prices!

The metal lunchboxes are so plentiful in all designs and colors that paying more than $40 for one in very good condition is foolish—you're sure to find one at a better price elsewhere. The eBay auction site provides a good example of that (and so does my attic). The plastic ones (not to be mistaken for vinyl) are new, and should not go for more than $5-8. Most have a PEANUTS decal.

Vinyl lunchboxes are more desirable because they are older and the material is very fragile. Yet they are available, and the price need not empty your wallet—though it is difficult to secure one in mint condition. You may find a lunchbox with the vinyl torn in places, or maybe the last kid to own it wrote his name in it, and it won't come out. The background on the vinyl lunchboxes came in several colors.

All of the lunchboxes, regardless of construction, came with a thermos. So many were made that you will never know if you have a thermos from the 1960s, the 1970s, or the 1980s.

74. Lunchboxes

•Doghouse-shaped. Printed: "Have Lunch With Snoopy." Front: Snoopy is lying on his back eating a sandwich. Reverse side: Snoopy is lying on his tummy reading a book.

Printed: "Go To School With Snoopy." The thermos pictures Charlie Brown, Linus, Lucy, Schroeder, and Snoopy playing baseball. Their names appear below each character. Metal. #658, King Seeley Thermos. 1968. $40-45

•Printed: "PEANUTS" on front and back. Charlie Brown, Linus, and Lucy watch Snoopy, as the Flying Ace, on top of his doghouse. Reverse side: Snoopy sits on Schroeder's piano as Charlie Brown, Linus, and Lucy watch Schroeder play. The top, bottom, left, and right sides feature comic strip panels. A metal thermos is included. Metal. #1448, King Seeley Thermos. 1969-1975. $25-40

•Printed: "PEANUTS" on front and back. Charlie Brown sits at Lucy's psychiatrist booth, as Lucy leans back in her seat behind the booth. Linus stands behind Charlie Brown. Woodstock and Snoopy, as the Flying Ace, appear in the foreground. Reverse side: Snoopy kisses Peppermint Patty on the nose. Lucy stands behind Snoopy, and Charlie Brown rests against a tree. The top, bottom, left, and right sides feature comic strip panels. A plastic thermos is included. Metal. #1448, King Seeley Thermos. 1974. $25-35

•Printed: "PEANUTS" on front and back. Charlie Brown leans back on the pitching mound, ready to throw a baseball. In the upper left-hand corner is a four-panel comic strip about baseball. Reverse side: Snoopy, Woodstock, and his friends, all dressed in scouting gear, are on a hike. In the upper right-hand corner is a four-panel comic strip about going on a hike. The top, bottom, left, and right sides feature comic strip panels. Available in other colors. A plastic thermos is included. Metal. #1448, King Seeley Thermos. 1974-1976. $25-38

75. Lunchboxes

•Printed: "PEANUTS" on front and back. Snoopy looks up into his open mailbox. A three-panel comic strip is to the right. Reverse side: Snoopy, wearing a baseball glove, covers his heart with his cap, as Woodstock plays an organ. A three-panel comic strip is to the right. Left side: Snoopy, walking, wears a motorcycle helmet. A three-panel comic strip is above. Right side: Snoopy swings a tennis racket. A three-panel comic strip is above. A plastic thermos is included. Vinyl. King Seeley Thermos. Mid-1970s. $50-60

•Printed: "PEANUTS" on front and back. Charlie Brown flies his kite as Linus, Lucy, and Snoopy watch. Reverse side: Charlie Brown stands on the pitcher's mound surrounded by Linus, Schroeder, Lucy, and Snoopy. Left side: Linus pats birds on the head, while Lucy and Charlie Brown peek out from behind a tree. Right side: Charlie Brown stands in front of Snoopy, as the Flying Ace, on his doghouse. Available in other colors. A plastic thermos is included. Vinyl. King Seeley Thermos. Mid-1960s. $50-60

•Printed: "PEANUTS" on front and back. Charlie Brown swings a baseball bat. Lucy gets ready to catch the ball from behind him, as Linus runs toward them. Reverse side: Lucy leans on Schroeder's piano as he plays. Charlie Brown and Linus stand in the background. Snoopy and Woodstock dance in foreground. Left side: Snoopy, as Joe Cool, stands in front of his doghouse as Linus walks by. Lucy looks up a tree at Woodstock and Snoopy, sitting in a nest. Available in other colors. A plastic thermos is included. Vinyl. #6168/3, King Seeley Thermos. 1973. $50-60

Lunch Bag

•Binocular-shaped bag, with a zipper and handle, this case depicts Snoopy and Woodstock dancing, as Charlie Brown watches. Printed: "PEANUTS." A plastic thermos, featuring

Charlie Brown swinging a baseball bat is included. Vinyl. #6638, King Seeley Thermos. 1975. $30-35

76. Thermos

Wide mouth. Individual characters are pictured on the lids. Available in different colors. Plastic. 3-2/3" diam. Thermos, a division of King Seeley. $3-4 ea.

- Charlie Brown. #1155. Late 1970s.
- Snoopy as the Flying Ace. #155/3. Early 1980s.
- Lucy. #1155. Late 1970s.

MAGNETS

77. Magnets

Plastic. Approximately 2"H. Butterfly. 1981-1982. $2-4 ea.

- Snoopy and Woodstock stand with a mug of root beer.
- Snoopy is wearing a helmet and carrying a football.
- Snoopy is sitting, holding a letter.
- Snoopy is wearing a goalie's glove.
- Snoopy is sitting, holding a telephone to his ear.
- Snoopy is holding a hockey stick.
- Snoopy is wearing a baseball cap and glove.

Magnets

Plastic. Approximately 2"H. Series #2402, Butterfly. 1979. $2-4 ea.

- Snoopy is sitting with a slice of watermelon on his lap.
- Snoopy, as Joe Cool, drinks root beer from a mug.
- Snoopy, dressed in formal attire, stands in front of a star.
- Snoopy is holding a tennis racket.
- Snoopy is lying on a heart.
- Snoopy, wearing a stocking cap, sleeps in a crescent moon.
- Snoopy, sitting, hugs Woodstock.
- Snoopy is dancing in front of a jukebox.
- Snoopy, wearing a raccoon coat, carries a flag that reads, "Rah."
- Snoopy, dressed as a chef, holds a pie.
- Snoopy rides on a skateboard.
- Snoopy is sitting on top of a CB radio.

Magnets

Plastic. Approximately 2"H. Series #1526050, Butterfly. 1984. $2-4 ea.

- Snoopy is dribbling a basketball.
- Snoopy, as Joe Cool, is throwing a Frisbee.
- Snoopy is holding a straw hat and cane.

- Snoopy is roller-skating.
- Snoopy is sitting, eating a hamburger.
- Snoopy is carrying Woodstock in his nest.
- Snoopy is dressed as a scout.
- Snoopy and Woodstock shake hands in front of a rainbow.
- Snoopy, as the Flying Ace, stands in front of his doghouse.
- Snoopy is lying on top of the word "Love."
- Snoopy is jogging. The number "1" appears on his running gear.
- Snoopy, wearing a beret, holds palette and paintbrush.

78. Magnets

Rubber. Available in different colors. Sizes vary from 1-1/4" to 2". Simon Simple. 1969-1970. $4-6 ea.

- Charlie Brown and Snoopy are walking.
- Linus is sitting with his blanket.
- Woodstock is sitting at a typewriter.
- Snoopy is standing.
- Charlie Brown stands with one hand under his chin; the other holds the opposite elbow.
- Lucy is sitting at her psychiatrist booth.
- Charlie Brown, with his head in his hands, and Lucy lean on a wall.
- Snoopy sits at a desk. Woodstock is on top of a book on the desk.
- Woodstock is smiling.
- Charlie Brown is throwing a baseball from the pitcher's mound.
- Lucy is jumping rope.
- Snoopy, with his head in his hands, rests his elbows on a tree stump.
- Schroeder is playing his piano as Lucy brings him flowers.

Magnets

Premium. Rubber. 1-5/6"H. Rival. 1974. $4-6 ea.

- Woodstock with outstretched wings.
- Snoopy, as the Flying Ace.

Magnets

Glitter. Plastic. 1-1/2" to 2-1/4". Series #7650-5, Butterfly. 1983. $2-4 ea.

• Snoopy, on his tummy, lies on a heart.

• Snoopy rides on a shooting star that has a rainbow tail.

• Snoopy is sitting next to a large apple.

• Snoopy is sitting in front of an ice cream cone.

• Snoopy and Woodstock sit in front of Snoopy's doghouse.

• Snoopy stands next to a treble clef.

• Snoopy, on his tummy, lies on a strawberry.

• Snoopy is sitting next to a pizza pie.

• Snoopy lies in a crescent moon which has stars underneath.

• Snoopy sits next to a large flower.

• Snoopy, on his tummy, lies across a slice of watermelon.

• Snoopy rests against two large cherries.

79. Magnets

Featured both early drawings of the characters' faces with their names below and full-figured drawings with no names. Full-figured magnets were sold in packages, four to a set. Magnets also came in yellow. Both types of drawings were available as pinback buttons in yellow and white. Metal. 7/8". Peanuts characters assorted—#MB-2. Snoopy assorted—#MB-3, Simon Simple. 1969-1970. $5-8 ea. Set: $40-45*

• Snoopy.

• Lucy.

• Pig-Pen (sic).

• Charlie Brown in baseball gear. Set #MB-2.

• Charlie Brown.

• Shermy.

• Patty.

• Linus sitting with his blanket. Set #MB-2.

• Schroeder.

• Linus.

• Violet.

• Snoopy sitting. Set #MB-3.

MISCELLANEOUS KITCHEN ITEMS

80. Cake Pans

Snoopy or Charlie Brown versions. A plastic face is included to transfer to the finished cake. Wilton Enterprises. 1986. $25-35 ea.

• Snoopy, as the Flying Ace atop his doghouse, wearing his scarf. 10" x 12". #1821-1319.

• Charlie Brown wears a baseball cap and glove. 13" x 11". #1821-1320.

81. Corn on the Cob Set

• Snoopy is depicted seated in the corn cob dish. Comes with two metal-pronged corn cob holders with Snoopy, as the Flying Ace, on top. Plastic. #60, Wecolite. 1989. $4-6*

Bottle Caps

• Woodstock, wearing a green scout hat, sits on top of each bottle cap. Bottle caps were also available with Lucy, Charlie Brown, and Snoopy as the Flying Ace. Plastic. #59, Wecolite. 1989. $4-6*

Ice Cream Scoop

• Snoopy, appearing to be lying on his tummy, is the handle of the scoop. Plastic. #57, Wecolite. 1989. $5-7*

82. Date Book with Coupons

• This mini book, free from Payless Drug Store, contains coupons for Ambassador cards and an order form for a free canvas coupon organizer. Paper. $1.00

Coupon Organizer

• Snoopy is pictured sitting and reading. Printed: "Greeting Cards With Heart!...Ambassador." Blue canvas. 7-1/2" x 3-1/2". Ambassador. 1990. $5-9

83. Gourmet Chef Outfit

• Apron and hat. Woodstock, with chef's hat, sits on a pepper mill watching Snoopy, also wearing a chef's hat, as he makes a salad. Cotton. Adult large: #8792. Child's medium: #8791. Child's small: #8790. Determined Productions. Mid-1970s. Adult $15-20** Child's $12-14**

Cutting Board

• Woodstock, with chef's hat, sits on a pepper mill watching Snoopy, also in a chef's hat, mix a salad. Pictured side is for serving; reverse side for cutting. Plastic. 8" x 10", with 5" handle. Brookpark. 1979. $45-50

Cake Plate on Pedestal

•Snoopy stands in front of bakery showcase, wearing a chef's hat and holding a cake. Woodstock and his friends complete the scene. Plastic. 12" diam. Brookpark. 1979. $50-55*

Ice Cream Maker

•Snoopy and Woodstock are pictured holding ice cream cones. Available in pink or blue. Plastic with metal. #17-WSP 4488817, Danvier/Nikkai Industries. 1988. $20-25 $30-38*

84. Placemats

•Snoopy is lying on top of his doghouse. Sold individually. Vinyl. 17-3/4" x 13". #4041, Determined Productions. 1974. $3-5 ea.

Recipe Box

•Hinged box with a different scene on each of five sides. Top: Snoopy, dressed as a chef, and sporting a handlebar mustache, throws a pizza in the air as Woodstock watches, seated at a cafe table. A sign hangs on Snoopy's doghouse printed "Snoopy's Pizza Palace." Front: Snoopy, as the Flying Ace, sits at a cafe table and is served his supper dish by Lucy, dressed as a waitress. Back: Lucy and Charlie Brown sit drinking lemonade. Lucy asks, "How Do You Like The Chocolate Lemonade?" Right side: Sally is scooping ice cream from a container printed "Spumoni" to make cones. Left side: Charlie Brown scoops food into Snoopy's supper dish. Metal. 3-1/2"H x 5"W x 3"D. #250EBC152-4, Hallmark. Late 1970s. $6-12

85. Pumpkin Carving Kit

•Snoopy, appearing to be lying on his tummy, is the handle of the serrated carver. A scoop for removing the pumpkin's insides is included. The blister package features Linus, Sally, Snoopy, and Woodstock sitting in a pumpkin patch. #554, Trade Source International. Late 1980s. $4-6*

Pumpkin Painting Magic

•The blister package, depicting Snoopy painting a jack-o'-lantern, contains red, white, yellow, green, blue, and black paint pots and a paintbrush. #552, Trade Source International. Late 1980s. $2-4*

86. Waffle Baker

•The waffles are shaped in the form of Snoopy's head. Instruction/recipe guide is included. #WM-2, Salton/MAXIM Housewares, Inc. 1991. $25-30 $40-60*

Sandwich Maker

•Makes sandwiches in the shapes of Charlie Brown's and Snoopy's heads. Instructions and a recipe guide are included. The box pictures the finished product. #SA-12, Salton/MAXIM Housewares, Inc. 1992. $25-30 $50-60*

PARTY GOODS

Hallmark does not have a complete archive, and since I've been collecting longer than the average age of most of their staff, it was difficult to determine the exact year a Hallmark item was manufactured. For the future, a good idea would be to mark the year on the item when you buy it new.

There are several ways to help you determine the age fairly accurately. We know that, of late, Woodstock usually appears with Snoopy. If you don't see Woodstock, it will be prior to 1971. In place of Woodstock you may see "birds." The birds were the forerunners of Woodstock. His beak changed drastically from the early 1970s through the 1990s. It went from very pointed to being slowly rounded out. The early items featured some of the older characters, such as Violet, Shermy, and Patty (not Peppermint Patty.) Look at Snoopy. Hasn't he changed in appearance?

In front of the letters on a Hallmark item, you can find numbers. These numbers represent the price. For example: 35TC404-1. In this case the price was 35 cents. If this were a card, you can be assured it's not from the 1990s!

Many of these hints will be helpful with other items as well. So, if there is some overlapping, such as late 1960s/early 1970s, you can now understand why.

87. Cake Decoration Kits

•The set includes Snoopy, as the Flying Ace, Woodstock and friends, ten candle hold-

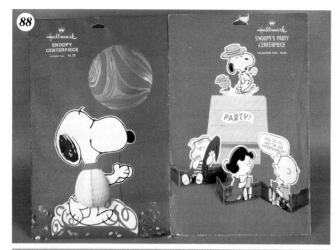

ers, and the words "Happy Birthday!" Sugar candy. #100PF97-2, Hallmark. Mid-1970s. $15-20**

•A center design features Sally, Schroeder, Lucy, and Charlie Brown carrying Snoopy, with Woodstock on his head in a supper dish, on their shoulders. Printed: "Hail! Hail! The Gang's All Here!" The kit includes ten candle holders and the words "Happy Birthday!" Sugar candy and paper. #150PCD97-4, Hallmark. Mid-1970s. $15-20**

•A center design features Charlie Brown and Snoopy dancing. Charlie Brown says, "Hooray for Birthdays!" The kit includes ten candle holders and the words "Happy Birthday!" Sugar candy and paper. #169PCD7521, Ambassador. Late 1970s. $15-20**

88. Centerpieces

•Snoopy is walking, holding a pink, orange, and red balloon. Printed on package: "Snoopy Centerpiece." Cardboard and tissue paper. 14"H. #175CP98-3, Hallmark. 1974. $10-12**

•Snoopy and Woodstock are dancing on Snoopy's doghouse, holding canes and wearing straw hats. Printed: "Party!" Linus, holding his blanket, and Lucy and Charlie Brown holding cups, sit on the grass below. Charlie Brown asks, "How Do You Like The Live Entertainment?" Printed on package: "Snoopy's Party Centerpiece." Cardboard. 14-1/4"H. #200CP97-4, Hallmark. Mid-1970s. $8-10**

89. Centerpieces

•Snoopy is holding a kite, and is tangled up in the kite's string. Printed on package: "PEANUTS Snoopy." Cardboard and tissue paper. 12"H. #150CP97-1, Hallmark. 1969. $10-14**

•Snoopy lies on top of his doghouse. Woodstock stands on his tummy. Cardboard and tissue paper. 15"H. Hallmark. 1969. $10-14**

90. Centerpieces

•Snoopy, as the Flying Ace, is sitting on top of his doghouse, which is riddled with bullet holes. Printed on package: "Snoopy and the Red Baron." Cardboard. 18"H. #150CP97-5, Hallmark. 1969. $10-14**

•Schroeder plays his piano while Snoopy dances on top and Woodstock watches. Printed on package: "Party with PEANUTS Centerpiece." Cardboard and tissue paper. 10-1/4"H. #189CP118J, Ambassador. Late 1970s. $7-9**

91. Centerpieces

•Schroeder plays his piano while Snoopy, Woodstock and his friends in party hats, and Charlie Brown and Sally dance around him. A birthday cake is on the piano. Printed on package: "PEANUTS Happy Birthday Centerpiece." Cardboard and tissue paper. 8"H. #350CP277-8, Hallmark. Early 1980s. $6-8**

•Snoopy dances on his doghouse as Lucy, Charlie Brown, and Linus stand in the grass and watch. Woodstock stands on Charlie Brown's head, while the others wear party hats. Printed on package: "Snoopy and Friends Centerpiece." Cardboard. 15-1/2"H. #150CP60J, Ambassador. Mid-1970s. $10-12**

•Snoopy as the Flying Ace, Charlie Brown, Linus, Woodstock, and Lucy ride on a Ferris wheel. Printed: "Happy Birthday." Printed on package: "PEANUTS Happy Birthday Centerpiece." Cardboard. 15-1/4"H. #300CP117-4, Hallmark. Early 1980s. $6-8**

92. Centerpiece

•Snoopy, Peppermint Patty, Charlie Brown carrying a kite, Marcie and Linus walk under a rainbow. Woodstock holds onto one of three balloons above the rainbow. Printed on package: "PEANUTS Rainbow Party Centerpiece." Cardboard. 10-1/4"H. #175CP116-2, Hallmark. Late 1970s. $5-8**

• Snoopy, wearing a hat and holding an ornament, decorates a Christmas tree. Woodstock, with a halo on his head, stands on the top of the tree. Woodstock's friends are pictured on the garland that encircles the tree. Printed on package: "Snoopy 'N Friends Christmas Decoration." Cardboard and tissue paper. 15"H. #350XHB632-3, Hallmark. Early 1980s. $7-9**

95. Centerpieces

• Snoopy, wearing a football helmet, watches as Woodstock attempts to kick a football. Printed on package: "Super Snoopy Centerpiece." Cardboard and tissue paper. 12-3/8"H. #150CP102-9, Hallmark. Late 1970s. $6-8**

• Snoopy, wearing a green leprechaun hat and holding a shamrock, dances in a patch of shamrocks. Printed on package: "Snoopy's Shamrock." Cardboard and tissue paper. 13"H. #125SHD7-2, Hallmark. Mid-1970s $6-8**

• Linus, with his head in his hands, leans his elbows on a pumpkin. Snoopy sits inside a pumpkin with the pumpkin's top on his head. He holds a sign that reads, "Welcome Great Pumpkin." Printed on package: "Linus and the Great Pumpkin." Cardboard and tissue paper. 13"H. #150HYP14-4, Hallmark. 1968. $18-22**

96. Centerpieces

• Snoopy lies on his tummy on top of a heart. Linus sits, and Charlie Brown and Lucy stand around the heart with smaller hearts at their feet. Printed on package: "Snoopy's Heart." Cardboard. 11-1/4"H. #150VCP3-2, Hallmark. Early 1970s. $10-12**

• Snoopy, as the Flying Ace, and Woodstock, wearing an army helmet, are shown walking. Snoopy is thinking, "I Shall Go Into The Village And Quaff A Few Root Beers…" Printed on package: "Snoopy Centerpiece." Cardboard and tissue paper. 17-1/2"H. #175CP97-2, Hallmark. Mid-1970s. $10-12**

93. Card Holder

• Snoopy, dressed as Santa, is the engineer of a two-car train that holds Christmas cards. Printed on package: "PEANUTS Express Card Holder." Cardboard. 11"H. #250XCH46-6, Hallmark. Late 1970s. $8-10**

Centerpieces

• Snoopy, wearing a stocking cap, scarf, and holding an ornament, and Woodstock, on top of a Christmas tree and holding a star, decorate the tree on top of Snoopy's doghouse. The doghouse has a snow-covered roof and is decorated with lights and stockings. Printed on package: "Snoopy Christmas." Cardboard and tissue paper. 15"H. #275XCP17-1, Hallmark. Late 1970s. $7-9**

94. Centerpiece

• Snoopy, wearing a stocking cap, and with a bag of candy canes at his feet, strings lights on the front of his doghouse. Woodstock stands on top of the doghouse, helping with the lights. Printed on package: "PEANUTS Holiday Trimmings Centerpiece." Cardboard. 10-3/16"H. #250XHD801-6, Hallmark. Late 1970s. $7-9**

•Snoopy, along with Woodstock and his friends, ride on a two-piece cart containing a large and small Easter Egg. Printed: "Happy Easter." Printed on package: "Easter Beagle-Mobile Table Decoration." Cardboard and tissue paper. 10"L. #350EHM251-6, Hallmark. Mid-1980s. $5-8**

•Snoopy stands behind a booth printed "Sensational Valentine Kisses" on top and "The Kisser Is In" on the bottom. Woodstock and his friends line up in front. Lucy stands next to the booth with her hands covering her face. Printed on package: "PEANUTS Valentine Celebration Centerpiece." Cardboard. 10-1/2"H. #175VCP1-2, Hallmark. Late 1970s. $8-10**

97. Coasters

Paper. Hallmark. Late 1970s. $3-4** ea.

•Snoopy and Woodstock are dancing. 3-1/4" diam. #75CO118J.

•Woodstock sips a drink with a straw from a rainbow-striped cup. 3-1/4" diam. #75CO1162.

•Woodstock, wearing a stocking cap, balances a candy cane on his beak. 3-1/4" x 3-1/4". #75XCO46.

•Snoopy putts a golf ball toward the hole. 3-1/4" diam. #75CO1194.

98. Coasters

Paper. 3-1/4" diam. Hallmark. Mid-1970s. $3-5** ea.

•Snoopy, as the Flying Ace, stands with his paw in the air. #50CO972.

•Snoopy and Woodstock, on top of the doghouse. Snoopy says, "Drinks are on the House." #50XCO233.

•Snoopy, wearing a stocking cap, rides on a sled with a large sack of gifts. Printed: "Merry Christmas to All!" #75XCO391.

99. Cups

•Snoopy sips Lucy's drink with a straw, and Charlie Brown, holding a cup, watches. Lucy says, "Yuk! Beagle Germs!" Six 9-oz. paper cups with handles. Hallmark. Mid-1970s. $4-6**

•Linus, head in hand, leans his elbows on a pumpkin. Snoopy sits on top of a pumpkin. A sign in the pumpkin patch reads, "Welcome Great Pumpkin." Eight 9-oz. paper cups with handles. #55-HDC-14-4, Hallmark. 1968. $6-8**

•Schroeder plays his piano, as Lucy brings him drink and a piece of cake with a heart on it. Flowers and hearts appearing as musical notes surround the cup. Six 9-oz. paper cups with handles. Hallmark. Mid-1970s. $5-7**

•Snoopy, as the Flying Ace, walks up to his doghouse, kisses it (Printed: "SMAK"), and then thinks, "I Love My Sopwith Camel!" Eight 9-oz. paper cups with handles. Hallmark. Mid-1970s. $5-7**

•A sea monster, spiders, and Lucy scare Snoopy and Woodstock, Linus, and Peppermint Patty riding in individual boats. Snoopy hugs Woodstock tightly thinking, "Yipes!" Printed: "Yiii!" and "Eeeck!" Eight 9-oz. paper cups. #DC117-4, Hallmark. Late 1970s. $3-4**

•Snoopy dances holding a lace-trimmed heart. Lucy and Linus, also holding hearts, watch along with Charlie Brown, who doesn't have one. Eight 9-oz. paper cups with handles. #65VDC3-2, Hallmark. Early 1970s. $5-7**

•Snoopy dances while flying a kite. Lucy and Linus walk behind him. Eight 9-oz. paper cups with handles. #49DC97-1, Hallmark. Early 1970s. $5-7**

100. Glasses

•Snoopy, featured with a pink, red, and orange balloon, poses differently on each glass. Woodstock and his friends appear with Snoopy on one glass. A different thought balloon appears on each. Plastic. Four 10 oz. #125DC60M, Ambassador. 1974. $24-28**

101. Glasses

•Snoopy dances holding a lace-trimmed heart. Lucy and Linus, also holding hearts, watch along with Charlie Brown, who doesn't have one. Plastic. Eight 10 oz. #150VDC3-2, Hallmark. Mid-1970s. $10-12**

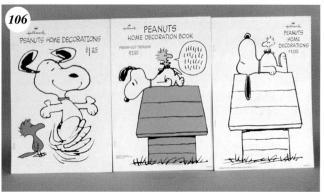

102. Glasses

•Snoopy dancing, Linus sitting with his blanket, Lucy frowning, and Charlie Brown with his baseball bat and glove, are pictured individually on each glass along with a thought or talk balloon. The packaging contains each character's name printed below the glasses. Plastic. Four 10 oz. #125DC60K, Ambassador. Mid-1970s. $18-22**

103. Cups

•Snoopy, as the Flying Ace, is pictured individually in various poses on and off his doghouse, with a different thought balloon on each glass. Woodstock appears on one glass. The packaging is printed "Adventures of W. W. 1 Flying Ace" and "Snoopy and his Mechanic Woodstock." Plastic. Four 10 oz. #125DC972, Hallmark. Mid-1970s. $20-25**

104. Cups

•Snoopy, as the Flying Ace, is pictured in various poses on and off his doghouse, with a different thought balloon on each glass. The packaging is printed "Snoopy and the Red Baron" and "Adventures of World War 1 Flying Ace." Plastic. Four 10 oz. #125DC97-5, Hallmark. Mid-1970s. $20-25**

105. Glasses

•Snoopy and Woodstock with tennis rackets are shown in various poses. Yellow tennis balls encircle the glass. Printed: "Anyone for Doubles?" Plastic. Four 16 oz. #200DC117-2, Hallmark. Late 1970s. $5-8**

•Snoopy, with tennis racket and tennis balls, seen in various poses. Green tennis balls encircle the glass. Printed: "Whap!" and "There's Nothing Like Service With A Smile!" Plastic. Four 16 oz. #200DC117-2, Hallmark. Late 1970s. $5-8**

106. Decoration Books

Press-out designs. Cardboard. 9"W x 13"H. Hallmark. 1969. $10-15 ea.

•Snoopy is dancing as a red Woodstock watches. #125HD97-7.

•Snoopy, on his tummy, lies on his doghouse, which is orange. Woodstock sits on Snoopy's back chirping. #100HD97-5.

•Snoopy lies on his back on his doghouse. Woodstock sits on his tummy. #100HD96-4.

107. Decoration Books

Valentine's Day theme press-out designs. Cardboard. Hallmark. $5-8 ea.

•Snoopy, standing on his toes, reaches up to give Woodstock, in his nest, a heart. Snoopy thinks, "Happy Valentine's Day." 8"W x 11-1/8"H. #100VHD1-2. Early 1980s.

•Snoopy, Woodstock, and friends are surrounded by hearts. Snoopy paints a heart with the words "Happy Valentine's Day!" 7-3/4"W x 12"H. #VHM66-3. Mid-1980s.

•Snoopy holds a Valentine and thinks, "There's Nothing More Romantic Than a Pizza-scented Valentine!" 8"W x 11-1/8"H. #125VHD250-7. Early 1980s.

108. Decoration Books

St. Patrick's Day theme press-outs. Cardboard. 7-3/4"W x 12"H. Hallmark. Late 1980s. $4-6 ea.

• Snoopy and Woodstock, wearing green leprechaun hats, jump over a pot of gold coins that's surrounded by shamrocks and more coins. Snoopy thinks, "If Your Irish Heart Is Happy, Let Your Irish Feet Show It!" #SHM69-6.

• Snoopy is lying on his doghouse, upon which Woodstock and his friends have painted "Happy St. Patrick's Day!" #SHM69-3.

109. Decoration Books

Easter theme press-outs. Cardboard. Hallmark.

• Snoopy, wearing a top hat, rides in an Easter basket on wheels surrounded by colored eggs. The basket is being pulled by Woodstock and his friend. Printed: "Easter Parade." 8"W x 11-1/4"H. #125EHD252-1. Mid-1980s. $4-6

• Snoopy lies on his doghouse with an Easter egg balanced on his nose and Woodstock sitting on his tummy. 8"W x 13"H. #100EHD16-9. Mid-1970s. $5-8

• Snoopy, surrounded by flowers, holds an Easter basket filled with colored eggs, and tosses one to Woodstock. He thinks, "Have A Hippity-Hoppity-Happy Easter!" 7-3/4"W x 12"H. #EHM608-3. Mid-1980s. $4-6

110. Decoration Books

Graduation theme press-outs. Cardboard. Hallmark. $4-6 ea.

• Snoopy, wearing a graduation cap and holding a diploma, thinks, "Congratulations Are In Order!" He is looking up at Woodstock and his friends standing on top of one another, wearing graduation caps and holding banners printed "Bravo!", "Hurrah!", and "You Did It!" 8"W x 11-1/4"H. #150GHM250-2. Mid-1980s.

• Snoopy and Woodstock, wearing graduation robes, toss their caps into the air. Snoopy thinks, "Hats Off To The Grads!" 7-3/4"W x 12"H. #GHM250-7. Mid-1980s.

• Snoopy, wearing a graduation cap and gown, looks at a sign printed "Good Times Ahead." 8"W x 11-1/4"H. #100GHD4-4. Mid-1970s.

111. Decoration Books

Press-outs. Cardboard. Hallmark. Mid-1980s. $4-6 ea.

• Snoopy and Woodstock wear football helmets. Woodstock, flapping his feathers, chirps at Snoopy, who holds a football and thinks, "Everybody Wants To Be Quarterback!" 7-7/8"W x 11-1/8"H. #125HD253-3.

• Snoopy plays soccer with Woodstock and his friends. Printed: "I Get A Kick Out Of School!" 7-1/8"W x 12"H. #FHM996-2.

112. Decoration Books

Halloween theme press-outs. Cardboard. Hallmark.

• Snoopy, wearing a witch's hat, and Woodstock ride a broomstick in front of a crescent moon. 7-3/4"W x 12"H. #HHM782. 1989. $5-8

• Snoopy, Linus, and Woodstock sit in a pumpkin patch. 7"W x 13"H. #100HHD4-9. Mid-1970s. $8-12

113. Decoration Books

Press-outs. Cardboard. Hallmark. $4-6 ea.

• Snoopy and Charlie Brown sit at a table in front of a Thanksgiving feast. Charlie Brown says, "Thanksgiving Means

Roasted Turkey, Mashed Potatoes, Pumpkin Pie..." Snoopy thinks "...Cranberry Pizza!" 8"W x 11-1/4"H. Late 1970s.

•Snoopy, dressed as President Abraham Lincoln, thinks, "Four Score and Seven Thousand Hours to Go Until Vacation..." 8"W x 11-1/4"H. #150HD251-1. Mid-1980s.

•Snoopy and Woodstock jump into a pile of leaves. Printed: "Cowabunga!" 7-3/4"W x 12"H. #HM995-6. Late 1980s.

114. Decoration Books

Christmas theme press-out designs. Cardboard. Hallmark. $5-8 ea.

•Snoopy lies on his doghouse, decorated with lights and garland, and thinks, "There's Holiday Happiness in the Air!" Woodstock, wearing a stocking cap, flies overhead pulling a banner that reads, "Season's Greetings." 8"W x 11-1/4"H. #125XHD251-9. Mid-1980s.

•Snoopy, dressed as Santa and holding a sack of toys, stands in front of a lit fireplace decorated with garland, candles, holiday cards, and Woodstock in a stocking. 7-7/8"W x 12"H. #XHM85-7. Late 1980s.

•Snoopy stands in the snow while listening to Woodstock and his friends sing. They are all wearing knit caps and scarves. Snoopy thinks, "Christmas Puts a Carol in Your Heart!" 8"W x 11-1/4"H. #XHM843-5. Late 1980s.

115. Decoration Books

Christmas theme press-out designs. Cardboard. Hallmark. $4-6

•Snoopy, Lucy, Linus, and Charlie Brown are depicted as the different ornaments that can be made from the press-out designs. 8"W x 11-1/4"H. #22XHD772-9. Late 1980s.

•Snoopy's head is seen through the center of a Christmas wreath. Printed: "Merry Christmas." 8"W x 11-1/4"H. #100XHD28-4. Late 1970s.

116. Party Picks

•Snoopy, dressed as a chef, is hitting a triangle, thinking, "Come And Get It!" Printed on packaging "Party Picks." Plastic. Set of eight. 3-1/8"H. #150PF751, Hallmark. Mid-1970s. $8-10**

•Snoopy sits on top of each party pick. Printed on packaging: "Snoopy Party Picks." Plastic. Set of twelve. 3-1/8"H. #100PF101-8, Hallmark. Mid-1970s. $8-10**

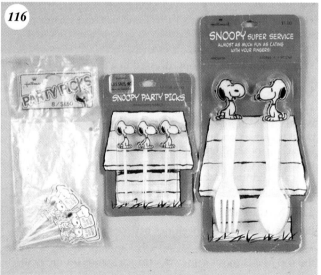

127. Luncheon Napkins

Paper. 13-1/2" x 13-1/2". $3-5** ea.

•Charlie Brown, Snoopy, and Lucy are pictured riding carnival bumper cars. Reverse side depicts Woodstock and friends in bumper cars. #NK1174, Hallmark. Early 1980s.

•Charlie Brown and Snoopy are dancing. Charlie Brown says, "Hooray For Parties!" #NK118J, Ambassador. Late 1970s.

•Snoopy and Woodstock are dancing as Snoopy thinks, "Happiness Is The Sound Of A Good Time." #80NK118-1, Hallmark. Late 1970s.

•Snoopy and Woodstock are dancing in front of a flag. Snoopy is thinking, "America, You're Beautiful!" #65NK118-1, Hallmark. Early 1970s.

128. Napkins

•Snoopy, in front of a decorated tree, is tangled up in Christmas lights. Woodstock, dressed as Santa, stands on a gift box. Paper. 13-1/2" x 13-1/2". #65XNK17-5, Hallmark. Mid-1970s. $3-6**

•Snoopy, as the Flying Ace, sits on his doghouse. Paper. 13-1/2" x 13-1/2". #65NK101-2, Hallmark. 1969. $5-6**

129. Luncheon Napkins

Paper. 13-1/2" x 13-1/2". Hallmark.

•Lucy, holding a sandwich up to Snoopy, shouts, "You call this peanut butter sandwich a party?" Snoopy and Woodstock are sitting atop the doghouse. #65XNK97-4. Mid-1970s. $3-5**

•Snoopy, in party hat, and Woodstock dance as Schroeder plays his piano. Printed: "Happy Birthday." #65NK116-3. Mid-1970s. $3-5**

•Snoopy and Woodstock, who is wearing an Uncle Sam hat, are dancing in front of a big red star. #65NK80-2. Mid-1970s. $3-5**

•Snoopy, as the Flying Ace, sits on his bullet-ridden doghouse thinking, "Rats!" while Woodstock observes from the ground. #65NK97-1. Early 1970s. $4-6**

130. Dinner Plates

Paper. 9" diam. Hallmark. Early 1970s. $4-7** ea.

•Woodstock is standing on Snoopy's supper dish. Snoopy, lying on his tummy atop the doghouse, peers down at him. #65DP97-1.

•Charlie Brown leans dejectedly against the mailbox as a triumphant Snoopy walks away with an armful of Valentine cards—walking all over Charlie Brown in the process. #49VDP1-l.

131. Dinner Plates

Snoopy flies a kite while lying flat on his back atop his doghouse. Paper. 9" diam. #49DP97-1, Hallmark. Early 1970s. $4-7**

•Snoopy, as the Flying Ace, hovers above the doghouse, and Woodstock falls off, landing on his head. A bull's-eye is painted on the house. Printed: "Ka-Bam!", "Whump!", "Ka-Chunk!", "Rip!", and "Clunk!" Paper. 9" diam. #65DP97-2, Hallmark. Mid-1970s. $4-7**

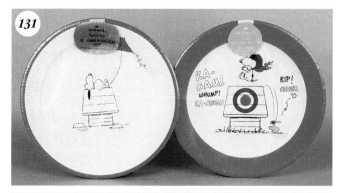

132. Dinner Plates

•Schroeder and Lucy at the piano, a dancing Snoopy, a sitting Rerun, and Woodstock sipping a soft drink through a straw, enjoy themselves at a party as Linus says, "Hooray for friends"—Sally says, "Hooray for parties"—Peppermint Patty says, "Hooray for fun"—and Charlie Brown says, "Hooray for everyone." Paper. 9" diam. #DP118J, Ambassador. Late 1970s. $4-5**

•Clockwise: Snoopy, Woodstock and friends, Linus, Lucy, Pigpen, Franklin, Marcie, Peppermint Patty, Sally, and Charlie Brown ride on a Ferris wheel. Printed: "HAPPY BIRTHDAY". Paper. 9" diam. #DP117-4, Hallmark. early 1980s. $3-5**

133. Deep Dish Plates

•Snoopy sits next to his Christmas tree on the roof of his snow-covered doghouse as he happily watches Woodstock place a gold star on top of the tree. Paper. 11" square. #349UDP33F, Ambassador. Late 1970s. $4-7**

Bowls

•Snoopy, with dog dish on his head, is being carried by Charlie Brown, Lucy, Schroeder, and Sally. Woodstock is perched on the dish. Printed: "The Gang's All Here!" Paper. 6-1/8" diam. #50DP97-4, Hallmark. Mid-1970s. $4-5**

134. Plates

•Snoopy, holding an ornament and wearing a Santa hat, sits next to his Christmas tree which is placed on the roof. Woodstock sits above the tree holding a gold star. Printed around the rim of the plates are the words, "MERRY CHRISTMAS." Paper. 11" diam. #150XDP17-1, Hallmark. Late 1970s. $4-7**

•Snoopy, wearing an apron and chef's hat, thinks, "A full stomach maketh a happy heart," as he watches Charlie Brown dance. Paper. 11" diam. #85DP12-9, Hallmark. Late 1970s. $4-7**

135. Plates

•Snoopy and Linus are sitting in a pumpkin patch. Snoopy thinks, "I think I heard my stomach growl." Linus says, "I think I heard pumpkin bells!" Paper. 7" diam. #50DP4-9, Hallmark. 1975. $4-7**

•Snoopy, wearing a graduation cap and holding a diploma, and Woodstock are dancing. Paper. 9" diam. #65GDP1-1. Early 1970s. $4-7**

136. Plates

•Snoopy, dressed as a vampire, stands behind a jack-o'-lantern with his arms outstretched. He emits the sound "OOOOOOO." Woodstock hangs upside from a tree decorated with ghosts. Silhouettes of a frightened Linus and Peppermint Patty appear in the background. Paper. 7" diam. #79HDP6G, Ambassador. Mid-1970s. $4-7**

•Schroeder and Lucy at the piano, a dancing Snoopy, a sitting Rerun, and Woodstock sipping a soft drink through a straw, enjoy themselves at a party as Linus says, "Hooray for friends"—Sally says, "Hooray for parties"—Peppermint Patty says, "Hooray for fun"—and Charlie Brown says, "Hooray for everyone." Paper. 7" diam. #DP118J, Ambassador. Late 1970s. $4-6**

137. Plates

Paper. 7" diam. Hallmark. $4-7** ea.

•Snoopy, as the Flying Ace, hovers above the doghouse and Woodstock falls off, landing on his head. A bull's-eye is painted on the house. The printed legends read, "Ka-Bam!" "Whump!" "Ka-Chunk!" "Rip!" and "Clunk!" #50DP97-2. Mid-1970s.

•Charlie Brown tries to fly his kite. Snoopy, Peppermint Patty, Linus, and Lucy walk, and Woodstock rides a bicycle. They are in a field with a red, yellow, and orange rainbow behind them. Lucy says, "A party! A party!" #80DP116-2. Late 1970s.

•Sally, Schroeder, Lucy, and Charlie Brown carry Snoopy, with Woodstock on his head in a supper dish, on their shoulders. Printed: "Hail! Hail! The Gang's All Here!" #55DP97-4. Mid-1970s.

138. Plates

•Schroeder plays his piano, which has a birthday cake on it. Charlie Brown and Peppermint Patty dance. Snoopy, wearing

a party hat and holding a horn, dances. Woodstock, wearing a party hat and blowing a horn, sits on top of a balloon. Printed: "Happy Birthday to You!" Paper. 7-3/4" diam. DPB2778, Hallmark. Early 1980s. $3-5**

•Inside a lace-trimmed heart, Peppermint Patty hugs Snoopy. He holds a heart that reads, "I Love You," and he thinks, "Every lover needs a lovee!" Paper. 9" diam. #65VDP1-2, Hallmark. Mid-1970s. $5-7**

139. Table Covers

Paper. 60"W x 102"L. Hallmark.

•Snoopy, Woodstock, and his friends are pictured riding a roller coaster. Linus and Sally are pictured in bumper cars. These two scenes continue throughout the table cover with Linus, Lucy, Charlie Brown, Sally, and more of Woodstock's friends. Printed on the packaging: "PEANUTS Carnival Capers." #TA1174. Early 1980s. $4-6**

•Patty gives Rerun a Valentine card, a freckle-faced girl gives cards to Charlie Brown, and Lucy leans on Schroeder's piano as he plays. Charlie Brown says, "Whoever heard of a Valentine addressed to 'Occupant'?" Lucy says "It's so hard for a beautiful person to decide whose Valentine to be!" #150VTA1-2. Mid-1970s. $7-9**

•Snoopy, as the Flying Ace, sits on top of his doghouse. Woodstock flies nearby. Printed: "RRRRRR." #100TA97-2. Mid-1970s. $7-9**

•Charlie Brown leans against a post under a mailbox. Snoopy sits on his tummy reading a Valentine's Day card. #100VTA2-5. Mid-1970s. $7-9**

140. Table Covers

Paper. 60"W x 102"L. Hallmark.

•Schroeder plays his piano, Sally carries a present, and Lucy sits sipping a drink. Woodstock and his friends walk in front of the piano. Linus, Snoopy, and Peppermint Patty dance. Peppermint Patty says, "Let's sit the next one out, Crazylegs." #125TA97-4. Mid-1970s. $5-7**

•Snoopy, Linus, Charlie Brown, and Peppermint Patty are sitting in a pumpkin patch. Marcie, not visible, says to Peppermint Patty, "What time is the Great Squash supposed to get here, Sir?" Snoopy thinks, "Make mine a pizza." Charlie Brown says, "Oh, good grief!" #150HTA4-9. Mid-1970s. $7-9**

•Snoopy is pictured walking and Woodstock is pictured lying in a plate. Printed: "Friends Of A Feather Welcome Good Times Together." Other scenes on the table cover depict Snoopy, Woodstock, and various food and drink. #195TA118-1. Early 1980s. $4-6**

PET ACCESSORIES

141. Pet Identification Tag

•Snoopy is sitting and hugging Woodstock. Metal. 1-1/2"H. #71-63118-4, ConAgra Pet Products Co. Sold exclusively at Sears. 1980. $4-8*

Bird Buddy

•This spring-action toy, featuring Snoopy hugging Woodstock, attaches to a bird cage. Plastic. 3"H. #71-63452-7, ConAgra Pet Products Co. Sold exclusively at Sears. 1980. $4-8*

Pet Toy

•Woodstock. Rubber. 7"H. #48275, ConAgra Pet Products. Early 1980s. $2-4*

Pet Memory Book

•Charlie Brown takes a picture of Snoopy, wearing a top hat and mustache. Woodstock, also wearing a mustache and top hat, sits on Snoopy's hat. Vinyl. 6"W x 4-1/2"H. #71-63126-7, ConAgra Pet Products Co. Sold exclusively at Sears. 1980. $4-7

Pet Toy

•Snoopy is lying on his doghouse. Rubber. 4"W x 7"H. ConAgra Pet Products Co. Sold exclusively at Sears. 1980. $3-4*

Pet Identification Tag

•Snoopy, as the Flying Ace, is on a reflective red heart. Comes with an insert for name and owner information. Plastic. 1-1/2"H. #42263, Geisler. Distributed by ConAgra Pet Accessories Division. 1980. $4-7*

Pet Toy

•Snoopy, wearing a stocking cap, is pictured on a red and white candy cane. Rubber. 7"H. #48143, ConAgra Pet Products Co. Early 1980s. $3-4*

Pet Toy

•Snoopy, dressed as a chef, holds a frying pan over a fire. Printed: "Snoopy Gourmet Dog Food." Vinyl. 3-1/2"H x 2-1/8" diam. #48259, Geisler. Distributed by ConAgra Pet Accessories Division. Early 1980s. $3-4*

142. Dog Dishes

•Snoopy kicks his supper dish and thinks, "To me, the ugli-est sight in the world is an empty dog dish!" Printed around the bowl are two other pictures, each with a quotation from Snoopy: "Just as I thought, he's cutting down on my rations!" and "How can I eat when I feel guilty?" Plastic. 8" diam. #362, Determined Productions. Early 1970s. $8-12

•A comic strip featuring Snoopy and Woodstock is printed around the bowl. Printed inside the bowl in raised lettering: "A Watched Supper Dish Never Fills." Plastic. 9-1/2" diam. ConAgra Pet Products Co. Sold exclusively at Sears. 1980. $18-25

•Snoopy is depicted around the bowl in various poses next to quotations. Printed: "I hate it when it rains on my French toast!"; "I never know what to do with the used tea bag..."; and "Eating out can be fun!" Plastic. 6" diam. #361, Determined Productions. Early 1970s. $7-10

•Snoopy, Lucy, and Sally are depicted around the bowl next to quotations. Printed: "Relaxation is an art—a full stomach helps!"; "One should begin each day with eggs benedict!"; and "When you're going to supper, you have no time for girls!" Plastic. 10" diam. #363, Determined Productions. Late 1970s. $14-18

•Snoopy, Woodstock, Charlie Brown, and Peppermint Patty are depicted around the bowl next to quotations. Printed: "I knew I smelled a picnic going by!"; "What's wrong with wanting to eat on the terrace?"; and "Just what I need, feathers in my soup!" Plastic. 6" diam. Determined Productions. Mid-1970s. $7-10

143. Pet Placemats

•Lucy, dressed as a maid, serves a bone in a dog dish to Snoopy, who is sitting on his doghouse. Snoopy thinks, "Room service! How delightful!" Paw prints and "Snoopy Suppertime" are printed on the edge of the mat. The packaging is printed "Snoopy Suppertime Splash Mat for Particular Pets." Vinyl. 19-7/8"W x 13-1/2"H. #71-63355-2, ConAgra Pet Products Co. Sold exclusively at Sears. 1980. $10-15**

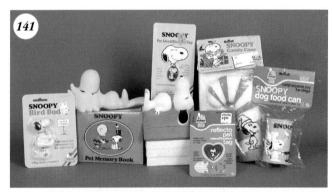

• Woodstock, dressed as a chef, has a barbecue in his nest and a spatula in his hand. Snoopy looks up at him and thinks, "Medium rare, if you please!" Paw prints and "Snoopy Suppertime" are printed around the edge of the mat. Vinyl. 19-7/8"W x 13-1/2"H. #71-63371-9, ConAgra Pet Products Co. Sold exclusively at Sears. 1980. $10-15**

TOWELS

144. Towels

Packaging depicts the towel design inside. Printed: "PEANUTS Pure Linen Towel." 16"W x 26"H. Determined Productions. 1976. $8-10 $15-18*

• Snoopy kisses a sitting Peppermint Patty on the nose. She says, "Thank goodness for people!" #6392.

• Snoopy sits in front of his dog dish with snow falling around him. He thinks, "I hate it when it snows on my French toast!" #6391.

• Snoopy, lying on his doghouse, and with Woodstock lying on his nose, thinks, "It's nice to have a home where guests feel welcome!" #6395.

• Charlie Brown, bringing a dancing Snoopy his supper dish, says, "I feel like I'm feeding Fred Astaire." #6394.

145. Towel

• Lucy, dressed as a maid, brings Snoopy his dinner. Snoopy, sitting on his doghouse, thinks, "How come my kind never gets to eat off the fine china?" Linen. 16"W x 26"H. #6393, Determined Productions. 1976. $8-10 $15-18*

TRAY TABLES AND SERVING TRAYS

146. Tray Table

•Lucy, Linus, Charlie Brown, Peppermint Patty, Sally, and Snoopy are shown standing. Tray can be removed from its stand. Metal. 21-1/2"W x 15-1/2"D x 23"H. Marshallan Products, Inc. Mid-1970s. $25-30

Lap Tray

•Snoopy is pictured in six panels. Top: Tennis player, Flying Ace, roller skater. Bottom: Baseball player, dancing, carrying a hobo pack. Tray legs fold out from underneath. Tray cannot be removed from its legs. Metal. 17-1/2"W x 12-1/2"D x 6"H. Marshallan Products, Inc. Mid-1970s. $12-15

147. Serving Trays

•Snoopy, dressed as a waiter, grins as he roller-skates through a restaurant, carrying covered trays. Woodstock flies behind him. Metal. 13" x 13". #41-0365, Determined Productions. 1979. $12-14

•Snoopy, dressed in an apron and grinning, wipes a counter with one hand and pours coffee with the other, as Woodstock sits on the counter holding a coffee cup. Printed: "Snoopy's Cafe." Metal. 12" diam. #41-0364, Determined Productions. 1979. $12-14

148. Serving Trays

•A four-panel comic strip with dialogue depicts Charlie Brown bringing Snoopy his dinner at his doghouse. Came in different color combinations. Metal. 13" x 13". Made in England for Determined Productions. Early 1970s. $15-25

•A four-panel comic strip with dialogue depicts Charlie Brown and Snoopy as Charlie Brown prepares Snoopy's supper. Came in different color combinations. Metal. 13" x 13". Made in England for Determined Productions. Early 1970s. $15-25

The demand for PEANUTS-related publications outside the United States is seemingly insatiable. As an example, PEANUTS comic strips appear in over 3,000 newspapers in 75 different countries. The number of hard and soft cover book titles published for overseas consumption run into the thousands, and this number is growing almost daily.

Pictured here is a small sampling of offshore books from just a few countries—Germany, Mexico, Israel, Finland, Japan, and England. Also shown are two items of interest from Japan: On the floor is an unusual wooden record holder (1984) configured like a double-decker bus. A wooden cassette holder is placed on the table.

Also on the table are two musical devices rarely seen in the United States. The small blue Snoopy "Play and Record" is a Japanese battery-operated instrument that allows the user to create, record, and play back simple melodies. The large box contains a Snoopy "Sing Along Music Centre," from England. In addition to allowing the user to create original music in either piano or organ mode, it includes a microphone that provides a sing-along capability—either with a new creation or with prerecorded melodies—that can then be played back for personal enjoyment.

The Library

Welcome to the place where reading is fun and listening to your favorite PEANUTS music is most pleasurable. Your choice of reading material will consist of more than the usual compilations of comic strips or additional works by Schulz based solely on the characters. There will also be books that explore some of the subject matters of the strip (The Gospel According to PEANUTS, by Robert L. Short); books about Schulz (Good Grief! by Rheta Grimsley Johnson); and other books related to the PEANUTS family. Collectors will find enjoyment in the many "general interest" books and magazines that include feature articles about Schulz and/or the PEANUTS gang.

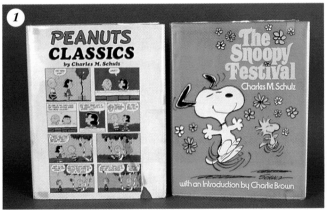

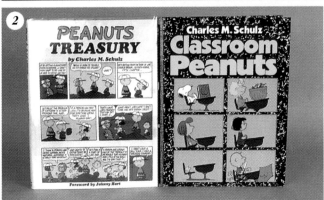

BOOKS

1. Books

• *PEANUTS Classics*, by Charles M. Schulz. Hardcover. Holt, Rinehart and Winston. 1970. $10-12

• *The Snoopy Festival*, by Charles M. Schulz. Introduction by Charlie Brown. Hardcover. Holt, Rinehart and Winston. 1974. $10-12

2. Books

• *PEANUTS Treasury*, by Charles M. Schulz. Foreword by Johnny Hart. Hardcover. Holt, Rinehart and Winston. 1968. $10-12

• *Classroom PEANUTS*, by Charles M. Schulz. Hardcover. Holt, Rinehart and Winston. 1982. $12-15

3. Baby Books

• *Belle Goes To A Party.* Interactive touch, smell, and squeeze pages. Heavy cardboard. Determined Productions. Early 1980s. $5-7*

• No title. Snoopy and Woodstock dance in front of the number "1." Packaging is printed "Snoopy Picture Book." Pages can be squeezed to make noise. Vinyl. Danara. Early 1980s. $4-6*

• *Pet Snoopy.* Interactive touch, smell, and squeeze pages. Heavy cardboard. Determined Productions. Early 1980s. $5-6*

4. Flip Books

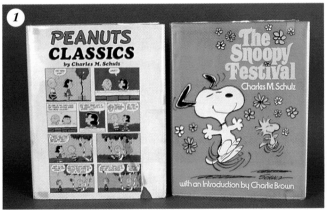

Pages depicting comic strips are held together on a metal ring. 3" x 3". Hallmark. Early 1970s. $10-15 ea.

• Lucy reads a piece of paper. Printed: "Lucy's Philosophy." #100RB2-4.

• Snoopy, as the Flying Ace, is sitting. Printed: "The Flying Ace." #100RB2-7.

• Linus sits at desk. Printed: "Live and Learn." #100RB2-6

• Snoopy dances. Printed: "Sayings of Snoopy." #100RB2-2.

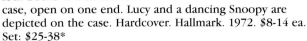

•Charlie Brown, head in hand, leans on a wall. Printed: "Charlie Brown's World." #100RB2-8.

•Lucy knocks Linus over backwards. Printed: "A Woman's World." #100RB2-3.

•Snoopy hugs Charlie Brown. Printed: "Love, Sweet Love." #100RB2-1.

5. Books

More Peanuts Philosophers, by Charles M. Schulz. A set of four books in a cardboard case, open on one end. Lucy and a dancing Snoopy are depicted on the case. Hardcover. Hallmark. 1972. $8-14 ea. Set: $25-38*

•*Charlie Brown's Reflections*

•*The Meditations of Linus*

•*Lucy Looks at Life*

•*The Wit and Wisdom of Snoopy*

Books

The Peanuts Philosophers, by Charles M. Schulz. A set of four books in a cardboard case. Lucy, Linus, Charlie Brown, and a dancing Snoopy are depicted on the case. Hardcover. Hallmark. 1972. $8-14 ea. Set: $25-38*

•*Linus on Life*

•*The World According to Lucy*

•*The Wisdom of Charlie Brown*

•*Snoopy's Philosophy*

6. Book

•*Snoopy's Daily Dozen—12 Physical Fitness Exercises.* On each page Snoopy watches one of the gang doing an exercise, and makes comments. By Charles M. Schulz, 15" X 10". Cardboard. Spiral bound at top. Late 1960s #150M-2, Hallmark. $15-20

7. Books.

A nine-volume set titled *The World of Charlie Brown*, packaged in a cardboard case depicting a dancing Snoopy. Each volume contains two titles. Hardcover. Mattel. 1979. $8-15 ea. Set: $45-60*

•*You Can't Win, Charlie Brown, & You're You, Charlie Brown*

•*Go Fly A Kite, Charlie Brown, & Snoopy*

•*You're Out of Your Mind, Charlie Brown, & But We Love You, Charlie Brown*

•*Peanuts Every Sunday, & The Unsinkable Charlie Brown*

•*You're Something Else, Charlie Brown, & We're Right Behind You, Charlie Brown*

•*You're Out of Sight, Charlie Brown, & Sunday's Fun Day, Charlie Brown*

•*You've Had It, Charlie Brown, & As You Like It, Charlie Brown*

•*It's A Dog's Life, Charlie Brown, & You Need Help, Charlie Brown*

•*You Can Do It, Charlie Brown, & You'll Flip, Charlie Brown*

8. Books

A five-volume set titled *Charlie Brown* is packaged in a cardboard case depicting Charlie Brown. Paperback. #6-4227, Fawcett Crest Books. 1978. $1-2 ea. Set: $15-18*

•*For The Love Of Peanuts*

•*That's Life, Snoopy*

•*Keep Up The Good Work, Charlie Brown*

•*It's All Yours, Snoopy*

•*Here Comes Snoopy*

Books

A five-volume set titled *Snoopy* is packaged in a cardboard case depicting Snoopy on his doghouse playing with his paw-pets. Paperback. #6-4228, Fawcett Crest Books. 1978. $1-4 ea. Set: $30-34*

•*You're So Smart, Snoopy*

•*All This And Snoopy, Too*

• *Good Ol' Snoopy*

• *It's Raining on Your Parade, Charlie Brown*

• *Fun With Peanuts*

9. Books

A six-volume set titled *Good Grief! It's Charlie Brown!* is packaged in a cardboard case with a handle depicting Lucy and Charlie Brown in baseball gear, and Snoopy as the Flying Ace. Printed on the box: "This Lunchbox Belongs to:_____". Paperback. Signet. Sold through Sears Catalog. Early 1970s. $1-4 ea. Set: $35-40

• *A Charlie Brown Christmas*

• *Charlie Brown's All-Stars*

• *He's Your Dog, Charlie Brown*

• *You're In Love, Charlie Brown*

• *It's The Great Pumpkin, Charlie Brown*

• *It Was A Short Summer, Charlie Brown*

The following hardcover books, originally published in the 1960s, were reprinted throughout the 1970s and 1980s. Considered children's toys, not books, the publication date remained the same as the first year they were published. The original publication date is listed below. Some titles were released in soft-cover in 1979.

10. Books

Hardcover with dust jacket. 5-3/4" x 5-3/4". Determined Productions.

• *Happiness Is A Warm Puppy.* 1962. $6-10

• *Happiness Is A Sad Song.* 1967. $8-10

• *Peanuts Cook Book.* 1969. $8-15

• *Peanuts Lunch Bag Cook Book.* 1970. $8-15

• *I Need All The Friends I Can Get.* 1964. $6-10

11. Books

Hardcover with dust jacket. 5-3/4" x 5-3/4". Determined Productions.

• *Happiness Is Walking Hand In Hand.* 1965. $6-10

• *Security Is A Thumb And A Blanket.* 1963. $6-10

• *Christmas Is Together-Time.* 1964. $6-10

• *Suppertime.* 1968. $8-10

• *Home Is On Top Of A Dog House.* 1966. $8-10

12. Books

Hardcover. 3-1/2"W x 5-3/4"H. Determined Productions. 1970. $9-15 ea.

• *Winning May Not Be Everything, But Losing Isn't Anything!*

• *It's Fun To Lie Here And Listen To The Sounds Of The Night!*

• *For A Nickel I Can Cure Anything!*

• *It Really Doesn't Take Much To Make A Dad Happy!*

13. Books

• *Dear President Johnson.* Letters selected by Bill Adler. Illustrated by Charles M. Schulz. Hardcover with dust jacket. William Morrow and Co. 1964. $10-14

• *A Big World II,* by Adaia and Abraham Shumsky. Charlie Brown, with baseball bat, cap, and ball, is depicted on lower left-hand corner of the book cover. The last chapter of this Hebrew textbook features illustrations of the PEANUTS characters. Hardcover. Union of American Hebrew Congregations and Central Conference of American Rabbis. 1977. $10-15

• *PEANUTS,* by Charles M. Schulz. In early editions of this book, opposite the first page of comic strip panels, a three-paragraph introduction to the PEANUTS characters can be found. Soft-cover. Rinehart & Co., Inc. 1952. With Intro: $15-18. Without Intro: $10-15

14. Books

•*Snoopy And 'It Was A Dark And Stormy Night,'* by Charles M. Schulz. Hardcover with dust jacket. Holt, Rinehart and Winston. 1971. $8-10

•*Snoopy's Secret Code Book,* by Charles M. Schulz and Kathryn Lumley. Includes rare appearances of Roy, Jose Peterson, and Thibault. Soft-cover. 107 pages. Holt, Rinehart and Winston. 1971. $15-18

•*You're A Good Man, Charlie Brown,* based on the comic strip "PEANUTS," by Charles M. Schulz. Hardcover. A Random House play. 1968. $8-10

•*Snoopy And The Red Baron,* by Charles M. Schulz. Hardcover with dust jacket. Holt, Rinehart and Winston. 1966. $6-10

15. Book

•*Snoopy And His Sopwith Camel,* by Charles M. Schulz. Hardcover with dust jacket. Holt, Rinehart and Winston. 1969. $6-10

16. Books

•*All I Want For Christmas Is…Featuring The Peanuts Characters,* by Charles M. Schulz. Hardcover. #150XTR8-4, Hallmark. 1972. $10-12

•*Yes, Santa, There Is A Charlie Brown,* by Charles M. Schulz. Hardcover. 5"W x 6-3/4"H. #150XBG9-7, Hallmark. 1971. $8-10

•*Yes, Santa, There Is A Charlie Brown,* by Charles M. Schulz. This version has one less two-page scene. Hardcover. 3"W x 4-1/2"H. #175HE1-1, Hallmark. 1972. $8-10

17. Books

•*The Peanuts Platform,* illustrated by Charles M. Schulz. Soft-cover. #150KF2, Hallmark. 1972. $6-9

•*What's It All About, Charlie Brown? Peanuts Kids Look At America Today,* by Jeffrey H. Loria. Hardcover with dust jacket. Holt, Rinehart and Winston. 1968. $15-20

18. Books

•*The Parables Of Peanuts,* by Robert L. Short. Hardcover with dust jacket (also available in soft-cover). Harper and Row Publishers. 1968. Hardcover: $6-10 Soft-cover: $4-6

•*The Gospel According To Peanuts,* by Robert L. Short. Hardcover with dust jacket (also available in soft-cover). John Knox Press. 1964. Hardcover: $6-10 Soft-cover: $4-6

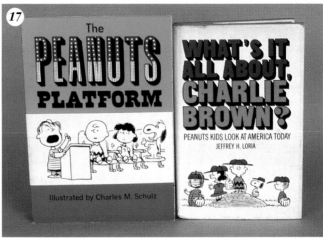

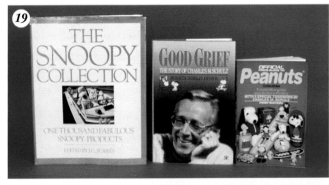

19. Books

•*The Snoopy Collection: One Thousand Fabulous Snoopy Products,* edited by J.C. Suares. Hardcover with dust jacket. Newspaper Enterprise Association, Inc., World Almanac Publications. 1982. $15-20

•*Good Grief— The Story of Charles M. Schulz,* by Rheta Grimsley Johnson. Authorized biography. Hardcover with dust jacket. Pharos Books. 1989. $8-10

•*Official Price Guide To PEANUTS Collectibles,* by Freddi Margolin and Andrea Podley. Soft-cover. 5"W x 8"H. House of Collectibles, a Random House division. 1990. $20-25

20. Books

•*The Graphic Art of Charles Schulz—The Oakland Museum.* From an exhibit organized by the Oakland Museum in Oakland, California, with a grant from United Media. Soft-cover. 1985. $18-22

•*Charlie Brown—A Boy For All Seasons: 20 Years On Television At The Museum Of Broadcasting.* From an exhibit at the Museum of Broadcasting November 15, 1984, through January 31, 1985. Soft-cover. 1984. $15-18

21. Books

Snoopy Little Books Set, by Charles M. Schulz. Set of 5 in a cardboard case featuring Snoopy reading a book on each side. Hardcover. 2-1/2"W x 2-3/4"H. #1069, Determined Productions. 1984. Set: $25-30*

•*Home Is On Top Of A Doghouse.* Snoopy lies on top of the title. $7-9

•*Security Is A Thumb And A Blanket.* Linus and Snoopy, sucking their thumbs, each hold on to one end of Linus's blanket. $7-9

•*Happiness Is. . . A Warm Puppy.* Snoopy sits between the words of the title. $4-6

•*I Need All The Friends I Can Get.* Snoopy lies on his doghouse, surrounded by Woodstock and his friends. $6-8

Love Is… Walking Hand-In-Hand. Charlie Brown and Peppermint Patty, holding hands, walk between the words of the title. $4-6

Book Plates

•Charlie Brown is standing with a book. Lucy is in a booth printed: "Books Reviewed 5¢" and "The Critic Is In." Also printed: "This Book Belongs To:" Paper. Antioch. 1987. $6-8**

BOOKS WITH SOUND

22. Book with Sound

•Snoopy and Woodstock, dressed as farmers, walk down a barnyard path. An electronic keyboard that makes animal sounds is included with the storybook. Printed: "PEANUTS Sound Story" and "Snoopy's Day at the Farm." Soft-cover. 24 pages. 9"W x 12"H. #64001, Sight & Sound, Inc. 1989. $8-15

Song Books

•Snoopy leans on his doghouse as Woodstock and his friends surround him, carrying musical notes. A color-coded electronic keyboard is included. Printed: "PEANUTS" and "Snoopy's Musical Adventures." Hardcover, spiral bound. 8"W x 10-3/4"H. #60160. Sight & Sound, Inc. 1988. $8-15

•Lucy, Linus, Charlie Brown, Peppermint Patty, Sally, Snoopy, and Woodstock stand on a hill with suitcases. A plane flies overhead. A color-coded electronic keyboard is included. Printed: "PEANUTS" and "Around The World With Charlie Brown." Hardcover, spiral bound. 8"W x 10-3/4"H. #60162. Sight & Sound, Inc. 1988. $8-15

COMIC BOOKS

23. Comic Books

Printed: "PEANUTS." Although the covers are signed by Schulz, the comics inside were not his drawings. Soft-cover. Dell Publishing Co. $12-15 ea.

•Charlie Brown bangs on a drum, which Snoopy carries on his back. #13. May-July 1962.

•Charlie Brown and Snoopy are roller-skating. #11. Nov.-Jan. 1962.

•Charlie Brown is carrying Snoopy in the hood of his coat. #12. Feb.-April 1962.

24. Comic Books

Printed: "PEANUTS." Although the covers are signed by Schulz, the comics inside were not his drawings. Soft-cover. Dell Publishing Co. $12-15 ea.

•Charlie Brown is walking in the rain with an umbrella over his head. Snoopy walks alongside, covered by his doghouse. #6. Aug.-Oct. 1960.

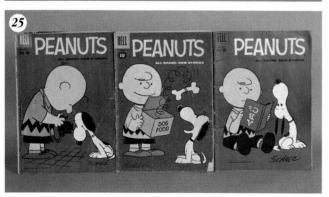

•Charlie Brown lies tummy down on a sled. Snoopy sits on his back. His ears are spinning like a propeller. #7. Nov.-Jan. 1961.

•Charlie Brown stands near Snoopy's doghouse, which has an antenna on the roof. Snoopy sits inside the doorway, as if watching television inside. #5. May-June 1960.

25. Comic Books

Printed: "PEANUTS." Although the covers are signed by Schulz, the comics inside were not his drawings. Soft-cover. Dell Publishing Co. $15-25 ea.

•Charlie Brown attempts to take a picture of Snoopy as Snoopy blocks the lens by looking through the front end of the camera. #4. Feb.-April 1960. Also published by Gold Key in 1964, excluding non-Peanuts features and including one additional Peanuts feature.

•Charlie Brown holds a jack-in-the-box type container which has a dog bone on a spring. Snoopy sits with his mouth open ready to catch the bone. #8. Feb.-April 1961.

•Charlie Brown is sitting, and reading an upside-down book. Snoopy is looking straight up in the air. #969. 1958. Also published by Gold Key in 1963.

26. Comic Books

Printed: "PEANUTS." Although the covers are signed by Schulz, the comics inside were not his drawings. Soft-cover. Dell Publishing Co. $15-25 ea.

•Snoopy clings to Charlie Brown as a wind-up mechanical turtle goes by. #9. May-July 1961.

•Charlie Brown sits on a club chair watching television. Snoopy peeks out from under the cushion Charlie Brown is sitting on. #878. 1958. Also published by Gold Key in 1963.

•Charlie Brown, dressed as a gold miner, walks alongside Snoopy, who is outfitted as a pack animal. #10. Aug.-Oct. 1961.

Many comic books were produced that featured PEANUTS characters on the cover, but which contained only a few pages of PEANUTS comics inside. Comic books were also produced that did not feature PEANUTS characters on the cover, but which still included a few pages of PEANUTS comics inside. While not pictured, a partial listing of these comic books follows. Cover descriptions, and the pages presenting the PEANUTS comics, are noted. These issues may cost more than a PEANUTS collector would want to pay for only four pages or so, but keep in mind that the Nancy comics and Tip Top Comics are collectible, too.

Tip Top Comic Books (Not pictured)

Printed: Tip Top Comics. Soft-cover. $12-15 ea.

• Charlie Brown, Lucy, Snoopy, and Schroeder are pictured in baseball scenes. Charlie Brown, running to catch the ball, says, "I got it!" Snoopy catches the ball in his mouth and Lucy says, "There must be a rule covering that catch!" Pages 12-15. #187, Tip Top Comics. July-Aug. 1954.

• Nancy and Sluggo sit in a forklift watching a baseball game over a fence. Pages 14-18. #191, St. John. October 1955.

• Nancy, dressed as Santa Claus, and Sluggo, sitting in a sack of toys wearing a pig-tailed wig, have their picture taken by a photographer. Pages 16-21. Vol. 2, #207, St. John. February 1957.

• Charlie Brown feeds a lollipop to a snowman, as Linus frowns. Other characters in scenes on the cover include Sluggo, Nancy, and the Captain and the Kids. Inside cover and pages 8-15. #211, Dell Publishing Co. Nov.-Jan. 1958.

• Snoopy relaxes in a rubber swimming pool as Charlie Brown, wearing bathing trunks and holding a towel, looks on, sweating. Other characters in the cover scenes include Sluggo, Nancy, and the Captain and the Kids. Inside cover and pages 9-16. #212, Dell Publishing Co. Feb.-April 1958.

• Charlie Brown, dressed in baseball gear, catches a baseball while bouncing on a pogo stick. Other characters in scenes on the cover include Sluggo, Nancy, and the Captain and the Kids. Pages 9-16. #217, Dell Publishing Co. May-July 1959.

• Charlie Brown is skiing, with Snoopy standing on the tip of one of the skis. Other characters in scenes on the cover include Sluggo, Nancy, and the Captain and the Kids. Inside cover and pages 8-15. #215, Dell Publishing Co. Nov.-Jan. 1959.

• Snoopy tries to lick Charlie Brown's candy apple. Other characters in scenes on the cover include Sluggo, Nancy, and the Captain and the Kids. Inside cover and pages 9-16. #219, Dell Publishing Co. Nov.-Jan. 1960.

"Nancy" Comic Books (Not pictured)

Printed: "Nancy." Soft-cover. Dell Publishing Co. $12-15 ea.

• Nancy brings a towel and soap to a bird in a bird bath. Pages 22-25. #154. May 1958.

• Sluggo tries to start a fire to cook hot dogs as Nancy, holding a hot dog on a long fork, watches. Pages 26-29. #157. August 1958.

• Nancy gives a dog an eye test using a chart with bones instead of letters. Pages 25-28. #160. November 1958.

• Nancy decorates a pool table with flowers as Sluggo looks on. Pages 19-22. #163. February 1959.

• Many dogs follow Nancy as she walks in the rain holding an umbrella. Pages 24-27. #168. July 1959.

• Nancy and Sluggo hold ice cream cones. Pages 22-25. #169. August 1959.

"Nancy and Sluggo" Comic Books (Not pictured)

Printed: "Nancy and Sluggo." Soft-cover. $10-15 ea.

• Nancy walks a toy elephant on ice. Sluggo has fallen through the ice. Pages 22-24. #142, St. John Publishing Co. March 1957.

• Nancy and Sluggo slide down a snow-covered hill in a saucer. Pages 13-16. #174, Dell Publishing Co. Jan.-Feb. 1960.

• Nancy washes a dog while Sluggo watches. Pages 14-17. #175, Dell Publishing Co. March-April 1960.

• Nancy washes dishes in a shower while Sluggo dries them. Pages 15-18. #178, Dell Publishing Co. Sept.-Oct. 1960.

• Nancy blows out the candles on a cake—right into Sluggo's face. Pages 19-22. #179, Dell Publishing Co. Nov.-Dec. 1960.

• Nancy flips a fence slat, which springs and hits Sluggo on the rear end. Pages 21-24. #183, Dell Publishing Co. July-August 1961.

• Nancy looks through a microscope as Sluggo positions a frog, dangling on a fishing pole, into her view. Pages 22-25. #185, Dell Publishing Co. Nov.-Dec. 1961.

• Nancy stands on a ladder holding a paint bucket while Sluggo, dipping a paintbrush into the paint, is suction-cupped to the ceiling. Pages 11-14. #188, Gold Key. October 1962.

• Sluggo carries a large piece of furniture from behind while Nancy, attempting to help from in front, succeeds only in pulling out a drawer. Pages 21-24. #189, Gold Key. January 1963.

"Fritzi Ritz" Comic Books (Not pictured)

• Fritzi Ritz is at the beach looking at a man reading a "Learn To Wrestle" book. He has gotten himself tied-up in knots, and says to Fritzi, "Quick Fritzi, turn the page and find out how to get me untied!" Printed on cover: "Fritzi Ritz." Pages 6-7. #22, United Comics. May-June 1952. $10-15

• Fritzi Ritz, dressed as a majorette, leads a member of the band carrying Nancy in his tuba. Fritzi Ritz says, "Stop complaining, Phil! Nancy's feet hurt." Printed on cover: "Fritzi Ritz." Soft cover. Pages 19-21. Vol. 1, #49, St. John Publishing Co. December 1956. $10-15

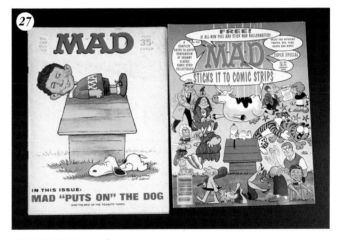

27. *MAD* Magazine

• Alfred E. Neuman lies on top of Snoopy's doghouse. Snoopy, on his tummy, lies on the ground. Printed: "MAD" and "In This Issue: Mad 'Puts On' The Dog (And The Rest Of The PEANUTS Gang)." Pages 20-23. Soft-cover. #137, E. C. Publications. October 1970. $12-15

• The cover features images of many comic strip characters surrounding Snoopy, who is lying on his doghouse. Printed: "MAD Sticks It To The Comic Strips." Pages 4, 10, 12, 13, 21-23, 30, 31, 33, 34, 48, 49, 53, 58, 59. 63. Soft-cover. #101, E. C. Publications. January 1995. $8-10

MAD *Magazine often satirized the PEANUTS characters in its pages. Below is a partial listing of issues which did not feature the characters on the cover, but which did feature one or more of the PEANUTS characters on inside pages. The covers are described, along with the pages the PEANUTS characters can be found on. Cracked Magazine also satirized*

PEANUTS *with depictions on the covers and inside the maga-* *zine. Some* Mad *Comic Magazines may cost more than you* *would wish to pay for one story, but* Mad *Comics is, in itself,* *a collectible magazine.*

If you like parodies, try these!

27. *MAD* Magazine. E. C. Publications (Not pictured)

•Alfred E. Neuman, in a football uniform, is kicked through a goalpost while holding onto a football. Table of contents and pages 4-7. Soft-cover. #117. March 1968. $10-12

•Alfred E. Neuman is depicted as a hippie. Printed: "Turn On Tune In Drop Dead." Table of contents and pages 9 and 45. Soft-cover. #118. April 1968. $10-12

•Cover shows Alfred E. Neuman's face surrounded by the words "This Copy Of MAD Is Number 1,376,485 In A Series Of 2,148,000. Collect Them All!" Table of contents and pages 4-6. Soft-cover. #123. December 1968. $10-12

•Alfred E. Neuman's head is being rolled onto a wall as if it were paint. Table of contents and pages 4-7. Soft-cover. #148. January 1972. $8-10

•The cover shows a sticker coming out of a man's ear. The sticker shows a dog being cemented into a curb with the caption: "Curb Your Dog." Page 49. Soft-cover. Special Issue #10. 1973. $8-10

•Cover shows panels from several different comic strips. Pages 2, 4, 5, 20-23, 30, 32, 33, 42, 46, 47, 50, 51, 59, 68-72. Soft-cover. Special Fall Issue #36. 1981. $8-10

•Cover depicts Roseanne, eating a sandwich and sitting on the high end of a seesaw, and Alfred E. Neuman, standing on the low end. Page 6. Soft-cover. #287. June 1989. $8-10

Cracked Magazine. Globe Communications Corp. (Not pictured)

•The Flintstones men are depicted as wild cavemen. Page 30. Soft-cover. #292. 1994. $6-7

•The cover shows famous dogs, including Snoopy, in a bathroom. Page 61. Soft-cover. Collectors' edition. #98. April 1994. $6-7

•The cover depicts a teenager with a CD player and several fake CD covers including one that depicts Snoopy on his doghouse, Sally with a net, and Charlie Brown and Linus as rappers. Color insert after page 50 and pages 66-67. Soft-cover. #4. Summer 1994. $6-7

COOKBOOKS

28. Cookbooks

Soft-cover. Determined Productions. $15-22

•*Snoopy & The Gang Out West.* Contains stories, recipes, and apparel. Illustrations were drawn by Charles M. Schulz. The text and recipes in the book were done by June Dutton. 1983.

•*The Snoopy Doghouse Cook Book—59 Recipes For Your Dog.* Illustrations for the book were drawn by Charles M. Schulz. Text was created by Evelyn Shaw, Ph.D. #0187. 1979.

•*Great Pumpkin Cookbook No Tricks…Just Treats.* Illustrations were drawn by Charles M. Schulz. Recipes in the book were the work of June Dutton. 1981.

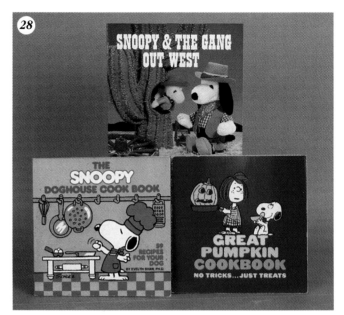

DICTIONARIES AND ENCYCLOPEDIAS

29. Dictionary

Charlie Brown Dictionary, by Charles M. Schulz. This dictionary was available in three formats: an eight-volume set, a six-volume set, and as one volume. The multi-volume sets were sold through supermarket promotions. Hardcover. Based on *The Rainbow Dictionary* by Wendell W. Wright. Published by World Publishing Co., New York and Nelson Foster & Scott Ltd., Canada.

•Advertisement. Safeway Supermarkets. 1976. $5-7

•Single Volume Format. 399 pages. 580 color pictures. 2,400 defined words. 1973. $10-15

•Eight-Volume Format. The cover of each volume is illustrated with the alphabet letters contained in the volume. 1976. $4-6 ea. Set: $30-40

•Six-Volume Format. The cover of each volume is illustrated with the alphabet letters contained in the volume. 1976. $4-6 ea. Set: $25-35 (Not pictured)

30. Book Rack

•Snoopy, as Joe Cool, standing in front of a pile of books, is depicted on a bookrack shaped like his doghouse. Holds all the volumes of the *Charlie Brown 'Cyclopedia* set. Plastic. Made by Butterfly Originals. Distributed by Funk & Wagnalls, Inc. 1980 $4-6 $7-10*

Encyclopedia Set

•*Charlie Brown's 'Cyclopedia.* Sold individually, or as a complete set of fifteen volumes in the pictured gift box. Hardcover. Published by Random House, New York, and Random House, Canada. Distributed by Funk and Wagnalls, Inc. 1980. $4-6 ea. Set: $50-65*

GREETING BOOKS

31. Greeting Books

Came with envelopes for mailing. Hardcover. 4"W x 5-1/2"H. Ambassador. $8-15 ea.

•*Cheery Sayings of Snoopy.* #100AEK4-3J. Early 1970s.

•*It's The Thought That Counts.* #100AEK45J. Early 1970s.

•*A Letter From Me.* #100AEK46J. 1972.

•*A Woman's World.* #100AEK4-1J. Early 1970s.

•*May I Offer You Some Free Advice?* #100AEK47J. Early 1970s.

32. Greeting Books

Came with envelopes for mailing. Hardcover. 4"W x 5-1/2"H. Hallmark. $8-15 ea.

•*Live And Learn: Thoughts About School, By The Peanuts Characters.* #100HEK4-4. Early 1970s.

•*All About Birthday: Thoughts On Growing Up, By The Peanuts Characters.* #125B109-1. Mid-1970s.

•*Help Stamp Out Things That Need Stamping Out! And Other Philosophical Gems Of Linus.* #GB506-P. Made in Western Germany. 1975.

•*A Friend Is…* #100HEK4-1. Early 1970s.

33. Greeting Books

Came with envelopes for mailing. Hardcover. 4"W x 5-1/2"H. Hallmark. $8-15 ea.

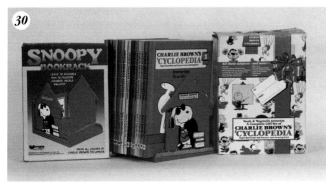

•*The Flying Ace. Great Moments With Snoopy And The Red Baron.* #100HEK4-5. Early 1970s.

•*It Shouldn't Happen To You … Let Alone A Dog!* #100HEK4-15. 1972.

•*All About Friendship. A Commentary On Friends, By The Peanuts Characters.* #100HEK4-3. 1971.

•*Thoughts On Getting Well. The Peanuts Manual For Prompt Recovery.* Yellow cover. #125C110-1. Early 1970s.

34. Greeting Books

Came with envelopes for mailing. Hardcover. 4"W x 5-1/2"H. Hallmark. $8-15 ea.

•*Everything I Do Makes Me Feel Guilty. And Other Wisdom Of Charlie Brown.* #125GBK114-1. Mid-1970s.

•*We All Have Our Hang-ups. And Other Thoughts Of Snoopy.* #125GBL112-1. Mid-1970s.

•*Thoughts On Getting Well. The Peanuts Manual For Prompt Recovery.* Pink cover. Part of the Thoughtfulness Library series. #100HEK4-2. 1971.

•*Happy Birthday Person To Person.* #100HEK4-8. Early 1970s.

35. Greeting Books

Came with envelopes for mailing. Hardcover. 4"W x 5-1/2"H. Hallmark. $8-15 ea.

•*It Always Rains On Our Generation. And More Of Lucy's Philosophy.* #125GBL113-1. Mid-1970s.

•*Snoopy's Home Medical Advisor. With Best Wishes For A Speedy Recovery.* #125HEK41-2. Mid-1970s.

•*Love, Sweet Love. Romantic Thoughts By The Peanuts Characters.* #100HEK4-6. 1971.

•*Help Stamp Out Things That Need Stamping Out! And Other Philosophical Gems Of Linus.* #125GBL115-1. Mid-1970s.

MAGAZINES

36. Magazines

•*Dynamite* Magazine. Snoopy is pictured lying on his dog-house. An airplane has written the words "This Is Your Life Snoopy" in the sky. Pages 2-5. Soft-cover. #TV2974, Scholastic Magazines. December 1974. $15-20

•*Ms.* Magazine. Lucy sits behind her lemonade stand with her feet propped up. The booth is printed "Lucy Inc. Lemonade 5¢" and "Ms. Lucy Van Pelt, Prop. Is In." Selling more than just lemonade, signs around the booth advertise for products such as lemon seeds, lemon burgers, and lemon lessons. Cover only. Soft-cover. April 1976. $10-12

•*Teen* Magazine. Snoopy, as the Flying Ace, is sitting on his doghouse. The face of the cover model is to his right. Pages 2, 5, 6, 11, 12, 28, 30, 32, 34, 40, 60, 62, 70-78, 84, 86, 88-90, 92, 93, 98, 100, 103. Soft-cover. September 1969. $15-25

•*Woman's Day* Magazine. Snoopy, as the Flying Ace, has his arms raised in the air as Charlie Brown walks him on a leash. Pages 58-59 and 110-112. February 1968. $8-10

•*J&B Scotch ProAm Program.* Snoopy is getting ready to swing at a golf ball. Lucy says, "I've had strange partners before, but this is ridiculous!" Page 61. Soft-cover. March 1982. $8-10

•*Nemo* Magazine. Lucy is kneeling on the ground holding a football. Charlie Brown, with arms outstretched, shouts "How long, O Lord?" Printed: "Charles Schulz Interview." Pages 3, 5-41. Soft-cover. #31-32. Jan/Winter 1992. $10-20

37. Magazines

•*Jack and Jill* Magazine. Snoopy dances while playing a fiddle. Woodstock and his friends dance along behind him with musical notes over their heads. Pages 16-17. Soft-cover. January 1977. $10-12

•*Children's Digest.* Charlie Brown, Lucy, and Linus hold hands while standing in front of a Christmas tree. Snoopy is sitting on top of the tree. Pages 8-11. Soft-cover. December 1970. $10-12

•*Sing Out! The Folk Song Magazine.* A four-panel comic strip featuring Charlie Brown and Roy at camp is depicted on the cover. Cover only. September 1965. $7-10

•*Time* Magazine. Snoopy and Linus sit on top of the dog-house. Schroeder plays his piano as Lucy, leaning on the piano, gazes at him. Charlie Brown, standing, watches them. Printed "Comment In The Comics" and "The World According To PEANUTS." Pages 19, 80-84. April 9, 1965. $12-15

38. *The Illustrator* Magazine

•The front cover depicts an oil painting of a young girl and boy in a field. The back cover is a full-color, thirteen-panel comic strip featuring Charlie Brown and Patty (not Peppermint). Inside the magazine (pages 13-19) is an article about Charles Schulz featuring more of his cartoons and comic strips. Summer 1954. Vol. 40, No 3. Published by Art Instruction, Inc., Minneapolis, MN. $35-40

POP-UP BOOKS

39. Pop-Up Books

Hardcover.

•*The Peanuts Philosophers,* by Charles M. Schulz. #400HEC33, Hallmark. 1972. $35-40

•*Snoopy's Secret Life,* by Charles M. Schulz. #400HEC34, Hallmark. 1972. $35-40

•*Snoopy And The Twelve Days Of Christmas,* by Charles M. Schulz. The cover depicts Snoopy and Woodstock on Snoopy's doghouse, wearing stocking caps and surrounded by Christmas gifts. Determined Productions. 1984. $25-35

40. Pop-Up Books

Hardcover. Hallmark. $35-40 ea.

•*Christmas Time With Snoopy And His Friends.* #495HEC80. 1978.

•*Love A La Peanuts,* by Charles M. Schulz. #400HEC35. 1972.

•*It's Good To Have A Friend,* by Charles M. Schulz. #400HEC36. 1972.

VIDEOS AND MUSIC

41. Promotional Display

• Lucy, with her head back and mouth wide open, promotes PEANUTS videos sold through Shell Oil gas stations. Printed: "AARGGGHH! Charlie Brown's All-New Video Is Only Available Until Dec. 25th, And Only At Shell. Only $4.99." Cardboard. 1992. $6-8

Videos

• Available as a promotion through Shell Oil for $4.99 with purchase of gasoline. Woodstock and his friends, wearing football helmets, throw a container of ice water on Snoopy. Printed: "You're In The Super Bowl, Charlie Brown." This PEANUTS film did not air on television until after the Shell promotion had ended. 1993. $4-6

• Available as a promotion through Shell Oil for $3.99 with purchase of gasoline. Charlie Brown looks at his scrawny Christmas tree, made top heavy by an ornament. Printed: "A Charlie Brown Christmas." 1991. $4-6

• Available as a promotion through Shell Oil for $4.99 with purchase of gasoline. Snoopy, wearing a top hat and bow tie, leans on a candy cane. Printed: "It's Christmastime Again, Charlie Brown." 1992. $4-6

42. 8-Track Cartridges

• "Merry Snoopy's Christmas With Snoopy and His Friends The Royal Guardsmen." Snoopy, wearing a red nightshirt and cap, holds a candle. He is pictured inside a Christmas wreath. Plastic. #8TMLP1238, Mistletoe Records, a product of Springboard International, courtesy of Laurie Records. 1978. $4-6

• Original cast album recording of "You're A Good Man, Charlie Brown." Charlie Brown reads a poster for the play. Plastic. #MCC 89, MGM. Early 1970s. $4-6

43. Records

• "Vince Guaraldi" and "Oh Good Grief!" Snoopy, wearing glasses and a mustache, stands in front of Schroeder and his piano. Cardboard sleeve and vinyl record. #1747, Warner Brothers-Seven Arts Records. 1968. $15-20

• Original soundtrack for the CBS-TV special, "A Charlie Brown Christmas Featuring The Famous PEANUTS Characters." Charlie Brown, Lucy, and Linus hold hands in front of a Christmas tree. Snoopy sits on top of the tree. In stereo. Cardboard sleeve and vinyl record. #8431, Fantasy Records. Mid-1960s. $12-15

• "Jazz Impressions Of A Boy Named Charlie Brown" and "Vince Guaraldi Trio." Linus and Charlie Brown play instruments and Snoopy dances. Lucy leans on Schroeder's piano, which is being played by Vince Guaraldi as Schroeder stands nearby. A set of twelve 8" x 10" posters, pictured on the back of the record, are included. In stereo. Cardboard sleeve and vinyl record. #85017, Fantasy Records. Late 1960s. $15-20

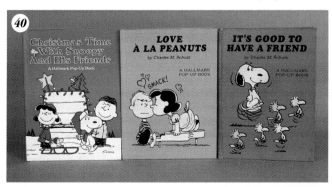

itting on the couch is a plush Snoopy from Japan. The Woodstock next to him is from Mexico. All of the items on the coffee table are from Japan. They include the metal tray, the tea set and cups behind the tray, and the red and the black music boxes. Also, the musicals: Snoopy kissing Lucy (on the left), Snoopy on a mushroom (front right), and Snoopy on an eggplant (back right, near the couch).

The characters with the green caps on the table behind the couch are nodders, from Japan. Immediately to their right are four banks featuring Lucy, Schroeder, Charlie Brown, and Linus, each playing an instrument (Japan). On the table to the right is a remarkable Japanese tableau of twelve miniature PEANUTS characters and three Woodstocks, each dressed in traditional Japanese ceremonial outfits. Next to it is a picture frame (Japan).

The cabinet in the rear is the repository for a number of decorative pieces, all from Japan unless otherwise noted. The top shelf holds a single piece containing five of the PEANUTS characters wearing traditional Japanese outfits. To its right is a

carousel that accepts miniature cassettes. The shelf below it has two rows. In the front row are various small musicals. The back row consists of decorative banks featuring Snoopy, Belle, and four of their brothers playing instruments.

Going down to the next shelf, we find, on the left, a decorative ceramic Snoopy in a blue kimono. This item also doubles as a bug repellent for outdoor use. Next to it is an Olaf mug, and then another Snoopy in a kimono bug repellent—this one in a green kimono. To its right is a Charlie Brown mug, and on the extreme right is a Snoopy flexible rubber doll from England, known as a "bendy."

The three banks on the left side of the bottom shelf are from Switzerland. To their right are four banks: Snoopy, Linus, Schroeder, and Lucy, all wearing baseball uniforms. The table clock on the right is from Germany.

The picture on the wall is an American lithograph commemorating the 1990 exhibit of "Snoopy in Fashion" at the Louvre, in Paris, and Charles Schulz receiving the Ordre des Arts et des Lettres from the French Ministry of Culture.

The PEANUTS Home Collection

The Living Room

As more and more family activity, including entertaining, moves into the den/recreation room/playroom, or into any room that houses a computer, the lesser-used living room is more apt to maintain its status as the showplace of the house.

One would expect to find decorative items in a showplace, and our living room is no exception as we display a large number of pieces in both ceramic and crystal. Far and away the most popular collectible in our living room is the musical. As the reader will discover, the selection is bountiful and the choices are endless.

One note about terminology. Although it is customary to use the terms "musical" and "music box" interchangeably, in reality there is a difference. A musical is any piece that will play a tune. Most musicals, upon winding, will play a tune and will either revolve around a base or the characters will become animated. In some cases both will happen. Only a relatively small category of musicals actually have their tune activated by the opening of a lid or the cover of a box. This is the only group of musicals that can truly be called "music boxes."

• "Snoopy Jr." Snoopy sits, looking ahead, with a red ribbon around his neck. 5"H. #M736/12-01. $140-150 $155-200*

• "Snoopy Sr." Snoopy sits, looking ahead, with a red ribbon around his neck. Produced in a limited edition of 1,000 signed pieces, this Snoopy did not come packaged in a graphic box. 7"H. #M736/18-01. $200-225

CRYSTAL

1. Crystal

Packaged in the pictured doghouse-shaped box. Made in Sweden by Marcolin. Distributed by Riedel of America. 1988.

• "Snoopy Snoozing." Snoopy is lying on his tummy. 7"L. #M740/18-01. $140-150 $160-180*

• "Sitting Snoopy." Snoopy sits with his head bowed down and a red bow around his neck. 5"H. #M734/12-01. $100-120 $130-150*

2. Crystal

• Snoopy is sitting. "UFS 1972" is etched on the bottom. 4-3/4"H. Determined Productions. 1972. $75-85

3. Crystal

• "Joe Cool Hockey." Snoopy, as Joe Cool, plays hockey. 4-1/4"H. #02814, Silver Deer. 1992. $130-150

• "Joe Cool Surfin'." Snoopy, as Joe Cool, rides a wave on a surfboard. 3-13/16"H. #02019, Silver Deer. 1990. $145-155

• "Golfing Snoopy." Snoopy plays golf. His golf bag stands nearby. 3". #02650, Silver Deer. 1991. $150-155

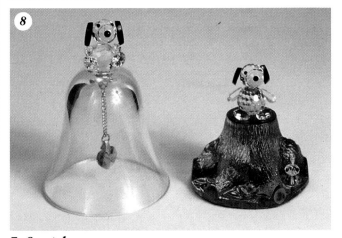

4. Crystal

•"Sledding With Snoopy." Snoopy and Woodstock share a sled. 1-11/16"H. #02648, Silver Deer. 1991. $85-95

•"Joe Cool Skiin'." Snoopy, as Joe Cool, is a skier. 2"H. #02020, Silver Deer. 1990. $90-100

•"Slugger Snoopy." Snoopy swings a baseball bat. 1-1/4"H. #04489, Silver Deer. 1993. $115-125

•"Flying Ace." Snoopy, as the Flying Ace, is in his Sopwith Camel. Produced in a limited edition of 1,500 pieces. 3-5/8"H. #02649, Silver Deer. 1991. $150-160

5. Crystal

•"Snoopy's Suppertime." Snoopy sits with his supper dish in front of him. Produced in a limited edition of 5,000 pieces. 75mm H. #01973, Silver Deer. 1990. $150-160

6. Crystal

•Woodstock sitting. 1-1/8"H. #04482, Silver Deer. 1993. $50-60

•Snoopy sitting. 21mm H. #01976, Silver Deer. 1990. $50-60

•Snoopy is standing with outstretched arms. 35mm H. #01975, Silver Deer. 1990. $50-60

•"Snoopy With Heart." Snoopy, with a red heart on his chest, is standing with outstretched arms. 1-3/16"H. #00131, Silver Deer. 1991. $50-60

•"Good Grief!" Snoopy sits on top of his doghouse. 52mm H. #01974, Silver Deer. 1990. $55-65.

7. Crystal

•"Joe Cool Skateboardin'." Snoopy, as Joe Cool, rides on a gold skateboard. 3-1/16"H. #02811, Silver Deer. 1992. $120-125

•Spike, wearing a gold hat, stands next to a cactus with red flowers. 3-1/16"H. #03147, Silver Deer. 1992. $145-155

•"Joe Cool Jammin'." Snoopy, as Joe Cool, plays the drums. 3"H. #02319, Silver Deer. 1991. $140-150

•"Joe Cool Croonin'." Snoopy stands behind a gold microphone. 2-1/16"H. #02324, Silver Deer. 1991. $125-135

•"Literary Ace." Snoopy sits at a gold typewriter with paper in it printed, "It was a dark and stormy night." 1-5/8"H. #02810, Silver Deer. 1992. $110-120

•"Toe Tappin' Snoopy." Snoopy sits on top of a gold piano while Woodstock sits on the gold bench playing the piano. 2"H. #03794, Silver Deer. 1993. $130-140

8. Crystal

•Snoopy sits on top of a glass bell with a pink crystal heart as the bell ringer. 3"H. #03817, Silver Deer. 1993. $50-55

9

10

11

12

13

•"Hide and Seek." Snoopy stands on a tree stump with Woodstock below. 2-1/4"H. #07164, Silver Deer. 1994. $50-60

9. Comic Strip Panel

•"Warm & Fuzzy." The three-panel comic strip features Charlie Brown towel drying Snoopy. Lucite. 8-7/8"L. #04739, Silver Deer. 1995. $45-50

Comic Strip Panel

"Literary Ace." The three-panel comic strip features Snoopy on top of his doghouse with his typewriter. Lucite. 9-1/8"L. Silver Deer. 1993.

•With crystal Snoopy. #03801. $75-85
•Without Snoopy. #03800. $45-50

10. Comic Strip Panel

"The Outfield." The three-panel comic strip features Charlie Brown on his pitcher's mound and Lucy in the outfield. Lucite. 9-1/8"L. Silver Deer. 1993.

•With crystal Snoopy. #03797. $75-85
•Without Snoopy. #03796. $45-50

Comic Strip Panel

"The Psychiatrist Is In." The two-panel comic strip features Charlie Brown with Lucy at her psychiatrist booth. Lucite. 5-3/32"L. Silver Deer. 1993.

•With crystal Snoopy. #03799. $75-80
•Without Snoopy. #03798. $40-50

11. Crystal

•"Joe Cool T-Bird." Snoopy, as Joe Cool, rides in a T-Bird convertible replica. Limited edition of 1,500 pieces. 10-1/2"L. #03804, Silver Deer. 1993. $200-250

•"Joe Cool Cruisin'." Snoopy, as Joe Cool, rides in a 1936 Mercedes 500K Roadster replica. Limited edition of 1,500 pieces. 10"L. #02018, Silver Deer. 1990. $250-275

12. Crystal

•"Snoopy and Woodstock Mercedes." Snoopy rides in a Mercedes Benz convertible, with Woodstock sitting on the back of the car above the spare tire. Limited edition of 1,750 pieces. The color of the car may vary. 7"L. #07163, Silver Deer. 1994. $250-275

13. Crystal

•"Joe Cool Jag." Snoopy, as Joe Cool, rides in a Jaguar convertible. 10"L. #04738, Silver Deer. 1994. $240-260

•"Joe Cool 'Vette." Snoopy, as Joe Cool, rides in a Corvette convertible. The hood, trunk and doors open. Limited edition of 1,500 pieces. 9-5/8"L. #02807, Silver Deer. 1992. $250-275

DECORATIVE ITEMS

14. Ceramic Eggs

Aviva. 1972. $12-20 ea.

•Snoopy lies on his tummy across a red heart, and looks over the edge at Woodstock. Printed: "I Love You."

•Woodstock sits on Snoopy's nose and sings musical notes. Printed: "Let's Be Friends."

•Snoopy is surrounded by red hearts. Printed: "A Little Love Goes A Long Way."

•Snoopy holds an ice cream cone against a yellow circle. Printed: "Hummm..."

•Snoopy kisses Lucy on the cheek against a yellow circle. Printed: "Smak!"

14

15. Ceramic Eggs

Aviva. 1972. $12-20 ea.

•Snoopy is biting his tennis racket, against a green circle. Printed: "Aaugh!"

•Snoopy is dressed as a Scout, with Woodstock and his friends sitting around the brim of his hat. Printed: "World's Greatest Dad."

•Snoopy, dressed as a chef, holds a frying pan and spatula. Printed: "Joe Gourmet."

•Snoopy leaps over the word "Mom." Printed: "World's Greatest Mom."

•Snoopy is biting his tennis racket. Printed: "Aaugh!"

16. Ceramic Eggs

Aviva. 1972. $12-20 ea.

•Snoopy is sitting in front of a rainbow with his arms outstretched. Printed: "You're The Cutest."

•Snoopy, grinning and holding his supper dish to his heart, against a yellow circle, thinks, "I'm So Cute!"

•Snoopy, grinning and holding his supper dish to his heart, thinks, "I'm So Cute!"

•Snoopy, standing among some flowers, winks. Printed: "Hi, Sweetie!"

17. Ceramic Eggs

Aviva. 1972. $12-20 ea.

•Snoopy and Woodstock share Woodstock's nest, against a blue circle. Printed: "Love Is For Sharing."

•Snoopy hugs Charlie Brown, against a yellow circle. Printed: "MMMMM."

•Snoopy is sitting and holding a flower, against an orange circle. Printed: "Gee!"

•Snoopy holds a bouquet of flowers, against a yellow circle. Printed: "Giving Is More Fun Than Receiving."

•Snoopy holds a heart and has a tear on his cheek, against a blue circle. Printed: "Snif!"

18. Ceramic Egg

•Snoopy and Woodstock are asleep, leaning back on a rock, against a blue circle. Printed: "ZZZZZ." Egg stands on its wider end. Aviva. 1972. $12-20

•Snoopy is dancing, with a basket of flowers in his hand. A ring of pink, blue, and white flowers encircles the egg. Printed: "I Feel Free!" The egg lies on its side, rather than standing on end. Determined Productions. Mid-1970s. $40-45

•Snoopy and Woodstock share Woodstock's nest. Printed: "You're The Best." Egg stands on its wider end. Aviva. 1972. $12-20

19. Ceramic Eggs

Aviva. 1972. $12-20 ea.

•Snoopy is lying on top of his doghouse. Musical notes come from inside. Printed: "Security Is A Happy Home."

•Snoopy sits at his typewriter as Woodstock looks on. Printed: "Work Is For The Birds."

•Snoopy and Woodstock share Woodstock's nest. Printed: "Love Is For Sharing."

20. Gift Boxes

Decorative bows top the lift-off lids on the boxes. Ceramic. Determined Productions. 1976.

•Snoopy lies in the ribbon of a six-sided gift box. 6"H. Blue bow: #8822. Pink bow: #8823. Gift box with blue bow: $160-175. Gift box with pink bow (rarer): $175-195

•Snoopy and Woodstock lie in the blue ribbon of a square gift box. 4-1/2"H x 4-1/2"W x 3-1/2"D. #8821. $140-150

21. Heart- and Letter-shaped Boxes

•Heart-shaped box. Snoopy lies on his tummy on the lift-off lid, which bears the word "Love" in raised lettering. Ceramic. 5-1/2"W. #8483, Determined Productions. Late 1970s. $60-70

•Heart-shaped box. Snoopy sits on the lift-off lid, which has the word "Love" in raised lettering. Silver, lined in red velvet. 2-1/2"W. #7, Leonard Silver. 1979. $15-25

•Heart-shaped box. Snoopy sits on the lift-off lid, which has the word "Love" in raised lettering. Ceramic. 2-1/2"W. #8835, Determined Productions. Late 1970s. $12-15

•Letter-shaped box. Snoopy, holding a letter with a heart on it, sits on the lift-off lid. The box resembles envelopes tied with an orange ribbon and bow. Ceramic. 5"L x 6"H x 4"D. #8827, Determined Productions. 1976. $175-195

22. Nut-shaped Dishes

Ceramic. Determined Productions.

•Large Peanut. 4" x 7-1/2". #8824. 1977. $65-75

•Small Peanut. 2-1/2" x 3". #8920. 1978. $185-195

•Walnut. 2-1/2" x 3". #8921. 1978. $155-160

FIGURES

23. Bronze Sculptures

Set of five figures depicts Snoopy and Woodstock in various scenes. Each figure is solid bronze and fits onto a 1-1/2" wooden base. Each base has a bronze plaque with the title of the scene, and is printed, "Solid Bronze Sculpture Derived From Original Art Of Charles M. Schulz Limited Edition." The set was limited to 7,500 pieces. Packaged in a red velvet-lined wooden box, the set included a certificate of authenticity, a history of the first edition, a photo sheet, and a statement by Charles Schulz. International Trading Technology, Inc., 1992. $275-300**

•"Dreaming." Snoopy leans against a tree with Woodstock in his nest above. 2"H.

•"Friends." Snoopy and Woodstock, dressed as Scouts, roast hot dogs and marshmallows over a campfire. 1-1/8"H.

•"Admiration." Snoopy and Woodstock face each other, sitting atop Snoopy's doghouse. 2-1/2"H.

•"Sharing." Snoopy and Woodstock are surrounded by cookies, ice cream, hot dogs, hamburgers, and doughnuts. 1-1/8"H.

•"Snow Buddies." Snoopy, with Woodstock sitting in his hat, skis past a tree. 2-1/8"H.

24. Figures

"PEANUTS Classic Moments." Each figure has the name of the scene on the underside of the base. Set of twelve, sold individually. Resin. Danbury Mint. 1993. $40-60 ea.

•"The Flying Ace." Snoopy, as the Flying Ace, and Woodstock are on top of Snoopy's doghouse, which is on a cloud base. 2-7/8"H.

•"Charlie Brown and Linus." Charlie Brown and Linus lean against a brick wall, on a grass base. 3-7/8"L.

•"Skate Mates." Snoopy and Woodstock play hockey on a birdbath. 3-1/2" diam.

•"Psychiatrist." Lucy sits behind her psychiatrist booth, advising Charlie Brown. 4" diam.

•"Baseball Mound." Schroeder and Charlie Brown, dressed in baseball gear, stand on the pitcher's mound. 4" diam.

•"Snoopy's Kiss." Snoopy kisses Lucy on the cheek. She is sticking out her tongue. 3" x 2" rectangular base.

25. Figures

"PEANUTS Classic Moments." Each figure has the name of the scene on the underside of the base. Set of twelve, sold individually. Resin. Danbury Mint. 1993. $40-60 ea.

•"Lovestruck Lucy." Schroeder plays his piano as Lucy reclines against it. Oval base 5"L.

•"Pumpkin Patch." Linus is sitting in a pumpkin patch. 4" x 3".

•"Fooled Again." Lucy has pulled the football out from under Charlie Brown, who lies on the ground. 4-7/8"L base.

•"Peppermint Patty." Peppermint Patty is asleep at her desk, with her school book open. 3-1/2" x 3" base.

•"Strung Out." Snoopy sits next to Charlie Brown, who is holding his kite. 3-1/2"L oval base.

•"Sally's Valentine." Linus runs from Sally as she tries to give him a Valentine. 4"L oval base.

26. Figurine

•Snoopy is dressed as a king, wearing a red crown and a red robe trimmed in white, and holding a scepter. One of a few samples, this item never went into production. It was also produced as a prototype of an ornament. Ceramic. 3-1/2"H. Determined Productions. Mid-1970s. $300-350

27. Figures

Set of five figures depict Snoopy performing a headstand. Ceramic. Determined Productions. Early 1980s.

•Snoopy is sitting. $35-40

•Snoopy leans back and starts to bring his legs up. $35-40

•Snoopy is on his back with his legs in the air. $45-50 (rarer)

•Snoopy is standing on his hands with his legs straight up. $35-40

•Snoopy begins to bring his legs down to the ground. $45-50

28. Figurines

Ceramic. Willitts Designs. 1989. $35-38*

•"Best Friends." Snoopy hugs Woodstock. 4"H. #9312.

•"Flying Ace." Snoopy, as the Flying Ace. 4"H. #9314.

•"The Good Life." Snoopy lies in his supper dish. 3"H. #9313.

•"World Famous Author." Snoopy sits at his typewriter. 3-1/2"H. #9311.

29. Figurine

The characters each ride on a porcelain carousel horse. The brass base has an inlaid coin featuring Snoopy, and printed "PEANUTS Playland Carousel." 5"H. Willitts Designs. 1989. $25-30*

•Lucy. #9589.

•Snoopy. #9587. (Not pictured)

•Charlie Brown. #9588. (Not pictured)

•Linus. #9590. (Not pictured)

30

31

32

•Schroeder. 2-1/2"H.

•Schroeder's piano. 1-7/8"L.

•Lucy. 3"L.

•Charlie Brown. 3"H.

•Marcie. 2-3/4"H.

•Peppermint Patty. 3"H.

•Linus. 2-1/2"H.

•Sally. 3"H.

30. Jointed Figure

•Snoopy's arms and legs are jointed and movable. Ceramic. 12"H in the sitting position. Determined Productions. Early 1980s. $400-500

31. Musical Jewelry Box with Figures

"40th Anniversary Gift Set." This set was a gift from United Media to some of the PEANUTS licensees. The music played is "Schroeder," by Vince Guaraldi. A bronze plate on the front of the music box features the 40th anniversary logo. The box is lined in velvet, and has a jewelry compartment beneath the figures. Numbered and limited to 500 pieces. Bone china figures and walnut box. The music box comes in a graphic cardboard box, with the 40th anniversary logo on the top and the characters on all four sides. 1990. $850-1000*

•Snoopy hugging Woodstock by Snoopy's doghouse. 3"H.

32. Nodders

The heads of the characters are attached to their bodies by a spring. The heads "nod" when moved. Each character stands on a base printed with his or her name and "Of The PEANUTS Comic Strip." Papier-mâché. 5-1/2"H. Lego. 1959.

•Pig Pen (sic). $160-190

•Linus. $85-165

•Schroeder. $85-165

•Lucy. $85-165

•Snoopy. $85-165

•Charlie Brown. $85-165

The material from which the nodders and bobbleheads were made had a tendency to crack, chip, and peel, especially with changes in the weather. The nodders fare the worst. It is difficult to find one in mint condition. If you do find it mint, or even very good condition, ask the seller how it was stored.

33. Bobbleheads

The heads of the characters are attached to their bodies by a spring. The heads "bobble" when moved. Papier-mâché. 4"H. Determined Productions. 1976.

•Sitting Snoopy. $30-35

•Lucy. $40-45

•Charlie Brown. $40-45

•Woodstock. $35-40

•Snoopy, dressed as Santa. $30-35

•Snoopy, as the Flying Ace. $25-32

•Snoopy, as Joe Cool. $25-32

34. Porcelain Baseball Team

The PEANUTS characters each wear a red baseball cap. The figures are approximately 2"H. They are posed on a hardwood baseball diamond with no PEANUTS graphics. Base measures 10"W x 1"H x 10-3/4"D. Willitts Designs. 1988.

• Set of six figures and baseball diamond. #8627. $145-155

• Baseball diamond. #8124. $15-20

• Schroeder dressed as a catcher. #8128. $25-35*

• Snoopy with Woodstock perched on his cap and bat in hand. #8127. $25-35*

• Linus holding his blanket. #8129. $25-35*

• Charlie Brown with baseball and glove. #8126 $25-35*

• Lucy with glove. #8125. $25-35*

• Peppermint Patty with glove. #8130. $25-35*

35. Snowfall Water Globe

• Lucy stands inside the globe with her mouth open and her arm extended. Printed on the base: "Will someone please tell me what's going on?" Resin base and figure. Glass globe. 4"H. #45065, Willitts Designs. 1992. $45-50*

Figurines on Bases

Resin. Willitts Designs. 1992. $35-40*

• Lucy stands on a base with her mouth open and her arm extended. Printed: "Will someone please tell me what's going on?" 3-3/4"W x 5"H. #45071.

• Lucy slouches in a chair that appears to be too big for her. Printed: "I'm tired, I'm crabby, I'm mad and this is a good day!" 2-5/8"W x 5"H. #45069.

• Snoopy stands in the center of a raised platform, with Woodstock and his friend on lower ground to each side. They all wear medals around their necks. Printed: "Gold Medal Friend." 4-1/4"W x 4-1/4"H. #45067.

• Sally stands at a bus stop with her brown bag lunch at her side. Printed: "Is it too late to call in sick?" 2-3/4"W x 4-1/2"H. #45072.

• Lucy lies on her back with her tongue sticking out. Printed: "Birthdays don't come and go so much as they hit and run." 3-3/4"W x 2-1/4"H. #45068. (Not pictured)

36. Thimbles

Hawaiian scenes atop pewter thimbles. Each of the eight thimbles was available in any of three different finishes: Series 6000 (#6001-6008)—an antique pewter finish; Series 6100 (#6101-6108)—spot-painted by hand; and Series 6200 (#6201-6208)—completely hand painted. (Examples from 6100 and 6200 depicted here.) Each thimble displays "Aloha" in raised lettering. Saratoga Mint, Ltd. 1989. $22-25 ea.

• Schroeder plays his piano, which has a pineapple and a watermelon slice on top.

• Charlie Brown reclines in a lounge chair.

• Sally has an inner tube around her waist.

• Snoopy, as Joe Cool, and Woodstock ride a wave on a surfboard.

37. Thimbles

Hawaiian scenes atop pewter thimbles. The thimbles came in three different finishes: Series 6000 (#6001-6008)—antique pewter finish (depicted here); Series 6100 (#6101-6108)—spot-painted by hand; and Series 6200 (#6201-6208)—completely hand painted. Each thimble has the word "Aloha" in raised lettering. Saratoga Mint, Ltd. 1989. $22-25 ea.

38

39

• Snoopy, as Joe Cool, and Woodstock ride a wave on a surfboard.

• Lucy, wearing goggles and fins, swims underwater with the fish.

• Linus builds a sand castle.

• Charlie Brown reclines in a lounge chair.

38. Thimbles

Hawaiian scenes atop pewter thimbles. The thimbles came in three different finishes: Series 6000 (#6001-6008)—antique pewter finish (depicted here); Series 6100 (#6101-6108)—spot-painted by hand; and Series 6200 (#6201-6208)—completely hand-painted. Each thimble displays the word "Aloha" in raised lettering. Saratoga Mint, Ltd. 1989. $22-25 ea.

• Marcie wears a grass skirt and does a hula dance.

• Sally has an inner tube around her waist.

• Schroeder plays his piano, which has a pineapple and a watermelon slice on top.

• Peppermint Patty rides a windsurfer.

MUSICALS

Question: If it plays music, what is it?

Answer: A musical.

Question: If it looks like a box, and the lid opens and it plays music, what is it?

Answer: A music box—which is one form of musical.

Question: If it doesn't look like a box and plays music, what is it?

Answer: A musical.

The point here is that most people (mistakenly) believe that any device that plays music is a music box. Not so! A device that plays music comes under the general heading of "musical." Only a device that is box-shaped and plays music when the lid is opened can truly be called a music box. A music box, therefore, is just one specific type of musical. In this book, I correctly use the word "musical" to describe any device that plays music. If it happens to be shaped like a box, I will call it a music box—but only if the lid opens.

I have not attempted to analyze why musicals are so popular. They just are. Unlike most items, where the packaging enhances the price, musicals do not lose monetary value if the box is missing. The Schmid musicals did not come in graphic boxes. I did not put an asterisk after the price. The unusual exception—the wooden musical depicting Snoopy as the Flying Ace on his doghouse—is pictured on page 213. The same goes for the companies Anri, Aviva, and Quantasia. On the other hand, more often than not, Willitts musicals did come in a graphic box. Although the price does not change, I noted this with an asterisk.

In the late 1960s and early 1970s, Anri, a division of Schmid, manufactured hand-painted, hand-carved, wood musicals in Italy. They were distributed by Schmid here in the United States.

Other companies that manufactured musicals from the 1970s through the early 1990s included Aviva, Quantasia, Schmid, and Willitts.

In addition to its regular line of musicals and music boxes, both wood and ceramic, Schmid produced dated Christmas musicals in 1980, 1981, and 1982, and Mother's Day musicals in 1981 and 1982. In 1983, Schmid began to manufacture an annual musical with a matching plate and bell, having no particular holiday theme, as was done prior to 1983. Each year was a different Limited Edition design. This continued through 1986. You will see the matching plates and bells in other chapters.

In 1987, the musical "Big Top Blast Off" was to be the "Fifth Limited Edition," but before production began, Schmid gave up its PEANUTS license and only a few prototypes made it into the hands of collectors, along with a matching bell and plate. There was one other Schmid musical, depicting Snoopy looking at a Christmas tree decorated with Woodstock and his friends, distributed in small quantities. Both of these musicals are pictured together on page 210. Note the high prices these command. They prove the old adage, "If I can't have it, I want it—and I'll pay for it".

Willitts, known for its carousel designs, became a new licensee and picked up where Schmid left off. In 1987, in addition to other PEANUTS collectibles, they began to manufacture musicals, some dated, but most undated. The dated musicals of 1987-1992 had a matching bell, plate, and ornament. In some years, a matching ceramic disk ornament and musical glitter dome was included.

Last, but not least, are the manufacturers Aviva and Quantasia. Although the quality in no way matches that of Schmid or even Willitts, they are sought after to complete a musical collection.

You will also notice that the music played does not vary all that much, and some musicals may play more than one tune.

They are a colorful and decorative collection to display, but if played all at once, they can, of course, prove very noisy.

ANRI

39. Display

• "PEANUTS Music Boxes By Anri." The display features pictures of three music boxes and a close-up of Charlie Brown. Cardboard. $20-25

39A. Musicals

Hand-painted and hand-carved wood musicals. Made in Italy by Anri. Distributed in the United States by Schmid. 1968.

40

41

42

•Lucy stands behind her psychiatrist booth. A non-Woodstock bird is perched on the booth. Plays "Try To Remember." 6-3/4"H x 4" diam. octagon base. #819-400. $225-265

•Charlie Brown stands in front of Lucy, who is behind her psychiatrist booth. A non-Woodstock bird and small flowers are on the base. Plays "Try To Remember." 8-1/2"H x 5" diam. base. #819-200. $275-295

40. Musicals

Hand painted and hand carved. Wood. Made in Italy by Anri. Distributed in the United States by Schmid.

•Snoopy, as the Flying Ace, is standing in a battlefield with barbed wire and a WWI helmet. 4"H x 4-1/4" diam. base. #819-010 plays "Pack Up Your Troubles." #819-020 plays "It's A Long Way To Tipperary." 1968. $95-130

•Snoopy, wearing a striped stocking cap and gloves, plays hockey as a non-Woodstock bird watches. A puck is on the ice and small flowers are on the base. Plays "My Way" or "Love Story." 5"H x 4-1/4" diam. base. #81907. 1971. $90-125

•Snoopy, wearing a striped stocking cap, ice-skates. A snow-covered tree, flowers, and a non-Woodstock bird encircle the base. Plays "Skater's Waltz." 5"H x 4-1/4" diam. base. #819-050. 1970. $90-125

•Charlie Brown, wearing a baseball cap, holds a bat over his shoulders. Two non-Woodstock birds and flowers encircle the musical. Plays "Take Me Out To The Ball Game." 6"H x 4-1/4" diam. base. #819-060. 1968. $125-135

41. Musicals

Hand painted and hand carved. Wood. Made in Italy by Anri. Distributed in the United States by Schmid.

•Snoopy, on all fours, comes up behind Linus, who holds his blanket. Small flowers are on the base. Plays "Please Release Me." 5"H x 4-1/4" diam. base. #819-040. 1968. $130-135

•Schroeder plays his piano on a checkered base. A bust of Beethoven is on the piano and non-Woodstock bird is on the base. Plays "Leitmotiv Kaiserkonzert," "Beethoven's Emperor's Concerto No. 5" or "Beethoven's Minuet." 4-1/2"H x 4-1/4" diam. base. #819-030. 1968. $160-175

•Schroeder at his piano. A bust of Beethoven is on top. A toy soldier and small flowers are on the base. Plays "Third Man Theme." 6"H x 4" diam. octagon base. Late 1960s. $275-350

42. Musicals

Hand painted and hand carved. Wood. Made in Italy by Anri. Distributed in the United States by Schmid.

•Linus is standing and holding his blanket. Small flowers encircle the base. Plays "Close To You." 6"H x 3" diam. base. #81982. 1972. $240-245

•Snoopy, as the Flying Ace, is surrounded by small flowers. Plays "The Impossible Dream." 5"H x 3" diam. base. #81980. 1972. $250-260

•Lucy stands with small flowers around her feet. Plays "Love Story." 5"H x 3" diam. base. #81981. 1972. $185-190

43. Musical

•Snoopy, as the Flying Ace, is on the surface of the moon standing next to the Lunar Module. Charlie Brown hovers above in the Command Module. Musical plays "Battle Hymn Of The Republic." Commemorating the Apollo 10 flight, the rare music box pictured here is courtesy of a private collector, who wishes to remain anonymous. Hand painted and hand carved. Wood. Made in Italy by Anri. Distributed in the United States by Schmid. 1969. $3,000-3,500

44. Musicals

Hand painted and hand carved. Wood. Made in Italy by Anri. Distributed in the United States by Schmid.

•Snoopy, Linus, and a non-Woodstock bird stand near a small doghouse. Plays "What The World Needs Now Is Love." 3"H x 3" diam. base. #81972. 1972. $170-185

•Snoopy and Lucy stand near a small doghouse. A non-Woodstock bird sits on top. Plays "Close To You." 3-1/2"H x 3" diam. base. #81971. 1972. $170-185

•Charlie Brown and Lucy stand under a mushroom-shaped tree with small flowers on the base. Plays "Rose Garden." 5"H x 3" diam. base. #81973. 1972. $175-190

•Snoopy stands under a mushroom-shaped tree next to a small doghouse with a non-Woodstock bird on top. Small flowers are also on the base. Plays "Yellow Bird." 5"H x 3" diam. base. #81970. 1972. $175-195

43

•Schroeder plays his piano under a mushroom-shaped tree with small flowers around the base. A non-Woodstock bird is on top of the piano. Plays "Emperor's Concerto No. 5." 5"H x 3" diam. base. #81974. 1971. $185-225

45. Musical Wall Hangings

Turn the knob at the bottom of the frame to hear the music. Hand painted. Wood. 6" x 8-1/4". Made in Italy by Anri. Distributed in the United States by Schmid. 1971.

•Schroeder plays his piano, while Snoopy dances on top. Three-dimensional flowers, trees, and fence in foreground. Plays "I Could Have Danced All Night." #72393/2. $295-350

•Linus sits in a pumpkin patch. Three-dimensional flowers, trees, and fences are in the foreground. Plays "Who Can I Turn To?" #72393/1. $355-395

•Snoopy kisses Lucy on the nose. Plays "Honey." #72393/3. $350-395

•Charlie Brown pats a sitting Snoopy on the head. Plays "Love Makes The World Go Round." #72393/5. $350-395

•Peppermint Patty tosses a baseball, ready to swing her bat. Snoopy, wearing a baseball cap and glove, watches. Plays "Take Me Out To The Ballgame." #72393/6. $375-425

•Snoopy is on his doghouse as Woodstock flies upside down. Plays "Yellowbird." #72393/4. $295-350 (Not pictured)

46. Music Boxes

Hinged lids open, revealing a different design inside. Hand painted. Wood. 7" x 4-1/4" x 2". Made in Italy by Anri. Distributed in the United States by Schmid. 1971. $230-265 ea.

•Snoopy kisses Lucy on the nose. Inside design: Snoopy is sitting on his doghouse as Woodstock flies upside down.

Plays "Honey." #33905/3.

•Schroeder plays his piano while Snoopy dances on top. Inside design: Snoopy kisses Lucy on the nose. Plays "I Could Have Danced All Night." #33905/2.

•Charlie Brown pats a sitting Snoopy on the head. Inside design: Peppermint Patty tosses a baseball, ready to swing her bat. Snoopy, wearing a baseball cap and glove, watches. Plays "Raindrops Keep Falling On My Head." #33905/5.

•Snoopy is on his doghouse as Woodstock flies upside down. Plays "Yellowbird." #33905/4. (Not pictured)

•Peppermint Patty tosses a baseball, ready to swing her bat. Snoopy, wearing a baseball cap and glove, watches. Plays "Take Me Out To The Ball Game." #33905/6. (Not pictured)

•Linus is sitting in a pumpkin patch. Inside design: Schroeder plays his piano while Snoopy dances on top. Plays "Who Can I Turn To?" #33905/1. (Not pictured)

47. Mini Music Boxes

These boxes do not open, and have a carved floral design on all four sides. Hand painted. Wood. 2-1/4" x 1-7/8". Made in Italy by Anri. Distributed in the United States by Schmid. 1971. $75-85 ea.

•Charlie Brown pats a sitting Snoopy on the head. Plays "Raindrops Keep Falling On My Head." #33908/5.

•Linus is sitting in a pumpkin patch. Plays "The Shadow Of Your Smile." #33908/1.

•Peppermint Patty tosses a baseball, ready to swing her bat. Snoopy, wearing a baseball cap and glove, watches. Plays "Hi Lilly Hi Lo." #33908/6.

•Snoopy is on his doghouse as Woodstock flies upside down. Plays "Edelweiss." #33908/4.

•Snoopy kisses Lucy on the nose. Plays "Honey." #33908/3. (Not pictured)

•Schroeder plays his piano while Snoopy dances on top. Plays "Lara's Theme." #33908/2. (Not pictured)

44

45

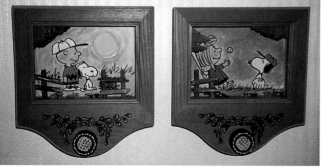

46

47

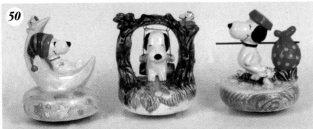

AVIVA

48. Musicals

Ceramic figures on composition base. The smaller figure of each musical has a magnet on its bottom, and moves independently of the base as it revolves. Aviva. 1975. $50-55 ea.

• Snoopy sits on a red base, wearing a straw hat and playing the mandolin for Woodstock. Plays "It's A Small World." 4-1/2" x 6-1/4".

• Snoopy stands on a green and white base playing a concertina for Woodstock. Plays "I'd Like To Teach The World To Sing." 4-1/2" x 6".

• Woodstock sits on Snoopy's snow-covered doghouse as Snoopy "skates" on the blue and white base. Plays "Skater's Waltz." 4-1/2" x 6-1/4".

• Woodstock, sitting in a tree, looks at Snoopy below on a green base. Plays "It's A Small World." 4-1/2" x 6-1/4".

49. Musicals

Ceramic. Aviva. $75-85 ea.

• Snoopy, wearing headphones, and Woodstock roller-skate on a pink base. Plays "Für Elise." 5"H. #212001. 1982.

• Woodstock sits on Snoopy's tennis racket as he is about to toss the tennis ball for a serve. Plays "Lara's Theme." 7-1/2"H. 1982.

• Woodstock sits on Snoopy's doghouse as Snoopy, sitting on the ground but at eye level with Woodstock, holds a pink heart. Plays "Love Story" or "Let's Fall In Love." 5"H. 1982.

• Snoopy wears a top hat and bow tie, and carries a cane on a red, white, and black base. Plays "Pennies From Heaven" or "Happy Days Are Here Again." 7-1/2"H. #213. 1979.

50. Musicals

Ceramic. 6"H. Aviva. 1974.

• Snoopy, wearing a stocking cap, lies in a crescent moon. Woodstock lies on the outside of the moon. Plays "Impossible Dream." $150-160

• Snoopy sits on a swing supported by a branch between two trees. Woodstock sits in his nest in one of the trees. Plays "Yellowbird." A similar design—one tree and Woodstock in a branch—was produced in 1982 (#212003). $95-100

• Snoopy wears his supper dish on his head and carries a hobo pack over his shoulder. Woodstock walks behind him. Plays "Born Free." $130-135

51. Musicals

Ceramic. Aviva. $30-35 ea.

• Snoopy is holding a bouquet of flowers. Multicolored hearts surround the white base. Plays "Somewhere, My Love." 5"H. 1974.

• Snoopy is lying on top of his doghouse with Woodstock sitting on his tummy. Multicolored flowers surround the white base. Plays "Für Elise." 5-1/2"H. 1982.

• Snoopy is wearing a party hat and holding a birthday cake with one candle on a white base. Plays "Happy Birthday" or "Fly Me To The Moon." A similar musical has the same figure of Snoopy, but the base is printed with "Happy Birthday" and musical notes. 5-1/2"H. 1974.

52. Musicals

Ceramic. Aviva. 1973.

• Snoopy, on skis with poles, wears a sweater, cap, and goggles on a white base. Plays "Edelweiss." A similar musical has the same figure of Snoopy, but the base is printed with "Ski Love." 5-1/4"H. $35-39

• Snoopy and Woodstock, sitting on the base, are wrapped in a blanket. Woodstock holds a paper pennant printed "Rah." Red pennants printed "State," "University," and "College" surround the white base. Plays "Raindrops Keep Falling On My Head." 5"H. $30-35

53. Musical

Ceramic. 5-1/4"H. Aviva. 1974. $25-30 ea.

• Snoopy, with Woodstock sitting on his tummy, lies on top of the multicolored word "Love," which circles the top of the base in tall letters. The base itself came either decorated with yellow flowers encircled in hearts, or in plain white. Plays "Theme From Love Story."

54. Music Boxes

Hinged lid. Lucite. 2-1/2"H x 3-1/2" diam. Aviva. 1982. $45-55

•Snoopy conducts, as Woodstock plays the violin on the lid. Printed: "Snoopy." Charlie Brown, Schroeder, Marcie, Sally, Lucy, Linus, Woodstock, and Snoopy play instruments around the circular box. Plays "Music Box Dancer." #211002.

•Snoopy rides a carousel horse, and Woodstock sits on a star on the lid. Linus, Lucy, Schroeder, and Marcie ride carousel horses around the circular box. Snoopy holds a cowboy hat, Woodstock flies upside down, and Charlie Brown has fallen off his horse. Plays "Für Elise." #211001.

Lift-off lids. Ceramic. Aviva. $75-85 ea.

•Snoopy lies on top of his doghouse, with Woodstock standing on his tummy. Plays "Candy Man." 8"H. #124. 1979.

•Snoopy, hugging Woodstock, sits on top of a heart-shaped box. "Love" is printed on the outside, "And Kisses" is printed on the inside of the heart. Plays "Love Makes The World Go Round." 6-1/2"H x 4-1/2"W. #215. 1982.

55. Music Boxes

•Snoopy, dressed as a cowboy, spells his name with a lasso. Woodstock, dressed as an Indian, sits on a cactus. Plays "Oh, What A Beautiful Morning." Hinged lid. Wood. 4-1/4" x 3-1/4" x 2-1/4". #216000, Aviva. 1982. $45-55

•The decal on the hinged lid features Snoopy, carrying a briefcase, and Woodstock walking in front of a city skyline. Printed: "Snoopy in New York." Snoopy, Charlie Brown, Linus, Sally, and Woodstock and his friends are featured walking around the music box in front of the city skyline, while Peppermint Patty and Marcie run to catch up. There is a mirror on the inside of the lid, and the music box is lined with velvet. Plays "Love Story." 4"W x 2-1/4"H. Plastic. Aviva. Early 1980s. $35-40

56. Music Boxes

Musical jewelry box. Ceramic figure; wood box. Aviva. 1974.

•Snoopy, on top of the box, revolves when the drawer is opened and music plays. Woodstock is asleep in bed. On the front of the drawer, Woodstock and his friends sing, with bars of music pictured above them. Plays "Beautiful Dreamer." 5-1/2" x 3-1/2". $75-85

•Snoopy, on top of the piano-shaped box, revolves when the drawer is opened and music plays. Woodstock is sitting at a red piano on top of the box. Plays "The Sound Of Music." 5-7/8" x 5-1/2" x 6". $55-60

57. Musical

•Snoopy, wearing a straw hat, sits on top of the musical picture frame. Plays "Candy Man." Ceramic figure; wood box. 3-1/4" x 6-1/2". 1974. $30-35

Music Box

•Snoopy, on top of the box, revolves when the hinged lid is opened and music plays. Woodstock flies a kite atop the box. Charlie Brown runs with his kite, as Snoopy is tangled in the string on the front of the box. Plays "Pennies From Heaven." Ceramic figure; wood box. 7-1/2" x 4-1/2" x 3". 1974. $75-85

QUANTASIA

58. Musical

•Snoopy sits on a red heart-shaped base, hugging Woodstock. Plays either "Swan Lake" or "Let Me Call You Sweetheart." Ceramic. 5-3/4"H. #141018, Quantasia. 1984. $70-80

Music Box

•Snoopy lies on his doghouse, with Woodstock sitting on his tummy. The music plays when the roof is lifted off. Plays "Home Sweet Home." Ceramic figures on plastic base. 3" x 6". #141013, Quantasia. 1984. $60-65

59. Musicals

Ceramic. Quantasia. 1984. $70-80 ea.

•Snoopy plays the bass, and Woodstock plays the trumpet, on a red base with raised musical notes. Plays "Feelings." 6"H. #141015.

•Snoopy holds a trumpet in one hand, and leans against a musical note on a pink base with raised musical notes. Plays "Für Elise." 6"H. #141017.

•Snoopy sits at his typewriter, with Woodstock perched on top. The pink base is printed "Love Is Sharing" in raised lettering. Plays "Feelings." 5-1/2"H. #141014.

•Snoopy, holding a bouquet of flowers behind his back, looks at Woodstock sitting in a tree mounted on a green base. Plays "Yesterday." 6-1/2"H. #141016.

60. Musicals

Available with Snoopy revolving, or not revolving, when the music plays. Fabric. Quantasia. 1983. Non-revolving: $50-55 ea. Revolving: $75-80 ea.

•Snoopy, dressed in dance attire, performs a split on a round base. Plays "Brahm's Lullaby." 8"H. Available in two color schemes: #141005 (lavender base with pink outfit); #141004 (pink base with lavender outfit).

•Snoopy, wearing a red and white beanie, sits on a multicolored alphabet block. Plays "Send In The Clowns." 9"H. #141001.

•Snoopy sits, with a green and orange beachball in his hands, on a square base printed "Snoopy." Plays "It's A Small World." 8"H. #141006.

61. Musicals

Available with Snoopy revolving, or not revolving, when the music plays. Fabric. Quantasia. 1983. Non-revolving: $50-55 ea. Revolving: 75-80 ea.

•Snoopy holds drum sticks, and sits on a red drum base. Plays "Send In The Clowns." 9"H. #141003.

•Snoopy, wearing a bib and a diaper, holds a bottle and sits on a base covered with an unattached yellow print fabric. Plays "It's A Small World." 8"H.

•Snoopy wears a red bow tie and sits on a black top hat base. Plays "Send In The Clowns." 8"H. #141002.

62. Musical Water Globes

Snoopy moves inside the globes when the music is played. The bases are printed "Snoopy," and available in different colors. Plastic. 3-1/2"H x 2-1/2" diam. Quantasia. 1985. $50-55

•Snoopy skis inside the globe, which is decorated on the outside like a ski resort. (I was unable to identify the tune played. Reader input is invited.) #141019.

•Snoopy sails inside the globe, which is decorated on the outside like a seaside resort. Plays "Blue Hawaii." #141020.

60

61

58

59

62

63

63. Music Boxes

Hinged lids. Plastic. Quantasia. 1985. $40-45

•A two-dimensional sitting Snoopy holds a musical note on the lid, which is decorated with more notes. "Snoopy" is printed on the box, which is available in red or blue. Plays "Für Elise." 3-1/2" x 2". #141021.

•A two-dimensional Snoopy sits next to Woodstock, who sits on a musical symbol. Musical notes decorate the lid. "Snoopy" is printed on the box, which is available in red or blue. Plays "It's A Small World." 3-1/2" x 2". #141021.

•Woodstock, singing, and Snoopy sit on the lid, surrounded by musical notes. Woodstock and his friends are on the front of the box printed "Snoopy & Woodstock." Plays "Yesterday." Available in translucent brown or red. 4-1/4" x 3" x 2-1/4". #141022.

•Snoopy and Woodstock, on the lid, play a tune on glasses filled with different amounts of water. Woodstock is on the front of the box, printed "Snoopy." Plays "The Way We Were." Available in translucent red or brown. 4-1/4" x 3" x 2-1/4". #141022.

64. Music Boxes

Hinged lids. Ceramic figures, plastic box and lid. Quantasia. 1984. $50-55 ea.

•Snoopy sits and holds a red musical note on the lid. Woodstock is pictured on the circular box above the words "Snoopy & Woodstock." Plays "Music Box Dancer." Available in black or red. 4-1/2"H. #141011.

•Snoopy, holding a red musical symbol, and Woodstock sit on the lid. Woodstock flies across the words "Snoopy & Woodstock." Plays "Für Elise." Available in black or red. 4" x 5-1/2". #141012.

SCHMID

65. Musicals

Ceramic. Schmid.

•"In Concert." Schroeder plays his piano. Snoopy stands on top, dressed as a circus ringmaster. Plays "Beethoven's Piano Concerto." First edition annual musical, limited to 15,000

numbered pieces. 6"H. #289-030. 1983. $150-160

•"Clown Capers." Sally, Charlie Brown, Lucy, Peppermint Patty, Schroeder, and Marcie—all dressed as circus clowns— ride in an open car. Snoopy lies across the hood, and Woodstock sits on the rear wheel fender. Plays "Be A Clown." Third edition annual musical, limited to 10,000 numbered pieces. 5-3/4"H. #289-052. 1985. $240-250

•"Flyin' Tamer Snoopy." Snoopy, dressed as a circus lion tamer, holds a whip in one hand as Woodstock, with a lion's mane, "jumps" over a stand. Plays "Pussycat, Pussycat." Fourth edition annual musical, limited to 15,000 numbered pieces. 6"H. #289-053. 1986. $150-160

66. Musicals

Ceramic. Schmid.

•Snoopy, as the Flying Ace, sits on top of his doghouse, which is on a cloud base with "Mom" in raised letters. "For Mother 1981" is printed on the back. Plays "It's A Small World." Limited to 10,000 numbered pieces. 7-1/2"H. #289-020. 1981. $95-110

•Snoopy and Woodstock, holding a flower, look at a sign-post with "Mom" written in five languages. "For Mother 1982" is printed on the back. Plays "Edelweiss." Limited to 10,000 numbered pieces. 7"H. #289-021. 1982. $130-140

64

65

66

• "Snoopy And The Beagle Scouts." Snoopy, Woodstock, and his friend, wearing back packs and red scout hats, are on a hike. Plays "Whistle A Happy Tune." Second edition annual musical, limited to 15,000 numbered pieces. 7"H. #289-051. 1984. $150-160

• Charlie Brown sits next to an opened present, with Snoopy, wearing a party hat, standing on top. Printed on the base: "Happy Anniversary 1950-1980." Plays "Anniversary Waltz." Limited to 15,000 numbered pieces. 6-1/4"H. #289-090. 1980. $130-140

67. Musicals

Dated Christmas musicals, limited to 15,000 pieces. Ceramic. 7-1/2"H. Schmid.

• "A Christmas Wish." Snoopy lies on top of his doghouse, which is covered with stockings. The base is decorated with holly leaves. "Christmas 1981" appears on the reverse side of the base. Plays "Silent Night." #289-001. 1981. $145-160

• "Waiting For Santa." Snoopy looks up at Woodstock in his nest in a tree hung with stockings, mounted on a white base. "Christmas 1980" appears on the reverse side of the base. Plays "O Tannenbaum." #289-000. 1980. $230-240

• Snoopy, wearing a stocking cap and scarf, is ice-skating. The base is decorated with holly leaves. "Christmas 1982" appears on the reverse side of the base. Plays "Skater's Waltz." #289-002. 1982. $150-155

68. Musicals

Ceramic. Schmid.

• Snoopy, dressed as Santa, moves up and down the snow-covered chimney when the music is played. Plays "Up On The House Top." 6"H. #253-723. 1984. $200-235

• Lucy, Charlie Brown, Snoopy, Sally, Woodstock, and Linus hold presents and sit or stand around the Christmas tree. When the music is played, the characters rotate on the base, but the tree does not move. Plays "Joy to The World." 8"H. #253-724. 1984. $235-250

• Snoopy, dressed as a clown, moves in and out of the musical when the music is played. The musical is decorated with multicolored stars. Plays "Be A Clown." 6-1/2"H. #253-731. 1985. $200-235

69. Musicals

Ceramic. Schmid.

• Snoopy, wearing a striped scarf and hat, looks at a Christmas tree decorated with Woodstock and his friends. Plays "O Tannenbaum." 7-1/2"H. #159-101. 1986. Rare. $500-550

• "Big Top Blast Off." Charlie Brown is inside a cannon. Woodstock, sitting on the back end, prepares to light the fuse,

and Snoopy, in top hat and tuxedo jacket, directs the action. Snoopy revolves independently of the base when the music is played. Plays "California, Here I Come." This was to be the 1987 annual musical, but Schmid gave up its license and it was never mass-produced. The pieces that are in circulation were intended for proof/sample purposes. 1987. $500-600

70. Musicals

Ceramic. Schmid.

• Snoopy, dressed as Santa and carrying a bag of gifts, looks down at Woodstock, who is holding a present. Woodstock revolves when the music is played. Plays "Here Comes Santa Claus." 5"H. #418-001. 1985. $160-170

• Snoopy and Woodstock, wearing red stocking caps, sit on a sled that moves back and forth when the music is played. Plays "Winter Wonderland." 5-1/2"H. #417-000. 1985. $165-175

• Snoopy—standing on Lucy's shoulders, with Lucy, in turn, standing on Charlie Brown's shoulders—reaches to put a star on top of the Christmas tree. Plays "We Wish You A Merry Christmas." 7"H. #417-004. 1986. $175-225

• Woodstock, wearing a Santa hat, sits on Snoopy's snow-covered and decorated doghouse. Snoopy, dressed as Santa, holds a gift up to him. Plays "Deck The Halls." 5-3/4"H. #417-005. 1986. $155-165

68

69

70

67

71. Musicals

Ceramic. Schmid.

•Lucy, wearing angel wings, holds a book of Christmas carols on a cloud base with multicolored stars. Plays "Silent Night." 6"H. #253-722. 1984. $145-150

•Snoopy, wearing a red stocking cap and holding poles, is on green skis which move back and forth when the music is played. Woodstock is nearby on red skis. Plays "Let It Snow." 6"H. #253-720. 1985. $170-180

•Snoopy, Belle, and Woodstock are ice-skating. They revolve independently of the rotating disk on top of the base when the music is played. Plays "Skater's Waltz." 4-3/4"H. #253-700. 1984. $155-165

•Snoopy, wearing a red and green striped cap and scarf, sits next to a gift with the word "Joy" on its wrapping. Plays "We Wish You A Merry Christmas." 5"H. #253-721. 1984. $110-125

72. Musical

•Charlie Brown is sitting with a gift printed "To Charlie Brown" between his feet. Plays "Joy To The World." Ceramic. 5"H. #417-001, Schmid. 1985. $115-130

73. Musicals

Ceramic. Schmid. 1985.

•Snoopy wears a pastel-colored striped nightshirt, a pink nightcap, and holds a teddy bear. Plays "My Favorite Things." 6-1/2"H. #253-726. $175-200

•Snoopy sits and wears a bib printed "Baby." Plays "Brahm's Lullaby." This musical comes with the bib and Snoopy's ears in light blue or pink. 5"H. #281-017. $65-75

•Snoopy, wearing a blue and white striped nightshirt and cap, sits in a swing suspended from a crescent moon with facial features. Snoopy swings back and forth when the music is played. Plays "Twinkle, Twinkle Little Star." 7"H. #281-020. $165-175

74. Musical.

Ceramic. 4"H. Schmid. 1974.

•Woodstock stands. Plays "Snow Bird." #253-011. $150-155

•Lucy is wearing a blue dress. Plays "My Way." #253-014. $150-155

•Charlie Brown is wearing his baseball cap and glove. Plays "Impossible Dream." #253-013. $155-160

•Linus is holding his blanket, with his thumb in his mouth. Plays "Tie A Yellow Ribbon." #253-016. $150-155

•Schroeder is playing his piano. Plays "I'd Like To Teach The World To Sing." #253-015. $160-165 (Not pictured)

•Snoopy is lying on top of his doghouse. Plays "It's A Small World." #253-012. $160-165 (Not pictured)

75. Musical

•Charlie Brown and Snoopy stand next to each other on a green base. Plays "It's A Small World." Ceramic. 7"H. #278-552, Schmid. 1974. $250-275

76. Musical

•Lucy, wearing a red dress and sitting on a green base, is kissed on the cheek by Snoopy. Plays "Close To You." Ceramic. 7"H. #278-550, Schmid. 1974. $285-300

77. Musicals

Ceramic. Schmid. $200-235 ea.

•Snoopy and Woodstock, who is holding a pink balloon, play on a seesaw, which moves up and down when the music is played. Plays "Playmates." 7"H. #253-709. 1984.

• Snoopy, as the Flying Ace, rides in a red airplane. Turn the propeller to play the music. Plays "Around The World In 80 Days." 5-1/4"H. #253-729. $165-175

• Snoopy plays the piano. Woodstock, sitting on top of the piano, revolves when the music is played. Snoopy and Woodstock wear purple hats, and Snoopy wears a matching vest. Plays "The Entertainer." 5-1/2"H. #253-732. $195-230

79. Musicals

Ceramic. Schmid. 1985.

• Snoopy, dressed as a sailor, is sitting and holding a sailboat. Plays "Anchors Away." 5-1/2"H. #253-727. $185-200

• Snoopy, dressed as the Easter Beagle, is standing and holding a basket of Easter eggs. Plays "Easter Parade." 7-1/2"H. #281-010. $155-165

• Snoopy, as Joe Cool, wears a green hat and a green shirt printed "Joe Cool" with a shamrock on it. Plays "With A Little Bit Of Luck." 7"H. #281-011. $145-150

• Snoopy, dressed as an engineer with a yellow neckerchief, is sitting and holding a toy train. Plays "I've Been Working On The Railroad." 5-1/2"H. #253-728. $185-225

80. Musicals

Ceramic. Schmid. 1985.

• Woodstock is sitting. Plays "Just The Way You Are." 6-1/2"H. #253-725. $75-80

• Snoopy is lying on top of his doghouse. Plays "Home Sweet Home." 5"H. #253-734. $75-80

• Snoopy, wearing a pink clown outfit, moves up and down out of a drum when the music is played. Woodstock, wearing a clown hat, sits on the edge of the drum. Plays "Put On A Happy Face." 7"H. #253-733. $185-225

81. Musicals

Ceramic. Schmid. 1985.

• Lucy wears yellow roller skates and a blue dress. Plays "Playmates." 6-1/4"H. #281-018. $130-140

• Snoopy lies atop his doghouse as Woodstock and his friends sit on the grass-covered base. The doghouse and base revolve in opposite directions when the music is played. Plays "Oh, What A Beautiful Morning." 7"H. #253-708. $140-150

• Charlie Brown, wearing his baseball cap and glove, has just thrown a pitch. Plays "School Days." 6-1/4"H. #281-019. $130-140

• Snoopy pushes a flower cart covered by a pink umbrella. Woodstock, sitting on top of the umbrella, revolves when the music is played. Plays "Younger Than Springtime." 7-1/2"H. #253-707. 1984.

• Snoopy, wearing a hat and holding a painter's palette and brush, sits at an easel painting. Plays "I Whistle A Happy Tune." 6"H. #253-000. 1986.

78. Musicals

Ceramic. Schmid. 1985.

• Snoopy is walking, wearing a blue party hat and carrying two pink balloons. Plays "Up, Up And Away." 7-3/4"H. #253-730. $160-165

82. Musicals

Ceramic. 12"H. Schmid. 1984. $400-450 ea.

•Charlie Brown is sitting. Plays "You've Got A Friend." #253-702.

•Snoopy is sitting. Plays "I'd Like To Teach The World To Sing." #253-700.

•Lucy is sitting. Plays "My Favorite Things." #253-701.

Ceramic. 5-3/4"H. Schmid. 1984. $95-130 ea.

•Charlie Brown is sitting. Plays "Somebody Loves Me." #253-705.

•Snoopy is sitting. Plays "When The Saints Come Marching In." #253-704.

•Lucy is sitting. Plays "Everybody Loves Somebody." #253-703.

83. Musical Steins

Music plays when the stein is lifted. Ceramic. 4-1/2"H. Schmid. 1971. $45-55 ea.

•Charlie Brown. Plays "Take Me Out To The Ball Game." #276-789.

•Snoopy, as the Flying Ace. Plays "Fly Me To The Moon." #276-787.

•Lucy. Plays "Honey." #276-788.

84. Musicals

Wood. Schmid.

•Snoopy, dressed as an astronaut, sits on his white doghouse, which has an American flag on the roof. Plays "Fly Me To The Moon." 8"H. #276-764. 1971. $155-165

•Snoopy, as the Flying Ace, sits on his yellow doghouse, which has a bull's-eye target on the roof. Plays "Over There." 8"H. #276-762. 1971. $100-110 $130-140*

•Snoopy, as the Flying Ace, moves in and out of the roof of his green doghouse when the music is played. Plays "Both Sides Now." 6-1/2"H. #277-352. 1973. $115-130

85. Musicals

Wood. 5-1/2"L. Schmid. 1971.

•The Red Baron pilots a red airplane. Plays "Auf Wiedersehen" when the propeller is turned. This piece has a Schmid copyright but no PEANUTS graphics or UFS copyright. It is treated as a companion piece to Snoopy, as the Flying Ace, in his green airplane. #276-763. $110-125

•Snoopy, as the Flying Ace, pilots a green airplane. Plays "When The Saints Come Marching In" when the propeller is turned. #276-759. $230-260

86. Musical Wall Hangings

Wood. 4-1/2" x 4-1/2". Schmid. 1972. $130-135 ea.

•Snoopy, as the Flying Ace, is on top of his doghouse thinking, "AH! Saint-Pol-Sur-Mer!" Plays "The Last Time I Saw Paris" when the orange ball on a string is pulled. #277-412.

•Charlie Brown holds an umbrella over Snoopy and his supper dish, as Snoopy dances in the rain. Plays "Raindrops Keep Falling On My Head" when the orange ball on a string is pulled. #277-414.

84

82

85

83

86

87. Music Boxes

Hinged lids. Wood. 4-1/2" x 3" x 2-3/8". Schmid. 1972.

•Schroeder, Lucy, Charlie Brown, Snoopy, Patty, and Linus stand on the pitcher's mound. Plays "Take Me Out To The Ball Game." #277-426. $95-120

•Snoopy, Sally, Linus, Franklin, and Patty stand in line at the movies. Sally says to Linus, "You know what I'm doing, Linus? I'm pretending that you're taking me to the movies." Linus replies, "Well, I'm not! We just happen to be standing in the same line!" Plays "Who Can I Turn To?" #277-427. $95-120

•Linus watches as Sally lets go of a balloon printed "Love." Linus says, "Maybe some great leader will find it and be inspired to seek world peace." Sally says "Go balloon! Carry your message of love!" Plays "What The World Needs Now Is Love." #277-428. $120-125

•Snoopy and Woodstock each walk under their own umbrellas in the rain. Plays "Raindrops Keep Falling On My Head." #277-429. $85-90

•Snoopy and Woodstock dance against a background of red, white, and blue stars and stripes. Snoopy is thinking, "America you're beautiful!" Plays "God Bless America." #277-430. $85-100

•Charlie Brown, patting Snoopy on the head and holding a piece of paper, says to Linus, "Who else do you know who's (sic) dog has just been promoted to 'Head Beagle'?" Plays "Camelot." #277-421. $65-70

88. Musicals

•Snoopy appears in various poses on each side of the cube—leaning on his golf club, carrying skis over his shoulder, carrying a fishing pole, smelling a flower, and ice-skating. A metal crank handle is used to wind the musical. Plays "Superstar." Wood. 3-1/4" x 4". #277-350, Schmid. 1972. $150-160

•Snoopy appears on each side of the cube with different characters. Snoopy kisses Lucy on the nose, Charlie Brown pats Snoopy on the head, Snoopy watches Peppermint Patty hit a baseball, and Snoopy dances on Schroeder's piano. A metal crank handle is used to wind the musical. Plays "I'd Like To Teach The World To Sing." Wood. 3-1/4" x 4". #277-351, Schmid. 1972. $150-160

WILLITTS DESIGNS

89. Musicals

Ceramic. Willitts Designs.

•"Takin' A Cool Drive." Snoopy, as Joe Cool, drives a light blue convertible, with Woodstock sitting on the spare tire. Plays "Puppy Love." 10-1/2"L x 4"H. #9360. 1989. $155-165*

•"Happiness Ride." Charlie Brown drives a red Volkswagen with Linus, Lucy, and Sally as passengers. Snoopy lies across the trunk, and Woodstock sits on the hood. Plays "King Of The Road." 9"L x 3-3/4"W x 3/12"H. #19016. 1990. $175-185*

•"Cruising!" Snoopy drives a red and white convertible, with Woodstock sitting on the hood and a license plate printed "Cool." Plays "Puppy Love." 10-1/2"L x 4"H. #8105. 1988. $165-175*

The carousel musicals by Willitts were of poor quality and durability, and the characters are not in proportion to their surroundings or to each other.

90. Musicals

The characters each ride a porcelain carousel horse that moves up and down when the music is played. The base has an inlaid coin featuring Snoopy and printed "PEANUTS Playland Carousel." Porcelain figures, brass posts, and wooden bases. 6"H. Willitts Designs. 1989. $40-50* ea.

•Linus. Plays "The Loveliest Night Of The Year." #9562.

•Lucy. Plays "Carousel Waltz." #9561. (Not pictured)

•Charlie Brown. Plays "Tales From The Vienna Woods." #9563. (Not pictured)

•Snoopy. Plays "When The Saints Go Marching In." #9564. (Not pictured)

The characters each ride a porcelain carousel horse against a porcelain "mini band organ" backdrop, with Woodstock in each upper corner. The carousel horse moves up and down when the music is played. The base has an inlaid coin featuring Snoopy and printed "PEANUTS Playland Carousel." Porcelain figures, brass posts, and wooden bases. 5-1/4" x 7"H. Willitts Designs. 1989. $40-50*

•Snoopy. Plays "The Loveliest Night Of The Year." #9794.

•Charlie Brown. Plays "Carousel Waltz." #9795. (Not pictured)

•Lucy. Plays "Tales From The Vienna Woods." #9796. (Not pictured)

(Linus was not produced in this configuration.)

91. Musicals

•Snoopy, Linus, Lucy, and Charlie Brown each ride a porcelain carousel horse under a merry-go-round canopy that revolves when the music is played. Turn the canopy to play the music. Plays "Tales From The Vienna Woods." Porcelain figures, brass posts, and hardwood base. 10"H x 7" diam. base. #8113, Willitts Designs. 1988. $175-185*

•Snoopy, holding an ice cream cone, rides a porcelain carousel horse that moves up and down when the music is played. Woodstock sits atop the brass post. Plays "The Loveliest Night Of The Year." Pine base. 9-1/2"H. #7858, Willitts Designs. 1988. $40-50*

92. Musicals

"Christmas Signature Collection." Part of a collection of dated plates, bells, and ornaments issued annually at holiday time. Ceramic. Willitts Designs.

•Snoopy, wearing a stocking cap and lying on his tummy, looks over the roof of his decorated doghouse at Woodstock, who is sitting on top of a Christmas tree. Printed on the back of the doghouse: "Christmas 1987." Plays "We Wish You A Merry Christmas." 5"H. #7704. 1987. $145-155*

•Snoopy, wearing a red top hat, coat, and green scarf, looks up at Woodstock, perched on a decorated lamppost. Printed: "Christmas 1988." Plays "God Rest Ye Merry Gentlemen." 7"H. #8428. 1988. $155-165*

•Snoopy, wearing a pink cap and sweater, carries a Christmas tree over his shoulder while he pulls Woodstock

on a sled. Printed: "Christmas 1989." Plays "O Tannenbaum." 4-1/2"W x 6"H. #9351. 1989. $165-170*

93. Musicals

"Christmas Signature Collection." Part of a collection of dated plates, bells, and ornaments issued annually at holiday time. Willitts Designs.

•Charlie Brown, Snoopy, and Woodstock share a toboggan in the snow. Plays "We Wish You A Merry Christmas." Resin. 5-1/2"H. #44028. 1991. $85-90*

•Woodstock decorates a Christmas tree on top of Snoopy's doghouse as Snoopy, wearing a Santa hat, hangs stockings on the roof. Printed: "Christmas 1992." Plays "Winter Wonderland." Resin. 6"H. #44041. 1992. $85-90*

•Snoopy, dressed as Santa, drives his decorated doghouse being led by Woodstock. Plays "Up On The Housetop." Ceramic. 7-1/2"H. #44006. 1990. $195-225* (Not pictured)

94. Musicals

Ceramic. Willitts Designs. $85-95* ea.

•Snoopy, dressed as Santa, is sitting with a bag of toys over his shoulder. Plays "Jolly Old St. Nicholas." 5"L x 4-3/4"H. #9687. 1989.

96

97

98

99

100

• Snoopy, wearing a stocking cap and scarf, rides a sled through the snow. Woodstock, out of view in the picture, sits beside Snoopy on the other side. Plays "Winter Wonderland." 5-1/2" x 6"H. #9685. 1989.

• Snoopy, wearing a green and white striped stocking cap, lies on top of his decorated doghouse. Woodstock is lying in the green bow. Plays "We Wish You A Merry Christmas." 5-1/2"H. #8437. 1988.

95. Musicals

Ceramic. Willitts Designs. $80-90* ea.

• "Trimming The Tree." Snoopy decorates a Christmas tree with Woodstock sitting on top. Plays "Joy To The World." 6-1/2"H. #44007. 1990.

• Snoopy and Woodstock, who is in Snoopy's lap, sit on top of the doghouse strung with lights. Plays "Jingle Bells." 3-1/2"W x 7"H. #9686. 1989.

• Snoopy, wearing a red scarf and a blue and yellow cap, and Woodstock face each other on a snow-covered base. Plays "Joy To The World." 5-3/4"H. #9688. 1989.

96. Musicals

Willitts Designs.

• "Snoopy Skates To Music." Snoopy ice-skates when the music is played. Woodstock watches from atop a snowman. Plays "Skater's Waltz." Ceramic. 6"W x 4"H. #7897. 1987. $135-140*

• "Christmas Express." Snoopy, dressed as Santa, looks at a globe with a magnifying glass. The globe revolves, and Woodstock rides a train through a tunnel around the base when the music is played. A toy bear and elephant stand near Snoopy. Plays "Santa Claus Is Coming To Town." Plastic. 5-1/4"H. #44024. 1990. $85-90*

• Snoopy, Charlie Brown, and Lucy, wearing ice skates, stand with their arms outstretched and their backs to a Christmas tree with Woodstock on top. Plays "Skater's Waltz." Ceramic. 6"H. #8436. 1988. $90-110*

97. Musical

• "Winter Frolic." Snoopy, wearing a green sweater and red cap, sits in the snow, watching as Woodstock, wearing a green stocking cap, ice-skates in Snoopy's supper dish. Woodstock revolves when the music is played. Plays "Love Makes The World Go Round." Ceramic. 5"W x 4-1/2"H. #7845, Willitts Designs. 1987. $135-140*

Musical Candle Holder

• Snoopy, Charlie Brown, and Lucy, wearing ice skates, stand with their arms outstretched and their backs to the candle holder. Plays "Let It Snow." Also came as a non-musical piece. Ceramic and glass. 4-1/2"H. #8622, Willitts Designs. 1988. $65-75*

Musical

• "Holiday Hug." Snoopy, sitting and wearing a Santa hat, is hugging Woodstock. Plays "White Christmas." Ceramic. 6"H. #44010. Willitts Designs. 1990. $65-75*

98. Musicals

Ceramic. Willitts Designs.

• "Snoopy Plays Snowman." Snoopy, wearing a Santa hat, stands behind the body of a snowman, with his head and arms where the snowman's should be. Plays "Have Yourself A Merry Little Christmas." 6-3/4"H. #44008. 1990. $65-70*

• "The Snowfight." Snoopy, wearing a green hat and gloves, and a red sweater, is getting ready to throw a snowball at Woodstock and his friend. When the music is played, Woodstock and his friend move up and down inside the igloo. Plays "Let It Snow." 8-3/4"L x 6-1/4"H. #7867. 1987. $175-185*

• Snoopy, wearing a blue sweater, looks up at a tall snowman wearing a pink scarf and hat. Plays "Let It Snow." 5-1/2"H. #9684. 1989. $75-85*

216

The PEANUTS Home Collection

101

102

99. Musicals

Ceramic. Willitts Designs. 1989. $75-85 ea.

•"Summertime Dream." Snoopy carries Woodstock in his nest on his head. Plays "Beautiful Dreamer." 7-3/4"H. #9303.

•Snoopy and Woodstock, sitting in the egg basket he carries, both wear bunny ears. Easter eggs and flowers are on the base. Plays "Peter Cottontail." 6-1/2"H. #40001.

100. Musicals

Ceramic. Willitts Designs.

•"Schroeder and Lucy." Schroeder is playing his piano while Lucy, holding her head in her hands and resting her elbow on the piano, gazes at him. Plays "Für Elise." 7"W x 4"H. #8102. 1990. $130-135*

•"Puppy Love." Snoopy is sitting and hugging Woodstock on top of a blue base printed "Puppy Love" in raised letters. Plays "Puppy Love." 6"H. #9304. 1989. $55-65*

•"Solo Flight." Snoopy, as the Flying Ace, sits on a cloud base. Plays "It's A Long, Long Way To Tipperary." 5-1/2"H. #9307. 1989. $55-65*

•"On Top Of The World." Snoopy lies in his supper dish. Plays "I'm Sitting On Top Of The World." 4-1/2"H. #9305. 1989. $55-65*

101. Musicals

Ceramic. Willitts Designs.

•"Sweet Dreams." Sally, wearing pink footed pajamas, carries Snoopy, wearing a blue night cap, under her arm. The cloud base is decorated with stars and crescent moons. Plays "Brahm's Lullaby." 7-3/4"H. #45002. 1989. $145-155*

•"Go Fly A Kite." Charlie Brown, wearing a sailor's hat, flies his kite. The base is decorated with red kites. Plays "Anchor's Away." 7"H. #45001. 1990. $130-140*

•"Trust Me." Lucy kneels on a grass-covered base, holding a football. Printed on the base: "Trust Me." Plays "The Impossible Dream." 7"H. #45004. 1990. $125-135*

102. Musicals

Ceramic. Willitts Designs.

•"Joe Surfer." Snoopy, as Joe Cool, leans against a surfboard with Woodstock on top. "Joe Surfer" is printed on the base in raised letters. Plays "In The Good Old Summertime" or "Feelin' Groovy." 7-1/2"H. #45003. 1989. $90-110*

•"Super Snoopy." Snoopy, wearing a helmet, and Woodstock ride a skateboard that revolves when the music is played. "Super Snoopy" is printed on the base. Plays "Spinning Wheel." 5"W x 7"H. #45008. 1990. $90-100*

•"Beaglescout." Snoopy, wearing a backpack, scout hat and red neckerchief, goes for a hike. Printed on the base: "Beaglescout." Plays "Climb Every Mountain." 6-1/2"H. #9310. 1989. $85-95*

•Snoopy, as the Flying Ace, sits on his doghouse, which has a propeller on the front. Turn the propeller to play the music. Plays "It's A Long, Long Way To Tipperary." 7"H. #8106. 1988. $90-100*

103. Musicals

Ceramic. Willitts Designs. 1989. $75-85* ea.

•Snoopy, wearing a cap, leans on a baseball bat. Woodstock sits on Snoopy's cap. Plays "Take Me Out To The Ball Game." 7-1/4"H. #9578.

•Snoopy dribbles a basketball. Plays "Luck Be A Lady." 5-3/4"H. #9581.

•Snoopy holds a golf club ready to hit the ball. Plays "Say A Little Prayer." 6"H. #9582.

•Snoopy, dressed in a hockey uniform, stands on the ice holding a hockey stick. Plays "Looks Like We Made It." 6"H. #9580.

•Snoopy kicks a soccer ball. Plays "Who Can I Turn To?" 6"H. #9577.

•Snoopy wears a visor and holds a tennis racket. Plays "In The Good Old Summertime." 6-1/4"H. #9579.

104. Musicals

Ceramic. Willitts Designs. 1989.

•"Literary Ace." Snoopy sits at his typewriter on top of a purple dictionary. Plays "Nine To Five." 4-1/2"W x 5"H. #9306. $55-65*

103

104

• "Home Sweet Home." Snoopy, lying on his tummy, leans over the roof of his doghouse, imprinted "Snoopy" on the roof and "Superbeagle" over the doorway. Plays "Home Sweet Home." 4-1/4"W x 5-1/2"H. #9308. $55-60*

• "Joe Scholar." Snoopy, as Joe Cool, leans against a pile of books with an apple at the top. Printed "Joe Scholar" on the base book and "English," "Reading," "Math," and "History" on the other books. Plays "Chariots Of Fire." 5"W x 6"H. #9309. $65-75*

105. 40th Anniversary Musical Cake

• Charlie Brown, Snoopy, Sally, Linus, Peppermint Patty, Marcie, Schroeder sitting at his piano, and Lucy—all wearing party hats and holding gifts, balloons, or cake—are arrayed around the cake. Woodstock appears on the disk printed "40 Years of Happiness." Plays "Love Makes The World Go Round." Part of the PEANUTS 40th Anniversary Signature Collection and limited to 1,500 numbered pieces. The reverse side of the disk bears the certificate of authenticity. Porcelain. 7"H x 6-1/4" diam. #19005, Willitts Designs. 1990. $225-240*

40th Anniversary Figurines

The characters shown on the cake were also available individually. Porcelain. Approximately 2-1/2"H. Willitts Designs.

105

1990. $18-25* ea. (Not pictured individually)

• Snoopy holds a gift. #19006.

• Charlie Brown holds a cake with a candle in it. #19007.

• Schroeder sits at his piano. #19008.

• Lucy holds a balloon. #19009.

• Sally holds a gift. #19010.

• Peppermint Patty holds a balloon. #19011.

• Marcie holds a balloon. #19012.

• Linus holds a balloon. #19013.

106. Musical

• Snoopy, dressed as an engineer, lies on top of a locomotive. Plays "Chattanooga Choo Choo." Ceramic. 7"L x 6"H. #45030, Willitts Designs. 1991. $45-50*

107. Musical

• Snoopy and Woodstock each read one side of a paper printed "PEANUTS Collector Club." Printed on the base: "Beaglefest July 1993." Plays "Memories." Resin. 4-1/2"H. Willitts Designs. 1993. $40-45*

108. Musical Snowfalls

"Christmas Signature Collection." Part of a collection of dated musicals, plates, bells, and ornaments issued annually at holiday time. 5-1/2"H. Willitts Designs.

• Snoopy, wearing a red coat and hat, stands near a decorated lamppost. Woodstock and his friend are pictured on the base. Printed: "Christmas 1988." Plays "We Wish You A Merry Christmas." Porcelain base. #8442. 1988. $70-75*

• Snoopy, wearing a pink sweater and hat, carries a Christmas tree over his shoulder. On the base, Snoopy is shown pulling Woodstock on a sled. Plays "Santa Claus Is Coming To Town." Porcelain base. #9352. 1989. $70-75*

• Snoopy, wearing a Santa hat, sits on top of his decorated doghouse. Printed: "Christmas 1990." Plays "Santa Claus Is Coming To Town." Porcelain base. #44005. 1990. $60-65*

106

107

108

109

110

111

•Snoopy and Woodstock share a toboggan. Printed: "Christmas 1991." Plays "We Wish You A Merry Christmas." Porcelain base. #44030. 1991. $60-65*

•Woodstock decorates a Christmas tree on top of Snoopy's doghouse while Snoopy hangs stockings on the roof. Printed: "Christmas 1992." Plays "We Wish You a Merry Christmas." Resin base. #44038. 1992. $60-65*

109. Musical Snowfalls

5-1/2"H. Willitts Designs.

•Snoopy lies on top of his snow-covered doghouse. Woodstock appears on the base, holding a snow shovel. Plays "Beautiful Dreamer." Porcelain base. #8110. 1988. $55-60*

•Snoopy, wearing a stocking cap, is ice-skating. Woodstock and his friends are ice-skating on the base. Plays "Skater's Waltz." Porcelain base. #8441. 1988. $55-60*

•Snoopy is dancing inside the globe. Portraits of the characters decorate the base. Plays "Everything Is Beautiful." Porcelain base. #19004. 1990. $55-60*

•Snoopy lies on top of a tent printed "Super Beaglescout." His hat hangs on the corner of the tent. Plays "On Top Of Old Smokey." Hardwood base. #8833. 1988. $70-75*

•Snoopy, as Joe Cool, wears a Santa hat and holds a gold star. Plays "Let It Snow." Pine base. #7850. 1987. $55-65*

110. Musical Snowfall

•Snoopy is dressed as a band leader inside the globe. Woodstock and his friends, holding band instruments, are above the base on a red disk that revolves when the music is played. Plays "When The Saints Go Marching In." Plastic. 6"H. #45035, Willitts Designs. 1991. $60-65*

Musical Kaleidoscope

•Lucy, Snoopy, and Charlie Brown ice-skate inside the water scope and revolve when the music is played. The characters can be viewed as they revolve by looking through one end of the scope. Plays "Skater's Waltz." Plastic. 8". #8131, Willitts Designs. 1988. $60-65

Musical Snowfall

•Snoopy, wearing an engineer's hat, lies on top of his doghouse inside the globe. Woodstock "engineers" a train, mounted on a red disk above the base, that revolves when the music is played. Printed on the base: "A-l-l Aboard..." Plays "I've Been Working On The Railroad." Plastic. 6"H. #45034, Willitts Designs. 1991. $70-75*

Musical Snowfall

•Snoopy, Lucy, Charlie Brown, and Linus ride carousel horses that move up and down when the music is played. Plays "Carousel Waltz." Plastic. #8111, Willitts Designs. 1988. $60-65*

111. Musical Snowfalls

Plastic. 5-1/2"H. Willitts Designs. 1989. $45-55 ea.

•Snoopy, wearing a stocking cap, rides in a sleigh being led by Woodstock. The base features Snoopy, lying on his tummy. Plays "Jingle Bells." #9595.

•Snoopy skates along with his hockey stick ready to hit the puck that Woodstock is sitting on. Plays "Let It Snow." #9596.

•Snoopy is tangled in the Christmas tree lights. Woodstock sits on top of the tree. The base features Snoopy, lying on his tummy. Plays "We Wish You A Merry Christmas." #9594.

The desk top is full of useful office paraphernalia. A red telephone (Japan) sits on the lower left hand corner. Behind the phone, partially hidden from view, is a wooden Rolodex-type file (Canada). Farther back is a red plastic office supply storage container with three drawers (Japan). A wooden Snoopy clock (Japan) sits on top of the container surrounded by stampers (Japan). Sandwiched between this box and another three-drawer storage box (Japan) are a blue file binder (Canada) and a large red file binder (Japan). To the right of the box is a pen holder with pen, and a note paper holder—both from Italy. The typewriter is from Japan. Behind the typewriter is a red plastic storage box with handle (cover and inner shelf are not shown), from Japan, which is pictured holding paper supplies. To the right of the typewriter is a calculator (Japan) and a bank passbook (England). Also, a wooden clip on a stand (Japan), holding greeting cards. To the rear is a globe from Japan.

On the left side of the map are stampers from Hong Kong, and a birthday calendar from England. A decorative ceramic tile (Japan) is affixed to the map's right frame. The map is obviously an American product. It is described on page 223. The blackboard on the wall is from Japan. On the shelf above the map are metal bookends (Canada), along with a pencil holder, plastic clock, Charlie Brown bank, black metal bank, and a miniature garbage can—all from Japan. The book is *Good Grief!*, a biography of Charles Schulz by Rheta Grimsley Johnson.

The Office

Are PEANUTS characters an aid or a distraction to a smooth-running office? We can only speculate. One thing is certain: With the exception of high-tech equipment, today's workplace is a major repository of PEANUTS office paraphernalia. Most of it, from pencils to adding machines (hand-held), are items that are universally found in any office. Whether they are really instrumental in creating a more efficient office environment is an entirely different matter.

BINDERS

1. Three-Ring Binders

•A flower on a very long stem reaches over Snoopy, who is lying on his doghouse. Snoopy is thinking "All right, who planted the flower?!" Vinyl. 10-1/2" x 11-1/2". #PN1-1/2. Manufactured by K & M for Simon Simple. 1974. $8-12

•Snoopy and Woodstock are sitting on top of the doghouse, blowing bubbles with their chewing gum. Vinyl. 10-1/2" x 11-1/2". #PN1-1/2. Manufactured by K & M for Butterfly Originals. 1976. $5-7

Note Pad Holder

•Snoopy is sitting on top of his doghouse, hugging Woodstock. Vinyl. 5-5/8" x 8-1/2". Manufactured by K & M for Butterfly Originals. 1976. $4-6

BOOKENDS

Bookends by Butterfly Originals were sold as a set or individually. They could be mixed and matched as bookends, or used singly as paperweights. Prices below reflect purchase of a matched set.

2. Bookends

•Snoopy is sitting. Ceramic. 5"H. #1522000, Butterfly Originals. Early 1980s. $50-55*

3. Bookends

•Snoopy is sitting and hugging Woodstock on a heart-shaped base and backdrop. Ceramic figures on rubber. 5"H. #1303, Butterfly Originals. 1981. $20-25*

4. Bookends

•Charlie Brown leans his back against a door on one bookend while Snoopy, supper dish in his mouth, kicks the door on the other bookend. Ceramic. Butterfly Originals. 1976. $145-175*

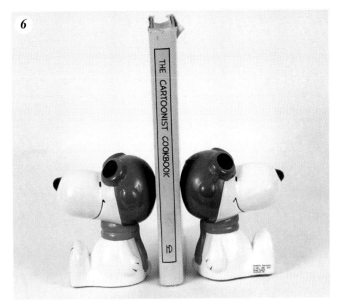

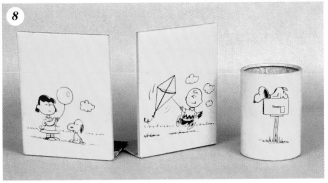

5. Bookends

•A sitting Snoopy wears a visor and holds a tennis racket. Ceramic. 5"H. #1301, Butterfly Originals. Early 1980s. $60-70*

•A sitting Snoopy wears a yellow raincoat and hat. Ceramic. 5"H. Butterfly Originals. Early 1980s. $60-70*

6. Bookends

•Snoopy as the Flying Ace. Ceramic. 5"H. #1323, Butterfly Originals. Early 1980s. $60-65*

7. Bookends

•Snoopy, wearing an engineer's hat, lies on his tummy on top of a locomotive. Woodstock, also wearing an engineer's hat, sits on the caboose. Ceramic. Locomotive: 7"H x 6"H. Caboose: 4-1/2" x 4-1/2". #45029, Willitts Designs. 1991. $30-35*

8. Bookends

•Lucy is holding a balloon as Snoopy sits nearby. Charlie Brown is flying his kite. Available in various colors. Leather-look paper covers metal bookends. 4-7/8" x 6-1/8". A&M Leatherlines, Inc. for Determined Productions. 1971. $25-35

Pencil Cup

•Snoopy lies on his tummy on top of a mailbox, looking over the edge. Available in various colors. Leather-look paper

covers cardboard. 4"H x 3" diam. A&M Leatherlines, Inc. for Determined Productions. 1971. $10-12

BULLETIN BOARDS AND MEMO BOARDS

9. Bulletin Boards

"Snoopy Bulletin Board." Felt appliqués on burlap. 18" x 36". Simon Simple. 1969-1970. $10-15

•Snoopy, Charlie Brown, and Linus play baseball. #BB-6.

•Snoopy, as the Flying Ace, sits atop his doghouse. #BB-5.

• "Snoopy Bulletin." Snoopy holds balloons printed "Love." The word "Love," surrounded by the characters, is printed directly on the bulletin board. Felt appliqués on burlap. 28" x 12". Simon Simple. 1968. $12-15

13. Bulletin Board

• "PEANUTS Cork Bulletin Board." Sally, Linus, Charlie Brown, and Snoopy sit at their school desks, and Lucy stands beside hers. Behind them, the alphabet is written on a blackboard. Woodstock sits on a stack of books in the lower right hand corner. Cork. 23" x 15". Butterfly Originals. 1977. $10-15

14. Bulletin Board

• Snoopy, Belle, Woodstock, and his friends are featured in different poses and outfits across a map of the United States. Cork. 35" x 23". #91119, Manton Cork Company. 1983. $45-65

15. Bulletin Board

• A four-panel comic strip on the right side of the bulletin board features Snoopy and Woodstock. Cork. 23" x 17". Butterfly Originals. 1977. $10-15

16. Bulletin Boards

• Snoopy and Woodstock are roller-skating across the board. Cork. 23" x 17". #91108, Manton Cork Company. 1983. $8-10

• Snoopy is sitting and hugging Woodstock. The word "Love" is printed along the left side of the board. Cork. 23" x 17". Butterfly Originals. 1971. $10-15

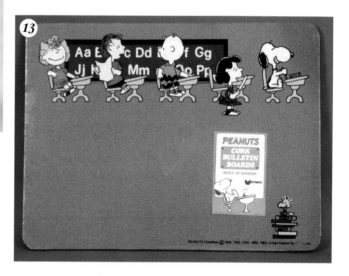

10. Bulletin Boards

"Snoopy Bulletin Board." Felt appliqués on burlap. 18" x 36". Simon Simple.

• Snoopy, dressed as an astronaut, dances on the moon. His doghouse is in the background. Came with pinback button featuring Snoopy, dressed as an astronaut, dancing on the moon. #BB-9. 1969-1970. $30-40

• Lucy watches as Charlie Brown flies his kite and Snoopy dances. Early 1970s. $10-15

11. Bulletin Boards

"Snoopy Bulletin Board." Felt appliqués on burlap. 18" x 36". Simon Simple. 1972. $10-15

• Snoopy dances among the flowers, as Woodstock watches.

• Snoopy lies on his tummy on top of his doghouse. Lucy and Charlie Brown are standing on each side of the doghouse.

12. Bulletin Boards

"Snoopy Bulletin Board." Felt appliqués on burlap. 18" x 36". Simon Simple.

• Snoopy hits a golf ball from the top of his doghouse. #BB-7. 1969-1970. $12-15

• Snoopy leans back in the seat of a bicycle, putting his feet up on the handlebars. Lucy stands near Snoopy's doghouse, and Charlie Brown stands under a tree. 1970. $10-15

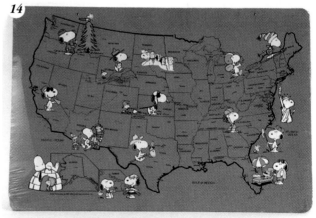

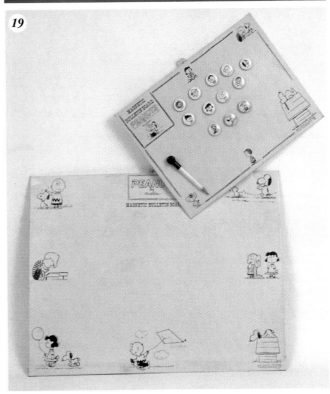

17. Bulletin Boards

•Snoopy, dressed as a soda jerk, is behind the counter of a soda fountain, serving ice cream to Woodstock and his friends. Printed: "Cool It!" Cork. 11" x 17". #91143, Manton Cork Company. 1984. $3-5

•Snoopy carries a stack of books, with a tray of food on top, over his head as Woodstock follows. Printed: "Brain Power!" Cork. 11" x 17". #91144, Manton Cork Company. 1984. $3-5

•Snoopy rides a hobby horse and thinks, "Here's the world's greatest scout delivering messages for 'The Beagle Express'." Cork. 11" x 17". Butterfly Originals. Late 1970s. $3-5

18. Bulletin Boards

•Snoopy, lying on his tummy, leans over the roof of his doghouse. Printed: "Why Have I No Friends In High Places?" Cork. 11" x 17". Butterfly Originals. Late 1970s. $4-7*

•"Snoopy Color Me Cork Board." Snoopy paints a portrait of Charlie Brown against an amusement park scene. A box of Snoopy Crayons is included. 8-1/2" x 11". Cork. #275-7949-6, Butterfly Originals. 1982. $4-7

19. Magnetic Bulletin Boards

"PEANUTS Magnetic Bulletin Board." The PEANUTS characters are pictured around the board. Paper, magnets, and a magnetic pencil are included. See Kitchen page 164 for a description of the magnets. Available in assorted colors. #MB-21, Simon Simple. 1969-1970.

•Small board. Includes three magnets featuring full-figure characters. 12" x 9". $30-35

•Large board. Includes six magnets featuring full-figure characters. 18" x 14". $35-48

20. Memo Boards

•"Magnetic Write And Wipe Board." Snoopy, dressed as a scout, leans over a cliff. Woodstock and his friends, standing on each other's scout hats on top of Snoopy's scout hat, extend out over the edge. Printed: "While You Were Out." Includes a magnet of Woodstock, sitting in a cloud, and a wipe-off pen. 11-1/2" x 12-1/8". #91400, Manton Cork Company. 1984. $3-6

•"Micro Memo Write And Wipe Board." Snoopy, standing next to a gum ball machine, blows bubbles, one of which has Woodstock inside. Printed: "Notes." Wipe-off pen is included. 4-3/4" x 6-7/8". #91325, Manton Cork Company. 1984. $2-4

•"Mini Wipe Off Memo Board." Snoopy, standing next to a sign printed "Joggers Track," puts on a jogging suit that is too big for him. Wipe-off pen is included. 4-1/8" x 5-3/4". #99-2023, Butterfly Originals. Early 1980s. $2-4

•"Snoopy Plastic Wipe-Off." Snoopy, sitting on top of his doghouse, holds a large hero sandwich with Woodstock walking on it. Wipe-off pen is included. Plastic. 8" x 12". #225-2103, Butterfly Originals. Early 1980s. $2-4

21. Memo Boards

"Snoopy Wood 'N Wipe-Offs." A plastic wipe-off board with pen hangs from the bottom of a wood design. Memo board—4-3/8" x 2-3/4". Butterfly Originals. 1977 $12-15* ea.

•Snoopy, wearing his supper dish on his head, carries a hobo pack over his shoulder. Woodstock follows behind him. 10"H. #PWW-0-010.

•Snoopy, wearing a red nightshirt and green nightcap, carries a candle. 10-1/2"H. #PWW-0-012.

•Snoopy, wearing a straw hat and holding a cane, is dancing. 12-1/2"H. #PWW-0-014.

22. Memo Boards

"Snoopy Wood 'N Wipe-Offs." A plastic wipe-off board with pen hangs from the bottom of a wood design. Memo board—4-3/8" x 2-3/4". Butterfly Originals. 1977. $12-16* ea.

•Snoopy sits at his typewriter. 10-1/4"H. #PWW-0-011.

•Snoopy is sitting and hugging Woodstock. 10-1/4"H. #PWW-0-013.

CALCULATORS

23. Calculator

•Snoopy, wearing headphones, roller-skates with Woodstock and his friends. Printed: "Snoopy & Woodstock." The packaging features Snoopy, Woodstock, and his friends dressed as scouts. Battery operated. Printed: "Snoopy & Woodstock"

and "Canon LC-401." A white vinyl case is included. Canon. Early 1980s. $12-15 $18-25*

Learning Aid

•"Snoopy Canon Math Learning Aid." Snoopy lies on top of the multi-function math game/calculator, shaped like his doghouse, next to the word "Snoopy." Plastic. 4" x 5". Canon. 1984. $15-25 $35-40*

Calculator

•"Snoopy & Woodstock Solar Calculator." Snoopy and Woodstock, dressed as astronauts, stand on the moon. Solar-powered. 2-7/8" x 4". Canon. 1984. $13-15 $16-25*

CALENDARS

24. Advent Calendars

•"Holiday Greetings From The PEANUTS Gang, An Advent Calendar Of Holiday Riddles." Charlie Brown, Sally, Linus, and Lucy stand in the snow looking at Snoopy's decorated doghouse. Snoopy and Woodstock sit on top, with a Christmas tree between them. A mailing envelope is included. #250XC1-3, Hallmark. Mid-1980s. $5-10

•"The PEANUTS Advent Calendar." Marcie and Violet sing, Sally pulls a sled, Snoopy and Charlie Brown decorate the Christmas tree, and Woodstock sits on top of the tree. A mailing envelope is included. #15-XC1-3, Hallmark. Late 1970s. $5-10

22

20

21

23

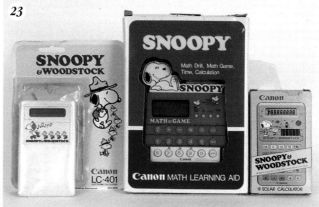

25. Advent Calendars

•"Let's Have Fun With The PEANUTS Gang, An Advent Calendar Of Holiday Riddles." Snoopy pulls a Christmas tree and Woodstock and his friends on a sled; Linus, Marcie, and Schroeder pull a Christmas tree with Lucy on it; and Charlie Brown, carrying an ax, and Sally, Pigpen, and Peppermint Patty walk along in the snow. 20-3/8" x 27-1/7". Mailing envelope is included. #250XC1-5, Hallmark. Late 1980s. $5-10

•"A PEANUTS Advent Calendar." Snoopy is dressed as a shepherd and holds a staff, while Charlie Brown, dressed in a suit, points to a sign on a stand printed "Presenting The Story Of The First Christmas." Mailing envelope is included. #225XC1-1, Hallmark. Late 1970s. $5-10

26. Calendar

•"Snoopy Around The World In 1991." Snoopy and Belle are dressed in clothes by French designer Angelo Tarlazzi, against a backdrop of Cairo, Egypt. The calendar features Belle and Snoopy dressed in designer outfits in different locations around the world. Sold exclusively by FAO Schwarz. Published by Harry N. Abrams, Inc., a Times Mirror Company. 1991. $15-18

27. Calendar

•"Charlie Brown 1973 Wall Hanging Calendar." Charlie Brown wears a baseball cap and glove. The calendar's pages are beneath Charlie Brown's baseball glove. The figure is punched out of the heavy cardboard. 18"H. Determined Productions. 1973. $10-12

28. Calendar

•"Snoopy 1983 Wall Hanging Calendar." Snoopy wears a visor and holds a tennis racket. The calendar's pages are beneath the tennis racket. Heavy cardboard. 14-1/2"H. Determined Productions. 1983. $10-12

DECORATIVE ITEMS

29. Mini Snowfalls

Plastic. 3"H. Willitts Designs. $10-15 ea.

•Snoopy wears a red bow tie and holds a heart. Printed on the red base: "Hugs 'N Kisses." #88035. 1988.

•Snoopy wears a green derby and holds a shamrock. Printed on the green base: "A Day O'Luck To You." #400890. 1990.

•Snoopy wears a blue bow tie and is dancing. Printed on the light green base: "Spring Fever." #400390. 1989

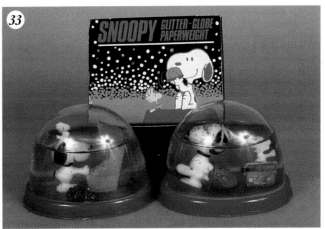

30. Mini Snowfalls

Plastic. 3"H. Assortment #88007, Willitts Designs. 1987. $10-15 ea.

•Snoopy, wearing a stocking cap, is ice-skating. Printed on the red base: "Cheers."

•Snoopy, as Joe Cool, is dressed as Santa. Printed on the red base: "Have A Cool Yule."

•Snoopy, dressed in a hat and coat, is hugging Woodstock. Printed on the red base: "Warm Wishes."

31. Mini Snowfalls

Plastic. 3"H. Willitts Designs. $10-15 ea.

•Snoopy, wearing a purple graduation cap and gown, is holding a diploma. Printed on the blue base: "Top Dog." #400490. 1989.

•Snoopy, wearing a party hat, holds a present. Printed on the pink base: "Happy Birthday." #450190. 1989.

•Snoopy wears a backpack, scout hat, and a red neckerchief. Printed on the red base: "Hup, Hup, Pup!" #88087. 1987.

32. Snowfall Paperweights

•Snoopy lies on top of his yellow doghouse. Plastic. #PW1/150, Simon Simple. 1969. $12-20 $32-38*

•Snoopy, wearing a stocking cap and a scarf, is ice-skating. Plastic. #PW3/200, Simon Simple. 1971. $15-20 $32-40*

33. Glitter-Globe Paperweights

Plastic. 4" x 3" x 3". #1522051, Butterfly Originals. 1984. $12-15 ea. $20-25* ea.

•Snoopy plays a video game with Woodstock sitting on his head.

•Snoopy, wearing headphones, is dancing, and Woodstock sits on top of a radio.

34. Sno-Globes

"PEANUTS Sno-Globe With Shake Action." Plastic. #4601, Butterfly Originals. 1981. $12-15 ea. $20-25* ea.

•Snoopy kisses Lucy on the cheek.

•Snoopy and Woodstock, dressed as scouts, toast marshmallows over a campfire.

DESK ACCESSORIES

35. Desk Blotter

•Snoopy, as the Flying Ace, is pictured in various scenes on each side of the blotter. Red, white, and black leather-look paper covers cardboard. 22" x 15". A&M Leatherlines, Inc. for Determined Productions. 1971. $20-35

Pencil Cup

•Snoopy, as the Flying Ace, is on top of his doghouse thinking, "Curse you, Red Baron." Leather-look paper covers cardboard. 4"H x 3" diam. A&M Leatherlines, Inc. for Determined Productions. 1971. $12-15

Note Pad

•Snoopy, as the Flying Ace, is on top of his doghouse thinking, "Here's the World War I Flying Ace zooming through the air in his Sopwith Camel." Leather-look paper covers cardboard. A&M Leatherlines, Inc. for Determined Productions. 1971. $10-15

Letter Holder

•Snoopy as the Flying Ace is pictured in various scenes around the letter holder. Leather-look paper covers cardboard. A&M Leatherlines, Inc. for Determined Productions. 1971. $20-30

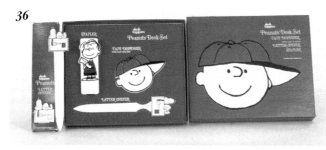

36. Letter Opener

•"Desk Toppers." Snoopy is lying on a mailbox at the top of the letter opener. Plastic. #DSK 1006, Springbok. Early 1970s. $18-20 $20-25*

Desk Set

•"Desk Toppers PEANUTS Desk Set." Boxed set features Linus holding a letter on the stapler; Charlie Brown wearing a baseball cap is the tape dispenser; and Snoopy lying on a mailbox at the top of a letter opener. The red and white box features Charlie Brown wearing his baseball cap. Each piece came boxed individually as well. Plastic. #DSK 1201, Springbok. Early 1970s. Individually out of original box: $18-22 ea. Set: $75-85*

37. Desk Set

•Set includes blotter, pen and pen holder, note paper holder, and address book. Snoopy, Charlie Brown, and Woodstock appear in outdoor scenes on each piece. Shrink wrapped 21-1/2" x 15". Butterfly Originals. Early 1980s. Pad: $6-8 Address Book: $6-8 Pen Holder: $6-8 Set: $30-35*

38. Desk Set

•Set includes a blotter, pen and pen holder, note paper holder, and address book. Snoopy, Charlie Brown, Sally, and Woodstock are featured in an office setting on each piece. Shrink-wrapped. 21-1/2" x 15". #1701, Butterfly Originals. Early 1980s. Pad: $5-8 Address Book: $6-8 Pen Holder/Pen: $6-8 Set: $30-35*

39. Erasers

•"PEANUTS Erasers." Set of three erasers features Snoopy dancing, Charlie Brown wearing baseball cap and glove, and Lucy. #50M999-3, Hallmark. Mid-1970s. $8-10*

40. Glue

"PEANUTS White Glue" and "PEANUTS School Glue." Plastic bottle. Duro Woodhill Chemical Sales Corp. 1975. $4-10 ea.

•White Glue. Charlie Brown is wearing his baseball cap and glove. 4 fl. oz.

•White Glue. Snoopy, as the Flying Ace, has one hand over his heart. 4 fl. oz.

•School Glue. Snoopy, as the Flying Ace, stands in front of a blackboard. 4 fl. oz.

•School Glue. Charlie Brown stands in front of a blackboard. 4 fl. oz.

•School Glue. Linus stands in front of a blackboard holding his blanket. 2 fl. oz.

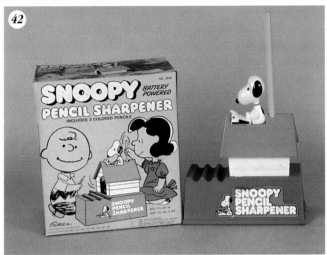

44. Scissors

•"Snoopy Snippers Cordless Electric Scissors." Scissors are shaped like Snoopy, lying on his tummy. Snoopy's mouth is the scissors. Battery operated. Plastic. #7410, Mattel. 1975. $12-15 $35-40*

FIGURESCENES

45. Figurescenes

Papier-mâché. This material, similar to that used for the nodders, tends to crack and peel with changes of moisture in the air, affecting the condition of the figurescene and, therefore, the price. Determined Productions. 1971.

•Snoopy, wearing an Uncle Sam hat, holds his hand over his heart. Printed on the base: "America You're Beautiful!" 6-1/2"H. #776. $30-45

•Snoopy, as Joe Cool, is wearing an orange sweater. Printed on the base: "Joe Cool." 5-1/4"H. $30-40

•Linus, with arms outstretched, wears a white baseball cap and holds a red blanket. Printed on the base: "To Know Me Is To Love Me." 5"H. #777. $30-35

•Charlie Brown, wearing his baseball cap and glove, is frowning. Printed on the base: "I've Made 120 Decisions Today... All Of Them Wrong." 5-1/4"H. #778. $30-40

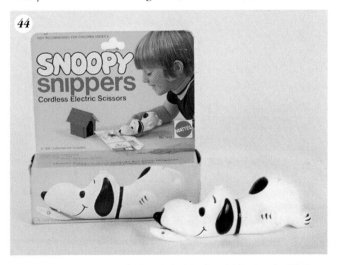

•White Glue. Linus, with his thumb in his mouth, holds his blanket. 4 fl. oz.

41. Pencil Cases

•Shaped like a school bus: Snoopy is the driver, Lucy stands in the doorway, and Peppermint Patty and Woodstock are the seated passengers. Includes pencils, colored pencils, an eraser, pencil sharpener and a ruler. Plastic. 4-1/4" x 2". #250-0774, Butterfly Originals. Late 1970s. $6-8

•Shaped like a school bus: Snoopy, as the Flying Ace, is the driver; Charlie Brown stands in the doorway; and Linus, Lucy, Franklin, and Peppermint Patty are the seated passengers. Includes pencils, colored pencils, tape, an eraser, pencil sharpener, and a ruler. Plastic. 8" x 4". Simon Simple. Early 1970s. $30-35*

42. Pencil Sharpener

•"Snoopy Pencil Sharpener." Snoopy sits at his typewriter on top of his doghouse, which is on a green base printed "Snoopy Pencil Sharpener." Three colored pencils are included. Battery operated. Plastic. #3550, Kenner. $8-12 $25-30*

43. Rulers

•"Snoopy's Fantastic Figure-Finder." The sliding part of the ruler features Snoopy, wearing a graduation cap, sitting behind a booth printed "Arithmetic Help 5¢" with Woodstock nearby. At the top of the ruler, Woodstock and his friends depict addition. The figure finder can add, subtract, multiply, divide, convert Fahrenheit to Centigrade, and convert numbers from the decimal system to the metric system. Plastic. #279PF791J, Ambassador. Late 1970s. $10-15*

•"Snoopy's Fantastic Figure-Finder." The sliding part of the ruler features Snoopy holding a blackboard. The top of the ruler features Lucy, Snoopy, and Charlie Brown. The figure finder can add, subtract, multiply, divide, convert Fahrenheit to Centigrade, and convert numbers from the decimal system to the metric system. Plastic. #225PF326-2, Hallmark. 1977. $10-15*

46

47

• Snoopy, as the Flying Ace, sits at a cafe table. Printed on the base: "Perhaps Some Dark-Haired Lass Will Share My Table." 5"H. #773. $25-30

• Snoopy sits next to Woodstock who holds a sign printed "?" Printed on the base: "He's A Nice Guy But I Don't Know Where He Stands." 4-1/2"H. #775. $35-40

48. Figurescenes

Papier-mâché. Determined Productions. 1971.

• Woodstock sits at a typewriter with Snoopy sitting behind him. Printed on the base: "My Secretary Isn't Worth Anything Before Coffee Break." 4-1/2"H. #767. $35-45*

• Charlie Brown and Linus, holding his blanket, sit together on a bench. Printed on the base: "I've Developed A New Philosophy—I Only Dread One Day At A Time." #766. $35-50*

• Schroeder plays his piano while Lucy leans on it. Printed on the base: "I Look Forward To The Day When I'll Understand Men." 4-1/2"H. #762. $40-60*

49. Figurescenes

Papier-mâché. Determined Productions. 1971.

• Linus, Schroeder, Charlie Brown, and Snoopy stand while Lucy is seated on a bench. They are all wearing baseball caps. Printed on the base: "How Can We Lose When We're So Sincere?" 4-1/2"H. #790. $135-185*

• Lucy, wearing a purple dress, sticks out her tongue. Printed on the base: "Bleah!" 5-1/4"H. #768. $25-30*

48

46. Figurescenes

Papier-mâché. Determined Productions. 1971.

• Snoopy, wears an award around his neck printed "Hero." Printed on the base: "It's Hero Time." 5-1/2"H. #771. $35-40*

• Snoopy is lying on his tummy on top of his doghouse. Printed on the base: "I'm Allergic to Morning." 4-1/2"H. #763. $18-22*

• Lucy sits behind her psychiatrist booth with a frazzled Charlie Brown sitting on a stool next to it. Printed on the base: "Even My Anxieties Have Anxieties." 5"H. #769. $75-85* Hard to find.

47. Figurescenes

Papier-mâché. Determined Productions. 1971.

• Linus, sitting in front of a tree, sucks his thumb and holds his blanket. Printed on the base: "I'm Thinking Of You." 5-1/2"H. #770. $30-35

• Lucy, wearing a pink dress, is standing with a scrunched look on her face. Printed on the base: "Look Out. I'm Going To Be Crabby All Day!" 5-1/4"H. #772. $30-35

• Snoopy leans against a standing Charlie Brown. Printed on the base: "Happiness Is Having Someone To Lean On." 5"H. #760. $30-35

• Linus and Sally smile and hold hands. Printed on the base: "Love Is Walking Hand In Hand." 5"H. #761. $18-25

49

GIFT WRAP AND GIFT TAGS

Hallmark and Ambassador have produced wrapping paper using the PEANUTS characters for many years. Wrapping paper alone could fill an entire book. Some of the older designs are pictured here packaged in sheets although they also came in rolls.

50. Gift Wrap

Hallmark. Late 1970s. $4-6* ea.

•Valentine's Day. Snoopy, Woodstock, and his friends are pictured in various scenes on a red background. Snoopy and Woodstock share a nest and hang a string of hearts printed "Happy Valentine's Day" in the tree; Woodstock sings to Snoopy; Snoopy hugs Woodstock; Woodstock is behind a booth printed "Pecks 5¢...The Beak Is In" as his friends line up in front; Snoopy as Cupid with a bow and arrow; Snoopy holds a handful of Valentines; Snoopy holds a heart; Woodstock delivers a Valentine. #65VW7514.

•All Occasion. The PEANUTS characters engage in various outdoor activities on a green background with rainbows. Lucy carries a golf bag; Schroeder watches as Woodstock fishes; Snoopy lies on top of a tent with Woodstock and his friends lying on its ropes; Peppermint Patty and Charlie Brown carry a picnic basket; Linus kicks a ball. #65EW1501.

•Christmas. Snoopy, Woodstock, and his friends are pictured among the shelves full of toys in Santa's workshop on a green background. #75XW2554.

•All Occasion. The PEANUTS characters engage in various outdoor activities on a green background. Woodstock plays hopscotch; Snoopy plays tennis; Woodstock sings in a birdbath; Linus and Peppermint Patty play Frisbee; Woodstock sails in Snoopy's supper dish; Sally and Rerun play in a sandbox; Lucy roller-skates; Charlie Brown flies his kite; Violet skips rope; Five and Roy are fishing; and Patty and Sophie play basketball. #65EW1522.

51. Christmas Gift Wrap 'N Trim

•The PEANUTS characters are featured outdoors on a white background. Lucy sits behind her psychiatrist booth dispensing Christmas advice; Snoopy, as the Flying Ace, pulls a present on a sled; Linus builds a snowman; Woodstock wears an oversized stocking cap; and Charlie Brown carries a gift. A gift tag—Charlie Brown holding a gift—is included with the wrapping paper. #75XE4055, Hallmark. Mid-1970s. $5-7*

All Occasion Gift Wrap

•The PEANUTS characters are featured at a party on a yellow background. Snoopy and Peppermint Patty are dancing; Woodstock and Charlie Brown carry gifts; Sally gives a gift to Linus; Violet gives a gift to Franklin; Lucy has climbed onto Schroeder's piano; and Patty gives a block to Rerun. #50EW1524, Hallmark. Mid-1970s. $5-7*

All Occasion Gift Wrap

•The PEANUTS characters are featured on an orange background. Lucy gazes at Schroeder across his piano; Charlie Brown, Lucy, and Linus watch TV; Linus skateboards; Snoopy throws a Frisbee; Charlie Brown flies his kite; Snoopy kisses Peppermint Patty on the cheek; Sally roller-skates; and a blue non-Woodstock bird looks up at Snoopy doing a handstand on top of his doghouse. #35EW3313, Ambassador. Late 1960s. $5-8*

Christmas Gift Wrap

•The PEANUTS characters are featured outdoors on a white background. Charlie Brown looks up at his kite stuck at the top of a decorated tree; Lucy and Linus build a snowman; Schroeder plays his piano with a bust of Beethoven wearing a Santa hat on top; Snoopy dreams of pizza; and Charlie Brown and Linus cover their ears as Lucy sings. #35XW300, Ambassador. Late 1960s. $5-8*

52. Gift Tags

•Lucy, sitting behind her booth printed "Good Luck Charms Today Only 25¢" wears a graduation cap. Lightweight cardboard. 5" x 6-1/8". #40GMT748-5, Hallmark. Mid-1970s. $2-4

•Charlie Brown is walking with a handful of presents. Lightweight cardboard. 5" x 5-3/4". #30XTM200-1, Hallmark. Early 1970s. $2-4

Gift Trim

Snoopy is lying on top of his doghouse. Lightweight cardboard. 4-1/8" x 3-1/2". #35TM46-2, Hallmark. Early 1970s. $2-3*

53. Gift Tags

•Snoopy and Woodstock on roller skates create rainbow-colored stripes behind them. Lightweight cardboard. Hallmark. 4-3/4" x 3-3/4". #65TM154-3. Early 1980s. $0.75-1.50

•Snoopy, grinning, carries a bouquet of patterned balloons. Lightweight cardboard. Hallmark. 4" x 6". #60TM156-1. Late 1970s. $0.75-1.50

•Snoopy, dressed as a beagle scout, walks in front of a rainbow, as Woodstock and his friends, also dressed as scouts, walk over the rainbow. Lightweight cardboard. Hallmark. 6-3/4" x 5-3/4". #50TM150-1. Mid-1970s. $2-3

GREETING CARDS

A popular way to send a card, was to send a "book card." These were discontinued in the 1990s, but if you look you can find some hanging about behind other cards.

54. Greeting Card Books

•"What Is A Baby?" Sally and Charlie Brown look into a baby carriage with Woodstock on top looking inside. 4-7/8" x 6-1/4". #275HEP410, Hallmark. Early 1980s. $3-5

•"Happy Birthday Gift Certificates For You." Snoopy, standing, grins and points to the title. 4-7/8" x 6-1/4". #250HEP20-7, Hallmark. Late 1970s. $3-5

•"A Collection Of Birthday Thoughts For You." Atop the pitcher's mound, wearing baseball caps and gloves, Charlie Brown says, "You're not getting older..." and Peppermint Patty finishes the thought saying, "You're getting better!" 4-7/8" x 6-1/4". #125HEP102, Hallmark. Late 1970s. $3-5

•"Keep Smiling! ... And Other Thoughts To Happy Up Your Day!" A baseball flies by Charlie Brown on the pitcher's mound, knocking his clothes off and sending him into the air. 4-7/8" x 6-1/4". #150HEP20-5, Hallmark. Late 1970s. $3-5

•"Christmas Gift Certificates For You." Surrounded by a string of Christmas lights, Snoopy, Lucy, Charlie Brown, and Sally stand with their arms outstretched. Woodstock stands on the title. 4-7/8" x 6-1/4". #225HEP80-0, Hallmark. Early 1980s. $3-5

•"Happy Father's Day To The Very Best Dad Of All." Lucy carries a large trophy cup as Snoopy sits behind her. 4-7/8" x 6-1/4". #125FTR3-7, Hallmark. Mid-1970s. $3-5

•Snoopy, lying on his doghouse, holds a sign printed "My Mother, by Charles M. Schulz." Charlie Brown and Lucy stand with their backs to each side of the doghouse. 5-1/8" x 7-1/8". #50MD201H, Ambassador. Late 1960s. $6-9

•"I Love You A Whole Bunch!" Snoopy, sitting on top of his doghouse, holds a very large bunch of bananas. A heart is pictured over his head. 4-7/8" x 6-1/4". #125HEP20-4, Hallmark. Late 1970s. $3-5

Musical Birthday Card

•Snoopy, wearing a party hat and blowing a party favor, dances against a background of confetti and streamers. The card plays "Happy Birthday" when opened. 6-3/4" x 8-3/4". #PRB173-1, Hallmark. Late 1980s. $6-9

55. Card Books with Songs

"The PEANUTS Book Of Pumpkin Carols." The following songs, in different combinations, can be found in the song books: "I'm Dreaming of the Great Pumpkin;" "Pumpkin Bells;" "Deck The Patch;" "The Twelve Days of Halloween;" "I Heard the Bells on Halloween;" "O Pumpkin Cards;" "Shivery Yells;" "Up in the Pumpkin Patch;" "Pumpkin Wonderland;" and "Great Pumpkin is Comin' to Town."

•Lucy, Linus, Snoopy, and Charlie Brown sing in the pumpkin patch. The song book is pumpkin-shaped. #100H20-1, Hallmark. Mid-1970s. $5-7

•Linus sits in the pumpkin patch. The song book is pumpkin-shaped. #100H20-1, Hallmark. Mid-1970s. $4-6

•Linus sits in the pumpkin patch. The song book is rectangular #125H20-3, Hallmark. Mid-1970s. $4-6

•Lucy, Charlie Brown, and Schroeder listen to Linus tell them about the Great Pumpkin, as Snoopy walks by on all fours. The song book is pumpkin-shaped. #75H20-1, Hallmark. Late 1960s. $6-10

•Schroeder plays his piano as Charlie Brown, Linus, Lucy, and Snoopy sing. The song book is pumpkin-shaped. #50H201H, Ambassador. Late 1960s. $6-10

56. Stand-up Greeting Cards

Each card comes with a box for mailing. Cardboard. 24"H. Hallmark. 1967. $12-20 ea.

•Lucy holds a paper banner, secured with yarn, printed "Merry Christmas To Someone I'm Immensely Fond Of." #250X203-6.

•Charlie Brown holds a paper Christmas ornament, secured with yarn, printed "Merry Christmas." Inside the ornament: "And Other Salutations Of The Season." #250X202-3.

Floor Stand

Snoopy, wearing a raccoon coat and a hat, carries a pennant printed "Rah!" Cardboard. 25"H. #200HD101-1, Hallmark. Late 1960s. $8-10

57. Greeting Cards in Frames

Cards feature molded, raised plastic scenes pasted onto the card, and a continued message inside. The cards were packaged in non-graphic boxes, and each included a white plastic frame. 8" x 10". Hallmark. 1969. $15-25* ea.

•Charlie Brown sits on a bench, frowning. Printed: "I've developed a new philosophy...I only dread one day at a time." #175M400-3.

•Snoopy is lying on top of his doghouse with a bunny lying on his tummy. Printed: "It's good to have a friend." Printed inside the card: "Especially one like you." #175M400-4.

•Snoopy is sitting and grinning. Printed: "Keep Smiling!" Printed inside the card: "It makes people wonder what you've been up to..." #175M400-1

•Snoopy, as the Flying Ace, sits on top of his bullet-riddled doghouse thinking "Curse you, Red Baron!" #174M400-2.

58. Pop-Up Greeting Cards

•The front of the card shows Charlie Brown flying his kite and saying, "Just a line to let you know..." Printed inside: "Things around here are about the same...!" Charlie Brown's kite is in a tree, and he hangs upside down from the tree tangled in the kite string. #50F400-6, Hallmark. Mid-1960s. $5-8

•The front of the card features Schroeder carrying his piano as Snoopy follows on all fours. Schroeder says, "Thought I'd wish you a happy birthday..." Printed inside the card: "And all

that jazz!" Frieda, Lucy, Sally, Charlie Brown, Violet, Linus, and Snoopy sing and play instruments around Schroeder playing his piano. #50B400-7, Hallmark. Mid-1960s. $5-8

•The front of the card shows Lucy, with her ear to a can attached to a cord going through a fence. Printed: "Waiting to hear...." Inside the card: "That you're feeling fine again!" Patty and Violet with cans to their ears; Snoopy and Charlie Brown stand in front of a fence. #50C103L, Ambassador. Mid-1960s. $5-8

59. Pop-Up Greeting Cards

•The front of the card features Lucy at her psychiatrist booth with Snoopy lying on his tummy in front of it. Printed: "So you're having another birthday... Well, that happens to a lot of people... And if you want my advice, there's only one thing you can do about it..." Printed inside the card: "Have a perfectly marvelous day!" Lucy and her booth pop up and Snoopy is sitting. #50B108L, Ambassador. Mid-1960s. $5-8

•The front of the card features Linus saying "As the Great Pumpkin always says..." Printed inside the card: "Happy Halloween!" Snoopy, Linus, Charlie Brown, Sally, Frieda, Lucy, and Schroeder are all sitting in a pumpkin patch. #50H206-4, Hallmark. $5-8

60. Puzzle Greetings

Each puzzle has space for a sender's signature. Mailing envelope included. 7" x 10-1/8". Hallmark. Late 1980s. $3-6 ea.

•Sally makes a popcorn garland—Charlie Brown is tangled in it, and Woodstock and his friends fly the garland around the Christmas tree. Lucy puts a star on top of the tree; Linus wraps a present; and Snoopy writes out his list to Santa.

Printed on the puzzle: "Hope Happiness Will Decorate Your Holidays!" and "Merry Christmas." #200X3103.

•Snoopy reads a Valentine card surrounded by cards, as Woodstock and his friends deliver more. Printed on the puzzle: "Everybody Wants To Be Your Valentine!" and "Happy Valentine's Day." #200V3103.

•Snoopy, dressed as a Pilgrim, holds a turkey drumstick. He is surrounded by baskets of fruit. Printed on the puzzle: "Have A Happy Thanksgiving!" #175TH3012.

61. Puzzle Greeting

•Pigpen hangs mistletoe; Charlie Brown and Lucy decorate the Christmas tree; Peppermint Patty and Schroeder carry gifts; Sally hangs stockings on the fireplace; Marcie and Linus sit at a table with milk and cookies; and Woodstock watches as Snoopy writes out his list to Santa. Printed on the puzzle: "Hope You're All Set For Your Best Christmas Yet" and "Merry Christmas from the PEANUTS Gang." #175X3101, Hallmark. Late 1980s. $4-6**

MINI DESK ACCESSORIES

62. Mini Desk Accessories

Assorted desk accessories and mini desk accessories by Butterfly Originals.

•Snoopy Mini Notes shaped like a strawberry with a plastic Woodstock mascot. Snoopy is eating. Series #0751. 1980. $1-2

•Snoopy Scratch 'N Sniff Telephone Book shaped like an ice cream sundae with a plastic Woodstock mascot. Snoopy and Woodstock sit in front of a dish of ice cream. 1-3/4" x 2". Series #1561002. 1984. $1-2

•Snoopy Mini Notes shaped like a bunch of bananas with a plastic Woodstock mascot. Snoopy is eating a banana as Woodstock watches. 2" x 1-1/2". Series #0751. 1980. $1-2

•Mini Address Book shaped like a heart with a plastic Woodstock mascot. Snoopy is sitting with Woodstock. 1-1/2"H. #0728. 1979. $1-2

•Desk Tray with two flip lids and front drawer. Snoopy, Charlie Brown, and Woodstock and his friends wear space suits and float in space. Printed: "PEANUTS In Space." Molded plastic. 6" x 8". #8764-6. 1982. $18-22

•Snoopy Stick-Up Pen and Holder. The pen slides into the holder under Snoopy, and is attached to the holder by a plastic coiled cord. Snoopy sits at his typewriter with Woodstock sitting on top. Series #6301. 1981. $2-3

•Snoopy Jumbo Yellow Clothespin. Snoopy as Joe Cool. Printed: "Joe Cool." Plastic. 5-3/4". Series #6005. 1981. $4-6

•Snoopy Jumbo Blue Clothespin. Snoopy is sitting. Printed: "Snoopy." Plastic. 5-3/4". Series #6005. 1981. $4-6

•Snoopy Jumbo Red Clothespin. Snoopy approaches Woodstock, who holds flowers. Printed: "Love." Plastic. 5-3/4". Series #6005. 1981. $4-6

•Snoopy Message Board. Message board is shaped like a house. Snoopy looks out a window at Woodstock, who is sitting on the roof. Includes a pencil. Plastic. #99 07390. 1980. $2-3

•Snoopy Scented Telephone Book shaped like a piece of wrapped candy with a plastic Woodstock mascot. Snoopy carries a dish of ice cream. 2-1/2" x 1-3/4". Series #1561002. 1984. $1-2

•Snoopy Fruit Address Book shaped like an apple with a plastic Woodstock mascot. Snoopy has his feet on a desk with an apple on it. 1-3/4" diam. #0802. 1981. $1-2

•Mini Autograph Book. Marcie and Peppermint Patty shake hands with Snoopy as the Flying Ace. Printed: "May I Have Your Autograph?" 4" x 3". Series #0717. 1980. $1-2

•Magic Memo Mate. Opens from both sides. Snoopy and Eudora are featured on the back and front. Contains a pad, address book, schedule sheet, and ID card. Available in different colors. #7801-1. 1983. $2-3

•PEANUTS Mini Address Book with mini telephone book attached by a chain. The address book features Peppermint Patty and Charlie Brown talking on the telephone. The telephone book features Snoopy on the telephone. Address book: 3-3/4" x 2-1/2". Phone book: 1-1/4" x 1". #0750. 1981. $1-2

•Snoopy Roll Memo. Snoopy and Woodstock ride in a red convertible. Pen is included and paper is refillable. Comes on a blister card featuring Snoopy driving a blue convertible. Plastic. 5"H. #8736-6. 1981. $2-4*

•Double Layer Memo Box. Snoopy and Woodstock wear

space suits and float in space. Printed: "UFO." Includes note paper and pen. Plastic. 3-1/2" x 2-1/2" x 2-1/2". #8737-6. 1982. $12-15

•PEANUTS Mini Binder with plastic Snoopy mascot. The clip features Snoopy at his typewriter with Woodstock on top. A mini pencil and pad is included. Sally and Linus are pictured on the pad. Designs on the note pad may vary. Plastic. #0713. 1979. $1-2

•PEANUTS Roll Call. Snoopy, Woodstock, and his friends are dressed as scouts on an orange background. Snoopy is calling attendance. Woodstock and his friends decorate the folder's clip. Vinyl. #0766. 1979. $2-3

•Snoopy Sentiment Clip. Oversized paper clip features Snoopy as a mailman. Printed: "Clip It." Plastic. 5-3/4"H Series #6009. 1981. $1-2*

•Snoopy Loose-leaf Reinforcements. Snoopy is pictured in various poses around the reinforcement holes. Package contains three sheets of 12 designs. #8302. 1984. $1-2*

•Mini School Bus Pencil Case. Snoopy drives the bus. Sally, Charlie Brown, Peppermint Patty, and Lucy appear in the windows. A pencil sharpener is part of the bus. Two mini colored pencils are included. Plastic. 2-3/4" x 1-3/4". #0748. $3-5

•PEANUTS Memo. Snoopy is kissing Peppermint Patty on the nose. A small pocket on the cover houses a pad featuring Sally on the cover. Plastic. 3-3/4" x 2-1/2". #0804. 1981. $1-2

•Snoopy Mini Pencil Case. Snoopy lies on his tummy watching as Woodstock falls off his supper dish. Includes five mini pencils and an eraser. Vinyl. 4-3/4" x 1-1/2". #0723. 1980. $1-2

•Snoopy Mailbox Letter Set. Snoopy looks inside a mailbox on one side. Woodstock and his friends peek out of a mailbox on the other side. The mailbox-shaped case contains envelopes, paper, an address book, and a pencil. Plastic. #0817-2. 1981. $2-4

•Snoopy Tape Dispenser. Snoopy and Woodstock are pictured on each side. Available in blue or pink tape and dispenser. Tape is refillable. Plastic. 3" x 2". #1727-2. 1982. $1-2*

•Snoopy Clip-Ons. Package of four clips feature Snoopy and Woodstock. Plastic. #0826-2. 1982. $1-2*

•Snoopy Mini Index. Snoopy is talking on a phone, which is in Woodstock's nest, against a red background. 1-3/4" x 2-1/2". 1980. $2-3

•Snoopy Cube Pencil Sharpener. Snoopy and Woodstock are featured on the sides of the cube. Available in red, yellow, and white. #2726. 1982. $1-2

•Snoopy Stapler. Snoopy stapling paper is featured on the stapler. Available in pink or blue. Packaged on a blister card with staples included. 3-1/2"L. #1728-2. 1982. $2-4*

MISCELLANEOUS ITEMS

63. Attaché Case

•Designer-like fabric features a repeating pattern of Snoopy standing with his arms outstretched. The case is trimmed in brown leather with key locks on both sides. The compartments inside are suede and leather. 16-1/2" x 13". Aviva. 1980. $185-250

PAPERWEIGHTS

64. Paperweights

Ceramic. 5"H. Butterfly Originals. Early 1980s.

•Snoopy, sitting, wears a cowboy hat, red neckerchief, and holds a lariat. $35-40*

•Snoopy sitting. $30-35*

•Snoopy, wearing a red and white striped baseball uniform, holds his bat. $35-40*

65. Paperweights

Ceramic. 3-1/2". Butterfly Originals. Mid-1970s. $15-20 ea.

•Snoopy sits at his typewriter on a red heart-shaped base. #300CPPW003.

•Snoopy wears a blue baseball cap and sits next to a red bat on home plate. #300CPPW001.

•Snoopy is sitting in his supper dish hugging Woodstock. #300CPPW004.

•Snoopy, wearing a backpack and red hat, is climbing a rock. #300CPPW005.

•Snoopy, with legs and arms crossed, sits in a green club chair. #300CPPW002.

66. Paperweights

Ceramic. Butterfly Originals. 1979.

•Snoopy is sitting with Woodstock between his feet. 4-1/4"H. #1009. $10-12*

•Snoopy, as Joe Cool, lies on his back with his head on a rock. 3-1/2"L. #1008. $10-12*

•Snoopy, lying on his tummy, is propped up on his elbows. 3"L. #1004. $12-15*

•Snoopy is lying on his tummy asleep. 4-1/2"L. #1007. $10-12*

•Snoopy is lying on his back. 3-1/2"L. #1005. $12-18*

67. Paperweights

Ceramic. 3"H. Butterfly Originals. 1979.

•Snoopy is sitting, wearing a yellow raincoat and hat. #1020. $15-20*

•Snoopy, as the Flying Ace, is sitting with Woodstock between his feet. #1023. $15-18*

•Snoopy is sitting, wearing a blue visor and holding a tennis racket. #1021. $15-20*

•Snoopy is sitting, wearing a red and white striped baseball uniform, red cap and holding a bat. #1022. $15-20*

68. Mini Paperweights

Ceramic. Butterfly Originals. Early 1980s. $9-15* ea.

•Snoopy, with his hands raised and clasped together, stands on a red base printed "Everybody Loves A Winner." 3"H.

•Snoopy rests his elbows on a green base printed "I Think Of You." 1-1/2"H.

•Snoopy, holding a tennis racket, and Woodstock sit back-to-back on a red base printed "Perfect Set." 2-1/2"H.

•Snoopy sits at his typewriter on a blue base printed "Love Letters." 2-1/4"H.

•Snoopy, with Woodstock lying on his tummy, lies on his back on a green base with yellow flowers printed "Daydreamin'." 2"H.

•Snoopy, wearing a yellow jacket, dances on a blue base printed "Disco." 3"H.

69. Paperweight

•Snoopy is sitting. Silver-plated—can tarnish beyond repair 3-1/2". #9677, Leonard Silver. 1980. $18-25

70. Paperweights

Dome-shaped glass with graphics on paper inside magnified by the glass. Butterfly Originals. 1977. $15-25 ea.

•Snoopy is lying on top of his doghouse. #250GPPW002.

•Snoopy tosses a tennis ball as he prepares to serve. #250GPPW003.

•Snoopy has just hit the baseball with his bat as Woodstock watches its flight. #250GPPW004.

•Snoopy, wearing a helmet, throws a football. Woodstock runs to catch it. Printed: "Go!" #250GPPW001.

71. Paperweights

•Snoopy is sitting and holding flowers. Stippled glass. 3-1/2" x 4-1/2". #8572, Determined Productions. 1978. $20-25

•Woodstock is sitting. Stippled glass. 2-1/2" x 3". #8576, Determined Productions. $18-25

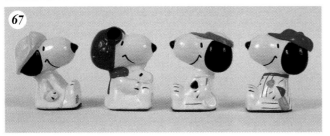

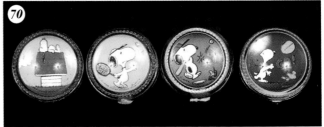

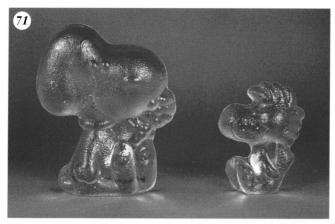

72. Paperweights

Designs are etched inside the glass. The box pictures the paperweight inside. 3" x 2-1/2". Butterfly Originals. Late 1970s. $35-40* ea.

•Snoopy holds a heart with "I Love You" etched above inside a heart-shaped paperweight. #1804.

•Snoopy is standing with Woodstock and his friends flying around him inside a round paperweight. #1803.

73. Paperweights

Designs are etched inside the glass. The box pictures the paperweight inside. Heart-shaped. 3" x 2-1/2". Butterfly Originals. Late 1970s. $35-42* ea.

•Snoopy and Woodstock sit back-to-back, with hearts above them. #1801.

•Woodstock presents a flower to a sitting Snoopy, with the word "Friends" etched above them. #1805.

•Snoopy is standing and sniffing flowers with very long stems. #1802.

PEN AND PENCIL HOLDERS

Pen/pencil holders were usually removed from their boxes before being put on store shelves. If customers asked, sometimes the boxes could be found for them.

74. Pen/Pencil Holders

Ceramic. Butterfly Originals. $22-28 ea.

•Snoopy and Woodstock are leaning against the trunk of a tree. 1976.

•Snoopy is sitting with a blue ink bottle between his feet (pen is not included). Printed: "Ink." 3-1/2"H. 1977.

•Snoopy stands against a blue ink bottle with a red cap. Printed: "Ink." 4"H. 1977.

75. Pen/Pencil Holders

Ceramic. Butterfly Originals.

•Snoopy wears a baseball cap and holds a bat on a green base printed "World's Greatest Baseball Player." Pen is included. 4"H. Late 1970s. $25-30

•Snoopy as Joe Motocross, wearing a red helmet, stands next to a stack of tires with his arms folded across his chest. 4"H. 1976. $22-25

•Snoopy, as Joe Motocross, wearing a red helmet, sits on a tire. 3-1/2"H. 1976. $18-25

•Snoopy wears a visor and holds a tennis racket. Pen is included. 4"H. Late 1970s. $25-30

76. Pen Holders

•Snoopy is sitting on a red heart-shaped base. Pen not included. Ceramic. 4"H. Butterfly Originals. Late 1970s. $25-30

•Snoopy is sitting at his typewriter with Woodstock on top. Pen is included. Lucite. 4"W. Butterfly Originals. Late 1970s. $22-25

Pen/Pencil Holder

•Snoopy, wearing a blue visor, sits next to an open red tennis bag with a tennis racket on its side. Pencils not included. Ceramic. 4"H. Butterfly Originals. Mid-1970s. $30-35*

• Snoopy, wearing a blue visor and talking on the telephone, sits on a yellow base printed "Hello."

• Snoopy, at his typewriter, sits on a blue base printed "Love Letters." #0200 0911.

• Snoopy is sitting and hugging Woodstock on a red base printed "Love."

• Snoopy is lying on his back. Woodstock, on his back, is lying on Snoopy's tummy on a green base printed "Daydreamin'."

79. Pen/Pencil Holders

Ceramic. Butterfly Originals. Late 1970s.

• Snoopy, his hands on his heart, stands in front of a red heart printed "I Love You." 3"H. $30-35

• Snoopy, hugging Woodstock, sits on a white base printed "Love." 2-7/8" x 2-7/8". $15-20

• Snoopy, with a red visor, leans on his tennis racket on a brown base printed "World's Greatest Tennis Player." 3" x 4". $25-32

80. Pen/Pencil Cups

The base rotates, allowing an arrow to point to a day of the week or an activity printed on the cup. Plastic. 3-1/2"H. #1170, Butterfly Originals. 1981. $7-9* ea.

• Snoopy is shown reading a newspaper; sitting at a typewriter; asleep on the typewriter; and holding a pencil and paper. The orange cup is printed "mon," "tue," "wed," "thu," "fri," "sat," and "sun."

• Snoopy is pictured holding a pencil and pad; sitting at a typewriter; deep in thought; and asleep at the typewriter. The blue cup is printed "I'm busy...do not disturb" and "writing," "reading," "typing," "thinking," and "relaxing."

77. Mini Pencil Holders

Snoopy sits beside the holder. Includes mini colored pencils. Ceramic. Approximately 1-1/2"H. Butterfly Originals. 1980. $10-12* ea.

• Snoopy sits at his typewriter.

• Snoopy is on the telephone. "Hello" is printed on the pencil holder.

• Snoopy, wearing a visor and holding a tennis racket, sits back to back with Woodstock. "Perfect Set" is printed on the pencil holder.

• Snoopy is hugging Woodstock. "Love" is printed on the pencil holder. #119 0717.

78. Pen Holders/Paperweights

A mini colored marker is included. Ceramic. 2" x 2-3/4". Butterfly Originals. Early 1980s. $10-12*

POSTCARDS

81. Postcard Books

Each book contains twenty identical detachable postcards. 6" x 4". Mid-1970s. $6-12 ea.

• Charlie Brown, standing on the pitcher's mound and wearing his baseball cap and glove, frowns and says, "Sigh." Ambassador.

• Woodstock, in his nest, reads a book out loud. Ambassador.

• Lucy pulls the football out from underneath Charlie Brown, sending him into the air. Printed: "Aaugh!" #100ST949, Hallmark.

•Snoopy is lying on top of his doghouse, as Woodstock flies upside down nearby. Printed: "Flitter Flitter Flitter Flutter." Ambassador.

•Snoopy is lying on top of his doghouse with a flower on a very long stem reaching over him. Snoopy thinks, "All right, who planted the flower?!" Ambassador.

•Snoopy lies on his tummy, thinking, "There's no sense in doing a lot of barking if you don't really have much to say." Also printed: "Line Dropper Postcards." #100ST950, Hallmark.

•Snoopy, lying on his doghouse with Woodstock lying on his tummy, is thinking, "Someday, I must give up this mad, carefree existence. #100ST945-1, Hallmark.

•Snoopy, playing in a circle with nine bunnies, is thinking, "It's good to have friends." Also printed: "Line Dropper Postcards." #100ST948, Hallmark.

•Charlie Brown says, "Just a note to say I think you're nice." Snoopy thinks "...and it's not even 'Be Kind to People Week'!" #100ST944-1, Hallmark.

•Snoopy grins as he walks and thinks, "Say something nice to everyone you meet today! It'll drive them crazy!" #100ST943-1, Hallmark.

•Woodstock and his friends each hold a sign with a word on it to spell out "Have A Nice Day!" #100ST946-1, Hallmark.

Oversize Postcard Book

•The top postcard features Snoopy lying on top of his doghouse, with Woodstock standing on his tummy. He is thinking "It's good to have a friend." Printed underneath the doghouse: "And it's fun to keep in touch with them on these 20 detachable Snoopy friend-to-friend cards." Contains 20 different postcards featuring Snoopy, Lucy, Charlie Brown, and Woodstock. 4-1/2" x 9-1/2". #200KF1-5, Hallmark. 1971. $10-22

SEALS, STICKERS, AND NAME TAGS

82. Seals

"PEANUTS Seals." Red, white, and blue seals. Hallmark. Late 1960s. $6-8** ea.

•Snoopy, Charlie Brown, Lucy and Linus are featured. Pack contains five sheets of six different designs. #35HD97-7.

•Snoopy is featured in various poses and thinking different thoughts. Pack contains four sheets of nine different designs. #50HD98-4.

•Snoopy, as the Flying Ace, is featured in various poses. Pack contains four sheets of twelve different designs. #50HD97-2.

•"Snoopy Seals." Snoopy and Woodstock are featured on seals with red, pink, blue, and yellow backgrounds. Pad-like package contains four sheets of nine different designs. #59HD97-1, Hallmark. Mid-1970s. $4-7

•Snoopy, Woodstock, Linus, Lucy, and Charlie Brown are featured on seals with red and yellow backgrounds. Package contains four sheets of nine different designs. #59SS118J, Ambassador. Mid-1970s. $5-7**

•"Snoopy World's Greatest Sports Hero." Snoopy is featured involved in various sports on seals with various light-colored backgrounds. Pack contains four sheets of twelve different designs. #50HD96-6, Hallmark. Early 1970s. $5-7**

•Snoopy is featured competing in various Olympic events on seals with light blue and light green backgrounds. Package contains four sheets of twelve different designs. #50HD96-1, Hallmark. 1972. $6-8**

Stickers

•"PEANUTS Postage Stickers." Snoopy, Woodstock, Charlie Brown, Lucy, Linus, and Schroeder are featured on seals with red and blue backgrounds. Pad-like packaging contains four sheets of nine different designs. #59KM600Q, Ambassador. Mid-1970s. $4-7

83. Seals

•Snoopy and Woodstock appear on seals that incorporate rainbows into their backgrounds. Package contains four sheets of six different designs. Hallmark. Late 1970s. $3-5**

Stamps

•"Snoopy Astronaut Stamps." Snoopy, dressed as an astronaut, is featured in two designs. Snoopy on his doghouse is surrounded by the words "First Landing On The Moon Commemorative 1969." Snoopy holding flight safety gear is surrounded by the words "All Systems Are Go! Snoopy." Forty eight red, white, and blue stamps. Determined Productions. 1969. $40-45**

Seals

•"Easter Egg Seals." Lucy, Snoopy, Linus, Franklin, Charlie Brown, and Schroeder are on oval-shaped seals with white backgrounds. Package contains three sheets of eighteen different designs. #50EHD14-4, Hallmark. Early 1970s. #7-9**

Seals

Hallmark. Mid-1970s. $6-8** ea.

•Charlie Brown, Snoopy, Sally, Lucy and Pigpen are featured on seals with red, yellow, green, and blue backgrounds. Package contains four sheets of nine different designs.

•Lucy, Snoopy, and Charlie Brown are featured on seals with a CB radio theme on pink, orange, white, and yellow backgrounds. Pack contains four sheets of six different designs.

•Charlie Brown, Snoopy, Woodstock, Sally, and Linus appear on seals with Christmas and winter scenes on red, green, and blue backgrounds. Package contains four sheets of six different designs.

84. Name Tags

•Snoopy is featured in two designs. Snoopy wears an orange jacket on a white background with pink trim. Snoopy, as Joe Cool, wears a pink shirt on a white background with orange trim. Package contains sixteen name tags. #59HD975, Hallmark. Mid-1970s. $3-5**

•Snoopy and Woodstock are featured in two designs. Woodstock holds a heart printed "Be Mine," and Snoopy holds a heart printed "Love." Package contains sixteen name tags. #59VNT12, Hallmark. Mid-1970s. $3-5**

•Snoopy is featured in two designs. Snoopy is dancing on a white background with red trim. Snoopy, as the Flying Ace, is walking on a white background with blue trim. Package contains twenty name tags. #50HD99J, Ambassador. Mid-1970s. $3-5**

•Snoopy and Woodstock appear in two designs. Snoopy holds his red and green stocking cap above his head. Woodstock stands among a row of snowmen. Package contains sixteen name tags. #75XNT165, Hallmark. Late 1970s. $3-5**

Stickers

•"PEANUTS Holiday Stickers." Four stickers feature Snoopy, Charlie Brown, Lucy, and Woodstock in Christmas scenes on red, white, and green backgrounds. Vinyl. #150XHD41-7, Hallmark. Mid-1970s. $4-6

•"PEANUTS Stickers." Linus, with his thumb in his mouth, is holding his blanket against a green background. Printed: "Don't Bug Me!" Contains seven other stickers featuring Snoopy, Charlie Brown, and Lucy, which are pictured on the back of the package. #100M400-3, Hallmark. 1968. $6-10**

Sticker Picture Book

•Snoopy and Woodstock sit on top of Snoopy's doghouse reading books. Stickers are included to put on the four scenes in the book. Paper. 7-3/4" x 9-3/4". #100HD100-2, Hallmark. Early 1970s. $4-8

85. Seals

•"Valentine Seals." Woodstock, wearing a cap, delivers Valentines. Package contains four sheets of six different designs. #100VS682 K 4205, Hallmark. Late 1980s. $2-3**

•"Snoopy Bicentennial Seals." Snoopy, Woodstock, Charlie Brown, Linus, and Lucy are featured on seals with red, white, and blue backgrounds. Package contains six sheets of eight different designs. #HD1198, Hallmark. 1976. $4-6**

•"Snoopy Seals." Snoopy is featured in various poses against red, white, and blue stars and stripes backgrounds. Package contains four sheets of nine different designs. #50HD99-1, Hallmark. Early 1970s. $6-10**

•Snoopy, Woodstock, Lucy, and Charlie Brown are featured on football-theme seals with red, yellow, and green backgrounds. Package contains four sheets of eight different designs. #75SS1919, Hallmark. Early 1980s. $3-5**

•Snoopy, Linus, Peppermint Patty, Lucy, Linus, and Charlie Brown appear on Halloween-theme seals with orange, yellow, and black highlights. Pack contains four sheets of nine different designs. #50HHD131, Hallmark. Early 1970s. $6-10**

•Snoopy, Woodstock, and Charlie Brown are featured on Thanksgiving-theme seals with red backgrounds. Package contains four sheets of six different designs. #100TSS2523 K 2095, Hallmark. Late 1980s. $2-4**

•Snoopy, Lucy, Charlie Brown, and Linus are featured on Christmas-theme seals with olive, red, white, and light blue backgrounds. Package contains four sheets of nine different designs. #50XHD309, Hallmark. Early 1970s. $6-8**

STATIONERY AND NOTE PADS

86. Stationery

"PEANUTS Stationery." The red, white, and black graphic box contains twelve decorated sheets and envelopes and six plain sheets. Box—10-1/4" x 7-1/4". 1969. $25-35** ea.

•Snoopy, as the Flying Ace, sits on top of his bullet-riddled doghouse. The sheets feature the Flying Ace on his doghouse, and the envelopes depict him walking toward his doghouse. #125ST922, Hallmark.

•"King Kite." Charlie Brown is holding his kite. The sheets feature Charlie Brown tangled in his kite string and hanging upside down next to his kite. The envelopes depict him flying his kite. #150ST989, Hallmark.

•Snoopy carries a tall stack of letters to an open mailbox. The sheets feature Snoopy writing a letter on top of his doghouse, and the envelopes depict him reading a letter on top of his doghouse. #125T901J, Ambassador.

•Snoopy lies on his tummy on top of an open mailbox. The sheets feature Snoopy looking at an envelope, and the envelopes depict Snoopy inside an open mailbox, looking out. #125ST910, Hallmark.

•"Pen Pal." The red, white, and black graphic box features Lucy leaning on her hands and knees in front of a mailbox, with Linus standing on her back mailing a letter. Printed on the box: "Dear Pen Pal." The box contains fifteen decorated sheets and envelopes, and a pen with a red cap. The sheets feature Lucy watching Linus write a letter. The back of the envelopes show Lucy licking an envelope. The pen features Snoopy, Lucy, Linus, and Charlie Brown, each pictured three times around. Box—10-1/4" x 7-1/4" #200ST937, Hallmark.

87. Pads

Paper. 7" x 10". Hallmark. $4-7 ea.

•Snoopy sits at his typewriter typing a letter on top of his doghouse against a red background. Printed: "PEANUTS Note Pad." The sheets inside show different designs with Charlie Brown, Linus, Frieda, and Snoopy in the upper left-hand corners. #89EFC204-6. Early 1970s.

•Snoopy is dancing against a red, white, and blue background printed "Snoopy For President Memo Pad" and "Happiness Is

The Best Policy." Snoopy dancing and "Snoopy For President" is on the top of each sheet inside. #100KF1-1. 1972.

•Charlie Brown writes a letter, with several crumpled sheets nearby. Snoopy leans over the edge of the table next to him, against a red background. Inside, the sheets show different designs with Charlie Brown, Linus, and Snoopy in the upper left-hand corners. Printed: "PEANUTS Memo Pad." #89EFC104-6. Early 1970s.

88. Stationery

Paper box—8-1/2" x 7". Hallmark.

•Snoopy lies on his tummy on top of an open mailbox. The sheets feature Snoopy reading a letter, and the back of each envelope shows him reading a letter with envelopes tossed all around. Contains eighteen tan and white decorated sheets and envelopes, and eighteen plain white sheets. #200ST963-1, Hallmark. Mid-1970s. $6-10**

•Snoopy and Lucy are featured in a four-panel comic strip against a blue background. The sheets feature the same comic strip. The envelopes have no graphics. Contains twenty decorated sheets, twenty red envelopes, and twenty plain white sheets. #200ST913-1, Hallmark. Mid-1970s $6-10**

•Snoopy, wearing a tail coat, plays the piano, while Woodstock sings, and five of his friends play musical instruments. The stationery paper resembles sheet music, and features Woodstock and a friend playing instruments in the upper left-hand corner. The envelopes have no graphics. Contains thirty decorated sheets and fifteen yellow envelopes. #ST427-2, Hallmark. Early 1980s. $4-7**

•Snoopy is sitting among potted plants and flowers that have a water-color look. The bottom of the sheets feature the same design. The envelopes have no graphics. Contains sixteen decorated sheets, sixteen yellow envelopes, and sixteen plain white sheets. #300ST107-8, Hallmark. Early 1980s. $4-7**

•Snoopy, standing by a tripod with a camera on it, against a red and white polka-dot background, thinks, "Watch the birdie!" He holds Woodstock on a stand in his hand. Woodstock, in turn, holds a sign printed "Smile." Design repeats in the upper left corner of each sheet. The envelopes show Woodstock holding a sign printed "Smile." Contains eighteen decorated sheets and envelopes, and eighteen plain white sheets. #250ST465-6, Hallmark. Late 1970s. $6-8**

•Snoopy sits at his typewriter on top of his doghouse as Woodstock flies in to deliver a letter, against an orange back-

ground. This design is repeated in the lower right-hand corner of each sheet. The envelope features Woodstock flying toward and open mailbox. Contains eighteen decorated sheets and envelopes, and eighteen plain white sheets. #200ST925-1, Hallmark. Mid-1970s. $6-10**

89. Stationery

Paper box—8-1/2" x 7". Hallmark. $5-8** ea.

•Snoopy, dressed as a mailman, walks along a path toward the mailboxes on his route. The sheets feature Snoopy holding a letter and walking toward mailboxes, where Woodstock sits holding a flower. The envelopes feature mailboxes and a house on the path. Contains sixteen decorated sheets and envelopes, and sixteen plain white sheets. #300ST108-8, Hallmark. Early 1980s.

•Snoopy dances diagonally across a striped pastel background, with musical notes all around him. The sheets show Snoopy dancing in the upper left-hand corner. The envelopes are plain. Contains thirty decorated sheets and fifteen yellow envelopes. #ST263-0, Hallmark. Late 1970s.

•Snoopy is sitting with an open box of crayons against multicolored vertical and horizontal lines. Sheets feature multicolored horizontal lines, with Snoopy sitting among the crayons in the lower right-hand corner. The envelopes are plain. Contains sixteen decorated sheets, sixteen orange envelopes, and sixteen plain sheets. #300ST721-7. Early 1980s.

•Snoopy, dancing on a blue background with small red and white flowers, is thinking, "Oh, happy day!" The sheets feature the same design without the flowers in the upper right-hand corner. The envelopes have no graphics. Contains sixteen decorated sheets, sixteen green envelopes, and sixteen plain sheets. #ST521-3. Late 1970s.

•Woodstock and many of his friends fly overhead, as Snoopy sits in the lower right-hand corner. The top of the sheets feature Woodstock and his friends flying in a pattern that spells "Hello." Snoopy sits in the lower right-hand corner. The envelopes have no graphics. Contains sixteen decorated sheets, sixteen yellow envelopes, and sixteen plain sheets. #300ST722-7. Early 1980s.

WASTEBASKETS AND MAGNETIC BOARD SETS

90. Wastebasket

•Snoopy and Woodstock dance as Schroeder plays the piano, Lucy sings, Sally plays the saxophone, Linus plays the

guitar, and Charlie Brown plays the drums printed "Snoopy and the C.B.s." Reverse side: Snoopy, wearing a pink and blue party hat, dances against a yellow and white background. Printed: "Let's Party." Metal. 19"H. #WB687LP, P & K Products, Inc. 1988. $25-35

Magnetic Bulletin Boards

•Snoopy, wearing a pink and blue party hat, dances against a yellow and white background. Printed: "Let's Party." Metal. 14" x 19-1/8". #PM687CB, P & K Products, Inc. 1988. $25-30

•Snoopy and Woodstock dance as Schroeder plays the piano, Lucy sings, Sally plays the saxophone, Linus plays the guitar, and Charlie Brown plays the drums printed "Snoopy and the C.B.s." Metal. 14" x 19-1/8". #PM687LP, P & K Products, Inc. 1988. $25-30 (Not pictured)

91. Wastebasket

•Snoopy peers out from the tree top, thinking, "Here's the Watchbeagle waiting for a litter bug..." Reverse side: Snoopy, dressed as janitor, holds a broom and stands next to a bucket and dust pan. Printed: "These Premises Are Maintained By The Resident Stationary Sanitation Engineer." Metal. 19"H. #WB688WB, P & K Products, Inc. 1988. $25-35

Magnetic Bulletin Boards

•Snoopy, dressed as janitor, holds a broom and stands next to a bucket and dust pan. Printed: "These Premises Are Maintained By The Resident Stationary Sanitation

92

93

94

Engineer." Metal. 14" x 19-1/8". #PM688ST, P & K Products, Inc. 1988. $25-30

•Snoopy peers from a tree, thinking, "Here's the Watchbeagle waiting for a litter bug..." Metal. 14" x 19-1/8". #PM688WB, P & K Products, Inc. 1988. $25-30 (Not pictured)

92. Wastebasket

•Snoopy, as Joe Cool wearing a red shirt and holding a cup, stands against a light blue polka-dot background. Printed: "Super Cool." Reverse side: Snoopy as Joe Cool, wearing a blue shirt and holding a cup, stands against a red polka-dot background. Printed: "Super Cool." Metal. 19"H. #WB686SC, P & K Products, Inc. 1988. $30-35

Magnetic Bulletin Boards

•Snoopy, as Joe Cool wearing a blue shirt and holding a cup, stands against a red polka-dot background. Printed: "Super Cool." Metal. 14" x 19-1/8". #PM686JR, P & K Products, Inc. 1988. $25-30

•Snoopy, as Joe Cool wearing a red shirt and holding a cup, stands against a light blue polka-dot background. Printed: "Super Cool." Metal. 14" x 19-1/8". #PM686JB, P & K Products, Inc. 1988. $25-30 (Not pictured)

93. Wastebasket Backboards

"Snoopy Waste Paper Basketball Backboard." Includes all necessary materials to make a basket to attach to any wastebasket. Plastic net and hard backboard. 9" x 13". P & K Products, Inc. 1988. $10-15** ea.

•Snoopy, Woodstock, and Charlie Brown play basketball against a blue background. #BBA688SB.

•Snoopy, running with the basketball, is followed by Woodstock against a maroon and white background. #BBA687SM.

•Snoopy attempts to shoot a basketball into Woodstock's nest, as Woodstock tries to block the shot, against a red background. #BBA686SR.

94. Magnetic Bulletin Boards

Metal. 14" x 19-1/8". P & K Products, Inc. 1988. $30-35 ea.

•Snoopy, wearing sunglasses and eating french fries, sits on top of his doghouse surrounded by junk food. His doghouse is printed "Dorm" with the University of Michigan's "Go Blue" logo above it. #PM545MD.

•Snoopy, wearing a suit and sunglasses, holds a mug of root beer and thinks "Party Time!" Printed: "Michigan." #PM545MP.

Here is just a small sampling of what kids who live in other countries get to play with:

The two yellow boxes near the front, labeled "Snoopy," feature a number of really creative activities for kids ages three to ten (France). The activity and coloring books in the front are from Japan. Next to the books on the left is a red wood "educational" wagon containing shaped blocks which can be inserted into corresponding holes—helpful in developing eye-hand coordination and dexterity (Japan). On top of the wagon is a pinball game (Japan), and next to it is a lacquered hardwood toy Sopwith Camel-style airplane (France), with Snoopy (hidden from view) at the controls.

The toy piano, which actually plays, is from Japan, and the green ball (partially shown in front of the piano) is from Spain. Next to the piano is a ring toss game, and behind it is a cable car-styled wagon loaded with building blocks decorated with PEANUTS characters—both from Japan.

The red table is also from Japan. The play dishes on top of it are from Hong Kong. Next to the table is a small child's chair (Japan), with Spike and Snoopy plushes (Mexico) sitting on it. Behind the table, on the right, is a Snoopy-shaped chair (Germany). A large Snoopy plush (Mexico) sits on it.

In the rear, a large Snoopy plush (Japan) rests on a magnificent Japanese-made combination hall stand/storage box. Returning to the row behind the front, on the right side, is a Japanese board game in a blue-sided box labeled "Snoopy." Above the board game is the pink box that housed the dishes.

Scattered throughout are parts of a marvelous child's kitchen set, decorated mostly in red, with oven, covered casserole dish, pot, frying pan, and toaster (Hong Kong).

Truly a United Nations of toy land!

The PEANUTS Home Collection

The Playroom

I f it is true that he who winds up with the most toys wins, then the kid who is lucky enough to have a playroom overflowing with PEANUTS toys is way ahead before the race even begins! Our PEANUTS playroom is truly a fantasy for kids of all ages. May we never grow up!

BIG STUFF FOR LI'L FOLKS

1. Toy Chest/Activity Center

•Charlie Brown and Snoopy are featured on sliding top-shelf doors. Snoopy, lying on his doghouse with Woodstock lying on his tummy; Woodstock's friends; and Charlie Brown are pictured on the front of the chest. Not pictured are the sliding chalkboard doors. Fiberboard. 41"H. Sold exclusively at Sears. 1983. $60-85

2. Toy Chest

•Snoopy, lying on his doghouse with Woodstock lying on his tummy; Woodstock's friend; and Charlie Brown are featured on all sides. Fiberboard on wheels, with metal handle bars. 22"H. Sold exclusively at Sears. 1983. $45-60

3. Toy Chest

•Shaped like Snoopy's doghouse, the roof is removable. Snoopy and Woodstock are part of the doghouse's doorway. Molded polyethylene. 23"L x 16"W x 22"H. Sold exclusively at Sears. 1983. $50-65

4. Tent

•"Snoopy Funhut Bed/Play Tent." Tent features Snoopy and Woodstock. For indoor/outdoor use. Fits over a twin-size bed. Includes all hardware necessary for assembly. Nylon taffeta. #825-0026, Ero Industries. 1989. $7-9 $10-15*

Playhouse

•Shaped like a house, the front has a door that opens featuring Charlie Brown holding Snoopy's supper dish. Snoopy sits outside the door, and Sally looks out the window. Woodstock and his friends fly over the roof. The back fea-

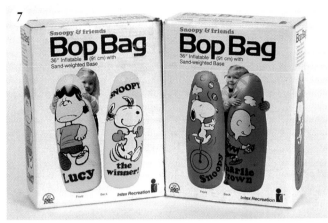

tures Lucy sitting behind her psychiatrist's booth, Woodstock falling off the roof of the house, and Charlie Brown flying his kite. One side of the playhouse features Schroeder playing his piano and a dizzy Snoopy. This side has an open window. Printed on the playhouse: "Snoopy." Printed on the packaging: "Snoopy Playhouse For Indoor/Outdoor Fun!" Includes all pieces necessary for assembly. Vinyl with plastic frame. 42"H x 38"L x 30"W. #44628, Intex Recreation Corp. 1989. $8-15 $20-25*

5. Table and Chair Set

•Table top shows Snoopy on his doghouse with Woodstock on his tummy. House is printed "SNOOPY." Charlie Brown and two of Woodstock's friends stand by. Top is vinyl laminated plastic with red molding. Chairs have molded plastic seats and backs, but no graphics. Comes unassembled. Chairs: 24"H with a seat height of 12". Table: 24" square, 20-1/2"H. Sold through Sears catalog, 1983. Set: $45-75

6. Pushover Inflatable Toy

•Charlie Brown is featured on the bag. Printed: "I Need All The Friends I Can Get." Heavy duty vinyl with a weighted base. 34"H. Determined Productions. 1973. $30-35

Bop Bag

•Snoopy, as Joe Cool, is featured on the inflatable bop bag. Printed: "Snoopy." Heavy duty vinyl with a weighted base. 36"H. #5530-1, Ideal Toy Company. 1978. $25-30 $30-35*

7. Bop Bags

•"Snoopy & Friends Bop Bag." Lucy is featured on one side, and Snoopy, wearing boxing gloves and dancing, is on the other side. Printed on the bag: "Lucy" and "Snoopy The Winner!" Heavy duty vinyl with a weighted base. 36"H. #44689, Intex Recreation Corp. 1989. $6-8 $12-15*

•"Snoopy & Friends Bop Bag." Snoopy, riding a unicycle and juggling Easter eggs, and Woodstock, sitting on Snoopy's head, are featured on one side. Charlie Brown flying his kite is on the other side. Printed on the bag: "Snoopy" and "Charlie Brown." Heavy duty vinyl with a weighted base. 36"H. #44689, Intex Recreation Corp. 1989. $6-8 $12-15*

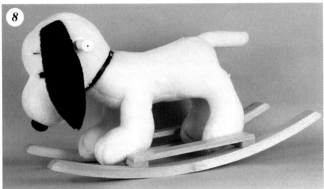

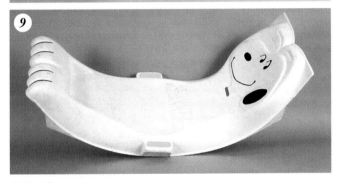

8. Rocker

•Plush Snoopy is a rocking horse on a wooden base. Plastic handles protrude from behind each ear. 31"L x 18"H x 14"W. FAO Schwarz catalog #359554. Made exclusively for FAO Schwarz. 1990. $450-600

9. Slide Rocker

•Snoopy's head and feet make up each end of this slide which has handles on each side. Printed in raised lettering in the middle: "Snoopy Rock 'N Slide." Molded plastic. Knickerbocker. 1980. $40-45

10. Inflatable TV Chair

•"PEANUTS Party Play Chair." Toddler-sized chair features Lucy, Linus, Charlie Brown, Snoopy, Peppermint Patty, Sally, and Schroeder playing his piano around the base. Printed on chair back: "PEANUTS." Vinyl. #5385-0, Ideal Toy Company. 1977. $25-30 $35-40*

Inflatable Toy

•Known as Fluttering Woodstock. Comes with an action spring. Printed on packaging: "PEANUTS" and "Woodstock

Lucy, and Woodstock are pictured with cubes that have their faces on each side. #4235, Golden Design. 1989. $15-20**

•"Snoopy Card Game." Snoopy, sitting on top of his doghouse, wears a visor and holds playing cards while Woodstock looks on. #4425, Milton Bradley/Determined Productions. 1975. $20-25**

•"Snoopy's Doghouse Game." Snoopy is pictured holding a hammer walking toward the game's pieces. #4704, Milton Bradley/Determined Productions. 1977. $20-25**

14. Game

•"Snoopy And The Red Baron" skill and action game. Snoopy, as the Flying Ace, is on top of his doghouse. #4067, Milton Bradley/Determined Productions. 1970. $20-30**

15. Game

•"Lucy's Tea Party Game." Lucy is pictured next to the set-up game along with Peppermint Patty, Charlie Brown, Sally, and Linus. #4129, Milton Bradley/Determined Productions. 1972. $30-40**

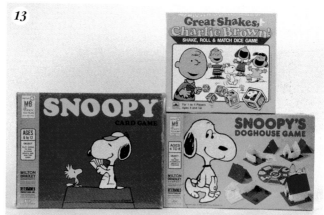

With Crazy Spring And Squeaker." Vinyl. 15"H. #5315-0, Ideal Toy Company. 1977. $5-10 $20-25*

CHAIRMAN-OF-THE-BOARD GAMES

11. Game

•"Charlie Brown's All-Stars" baseball game. Schroeder, Snoopy, Charlie Brown, Pigpen, Lucy, and Woodstock are pictured playing baseball. #410, Parker Brothers. 1974. $30-35**

12. Table Top Action Game

•"Snoopy And His Pals Play Hockey." Snoopy, Lucy, and Charlie Brown, all wearing ice skates and holding hockey sticks are pictured above the ice hockey game. Metal hockey rink. Munro Games/Determined Productions. 1972. $60-85 $125-160*

13. Games

•"Great Shakes, Charlie Brown! Shake, Roll, and Match Dice Game." Charlie Brown, Snoopy, Linus, Peppermint Patty,

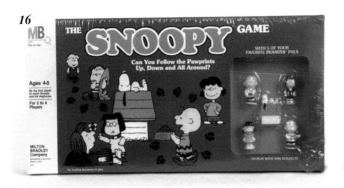

16

18

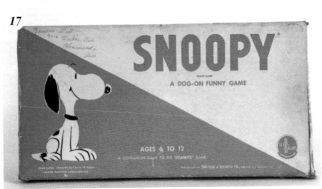

17

19

20

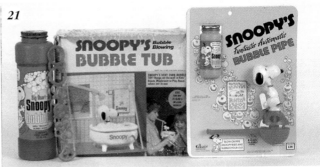

21

16. Game

•"The Snoopy Game." The game pieces are showing through a window on the packaging. Schroeder, Linus, Snoopy lying on his doghouse, Lucy, Charlie Brown, Marcie, and Peppermint Patty are pictured, surrounded by paw prints. #4413, Milton Bradley. Late 1980s. $25-30**

17. Game

•"Snoopy A Dog-On Funny Game." A sitting Snoopy is pictured on a red and white box. Game pieces and the game board contain no PEANUTS graphics. #66, Selchow & Richter Co. 1967. $40-45**

18. Game

•"PEANUTS The Game Of Charlie Brown And His Pals." Snoopy, holding a ball in his mouth, is being chased by Linus, Schroeder, Lucy, Charlie Brown, Pigpen, and others. #86, Selchow & Richter Co. 1967. $30-40**

19. Game

•"Snoopy Come Home Game." Snoopy is pictured with his supper dish on his head and a hobo pack over his shoulder as Woodstock walks behind him. #4303, Milton Bradley/Determined Productions. 1973. $20-30**

20. Game

•"Good Ol' Charlie Brown' Game." Charlie Brown is pictured next to Woodstock, who is standing in a birdbath holding a hockey stick. #4139, Milton Bradley. 1972. $25-35**

D-I-Y (DO-IT-YOURSELF TOYS)

21. Bubble Blowing Liquid and Wand

•"Big Quart-O-Snoopy Bubbles." Snoopy dances on the bottle thinking, "This is my big bubble dance." Lucy, Charlie Brown, Snoopy, and Woodstock form the handle of the plastic bubble wand. 32 fl. oz. Chemtoy. 1976. $8-12

Bubble Tub

•"Snoopy's Bubble Blowing Bubble Tub." Snoopy, surrounded by bubbles sits in a bathtub with "Snoopy" printed on the side. The cardboard packaging features a bathroom scene. Plastic. Chemtoy. 1976. $3-5 $18-22*

Bubble Blowing Liquid and Pipe

•Snoopy stands on the end of a bubble-shaped pipe. Snoopy rises when bubbles are blown. A bottle of bubble blowing liquid featuring a dancing Snoopy is included. Plastic. Chemtoy. Late 1970s. $2-4 $8-12*

22. Snoopy Ball Darts and Snoopy All-Star Catch Mitts

Games include Velcro-covered balls that are thrown at targets or caught with mitts. In order to present all the available designs, pictures here show the backs of boxes; therefore, some designs may be duplicated. Targets and mitts are made of sponge-like material that will eventually dry out and crumble once packaging has been opened. Synergistics Research Corp. 1981. $15-25** ea.

Ball Darts

•Snoopy and Woodstock roller-skate past a sunburst target. #SD-65.

Catch Mitt

•Circle target. Snoopy, Peppermint Patty, Charlie Brown, Linus, and Lucy are pictured on the fingers of the mitt. #SM-10.

Ball Darts

•Snoopy sits and hugs Woodstock in front of heart targets. #SD-55.

•Snoopy lies on top of a bulls-eye target. #SD-15.

•Snoopy rides in a hot air balloon target. Woodstock and his friends fly nearby. #SD-35.

•Snoopy, Charlie Brown, and the gang are pictured on a baseball diamond target. #SD-25.

•The targets are balloons. Snoopy, Peppermint Patty, Sally, and Charlie Brown dance. Woodstock holds balloons and Lucy leans against Schroeder's piano. #SD-45.

Catch Mitt

•Baseball diamond target. Snoopy, Peppermint Patty, Charlie Brown, Linus, and Lucy are pictured on the fingers of the mitt. #SM-20. (Not pictured)

23. Puppets

Games include a velcro-covered ball that is caught with hand puppets. Printed on packaging: "PEANUTS Magic Catch Puppets." Synergistics Research Corp. 1981. $4-7 $12-15* ea.

•Woodstock. #SP-30.

•Snoopy. #SP-20.

•Lucy. #SP-40.

•Charlie Brown. #SP-10.

24. Puppet

•Snoopy wears a red shirt printed "Snoopy," blue denim pants and a baseball glove. 27"H. Hard plastic composition.

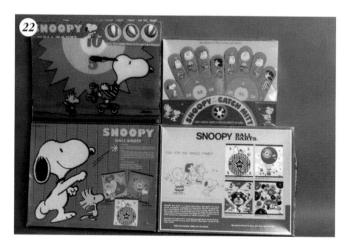

#DP10, made in England by Pelham. Distributed by Tiderider. 1979. $750-1000

25. Puppets

•Woodstock. Velveteen. 10"H. #898, Determined Productions. 1977. $8-14

•Snoopy. Plush. 10"H. #893, Determined Productions. 1975. $8-15

•A full-figure Snoopy wears a black tee-shirt printed "Hee Ha Ha Hee Hee." 14"H. #15815, Applause. 1989. $10-12

•A full-figure Woodstock wears a red tee-shirt printed with his bird-talk markings and "Ha." 9"H. #15816, Applause. 1989. $8-12

26. Puppets

"PEANUTS Pelham Puppets." Technically, a marionette. Hard plastic composition. 8"H. Made in England by Pelham. Distributed by Tiderider. 1979. $65-75 $100-140* ea.

• Woodstock. #SS20.

• Charlie Brown. #SS19.

• Snoopy. #SS18.

27. Toy

• "Stick-em Up." Snoopy, with a supper dish on his head, sits inside a cone. A wooden stick with a ball on the end comes out of the bottom. When the stick is pushed upward, Snoopy pops out. Snoopy is felt, his supper dish is plastic, and the cone is fiberboard. 17"H. First PEANUTS toy made by Aviva. 1971-1972. $25-30

28. Stackables

• "PEANUTS Stackables." Set of five includes Charlie Brown, Snoopy, Woodstock, Lucy, and Peppermint Patty dressed in athletic gear. Printed on packaging: "Meet The Latest Acrobatic Headliners." 2" to 3" pieces. #8642, Determined Productions. 1979. $20-30 $35-45*

• "Snoopy Stackables." Set of three Snoopys in various acrobatic positions. 3" pieces. #8641, Determined Productions. 1979. $25-30 $35-40*

29. Top on a Pedestal

• "Charlie Brown & Snoopy Poppin' Top." Small balls are inside the top where Snoopy is seen hugging Woodstock. Snoopy, Woodstock, Charlie Brown, Linus, Lucy, and Peppermint Patty are pictured around the base of the cone. Printed on the top: "Charlie Brown & Snoopy." Printed on the packaging: "Balls Pop Crazily As Top Turns!" Plastic and metal. 11-1/2"H. #322, Ohio Art Co. 1984. $10-15 $20-30*

Top

• "Snoopy & The Gang Spinning Top." Snoopy, Woodstock, Charlie Brown, Linus, Lucy, and Peppermint Patty are pic-

tured dancing. Printed on the top: "Snoopy & The Gang." Metal and plastic. 5-1/2" diam. #305, Ohio Art Co. 1984. $10-12 $15-22*

30. Tops

• "PEANUTS Top." Snoopy, Charlie Brown, Linus, Lucy, Schroeder, and Peppermint Patty are pictured around the top between blue, red, and orange circles. Metal. 9" diam. Chein. Late 1960s. $35-40 $50-55*

• "PEANUTS Top." Snoopy, Charlie Brown, Linus, and Lucy are pictured around the top with a multicolored patterned and dotted background. Metal. 9" diam. #263, Chein. Late 1960s. $35-40 $50-55*

31. Yo-Yo

• Snoopy is roller-skating and playing with a yo-yo at the same time. The sides of the yo-yo are flat. Plastic. 2-1/8" diam. Ambassador. Mid-1970s. $3-5 $6-8*

Yo-Yos

"PEANUTS Yo-Yo." Four designs available in different colors with colored strings. The sides of the yo-yos are rounded.

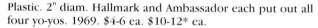

Plastic. 2" diam. Hallmark and Ambassador each put out all four yo-yos. 1969. $4-6 ea. $10-12* ea.

•Snoopy, as the Flying Ace, is sitting.

•Charlie Brown, dressed in baseball gear, stands on the pitcher's mound.

•Linus is sitting with his thumb in his mouth holding his blanket.

•Lucy is standing and smiling (pictured on packaging).

32. Yo-Yos

"Snoopy Champion Yo-Yo." The sides of the yo-yos are rounded. Plastic. 2" diam. Hallmark. 1975. $4-6 ea. $10-12* ea.

•Snoopy as Joe Cool. #125PF103-7.

•Snoopy wears an Uncle Sam hat and dances. #125PF103-8.

•Snoopy, as the Flying Ace, sports a handle bar mustache. #125PF103-5.

Yo-Yo String

•Charlie Brown, Snoopy, Linus, and Lucy are pictured on the package. Printed on front of package: "PEANUTS Yo-Yo Strings For All Designs Of PEANUTS Yo-Yos 4 Strings 25¢ 1 String Each Of: Fuss Budget Blue, Good Grief Green, Red Baron Red, Great Pumpkin Orange." Instructions appear on the reverse side. Hallmark. 1969. $6-8**

33. Puzzler Yo-Yos

"PEANUTS Puzzler Yo-Yo." The rounded sides of the yo-yos feature "get the balls in the holes" puzzles. Printed on packaging:

"Includes An Extra Little Puzzle For A Lot Of Extra Fun!" Plastic. 2-1/8" diam. Hallmark. 1977. $4-6 ea. $10-12* ea.

•Woodstock and his friends hold a flower, kick a ball, sit in a nest, and carry a flag. #200PF117-8.

•Snoopy in tennis gear is shown in various poses with his tennis racket. #200PF184-3.

•Snoopy, holding a bunch of balloons, and Woodstock float through the sky. #200PF276-5

34. Yo-Yos

•"Snoopy Yo-Yo for Beginners." Snoopy is pictured on a decal playing with a yo-yo. Wood. 1-5/8" diam. Hallmark. Early 1970s. $4-6 $10-12*

•"Snoopy Yo-Yo for Beginners." Snoopy is pictured on a decal playing with three yo-yos at the same time. Wood. 1-5/8" diam. Hallmark. Early 1970s. $4-6 $10-12*

35. Toys

•"Woodstock Trigger Action Toy." Woodstock's mouth opens when the trigger is pulled. Snoopy and Woodstock, who is flying over Snoopy's supper dish, are featured on the blister package. Plastic. 12"L. Series #70460, Aviva/Hasbro. 1982. $3-5 $10-15*

•"Snoopy Trigger Action Toy." Snoopy's mouth opens when the trigger is pulled. Snoopy and Woodstock, who is flying over Snoopy's supper dish, are shown on the blister package. Plastic. 12"L. Series #70460, Aviva/Hasbro. 1982. $3-5 $10-15*

36. Trapeze Toys

Characters flip over trapeze bar when buttons on side are squeezed in. Plastic. 5-1/2"H. Aviva.

•Snoopy. Connected to the trapeze with string. Printed: "Snoopy Flying Trapeze Toy." 1980. $12-15

• Snoopy. Connected to the trapeze by a plastic rod. Printed: "Snoopy Flying Trapeze Toy." Boxed: #2000. Loose: #1999. 1978. $10-15 $18-22*

• Woodstock. Connected to the trapeze with string. Printed: "Woodstock Flying Trapeze Toy." 1980. $12-15

• Woodstock (Not pictured). Connected to the trapeze by a plastic rod. Printed: "Woodstock Flying Trapeze Toy." Boxed: #2000. Loose: #1999. 1978. $10-15 $18-22*

37. Push Puppets

Jointed characters standing on a base move around when their bottoms are pushed in. Came in blister packages or loose. Plastic. 4"H. Loose assortment with display case: #5350-4. Blister packages: #5348-8. Ideal Toy Company. 1976. $35-40 ea. $45-50* ea.

• Snoopy as the Flying Ace.

• Snoopy is dressed as a sheriff.

• Snoopy as Joe Cool.

• Snoopy is dressed in a tuxedo and top hat.

• Charlie Brown wears a baseball cap and "Manager" shirt.

• Lucy is dressed as a nurse.

38. Super Slates

Includes film to write on and a writing implement. Cardboard. Saalfield.

• "PEANUTS Super Slate Fun." Snoopy, Linus, Lucy, and Charlie Brown are walking along side a rocket on wheels, printed "Super Slate Fun." Mid-1960s. $14-20

• "PEANUTS And Snoopy Super Slate." Snoopy is sitting in a wagon about to roll by Charlie Brown. Cardboard. Late 1960s. $14-20

• "PEANUTS Super Slate Fun With Snoopy." Snoopy is lying on his doghouse which has "Head Beagle" printed on the side. Early 1970s. $4-6

THE DOLL HOUSE

39. Display

• Cardboard. Japan, 1996. $15-20

Daisy Hill Puppies

Each plush has a red tag which includes a biography and pictures of the siblings inside, a silver cardboard name tag attached to their collars, and a plastic Knott's Berry Farm tag attached to one ear. 10"H. Designed by Determined Productions for Knott's Berry Farm. 1993. $25-30 ea.

• Belle.

• Spike.

• Marbles.

• Andy. #1368.

• Olaf.

40. Plush

"Belle." She is customarily dressed in a pink dress, printed with her name and picture, with a red ribbon tied around one ear. Available in five sizes. Determined Productions.

• Small. 10"H. #8734. 1982. $15-25

• Medium. 15"H. #822. 1980. $25-35

• Medium/Large. 25"H. #8737. 1982. $140-175

• Large. 32"H. #0787. 1982. $175-225

• Extra Large. 45"H. #8738. $350-450

Hat Box

• Carrying case for Belle's clothes matches her dress. Vinyl. 11" diam. #4460, Determined Productions. 1981. $30-35

41. Plushes

• "Levi's Belle." Belle is dressed in a red, white and blue jogging suit and headband with Levi's emblems. 12"H. #0710, Determined Productions. Released in conjunction with the 1984 Summer Olympic Games in Los Angeles. $20-25 $25-35*

• "Levi's Snoopy." Snoopy is dressed in a red, white and blue jogging suit and headband with Levi's emblems. 12"H. #0709, Determined Productions. Released in conjunction with the 1984 Summer Olympic Games in Los Angeles. $20-25 $25-35*

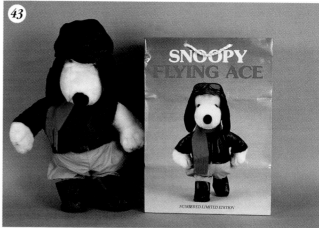

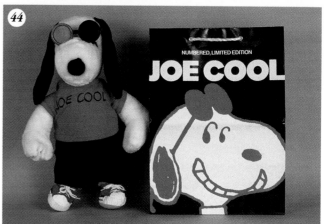

42. Plush

• Snoopy, as "Boy Snoopy," has long braids and wears a hat, white shirt with numbers on it, black pants, and a red tie bearing the words "Culture Club." The packaging features a picture of Boy George, and is printed "Boy Snoopy." 13"H. #0793, Determined Productions. 1984. $25-35 $35-40*

Display

• Mr. T is pictured holding Snoopy as Mr. S. Printed: "Mr. T's Little Buddy 'Mr. S'". Cardboard. 16"W x 20"H. 1984. $15-20

Plush

• Snoopy as "Mr. S" has a Mr. T haircut and wears jeans, bracelets, earrings, and gold chains. The packaging features a picture of Mr. T holding Mr. S and is printed "Mr. T's Little Buddy 'Mr. S'" 13"H. #0794, Determined Productions. 1984. $20-25 $25-35*

43. Plush

• Snoopy, as the Flying Ace, wears a helmet and goggles, jacket, boots, jodphurs, and a red scarf. Produced as a limited edition, a numbered certificate of authenticity is included. Packaged in shopping bag that pictures Snoopy as the Flying Ace. Printed: "Snoopy Flying Ace" and "Numbered, Limited Edition." 18"H. #4450, Determined Productions. 1986. $65-75 $80-90*

44. Plush

• Snoopy, as Joe Cool, wears sunglasses, black pants, sneakers, and a red shirt that reads, "Joe Cool." Produced as a limited edition, a numbered certificate of authenticity is includ-

ed. Packaged in a shopping bag that pictures a grinning Snoopy with sunglasses on his head. Printed: "Joe Cool" and "Numbered, Limited Edition." 18"H. #7527, Determined Productions. 1988. $35-40 $45-50*

45. Plush

• Snoopy wears a gold and silver tuxedo in honor of the 35th anniversary of PEANUTS. Produced as a limited edition, a numbered certificate of authenticity is included. Packaged in a shopping bag that pictures Snoopy wearing a gold and silver tuxedo. Printed: "35th Anniversary Snoopy" and "Numbered, Limited Edition." 18"H. #0806, Determined Productions. 1985. $75-95 $100-130*

48. Plushes

•Belle wears a red poodle skirt with Snoopy on it, a blue blouse with a rocking horse logo, and a multicolored ribbon on her ear. A plastic plaque with Belle's name on it is attached to her bottom. 15"H. Made by Applause exclusively for FAO Schwarz, catalog #352054. 1990. $55-65

•Snoopy wears a multicolored cap and a jacket with his picture on it. The rocking horse logo appears on the jacket's sleeve. A plastic plaque with Snoopy's name on it is attached to his bottom. 18"H. Made by Applause exclusively for FAO Schwarz, catalog #352112. 1990. $55-65

49. Dolls

Tricot fabric bodies, yarn hair, and cotton clothing. Their clothing is not removable except for Charlie Brown's baseball cap. 12"H. Determined Productions. 1983. $30-35 ea.

•Charlie Brown. #7442.

•Peppermint Patty. #7441.

•Lucy. #7440.

•Linus. #7443.

50. Dolls

Plush bodies, yarn hair, and cotton clothing. Their clothing is removable except for Linus's baseball cap. 15"H. Determined Productions. 1982. $35-40 ea.

•Charlie Brown. #7452.

•Peppermint Patty. #7451.

•Linus. #7453.

•Lucy. #7450.

46. Display

•Charlie Brown, Woodstock, and Snoopy wear red bow ties signifying the 40th anniversary logo. Printed on the top and bottom: "40 Years Of Happiness." Cardboard. 28"W x 20"H. 1990. $10-12

Plush

•Snoopy wears a black tail coat with a red flower on the lapel, a white shirt, a red cummerbund, and the red bow tie that signifies the 40th anniversary of PEANUTS. A plaque that reads, "Snoopy" is attached to his behind. 18"H. Applause. 1990. $15-25

47. Plushes

•Snoopy wears a red and green scarf, and a red, green, and white stocking cap printed "Macy*s." This plush was made for and sold exclusively at Macy's for $10.95 with any $50 purchase. 18"H. 1987. $30-35

•Snoopy wears, sunglasses, red shorts, and a green sleeveless shirt printed "Bullock's Recreation Club." This plush was made for and sold exclusively at Bullock's for $10.95 with any $50 purchase. 18"H. 1987. $25-30

•Snoopy wears earmuffs decorated with Woodstock and a red, green, and white sweater printed "Macy*s." This plush was made for and sold exclusively at Macy's for $12.95 with any $50 purchase. 18"H. 1988. $30-35

51. Outfit for Belle

•Belle wears a pink Chinese-style dress with black piping, and black cotton shoes. Made only for the 15" doll. Sold exclusively at Bloomingdale's during their China promotion. 1983. $35-40**

Outfit for Snoopy

•Snoopy wears a blue Chinese-style quilted jacket and pants with black piping, and black cotton shoes. Made only for the 18" doll. Sold exclusively at Bloomingdale's during their China promotion. 1983. $35-40**

52. Plush

•Snoopy wears a light blue hat, bib and booties, a yellow diaper, and holds a plush baby bottle. His bib is printed "Baby Snoopy." Knickerbocker. 1981. $5-8

50

51

52

Clip-Ons

Hands open and close when their bodies are squeezed. Plush. 3"H. Assortment #8352, Determined Productions. 1983.

•Snoopy. $4-6
•Spike. $6-9
•Lucy. $5-7
•Linus. $5-7
•Peppermint Patty. $6-9
•Belle. $4-6

53

Plush

•Snoopy, lying on his tummy, is known as Sleepy Snoopy. #8344, Determined Productions. 1981. $8-15

53. Plush

•Woodstock chirps when the string is pulled. A 9-volt battery is required. Determined Productions. Late 1970s. $30-40

54. Plush

•Talking/animated. Snoopy's ears, eyes, and mouth move in conjunction with the story cassette placed in his back. A story book and a cassette are included. Outfits are sold separately. Battery-operated. Printed on the front of the packaging: "Snoopy He Talks!" "The World of Snoopy" and "A Friend For Life Has Come To Life." The sides feature Snoopy talking to Charlie Brown, who flies a kite, and Lucy, with Linus, disbelieving that a beagle can talk. Marcie and Peppermint Patty are pictured on the back. 23"H. #701100-00, Worlds of Wonder. 1986. $50-75 $80-95*

Outfit for Worlds of Wonder Snoopy

•Snoopy wears a red pajama and nightcap set that is patterned with dog bones. He holds a red blanket trimmed in white. #701602-00, Worlds of Wonder. 1986. $22-30 $35-40*

55. Outfits for Worlds of Wonder Snoopy

•The Flying Ace outfit includes a helmet with goggles, a brown jacket, and a red scarf. #701601-00, Worlds of Wonder. 1986. $25-35 $40-45*

•The jogging outfit includes a blue jacket and pants with white stripes, a headband, and footwear. #701603-00, Worlds of Wonder. 1986. $22-30 $35-40*

54

Plush

Woodstock opens his mouth, flaps his wings, and chirps when his sides are squeezed. Printed on the front of the packaging: "Woodstock He Chirps!" and "The World of Snoopy." Charlie Brown, Snoopy, Linus, and Lucy are pictured on the sides. Marcie and Peppermint Patty are pictured on the back. 9-1/2"H. #701111-00, Worlds of Wonder. 1986. $8-10 $15-18*

56. Story Book and Cassette Tape Sets

For the "Worlds of Wonder" Snoopy. The title of each is printed on the story book, which is visible through the packaging. Printed on the packaging: "Snoopy Tales" and "The World of Snoopy." Worlds of Wonder. 1986. Book: $5-8 Tape: $4-8 Set: $15-25* ea.

• *Snoopy's Land of Make Believe.*

• *Snoopy and the Great Pumpkin.*

• *Snoopy, Spike and the Cat Next Door.*

Other titles (Not pictured):

• *Rock-A-Bye Snoopy.*

• *Snoopy's America.*

• *Snoopy at the Dog Show.*

• *Snoopy's Birthday Party.*

• *Snoopy Hits the Beach.*

• *Snoopy's Talent Show.*

• *Snoopy's Show & Tell.*

• *Snoopy Goes Camping.*

• *Snoopy's Band.*

• *Snoopy's Baseball Game.*

57. Pup Tent

Snoopy is pictured lying on top of a tent, under the moon and stars. Woodstock and his friends sleep on the support ropes. Printed: "Happiness Is Camping." The tent has tie-back flaps and a screen window with a roll-down flap. Includes wooden dowels with rubber tips. Orange linen-embossed vinyl. Determined Productions. 1978. $8-10 ea.

• Tent for 18" plush Snoopy. 21"L x 13"H. #8226.

• Tent for 11" plush Snoopy. 13"L x 9"H. #8225.

Sleeping Bags

Snoopy, as a Scout, thinks, "Okay rise and shine" as Woodstock and his friends are asleep in sleeping bags. Red with blue trim and yellow lining. Quilted cotton with polyester fill. Determined Productions. 1978. $6-10 ea.

• Sleeping bag for 18" plush Snoopy. 15-1/2" x 22 1/2". #0559.

• Sleeping bag for 11" plush Snoopy. 11-1/4" x 14". #0558.

• For plush Woodstock. Snoopy hugs Woodstock inside a white heart. Printed above the heart: "Gee, somebody cares!" Red with blue trim and yellow lining. Quilted cotton with polyester fill. 8" x 10". #0560, Determined Productions. 1978. $6-8

58. Wardrobe Trunk

Snoopy is pictured in various outfits on the outside of the red and yellow trunk. Assembly is required. Four plastic hangers depicting Snoopy in various poses are included. Came unassembled, wrapped in cellophane. Clothes and plush are not included. Cardboard with plastic handle. Determined Productions. 1980.

• Trunk for 11" plush Snoopy. 6-1/2" x 12". #4457. $20-25

• Trunk for 18" plush Snoopy. 18" x 10". #4467. $30-35

59. Deck Chairs

The blue cotton fabric of the chair is printed "Snoopy," and features Snoopy lying on the chair. Plastic frame. Determined Productions. 1978-1979.

•Chair for 18" plush Snoopy. Folded: 21-1/2" x 10". #6686. $15-20

•Chair for 11" plush Snoopy. Folded: 15-1/2" x 8". #6685. $12-15

The multicolored cotton fabric seat features Snoopy and Woodstock wearing bathing trunks and jogging past each other on a beach. Plastic frame. Determined Productions. 1980.

•Chair for 11" plush Snoopy. Folded: 15-1/2" x 8". #8233. $12-15

•Chair for 18" plush Snoopy. Folded: 21-1/2" x 10". #8234. $15-20

60. Chairs

A sitting Snoopy is featured on the seat, with "Snoopy" printed above his head. Vinyl with coated plastic-covered metal frame. Determined Productions. 1978.

•Chair for 18" plush Snoopy. 9" x 9" x 12". #0878. $5-7

•Chair for 11" plush Snoopy. 7" x 7" x 7". #0874. $4-6

61. School Bag Backpacks

Snoopy sits on top of his name, surrounded by books and an apple. Red jersey-backed vinyl with shoulder straps. Determined Productions. 1980.

•School bag for 11" plush Snoopy. 3-1/4" x 3-1/4". $4531. $2-3

•School bag for 18" plush Snoopy. 4" x 5". $4541. $3-4

62. Umbrellas

Snoopy and Woodstock are pictured around the see-through vinyl umbrellas walking with open red umbrellas. Metal frame with hard plastic end points. Determined Productions. 1978.

•Umbrella for 11" plush Snoopy. Closed: 10"H. Open: 13" diam. #4861. $5-8

•Umbrella for 18" plush Snoopy. Closed: 13"H. Open: 18" diam. #4881. $7-9

63. Doll Outfits

Doll clothing is designed to fit Barbie, Lindsey, Young 'n Lovely, and all other 11-1/2" dolls. Packaging features Snoopy and Woodstock wearing sunglasses, and a doll modeling a Joe Cool shirt. Fabric clothing with velcro fasteners. All shoes, handbags,

59

60

61

62

63

jewelry and other accessories are plastic. Printed: "Snoopy." Assortment #33331, M. & S. Shillman, Inc. 1989. $6-10** ea.

•Outfit includes a shirt featuring Snoopy on a telephone; a skirt featuring Charlie Brown, Snoopy and Sally on telephones; pink stockings; shoes; and a hanger.

•Outfit includes a blue and white striped vest printed with an "S"; a skirt featuring Charlie Brown, Lucy, Linus, and Snoopy cheering; a red shirt; a handbag; and pink shoes.

•Outfit includes a blue shirt printed with paw prints and "Snoopy"; a blue skirt featuring paw prints and Snoopy dancing; pink tights; shoes; and a mirror.

Other Outfits (Not pictured):

•Outfit includes a light blue skirt featuring Woodstock and his friends; a long-sleeved pink and light blue jacket featuring Woodstock superimposed on a "W"; pink shoes; and a camera.

•Outfit includes a checkered vest; a yellow and white dress featuring Snoopy, as Joe Cool, standing against a palm tree with Woodstock high up in the tree and printed "Cool"; a handbag; and pink shoes.

•Outfit includes a shirt featuring Snoopy, as the Flying Ace, on his doghouse; red and white striped pants; a red scarf; pink sunglasses; and shoes.

•Outfit includes a shirt featuring Snoopy, as Joe Cool, repeated three times and printed "Joe Cool"; red pants; two barbells; and pink shoes.

•Outfit includes a yellow and white striped shirt; black sun dress with checkered straps with Snoopy, as Joe Cool, and Woodstock on the front; a necklace; earrings; and pink shoes.

64. Rag Doll

•Snoopy, as the Flying Ace, wears removable brown pants, jacket, a helmet, and a blue scarf. 27"H. #3P1011, Ideal Toy Corp. 1976. $150-175 $185-250*

65. Autograph Doll

Snoopy is seated. Made of a smooth material meant to be written on. Pen is included. Packaging is printed "Autograph Snoopy." 10-3/4"H. #838, Determined Productions. 1971. $30-35**

Autograph Doghouse

Snoopy is lying on top of a stuffed doghouse. Made of a smooth material meant to be written on. Pen is included. #2125, Determined Productions. 1983. $15-20

66. Plushes

Snoopy is sitting. He has felt eyes, nose, and eyebrows, and a black spot on his back. A red tag around his neck is printed "A PEANUTS Character Plush Dog From The PEANUTS Comic Strip." Printed on packaging: "Playmate." Determined Productions. 1971.

•15"H. #833. $5-8 $18-20*

•12"H. #835. $4-6 $10-12*

67. Rag Doll

•Known as "Learn to Dress Snoopy," he is multicolored and designed to teach children various dressing skills, as well as numbers, words, and colors. Cotton. 13"H. #8815, Determined Productions. 1985. $6-9

Plush

•"Dress Me Snoopy." Snoopy is designed to teach children various dressing skills. Cotton. 12"H. #0544, Knickerbocker. 1980. $3-4 $8-10*

Rag Doll

•Known as "Learn to Dress Belle," she is multicolored and designed to teach children various dressing skills, as well as numbers, words, and colors. Cotton. 13"H. #8816, Determined Productions. 1985. $6-9

68. Rag Dolls

Cotton. Determined Productions. Mid-1970s.

•14"H. Snoopy wears blue jeans and a red shirt featuring the characters, and printed "The Gang's All Here." Sold in red cardboard packaging, which features Snoopy thinking, "I'm adorable! I'm lovable! I'm huggable!" and "I'm your cuddly Snoopy rag doll." $5-15 $45-50*

•11"H. Snoopy wears blue jeans and a red shirt featuring the characters, and printed "The Gang's All Here." Sold in a clear plastic sealed bag printed "Snoopy Rag Doll." Rare. $15-25 $40-45*

•7-3/4"H. Snoopy wears blue jeans and a red shirt printed "Snoopy." Sold in a clear plastic sealed bag printed "Snoopy Rag Doll." $3-5 $12-18*

69. Rag Dolls

•Snoopy wears blue jeans and a red shirt printed "Snoopy." The cardboard packaging features a see-through front with a picture of Snoopy lying on his doghouse in the corner. Cotton. 7-1/2"H. 1400-1, Ideal Toy Company. 1976. $3-5 $30-35*

•Snoopy wears blue jeans and a red shirt featuring the characters, and printed "The Gang's All Here." The cardboard packaging features a see-through front, with a picture of Snoopy lying on his doghouse in the corner. Cotton. 14"H. #1410-0, Ideal Toy Company. 1976. $5-10 $45-50*

•Snoopy wears blue jeans and a red shirt featuring the characters, and printed "The Gang's All Here." The blue and green cardboard packaging, featuring Snoopy and Woodstock dancing, has a see-through front shaped like a semi-circle. Cotton. 14"H. #1410-0, Ideal Toy Company. 1977. $5-8 $40-50*

70. Rag Dolls

Cotton. 14"H. Ideal Toy Company.

•"Greaser." Snoopy wears a black jacket with printed zippers, blue jeans, and a black plastic hat with a printed silver chain. Printed on the back of the jacket: "The Snoop." #1441-5. 1977. $25-50 $185-200*

•"Astronaut." Snoopy wears a plastic helmet and a silver space suit printed with patches and space gear. #1441-5. 1977. $25-50 $165-175*

•"Magician." Snoopy wears a black cape and pants, and a black plastic mustache and top hat. #1448-0. 1977. $25-50 $165-175*

•"Rock Star." Snoopy wears a reddish-brown wig, a multicolored jumpsuit, blue plastic boots, and holds a gray microphone. #1446-4. 1977. $25-50 $165-175*

•"Tennis Player." Snoopy wears a tennis outfit and holds a tennis racket. #1446-4. 1977. $30-50 $185-200* (Not pictured)

•"Reporter." Snoopy, wearing a trench coat and hat, carries a notebook and a pencil. #1441-5. 1977. $30-50 $185-200* (Not pictured)

•"CB Trucker." Snoopy, wearing a hard hat, work boots, pants, and a shirt printed "10-4 good Buddy," holds a CB radio. #1436-5. 1978. $30-50 $185-200* (Not pictured)

•"Boxer." Snoopy wears a robe, boots, and boxing gloves. #1435-7. 1978. $30-50 $185-200* (Not pictured)

71. Rag Dolls

•Snoopy wears red overalls, a green shirt patterned with candy canes, and black shoes. His clothes are not removable. Cotton. 12"H. #3440, Determined Productions. 1983. $35-45

•Belle wears a green dress patterned with candy canes, stockings patterned with holly, and red shoes. Her clothes are not removable. Cotton. 11"H. #3441, Determined Productions. 1983. $35-45

72. Rag Dolls

•Lucy wears a red dress and blue bloomers. Her clothes are removable. Cotton. 14"H. #1411-8, Ideal Toy Corp. 1976. $12-15 $40-45*

•Charlie Brown wears an orange shirt with a black zigzag and black shorts. His clothes are removable. Cotton. 14"H. #1412-6, Ideal Toy Corp. 1976. $12-15 $40-45*

73. Rag Dolls

•Linus wears a green and blue striped shirt and black shorts. His clothes are removable. Cotton. 14"H. #1414-2, Ideal Toy Corp. 1976. $12-15 $40-45*

•Peppermint Patty wears a green and white striped shirt and black shorts. Her clothes are removable. Cotton. 14"H. #1413-4, Ideal Toy Corp. 1976. $12-18 $40-50*

74. Pillow Dolls

Shaped like the character each pillow represents. Came in a sealed plastic bag with the name of the character on the front. Cotton, stuffed with kapok. Determined Productions. 1967.

•Lucy wears a pink dress. Her mouth is opened wide. 17-1/2"H. #812. $8-15 $45-50*

•Charlie Brown wears a blue shirt with a black zigzag and a baseball glove. 16"H. #810. $8-15 $45-50*

•Schroeder wears a blue shirt featuring Beethoven. 17-1/2"H. #814. $10-22 $10-15 $50-55*

75. Pillow Dolls

Shaped like the character each pillow represents. Came in a sealed plastic bag with the name of the character on the front. Cotton, stuffed with kapok. Determined Productions. 1967.

•Linus wears a pink striped shirt, holds a red blanket, and is sucking his thumb. 15-1/2". #811. $8-15 $45-50*

•Snoopy. 14"H. #813. $8-15 $45-50*

76. Bean Bag Dolls

Felt. #BN50R, Simon Simple. 1969-70. $18-25 ea.

•Charlie Brown wears a red shirt with a black zigzag. 7-1/2"H.

•Snoopy, as the Flying Ace, is on his doghouse. 6-3/4"H.

•Lucy wears a pink dress with a white collar. 7-1/2"H.

•Linus wears a blue striped shirt and holds a yellow blanket. 7-1/2"H.

77. Greeting Dolls

Each doll comes with a tag that has a shape and saying which reflects the way the character is dressed. Cotton. 6"H. Determined Productions. 1979. $5-7 ea.

77

78

79

• Lucy wears a red dress and blue bloomers.

• Peppermint Patty wears a green and white striped shirt and black shorts.

79. Mini Mascot Dolls

A string is attached for hanging. Packaged in clear plastic, with a red and white cardboard closure printed with each character's name on one side and "PEANUTS Mini Mascot" on the other side. Cotton. Determined Productions. 1973. $4-6 $8-10*

• Snoopy lies on a red heart. 4"H.

• Lucy wears a pink dress and holds her hands together. 4-1/8"H.

• Snoopy is sitting and wears a red bow tie. 3-1/8"H.

• Snoopy lies on top of his doghouse. 4-1/8"H.

• Snoopy is walking. 3-7/8"H.

• Woodstock is standing. 3-1/2"H.

• Sally wears a blue shirt and red polka-dot pants. 4"H.

• Charlie Brown wears an orange shirt with a black zigzag. 4-1/2"H.

• Peppermint Patty wears a green and black striped shirt. 4-1/2"H.

80. Paper Doll

• A paper Snoopy comes with ten outfits. An adhesive crayon is included to attach the outfits to Snoopy. The front of the packaging depicts Snoopy in the different outfits, and is printed "Snoopy Paper Doll." The reverse is printed: "Your favorite dog, Snoopy, has a whole new wardrobe... 10 separate outfits to cut out and stick on with the enclosed adhesive crayon." #274, Determined Productions. 1976. $30-40**

81. Dolls

Packaged in clear plastic with a yellow cardboard closure that features a four-panel comic strip. Clothes are painted on. Vinyl. Hungerford Plastics Corp. 1958.

80

• Charlie Brown is dressed in a baseball uniform. The baseball glove tag says, "You're A Winner!" #4288.

• Linus is dressed in suit with a bow tie and he wears a party hat. The gift box tag says, "You're The Life Of The Party!" #4289.

• Peppermint Patty is dressed in overalls and has a flower in her hair. The watering can tag says, "Let Me Grow On You." #4292.

• Snoopy is dressed as a pirate and wears a bandanna on his head. The treasure chest tag reads, "You're My Treasure." #4285.

• Snoopy is dressed as a magician with a cape and top hat. The playing cards tag reads, "For All Those Magic Moments." #4284.

• Snoopy, as a vaudeville performer, wears a striped jacket and hat with an old-time radio-shaped tag. #4287.

• Snoopy wears a chef's hat and apron. #4281.

• Snoopy wears an orange jumpsuit and blue sunglasses. The record-shaped tag reads, "You're A Superstar." #4291.

• Snoopy is dressed as a cowboy with a cactus-shaped tag. #4283.

• Snoopy, dressed as a clown, wears a multicolored polka-dot outfit with matching cone-shaped hat. #4282.

• Lucy, dressed as a cheerleader, holds a megaphone. #4290. (Not pictured)

78. Rag Dolls

Packaged in clear plastic with a yellow, green, and red cardboard closure featuring Lucy, Charlie Brown, Peppermint Patty, and Linus on the front. Printed: "PEANUTS." Cotton. 7-8"H. Series TP-0535, Ideal Toy Company. 1976. $3-6 ea. $15-20* ea.

• Linus wears a green and blue striped shirt and black shorts.

• Snoopy wears a red shirt printed "Snoopy" and blue jeans.

• Charlie Brown wears an orange shirt with a black zigzag and black shorts.

81

84

82

85

83

•Lucy wears a yellow dress and a yellow beanie. 8-1/2"H. $55-75 $195-225*

•Pigpen wears blue overalls. 8-1/2"H. $125-165 $225-250*

•Linus wears a red and black striped shirt and holds a white blanket. 8-1/2"H. $55-65 $195-225*

82. Dolls

Packaged in clear plastic, with a yellow cardboard closure that features a four-panel comic strip. Clothes are painted on. Vinyl. Hungerford Plastics Corp. 1958.

•Snoopy is sitting. 7"H. $65-75 $185-225*

•Sally, wearing a red sleeper and a bow in her hair, is sitting. 6-1/2"H. $65-80 $190-235*

•Charlie Brown wears a red shirt with a black zigzag and black shorts. 8-1/2"H. $55-75 $185-225*

•Schroeder, wearing a red shirt, sits with his piano. The piano, with a bust of Beethoven on it, is separate from the doll. 7"H. $200-250 (with piano) $20-25 (without piano) $350-400*

83. Dolls

Packaged in clear plastic, with a yellow cardboard closure that features a four-panel comic strip. Clothes are painted on. Vinyl. Hungerford Plastics Corp. 1958.

•Linus wears a red shirt and is pictured with a red blanket. The original blanket is white. 7"H. $60-65 $200-225*

•Lucy wears a yellow dress and a red beanie. 7-1/4"H. $60-65 $200-225*

•Snoopy is sitting. 5-1/2"H. $65-75 $225-235*

•Charlie Brown wears a red shirt with a black zigzag and black shorts. 7-3/4"H. $60-65 $200-225*

84. Dolls

"Playables." Made of bendable rubber. Packaged in a blue and white cardboard blister package with each character's name on it and printed "A PEANUTS Playable Twist It! Bend It! From America's Favorite Comic Strip 'PEANUTS' By Charles M. Schulz." Determined Productions. 1969. $7-9 ea. $20-25* ea.

•Lucy wears a pink dress. 5"H. #842.

•Charlie Brown wears a red zigzag shirt, orange cap, and a baseball glove. 5-1/4"H. #840.

•Snoopy. 4-1/4"H. #843.

•Linus wears a red and white striped shirt and holds a red blanket. #5"H. #841.

85. Dolls

Jointed action dolls with removable clothes. Packaging is printed with the character's name and "Jointed Action Playfigure Pose In Any Position." Plastic. 7-1/2"H. Determined Productions. 1976-1977. $20-30 ea. 55-75*ea.

•Lucy wears a red dress and saddle shoes. #378.

•Snoopy. #376

•Charlie Brown wears a yellow shirt with a red zigzag.

86. Outfits with Accessories for Jointed Dolls

Each blister pack shows the character dressed in the outfit. Printed with the character's name and the outfit-related activity. Determined Productions. 1976-1977. $30-45** ea.

•"Charlie Brown Plays Hockey." Includes a hockey stick, puck, skates, and a hat and scarf. #664.

•"Charlie Brown Goes Surfing." Includes a surfboard, flippers, bathing trunks, a towel, and goggles. #663.

•"Snoopy Goes Surfing." Includes a surfboard, flippers, bathing trunks, a towel, and goggles. #653.

•"Snoopy Plays Baseball." Includes a glove, cap, bat, ball, shirt, and shoes. #651.

•"Charlie Brown Plays Baseball." Includes a glove, cap, bat, ball, shirt, and shoes. #661.

•"Lucy Plays Baseball." Includes a glove, cap, bat, ball, shirt, and shoes. #671.

•"Lucy Nurse Set." Includes a nurse's bag, stethoscope, cap, shoes, and jacket. #672. (Not pictured)

•"Lucy Goes Surfing." Includes a surfboard, flippers, bathing suit, a towel, and goggles. #673. (Not pictured)

•"Lucy Plays Hockey." Includes a hockey stick, puck, skates, and a hat and scarf. #674. (Not pictured)

•"Snoopy Doctor Set." Includes a doctor's bag, stethoscope, mirror on a head piece, shoes, and lab coat. #652. (Not pictured)

•"Snoopy Plays Hockey." Includes a hockey stick, puck, skates, and a hat and scarf. #654. $25-35** (Not pictured)

•"Charlie Brown Doctor Set." Includes a doctor's bag, stethoscope, mirror on a head piece, shoes, and lab coat. #662. $25-35** (Not pictured)

87. Inflatable Doll

•Lucy, wearing a blue dress, stands with her arms outstretched. Vinyl. 16"H. Assortment #5380-1, Ideal Toy Company. 1977. $6-12 $18-22*

88. Pocket Dolls

Jointed dolls came in plastic bags with a black plastic closure. The character's name appears on the bag. Rubber. 7"H. Boucher and Company. 1968. $18-28 ea. $30-40* ea.

•Lucy wears a pink dress and has her mouth open wide. #802.

•Linus wears a red and white striped shirt and holds a red blanket. #801.

•Schroeder wears an orange shirt with Beethoven on it and black pants. #804.

•Snoopy, as the Flying Ace. #803.

•Lucy wears a pink dress and is smiling. #802.

•Charlie Brown wears a red shirt with a black zigzag, black pants, and a baseball cap. #800.

89. Philosophy Dolls

Jointed dolls with removable clothing stand. Base printed with words reflecting the character's philosophy. Vinyl doll, cardboard base. 5-1/2"H. Series #15976, Applause. 1990. $15-20 ea. On base: $22-26 ea.

•Peppermint Patty wears a green and black striped shirt and black pants. Printed on a yellow base: "They say that every broken heart takes a year off your life."

•Snoopy wears a white shirt and blue jeans. Printed on a red base: "I think I'm allergic to morning."

•Charlie Brown wears an orange shirt with a black zigzag and black pants. Printed on a blue base: "I have very strong opinions, but they don't last very long."

•Snoopy wears a white shirt and blue jeans. Printed on a yellow base: "I feel funny! It's either love or the flu!"

•Lucy wears a red dress. Printed on a yellow base: "When you're perfect you have to do everything yourself."

•Linus wears a yellow and black striped shirt and black pants. Printed on a green base: "I love mankind; it's people I can't stand."

Philosophy Dolls Display

•The backdrop features Snoopy standing on a soap box, Charlie Brown, Lucy, Linus, and Peppermint Patty. The base that holds 14 philosophy dolls features the characters talking and thinking their respective philosophies. Printed on backdrop: "Applause Presents The PEANUTS Gang Philosophy." 16"W x 12"H x 6-1/2"D. Cardboard. Applause. 1990. $15-20

90. Dolls

Each doll came with a folded tag with the character's name and picture on the outside and a biography on the inside. Removable clothing. Metal stands were sold separately. Rubber hands, feet, legs, and head; stuffed body. Applause. 1990. $30-35 ea.

•Charlie Brown wears an orange shirt with a black zigzag, black pants, and a blue baseball cap. 10"H. #36012.

•Snoopy wears a red shirt printed "Snoopy" and blue jeans. His ears are plush. 9"H. #36016.

•Woodstock wears a green shirt printed "Woodstock" and blue jeans. 7"H. #36017.

Doll Stand

•Two-piece stand, available in two sizes, features the 40th Anniversary logo on the base. #36059, Applause. 1990. $7-9

91. Dolls

Each doll came with a folded tag with the character's name and picture on the outside, and a biography on the inside. Removable clothing. Metal stands were sold separately. 10"H. Rubber hands, feet, legs, and head; stuffed body. Applause. 1990. $20-25 ea.

•Linus wears a blue and black striped shirt, black pants, and holds a blue blanket. #36013.

•Peppermint Patty wears a pink and black striped shirt, blank pants and holds a paper lunch bag printed "Brown Bagger." #36014.

•Lucy wears a red dress and carries a black handbag. #36015.

Doll Stand

•Two-piece stand, available in two sizes, features the 40th Anniversary logo on the base. #36059, Applause. 1990. $7-9

92. Doll

•Snoopy, as an astronaut, is dressed in a silver space suit and bubble helmet. He carries a life support system. The space suit's fabric is the same as used by NASA for their space suits. The cardboard packaging is printed "Snoopy Astronaut A PEANUTS Pocket Doll From America's Favorite Comic Strip PEANUTS By Charles M. Schulz." Rubber head with a hard plastic body. 9"H. #808, Determined Productions. 1969. $75-125 $130-200*

93. Dolls

Known as "Collector Dolls," they have movable joints and plush ears and tails. 8"H. Hard plastic. Determined Productions. 1982.

•Belle, as a bride, wears a wedding dress and veil. $35-65*

•Snoopy, as a groom, wears a tail coat, gray vest and striped formal pants. $55-65*

•Snoopy wears headphones attached to a Walkman, blue pants, and a red jacket printed with an "S". $25-30 $35-40*

•Belle wears headphones attached to a Walkman, and a red sweat suit with a paw print on the front. $25-30 $35-40*

94. Dolls

Known as Collector Dolls, they have movable joints and plush ears and tails. 8"H. Hard plastic. Determined Productions. 1982. $25-35 ea. $40-45* ea.

•Snoopy wears a yellow visor, white shirt and green pants, and carries a golf bag with clubs in it.

•Snoopy wears a red and white striped shirt, red shirts, and carries a soccer ball inside a netted bag. #3404.

•Snoopy wears a blue visor, white shorts and shirt, and carries a blue bag with a tennis racket inside. #3403.

•Snoopy wears a blue and white striped baseball uniform and cap both printed with an "S," and a baseball glove. #3405.

95. Dolls

Known as Collector Dolls, they have movable joints and plush ears and tails. 8"H. Hard plastic. Determined Productions. 1982.

•Belle wears a red and white colonial-style dress and bonnet. $35-40

•Snoopy wears a red and white striped shirt, blue shorts, and a white windbreaker with an anchor design. #3406. $20-25 $35-40*

•Snoopy wears a two-piece tan jogging suit and a yellow sweatband. #3402. $20-25 $30-35*

•Snoopy wears a red shirt printed with an "S," blue pants and roller skates. #3401. $20-25 $35-40*

96. Carry Case/Playhouse

•The plain blue case holds the "Dress Me Belle" and Snoopy dolls and their outfits. Also included are inserts that convert the inside of the case into four different scenes, with no PEANUTS graphics: Show Time, Country, Kitchen, and Bedroom. The packaging features Snoopy in a tuxedo, and Belle, as a beauty pageant contestant, holding a trophy against the Show Time backdrop. Printed: "The Snoopy & Belle Collection Show 'N Go House Portable Carry Case/Playhouse." Plastic case, cardboard inserts. 7-5/8" x 8-7/8" x 4". #1582, Knickerbocker. 1983. $5-8 $10-15*

97. Outfits with Accessories for Dress Me Snoopy

There are two categories of outfits: "Snoopy Fun Fashions" and "Snoopy Fancy Fashions." Fun Fashions (#1594, 1595 & 1596) are part of Assortment #9751. Fancy Fashions (#1597, 1598 & 1599) are part of Assortment #9752. Item numbers for the individual outfits appear on the back of the blister packaging. Fabric clothing, plastic accessories. Knickerbocker. 1983. $15-20** ea.

•Beach outfit includes a multicolored shirt, blue bathing trunks, sandals, and sunglasses. #1596.

•Western outfit includes a red and white checked shirt, a blue bandanna, a brown vest, chaps, boots, and a cowboy hat. #1598.

•Formal outfit includes tuxedo pants and jacket, red bow tie and cummerbund, white shirt, shoes, and a bouquet of flowers. #1597.

•Rock Star outfit includes purple pants, a fringed fuschia shirt, and a yellow and red guitar. #1599.

Doll

•Snoopy comes dressed in a red and yellow sweatshirt and blue jeans. A 2" Woodstock is included. The blue packaging pictures Belle and Snoopy in different outfits. Printed on packaging: "The Snoopy & Belle Collection" and "Fun & Fashion Dress-Up Doll Snoopy." Hard plastic. 8-1/2"H. #1580. Knickerbocker. 1983. $10-12 $25-35*

Outfits with Accessories for Dress Me Snoopy

There are two categories of outfits: "Snoopy Fun Fashions" and "Snoopy Fancy Fashions." Fun Fashions (#1594, 1595 & 1596) are part of Assortment #9751. Fancy Fashions (#1597, 1598 & 1599) are part of Assortment #9752. Item numbers for the individual outfits appear on the back of the blister packaging. Fabric clothing, plastic accessories. Knickerbocker. 1983. $15-20** ea.

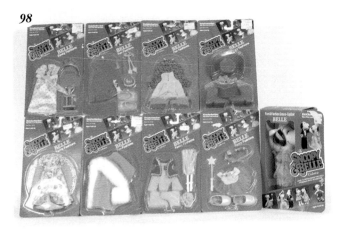

98

•Bathrobe outfit includes a burgundy robe trimmed in tan, a yellow back scrubber, and yellow slippers. #1595.

•Sport outfit includes a yellow shirt, blue pants and shoes, and a yellow tennis racket. #1594.

98. Outfits with Accessories for Dress Me Belle

There are two categories of outfits: "Belle Fun Fashions" and "Belle Fancy Fashions." Fun Fashions (#1574, 1575, 1576, 1577, 1583 &1585) are part of Assortment #9758. Fancy Fashions (#1578, 1579, 1584, 1586, 1587 & 1588) are part of Assortment #9759. Item numbers for the individual outfits appear on the back of the blister packaging. Fabric clothing, plastic accessories. Knickerbocker. 1983. $15-20** ea.

•Miss Hollywood outfit includes a light pink gown, silver tiara, gold trophy, and a sash printed "Miss Hollywood." #1586.

•Jewels outfit includes a dark pink gown, and pink earrings, necklace, ring, and shoes. #1577.

•Old Fashioned outfit includes a yellow and floral print dress, a floral print colonial-style hat and tan shoes. #1574.

•Western outfit includes a fringed red and white checked skirt, a red fringed skirt, and cowboy boots and hat. #1588.

•Southern Belle outfit includes a floral print dress, a pink bonnet, and a yellow basket. #1579.

•Cape outfit includes a pink cape trimmed in white faux fur and a matching white faux fur hand muff. #1576.

•Cheerleader outfit includes a red and yellow dress printed with a "B," a red vest trimmed in gold, yellow bloomers, and yellow pompoms and boots. #1578.

•Ballet outfit includes a light blue tutu with matching head piece, light blue shoes with ribbon ankle straps, and a pink wand with a star on top. #1584.

(Additional outfits not pictured):

•Tennis outfit includes a white dress trimmed in blue, shoes, a sun visor, and a yellow tennis racket. #1583.

•Nightgown outfit includes a nightgown, slippers, and a hand mirror. #1585.

•Beach outfit includes a bathing suit, skirt, sunglasses, and sandals. #1575.

•Roller Disco outfit includes a blue dress with gold stars and printed "Belle," white stockings, a gold handbag, a headband, and blue roller skates. #1587.

Doll

Belle comes dressed in a pink dress with a white ribbon on her ear. A 2" Woodstock is included. The pink packaging pictures Belle and Snoopy in different outfits. Printed on packaging: "The Snoopy & Belle Collection" and "Fun & Fashion Dress-Up Doll Belle." Hard plastic. 8"H. #1581. Knickerbocker. 1983. $10-12 $25-30*

Plush Snoopy Outfits (not pictured)

Most of Snoopy's outfits, mint in the package, sell for $8-15. Seasonal outfits and those which are difficult to find are priced below.

Description	Pcs.	11" Snoopy		18" Snoopy		Year
Baseball	3	#4241	$25-30	#4261	$25-30	1976
Basketball	2	#4932		#4952		1979
Beach Set	3	#4412		#4432		1974
Beagle Scout	3	#4245		#4265		1976
Blue Sleepers	1	#4487		#4497		1978
Boxing	3	#4536		#4546		1982
Call Me Cool T-shirt	1	#4481		#4491		1978
Camping *	2	#4254		#4274		1976
Candy-Stripe Nightshirt	2	#4489		#4499		1978
Cap and Gown	2	#4255	$10-15	#4275	$15-20	1977
Chef	2	unknown		#4443		1974
Chinese	3	#4927		#4947		1979
Clown (green/orange)	2	#4424		#4444		1976
Comic Strip	1	#4360		#4380		1983
Clown (red/blue)	2	#4078		#4208		1983
Cowboy	5	#4418		#4438		1976
Cyclist	2	#4930		#4950		1979
Denim Jacket/Jeans	2	#4417	$20-25	#4437	$25-30	1976
Denim Pants	1	#4361		#4381		1977
Disco Suit *****	3	#4935		#4955		1979
Down Vest	1	#4079		#4209		1983
Easter Beagle	1	#4967	$15-20	#4977	$20-25	1981
Engineer	3	#4400		#4401		1972
English	2	#4924		#4944		1978
Explorer	2	#4540		#4550		1981
Fireman**	2	#4539		#4949		1979
Flying Ace	3	#4420		#4440		1976
Football Jersey	1	#4537		#4547		1982
French	3	#4928		#4948		1979
Frontier	2	#4553		#4573		1981
Green Pajamas	2	#4243		#4263		1976
Gray Flannel Suit	3	#4535	$25-35	#4545	$35-40	1979
Handsome Dog T-shirt	1	#4534		#4544		1979
Happy Birthday T-shirt	1	#4533		#4543		1979
Hawaiian	2	#4532		#4542		1981
Hula Outfit	3	#4456		#4466		1981
Indian	3	#4926		#4946		1979
Letter Sweater	1	#4554		#4574		1982
Lifeguard	1	#4421		#4441		1976
Pink Sleepers	1	#4934		#4954		1979
Preppy T-shirt	1	#4538		#4548		1982
Racing Outfit****	2	#4440		unknown		1976
Rain	2	#4244		#4264		1976
Red Nightshirt	2	#4411		#4431		1976
Referee*	4	#4488		#4498		1978
Rock Star	3	#4253		#4273		1977
Runner	2	#4931		#4951		1979
Sailing	2	#4966		#4976		1980
Sailor	3	#4242		#4262		1977
Santa	4	#4419		#4439		1976
Scottish	4	#4923		#4943		1979
Signature Overalls	1	#4369	$15-20	#4389	$20-25	1978

Description	Pcs.	11" Snoopy	18" Snoopy	Year
Sherlock Holmes	2	#4368	#4388	1978
Skeleton	1	#4557 $12-16	#4577 $18-20	1982
Skiing	4	#4965	#4975	1980
Snoopy for Pres. T-shirt	1	#4963	#4973	1980
Soccer	2	#4933	#4953	1979
Spanish	3	#4922	#4942	1978
Square Dance Shirt	2	#4556	#4576	1982
Striped Overalls	1	#4864	#4884	1979
Striped Sleepers	1	#4555	#4578	1982
Surgeon	3	#4251	#4271	1976
Sweater and Cap	2	#4252	#4272	1976
Tank Top & Shorts	2	#4862	#4882	1979
Tennis	2	#4414	#4434	1974
Tennis Accessory Set***	2	#8245	#8255	1981
Tennis Warm-up	2	#4968	#4978	1981
Terry Robe	1	#4425 $15-20	#4445 $18-22	1976
Thermal Pajamas	2	#4962	#4972	1980
Tuxedo	4	#4247	#4267	1976
Tyrolean	2	#4925	#4945	1978
Uncle Sam	4	#4964 $15-20	#4974 $25-30	1980
Varsity Jacket	1	#4559	#4579	1983
Warm-Up Suit	2	#4374	#4394	1978
Yellow Nightshirt	2	#1671	#1684	1974

*Originally came with a whistle which was removed for safety reasons

**Fireman's hat #8958 for 11" and #8959 for 18" sold separately by Determined. Plastic. No Snoopy or PEANUTS markings

***Visor and one pair of sneakers

****This outfit has only been seen in the 11" size

***** This outfit had the "S" necklace removed after the first shipment for safety reasons

Description	Pcs.	30" Snoopy	60" Snoopy
Baseball*	3	unknown	$140-150
Blue Sleepers	1	#4903 $90-100	#4913 $130-135
Clown (green/orange)*	2	unknown	$125-135
Cowboy	5	#4917 $90-100	#4907 $135-145
Easter Beagle	1	#4904 $90-110	#4914 $145-150
Flying Ace**	3	#4937 $125-135	#4957 $175-195
Jogging Suit	2	#4936 $90-100	#4956 $135-140
Red Nightshirt	2	unknown $75-85	unknown $100-120
Santa	3	#4248 $125-135	#4268 $200-235
Tuxedo***	4	unknown	$250-300

*This outfit has only been seen in the 60" size

**The Flying Ace did not come with goggles

***Only available in the 60" size

Belle's Outfits

Most of Belle's mint-in-the-package outfits sell for $8-15. Seasonal outfits and those which are difficult to find are priced below.

Description	Pcs.	10" Belle	15" Belle	Year
Baby Doll Pajamas	2	#9246	#9256	1980
Ballerina***	3	#9248	#9258	1980
Bikini	2	#9272	#9253	1980
Bridal Gown	2	#9273 $15-20	#9293 $20-25	1983
Candy Striper	2	#9090	#9290	1982
Career Girl*	3	#9092	#9270	1982
Comic Strip Overalls	2	#9274	#9284	1983
Cheerleader*	3	#9086	#9264	1982

Description	Pcs.	10" Belle	15" Belle	Year
Clown	2	#9275		unknown
Cowgirl	3	#9088	#9266	1982
Dance Outfit*/**	4	#9098	#9298	1983
Easter Beagle	1	#9247 $15-20	#9257 $18-22	1980
Evening Gown**	3	#9097	#9297	1983
Hawaiian Muumuu	1	#9087	#9261	1982
Heart Top & Split Skirt**	3	#9099	#9299	1983
Hula**	4	#9249	#9259	1980
Jogging Suit	2	#9245	#9255	1980
Lingerie	2	#9080	#9281	1980
Leotard	1	#9095	#9295	1982
Mrs. Santa	3	#9082 $15-18	#9262 $18-22	1982
Party Dress	1	#9244	#9254	1980
Raincoat	1	#9085	#9263	1982
Roller Disco Outfit***	1		#9252	1980
School Girl	4	#9089	#9267	1982
Shoes and Purse	2	#9081	#9281	1980
Square Dance	2	#9094	#9283	1982
Signature Jeans/T shirt	2	#9083	#9260	1980
Tennis Accessories Set	2	#9096	#9296	1982
Tennis Outfit	2	#9084	#9251	1980
Witch	2	#9093 $12-18	#9282 $18-20	1982

*Number of pieces includes one pair of shoes

**Contains an unusual headpiece such as a headband, flower or tiara. Does not include hats that match the outfit such as a veil or a witch's hat.

***This outfit has only been seen in the 15" size

Description	Pcs.	25" Belle	45" Belle
Easter Beagle	1	#8622 $90-100	#8632 $145-150
Mrs. Santa	3	#8623 $95-120	#8633 $185-200

Woodstock's Outfits

Most of Woodstock's outfits, mint-in-package, sell for $10-12. Seasonal outfits and difficult to find items are priced below.

Description	Pcs.	9" Woodstock	Yr.
Birthday T-shirt	1	#0538	1979
Blue T-shirt	1	#0535	1979
Clown	2	#0695	1983
Cowboy	4	#0693	1981
Down Vest	1	#0696	1983
Engineer	3	#0539	1979
Great Pumpkin Costume	2	#0613 $15-20	1981
Jogging	2	#0608	1981
Letter Sweater	1	#0614	1981
Preppy T-shirt	1	#0603	1981
Red Nightshirt & Cap	2	#0536	1979
Santa	2	#0533 $15-20	1979
Scout	4	#0537	?
Tennis Warm-Up	2	#0540	?

Spike's Outfits

Most of Spike's mint-in-package outfits sell for $10-12. The plush Spike also came in 28" and 62" sizes, but no clothes were made for them.

Description	Pcs.	12" Spike	Yr.
Cowpoke	4	#7737	1982
Cut-off Pants	1	#7736	1982
Desert Overalls	1	#7735	1982
Long-johns	1	#7738	1982
T-shirt	1	#7734	1982

GO FIGURE!

Fun Figures. PVCs. Whatever you choose to call them, they are one hot collectible. Why? They are small, relatively inexpensive, colorful, well made, unbreakable, and although most are of Snoopy, the other characters are represented. After the Smurfs came on the market, Determined Productions, in the early 1980s, started manufacturing PEANUTS Fun Figures. They did not really become a hot item until the late 1990s. During the 1990s Determined sub-licensed the fun figures to Applause, who called them PVCs, which is the name that has stuck. PVCs from foreign countries such as Spain, France, Germany, and Hong Kong have been appearing on the secondary market at major toy shows. These foreign PVCs go for a relatively higher price but it all balances out.

99. Fun Figures

Christmas theme. PVC. #21792, Applause. 1991. $15-20 ea.

•Charlie Brown wears a red hat and scarf, snow boots, and a blue coat. He is carrying many Christmas gifts.

•Lucy wears a yellow dress and leans on a Christmas present. Woodstock sits on her head.

•Linus wears a green and white striped shirt and holds a red blanket. He has been strung with Christmas lights.

•Snoopy wears a red cap, sweater, and snow boots. He carries a Christmas tree, decorated with Woodstock and his friends, over his shoulder.

Halloween theme. PVC. #55041, Applause. 1990. $40-50 ea.

•Snoopy pops out of a jack-o'-lantern. He wears a purple shirt printed "Boo!"

•Lucy, dressed in a blue witch's costume, rides on a broomstick.

•Snoopy, dressed as a vampire, wears a tuxedo and a black cape. The cape's red lining is printed "Happy Halloween."

•Snoopy, dressed as a red devil, carries a jack-o'-lantern with a masked Woodstock coming out of the pumpkin's eye.

99

100. Fun Figures

Easter theme. PVC. #53057, Applause. 1990. $10-15 ea.

•Linus sits with a basket of eggs in front of him. He holds an egg which Woodstock sits in.

•Lucy, wearing a red dress, sits with a large Easter egg with a bow on it in front of her.

•Snoopy as the Easter Beagle wears a mint green bunny outfit. He holds Woodstock in his nest sitting on an egg.

101. Fun Figures

St. Patrick's Day theme. PVC. #20820, Applause. 1990. $10-15 ea.

•Snoopy, dressed in green coat and hat, stands beside a pot of gold with Woodstock sitting in the gold.

•Snoopy wears a yellow sweater with a green shamrock on it, a green hat, and holds the Irish flag.

•Snoopy, in green coat and hat, holds a shamrock bouquet.

Easter theme. PVC. #20493, Applause. 1991. $10-15 ea.

•Snoopy sits between two pieces of a cracked eggshell. Woodstock sits on top.

•Snoopy, wearing a blue beret, is painting an Easter egg.

•Snoopy carries an Easter basket filled with eggs in one hand and a pink Easter egg in the other.

Fun Figures

•Snoopy lifts the lid of a red and purple gift box to find Woodstock inside. PVC. #20988, Applause. 1990. $6-8

•Snoopy wears a hat, suit, glasses and carries a brief case. He stands on a black, yellow, and white base printed "Top Pop!" PVC. #54042, Applause. 1990. $15-20

102. Fun Figures

Graduation theme. PVC. Applause. $15-20 ea.

•Snoopy, as Joe Cool, in red graduation cap and shirt printed "Class of Cool," leans on a stack of books. #54219. 1991.

101

102

103

104

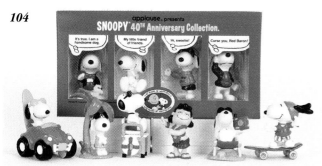

•Snoopy, holding a diploma, wears a blue cap and gown, sandals, shorts, and an orange shirt printed "I'm Out of Here!" #54075. 1990.

•Snoopy, wearing a blue cap and gown, adjusts his red bow tie while Woodstock stands behind him. #54075. 1991.

•Snoopy, wearing a red cap and gown, stands at a blue podium. #54219. 1991.

Birthday theme. PVC. Applause. 1990. $6-9 ea.

•Lucy wears a yellow dress, a striped party hat and holds an armful of gifts. #15992.M•Linus, wearing a party hat, holds his blanket and a bouquet of balloons. #15991.

•Charlie Brown, wearing party hat and red shirt, holds an empty plate. A piece of cake is on the ground in front of him. #15990.

•Snoopy, wearing a green shirt, an orange lei, and a party hat, holds a plate with birthday cake on it in one hand and a fork in the other. #15988.

•Woodstock stands on top of a light blue gift box, blowing a party favor. #15993.

•Snoopy wears a black tail coat, and a red bow tie and cummerbund. #15989.

103. Fun Figures

PVC. Applause. 1989.

•Snoopy lies on top of his doghouse. #15917. $5-8

•Snoopy, dressed as a cowboy, holds a brown lariat. #15913. $5-8

•Belle, dressed as a nurse, wears a light green nurse's uniform and cap, and holds a syringe. #15920. $5-8

•Snoopy, dressed as an astronaut, holds a pink moon rock. #15914. $5-8

•Snoopy, dressed as a groom, wears a black tuxedo jacket, a pink vest and bow tie, and gray pants and top hat. # 15918. $12-15

•Snoopy, holding a green towel and wearing slippers, is brushing his teeth. #15922. $5-8

•Snoopy, as the Flying Ace, wears a helmet with goggles and

105

a red scarf. #15924. $4-6

•Snoopy holds a large red heart. #15916. $4-6

•Belle, dressed as a bride, wears a pink gown and veil and holds a bridal bouquet. #15919. $12-15

•Snoopy, in a chef's hat, holds a pink cake. #15915. $6-9

•Snoopy, wearing a yellow shirt and blue shorts, is ready to release a bowling bowl. #15923. $5-8

Fun Figure

•Snoopy, as the Flying Ace, wears a bomber jacket, helmet with goggles, and a red scarf. PVC. Applause, 1990. $6-9

104. Fun Figures

40th Anniversary collection. The anniversary logo appears on the package. A different quote is printed on the red box above each figure. Printed on the package: "Applause Presents Snoopy 40th Anniversary Collection." Cardboard box. PVC. #15987, Applause. 1990. Set: $25-28*

•Snoopy wears a black tail coat, and a red bow tie and cummerbund. The quote on the box reads, "It's true. I am a handsome dog." $10-12

•Snoopy is sitting and hugging Woodstock. The quote on the box reads, "My little friend of friends." $5-7

•Snoopy, as Joe Cool, wears sunglasses and a blue shirt printed "Joe Cool." The quote on the box reads, "Hi, sweetie!" $5-7

•Snoopy, as the Flying Ace, wears a bomber jacket, helmet with goggles, and a red scarf. The quote on the box reads, "Curse you, Red Baron!" $4-6

Hawaiian theme. PVC. #36093, Applause. 1991. $12-20 ea.

•Snoopy, wearing sunglasses, drives a pink convertible with a surfboard behind him.

•Snoopy, as Joe Cool, leans against a palm tree with Woodstock sitting in its leaves.

•Snoopy, as Joe Cool, sits in a lifeguard chair with a whistle around his neck.

•Lucy, wearing a green grass skirt, a red lei, and sandals, does a hula dance.

•Snoopy, as Joe Cool, reclines in a red lounge chair on the beach listening to a radio.

•Snoopy, wearing a blue hat, red shirt, and blue and white striped shorts, rides a skateboard.

105. Fun Figures

Sports theme. PVC. Determined Productions. 1981.

•Snoopy, wearing a yellow cap, blue shorts and an orange shirt with "1" printed on it, is jogging. #2543. $4-6

•Snoopy, wearing a green and yellow hat, a yellow shirt and green shirt, rides a bicycle with training wheels. #2540. $5-7

•Snoopy, wearing blue shorts and a red and blue shirt, kicks a soccer ball. #2542. $8-10

•Snoopy, wearing a yellow shirt and green shirt, and a blue

visor, holds a tennis racket. #2546. $4-6

•Snoopy, wearing tan shorts and a blue shirt, with "2" printed on it, holds a basketball. #2548. $4-6

•Snoopy, wearing a purple turtleneck sweater and yellow pants, is skiing on red skis with poles. #2550. $5-7

106. Fun Figures

PVC. Determined Productions. 1981. $5-8 ea.

•Snoopy wears a red nightshirt and stocking cap, and holds a candle. #2551.

•Snoopy, dressed as Sherlock Holmes, wears a blue jacket, a green hat, smokes a pipe, and holds a magnifying glass. #2547.

•Snoopy wears a blue shirt and yellow shorts, and holds a blue briefcase while roller-skating. #2544.

•Snoopy wears an orange jacket, yellow shirt, and black pants, and is disco dancing. #2545.

•Snoopy, as the Flying Ace, wears a green jacket, red scarf, helmet with goggles, and sports a handlebar mustache. #2549.

•Snoopy, wearing a purple cropped shirt and his dog dish on his head, with Woodstock sitting on his nose, carries a suitcase printed "Snoopy." #2541.

107. Fun Figures

PVC. Determined Productions. 1981. $8-10 ea.

•Snoopy, dressed in scuba gear, wears an orange wet suit and goggles, and carries an air tank on his back, a flashlight, and a harpoon. #2564.

•Snoopy wears a green baseball cap, a blue and white uniform, and stands ready to swing the bat in his hand. #2558.

•Snoopy, dressed in lime green with orange goggles, is strapped into a red and orange hang glider. #2565.

•Snoopy, holding a green towel and wearing slippers, is brushing his teeth. #2560.

•Snoopy wears a yellow helmet and a red and yellow foot-

ball uniform, and stands ready to throw a football. #2556.

•Snoopy wears an open blue robe, purple shorts, and yellow boxing gloves. #2557.

108. Fun Figures

PVC. Determined Productions. 1981. $8-10 ea.

•Snoopy wears a blue sailor suit and hat and carries a yellow duffel bag. #2559.

•Snoopy wears a red raincoat and a yellow rain hat. #2553.

•Belle is a ballerina, wearing a pink tutu and ballet shoes. # 2562.

•Belle, dressed as a nurse, wears a white nurse's uniform and cap trimmed in blue, and holds a syringe. #2563.

•Snoopy wears a red bathing suit and carries a blue and white life preserver. #2555.

•Snoopy, on red roller skates, wears a green shirt, blue pants, and a Walkman with headphones. #2561.

109. Fun Figures

PVC. Determined Productions. 1983.

•Snoopy, dressed as an astronaut, holds a pink moon rock. #14-2529-7. $4-6

•Snoopy, wearing a red beret and purple smock, holds an artist's palette and brush. #14-2532-5. $5-7

•Snoopy, wearing a blue hat, red shirt, and black waders, holds a fishing rod with a hooked fish. #14-2531-4. $8-10

•Snoopy, dressed as a pirate, wears a red shirt, tan boots, a black hat and an earring, and holds a sword. #14-2534-7. $10-12

•Snoopy, wearing a green cap, yellow vest, and green pants, holds a club ready to hit a golf ball. #14-2530-3. $5-7

•Snoopy, wearing a yellow hat, blue shirt, and red pants, plays a guitar. #14-2528-6. $8-10

110. Fun Figures

PVC. Determined Productions. 1983. $15-18 ea.

•Belle, dressed in a blue dress with pink ribbons on her ears, is square dancing. #14-2537-0.

•Snoopy, wearing a red neckerchief, yellow shirt, blue pants, and black boots, plays a fiddle. #14-2533-6.

•Spike, wearing a red neckerchief, red hat, blue vest, and light blue pants, plays a banjo. #14-2539-2.

•Snoopy, dressed as a cowboy, holds a yellow lariat. #14-2536-9.

The PEANUTS Home Collection

111

112

113

• Belle, dressed in a pink dress, blue vest, brown boots, and a yellow hat, holds a coffee pot. #14-2538-1.

• Snoopy, dressed as an Indian, wears a feather headdress, tan fringed shirt and red pants. #14-2528-8.

111. Fun Figures

Olympic sports theme. Produced during the 1984 Olympic year. PVC. Determined Productions. 1984. $22-30 ea.

• Snoopy, wearing red swim trunks, stands on a diving block printed "1".

• Snoopy, wearing a white outfit, holds his mask in one hand and a fencing sword in the other.

• Snoopy leans forward on skis, dressed in a yellow cap, goggles, a red sweater, a white bib printed "4" on the back, and black pants.

• Snoopy, wearing an orange shirt and a yellow helmet, sits in a red kayak holding a two-sided oar.

• Snoopy, wearing a yellow helmet, blue shirt, red pants and gloves, and black ice skates, holds a hockey stick.

• Snoopy is a speed skater dressed in a one-piece blue outfit from his head to his ice skates.

112. Fun Figures

Olympic sports theme. Produced during the 1984 Olympic year. PVC. Determined Productions. 1984.

• Snoopy and Woodstock, wearing blue and white helmets, are sitting in a bobsled. $22-30

• Snoopy, wearing a green shirt and shorts, holds a silver barbell over his head. $25-30

114

• Snoopy, wearing a blue shirt and red shorts, stands ready to throw a yellow shot put. $25-30

• Snoopy, wearing a yellow shirt and green shorts, leaps over an orange hurdle. $25-30

• Snoopy, wearing a red shirt and yellow shorts, stands ready to hurl a javelin. This figure was dropped from the set because it was felt that the javelin could injure children. Rare—but a few are out there. $30-40

• Snoopy, wearing a red shirt, holds two oars as he crews a scull. $25-30

LET THE GANG ENTERTAIN YOU!

113. Drums

The characters march with different instruments around the drums. Sally plays the trumpet; Frieda playing a guitar, pulls Linus's drum on a wheeled platform; Pigpen, carrying an American flag, pulls Schroeder playing his piano in a wagon; Charlie Brown plays a trombone; Lucy carries a baton; and Snoopy walks along on all fours. The characters' names are printed beside their pictures. Linus's drum is printed "PEANUTS Marching Band And Good Grief Society." Two drumsticks are included. Metal. J. Chein. 1970.

• Small Drum. 8-1/2" diam. #1713. $45-50 $65-70*

• Large Drum. 10-3/4" diam. #1813. $45-55 $75-80*

• Charlie Brown, Linus, Sally, Schroeder, Lucy, Frieda, Pigpen, and Snoopy sit in director's chairs with their names printed on the backs. Printed around the drum under the chairs: "Stars of the Movie, A Boy Named Charlie Brown." Printed on the box: "PEANUTS Parade Drum With Snares" and "Featuring Unbreakable Drum Heads Hardwood Drumsticks Vinyl Carrying Strap." Two drumsticks are included. Metal. 9"H x 11" diam. #1798, J. Chein and Co. 1970. $50-55 $80-85*

114. Rhythm Set

• "PEANUTS Kindergarten Rhythm Set." The set includes a drumstick and a drum picturing Snoopy as a drum major, a tambourine picturing Woodstock, a triangle and striker, and two cymbals picturing head shots of Sally, Linus, Lucy, and Charlie Brown. The packaging features Charlie Brown playing a drum, Lucy playing a tambourine, Snoopy playing the cymbals and Woodstock playing the triangle. Printed on the packaging: "Set Contains 9" Drum & Beater 6" Tambourine Triangle & Striker Two Cymbals." Metal. #327, J Chein and Co. 1972. $65-85 $150-200*

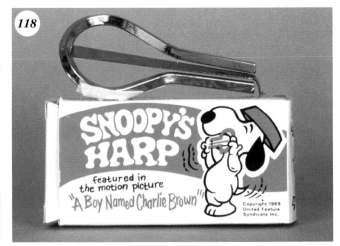

115. Drum Set

•A cymbal, tambourine (not shown) and snare drum attach to bass drum which has a foot pedal striker. Snoopy is pictured sleeping in the bottom of the drum. The snare drum has yellow stripes and black paw prints around it. Two drumsticks are included. 21"H x 16" diam. Metal. J. Chein and Co. 1970. $200-300

116. Guitars

•"Mattel Preschool Snoopy Musical Ge-tar." Snoopy is pictured on the guitar sitting in a tree with a baseball in his mouth. Charlie Brown and Lucy, wearing baseball gloves, are in the background. The guitar is played by turning a hand crank on the body of the guitar. The guitar is pictured in color on the packaging. Plastic. #4715, Mattel. 1969. $20-35 $60-75*

•"Snoopy Musical Guitar." A raised Snoopy and Woodstock on the body of the guitar move when the hand crank is turned to play the music. The heads of Charlie Brown, Lucy, and Linus appear over the words "Snoopy Musical Guitar" on the instrument's body. Small three-dimensional heads of Charlie Brown, Snoopy, Woodstock, and Lucy appear on the neck under the word "Snoopy." The packaging has a window on the side for the crank to protrude through. Plastic. #444, Aviva. 1980. $15-25 $55-60*

117. Piano

•Working piano features 30 black and white keys, and a color-coded decal above the keys. The top of the piano features Schroeder sitting at his piano with Lucy leaning on it; Snoopy playing a fiddle while standing on the piano; and Charlie Brown and Linus looking on. Printed on top: "PEANUTS." Printed on a decal on the piano's front below the keys: "Ely Mello-Tone Chime Pianos." 18"W x 11"H. Wood, fiberboard and plastic. T. J. Ely Mfg. Co. Late 1960s. $275-350

118. Mouth Harp

•The harp has nothing on it to connect it to PEANUTS. Graphic red, white, and black box features Snoopy with his dog dish on his head playing the instrument. Printed: "Snoopy's Harp Featured In The Motion Picture 'A Boy Named Charlie Brown.'" Metal harp, cardboard box. Trophy Music Co. 1969. $10-15**

119. Drum Majorette and Cheerleader Set

•Set includes a chrome baton with Snoopy's head on top, a blue and white whistle with Snoopy's head imprinted on each side, two blue and white pompoms, and a paper megaphone picturing Snoopy as a drum major and printed "Snoopy on Parade." The packaging features Snoopy, Charlie Brown, Lucy, and Linus wearing band uniforms and Woodstock blowing a whistle. Printed: "Snoopy on Parade" and "Drum Majorette And Cheerleader Set." #PMS-15, Synergistics Research Corp. 1982. $5-8 $25-30*

Megaphone

•Orange, yellow, and white megaphone printed "Head Beagle." Reverse shows Snoopy—wearing a beret, sunglasses, and holding a megaphone—plus Lucy and Charlie Brown. Printed under the characters: "Stars of the Movie 'A Boy Named Charlie Brown.'" Metal. 6"H. J. Chein and Co. 1970. $10-20

120. Whistles

•Woodstock's tail is the whistle. Printed on blister package: "'Woodstock' Whistle" and "A Perfect Gift Or Party Prize." Plastic. 3"H. #125PF120-4, Hallmark. $3-5 $15-20*

• Snoopy holds his dog dish, which is the whistle, behind his back. Printed on blister package: "'Snoopy' Whistle" and "A Perfect Gift Or Party Prize." Plastic. 3"H. #100PF119-2, Hallmark. Mid-1970s $3-5 $15-20*

121. Piano

• Working piano has 20 black and white keys. The piano also plays pre-set songs. On top of the piano, three-dimensional figures of Snoopy, Lucy, Schroeder, and Charlie Brown move and sway when the piano is played. A microphone is included. Printed on packaging: "Battery Operated Schroeder Piano." Available in two colors. The black piano was sold exclusively by QVC and "Exclusive For QVC" appears on the packaging. The blue piano was sold through retail outlets. Plastic. 11"W. #777, International Trading Technology. 1993. $40-45 $55-65*

122. Cassette Recorder

• "Snoopy Cassette Recorder." Snoopy is pictured dancing on the front of the unit. The packaging features a picture of the recorder and Snoopy holding one ear up listening to it. Battery operated. Plastic casing. 9"W x 9-1/4"H x 4" diam. #DP1560, Determined Productions. 1985. $30-35 $55-60*

123. Phonograph

• "Snoopy Solid State Phonograph." Inside the lid of the phonograph is a paper decal featuring Snoopy, Peppermint Patty, Lucy, Linus, Woodstock, and Charlie Brown dancing with stars and music notes all around them. Printed: "Snoopy Disco." Contained in a white carrying case, it has no outer markings connecting it to PEANUTS. The packaging

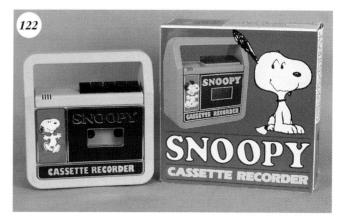

features a picture of the open phonograph. Electrically operated. Molded plastic. #66, Vanity Fair, a subsidiary of Walter Kidde & Co. 1979. $35-45 $50-60*

124. Phonograph

• Shaped like Snoopy's doghouse. The roof is hinged. When opened, the 45 rpm yellow turntable is exposed. Snoopy is dancing next to the on-off switch. The playing arm and needle is attached to the underside of the roof. The record plays when the roof is closed. The closed roof acts as a carrying handle. Decals of Lucy, Snoopy, Charlie Brown, Schroeder, Woodstock, and Peppermint Patty adorn the sides of the doghouse. A speed control switch is on the outside of the house. Records were not included. Plastic 9-1/4" x 8-1/4" x 7"H. Sold by Montgomery Ward Catalog. Determined Productions. 1975 $225-250

125. View-Master Set

• "GAF View-Master Charlie Brown Theatre." The set includes a GAF View-Master Stereo Viewer, a 2-D Entertainer Projector and ten picture reels featuring stories with the PEANUTS characters. The set comes in a cardboard container which pictures Snoopy as the Flying Ace, Woodstock, Linus, Charlie Brown, and Lucy. Printed on the container: "The Exciting World Of The PEANUTS Gang." Electrically operated. Plastic and celluloid. 12"H x 8" diam. #2438, GAF Corporation. 1976. $40-45**

126. View-Master Deluxe Gift Pak

•"GAF View-Master Charlie Brown Deluxe Gift Pak." This set includes a blue GAF View-Master Stereo Viewer and seven picture reels. The set comes in a cardboard container which pictures Snoopy dancing, Sally, Charlie Brown holding Snoopy's dog dish, and Lucy kneeling. Woodstock appears to be standing on Lucy's head. Plastic and celluloid. #2380, GAF Corporation. 1976. $30-35**

View-Master Gift Pak

•"GAF View-Master Gift Pak/Charlie Brown." This set includes a red GAF View-Master Stereo Viewer and seven picture reels. The set comes in a cardboard container which pictures Snoopy, Linus, Charlie Brown, and Lucy. Plastic and celluloid. #2360, GAF Corporation. 1976. $15-20**

View-Master Collector Set

•"View-Master Charlie Brown Collector's Set." Set includes a carrying case, a 3-D viewer, six picture reels and a personal

ID tag. The case is available in red and blue. The packaging features Snoopy dressed as a referee blowing a whistle, and Lucy holding a football as Charlie Brown gets ready to kick it. Printed in raised letters on the case: "View-Master Collector's Case." Plastic and celluloid. 13-1/2" x 4-3/4". #2501, View-Master International Group, Inc. Late 1980s. $15-20**

127. 3-D Picture Reels

•Package contains three View-Master reels of "It's Your First Kiss, Charlie Brown." On the package, Charlie Brown is pictured dreaming that he is floating through the air above the clouds. Cardboard and celluloid. #4210, View-Master International. 1980. $5-7*

•Package contains three View-Master reels of "Bon Voyage, Charlie Brown (and don't come back!)." The reels are in a paper packet stapled to a cardboard backing that is printed "Charlie Brown." Packet features Woodstock, Snoopy wearing a beret, Marcie, and Peppermint Patty, Linus, and Charlie Brown carrying suitcases. A 16-page storybook is included. Cardboard and celluloid. GAF Corporation. 1980 $5-7*

•Package contains three View-Master reels of "Snoopy And The Red Baron." The reels are in a paper packet which features Snoopy, as the Flying Ace, lying on his doghouse and a silhouette of the Red Baron's plane flying nearby. A 16-page storybook is included. Cardboard and celluloid. #B544, GAF Corporation. 1970s. $6-8*

•Package contains three View-Master reels of "It's A Bird, Charlie Brown." The reels are in a paper packet which features Snoopy, with a thermometer in his mouth, lying on his doghouse. Woodstock flies nearby. A 16-page storybook is included. Cardboard and celluloid. #B556, GAF Corporation. 1970s. $6-8*

•Package contains three View-Master reels of "PEANUTS." The reels are in a paper packet which features Charlie Brown, Pigpen, and Snoopy sitting in Schroeder's baseball glove with the baseball on the ground. A 16-page story book is included. Cardboard and celluloid. #B536, GAF Corporation. 1969. $6-8*

•Package contains three View-Master reels of "Charlie Brown's Summer Fun." The reels are in a paper packet which features Charlie Brown pulling Snoopy in a wagon and flying a kite, and Linus shooting an arrow at Snoopy's doghouse. A 16-page story book is included. Cardboard and celluloid. #B548, GAF Corporation. 1970s. $6-8*

128. 3-D Picture/Sound Reels

Packages includes three reels each that combine both sight and sound and require the use of an older-model Talking View-Master. Cardboard and celluloid. GAF Corporation. 1974. $12-20** ea.

•It's A Bird, Charlie Brown. #AVB556.

•Snoopy And The Red Baron. #AVB544.

•Charlie Brown's Summer Fun. #AVB548.

•PEANUTS. #AVB536.

3-D Picture/Sound Cartridge

•Package includes three cartridges that combine sight and sound and require the use of a newer-model Talking View-Master. On the package, Charlie Brown is pictured floating through the air above the clouds. Packaging is printed: "It's Your First Kiss, Charlie Brown" and "Talking View-Master 3-D Cartridges." (Talking View-Master, sold separately, had no PEANUTS graphics.) Cardboard, plastic, and celluloid. #4416, View-Master International Group, Inc. 1983. $8-10*

129. Movie Viewer Cartridges

Plastic. Fisher-Price. Early 1980s $6-9* ea.

- "Joe Cool On Campus." #488.
- "Snoopy Meets The Red Baron." #482.
- "A Snoopy Tennis Classic." #473.
- "It's A Hit, Charlie Brown." #494.
- "Snoopy To The Rescue." #492.
- "Peppermint Patty On Ice." #493.

Movie Viewer

- "Snoopy Movie Viewer." Set includes the movie viewer and one cassette, "Slide Snoopy Slide." Insert the cassette and turn the handle to view the movie. Snoopy dressed as a director, wearing a beret and sunglasses, and holding a megaphone, appears on the side of the viewer. Snoopy, as a director, is pictured on the packaging. Plastic. #35900, Kenner Products. 1975. $12-15 $30-35*

130. Movie Cassettes

"Snoopy Movie Cassette Color Show." Can be used with both the Snoopy Movie Viewer and the Snoopy Drive-In Movie Theater. Plastic. #35980, Kenner. 1975. $1-12 ea. $20-25* ea.

- "I'll Be A Dirty Bird!" #1.
- "Good Grief!" #2.
- "Roll Over, Beethoven!" #3.
- "Snoopy's Garage Sale." #4.

- "Chow Hound Snoopy." #5.
- "Skateboard Olympics." #6.
- "Blockhead's Bobble." #7.
- "Hang On, Snoopy!" #8.
- "The Easter Beagle." #9.
- "Sherlock Snoopy." #10
- "Lucy vs. Masked Marvel." #11.
- "Curse You, Red Baron!" #12.

Display

- All sides feature Snoopy as a director, wearing a beret, sunglasses, and holding a megaphone. The base holds 24 movie cassettes. Printed: "Snoopy Movie Cassette Color Shows." 13"W x 13"H x 6-3/4"diam. Cardboard. Kenner. 1975. $15-25

Drive-In Movie Theater

- "Snoopy Drive-In Movie Theater." Set includes the movie viewer and one cassette, "Woodstock's Dream House." Insert the cassette and turn the handle to view the movie. Snoopy sits in a convertible looking up at the screen. Woodstock is seen on a decal of a concession stand beneath the screen. Printed on the movie viewer: "Snoopy Drive-In." Battery-operated. Plastic. #39570, Kenner. $75-95 $250-275*

LET'S PLAY HOUSE

131. Dish Set

- The set includes four place settings and a toaster (13 pieces total). Lucy and Charlie Brown, bringing food and tea to Snoopy on his doghouse, are pictured on the plates and the toaster. The saucers feature Snoopy drinking tea on top of his doghouse. "Charlie Brown & Snoopy" is printed on each

plate, saucer, and on the toaster. The cups are white, with no graphics. Printed on the packaging: "Breakfast Set 4 Place Settings 13 Pieces" and "Charlie Brown & Snoopy." Metal plates, plastic cups. #452, Ohio Art. 1984. Dishes: $3 ea. Toaster: $10-25. Set: $60-70*

132. Tea Sets

• The set includes four place settings, silverware, and a teapot (26 pieces total). Lucy and Charlie Brown are pictured on the plates bringing food and tea to Snoopy on his doghouse. The saucers feature Snoopy drinking tea on top of his doghouse. "Charlie Brown & Snoopy" is printed on each plate and saucer. The cups, silverware and teapot have no graphics. Printed on the packaging: "4 Place Settings 26 Pieces" and "Charlie Brown & Snoopy." Metal plates, plastic cups, silverware, and teapot. #422, Ohio Art. 1984. Dishes: $3 ea. Set: $35-40*

• The set includes two place settings, silverware, and a teapot (14 pieces total). Lucy and Charlie Brown are pictured on the plates bringing food and tea to Snoopy on his doghouse. The saucers feature Snoopy drinking tea on top of his doghouse. "Charlie Brown & Snoopy" is printed on each plate and saucer. The cups, silverware, and teapot have no graphics. Printed on the packaging: "Charlie Brown & Snoopy." Metal plates, plastic cups, silverware, and teapot. #409, Ohio Art. 1984. Dishes: $3 ea. Set: $25-30*

133. Cook 'N Serve Set

• The set includes four place settings, silverware, teapot, pots and pans with lids, a strainer, serving utensils, napkins, and napkin rings. (45 pieces total). Lucy and Charlie Brown are pictured on the plates and inside the pots and pans bringing food and tea to Snoopy on his doghouse. The saucers feature Snoopy drinking tea on top of his doghouse. "Charlie Brown & Snoopy" is printed on each plate, saucer, and inside the pots and pans. The cups, silverware, and teapot have no graphics. Packaged in a corrugated box. Metal plates, plastic cups, silverware, and teapot. #468H, Ohio Art. Sold exclusively through Sears. 1984. Dishes: $3 ea. Pots and Pans: $6-10 ea. Set: $55-60*

134. Tea Sets

• "PEANUTS Tea Set." The set includes two place settings, silverware, and a tray (9 pieces total). The tray features Pigpen, Linus, Schroeder, Frieda, Sally, Snoopy, Charlie Brown, and Lucy. One plate pictures Schroeder, the other pictures Peppermint Patty. The cups, saucers and silverware have no graphics. The packaging features the faces of Lucy, Snoopy, Sally, Linus, Frieda and Charlie Brown. Metal. #208, J. Chein and Co. 1970. Tray: $15-25 Plates: $8-12 Set: $140-150*

• "Snoopy Tea Set." The set includes a tray, a plate, two cups and two saucers (6 pieces total). The tray features Pigpen, Linus, Schroeder, Frieda, Sally, Snoopy, Charlie Brown, and Lucy. The plate pictures Linus sucking his thumb and holding his blanket. The cups and saucers have no graphics. A cardboard insert between the cups and saucers features Snoopy as the Flying Ace holding a cup. Printed on the packaging: "Everything For Snoopy's Party." Metal. #276, J. Chein and Co. 1970. Tray: $15-25 Plate: $8-12 Set: $130-140*

135. Housekeeping Set

• "Snoopy Floor Care Play Set." The set includes an apron, broom, dust pan, sponge mop, and sponge. All pieces are child-sized. A decal of Snoopy and Woodstock appears on each piece. Snoopy is pictured on the packaging holding a broom and dancing. Plastic. #1636, A.R.C. 1988. $10-12**

136. Sno-Cone Machine

• "Snoopy Sno-Cone Machine." Ice is added and crushed when the handle is turned. Snoopy sits on top of the doghouse-shaped machine. Woodstock stands in front of a snowman on one side and a shovel leans against the other side. Charlie Brown and Lucy are pictured on the front. Includes a recipe, paper cups, and flavorings for the sno-cones. Plastic with metal ice compartment. Originally made in 1961 by Playskool, it has been continually produced every year thereafter with minor modifications. Playskool is now a division of Hasbro, Inc. The Sno-Cone Machine is still being made. Buy it new.

The PEANUTS Home Collection

PEANUTS PRESCHOOL TO GRADE 3

137. Clock

"Tell-Time Clock." Clocks can be taken apart and put together again. Once wound, the clocks will tell time for 8 hours. A character appears in the center of the clock holding its hands. The inner workings of the clock can be seen through the clear face. The bells are decorative and do not ring. Packaging is printed with the character's name. Plastic. Concept 2000. Early 1980s. $8-12 $20-30* ea.

- Snoopy. #171.
- Woodstock. #173.
- Charlie Brown. #172.

138. Toys

- "Push 'N Fly Snoopy," Snoopy, as the Flying Ace piloting his plane, rises up the handle as the toy is pushed along. Woodstock appears to be sitting in a tank looking through binoculars at Snoopy. His friends appear on its sides. Plastic. #821, Romper Room/Hasbro. 1983. $20-35

- "Snoopy Whirl N' Twirl Phone." Snoopy stands on the base of a rotary dial telephone holding the receiver. When the phone is dialed, Snoopy spins around. Plastic. 5-7/8" x 5-1/2" x 10". #823, Romper Room/Hasbro. 1981. $5-10 $25-35*

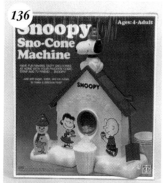

136

139. Toy

- "Snoopy Soft House." A quilted fabric house opens into a play area for the cloth Snoopy and Woodstock dolls, which are included. Accessories include a night-shirt, stocking cap, vest and scarf, and a sleeping bag and chair. The closed house has a handle for carrying. Cotton.

137

138

139

140

#0573, Knickerbocker. 1980. $35-40**

140. Toys

- "Stack-Up Snoopy." Snoopy, dressed as a Beagle Scout, comes in six pieces that are assembled on a pole to form the doll. The stay-together pieces will not come apart during play. Plastic. 5-1/2" x 5-1/2" x 9-1/2". #818, Romper Room/Hasbro. 1980. $8-12 $30-35*

- "Snoopy Take-A-Part Dog House." Snoopy's doghouse is on wheels, with Snoopy rising from the roof top. The doghouse can be taken apart and put together with a special Snoopy screwdriver, which is included. Plastic. #51705, Gabriel/Child Guidance. 1979. $8-12 $30-35*

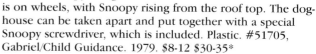

141

141. Toy

- "Electronic Snoopy Playmate." Snoopy, as a drum major, with Woodstock on the end of his baton, are featured on the front of this toy, which can be used to play games and songs, and record music. Musical notes are buttons that can be depressed. Knobs and buttons under Snoopy allow you to change activities. A songbook is included. Battery operated. Plastic. 11" x 13" x 6". #830. Romper Room/Hasbro. 1980. $45-60 $135-145*

142. Toys

- "Push And Play With The PEANUTS Gang." This toy features a house with a tree next to it and wagons in the front. Lucy, Linus, Charlie Brown, Peppermint Patty, and Snoopy can be found inside the house and the tree. When buttons are pushed the characters come out of hiding. Each character rides in a wagon which can all be hitched together to form a chain. Plastic. #1700, Child Guidance. 1975. $25-30 $55-65*

- "Snoopy's Shape Register." Eight geometric shapes sit in corresponding openings on top of the register. Each button on the front has a picture that matches each shape. When the button is depressed, the shape falls into the register. Snoopy, hugging Woodstock, is the handle of the register. When the handle is pulled, a bell rings and a drawer opens, revealing the shapes inside. Plastic. #51740, Gabriel/Child Guidance. 1980. $10-20 $40-50*

143. Toy

•"Snoopy And His Dog House Playset." Set includes a jointed Snoopy, his supper dish printed "Snoopy," his doghouse, and Woodstock. Woodstock fits on the edge of the supper dish and a clear plastic support enables Snoopy to lie on his doghouse. Plastic. #176, Determined Productions. 1975. $15-20 $30-35*

144. Toy

•"Snoopy Snack Attack." Snoopy hides behind the door of his doghouse. A bowl of bones is at the door. Includes a pop-o-matic device. Plastic. #70345, Gabriel. 1980. $20-25 $40-50*

145. Toy

•"My Friend Snoopy." A ball is placed in Snoopy's cupped hand. When his arm is pulled back and let go of, he releases the ball. Includes two balls, ten bowling pins, and a mat. Plastic. 14"H. #825, Romper Room/Hasbro. 1979. $5-10 $20-30*

146. Toys

•"Snoopy Counting Camera." Snoopy is shown holding a camera on the front. A 3-D Woodstock sits on the orange camera. Their tails operate the camera and change the images of the PEANUTS characters in the viewfinder. Plastic. 9-1/8" x 4-1/8" x 6-5/8". #821, Romper Room. 1981. $8-10 $20-25*

•"Snoopy Copter Pull Toy." A sitting Snoopy, with Woodstock in his lap, is on wheels. When Snoopy is pulled along, his

ears spin around and make noise. Plastic. #822, Romper Room. 1981. $5-8 $10-15*

147. Toys

A jointed Snoopy is dressed to participate in various activities. A small Woodstock is included. Vinyl doll, plastic accessories. 5"H. Knickerbocker. 1978. $10-20 ea. $60-70*ea.

•"Snoopy The Sport." Includes two tennis rackets, a soccer ball, towel, tote bag, visor, socks, sneakers, a sweat suit, and a tennis outfit. #9740-6541.

• "Snoopy The Chef." Includes a sink and stove, frying pan, pot with lid, coffee pot, cake, spoon, apron, and chef's hat. #9740-0542.

•"Snoopy The Astronaut." Includes a space suit, moon boots, helmet, life support system, camera, moon rover, and an American Flag. #9740-0540.

147

148

149

150

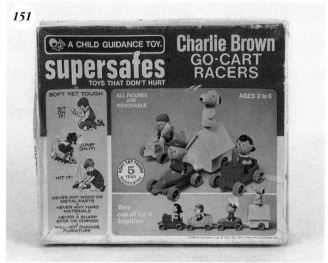

151

152

the clock. Snoopy's hands tell the time. The clock's numbers are printed on removable geometric shapes. Plastic. #819, Romper Room. 1983. $10-12 $15-20*

•"Snoopy & The 5 Balancing Woodstocks." Snoopy balances Woodstock and his friends in many different combinations. Plastic. Snoopy—5"H. Woodstocks—4"H. #826, Hasbro Preschool. 1983. $6-8 $12-15*

151. Toy

•"Charlie Brown Go-Cart Racers." Snoopy, Linus, Lucy, and Charlie Brown each ride a different go-cart. The characters are removable. The go-carts can be hooked together. Rubber. #1680, Questor Education Products/Child Guidance. Late 1970s. $20-25 $50-58*

152. Toys

•"Snoopy's Scooter Shooter." Set includes a scooter launcher and a ramp that allows Snoopy and Woodstock, wearing helmets, to perform stunts in their scooter. Plastic. #1720, Child Guidance. 1977. $12-15 $40-45*

•"Snoopy's Stunt Spectacular." Snoopy rides a break-apart stunt motorcycle with Woodstock in the side car. Set includes a cycle launcher, obstacles, and a double-sided ramp with the characters' faces at the top. Plastic. #1750, Child Guidance. 1978. $12-15 $60-70*

153. Toys

•"Snoopy's Beagle Bugle." Push the mouthpiece and the bugle call is played. Snoopy and Woodstock, dressed as scouts, sit on top of the bugle. A decal on the side features Snoopy, Woodstock, and Charlie Brown. Difficult to find in working condition. Plastic. #1730, Child Guidance. 1977. $50-75 $90-140*

•"Schroeder's Piano." Schroeder, Peppermint Patty, Charlie Brown, Snoopy, Linus, and Lucy sit in openings on the top of the piano. They pop up when the piano is played.

148. Toy

•"Snoopy's Dog House." Snoopy's doghouse is on a green base with a birdbath and a ramp. Includes wind-up Snoopy and Woodstock walkers, and an ice cream truck. Plastic. #815, Romper Room. 1978. $15-20 $40-45*

149. Toy

•"Camp Kamp." Lucy, Linus, Snoopy, Schroeder, Peppermint Patty, and Charlie Brown play inside and outside a cabin with bunk beds, a fireplace, a campfire, two canoes, and a picnic table and bench. Rubber. #1683, Child Guidance. Late 1970s. $30-40 $85-95*

150. Toys

•"Snoopy Shape Clock." Snoopy, dressed as a magician, and Woodstock, sitting in a top hat, are featured in the center of

Difficult to find the piano working. Plastic. #1710, Child Guidance. 1975. $50-60 $145-165*

154. Toy

•"Snoopy Playhouse." A jointed Snoopy and Woodstock come with Snoopy's doghouse in a yard with a mailbox and a white picket fence. The doghouse opens from the roof and sides to show the furnishings inside on two floors connected by stairs. The set includes a bed, piano, lamps, pictures on the walls, a table and chairs, and a dresser. The playset is portable. Plastic. #120, Determined Productions. 1977. $45-60 $175-185*

155. Toy

•"Can You Catch It, Charlie Brown?" This pinball-type game pictures Charlie Brown, Snoopy, Woodstock, Lucy, and Linus

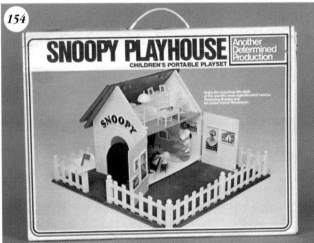

playing baseball on a decal insert. Oversized baseball gloves are on the field to catch the ball released by a spring-action trigger. Plastic. #8282-6, Ideal Toy Corp. 1976. $40-45 $135-145*

156. Toy

•"Snoopy's Pound-A-Ball." Charlie Brown, Snoopy, Woodstock, Lucy, and Linus are pictured sitting in a tree, and Peppermint Patty leans against the tree trunk. As the ball goes into a slot of this vertical pinball-type game, the bell rings and the proper character comes into the center of the tree. Plastic. #51702, Gabriel/Child Guidance. 1979. $50-60 $130-150*

157. Toys

•"Snoopy In The Music Box." The music box features a yellow and white top with "Mattel" printed in a red circle. The front features Snoopy playing an accordion, while a bluebird holds sheet music in front of him. Printed: "Snoopy In The Music Box." Other characters are featured around the music box in different scenes. Music plays when the hand-crank is turned. A cloth Snoopy with felt ears pops out when the music stops. The cardboard packaging is red and white, and features Snoopy with outstretched arms. Metal. #4745, Asst. #4738, Mattel. 1972. $20-25 $60-75*

•"Snoopy Jack-In-The-Music-Box." The music box features a yellow and white top with "Mattel" printed in different colored circles. The front features Snoopy playing an accordion, while a bluebird holds sheet music in front of him. Printed: "Snoopy In The Music Box." Other characters are featured around the music box in different scenes. Music plays when the hand-crank is turned. A cloth Snoopy with felt ears pops out when the music stops. The cardboard packaging alternates with pink and orange sides. Snoopy is pictured conducting music with a baton and popping out of the music box. The *Good Housekeeping* Magazine seal and the *Parents* Magazine seal appear on the packaging. Metal. #4745, Mattel. 1969. $25-35 $100-125*

158. Toys

•"Snoopy In The Music Box." The music box features a yellow top with "Mattel" printed in raised letters. The paper decal front features Snoopy playing an accordion while a bluebird holds sheet music in front of him. Printed: "Snoopy In The Music Box."

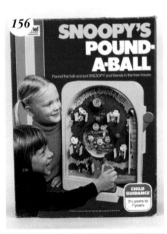

Other characters are featured around the music box in different scenes on paper decals. Music plays when the hand-crank is turned. A cloth Snoopy with felt ears pops out when the music stops. Plastic. Mattel. Late 1970s. $8-10 $15-20*

•"Snoopy Jack-In-The-Box." Music plays when the hand-crank is turned. Woodstock pops out of his nest on top of Snoopy's doghouse. Snoopy pops out of the entrance to the doghouse. Plastic. #818, Romper Room. 1979. $8-10 $15-25*

•"Snoopy Musical Jack-In-The-Box." Music plays when the hand-crank is turned. A sitting Snoopy pops out when the music stops. The music box is yellow with a white handle and a red top. Snoopy dancing and Woodstock flying, and Snoopy's doghouse are pictured on the sides. Plastic. 6-3/4" x 5-3/4" x 5-3/4". #319, Hasbro Preschool. 1984. $8-10 $15-18*

159. Toy

•"Deluxe Peanuts Playset." Set includes jointed action play-figures of Charlie Brown, Lucy and Snoopy, a psychiatrist's booth, and a stool. Their clothes are removable. The dolls were also sold separately as were their clothes. See Playroom, page 262 . Plastic. #575, Determined Productions. 1975. $75-100 $140-150*

160. Toy

"Peanuts Show Time Finger Puppets." The characters come in blister packages that look like a stage with an audience in front. They were sold individually, in twin packs and in a set of six. Vinyl. Ideal Toy Corp. 1976. 5-8 ea. 15-20*ea.

Individual Characters. Assortment #5369-4.

•Snoopy.

•Charlie Brown.

•Lucy.

•Linus.

•Schroeder.

•Peppermint Patty.

•Woodstock.

•Sally.

Set of six characters. Characters' names are printed on the box. (While Schroeder is pictured in the set shown here, he was only sold individually and does not belong in this set.) Peppermint Patty does belong in the set. Assortment #5379-3. $5-8 ea. Set: $40-45*

•Snoopy.

•Charlie Brown.

•Peppermint Patty (replaces Schroeder)

•Linus.

•Lucy.

•Woodstock.

Twin Packs. Assortment #5372-8 . $5-8 ea. $15-22* (Not pictured)

•Snoopy and Woodstock.

•Charlie Brown and Lucy.

161. Toys

•"Charlie Brown's Backyard." Charlie Brown, Lucy, and Snoopy, as the Flying Ace, in a blister pack that looks like a yard. Package depicts Snoopy's doghouse, trees, and a stool. Linus, spraying Peppermint Patty with a hose, and Sally, playing in a sandbox, are shown on the reverse side. Toy's name and other information are printed on the package bottom. Rubber. #1733, Child Guidance. Late 1970s. $25-35**

•"Charlie Brown's All Stars Dugout." Charlie Brown, Lucy, and Snoopy are dressed in baseball gear. They come in a blister package that looks like a dugout with a scoreboard on top. Lockers, mitts, hats, bats and the ball game's line-up are depicted in the dugout. Woodstock in his nest in a tree is next to the dugout. Schroeder, Linus, Marcie and Peppermint Patty are pictured on the reverse side. Rubber. #1736, Child Guidance. Late 1970s. $25-35**

162. Talking Storybook

•"Speak Up, Charlie Brown." Lucy, Charlie Brown, and Linus are leaning on a brick wall. Snoopy, as the Flying Ace, stands below next to a dial with an arrow on it. The arrow on the dial is turned to match the arrow on each page of the book.

158

159

160

161

162

163

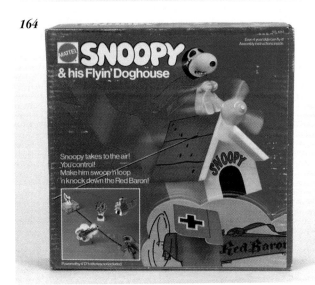

164

• "Snoopy Says See 'N Say." Eleven pictures of various characters are depicted around the toy. Snoopy is in the center. Point his arm to a picture of Charlie Brown, Snoopy, Peppermint Patty, Linus, Pig-Pen (sic), Frieda, Sally, Lucy, Schroeder, or Violet, pull the string, and the characters talk. Came packaged in a cardboard box that was open in the front. Rarely found in working condition now. Plastic. #4864, Mattel. 1969. $250-300*

163. Toy

• "Snoopy Playland." Interlocking tracks form an amusement park. Lucy, Linus, and Schroeder ride in a ferris wheel. Peppermint Patty is in a tree swing, Woodstock is in his nest above Snoopy's doghouse, and Charlie Brown operates a turn-table. Snoopy sits on a bus that follows tracks around the park. Also included are benches and flowers. Battery-operated. Plastic. #888, Aviva. 1978. $105-120**

PLANES, TRAINS, AND AUTOMOBILES . . . AND OTHER THINGS THAT MOVE

The production of the die-cast vehicles by Aviva Toy Company began in 1977. The packaging had the company's name printed on it. In 1980, Aviva gave up the toy division to Hasbro. The packaging was then printed with Hasbro's name, as well as with Aviva. In the Mid-1980s, when Aviva was no longer in business, their name was removed from the packaging. The die-cast vehicles still had "Aviva" printed on the bottom because the original molds were still being used by Hasbro. Out of the package, it is impossible to determine when the vehicle was made. Hasbro continued to produce the die-cast cars, but added to the series by creating a line of die-cast vehicles with characters that had slightly larger heads. These vehicles can be found in packages printed "Hasbro Preschool."

In 1989, International Trading Technology used some toy molds to reproduce old Aviva toys. Most of the toys are different in some minor way. Look on the undersides of all of these types of toys for hints as to who the manufacturer was if you are purchasing the item out of its original packaging. For example, the Aviva wind-up train is stamped "Aviva/Hasbro" and "Made in Hong Kong" on the underside of the train cars, while the International Trading train is stamped only "Made in China." Also, the manufacturers used different decals on each train car.

164. Toy

• "Snoopy & his Flyin' Doghouse." Snoopy, as the Flying Ace on his doghouse, zeros in on the Red Baron. The doghouse is attached to a control unit with a wire which the user operates. Battery-operated. Plastic and cardboard. #8263, Mattel. 1974. $35-50 $100-135*

165. Toy

• "Snoopy Skediddler And His Sopwith Camel." The carrying case opens into a baseball field and a backyard with Snoopy's doghouse in it. The toy includes Snoopy as the Flying Ace and his WWI plane. Snoopy can be removed from the plane. A wheel attachment to his back allows Snoopy to walk when it is pushed. The carrying case came in blue and black. Plastic. #4954, Mattel. 1969. $95-125**

166. Toys

• "Snoopy vs. The Red Baron." Snoopy, as the Flying Ace, sits on top of his doghouse. When the metal key attached to the doghouse is wound, the house jumps up and down and

When the string is pulled, the text on that page is heard. Rarely found working now. Printed on the storybook: "PEANUTS A See 'N Say Talking Storybook." Cardboard with vinyl-like pages. #4812, Mattel. 1969. $250-300*

Toys

• "Snoopy The Critic." Snoopy stands on top of his doghouse. Woodstock, in his nest, is on one side of him, and a sign printed "Snoopy The Critic" is on the other side. A microphone is attached to the doghouse. Snoopy claps and Woodstock hops up and down when the microphone is used. Plastic. #222, Aviva. 1977. Manufactured for one year and only 1,000 were produced. $175-195 $200-250*

165

167

166

168

169

around. Cardboard Snoopy, plastic doghouse. #139, Chein. Late 1960s. $25-30 $40-45*

•"Snoopy And Charlie Brown Copter." Snoopy and Charlie Brown, both with propeller blades attached to their heads, fly when they are launched by a spring action pull string from Snoopy's doghouse. Plastic. #600, Aviva/Hasbro. 1979. $12-18 $30-35*

167. Toys

•"Snoopy's Good Grief Glider." Snoopy, as the Flying Ace, flies in his Sopwith Camel up to 20 feet when it is launched from a spring action launcher. Plastic. #1775, Child Guidance. 1978. $55-65**

•"Snoopy's Daredevil Flyer." Snoopy, as the Flying Ace, pilots a hang glider which will soar up to 25-feet when launched. Plastic. #51748, Gabriel/Child Guidance. 1978. $65-75**

168. Toys

•"Snoopy's Dream Machine!" Suspended like a mobile, Snoopy, as the Flying Ace on his doghouse, chases the Red Baron in his Fokker triplane. The set includes all necessary parts for assembly. Batteries are required to operate pro-pellers. Does not have blinking lights. Laminated fiberboard. #417-M, D.C.S. 1980. $60-70**

•"Snoopy's Dream Machine!" Suspended like a mobile, Snoopy, as the Flying Ace on his doghouse, chases the Red Baron in his Fokker triplane. The set includes all necessary parts for assembly. Batteries are required to operate pro-pellers and blinking lights. Laminated fiberboard. D.C.S. 1979. $125-145**

169. Toys

•"Snoopy Push N' Pull Biplane." When the plane is pushed or pulled, the character in the plane moves. Set includes the biplane, Snoopy as the Flying Ace, Snoopy wearing a top hat, Charlie Brown, and Woodstock. The characters are inter-changeable in the plane. Plastic. #70866, Aviva/Hasbro. 1982. $12-15 $35-40*

•"Snoopy Push N' Pull Locomotive." When the train is pushed or pulled, the character in the train moves. Set includes the train, Snoopy as the Flying Ace, Snoopy wearing a top hat, Charlie Brown, and Woodstock. The characters are interchangeable in the locomotive. Plastic. #70877, Aviva/Hasbro. 1982. $12-15 $35-40*

170. Toys

•"Snoopy and Woodstock Handcar." Plastic. 3-1/2" x 3". #6-18407, Lionel Trains, Inc. 1990. $65-85 $95-115*

•"Charlie Brown and Lucy Handcar." Plastic. 3-3/4" x 3-1/2". #6-18413, Lionel Trains, Inc. 1991. $65-85 $85-110*

171. Toy

•"Snoopy Express Station Set." Snoopy rides in the locomotive waving a lantern. Charlie Brown and Woodstock wait for Snoopy to pull into the doghouse station. They move when Snoopy enters the station. Set includes all necessary parts for assembly. Battery-operated. Plastic. #988, Aviva. 1977. $75-85**

172. Toy

•"Snoopy Train Set." Schroeder rides in the locomotive, Charlie Brown rides in the tender, Snoopy rides atop his doghouse, and Woodstock rides in his nest in a tree. Each car is printed with its character's name. Set also includes tracks, a tunnel, signs, and a ticket office. It was sold in different packaging, as shown here. The contents are identical. Battery-operated. Plastic. #3000, Aviva. 1977. $75-85**

173. Toy

•"Snoopy Mechanical Wind Up Wood Train." The three-piece set includes a locomotive and two cars. Snoopy is the engineer, as well as a passenger in the last car. Other passengers depicted include Charlie Brown, Peppermint Patty, and Woodstock. Wood. #911, Aviva. 1977. $20-25 $45-50*

174. Toys

"Snoopy Die Cast Metal Toy." 4-3/4". #700, Aviva. 1977.

•Locomotive. Snoopy is the engineer of a blue, red, and yellow locomotive. $20-30 $40-45*

•Biplane. Snoopy, as the Flying Ace, pilots the yellow plane with red wings. "Snoopy" is printed on the side of the plane, and Woodstock is pictured on the plane's tail. $15-25 $33-40*

•Fire Engine. Snoopy drives the red fire truck with yellow ladders. Woodstock rides in the rear of the truck. $15-25 $35-40*

175. Toys

"Snoopy Die Cast Metal Toy." 4-3/4". #700, Aviva. 1977.

•Family Car. Charlie Brown drives an orange convertible. His passengers, Peppermint Patty, Snoopy, and Woodstock, ride in the back seat. $20-25 $40-50*

•Race Car. Snoopy, wearing a red helmet, drives a blue race car with "Snoopy" printed on the side. $20-30 $50-55*

•Sports Car. Snoopy drives a yellow convertible with red fenders. Woodstock sits on the back of the car. $20-30 $40-50*

176. Toy

•"Snoopy Racing Car Stickshifter." Snoopy, as a race car driver, sits in his yellow hot rod. Woodstock, in his nest, is on

173

170

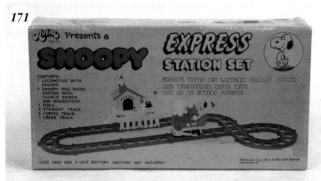

171

174

172

175

the front of the car. The car is placed on the ramp and a gearshifter moved into first, second, third, and fourth gear builds up speed. The car is automatically released when fourth gear is reached. Battery-operated. Plastic. #2500, Aviva. 1978. $70-85 $155-160*

177. Mini Die-Cast Toys

"Snoopy Handfuls." Snoopy and Woodstock drive different vehicles. Metal. 2-1/2". Series #72036, Aviva/Hasbro. 1982. $6-10 ea. Set: $40-55* ea.

•Snoopy rides in the yellow cherry-picker bucket of a purple snorkel.

•Snoopy drives red fire engine with yellow ladders and trim.

•Snoopy drives a gray wrecker with red equipment on the back.

•Snoopy drives a red buggy with a yellow surfboard on top.

•Snoopy drives a red and yellow truck printed "Cat Catcher."

•Snoopy drives a blue van printed "Fun Van."

•Woodstock drives a white ice cream truck.

•Snoopy drives a green car with his doghouse attached over the back seat.

•Snoopy drives a mail truck.

178. Mini Die Cast Toys

"Snoopy Handfuls." Snoopy and Woodstock with oversized heads drive different vehicles. Metal. Assortment #72036, Hasbro Preschool. 1984. $6-8 ea. Set: $35-45* ea.

•Snoopy drives a gray wrecker with red equipment on the back.

•Snoopy rides in the yellow cherry-picker bucket of a red snorkel.

•Snoopy drives a red fire engine with yellow ladders.

•Snoopy drives a red and yellow dune buggy.

•Snoopy drives a blue van printed "Fun Van."

•Snoopy drives a red and yellow truck printed "Cat Catcher."

•Snoopy drives a mail truck.

•Snoopy drives a green car with his doghouse attached over the back seat.

•Woodstock drives a white ice cream truck.

179. Mini Die-Cast Racing Set

•"Snoopy Free Wheeling Action." Set of four includes Lucy in a yellow racer, Woodstock in a white racer, Snoopy in a red racer, and Woodstock in a green racer. Metal. #2038, Aviva. 1980. $6-10 ea. Set: $50-60*

180. Mini Die-Cast Toys

Snoopy, Woodstock, Lucy, and Charlie Brown drive different vehicles. Metal. 2-1/2". Series #2033, Aviva/Hasbro. 1982. $6-10 ea. $12-15* ea.

•Lucy drives a yellow racing car printed "15" on the front.

•Charlie Brown rides in a red and blue locomotive.

•Snoopy drives a red and yellow truck printed "Cat Catcher."

•Snoopy drives a green car with his doghouse attached over the back seat (also in series #2030).

•Woodstock drives a pink land rover.

•Snoopy drives a blue van printed "Fun Van."

•Snoopy drives a yellow buggy with a pair of skis on top.

• Snoopy drives a red race car.

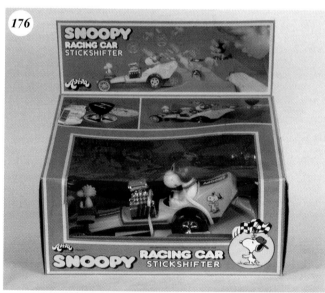

(Not pictured):

•Snoopy drives a green truck.

•Snoopy drives red fire engine with yellow ladders and trim (also in series #2030).

•Snoopy rides in the yellow cherry-picker bucket of a purple snorkel (also in series #2022).

•Woodstock drives a green race car.

181. Mini Die-Cast Toys

Snoopy, Woodstock, Lucy, and Charlie Brown drive different vehicles. Metal. 2-1/2". Series #2030, Aviva/Hasbro. 1982. $6-10 ea. $12-15* ea.

•Snoopy drives a red race car.

•Woodstock drives a forklift.

•Snoopy drives a blue race car.

•Snoopy drives a red and yellow tow truck.

•Charlie Brown drives a red and white race car.

•Snoopy drives a red and yellow dune buggy.

•Woodstock rides in a blue and yellow covered wagon.

•Woodstock drives a white ice cream truck.

•Snoopy drives red fire engine with yellow ladders and trim (also in series #2033).

•Charlie Brown drives a blue pick-up truck.

•Snoopy drives a green car with his doghouse attached over the back seat (also in series #2033).

•Lucy drives a truck that resembles her psychiatrist booth.

182. Mini Die-Cast Toys

Snoopy, Woodstock, Lucy, and Charlie Brown drive different vehicles. Metal. 2-1/2". Series #2022, Aviva/Hasbro. 1982. $6-10 ea. $12-15* ea.

•Snoopy drives a blue van printed "Fun Van." (Good Grief! This van does not belong in this series, even though it is pictured here. It belongs only in series #2033)

•Lucy drives a purple jeep.

•Snoopy rides in the yellow cherry-picker bucket of a purple snorkel (also in series #2033).

•Woodstock drives a white race car with a red stripe down the front.

•Snoopy drives a farm truck filled with dirt.

•Snoopy drives a mail truck.

•Woodstock drives a white race car printed "Woodstock" on the back.

•Snoopy drives a gray wrecker with red equipment on the back.

(Not pictured):

•Charlie Brown drives a tractor.

•Woodstock drives in a convertible known as a love car.

•Snoopy drives a red buggy with a yellow surfboard on top.

•Snoopy rides in a locomotive.

•Snoopy drives a land rover.

183. Large Die-Cast Toys

Snoopy rides in different vehicles. Metal. 4-3/4". Aviva/Hasbro. 1982.

•Biplane. Snoopy, as the Flying Ace, pilots a yellow plane with red wings. "Snoopy" is printed on the side of the plane and Woodstock is pictured on the plane's tail. #72039/2. $10-20 $25-30*

•Race Car. Snoopy, wearing a red helmet, drives a blue race car with "Snoopy" printed on the side. #72039/3. $18-25 $35-40*

•Sports Car. Snoopy drives a yellow convertible with red fenders. Woodstock sits on the back of the car. #72039/4. $18-25 $35-40*

•Fire Engine. Snoopy drives the red fire truck with yellow ladders. Woodstock rides in the rear of the truck. #72039/1. $12-20 $30-35

184. Happy Die-Cast Toys

Snoopy, Charlie Brown and Woodstock ride in different vehicles. The characters have oversized heads and bodies. 2-1/2". Hasbro. Early 1980s. $8-12 ea. $15-20* ea.

• Woodstock drives a truck with a picture of a clown on the side and printed "Circus." #72044-4.

• Snoopy, as the Flying Ace, drives a red race car printed "61" on the front and "Snoopy" on the back. #72044-6.

• Snoopy drives a red truck with a picture of a cat on the side and printed "Cat Catcher." #72044-5.

• Snoopy, wearing a tuxedo and top hat, drives a yellow convertible. #72044-2.

• Snoopy drives a red fire engine with yellow ladders and trim. #72044-3.

• Charlie Brown, wearing his red baseball cap to the side, drives a yellow convertible. #72044-1.

185. Push 'N' Pull Toys

Sold in individual packages. Snoopy and Lucy ride in different vehicles. As the vehicle is pushed or pulled, the character moves up and down. The characters are interchangeable. Packaging is red and yellow with a window. Printed: "Aviva Presents A Snoopy Push N Pull Toy." Plastic. Style #855, Aviva. 1977. $4-6 ea. $10-15* ea.

184

185

186

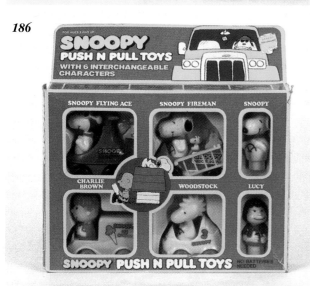

• Snoopy's blue ice cream truck.

• Lucy's yellow car.

• Snoopy's green helicopter.

• Snoopy's red rescue squad truck.

(Not pictured):

Boxed set of four Push 'N Pull Toys. Red and yellow package, with a window. Printed: "Aviva Presents Snoopy Push 'N Pull Toys." Plastic. Style #850, Aviva. 1977. $4-6 ea. Set: $35-45*

• Snoopy's blue ice cream truck.

• Lucy's yellow car.

• Snoopy's green helicopter.

• Snoopy's red rescue squad truck.

Toy

"Snoopy's Gyro Cycle." Snoopy as the Flying Ace rides a motorcycle. Woodstock and Charlie Brown ride along in the side car. This is a friction action toy. Plastic. #70440, Aviva/Hasbro. 1982. $30-50 $80-90*

186. Push N' Pull Toys

Snoopy, Woodstock, Lucy, and Charlie Brown ride in different vehicles. As the vehicle is pushed or pulled the character moves up and down. The set includes 4 vehicles and 6 interchangeable characters. Packaging is red and yellow with windows. Printed: "Aviva Presents Snoopy Push N' Pull Toys." Plastic. Style #70850, Aviva/Hasbro. 1982. $30-40**

• Snoopy's blue helicopter.

• Snoopy's red rescue squad truck.

• Snoopy's yellow ice cream truck.

• Snoopy's white car.

187. Toys

• "Snoopy Gravity Raceway." Snoopy, Charlie Brown, Woodstock, and Lucy race cars around a double track starting from the top of the holding tower to the bottom of the track. Batteries aren't needed. Plastic. #990, Aviva. 1977. $25-40 $65-75*

• "Snoopy Speedway." Snoopy, Charlie Brown, Woodstock, and Lucy race cars around a double track, starting from the top of the holding tower and moving to the bottom of the track; then the cars climb back up to the top. Battery-operated. Plastic. #999, Aviva. 1977. $35-50 $85-95*

188. Toys

• "Snoopy Formula 1 Racing Car." Snoopy sits in his race car, which is white with yellow, orange, and purple accents. "Snoopy" and "4" are printed in various places on the car. "Snoopy" and "Woodstock" are printed on the tires. A decal on the front of the car depicts Snoopy waving a checkered flag. Battery-operated. Plastic. 11-1/2". #950, Aviva. 1978. $20-30 $75-85*

(Not pictured):

• "Woodstock Formula 1 Racing Car." Woodstock sits

187

in his race car, which is white with yellow, orange, and purple accents. "Woodstock" and "3" are printed in various places on the car. "Snoopy" and "Woodstock" are printed on the tires. A decal on the front of the car depicts Snoopy waving a checkered flag. Battery-operated. Plastic. 11-1/2". #950, Aviva. 1978. $20-30 $75-85*

189. Toy

•"Talking Peanuts Bus." Snoopy drives the bus. Linus, Schroeder, Pigpen, and two bunnies look out the windows. On the reverse side Lucy, Charlie Brown, Frieda, Five, Sally, and non-Woodstock birds look out the windows. Printed on the bus: "Happiness Is An Annual Outing." The cardboard packaging exposes the sides of the bus. Talk balloons are positioned over the characters. An opening in the top of the box allows the user to press a button to hear the characters sing and talk. An opening in the bottom of the box allows batteries to be inserted into the bus. Metal. #261, J. Chein and Co. 1967. $500-700*

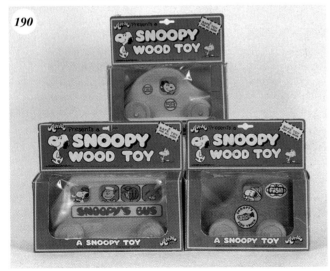

190. Toys

"Snoopy Wood Toy." Decals depict Snoopy driving various vehicles. Wood. Aviva. 1977. $5-8 ea. $12-15* ea.

•Snoopy, as the Flying Ace, drives a car with decals printed "59." Style #100, WT001.

•Snoopy, wearing a red cap, drives a bus with Charlie Brown, Peppermint Patty, and Woodstock as passengers. A "Snoopy's Bus" decal is on the side and a "USA" decal is on the front. Style #600, WT501.

•Snoopy, wearing a rain slicker and hat, drives a truck with decals printed "Fish" and "Snoopy's Fish Truck." Style #100, WT003.

191. Toy

•"Snoopy Wood Toy." A decal on the car depicts Snoopy as Joe Cool. Decals printed "Joe Cool" are on the sides and a decal printed "Rah" is on the back. Wood. Style #100, WT002, Aviva. 1977. $5-8 $12-15*

Toys

"Snoopy Wood Toy Mini Collector's Series." Decals depict Snoopy driving various vehicles which have red plastic wheels. Series #944, Aviva. 1977. $4-6 ea. $10-12* ea.

•Snoopy drives a mail truck with red and blue stripes and "Snoopy USA" decals on the sides. "USA" decals are on the front and back of the truck.

•Snoopy, wearing a rain slicker and hat, drives a truck with decals printed "Fish" and "Snoopy's Fish Truck."

•Snoopy, wearing an engineer's cap, drives a locomotive.

•Snoopy, as Joe Cool, drives a car with "Joe Cool" decals on the sides and a decal printed "Rah" on the back.

•Snoopy, wearing a red cap, drives a truck with a decal printed "Snoopy's Cement Truck" on the side, decals of lights on the front, and a decal printed "Snoopy" on the back.

192. Toys

"Snoopy Motorized Toy." Set of four wheeled toys. Packaging is printed "Snoopy Mini Friction Toys." Plastic. #810, Aviva. 1977. $4-6 ea. Set: $35-45*

•Snoopy scrubs his back in a bathtub filled with bubbles.

•Snoopy, as the Flying Ace, flies his doghouse.

•Snoopy rides in the cab of a locomotive.

•Snoopy drives a taxi with Woodstock in the back seat.

•"Snoopy Express Mechanical Wind Up Train." Three-piece set includes a locomotive and two cars. All are red and white

with yellow wheels. Snoopy is in the cab of the locomotive. Woodstock sits on top of the next car with Peppermint Patty, Charlie Brown, and Snoopy as passengers looking out the windows. The last car is Snoopy's doghouse with Snoopy lying on top. Plastic. #70911, Aviva. 1982. $15-20 $35-45*

•"Snoopy Family Car." Also known as the Mystery Car. Snoopy drives a yellow convertible with pink sideboards. Woodstock sits on the front of the car. Lucy sits next to Snoopy, and Peppermint Patty and Charlie Brown ride in the back seat. The car's lights flash and when the car hits an obstacle, it reverses itself, and keeps going. Battery-operated. Plastic. #2700, Aviva. 1978. $40-50 $70-80*

193. Toy

•"Snoopy Carry Case Garage." The carrying case can hold twenty four 3" vehicles. Detachable ramps and decals. Case converts into a garage when opened. Vehicles not included. Plastic. #73000, Aviva/Hasbro. 1982. $20-25 $30-35*

194. Toys

•"Snoopy Biplane Mini Die-Cast Toy." Snoopy flies a yellow biplane with red wings. "Snoopy" is printed on the sides. It comes packaged sitting on a cardboard base with a plastic cover extending over the base. Metal and plastic. #2024, Aviva. 1977. $10-15 $18-20*

•"Snoopy Family Car Mini Die Cast Toy." Also known as the Mystery Car. Snoopy drives the yellow convertible with pink sideboards. Charlie Brown sits next to Snoopy, and Lucy and Woodstock ride in the back seat. It comes packaged sitting on a cardboard base with a plastic cover extending over the base. Metal and plastic. #2028, Aviva. 1977. $15-20 $25-35*

•"Snoopy Biplane Mini Die Cast Toy." Snoopy flies a red biplane with yellow wings. "Snoopy" is printed on the sides. It comes packaged sitting on a cardboard base with a plastic cover extending over the base. Metal and plastic. #2024, Aviva. 1977. $10-15 $18-20*

195. Toy

"Snoopy Motorized Toy." Wheeled friction toys. Individually packaged in blue and yellow boxes with windows. Plastic. Series #800, Aviva. 1977. $4-6 ea. $12-15* ea.

•Snoopy rides in the cab of a locomotive.

•Snoopy, as the Flying Ace, drives his doghouse.

•Snoopy drives a taxi with Woodstock in the back seat.

•Snoopy, wearing a rain slicker and hat drives a boat.

•Snoopy scrubs his back in a bathtub filled with bubbles.

196. Toy

"Snoopy Motorized Toy." Wheeled friction toys. Individually packaged in green and yellow boxes with windows. Plastic. Series #966, Aviva. 1977. $20-35 ea. $45-50* ea.

•Snoopy, as the Flying Ace, drives his doghouse printed "Snoopy."

•Snoopy drives a red desk printed "Snoopy."

•Schroeder drives his white piano-mobile printed "Schroeder."

197. Toy

"Snoopy Motorized Toy." Wheeled friction toys. Individually packaged in green and yellow boxes with windows. Plastic. Series #966, Aviva. 1977. $20-35 ea. $45-50* ea.

•Linus drives his blue blanket-mobile printed "Linus."

•Lucy drives her orange psychiatrist booth printed "Psychiatric Help 25¢" and "The Doctor Is In."

•Charlie Brown drives his pitcher's mound printed "Charlie Brown."

198. Toys

•"Snoopy Tug Boat Motorized Toy." Snoopy, wearing a captain's hat, steers the tug boat. Charlie Brown is with him on the bridge. Woodstock, also wearing a captain's hat, sits on the bow of the red and white boat. When the wheeled friction boat is pushed, the smoke stacks move. Packaged in a yellow and red box with a window. The reverse side of the packaging pictures the two boats in the series. Plastic. #575, Aviva/Hasbro. 1978. $20-35 $40-45*

•"Snoopy Show Boat Motorized Toy." Snoopy, wearing a captain's hat, sits on the bow of the red, white, and blue boat with Lucy. Woodstock, also wearing a captain's hat, sits on the bridge. When the wheeled friction boat is pushed, the smoke stacks move. Packaged in a yellow and red box with a window. The reverse side of the packaging pictures the two boats in the series. Plastic. #575, Aviva/Hasbro. 1978. $20-35 $40-45*

199. Toys

•"Snoopy Radio Controlled Fire Engine." Snoopy, Charlie Brown, and Lucy, wearing firemen's hats, sit in a red fire engine with a yellow ladder. Woodstock sits on top of the fire truck's cab near the ladder. A Woodstock transmitter controls the fire engine, which has forward, turning, and reverse capabilities. The reverse side of the packaging is pictured. Snoopy is pictured carrying a hose and ladder on the front of the packaging, which has a window. Battery-operated. Plastic. #988 R/C, Aviva. 1980. $25-40 $55-60*

•"Snoopy Radio Controlled Dog House." Snoopy lies on his doghouse. A Woodstock transmitter controls the house which has forward, turning, and reverse capabilities. The reverse side of the packaging is pictured. The front of the packaging features Charlie Brown, Lucy, Snoopy, and Linus with Woodstock sitting on his head. The packaging has a window. Battery-operated. Plastic. #980 R/C, Aviva. 1980. $25-35 $50-60*

200. Toy

"Snoopy Skis Wind Up Action Toy." The characters move their arms up and down, and turn on their skis when the toy is wound. The window packaging features Snoopy skiing downhill and carrying his skis over his shoulder. Plastic. Style #711, Aviva. 1979. $25-35 ea. $40-45* ea.

•Snoopy wears a red sweater and hat. Woodstock rides along on Snoopy's skis.

•Charlie Brown wears a yellow sweater with a black zigzag, black pants, and a red hat. Woodstock rides on his skis.

•Lucy wears a blue sweater, and a pink hat and pants. Woodstock rides along on her skis.

201. Toy

"Snoopy Jump Cycle Motorized Toy." The characters ride friction-powered motorcycles. Plastic. 3-1/2" x 3". Series #550, Aviva/Hasbro. 1982. $8-10 ea. $15-20* ea.

•Snoopy, wearing a blue helmet, rides a blue and white motorcycle printed "Snoopy" on the side.

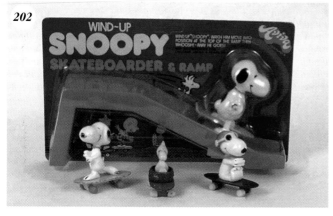

202

204

203

205

•Charlie Brown, wearing a green helmet, rides a green and white motorcycle printed "Charlie Brown" on the side.

•Woodstock, wearing a red helmet, rides a red and white motorcycle printed "Woodstock" on the side.

202. Toy

•"Wind Up Snoopy Skateboarder & Ramp." Set includes Snoopy on a skateboard and a red ramp. Wind Snoopy and he skates down the ramp. Plastic. Aviva. 1977. $6-8 $12-20*

Toys

"Skate 'N' Surf Mini Die Cast." The characters ride on skateboards. Metal skateboard, plastic characters. #2040, Aviva. 1977. $6-10 ea. $15-18* ea.

•Snoopy poses like a disco dancer on a yellow skateboard.

•Woodstock rides in his nest on a red skateboard.

•Snoopy, as the Flying Ace, sits on a blue skateboard.

(Not pictured):

•Snoopy, as Joe Cool, rides on a red skateboard.

•Snoopy, smiling and wearing shorts, on a green skateboard.

•Charlie Brown, in a red baseball cap, on a red skateboard.

203. Toy

•"Snoopy Mini Skateboard." Snoopy and Woodstock sit on a blue skateboard. Plastic. #752, Aviva. 1977. $5-7 $12-15*

Toys

"Snoopy Free Wheeling Action Mini Skateboard." The characters ride skateboards with their names on them. Packaged in a set of four. Also sold individually as shown above to the left. Plastic. #754, Aviva. 1977. $5-7 Set: $40-45*

•Woodstock rides in his nest on a blue skateboard.

•Snoopy, as the Flying Ace, sits on a yellow skateboard.

•Charlie Brown, wearing a red baseball cap, rides on a yellow skateboard.

•Snoopy and Woodstock sit on a blue skateboard.

204. Toy

"Snoopy And Friend On Skateboard." The characters ride two and three to a curved skateboard. Individually packaged in boxes and blister cards, and packaged two to a box with trees lining the inside. Plastic. #757, Aviva. 1977. $5-7 ea. $12-18* ea. Twin pack: $20-25* ea.

•Snoopy, as the Flying Ace, sits on the back end of a red skateboard. Woodstock in his nest rides at the front.

•Snoopy, wearing shorts, rides on the back end of a blue skateboard. Woodstock in his nest rides at the front.

•Snoopy as Joe Cool rides on the back end of a yellow skateboard. Woodstock in his nest rides at the front.

•Charlie Brown, in a red baseball cap, rides on the back end of a blue skateboard. Snoopy and Woodstock sit at the front.

•Snoopy, as the Flying Ace, sits on the back end of a yellow skateboard. Charlie Brown sits at the front.

•Charlie Brown, in a red baseball cap, rides on the back end of a red skateboard. Woodstock in his nest rides at the front.

205. Toy

•"Radio Control Snoopy Skateboard." Snoopy, as the Flying Ace, and wearing knee and elbow pads, performs stunts. The pistol-grip remote control enables the skateboard to go forward, reverse, left, and right. Snoopy is jointed and can be posed, but once attached to the skateboard he cannot be removed. Battery-operated. #6060, Matchbox. 1988. Assembled with remote: $85-100 Assembled, missing remote: $40-50 $175-250*

206. Toy

"Woodstock Wheelies" and "Snoopy Wheelies." The characters ride friction-powered scooters. Plastic. #777, Aviva/Hasbro. 1979. $8-10 ea. $20-30* ea.

•Woodstock, wearing a green hat, rides an orange scooter printed "Woodstock" and "Ice Cream."

•Woodstock rides a red scooter printed "Woodstock" and "Scooter."

•Snoopy rides a blue scooter printed "Snoopy" and "Scooter."

•Snoopy, wearing a yellow hat and jacket, rides a green scooter printed "Snoopy" and "Speedy Delivery."

207. Toy

"PEANUTS Motorized Toy." The friction-powered wheels are hidden underneath the characters. Packaged individually (#500) or in a set of three (#503). The packaging is orange with a window. The packaging for the set has the characters' names printed on the box. Plastic. Aviva. 1979. $7-10 ea. $15-20* ea. Set of three: $35-40* ea.

•Woodstock sitting in his nest.

•Charlie Brown.

•Snoopy as the Flying Ace.

208. Toy

"Skediddlers." A wheel attachment to the characters' backs allow them to walk when pushed. They are packaged in boxes with windows. Their names and pictures are printed on the box. Other characters also appear on the boxes. Printed on the box: "I Walk! Watch Me Move Along!" Rubber. 1969. $20-25 ea. $40-50* ea.

•Lucy wears a blue dress. #3631.

•Snoopy as the Flying Ace. #3630.

•Charlie Brown wears a yellow shirt with a black zigzag. #3632.

•Linus wears a red and white striped shirt and holds his blue blanket. #3634.

209. Toys

•"Charlie Brown Balance Bar." Charlie Brown, standing on a blue pedestal, balances Snoopy and Woodstock, who sit in red swings on each end of the balance bar. Plastic. #150, Aviva. 1979. $10-20 $25-30*

208

206

207

209

210

The PEANUTS Home Collection

•"Snoopy Balance Bar." Snoopy, standing on a blue pedestal, balances Lucy and Charlie Brown, who sit in swings on each end of the balance bar. Plastic. #155, Aviva. 1979. $10-20 $25-30*

210. Balance Toys

The characters are on one side of a balance bar that has a counter-balance weight on the other side. A pointed extension from the middle of the bar is placed on the red pedestal to allow the toy to balance and revolve on the pedestal. Plastic. Series #555 (blister packed) or #560 (boxed), Aviva/Hasbro. 1980. $15-20 ea. Blister: $22-25* Box: $30-35* ea.

•"Snoopy & Woodstock on Skis." Snoopy is on blue skis with Woodstock sitting on the tip. They both wear red stocking caps.

•"Snoopy & Woodstock Scouting." Snoopy with Woodstock and his friends behind him in a row wear green scout hats.

•"Snoopy Biplane." Snoopy, as the Flying Ace, pilots a red and yellow plane.

•"Snoopy & Woodstock On Dog House." Snoopy lies on top of his doghouse with Woodstock sitting on his tummy.

211

•"Charlie Brown & Woodstock on Skis." Charlie Brown is on red skis with Woodstock sitting on the tip. They both wear red stocking caps. (Not pictured)

211. Toy

"Snoopy Gyroscope." The characters sit on top of a sphere. When the attached cord is pulled all the way out, the gyroscope spins. Place it on its stand or bal-

ance it anywhere. Comes in a blue and yellow window box. Plastic. Style #400, Aviva. 1979. $8-12 ea. $18-22* ea.

•"Snoopy Gyroscope Featuring Snoopy." Snoopy sits on a red and yellow gyroscope with a yellow base.

•"Snoopy Gyroscope Featuring Woodstock." Woodstock sits on a red and blue gyroscope with a red base.

•"Snoopy Gyroscope Featuring Charlie Brown." Charlie Brown sits on a red and yellow gyroscope with a yellow base. (Not pictured)

212. Parachute Toy

The characters are attached to parachutes which display their individual pictures and their names. The blister card is printed "Snoopy, World's Greatest Paratrooper." Styrene characters and plastic parachute. Style #666, Aviva. 1977. $20-25** ea.

•Snoopy as the Flying Ace.

•Charlie Brown.

•Woodstock.

•Snoopy wearing a parachute harness. (Not pictured)

213. Toy

"Snoopy Action Toy." Plastic. #200, Aviva. 1977. $10-15 ea. $20-30* ea.

•"Snoopy Action Toy Starring Snoopy." Snoopy stands on a base holding a hockey stick. Press his helmet, and he hits the hockey puck.

•"Snoopy Action Toy Starring Snoopy." Snoopy stands on a base. Press his helmet, and he kicks the football.

•"Snoopy Action Toy Starring Charlie Brown." Charlie Brown is seen standing on a base, holding a baseball bat. Press his cap, and he hits the baseball which is perched on a stand on the base.

214. Toy

"Snoopy Wind Up Action Toy." Snoopy, standing on a green base, performs various actions when he is wound with a yellow key. Plastic. Aviva. 1977.

•"Snoopy The Drummer." Snoopy hits the drum when the toy is wound. Woodstock stands on the edge of the drum. #833. $15-20 $40-50*

•"Snoopy The Champ." Snoopy hits a punching bag when the toy is wound. Woodstock sits on top of the punching bag. #836. $15-20 $40-50*

212

213

214

•"Snoopy The World's Greatest Chef." Snoopy flips eggs in the frying pan he holds over a stove when the toy is wound. #835. $8-12 $30-40*

215. Toy

"Snoopy Pop-Up Toys." When the side of Snoopy's doghouse is pressed, the roof pops open to reveal the characters in different poses. In 1979, the inside of the doghouse was yellow and the roof identified the character inside by name. In 1980, the inside of the doghouse was blue and the roof identified the character inside by name and picture, and the package graphics were changed slightly. Plastic. #100—sold loose in a counter display. #111—sold individually packaged. Aviva. $5-10 ea. $10-15* ea.

•Woodstock is sitting in his nest.

•Snoopy is taking a bubble bath.

•Charlie Brown is lying in a hammock.

•Snoopy is sitting with a plate with a bone on it in his lap.

216. Toy

215

216

217

"Snoopy Walkers." The characters walk when wound. Plastic. Walkers were produced from 1976 to 1983 with new designs added periodically. Walkers came loose or packaged individually in blister cards or boxes. Graphics on the packaging were restyled periodically.

•Woodstock wears an Indian feather headband. 3-1/2"H. $8-10

•Woodstock wears a red stocking cap. 3-1/2"H. $8-10

•Belle. 3"H. $4-6

•Snoopy wears a red stocking cap. 3-1/2"H. $8-10

•Snoopy. 3"H. $4-5

•Snoopy as Joe Cool. 4-1/4"H. $8-10*

•Snoopy as Joe Cool. 3"H. $6-8

•Snoopy as a tennis player. 3"H. $6-8

•Snoopy as a football player. 3"H. $6-8

•Snoopy as the Flying Ace. 3"H. $6-8

•Snoopy as a bullfighter. 3"H. $8-10

•Snoopy as a sheriff. 3"H. $6-8

•Snoopy wears a top hat and tuxedo. 3-1/2"H. $6-8

(Not pictured):

•Woodstock holding a pink flower. $6-10

217. Toys

•"Chirping Woodstock Electronic." By maneuvering Woodstock's tail, five different bird calls can be heard. Battery-operated. Plastic. #477, Aviva. 1980. $12-15 $35-40*

•"Woodstock Climbing String Action." Pull the string, and Woodstock climbs up and down the string, chirping and flapping his wings. Plastic. #667, Aviva. 1977. $8-10 $25-35*

•"Chirping Woodstock." Woodstock, with feather wings, chirps and bounces on a 36" coil spring. Battery-operated. Plastic. #115, Determined Productions. 1973. $12-15 $35-40*

218. Toys

•"Snoopy Jump For Joy." A jointed Snoopy with floppy ears bounces on a 6" coil spring. Plastic. 5"H. #4505, Determined Productions. Late 1970s. $8-10*

•"Woodstock Jump For Joy." Woodstock, with jointed legs, bounces on a 6" coil spring. Plastic. 4-1/2"H. #4506, Determined Productions. Late 1970s. $8-10*

See Aviva sidebar on page 282 for a discussion of the difference between toys manufactured by International Trading and Aviva.

218

219. Toys

International Trading Technology. 1989.

"Snoopy Free Wheeling Action Die Cast Vehicle." Set of three vehicles. Metal. 2-1/8"L. $6-8 ea. Set: $15-18*

•Snoopy drives a green tank.

•Snoopy, wearing a green scout hat, drives a car with Woodstock and his friends as passengers.

•Snoopy drives a yellow truck printed "Snoopy Towing."

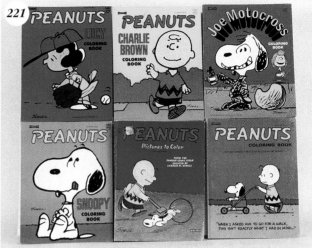

"Snoopy Mini Walkers." Set of three walkers. Plastic. #230. $5-7 Set: $12-14*

• Snoopy wears a top hat and tuxedo.

• Woodstock holding a green flower.

• Snoopy as the Flying Ace.

• "Snoopy Skateboard With Freewheeling Action." Snoopy, as Joe Cool, rides a skateboard printed "Snoopy." Plastic. 4" x 2". #550. $5-7*

• "Snoopy Die Cast Vehicle." Snoopy drives a blue ice cream truck. Metal. 2-1/2" x 2". #1010. $6-8*

• "Snoopy Wind-Up Train." Three-piece set includes a locomotive and two cars. All are red and white. Snoopy is in the cab of the locomotive. Woodstock in his nest sits on top of the next car with Snoopy and Woodstock as passengers looking out the window. The last car is Snoopy's doghouse with Snoopy lying on top. Plastic. 10-1/2"L. #711. $8-10 $15-20*

• "Snoopy Shape Clock." The center of the clock features Snoopy on his doghouse, lying on his tummy and looking over the edge of the roof. The hands of the clock are on the doghouse. The clock's numbers are printed on removable geometric shapes. Plastic. 9" x 11". $7-9*

RAINY DAY FUN

220. Coloring Books

Paper. Saalfield.

• "PEANUTS Pictures To Color." Snoopy hugs Charlie Brown. Small drawings of Lucy, Linus, Patty, Schroeder, and Violet appear around them. #4523. 1959. $40-50

• "PEANUTS Coloring Book Featuring Linus." Linus holds a triple scoop ice cream cone as Charlie Brown stands nearby. Printed: "There are times when life is pure joy." #4594. 1970. $18-25

• "PEANUTS Coloring Book Featuring Linus." A four-panel comic strip features Linus and Lucy playing tic-tac-toe. #9511. 1967. $30-40

• "PEANUTS Coloring Book Featuring Snoopy." Snoopy, as the Flying Ace, sits on top of his doghouse, which is being carried by Charlie Brown and Lucy. #9574. 1967. $30-40

• "PEANUTS Pictures To Color." As Lucy and Charlie Brown look on, Snoopy, sitting in a train car behind a locomotive, is about to enter a tunnel which is too small for him. #5626. 1959. $40-50

• "PEANUTS A Book To Color." Snoopy and Charlie Brown, wearing baseball caps, ride a skateboard. The coloring book has an irregular shaped cover and pages which follow Charlie Brown's outline—#4629. It also came with a straight-edged cover and pages—#4549. 1965. Irregular— $40-45 Straight—$35-40

221. Coloring Books

Paper. Saalfield.

• "PEANUTS Lucy Coloring Book." Lucy, wearing a baseball hat and glove, bends down to catch a ball that has just rolled by. #A1865. 1972. $18-25

• "PEANUTS Charlie Brown Coloring Book." Charlie Brown walks along a path waving. #A1851. 1972. $18-25

• "Joe Motocross Coloring Book." A disheveled, shaking Snoopy, his helmet on the ground, holds a trophy while Peppermint Patty claps in the background. #A1815. 1976. $18-22

• "PEANUTS Snoopy Coloring Book." Snoopy is sitting, holding his hands together and licking his lips. #A1852. 1972. $18-22

• "PEANUTS Pictures To Color." Charlie Brown rolls a hoop with a stick while Snoopy jumps through it. #A5331. 1960. $40-45

• "PEANUTS Coloring Book." Charlie Brown is pushing Snoopy in a purple stroller. Printed: "When I asked him to go for a walk, this isn't exactly what I had in mind." #5695. 1969. $35-40

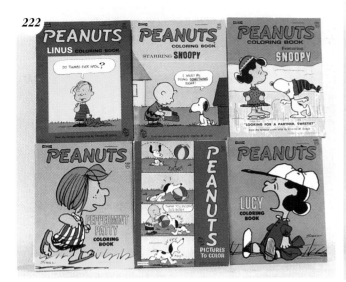

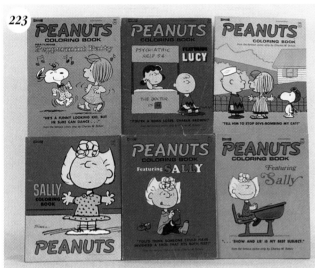

222. Coloring Books

Paper. Saalfield.

•"PEANUTS Linus Coloring Book." Linus, holding his blanket and looking at his thumb, says, "Do thumbs ever spoil?" #4563. 1968. $30-40

•"PEANUTS Coloring Book Starring Snoopy." Charlie Brown is putting two supper dishes down in front of Snoopy who is thinking, "I must be doing something right!" #4561. 1968. $30-40

•"PEANUTS Coloring Book Featuring Snoopy." Lucy, wearing skates, stands on the ice as Snoopy, wearing a stocking cap, glides up to her. Printed: "Looking for a partner, Sweetie?" #C0942. 1970. $25-30

•"PEANUTS Peppermint Patty Coloring Book." Peppermint, wearing a red and white striped shirt and sandals, is running. #A1836. 1972. $25-30

•"PEANUTS Pictures To Color." A four-panel comic strip featuring Snoopy, Charlie Brown, and a beach ball is on the cover. #5629. 1968. $35-40

•"PEANUTS Lucy Coloring Book." Lucy, wearing a purple dress and white baseball cap, is sitting on the ground and shouting. #A1853. 1972. $18-22

223. Coloring Books

Paper. Saalfield. $20-25 ea.

•"PEANUTS Coloring Book Featuring Peppermint Patty." Snoopy and Peppermint Patty are disco dancing. Printed: "He's a funny looking kid, but he sure can dance..." #3695. 1971.

•"PEANUTS Coloring Book Featuring Lucy." Charlie Brown sits in front of Lucy and her psychiatrist booth. Printed: "You're a born loser, Charlie Brown." #4648. 1971.

•"PEANUTS Coloring Book." Peppermint Patty talks to Charlie Brown, while Snoopy, as the Flying Ace, stands nearby. Printed: "Tell him to stop dive-bombing my cat!" #3996. 1970.

•"PEANUTS Sally Coloring Book." Sally, wearing a yellow dress with black polka dots, stands with her arms outstretched. #A1835. 1972.

•"PEANUTS Coloring Book Featuring Sally." Sally sits on the ground trying to put on her shoes. Printed: "You'd think someone could have invented a shoe that fits both feet." #4651. 1972.

•"PEANUTS Coloring Book Featuring Sally." A smiling Sally sits at her school desk. Printed: "'Show and Lie' is my best subject." #3966. 1971.

224. Coloring Books

•"Parade Of The Comics." Charlie Brown's face appears on the cover along with the faces of 14 other comic book characters. Thirty-three artists contributed to the coloring book. There are four PEANUTS pictures to color inside. Paper. #4644, Artcraft. 1966. $40-50

•"PEANUTS 'Great Pumpkin' Coloring Book." Snoopy and Linus are sitting in a pumpkin patch. Paper. #100HPF901-6, Hallmark. 1978. $20-22

•"PEANUTS Coloring Book For Preschoolers." Snoopy, holding a bouquet of balloons, looks at Woodstock. The coloring book includes 48 stickers that match each page. Paper. #125PF121-5, Hallmark. 1976. $30-35

•"PEANUTS Coloring Book." Charlie Brown is talking to Snoopy, Linus, and Shermy. A baseball bat, glove, and ball are on the ground in front of them. Printed: "Winning is everything... losing isn't anything." Paper. #3995, Saalfield. 1970. $30-40

• "PEANUTS Coloring Book Featuring Lucy." Charlie Brown lies dazed on the sidewalk as Lucy walks away holding a football. Printed: "No one's perfect, Charlie Brown." Paper. #3993, Saalfield. 1970. $30-40

225. Coloring Book Sets

"PEANUTS Trace And Color." Set of five trace and color books comes packaged in a box featuring Charlie Brown talking to a disheveled Snoopy. Printed: "Never pick a fight with a hundred pound cat!" Paper. #6122, Saalfield. Late 1960s. $45-55**

Pictured Trace And Color Set titles:

• "Snoopy The Head Beagle." Snoopy leans on a croquet mallet.

• "Lucy Does It Again." Charlie Brown tries to find change to buy 'GOOP' from Lucy for 5¢.

• "Peppermint Patty's Busy Day." Peppermint Patty, wearing a baseball cap, carries a bat and glove over her shoulder as Snoopy, wearing a glove and cap, walks behind her.

• "Linus Looks At The World." Linus, standing, holds his blanket.

• "Sally's School Days." Sally, standing, wears a pink dress.

"PEANUTS Coloring Books." Set of five coloring books comes packaged in a box (pictured) featuring Charlie Brown and Schroeder on the pitcher's mound, and Lucy, Snoopy, and Peppermint Patty walking by. All the characters are dressed in baseball gear. Paper. #6546, Saalfield. 1970. $45-55**

Individual titles included in set (not pictured):

• "Let's Play Ball." Charlie Brown and Schroeder are on the pitcher's mound. Lucy, Snoopy, and Peppermint Patty walk

by. All the characters are dressed in baseball gear. #4574.

• "Life Is Difficult, Charlie Brown." Charlie Brown, tangled in his kite string, stuck in a tree, thinks, "Good Grief!" Snoopy watches with his ears standing up straight. #4560.

• Peppermint Patty talks to Charlie Brown while Snoopy, as the Flying Ace, stands nearby. Printed: "Tell him to stop dive-bombing my cat!" #4596.

• "Typically Lucy." Lucy says to Linus, "Why shouldn't I complain?" #4562.

• The cover features Snoopy lying on his doghouse, Lucy, Charlie Brown, and Linus sucking his thumb. #4564.

226. Coloring Books

"The Colorful World of Snoopy, Linus, Schroeder, Lucy, and Charlie Brown." The green and orange cover has miniature pictures of the characters in the bottom of the word "Snoopy." Paper. Determined Productions. 1969.

• Large Coloring Book. Each page has a story told in panels, reminiscent of a Sunday strip. 19-1/2"H x 14"W. $35-45

• Small Coloring Book. Each page features a one-frame picture with a caption. 12-1/2"H x 10"W. $25-35

227. Toys

• "What's On Sale, Snoopy? Colorforms Set." Snoopy, wearing a grocer's apron, is pictured ringing up groceries on a cash register. Cardboard and plastic. #755, Colorforms, Inc. 1974. $20-30**

• "Hit The Ball, Charlie Brown! Colorforms Set." Charlie Brown swings a baseball bat as Linus and Lucy, wearing baseball caps and gloves, stand in the background. Cardboard and plastic. #750, Colorforms, Inc. 1972. $20-35**

• "Snoopy & Woodstock Play Set." Snoopy rides a skateboard and Woodstock rides a bicycle. Cardboard and plastic. #760, Colorforms Inc. 1981. $20-25**

228. Toys

• "Hold That Line, Charlie Brown! Colorforms Set." Charlie Brown, wearing a helmet, runs with a football tucked under his arm. Lucy, dressed as a cheerleader, roots for him in the background. Cardboard and plastic. #753, Colorforms, Inc. 1974. $20-30**

• "Carry On, Nurse Lucy! Colorforms Set." Lucy, dressed as a nurse, examines Woodstock with her stethoscope. Cardboard and plastic. #754, Colorforms, Inc. 1972. $20-35**

• "How's The Weather, Lucy? Colorforms Set." Lucy, wearing a rain slicker and hat, holds an umbrella. She stands near a window where Woodstock sits in a tree in the rain on the other side. Cardboard and plastic. #752, Colorforms, Inc. 1972. $20-35**

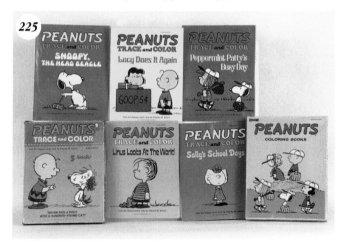

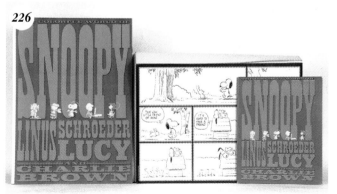

228

231

232

229

233

234

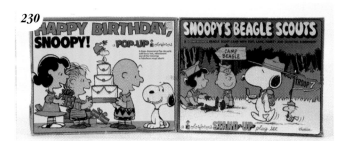

230

235

229. Toys

•"Snoopy How's The Weather? Dress-Up Set." Snoopy and Woodstock dance under umbrellas. The pieces for outfits worn in different kinds of weather are shown on the box. Cardboard and plastic. #2362, Colorforms, Inc. 1981. $30-40**

•"Let's Go To The Beach, Snoopy! Colorforms Set." Snoopy and Woodstock, sharing a surfboard, ride a wave. Lucy and Charlie Brown sit under a large umbrella on the beach. Cardboard and plastic. #7401, Colorforms, Inc. 1973. $35-40**

230. Toys

•"Happy Birthday, Snoopy! Pop-Up Colorforms." Lucy, holding a present, and Linus and Charlie Brown, holding a birthday cake with Woodstock on top, approach Snoopy, who is sitting with a big grin on his face. Cardboard and plastic. #4701, Colorforms, Inc. 1974. $35-40**

•"Snoopy's Beagle Scouts Stand-Up Play Set." Lucy and Charlie Brown, dressed in scout gear, light a fire as Snoopy, looking at a compass and wearing a backpack, and Woodstock, holding a "Troop 7" banner, go hiking. Cardboard and plastic. #4108, Colorforms, Inc. 1975. $30-40**

231. Toy

•"Lucy's Winter Carnival Colorforms Set." Charlie Brown, Lucy, and Snoopy, all dressed in winter clothes, are ice-skating on a lake in front of a snow-covered hill. Cardboard and plastic. #7400, Colorforms, Inc. 1972. $35-40**

232. Toy

•"Star Snoopy." Snoopy wears a space helmet and holds a light saber as Woodstock approaches in a spaceship. Cardboard and plastic. 16" x 12-1/2". #2358, Colorforms, Inc. 1979. $45-55**

233. Toy

•"PEANUTS Play Set." Snoopy and Woodstock stand on Snoopy's doghouse. A rainbow is behind them. Charlie Brown and Lucy stand on each side of the doghouse. Cardboard and plastic. 15-1/2" x 12-1/2". #8110, Colorforms, Inc. 1980. $25-30**

234. Toy

•"Batter-Up, Snoopy! Play Set." Snoopy swings a baseball bat. Woodstock appears to be running to catch the ball. Cardboard and plastic. #304, Colorforms, Inc. 1979. $25-30**

•"You're A Pal, Snoopy! Colorforms Set." Charlie Brown, sitting on his knees, hugs Snoopy. Cardboard and plastic. #758, Colorforms, Inc. 1977. $20-30**

235. Toys

•"Yankee Doodle Snoopy Colorforms Set." Snoopy, wearing a tri-cornered hat with a feather in it, holds an American flag. Woodstock holds an Uncle Sam hat. Cardboard and plastic. #756, Colorforms, Inc. 1975. $20-30**

•"Disco Snoopy Colorforms Set." Woodstock and Snoopy dance in front of a large pink circle surrounded by twinkling stars. Cardboard and plastic. #759, Colorforms, Inc. 1979. $20-25**

236

238

237

•"Come Home, Snoopy! Colorforms Set." Snoopy, carrying a hobo pack over his shoulder, walks in front of his doghouse. His supper dish, with Woodstock in it, is in Snoopy's mouth. Cardboard and plastic. #751, Colorforms, Inc. 1980. $15-25**

236. Toy

•"Tell Us A Riddle, Snoopy! Snoopy's Fantastic Riddle Machine!" Snoopy stands in the center holding a pointer surrounded by Lucy, Woodstock, Charlie Brown, and Linus. #2397, Colorforms, Inc. 1974. $55-65**

237. Toy

"Kaleidoscopes." Images are created by turning the cylinder, and are viewed by looking through an opening at one end. Cardboard. $15-25 ea.

•Snoopy is shown in various poses around the blue kaleidoscope. 9"H. #88030, Willitts Designs. 1987.

•Snoopy and Woodstock dance around the multicolored kaleidoscope printed "Snoopy Disco." #4961, Determined Productions. 1979.

•Lucy, Linus, Sally, Charlie Brown, Marcie, Peppermint Patty, Snoopy, and Woodstock play around the kaleidoscope in a green field with a rainbow. 8-3/4"H. #200PF500-2, Hallmark. 1977.

238. Toy Accessories

•"Lite-Brite Picture Refill Featuring Snoopy." Snoopy dancing, Lucy, Charlie Brown, Woodstock, and Peppermint Patty are pictured above a Lite-Brite image of Snoopy. The set includes 12 Lite-Brite pictures and 24 guide sheets. #5479, Hasbro. 1984. $15-20**

•"Lite-Brite Pictures & Pegs Accessory Pack Another PEANUTS Toy Featuring Snoopy." Charlie Brown, holding a magnet, and Snoopy and Woodstock, being pulled toward him, are pictured. A Lite-Brite image of Snoopy and Woodstock is also on the box. The set includes 12 Lite-Brite pictures and 240 pegs. #5471, Hasbro. 1981. $25-30**

239. Door Knob Caddies

•"PEANUTS Artist Door Knob Caddy." The blue caddy with red trim comes with art supplies in its pockets. The white pockets have comic strips printed on them. Cotton. 21"H x 12"W. #Y-11, Simon Simple. 1969-1970. $25-30

•"PEANUTS Desk Caddy." Appliqués of Snoopy sitting at his typewriter, Woodstock on a pink pocket, pencil, and a white pocket with a comic strip on it, decorate this blue caddy. The words "Pencil," "Ruler," "Pad," and "Stationery" surround the pink pocket and the pencil. Felt and cotton. 29"H x 11-1/2"W. Simon Simple. 1973. $20-35.

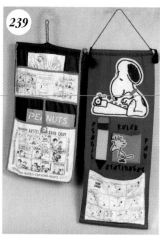

239

240. Toys

•"Snoopy Tennis Game & Watch." Hand-held electronic game of Snoopy playing tennis. The silver box shows the toy and is printed "Wide Screen." Battery-operated. Plastic. 4-1/2" x 3 1/2". #6000, Nintendo. 1983. $25-32 $40-50*

•"Snoopy Table Top Game & Watch." Electronic game. As Schroeder plays his piano, Snoopy tries to hit the notes with a hammer so the music doesn't wake up Woodstock. The orange box shows the toy, and pictures Snoopy, standing on his doghouse, hammering musical notes while Woodstock sits in his nest on a branch. Battery-operated. #SM-73, Nintendo. 1983. $75-95 $155-160*

240

Seated on the wicker chairs, and holding fans from Japan, are Spike and Belle (United States. See Playroom chapter for lists of plush toys and plush clothes sizes). Two vases, one from Hong Kong and one from Japan, are on the table to the left of Spike. On the table between the chairs, from left to right, is a vase, a planter, and another vase—all from Japan.

In the back are two roll-up shades bought in Italy. One depicts the PEANUTS gang on a boat, passing the Statue of Liberty. The other shows Snoopy serving something to the characters who are seated around a large table. Pizza pie and root beer, no doubt!

The Sunroom

Since the sun porch is used mostly in the summer, it follows that the room has a lot of sunlight and warmth—ideal for growing—which is why we keep our planters out there. But to help us deal with the sun, we also need fans and window blinds—all adorned with PEANUTS characters, of course!

HAND FANS AND BLINDS

1. Fan

• Sally, wearing a blue dress and looking frazzled, is sitting with a ball and jacks in front of her. She says, "Thought for the summer." On the reverse side Sally says, "Never play jacks on a hot sidewalk!" Cardboard fan, wood handle. 8-3/4"W x 9-1/4"H. #100S1P202-4, Springbok. 1974. $12-15

2. Poster Blind

• Snoopy, as the Flying Ace, is sitting on top of his doghouse thinking, "Up and at 'em!!" on a light blue rice paper background. Wood slats and metal hardware. 30"W x 72"H. Determined Productions exclusively for JC Penney, Catalog #736-2221C. 1986. $55-65

PLANTERS

3. Planters

Ceramic. Determined Productions. Mid-1970s.

• Snoopy, wearing a Santa hat, leans against a chimney decorated with a wreath. 7-1/2"H. #1106. $60-65

• Snoopy, dressed as Santa, sits with a gift bag with a red bow around it. Woodstock sits next to the gift bag. 4"H. $50-55

• Snoopy, wearing a Santa hat, leans against a cylindrical planter printed "Merry Christmas." 4-1/2"H. #1117. $35-40

• Snoopy, wearing a Santa hat, sits on the front of a sleigh; Woodstock sits on the back. 4-1/2H" x 5"L. #1529. $60-65

4. Planters

• Snoopy, standing on a stage with a red curtain, is wearing a bow tie and striped jacket. He holds a straw hat in one hand

and a bouquet of flowers, which he is giving to Woodstock. Ceramic. 4-1/4". Determined Productions. Mid-1970s. $45-50

• Snoopy, as Joe Cool, wearing an orange sweater and sunglasses, is raised from the surface of the planter against a rainbow background. Ceramic. 4-1/4". Determined Productions. Mid-1970s. $45-50

5. Planters

Ceramic. Determined Productions. Mid-1970s.

• Snoopy is sitting. The cylindrical planter comes out of Snoopy's back. 5"H. #1118. $35-42

• Snoopy and Woodstock sit against the doorway of the doghouse. The roof is open. Printed: "Snoopy." 3-1/2"H x 5"W x 5-1/2"D. $60-65

•Snoopy, wearing a red and green award ribbon printed "Hero," is raised from the surface of the star-shaped yellow planter. 4-1/4"H. #1126. $45-50

6. Planters

Snoopy is lying on top of his doghouse, which has an opening in one side of the roof. Available in three sizes. Ceramic. Determined Productions. Mid-1970s.

•Large. 7-3/4"H. #1103. $40-45

•Medium. 6-1/4"H. #1111. $35-40

•Small. 4-3/4"H. #1113. $22-30

7. Planters

Ceramic. Determined Productions. Mid-1970s.

•Snoopy is leaning against a cylindrical planter with "Snoopy" printed on the planter. 6-3/4"H. #1105. $60-65

•Snoopy is leaning against a cylindrical planter with "Snoopy" raised on the surface of the planter. 4-1/4"H. #1115. $42-48

8. Planters

Ceramic. Determined Productions. Mid-1970s.

•The cradle-shaped planter features Woodstock flying and holding Snoopy, lying on his tummy, in a blanket. Woodstock's

friends fly in a row up to Snoopy's nose. Image appears on both sides of cradle. 2-1/2"H x 3"W x 3-1/2"D. #1293. $50-55

•Snoopy and Woodstock are featured in scenes around the drum-shaped planter. 3"H x 4" diam. #1292. $40-45

•Snoopy is featured on each side of the block-shaped planter with an object representing a letter of the alphabet —A, B, C, and D. 3"H. #1291. $38-42

9. Planters

Ceramic. Determined Productions.

•Snoopy pushes a baby carriage as Woodstock flies in front of him on the baby-shoe planter. The reverse side features Woodstock in the baby carriage. The shoe is trimmed around the bottom with flowers. Available with blue or pink laces. 3-1/2"H. #1290. Mid-1970s. $45-48

•"Baby's First Cup." The mug-shaped planter features Woodstock flying and holding Snoopy, lying on his tummy, in a blanket. Woodstock's friends fly in a row on the reverse side. 2-1/4"H. #3696. Early 1980s. $12-14

•"Riding High Mug." The mug-shaped planter features Woodstock flying and carrying Snoopy, who is cradled in a blanket. Woodstock's friends fly in a row on the reverse side. 3-1/4"H. 1977. $15-17

10. Planters

Ceramic. Determined Productions. Mid-1970s.

•Snoopy, leaning against a basket-shaped planter, is holding a flower. 4-1/2"H. $60-65

•Snoopy lies on the handle of the basket-shaped planter which has the look of being woven. 5-3/4"H. #1120. $60-65

•Woodstock is looking over the edge of the basket-shaped planter. 4-1/2"H. $60-65

11. Planters

Ceramic. 2"H. Determined Productions. Mid-1970s. $17-24 ea.

•Woodstock gives a flower to Snoopy, who is wearing a green and red award ribbon printed "Hero." Printed: "I'm Not Perfect, But I'm Pretty Perfect!"

•Snoopy, sitting on the ground, is surrounded by red, yellow, and orange flowers and butterflies. Kidney-shaped. #1917.

12. Planters

Ceramic. 3-1/2"W x 4-3/4"D. Determined Productions. Mid-1970s. $45-55 ea.

•Snoopy, wearing an apron and gloves, waters flowers with a watering can as Woodstock flies above. Printed: "Jardinier." The reverse side features Woodstock sitting on Snoopy's head and holding a flower. Also printed: "Jardinier." #1210.

•Woodstock holds long-stemmed red flowers as butterflies fly nearby. The reverse side features Snoopy pushing an umbrella-covered flower cart. #1122.

13. Planters

Ceramic. 4-1/2"W x 2-1/4"D. Determined Productions. Mid-1970s. $17-24 ea.

•Snoopy, posing with different flowers, and Woodstock alternate on the eight-sided planter. #1525.

•Snoopy and Woodstock are featured in scenes with flowers on every other side of the eight-sided planter. #1197.

14. Planters with Saucers

Ceramic. Determined Productions. Mid-1970s.

•Snoopy is sitting and hugging Woodstock among flowers and surrounded by hearts. Printed on the reverse side in a thought balloon: "Surprise a friend with a hug." Planter: 3-1/4"H. Saucer: 3-3/4" diam. #1195. $45-50

•Woodstock is holding a bouquet of long-stemmed flowers. The reverse side features Snoopy sitting with his hands outstretched. Planter: 3"H x 2" diam. Saucer: 4" diam. #1196. $30-35

15. Planters

Ceramic. Series #1190, Determined Productions. Mid-1970s. Set: $50-60

•Snoopy and Woodstock are sitting and holding long-stemmed flowers. 2-1/2"H. $20-22

•Snoopy is sitting and hugging Woodstock among flowers and surrounded by hearts. 3-1/4"H. $25-30

•Snoopy dances among the flowers as Woodstock flies nearby. 2"H. $18-20

16. Planters

Ceramic. Determined Productions. Mid-1970s.

•Woodstock is giving a bouquet of long-stemmed flowers to Snoopy, sitting with his hands outstretched on the watering can-shaped planter. 4-3/4"H. #1123. $45-50

•Snoopy, wearing an apron and gloves, waters flowers with a watering can as Woodstock flies above on the watering can-shaped planter. The planter comes with three miniature gardening tools. 3"H. #1119. $55-60

17. Mini Planters with Wire Handles

Ceramic. Determined Productions. Mid-1970s.

•Snoopy, sitting on top of his name, reaches back to touch a flower on the tea pot-shaped planter. 2-3/4"H. $15-20

•Snoopy, with his hands over his heart, looks at yellow flow-

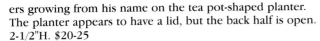

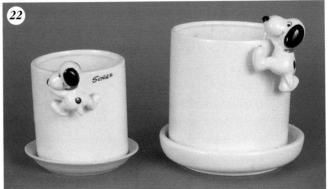

ers growing from his name on the tea pot-shaped planter. The planter appears to have a lid, but the back half is open. 2-1/2"H. $20-25

• Snoopy, standing on his name, is surrounded by an arch of flowers on the milk can-shaped planter. The planter appears to have a lid, but the back half is open. 3"H. $20-25

18. Mini Planters with Wire Handles

Ceramic. 3"H. Determined Productions. Mid-1970s. $15-20 ea.

• Snoopy, lying atop his name, sniffs a flower on the kettle-shaped planter.

• Snoopy stands on his name next to a large red tulip on the bucket-shaped planter.

• Snoopy lies on top of his doghouse over his name with two yellow flowers growing alongside on the pitcher-shaped planter.

19. Planters

Ceramic. Determined Productions. Mid-1970s. $20-25 ea.

• Snoopy, raised from the surface of the planter, sits under a long-stemmed yellow flower which curves over his head. 3-3/4"H. #1194.

• Snoopy and Woodstock dance around the bucket-shaped planter with wire handle. "Flowers" is printed in red and pink letters. 4-3/4"H. #1209.

• Snoopy and Woodstock sit against a haystack with a rake in it on the milk can-shaped planter. 4-3/4"H.

20. Planters

Ceramic. Determined Productions. Mid-1970s.

• Snoopy is featured in various poses with a slice of watermelon, a pineapple, a banana, and a strawberry on the sides of the square planter. 3"H. #1763. $44-48

• Snoopy, holding a green flag with a heart on it, is surrounded by Woodstock and his friends on a planter shaped like a tote bag. 4-3/4"H. $44-48

• Snoopy stands in front of a book case with several books at his feet on one side of the book-shaped planter. The other side is printed: "Ah! Here it is! 'A Beagle's Blooming Garden Guide'!" 3-1/2"H x 5"W. #1278. $40-44

21. Planters

Ceramic. Determined Productions. Mid-1970s.

• Snoopy, with his back arched, forms the handle of the cylindrical planter. 4"H. $55-60

• Snoopy, wearing an award ribbon printed "Hero," is standing. Ceramic. 7"H. #1127, Determined Productions. Mid-1970s. $50-55

• Snoopy lies on the top half of the handle of the cylindrical planter. 3-1/2"H. $50-55

22. Planters with Saucers

Snoopy hangs off the edge of the planter, which has an opening on the bottom for drainage. Comes with saucer. Ceramic. Determined Productions. Mid-1970s.

• Small Planter. 3-1/4"H. #1198. $45-50
• Large Planter. 4-1/4"H. #1199. $55-60

23. Planters

Ceramic. Determined Productions. Mid-1970s. $35-40 ea.

• Snoopy, lying on his tummy, looks over the edge of a mail box. Woodstock stands on the side near the door. "U.S." is printed on the side in raised letters and "Mail" is printed on the door. 3-1/4"H. #1528.

• Snoopy lies on top of the red and blue mailbox printed "US Mail" on the sides as well as under Snoopy. The front of the mailbox features the mail pick-up schedule. 3-1/2"H.

24. Planter

• Snoopy, standing with a bouquet of flowers behind his back, looks at Woodstock on the pitcher-shaped planter. Ceramic. 4"H. #1297, Determined Productions. Mid-1970s. $40-45

25. Planters

• Snoopy, dressed in Western gear and holding a lariat, and Woodstock, wearing a feather headband, are featured on the cowboy boot-shaped planter with a handle. Ceramic. 4-3/4"H. Determined Productions. 1980. $50-60

26. Planters

Snoopy, transporting Woodstock on his nose and his supper dish on his head, carries a yellow suitcase in one hand. "Snoopy" is printed on the green supper dish. Ceramic. Determined Productions. Mid-1970s.

• Large Planter. 7-1/2"H. #1102. $30-35
• Small Planter. 4-1/2"H. #1101. $18-22

27. Planters

• Snoopy lies on top of a red heart-shaped planter. "Love" is printed on the heart in raised white letters. Ceramic. 4-1/2"H x 3-1/2"W. #1572, Determined Productions. Mid-1970s. $40-45

• Snoopy lies on top of a gold-tone heart-shaped planter. "Love" is printed on the heart in raised letters. Silver-plated. (Over time this may tarnish beyond cleaning.) 4-1/2"H. #9696, Leonard Silver. 1979. $45-50*

• Snoopy, sitting with Woodstock, is sniffing a flower on a lace-trimmed red heart background. The planter is heart-shaped with legs. Ceramic. 3-1/4"H. Determined Productions. Mid-1970s. $40-45

28. Planters

• Snoopy, raised from the surface of the red heart-shaped planter, is smiling and holding his hands together over his heart. Ceramic. 4"H. Determined Productions. Mid-1970s. $42-45

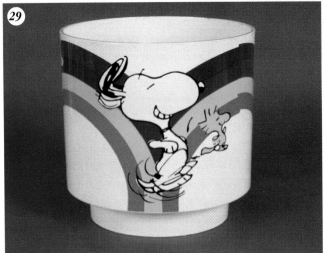

•Snoopy, standing and wearing a red bow tie, is smiling and holding his hands together over his heart, with a red heart-shaped planter behind him. Printed: "I Love You." Ceramic. 5-1/2"W x 5-1/4"H. #8132, Willitts Designs. 1988. $40-45

•Woodstock looks over the top of the red heart-shaped planter at Snoopy, who is below and raised from the surface of the planter, holding a bouquet of yellow flowers. Ceramic. 4"H. #1530, Determined Productions. Mid-1970s. $42-45

29. Planter

•Snoopy and Woodstock are featured in different poses around the planter against a blue, green, yellow, and red rainbow. Plastic. 6-3/4"H. #1274, Determined Productions. Mid-1970s. $25-35

30. Display Poster

•The poster is an advertisement for a Teleflora Valentine's Day bouquet, and features a plush Snoopy sitting on his doghouse. Printed: "Send Snoopy On A Mission Of Love." 1990. $5-7

Planter

•A plush Snoopy, as the Flying Ace, sits on his doghouse, which is the planter. Snoopy, wearing a red scarf and helmet and heart-shaped goggles, can be removed from the doghouse. Plastic. Doghouse: 5-1/2"H. Plush: 6-1/2"H. Teleflora. 1990. $6-8

STAINED GLASS AND WINDOW HANGINGS

31. Stained Glass

Leaded stained glass. Oden. 1980.

•Snoopy, sitting on a yellow crescent moon, is howling. 6"H. #4816. $50-55

•Snoopy, as the Flying Ace, wearing a red scarf and helmet, is walking. 6"H. #4808. $55-60

•Snoopy and Woodstock are sitting back-to-back. 4-1/2"W x 5"D. #4860. $45-50

•Woodstock, sitting in Snoopy's supper dish, smiles as Snoopy rolls his eyes. 5-1/2"W x 4-5/8"D. #4800. $45-50

•Snoopy lies on top of his doghouse, with Woodstock sitting on his tummy. 6-3/4"H. #4822. $45-50

32. Stained Glass

Leaded stained glass. Oden. 1980.

•Snoopy is sitting and holding a blue present. 3-3/4"H. #4809. $38-42

•Snoopy is sitting and holding a red heart. 3-3/4"H. #4818. $38-42

•Snoopy is sitting. 3-3/4"H. #4828. $38-42

•Snoopy, lying on his tummy, looks over the edge of a large red heart. 7-1/2"H. #4820. $50-55

•Snoopy is sitting. 5-3/4"H. #4827. $40-45

•Snoopy is dancing. 8"H. #4812. $50-55

•Snoopy is sitting and holding a red heart. 5-1/2"H. #4810. $45-50

33. Window Hangings

"Snoopy Sunshiners." Plastic. Aviva. Late 1970s. $8-10 ea. $12-15* ea.

• Snoopy, as the Flying Ace, walks past clouds as Woodstock and his friend float in parachutes in the background.

• Snoopy, as Joe Cool wearing sunglasses, stands against a green school locker. Woodstock, also wearing sunglasses, stands on a pile of school books next to Snoopy.

• Snoopy is lying on his tummy on top of a red, yellow, and orange rainbow with Woodstock sitting on his back.

• Woodstock is in his nest in a tree, with Snoopy sitting on the ground leaning against the tree trunk.

• Snoopy lies on top of a large red heart, with Woodstock sitting on his tummy.

34. Window Hangings

Painted glass. 5"W x 7"H. Aviva. 1981. $45-50 ea.

• Snoopy, as the Flying Ace, is sitting on his doghouse in front of a red, yellow, and orange rainbow.

• Snoopy, as Joe Cool wearing sunglasses, stands against a blue and yellow diamond-patterned background. Printed: "Joe Cool."

• Snoopy is walking and carrying a bouquet of balloons as Woodstock flies in front of him holding one balloon.

• Snoopy, wearing a chef's hat and apron, holds a frying pan in one hand and utensils in the other. Salt and pepper shakers are beside him against an orange background.

VASES

35. Vases

Ceramic. 5-1/2"H. Determined Productions. Mid-1970s. $34-38 ea.

• Snoopy, wearing a ski cap and goggles, carries a pair of skis over his shoulder as Woodstock, also wearing a ski cap, follows. The vase has a handle.

• Sally and Linus are walking and holding hands. Printed on the reverse side: "Love Is Walking Hand In Hand." #1573.

36. Vase

• Snoopy looks on as Woodstock gives Harriet a kiss. Printed on the reverse side: "Love Is What It's All About!" Ceramic. 5-1/2"H. Determined Productions. Early 1970s. $60-65

37. Vases

Ceramic. Determined Productions. Mid-1970s.

• Snoopy, kissing Sally on the cheek, thinks, "All girls look forward to their first kiss!" 5-1/2"H. #1218. $34-38

• Snoopy, lying on top of his doghouse, is grinning and kicking his feet in the air. Printed: "It's Hard To Feel Sorry For Yourself When Your Happy." 7-1/4"H. $32-36

• Snoopy, sitting on the ground, holds a flower. Printed: "How nice..." 7-3/4"H. #1281. $25-30

• Snoopy is lying on top of his doghouse with a long-stemmed flower curving over his face. Snoopy thinks, "All right, who planted this flower?" 8-1/2"H. #1283. $60-65

38. Vases

Ceramic. Determined Productions. Mid-1970s.

• Snoopy, sitting on the ground, has a flower inserted in his collar. Woodstock flies nearby. 6-1/2"H. Printed: "I Hate Not Having A Lapel!" $35-38

• Snoopy is lying on his doghouse, with Woodstock in his nest on his tummy. Printed on the reverse side: "This Has Been A Good Day." 5"H. #1128. $32-35

• Snoopy is sitting and sniffing a flower against a yellow background with a floral design. 7-1/4"H. $32-35.

• Snoopy is standing and holding a bouquet of balloons. 6-1/2"H. #1124. $35-38

39. Mini Vases

Ceramic. Approximately 2"H. Determined Productions. Mid-1970s. $24-28 ea.

• Charlie Brown is standing.

• Linus is standing.

• Lucy is walking on a milk can-shaped vase.

• Snoopy kisses Woodstock. Both of them are wearing Hawaiian leis.

• Snoopy, hugging Woodstock, sits between tulips on a milk can-shaped vase.

• Snoopy sits with his hands outstretched in front of a rainbow on a stein-shaped vase.

• Peppermint Patty is standing with her arms outstretched on a stein-shaped vase.

40. Vase

"Snoopy Bud Vase." Snoopy clings to the rim of the base. (This vase can tarnish beyond repair.) Silver-plated. 8"H. #9697, Leonard Silver. 1979. $45-50*

41. Vases

Glass. 31 oz. 6-3/4"H. Anchor Hocking. 1978.

• The vase features four panels with captions and the character's name. Lucy at her psychiatrist booth: "For A Nickel, I Can Cure Anything." Snoopy grinning: "Smile." Charlie Brown: "I Need All The Friends I Can Get." Linus without his blanket: "To Know Me Is To Love Me." $23-30

• Snoopy, standing on one foot, raises a bandaged foot in the air against a yellow and blue checkered background. The image appears on each side of the vase. Printed: "Get Well Soon!" $10-12

• Lucy, Linus, Woodstock, and Snoopy are pictured on one side of the vase, and Charlie Brown, Snoopy, and Sally are on the other side. They are all laughing, against a repeated background of "Hee Hee" and "Ha Ha." $10-12

42. Vases

The image appears on both sides of the vase. Glass. 31 oz. 6-3/4"H. Anchor Hocking. 1978. $10-12 ea.

• Snoopy, dressed in a tuxedo and top hat, gives Woodstock a bouquet of flowers against a light blue background. Printed: "For You, On A Special Day!"

• Snoopy is sitting with his arms outstretched as Woodstock brings him a bouquet of flowers. Depicted on a red and blue background. Printed: "How Nice!"

• Snoopy is dancing as he tosses flowers from a basket against a red background. Woodstock is turned upside down in the air. Printed: "Love Drives Me Crazy!"

42

44

43

45

43. Vases

Glass. 31 oz. 6-3/4"H. Anchor Hocking. 1978. $12-15 ea.

•Snoopy, wearing exercise clothes, and Woodstock stand in front of an instructional exercise sign on a fitness trail. Woodstock's friend sits on top of the sign. Printed on the reverse side: "We Superstars Stay In Shape."

•Snoopy, wearing a cowboy hat, sings and plays the guitar as Woodstock plays the fiddle against a blue background. Printed on the reverse side: "There's A Little Country In All Of Us."

•Snoopy, dressed as a cowboy, is on the ground looking dazed, having just fallen out of the saddle, as Woodstock flies nearby. Printed on the reverse side: "Nothing Is As Easy As It Looks."

44. Vases

The image appears on both sides of the vase. Glass. 31 oz. 6-3/4"H. Anchor Hocking. 1978. $10-15 ea.

•Lucy, Snoopy, and Peppermint Patty look at Woodstock under a blanket in a cradle. Printed: "What A Cutie!"

•Snoopy is sitting and hugging Woodstock against a pink background with small white hearts. Printed: "Gee, Somebody Cares!"

•Woodstock is flying and carrying Snoopy, who is in a blanket and looking behind him. Six of Woodstock's friends fly beneath them. Printed: "Congratulations."

45. Vases

Glass. 31 oz. 6-3/4"H. Anchor Hocking. 1978. $12-15 ea.

•Snoopy and Woodstock, wearing party hats, sit on top of Snoopy's doghouse with a cake between them. Printed on the reverse side: "Happy Birthday!"

•Snoopy, wearing a Santa hat, gives a candy cane to Woodstock, who is standing on a present, against a red background with yellow stars. The image appears on both sides of the vase.

The big red pillow on the top step is from Japan. On the next step down we find Snoopy standing next to the blue striped "cabana," which turns out to be a night light (Italy). The remaining four items are all clocks: Snoopy standing in a shoe (Japan); Snoopy on his house (Japan); Snoopy holding a tennis racket (Japan); and an alarm clock (Germany).

The black pillow (Spain) rests to the left of three clocks from Japan and a fourth clock from Germany. Almost hidden behind the German clock is a wooden Snoopy, holding Woodstock (Japan), which can be manipulated to reveal a mirror. Everything on the next-to-last step is from Japan, except for the colorful radio (third from left), which is from Germany. The remaining items include a picture frame; a night light shaped like a baseball, with Charlie Brown on the top; a Coca-Cola can radio; another picture frame; and two more night lights.

In the front row of the bottom step are five candles, all from Japan, except the middle one, which is from Holland. Behind them are a night light, disguised as Snoopy lying on his house; a picture frame; two plaques; and a decorative mirror—all from Japan.

PEANUTS!
Perfect Throughout the House

Some collectibles are "room specific." For example, cookware in the kitchen or toothbrush holders in the bathroom. Others are specifically designed for use almost everywhere, which is why we refer to them as perfect throughout the house. A partial list of these items, many of which appear in this section, includes smoke alarms, telephones, lamps, switch plates, mirror pictures, and radios.

CANDLES

1. Candle

• Snoopy is holding a pink and orange balloon on a brandy snifter-shaped glass covered with sparkles. 5"H. #250CD98, Hallmark. 1976. $15-20

2. Candles

• The continuous scene around the candle features Charlie Brown sticking his tongue out, as Woodstock and Snoopy, wearing straw hats, dance, and Lucy leans on Schroeder's piano. 6"H x 3" diam. #CDD259M, Ambassador. Mid-1970s. $6-10

• Snoopy, wearing a green and red striped stocking hat, sits with Woodstock at his feet. On the reverse side, Snoopy is skating. 6"H x 3" diam. #350CDD6583, Hallmark. Mid-1970s. $5-8

• Snoopy, sitting with Woodstock at his feet, and Charlie Brown, standing, are pictured on each side of Lucy. Continuing around the candle, Linus and Sally are pictured. 6"H x 3" diam. #CDD20R, Ambassador. Mid-1970s. $6-10

• Snoopy kisses Peppermint Patty on the nose. Printed: "Smak!" Charlie Brown and Lucy are pictured on the reverse side. 6"H x 3" diam. Hallmark. 1974. $6-10

• Snoopy, as Joe Cool, is featured in different poses around the candle. 6"H x 3" diam. #CDD6993, Hallmark. 1974. $5-8

3. Candles

• Snoopy stands next to a cake topped by the numbers 1, 2, 3, 4, and 5 on top of each other. 6-7/8"H. Hallmark. Early 1980s. $8-12

• Charlie Brown is surrounded by Snoopy kissing Marcie, and Linus patting Woodstock and his friend on their heads. 4"H x 3" diam. Hallmark. 1974. $5-8

• Snoopy is sitting. 5-1/2"H. Hallmark. Early 1970s. $6-8

4. Candles

• Woodstock blows a medieval trumpet as Snoopy thinks, "Hark! What light through yonder window breaks?" Lucy replies, "Tis just sweet precious me up in the balcony." Ceramic. 2-1/4"H x 1-3/4" diam. #CDM8700, Hallmark. Mid-1970s. $6-10

• Snoopy, pictured with his supper dish on his head, and Woodstock, stick their tongues out. Reverse side: Charlie

Brown looks on from the left and Lucy, on the right, is the object of the tongue-wagging. Printed: "Bleah!" Ceramic. 1-3/4"H. Hallmark. Mid-1970s. $6-10

•Snoopy holds a candle and thinks, "Everyone looks better by candlelight!" Around the candle, Woodstock, with a candle on his head, looks into a mirror; Peppermint Patty holds a candle; and Lucy gives a candle to Schroeder at his piano. Ceramic. 2-1/4"H x 1-3/4" diam. #CDM8701, Hallmark. Mid-1970s. $6-10

•Linus, sitting in a pumpkin patch, has his hands over his mouth, and his hair stands straight up. Frosted glass. 2-3/4"H. Hallmark. Early-1970s. $30-35

5. Candle

•Linus, Thibault, Five, Charlie Brown, Snoopy, Schroeder, Lucy, Peppermint Patty, and Woodstock, dressed in baseball uniforms, are on the baseball field. Frosted glass. 2-1/2"H. Hallmark. Early 1970s. $35-40

6. Candles

•Charlie Brown, frowning, wears a red baseball cap and a red shirt printed "Manager." 4-1/2"H. #325CDD7413, Hallmark. Late 1970s. $5-8

•Lucy, wearing a blue dress, kneels next to a football. 3-3/4"H. #325CDD74717, Hallmark. Late 1970s. $5-8

7. Candles

•Snoopy stands with his arms outstretched. The image appears on each side of the 2" thick candle. 3-3/4"H. #CDD6820, Hallmark. Mid-1970s. $4-6

•Charlie Brown stands with one hand touching his face. The image appears on each side of the 2" thick candle. 4-1/4"H. #CDD6819, Hallmark. Mid-1970s. $4-6

8. Candles

•Charlie Brown, frowning, sits with his knees pulled up to his chest, elbows resting on his knees and hands on his face.

5-3/4"H. Ambassador. Late 1970s. $10-12

•Charlie Brown, wearing a red baseball cap, and holding a bat and glove, is sitting. His cap is open at the top. The candle fills his body up to the cap. Ceramic. 5-1/4"H. Hallmark. Mid-1970s. $15-20

•Charlie Brown, standing, wears black pants and a red shirt with a black zigzag across the front. 7"H. Hallmark. Late 1970s. $10-12

9. Candles

•Snoopy sits on a red heart-shaped base, hugging Woodstock. 2-1/2"H. #CDD8718, Hallmark. Mid-1980s. $4-5

•Charlie Brown, with his arms outstretched, wears a green shirt and green baseball cap, and his baseball glove. 2-1/4"H. Hallmark. Late 1980s. $4-5

•Snoopy is sitting, holding Woodstock. 1-3/4"H. Hallmark. Mid-1980s. $4-5

•Snoopy, wearing a red scarf, holds a green and red present. 2"H. #CDD9009, Hallmark. Mid-1980s. $4-5

•Woodstock sits on a red and white present. 2-1/4"H. #CDD9010, Hallmark. Mid-1980s. $4-5

•Snoopy stands next to, and holds onto, an oversized bone. 2-1/4"H. Hallmark. Late 1970s. $4-6

10. Candles

•Snoopy, wearing a Santa hat, lies on his tummy on top of his snow-trimmed doghouse, which is decorated with a wreath. 3-1/2"H. #7863, Willitts Designs. 1987. $5-8

•Snoopy, as the Flying Ace, sits on his doghouse. 3-1/4"H. #CDD8719, Hallmark. Mid-1980s. $4-6

•Snoopy wears a yellow visor and holds a yellow tennis racket. 325CDD7416, Hallmark. Late 1970s. $4-5

11. Candle

•Snoopy is sitting, with Woodstock seated on Snoopy's feet. 6"H. Hallmark. Mid-1970s. $6-10

12. Candle Holder

•"Keepsake Candle Holder." Snoopy, dressed as a chef, stands next to a three-tier cake printed "Happy Birthday." Woodstock is above the printing with icing on his nose. 2-1/4"H. #125CD8861, Hallmark. 1981. $25-30*

13. Candles

"Love Lights." Replaceable candle in holder. The design on the box matches the design on the candle holder. Plastic. 1-1/2"H x 1-1/2" diam. Dick de Rjk Prod., Holland. Sold in the United States. Late 1980s. $5-8* ea.

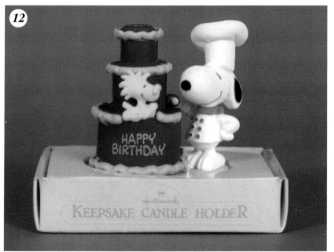

•Snoopy carries Woodstock. Printed: "Get Well Soon."

•Snoopy leans against the side of his doghouse thinking of a red heart.

•Snoopy is sitting and holding a pen. Printed: "Thanks!"

•Snoopy and Woodstock, holding a flower, are sitting. Printed: "Just For You."

•Snoopy draws a line under the word "Congratulations" with a paintbrush.

•Snoopy is standing, and hugging Woodstock. Printed: "You Make Me Happy!"

•Snoopy is walking, with bars of music behind him. Printed: "Happy Birthday."

•Snoopy, wearing a baseball cap, flies a heart-shaped kite. Printed: "I Love You."

•Snoopy lies on top of his doghouse. Printed: "Thinking Of You."

•Charlie Brown has his head back, mouth open, and arms in the air. Printed: "I Miss You."

14. Candle Holders

Composition material. Candle is not included. Hallmark. Early 1970s. $18-25 ea.

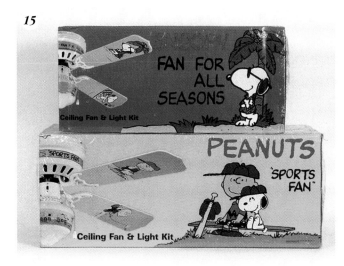

Linus, Lucy, Sally, Peppermint Patty, Schroeder, Snoopy, and Woodstock holding banners and pompoms. #4224SP.

16. Light Kits

•"Snoopy Light Kit." Snoopy, as the Flying Ace, is depicted on a globe-shaped fixture, sitting at a cafe table drinking root beer. Fits all standard ceiling fans. #Y-RG-PB, Key Largo. Late 1980s. $25-30 $35-40*

•"Snoopy Light Kit." Snoopy, as the Flying Ace, sits on his doghouse against a multicolored geometric design. Fits all standard ceiling fans. #Y-CL-PB, Key Largo. Late 1980s. $25-30 $35-40*

Ceiling Fan

•"Snoopy 48" Ceiling Fan." Each blade has a paw print and is printed "Snoopy." Scenes on the blades feature Snoopy as the Flying Ace, with Belle dressed as a nurse, and Spike dressed as a soldier. Light kit is not included. #&AO 0009, Key Largo. Late 1980s. $60-70 $75-85*

CLOCKS

17. Clocks

•"Snoopy & Charlie Brown Talking Alarm Clock." Snoopy is sleeping in Charlie Brown's lap. Printed: "Zzzz." Charlie Brown's voice is the alarm. He says "Hey Snoopy, I know you're allergic to morning! I'm losing my patience! Take warning! The gang and I have places to go. Hurry! Wake up! Don't be slow! We'll leave you behind, good friend of mine, since happiness is being on time." Battery-operated. 6-1/2" x 6-1/2". #8002, Equity/Determined Productions. Late 1970s. $90-110 $175-235*

•The plush, sitting Snoopy has the clock in his tummy. Battery-operated. 8-1/2"H. #900/55, Armitron/E. Gluck. 1988. $45-60 $75-85*

18. Large Twin-Bell Alarm Clocks

•Snoopy dances, as his arms move around the clock to tell the time. Charlie Brown, Lucy, and Linus are pictured on the background. Available in different color combinations. Metal. 10-1/2". #355, Blessing/Determined Productions. 1972. $70-85

Small Twin-Bell Alarm Clocks

•Snoopy dances, as his arms move around the clock to tell the time. Available in different color combinations, with black

•Linus sucks his thumb and holds his red blanket. 7-1/2"H.

•Lucy, wearing a red dress, leans her elbow on the candle holder printed "The Doctor Is In." 7"H.

•Charlie Brown, with the candle holder in his hands, wears a red baseball cap tilted to the side. 8"H.

•Snoopy, with the candle holder in his hands, wears a red hat. 7-7/8"H.

CEILING FANS & LIGHT KITS

15. Ceiling Fans with Light Kits

Sisco, Inc. Late 1980s. $80-100 ea. $140-150* ea.

•"Snoopy Fan For All Seasons." The scenes on each blade represent the four seasons: Snoopy in the snow; Snoopy at Halloween; Snoopy, as Joe Cool under a palm tree; and Snoopy with a basket of Easter eggs. Includes a 7" translucent globe picturing Woodstock during the different seasons. 42". #4225SP.

•"PEANUTS Sports Fan." The scene on each blade depicts the characters involved in sports activities: Charlie Brown stands on the pitcher's mound; Charlie Brown flies his kite; Snoopy plays tennis; and Lucy pulls the football away before Charlie Brown can kick it. The translucent globe features

and white being the most common. Metal. 3-1/2" x 5-1/2". #353, Blessing/Determined Productions. 1972. Black and white: $25-30. Other color combinations: $30-40

19. Clocks

•"Snoopy Alarm." Snoopy, with net in paw, chases a butterfly on the face of the clock. Metal. 4-1/8". #593, Equity. Early 1980s. $30-40 $50-60*

•"Snoopy Alarm." Snoopy, wearing a helmet, and Woodstock play football on the face of the clock. Metal. 4-1/8". #595, Equity. Early 1980s. $30-40 $55-60*

•"Snoopy Quartz Alarm." Snoopy and Woodstock ride a skateboard on the face of the clock. Battery-operated. Metal. #SN891, Equity. 1982. $30-40 $50-60*

•"Snoopy Alarm." Snoopy holds a bat while standing at home plate on the face of the clock. The baseball itself is the second hand on the clock. Metal. 4-1/8". #594, Equity. Early 1980s. $30-40 $55-60*

•Twin-Bell Alarm Clock. "Snoopy Alarm." On the face of the clock, Snoopy is seen lying on his tummy on top of his doghouse. Printed above Snoopy are the words: "I'm Allergic To Morning." Metal. 4-1/8". #596S, Equity. Early 1980s. $30-40 $50-60*

•"Snoopy Alarm." Snoopy holds a checkered racing flag on the face of the clock. Woodstock, seen driving a race car, is the second hand on the clock. Metal. 4-1/8". #593, Equity. Early 1980s. $30-40 $50-60*

•"Snoopy Alarm." Snoopy holds a tennis racket on the face of the clock. The tennis ball is the second hand. Metal. 4-1/8". #592, Equity. Early 1980s. $30-35 $50-60*

20. Clock

•"Snoopy Quartz Wall Clock." Snoopy, wearing an apron and a chef's hat, carries a covered tray over his head. Woodstock walks behind him. Printed: "Bon Appetit." Battery-operated. Plastic. 7" diam. #602-25Q, Equity. 1982. $30-40 $45-50*

•Mini Quartz Alarm Clock. Snoopy, as the Flying Ace, and Woodstock are featured on the face of the clock. Battery-operated. Plastic. 3" x 2-1/2". #SN811, Equity. 1982. $30-40

•Twin-Bell Alarm Clock. "Snoopy Quartz Alarm Clock." Woodstock flies out of a box. Snoopy sits beside the box, holding playing cards. Printed: "Snoopy." Battery-operated. Plastic case. 5" x 4-1/4" x 2-3/8". #QHB 5024-A, Citizen. Late 1980s. $15-18 $20-28*

•Twin-Bell Alarm Clock. "Snoopy Quartz Alarm Clock." Snoopy sits at his typewriter. Printed: "Snoopy." Battery-operated. Heart-shaped plastic case. 5-7/16" x 4-1/8" x 2". #QHB 5032-B, Citizen. Late 1980s. $15-18 $20-28*

21. Wall Clocks

"Snoopy Quartz." "Snoopy" is printed on the face of each clock. Battery-operated. Plastic case. Citizen. Late 1980s. $20-25 ea. $30-35* ea.

•Snoopy holds a tennis racket on the face of the clock. The tennis ball is the second hand. 9-7/8" diam. #QA 2234-A.

•Snoopy wears a jacket and bow tie. A briefcase is at his side. 9-1/2" x 10". #QK 2264-C.

•Snoopy and Woodstock ride a skateboard. 9-7/8". #QA 2234-B.

•Snoopy, wearing a baseball glove and cap, looks at the baseball between the "8" and the "9." 9-7/8". #QA 2148-B.

22. Wall Clocks

•"Snoopy Quartz." Snoopy sits at the piano with Woodstock on top, while Schroeder, Linus, Peppermint Patty, and Charlie Brown sing in the background. Printed: "Snoopy." Battery-operated. Plastic case. 9-1/2" x 10". #QK 2264-B, Citizen. Late 1980s. $20-28 $30-35*

•"Snoopy Quartz." Snoopy, dressed as an artist, sits at an easel painting Woodstock, who poses on a branch. Printed: "Snoopy & Woodstock." Battery-operated. Plastic heart-shaped case. 9-1/8" x 10-3/8". #QH 2399-C, Citizen. Late 1980s. $20-28 $30-35*

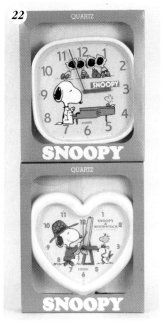

23

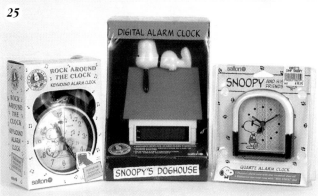

25

24

26

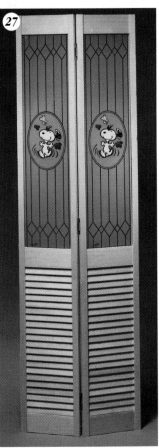

27

23. Clocks

Bell alarm. Battery-operated. Plastic. Citizen. Late 1980s. $15-18 ea. $20-25* ea.

•Snoopy and Woodstock hold tennis rackets. Printed: "Snoopy & Woodstock." 3-1/4" x 4-1/2" x 2-3/8". #QKB 5008-C.

•Snoopy kicks a soccer ball. 3-1/2" x 4-1/4" x 2-3/8". #QKB 5010-AO.

•Snoopy, wearing a bow tie, and Woodstock carry briefcases. Printed: "Snoopy." 3-1/2" x 4-1/4" x 2-3/8". #QKB 5010-BO.

•Snoopy, Woodstock, and his friends, dressed as scouts, are hiking. Printed: "Snoopy And Woodstock." 3-1/2" x 4-1/8" x 2-3/8". #QKB 5009-B.

•Snoopy and Woodstock are jogging. Printed: "Snoopy & Woodstock." 3-1/2" x 4-1/8" x 2-3/8". #QKB 5009-CW.

24. Pendulum Wall Clocks

•Snoopy, Woodstock, and his friends are dressed as scouts. Woodstock appears on the pendulum. Printed: "Snoopy & Woodstock." Plastic case and pendulum. 11-7/8" x 8-5/8" x 2-1/4". #QA 2149-D, Citizen. Late 1980s. $25-30 $32-35*

•Snoopy carries a tray of food. Woodstock appears on the pendulum. Printed: "Snoopy." Plastic case and pendulum. 11-7/8" x 8-5/8" x 2-1/4". #QA 2149-B, Citizen. Late 1980s. $25-30 $32-35*

25. Clocks

Salton Time, Ltd. Early 1990s.

•"Rock Around The Clock." Twin-bell alarm clock. Snoopy is in his dancing pose on the face of the clock. Woodstock rocks back and forth as the clock ticks. Metal. #ST-2283. $15-18 $20-25*

•"Snoopy's Doghouse Digital Alarm Clock." Snoopy lies on top of his doghouse. The digital clock is in the side of the

doghouse below the roof. Battery-operated. Plastic. #ST-2030. $12-15 $18-20*

•"Snoopy And His Friends Quartz Alarm Clock." Snoopy, as Joe Cool, is featured on the face of the clock. "Joe Cool" is printed 12 times from the top of the face to the bottom, behind Snoopy. Battery-operated. Plastic. 3-1/4" x 3-1/2". ST-2280. $12-15 $18-20*

26. Twin-Bell Alarm Clock

•"It's The Great Big Alarm Clock, Charlie Brown." Snoopy is sitting next to Charlie Brown, as Woodstock flies overhead. Clock can be mounted on a wall. Metal. 14-1/4"H x 11"W x 4" diam. #ST-2284, Salton Time, Ltd. Early 1990s. $30-35 $40-45*

DOOR & DOOR ACCESSORIES

27. Door

•"Two Friends Bi-Fold Door." Snoopy dances, as Woodstock

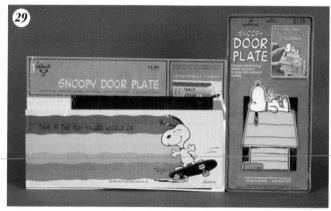

flies overhead. Wood and glass. 29-1/2"W x 78-1/2"H x 1" diam. #2900-3080, Wing Industries. 1988. $350-375

28. Doorknob Caddy

• "Snoopy Doorknob Caddy." Snoopy looks out a window at Woodstock sitting on the red shingled roof of a house with a chimney. The caddy comes with three interchangeable signs—"Studying," "I'm Out," and "Sleeping"—to indicate what the room's occupant is doing. Plastic. 5-1/2" x 4". #250-3301, Butterfly Originals. 1980. $5-8 $10-12*

29. Door Plates

• "Snoopy Door Plate." Snoopy rides on a skateboard, with horizontal rainbow colored stripes trailing behind him. Included with the door plate are self-sticking letters so the plate can be personalized. Cardboard. #100PF276J, Ambassador. Mid-1970s. $2-3**

• "Snoopy Door Plate." Snoopy is lying on his back on top of his yellow doghouse, with Woodstock lying on his tummy. Self-sticking letters are included to personalize the door plate. Plastic. #175SPF407-5, Hallmark. Mid-1970s. $6-10**

GRAPHIC PRINTS

30. Snoopy Gallery Print

• "Downhill Racer." Snoopy is skiing down a snow-covered mountain, with Woodstock riding along on the end of Snoopy's stocking cap. On the reverse side is a sticker with the name of the print and a biography of Charles Schulz. The print came matted and shrink-wrapped against cardboard, or matted and framed. Paper. 16"H x 20"W. Aviva. 1981. Unframed: $35-40 Framed: $45-50

31. Snoopy Gallery Print

• "The Flying Ace." Snoopy, as the Flying Ace, sits on top of a rainbow. On the reverse side is a sticker with the name of the print and a biography of Charles Schulz. The print came either matted and shrink-wrapped against cardboard, or matted and framed. Paper. 16"H x 20"W. Aviva. 1981. Unframed: $35-40 Framed: $45-50

32. Snoopy Gallery Print

• "Friends." Charlie Brown, sitting on a cushion, watches television with Snoopy lying on his head. On the reverse side is a sticker with the name of the print and a biography of Charles Schulz. The print came matted and shrink-wrapped against cardboard, or matted and framed. Paper. 16"H x 20"W. Aviva. 1981. Unframed: $35-40 Framed: $45-50

33. Snoopy Gallery Print

• "The Joe Coolest." Snoopy, as Joe Cool, arms folded across his chest, stands against a locker. On the reverse side is a

sticker with the name of the print and a biography of Charles Schulz. The print came matted and shrink-wrapped against cardboard, or matted and framed. Paper. 16"H x 20"W. Aviva. 1981. Unframed: $35-40 Framed: $45-50

34. 3-D Holusion Art Print

•"Space Ace." Stare at the dozens of miniature Flying Ace Snoopys, and Snoopy will appear sitting atop his dog-house with his scarf waving in the air behind him. Don't expect to see a white Snoopy or a red doghouse. These objects will appear made up of the miniature Snoopys. Paper. 28"W x 22"H. NVISion Grafix, Inc. 1994. Unframed: $25-30 Framed: $40-45

LIGHTING

35. Hurricane Lamps

Snoopy dances among flowers on a blue background. Milk glass. Kamco. 1978.

•Small. 10-1/2"H. #004809. $60-65

•Large. 13-1/4"H. #004817. $65-70

36. Hurricane Lamp

•Snoopy dances among flowers on a blue background. Blue metal candle-stick-shaped base and milk glass. 10-7/8"H. #004808, Kamco. Late 1970s. $60-70

37. Lamp

•Snoopy and Woodstock sit back-to-back on top of the dog-house, surrounded by hearts. Glass globe, wood and metal base. The globe design was also available with Snoopy dancing, surrounded by flowers. 15-1/2"H. #004805, Kamco. Late 1970s. $42-48

Hurricane Lamp

•Snoopy and Woodstock sit back-to-back on top of the dog-house, surrounded by hearts on each section of the lamp.

The lamp can be used as a nightlight with only one sec-tion of the lamp lit. Milk glass. 18"H. #4804, Kamco. 1978. $155-200

38. Goose-Neck Lamp

•Snoopy sits at his typewriter on top of a book. He wears a green bow tie with blue polka dots. Metal shade and chrome goose-neck on a ceramic base. 13-3/4"H fully extended. #6D3292, C.N. Burman Company. 1988. $20-25 $30-35*

Lamp

"Snoopy Lamp." Snoopy, standing on a round base with his arms folded across his chest, is wearing a red bow tie with white polka dots. The shade is white, with red trim. Ceramic base. 14-1/2"H with shade. #6B3290, C.N. Burman Company. 1988. $20-25 $30-35*

39. Lamp and Nightlight

•The base features Snoopy lying on top of his doghouse; Charlie Brown walking toward Snoopy holding his supper dish; and Lucy looking on. Snoopy's doghouse has a small bulb inside. Wood. 15-34/"H. Lights Fantastique. Early 1970s. $110-130

stars. Lucy, Linus, Schroeder, Snoopy, and Woodstock are also asleep around the rest of the lamp shade. Candlestick-shaped base. 15"H with shade. #004806, Kamco. Mid-1970s. $50-60

•Snoopy and Woodstock, in front of a pink, yellow, and orange rainbow. Yellow-trimmed shade features Woodstock and his friends around the bottom edge, each holding a flower. Plastic. 15"H with shade. #110-360, Nursery Originals. 1982. $25-30

43. Nightlights

•Snoopy is sitting and hugging Woodstock. 4.5-watt light bulb is included. Porcelain. 5-1/2"H. #8122, Willitts Designs. 1988. $25-30 $35-40*

•Linus is sitting, thumb in his mouth and holding his blanket. 7-watt light bulb is included. Porcelain. 7-1/2"H. #45024. Willitts Designs. 1989. $32-40 $42-48*

•Snoopy and Woodstock, dressed as scouts, toast marshmallows over a campfire on the base. The "fire" has a small bulb inside. Wood. 15-3/4"H. Lights Fantastique. 1974. $110-130

40. Wall Lamp

•Snoopy dances among flowers against a blue background on the shade and on the wall mounting. Wood, with metal fixture for mounting. 19"H with shade. Rare. Lights Fantastique. 1974. $65-75

Lamp

•The base features Lucy behind her psychiatrist booth, counseling Charlie Brown to the right. Snoopy, as the Flying Ace, walks toward them from the left. Wood. 15-3/4"H. Lights Fantastique. Early 1970s. $125-135

41. Wall Lamp

•Snoopy and Woodstock sit back-to-back on top of the doghouse, surrounded by hearts. Glass globe, with brass base and bracket for mounting. #5318, Kamco. Late 1970s. $95-110

42. Lamps

•The multicolored shade features Peppermint Patty and Charlie Brown asleep against a tree, under the moon and

Lamp

•Snoopy stands on the green base, holding red, yellow, and green plastic balloons. Woodstock stands next to Snoopy, holding a felt flower. The shade features Charlie Brown, Lucy, Sally, and Peppermint Patty holding pink and blue kites and balloons. Can use a light bulb with three wattage settings. Ceramic figures. 16"H with shade. #120-365, Kamco. 1982. $40-50

44. Lamp

•"Snoopy's Doghouse Decorative Lamp." Snoopy lies on top of his doghouse, on a sculptured grass-covered base with flowers, dog bones, and a window. From the doorway, a table can be seen which has Snoopy's supper dish and a candle on it. When the light is switched on, the inside of the doghouse glows. A 4-watt light bulb is included. Plastic. 4" x 6-7/8". #QHD361-2, Hallmark. 1984. $40-45 $50-55*

45. Lamp

•Snoopy is sitting. Uses a 25-watt light bulb, not included. Molded plastic. 18"H. 6-foot cord. #81605-9, Gladys Goose and Company. 1984. $65-75

46. Nightlights

"Snoopy Nite Lite." Plugs directly into electrical outlet. Raised, multicolored hand-painted design. Molded plastic. 2" diam. Assortment #50100, Monogram Products, Inc. 1980. $2-3* ea.

•Snoopy, wearing a nightshirt and nightcap, is walking and carrying a candle. #50105.

•Woodstock is sleeping in his nest in a tree. #50102.

•Charlie Brown, on the pitcher's mound, is ready to throw the baseball.

•Lucy, dressed as a cheerleader, holds pompoms. Woodstock holds a banner printed "Rah."

•Linus, sitting, sucks his thumb and holds his blanket.

•Snoopy reads "Ghost Stories."

•Snoopy is sitting and hugging Woodstock. #50106.

•Snoopy, as the Flying Ace, is sitting.

•Snoopy and Woodstock toast marshmallows over a fire.

47. Flashlight

•"Snoopy Flashlight." Snoopy, as Joe Cool. Battery-operated. Plastic. 4"H. #250PF117-1, Hallmark. 1977. $4-6 $10-15*

Nightlight

•Snoopy lies on top of his doghouse. Printed: "Rival." Plugs directly into electrical outlet. Available as a by-mail premium. Rival Dog Food. 1974-75. $8-10

48. Telephone with Lamp

•"Snoopy & Woodstock PhoneLamp." Snoopy stands on a red base with wood-grain trim. He has one arm extended, which holds the yellow receiver. Woodstock stands next to him. Touch-tone buttons on the dial pad. Also available with a rotary dial. Shown with the original lamp shade and receiver. Plastic. Approximately 30"H with shade. Comdial/American Telecommunications Corporation. Early 1980s. $110-135 $150-175*

MIRROR PICTURES

49. Mirror Pictures

Design is painted on the glass surface. Wood frame. 9-1/8" x 13-1/8". Determined Productions. Mid-1970s. $18-22 ea.

•Snoopy, lying on his tummy on top of his doghouse and looking to the left of the mirror, thinks, "I think I'm allergic to morning!"

•Snoopy, lying on top of his doghouse with Woodstock sitting on his tummy and singing, thinks, "I hate people who sing in the morning!"

50. Mirror Pictures

The design is painted on the glass surface. Wood frame. 8" x 10-1/2". Determined Productions. Mid-1970s.

•Snoopy and Woodstock, wearing tuxedos, top hats, and holding canes, are dancing with musical notes and instruments around them. Printed: "Razzle N' Dazzle." $25-30

•Snoopy is sitting and hugging Woodstock, surrounded by red hearts. $20-25

51. Mirror Pictures

The design is painted on the glass surface. Wood frame. 9-1/8" x 13-1/8". Determined Productions.

•Snoopy, lying on his tummy on top of his doghouse, and looking toward the front of the mirror, thinks "I think I'm allergic to morning!" Mid-1970s. $18-22

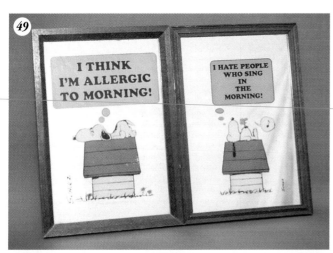

•Snoopy, wearing a yellow and green baseball cap, and signing an autograph, is surrounded by Woodstock and his friends. Snoopy thinks "It's great to be a superstar!" Early 1970s. $22-25

52. Mirror Picture

•Snoopy, wearing a helmet and sitting in the driver's seat of a race car, kisses Lucy on the cheek. Woodstock, wearing a helmet, sits on the back of the race car which is surrounded by the pit crew: Sally holding a checkered flag, Peppermint Patty, Linus, and Charlie Brown. Printed: "Grand Prix." The design is painted on the glass surface. Wood frame. 9-1/8" x 13-1/8". Determined Productions. Mid-1970s. $25-30

53. Mirror Picture

•Snoopy, dressed as a chauffeur, holds open the door of a Rolls Royce for Woodstock dressed in formal attire. The design is painted on the glass surface. Wood frame. 8" x 10-1/2". Determined Productions. Mid-1970s. $18-22

54. Mirror Picture

•Snoopy, walking, wears a top hat and cape and carries a cane. The design is painted on the glass surface. Wood frame. 9-1/8" x 13-1/8". Determined Productions. Mid-1970s. $18-22

55. Mirror Picture

•Snoopy holds a bouquet of balloons, and Woodstock holds one balloon with the word "Love" on it. The design is painted

on the glass surface. Wood frame. 9" x 12-3/4". Determined Productions. Mid-1970s. $30-35

56. Mirror Picture

•Snoopy, the driver of a double-decker bus printed "London," stands in the door of the bus. Woodstock and his friends can be seen in the windows. Sally, Charlie Brown, Peppermint Patty, Lucy, Schroeder, and Linus wait at the bus stop. The design is painted on the glass surface. Wood frame. 9-1/4" x 13-3/4". Determined Productions. Mid-1970s. $30-40

57. Mirror Picture

•Snoopy, as the Flying Ace, sits on top of his doghouse. The design is painted on the glass surface. Wood frame. 9" x 13-1/4". Determined Productions. Mid-1970s. $18-22

58. Mirror Picture

•Peppermint Patty and Charlie Brown are holding hands, and Snoopy is hugging Woodstock. Printed: "Love!" Large hearts are above the characters. The design is painted on the

glass surface. Wood frame. 10-1/2" x 8". Determined Productions. Mid-1970s. $22-28

59. Mirror Pictures

The design is painted on the glass surface. Wood frame. Determined Productions. Mid-1970s. $18-22 ea.

•Snoopy is walking and thinking "I'm so cute!" 9-1/4" x 13-1/4".

•Snoopy rides in a hot air balloon, as Woodstock and his friends fly around the balloon's basket. 8" x 10-1/2".

PICTURE FRAMES

60. Frames

Plastic. Holds a 2" x 2" photo. Hallmark. Late 1970s. $6-10

•Snoopy sits at his typewriter in a corner of the frame, thinking "A real inspiration!" #PP30342.

•Snoopy stands on the side of the frame, thinking of a big red heart. #PP3046.

•Snoopy, wearing a beret, and holding a paintbrush and palette, stands on the side of the frame, which is shaped like an easel. Printed: "A True Masterpiece!" #PP3045.

•Lucy stands with her hands clasped against her chest on the right side of the frame. She says, "Perfect, like me!" #PP3044.

61. Frames

Plastic. Holds 2" x 2" photo. Hallmark. Late 1970s. $6-10 ea.

• Snoopy and Woodstock, wearing party hats, dance on each side of the frame. Printed: "Let The Good Times Roll!" #PP3040.

• Snoopy, wearing a disco outfit, dances on the side of the frame and thinks "Born to boogie!!" #PP3041.

• Woodstock, in his nest in a tree, is thinking of a red heart. #PP4343.

62. Frames

• Snoopy, standing with his paws clasped, thinks, "Sigh!" The design is on paper, under glass. Metal frame: 6" x 5". Picture size: 2" x 3". Manufacturer unknown. Mid-1980s. $4-5

• Printed: "Smile!" Snoopy winks, and is thinking, "It makes people wonder what you've been up to!" Metal frame: 4" x 5-3/4". Picture size: 2" x 3". #PP3018, Hallmark. Early 1980s. $10-12

• Snoopy, winking and grinning, thinks, "Lookin' good!" The design is on paper under glass. Wood frame: 8-1/2" x 6-1/2". Picture size: 3" x 4". Manufacturer unknown. Mid-1980s. $4-5

• Snoopy sits on top of his doghouse, holding a red heart and thinking, "Love makes a day beautiful." Metal frame: 4" x 5-3/4". Picture size: 2" x 3". #PP3021, Hallmark. Early 1980s. $10-12

63. Frames

Enameled metal. Butterfly Originals. 1979.

• Snoopy, holding three balloons, and Woodstock wear party hats. 3" x 4-1/2". #3925. $8-15

• Snoopy, grinning, holds a pink heart. He sits next to a large pink and red heart. 3" x 3-1/4". #3928. $8-12

• Snoopy, wearing a visor and holding a tennis racket, looks over at Woodstock standing on a trophy printed "Top Seeded." 3-1/2" x 3-1/4". #3922. $8-15

64. Frames

Enameled metal. Butterfly Originals. 1979.

• Snoopy lies on top of his doghouse. 2" x 3-1/2". #3921. $8-10

• Snoopy lies on his tummy on top of a frame that spells out "SNOOPY." 7" x 3". #3935. $12-18

65. Frames

The paper insert where the photo goes features Snoopy, Woodstock, Lucy, Peppermint Patty, Charlie Brown, Marcie, Linus, Franklin, Schroeder, Sally, Eudora, and Pigpen.

Packaged in graphic boxes featuring the 40th Anniversary logo on the top and bottom. The frame in the box is pictured on the back. Silver plated. Godinger Silver Art Company, Ltd. 1990.

•"PEANUT (sic) Musical Theme Frame." Woodstock is in his nest in a tree, singing, with musical notes all around him. Snoopy lies on a double bar of music. In the lower left hand corner, Schroeder plays his piano as Lucy leans back on it. Frame: 9"H. Picture size: 5" x 7". #509. $15-20 $25-30*

•"Snoopy Album Frame." Snoopy stands behind a tripod with a camera on top. Woodstock, sitting in front of the tripod, watches. A tree is on each side of the frame. The cover of the album holds a 5" x 7" picture. Inside the album there is room for 48 4" x 6" pictures. Also available as a frame only. Album size: 9"H. Album: #511A. Frame: #511. Album: $20-30 $30-40* Frame: $15-20 $25-30*

•"Snoopy Oval Frame." Snoopy is pictured around the frame in different poses. Frame size: 8"H. Picture size: 4" x 6". #513. $10-15 $18-20*

•"Snoopy Birth Record Frame." Snoopy, Woodstock, and Lucy stand on each side of the frame, which represents a maternity ward. "Maternity Ward" is engraved on the frame. Also engraved are "Time," "Date," "Weight," "Height," and "Name," with space for the information to be engraved. Frame size: 6"H. Picture size: 3" x 5". #510. $10-12 $17-20*

•"Snoopy Frame." Snoopy is sitting and holding the frame between his feet. Frame size: 5"H. Picture size: 2" x 3". #508. $8-10 $10-14*

66. Frames

•Snoopy and Woodstock sit back-to-back on a paper decal that frames the picture. Printed: "Let's Be Friends." Plastic. Frame size: 2-3/4" x 3-1/2". Picture size: 1-3/4" x 2-1/2". Butterfly Originals. 1980. $1-2

•Snoopy sits, with small hearts around him, on a paper decal that frames the picture. Printed: "Super Mom." Plastic. Frame size: 2-3/4" x 3-1/2". Picture size: 1-3/4" x 2-1/2". Butterfly Originals. 1980. $1-2

•Snoopy stands beside a booth printed "Friendly Advice to Your Friend Is Always In." Pewter. 4-7/8"H. Burnes of Boston. Early 1980s. $22-25

•Snoopy, on one knee with his arms outstretched, is next to a star-shaped frame. Printed on the star's inner circular rim: "A Real Star." Pewter. Burnes of Boston. Early 1980s. $20-24

67. Mini Picture Frames

•Snoopy is sitting and hugging Woodstock. Printed: "Snoopy & Woodstock." Clear plastic. Frame size: 1-1/2" x 1-5/8". Picture size: 1-1/8" x 1-1/8". #79-3910, Butterfly Originals. 1979. $2-4*

•Snoopy lies on his tummy in front of his doghouse. Printed: "Snoopy's Friend." Clear plastic. Frame size: 2" x 1-7/8". Picture size: 1-1/4" x 1-1/4". #79-3910, Butterfly Originals. 1979. $2-4*

68. Frames

"Snoopy Picture Your Pet Frame." Plastic. 4" x 5". ConAgra Pet Products Co. Late 1970s. $6-10* ea.

•Lucy is holding a purring cat. Printed: "World's Greatest Cat."

•Snoopy is sitting and hugging Woodstock. Printed: "Love My Pet."

•Snoopy kisses Charlie Brown on the cheek. Printed: "Smak!" and "World's Greatest Dog."

69. Compact Frame

•Snoopy is sitting and hugging Woodstock. The inside of the case has room for two photos. Metal. 2-1/2" x 2-7/8". #1000PP3051, Butterfly Originals. Early 1980s. $12-15

PILLOWS
70. Sweatshirt Pillows

Cotton and acrylic knit, stuffed with 100% polyester. 15" x 13-1/2". Series #42-2100, Determined Productions. 1982. $15-18 ea.

70

71

72

73

73. Sweatshirt Pillows

Acrylic knit, stuffed with kapok. 16" x 16". Series #42-2200, Determined Productions. 1982. $15-20 ea.

•Snoopy lies on top of his doghouse, against a pink background. Printed around the pillow: "It's Nice To Get Home To One's Own Bed."

•Sally tickles Linus against a red background. Printed around the pillow: "Love Is Tickling."

74. Pillow

•Snoopy, dressed as an astronaut, stands on the moon with his arms outstretched, against a red background. Printed around the pillow: "The Moon Is Made Of American Cheese!" Cotton flannel. 16" x 16". Determined Productions. 1969-70. $35-50

75. Pillows

Known as "patch pillows" because the designs matched the sew-on patches made at the same time. Cotton, stuffed with kapok. 16" diam. Determined Productions. 1972. $20-25 ea.

•Snoopy leans against a golf club, on a yellow background. Printed: "You're Away." #669.

•Snoopy is poised to release a bowling ball, on a green background. Printed: "Strike." #663.

76. Pillows

Known as "patch pillows" because the designs matched the sew-on patches made at the same time. Cotton, stuffed with kapok. 16" diam. Determined Productions. 1972. $20-25 ea.

•Snoopy, standing against a blue background, wears a ribbon that reads "Hero." Printed: "It's Hero Time." #664.

74

75

•Snoopy is dancing against a red background. Printed: "Live It Up A Little!"

•Snoopy sits on top of his doghouse, against a blue background. Printed: "I'm Allergic To Morning!"

71. Sweatshirt Pillows

Cotton and acrylic knit, stuffed with 100% polyester. 15" x 13-1/2". Series #42-2100, Determined Productions. 1982. $15-18 ea.

•Snoopy lies on top of his doghouse, with Woodstock sitting on his tummy, against a yellow background. Printed: "I Love My Home."

•Snoopy, standing against a green background, wears a ribbon that says "Magna Cum Laude." Printed: "I'm Not Perfect, But I'm Pretty Perfect!"

72. Sweatshirt Pillows

Acrylic knit, stuffed with kapok. 16" x 16". Series #42-2200, Determined Productions. 1982. $15-20 ea.

•Linus kneels at the side of his bed against a yellow background. Printed around the pillow: "Security Is Knowing You're Not Alone."

•Linus sleeps on top of Snoopy's doghouse, while Snoopy lies on his tummy in the doorway, against a pink background. Printed around the pillow: "I Suppose I'll Just Have To Sleep In The Guest Room . . . ."

• Snoopy dances against an orange background. Printed: "Come Dance With Me Baby." #665.

77. Pillows

Known as "patch pillows" because the designs matched the sew-on patches made at the same time. Cotton, stuffed with kapok. 16" diam. Determined Productions. 1972. $20-25 ea.

• Snoopy kicks a football against an orange background. Printed: "The Mad Punter." #661.

• Snoopy holds a hockey stick, against a red background. Printed: "Hat Trick." #660.

78. Pillows

Known as "patch pillows" because the designs matched the sew-on patches made at the same time. Cotton, stuffed with kapok. 16" diam. Determined Productions. 1972. $20-25 ea.

• Snoopy, wearing a red stocking cap, goggles, and scarf, skis against a green background. Printed: "World Famous Ski Champion." #671.

• Snoopy, wearing a red stocking cap and scarf, ice-skates against a blue background. Printed: "Ice Is Nice." #668.

79. Pillows

Known as "patch pillows" because the designs matched the sew-on patches made at the same time. Cotton, stuffed with

kapok. 16" diam. Determined Productions. 1972. $20-25 ea.

• Lucy, wearing a green dress, stands against a pink background. Printed: "World's Crabbiest Female." #667.

• Snoopy, who is wearing a blue helmet and green scarf, roller skates against a red background. Printed: "Jamming." #670.

• Linus sucks his thumb and holds his blanket. Printed: "To Know Me Is To Love Me." #662. (Not pictured)

• Snoopy wears a visor, and carries a tennis racket. Printed: "Tennis Anyone?" #666. (Not pictured)

80. Decorative Pillow Cover

• Snoopy and Woodstock are sitting, facing each other, on the grass. A dark pink heart is on the light pink background. Plush material with zipper. Machine washable. 24"L x 19"H. Sold exclusively through Sears. 1981. $10-12

81. Decorative Pillow Cover

• Snoopy, his ear hanging loose, lies on top of his doghouse, with Woodstock lying on Snoopy's tummy, against a blue

79

76

80

77

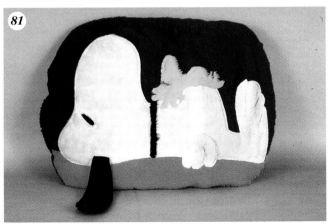

81

78

background. Plush material with zipper. Machine washable. 24"L x 19"H. Sold exclusively through Sears. 1981. $10-12

82. Toss Pillow

•"To The Beach." Woodstock, wearing oversized sunglasses, walks in the sun carrying a beach umbrella. Hand-printed, removable quilted cotton cover. 15" x 15". #F217-15, Import Specialties. 1988. $12-15

Floor Pillow

•"Type Away." Snoopy sits atop his doghouse at his typewriter, under a crescent moon, while Woodstock watches. Removable cover. Hand-printed, removable quilted cotton cover. 24" x 24". #F223-24, Import Specialties. 1988. $20-30

Toss Pillow

•"Fly A Kite." Snoopy flies a red kite. Hand-printed, removable quilted cotton cover. 15" x 15". #F219-15, Import Specialties. 1988. $12-15

PLAQUES

83. Wall Plaques

9-1/2"W x 18-1/2"H. Manufactured by Sanford J. Heilner, and sold through Hallmark stores. 1969. $14-18 ea.

•Linus holds a sign that says "Help Stamp Out Things That Need Stamping Out!"

•Lucy wears a blue dress, sunglasses, a baseball cap, and glove. Printed: "Cool It!"

•Charlie Brown and Snoopy sit on a bench. Printed: "I've Developed A New Philosophy. . . I Only Dread One Day At A Time!!"

84. Wall Plaques

4-1/8"W x 9-1/2"H. Manufactured by Sanford J. Heilner, and sold through Hallmark stores. 1969. $7-10 ea.

•Linus, sitting, holds his blanket and sucks his thumb. He says, "I love mankind. . . It's people I can't stand!!"

•Charlie, sitting on a log, says, "How can you do 'new math' with an 'old math' mind?"

•Charlie Brown, wearing a baseball cap and glove, and standing on the pitcher's mound, says, "We can't even win enough games to have a slump!"

•Snoopy is standing and thinking, "Nobody ever calls me 'sugarlips'."

85. Wall Plaques

4-1/8"W x 9-1/2"H. Manufactured by Sanford J. Heilner, and sold through Hallmark stores. 1969. $7-10 ea.

•Lucy and Charlie Brown, wearing baseball caps and gloves, stand on the pitcher's mound. Lucy says, "You know why we lost 123 to 0? We never got any breaks!"

•Snoopy, walking, with a tree in the background, thinks, "There is no sense in doing a lot of barking if you don't really have anything to say."

•Snoopy lies on top of his doghouse and thinks "I always thought you got a headache because your ears were too tight!"

86. Wall Plaques

Wood. 5-3/8" x 5-3/8". Hallmark. 1980s. $5-7 ea.

•Snoopy lies on a hammock strung between two trees, wearing headphones and listening to music. Food and books are

on the ground beneath the hammock. Printed: "Genius At Work." #DE8075.

•Snoopy and Woodstock lie against pillows on top of Snoopy's doghouse. Printed: "Keep Smiling! It Makes People Wonder What You've Been Up To!" #DE8090.

•Snoopy and Woodstock sit back-to-back. Printed: "A Friend Likes You. . . Just Because." #8091.

87. Wall Plaques

Wood. 5-7/8" x 6-1/4". $5-7 ea.

•Snoopy jogs on a path next to a stream, with a footbridge in the background. Printed: "The Secret Of Staying Young Is To Find An Age You Really Like And Stick With It." #DE474N, Ambassador. Late 1980s.

•Snoopy and Woodstock sit on top of Snoopy's doghouse. Printed: "Keep Smiling! It Makes People Wonder What You've Been Up To!" Hallmark. Early 1980s.

•Snoopy dances on background of red hearts. Printed: "Love Makes Monday Morning Feel Like Friday Afternoon." Ambassador. Early 1980s.

88. Wall Plaques

Wood. Springbok. $7-9 ea.

•Charlie Brown and Snoopy are hugging each other. Printed: "Happiness Is Having A Friend . . . " 5" x 6-7/8". #400DE111. 1971.

•Linus, sitting, holds his blanket and sucks his thumb. He says, "I love mankind...It's people I can't stand!!" 5-7/8" x 6-1/4". #DE310. 1974.

•Snoopy and Woodstock are dancing. Snoopy is thinking, "Start Each Day With A Smile On Your Lips And A Song In Your Heart!" 5-7/8" x 6-1/4". 1972.

•Snoopy, kissing Peppermint Patty on the cheek, is thinking, "We all need someone to kiss away our tears." Printed: "Smak." 5-7/8" x 6-1/4". #400DE113. 1972.

89. Wall Plaques

•Snoopy, wearing a visor, and holding a tennis racket on a tennis court, thinks "It doesn't matter if you win or lose . . . Until you lose." Wood. 6" x 8-1/4". #850DE770J, Ambassador. Late 1980s. $5-7

•Lucy, wearing a hard hat, holding a shovel, and pulling a wagon, says, "Amazing! Industry has just discovered something that will do the work of two men! One woman." Wood. 6" x 8-1/4". #DE773L, Ambassador. Late 1980s. $5-7

•Snoopy lies on top of his doghouse, with Woodstock and his friend standing one on top of the other on Snoopy's feet. Snoopy is thinking, "Mine is the sort of home where friends feel they can just drop in any time." Wood. 6" x 8-1/4". #600DE210, Springbok. 1971. $7-10

90. Wall Plaques

•Snoopy is sitting, and hugging Woodstock on a grassy hill. Printed: "A Friend Likes You Just The Way You Are." Wood. 7" x 7-1/4". #DE2041, Hallmark. Late 1980s. $5-7

•Charlie Brown stands on the pitcher's mound, as Woodstock, sitting on the baseball, Snoopy, and Lucy look at him angrily. Charlie Brown is thinking, "When you're right, no one remembers. When you're wrong, no one forgets!" A

scoreboard is in the background. Wood. 7" x 7-1/4".
Hallmark. Early 1980s. $5-7

91. Wall Plaques

•Woodstock sits in his nest filled with a TV, sports equipment, clothes, and other stuff, with a kite and headphones hanging off the side. Printed: "Bless This Mess!" Wood. 5" x 6-7/8". #DE570J, Ambassador. Late 1970s. $5-7

•Snoopy jogs on a hill, surrounded by flowers and trees. Snoopy's figure is raised off the plaque as if there were an air bubble underneath. Printed: "The Secret Of Staying Young Is To Find An Age You Really Like And Stick With It." Wood. 5-3/8" x 5-7/8". #DE1117, Hallmark. Early 1980s. $5-7

•Snoopy and Woodstock ride in a multicolored hot air balloon. Printed on the balloon: "When You've Got A Friend, The Sky's The Limit!" Wood. 4-1/2" x 6-1/4". #DE4109, Hallmark. Late 1970s. $5-7

92. Wall Plaques

•Snoopy, holding a flower behind his back, leans over to look at Woodstock in his nest. Printed: "It's So Nice To Know You're Loved." Wood. 6-7/8" x 5". #DE3044, Hallmark. Mid-1980s. $5-7

•Snoopy and Woodstock dance on a grassy hill, with a rainbow in the background. Printed: "Smiling Is Happy And Fun And Feels Good, Looks Nice, And Doesn't Cost Anything." Wood. 5-7/8" x 6-1/4". #700DE411J, Ambassador. Late 1980s. $5-7

93. Wall Plaques

A gold seal, embossed with Woodstock, appears in the lower right corner of each plaque. Wood. 5" x 7". Hallmark. Late 1980s. $3-4 ea.

•"The World's Best Roomie Award." Snoopy hugs Woodstock in his nest. Printed: "For possessing the perfect personality to put up with the world's worst roomie!" #DE8066.

•"The 'You Did It!' Diet Award." Snoopy and Woodstock ride a seesaw. Printed: "For tipping the scales in your favor." #DE8062.

•"The Party Person Award." Snoopy, Woodstock, and his friend, wearing party hats, are dancing amid confetti. Printed: "For cutting up, carrying on, and cavorting above and beyond the call of duty." #DE8064.

•"The All-Weather Friend Award." Charlie Brown hugs Snoopy. Printed: "For being such a warm person who's always a comfort to have around." #DE8068.

94. Wall Plaques

Wood. 4-5/8" x 3-1/4". Hallmark. Early 1980s.

•Snoopy and Woodstock, wearing red stocking caps, each pull a sled with a Christmas tree on it. Printed: "Special Friends Bring Special Joys To Christmas." #DE2069. $5-7

•Schroeder plays his piano in the snow, surrounded by Charlie Brown, Peppermint Patty, Sally, Linus, Woodstock, Snoopy, and Lucy, as they sing "Joy To The World." A Christmas tree is in the background. #DE1070. $5-8

•Charlie Brown, tangled in his kite string, hangs upside down from a tree. Printed: "Don't Let Life's Little Hang-Ups Get You Down." #DE8044. $6-9

•Snoopy and Woodstock dance, with canes and straw hats in their hands. Printed: "Every Dog Has His Day . . . Mine's Friday!" $4-6

•Snoopy and Charlie Brown hug each other. Printed: "Have You Hugged Your Dog Today?" #DE8053. $4-6

•Snoopy and Woodstock, wearing green derby hats, dance, with shamrocks in their hands. Printed: "Keep A Twinkle In Your Eye And A Song In Your Heart!" #DE2082. $3-4

95. Wall Plaques

•Pigpen walks in a cloud of dust. Printed: "Cleanliness Is Next To Impossible!" Wood. 4-5/8" x 3-1/4". Hallmark. Mid-1970s. $6-8

•Snoopy, as Joe Cool, stands in front of a blackboard. Woodstock flies in front of the board, and his friend stands near Snoopy, holding a megaphone. Printed on the blackboard: "The Grade 'A' Teacher Award For Making

School So Super Cool!" Wood. 4-1/2" x 3-1/8". #DE2204, Hallmark. Early 1980s. $3-4

•Snoopy chomps on a tennis racket. Printed: "Crunch!" and "Losing Is Nature's Way Of Keeping You From Winning!" Wood. 3-1/4" x 4-1/2". Hallmark. Mid-1970s. $4-6

•Snoopy, as Joe Cool, wears braces on his teeth. Printed: "Braces Make Beautiful Faces." Wood. 3-1/8" x 4-1/2". #DE1203, Hallmark. Early 1980s. $3-4

•Snoopy is sitting on top of his doghouse, surrounded by Woodstock and his friends holding flowers, who are flying overhead, and sitting in his lap. Printed: "With Good Friends Around, You Feel Good All Over!" Wood. 3-1/8" x 4-1/2". #DE110J, Ambassador. Early 1980s. $5-7

•Lucy sits behind a desk covered with office supplies and a telephone. Printed: "I Gave Up Soaps For This?!" Wood. 3-1/8" x 4-1/2". #DE1024, Hallmark. Early 1980s. $3-4

96. Wall Plaques

•Snoopy, wearing eyeglasses, sits at a desk with an apple on it, in front of a blackboard. Woodstock and his friends can be seen around the blackboard, which is printed "Merry Christmas Teacher." "1982" is printed at the bottom of the plaque. Wood. 3-7/8" diam. #DE9026, Hallmark. 1982. $3-4

•Snoopy and Woodstock are dancing. Printed: "Happy Today!" Wood. 4-1/2" x 3-1/8". Hallmark. Mid-1970s. $3-5

•Snoopy and Woodstock are sitting on top of Snoopy's doghouse, with clouds in the background. Woodstock is chirping. Printed: "A Friend Makes Things Better Just By

Listening." Wood. 3-5/8" x 3-5/8". #DE133L, Ambassador. Mid-1970s. $4-6

•Schroeder plays the piano, and Lucy leans on it, thinking "It's amazing how stupid you can be when you're in love." Wood. 3-5/8" x 3-5/8". Hallmark. 1981. $5-7

•Snoopy, standing on a platform and wearing a ribbon around his neck, holds a trophy cup with Woodstock inside. Printed: "You're always a winner when you do your very best!" 3-1/8" x 4-1/2". Hallmark. Mid-1980s. $3-4

97. Wall Plaques

"Snoopy Framed Stained Glass." These pieces give the illusion of having depth because the design on the glass is 1/4" from the background image. Production was limited to one year. 5-1/2" x 7-1/2". Aviva. 1983. $35-40* ea.

•Snoopy lies on top of his doghouse, with Woodstock sitting on his tummy. A rainbow and clouds are in the background. Printed: "Home Sweet Home."

•Snoopy is standing, and is surrounded by hearts and flowers on very tall stems. Printed: "Hearts & Flowers."

•Snoopy, wearing a cowboy outfit, lassos the cactus that Woodstock, dressed as an Indian, is sitting on. Printed: "Happy Trails."

•Snoopy, in an apron and a chef's hat, holds a frying pan. The smoke from the frying pan spells out "Joe Gourmet."

98. Wall Plaques

Three-dimensional characters, raised on a framed base. Each plaque came with background colors of light brown or light blue/green. Plastic. 8" x 14". Manufacturer unknown. Late 1960s. $25-35 ea.

•Lucy is wearing a yellow dress and beanie.

•Snoopy is sitting.

•Charlie Brown is wearing black shorts, and a red shirt with a black zigzag.

•Linus is sitting with his thumb in his mouth, and holding his blanket.

99. Plaquettes

Each has a cardboard back, with fold-out stand. Metal. 5" x 7". Hallmark. Mid-1970s. $10-12 ea.

•Snoopy, holding a tennis racket against a green background, thinks, "Everybody loves a natural athlete." #200HD99-9.

•Woodstock is asleep on top of Snoopy's doghouse. Snoopy, standing on the ground against a blue background, thinks, "A night out calls for a day in." #200HD97-7.

•Snoopy, sitting on top of his doghouse, set against a pink background, holds a large bunch of bananas and thinks "I can't stand this diet much longer." #200HD97-3.

Plaquettes

Each has a cardboard back, with fold-out stand. Metal. 3-1/2" diam. Hallmark. Mid-1970s. $8-10 ea.

•Snoopy and Woodstock, wrapped in a blanket and holding banners printed "Rah," sit on a bench set against an orange background. Printed: "It's Nice To Have A Friend You Can Lean On!"

•Snoopy, as Joe Cool, leaning on his doghouse set against a yellow background, thinks, "Some day I must give up this gay, mad, carefree existence."

•Snoopy and Woodstock play chess on top of Snoopy's doghouse, set against a pink background. Snoopy is thinking, "It's hard to solve chess problems with a checkers mentality."

100. Plaquettes

"PEANUTS Plaquettes." Each has a cardboard back with fold-out stand. 3-1/4" x 4-1/2". Hallmark. 1972. $5-7 ea.

•Snoopy lies on top of his doghouse and thinks, "Some day I must give up this mad carefree existence!" Blended pink and yellow background. Plastic covering metal. #125AWB985-5.

•Snoopy lies on his tummy and thinks, "Work is the crab grass in the lawn of life!" Blended green, red, and yellow background. Fabric covering metal. #150AWM36-1.

•Charlie Brown and Snoopy hug each other against a blended blue, green, and yellow background. Charlie Brown says,

"The only way to have a friend is to be one." Plastic covering metal. #125AWB985-6.

•Lucy, wearing a white dress and standing against a blended blue, green, and yellow background, says, "Smile…It's good for the environment!" Plastic covering metal. #125AWB185-1.

•Snoopy kisses Peppermint Patty on the cheek, against a pink and purple background. Printed: "A Kiss A Day Keeps The Blahs Away" and "Smak." Plastic covering metal. #125AWB185-3.

•Lucy, wearing a blue dress against an olive green background, says, "If you can't be right, be wrong at the top of your voice!" Fabric covering metal. #150AWM36-2.

POSTERS

101. Poster Books

•"PEANUTS Election Posters." Snoopy, as the Flying Ace sitting on top of his doghouse, is featured on the cover. Printed underneath the doghouse: "A Distinguished Combat Hero!" The spiral-bound book contains six color posters. 9-1/2" x 19-1/2". #150KF1-1, Hallmark. 1972. $10-15

•Linus carries a sign on the cover printed "PEANUTS Posters Six Different Posters With Words Of Wisdom From The PEANUTS Characters." Spiral bound. 9-1/2" x 19-1/2". #200M400-1, Hallmark. Early 1970s. $10-15

102. Posters

Posters are rolled-up and packaged in clear wrapping. Very thin paper. 28" x 20-1/2". Springbok. Early 1970s. $8-12 ea. $15-20* ea.

•Charlie Brown and Snoopy hug each other against a blue background. Charlie Brown says, "Dogs accept people for what they are."

•Snoopy, catching a wave as he rides a surfboard against a blue background, thinks, "Cowabunga!"

•Snoopy, walking with Woodstock and his friends against a yellow background, thinks, "Life is one big thrill after another!"

•Charlie Brown, sitting at his school desk against a yellow background, says, "How can you do 'new math' problems with an 'old math' mind?"

•Snoopy as a vulture in a tree against an olive green background thinks, "We all have our hang-ups."

•Linus, sitting, sucking his thumb, and holding his blanket against an olive green background, says, "I love mankind…It's people I can't stand!"

•Lucy, wearing an orange dress and standing against an olive green background, says, "No one understands us crabby people!"

•Snoopy, lying on his doghouse with Woodstock standing on his tummy, against an olive green background, thinks "It's good to have a friend."

103. Posters

Posters are rolled-up and packaged in clear wrapping. Very thin paper. 28" x 20-1/2". Springbok. Early 1970s. $8-12 ea. $15-20* ea.

•Pigpen, walking in a cloud of dust against an orange background, says, "If you're going to be an ecologist, you've got to stir things up a little!"

•Linus, holding his blanket and pointing against a magenta background, says, "No problem is so big or so complicated that it can't be run away from!"

•Snoopy, lying on his doghouse with Woodstock standing on his feet, against a blue background, thinks, "I have more to do than sit around and rap with a bird!"

•Snoopy, sitting against a magenta background, thinks, "A kiss on the nose does much toward turning aside anger!"

•Lucy, wearing a blue dress, against an olive green background, says, "If you can't be right, be wrong at the top of your voice!"

•Snoopy, kissing Peppermint Patty on the cheek against a blue background, thinks, "We all need someone to kiss away our tears."

•Charlie Brown lays on his back against an orange background as Lucy, holding a football, says, "A woman's handshake is not legally binding."

•Snoopy, lying on his tummy on top of his doghouse, against an olive green background, thinks, "Work is the crab grass in the lawn of life!"

POTPOURRI HOLDERS

104. Pomander

•Snoopy is sitting. Country spice-scented sachet is included. Snoopy has holes in his back for the scent to come out of, and an opening on the bottom to replace the potpourri. Porcelain. 3-1/2"H. #88038, Willitts Designs. 1988. $12-15

Potpourri Brewers

Includes potpourri and candle. Three-piece porcelain brewer. Willitts Designs.

•Snoopy, as the Flying Ace, sits on top of his decorated doghouse. Woodstock sits in the gift sack behind him. 7-1/2"H. #7866. 1987. $25-35 $35-45*

•Snoopy, wearing a red and green stocking cap, rides in a sleigh being led by Woodstock. 6"H. #8443. 1988. $18-22 $25-35*

•"California Dreamin'." Snoopy and Woodstock lounge in a hot tub. 5-3/4"H. #8119. 1988. $18-22 $25-35*

RADIOS

105. Radios

"Snoopy Radio." The radio is the shape of a sitting Snoopy, and came packaged in two different boxes. Battery-operated. Plastic. #351, Determined Productions. 1974.

107

108

109

in the clear nose section. Battery operated. Plastic. #4443, Concept 2000, a Mattel Company. 1978. $85-130 $150-175*

109. Radios

•"Joe Cool Wet Tunes." Snoopy, as Joe Cool, holding a towel and brush, stands next to a musical symbol. Printed: "Joe Cool Shower Radio With TV." This AM/FM radio can also tune in TV and weather alert channels. Battery operated. Plastic. 7-1/2"H. #WT-11, Salton/Maxim Housewares. 1993. $5-8 $10-12*

•"Snoopy AM Headphone Radio." Snoopy is dancing on the front of the radio. Printed: "Snoopy Flashbeagle." Snoopy is featured on the ear pieces of the headphones. Battery operated. Plastic. 3-1/2" x 3-1/2". #DP1562, Determined Productions. 1984. $25-30 $40-45*

•"Snoopy Plush Radio." Snoopy is sitting. The radio's controls are on Snoopy's back. A zipper opens in the back to reveal the battery compartment. 8-1/2"H. #8819, Determined Productions. Sold exclusively by Radio Shack. 1985. $8-12 $18-25*

110. Radio

•"Snoopy Doghouse Radio." Snoopy is lying on top of his doghouse. His body lifts up to form a handle. The radio's dials are under the roof's edge. "Snoopy" is printed over the doorway. Battery operated. Plastic. #354, Determined Productions. Mid-1970s. $30-35 $50-60*

111. Radios

•"Snoopy Woodstock Charlie Brown Portable AM Radio." Woodstock leans against Snoopy, who leans against Charlie Brown. The radio is pictured on the box. Battery operated. Plastic. #353, Concept 2000, a Mattel Company. Late 1970s. $30-40 $50-60*

110

111

•Rectangular Box: 5-1/2" x 7". $12-18 $25-35*

•Doghouse-Shaped Box: 7-1/8" x 8". $12-18 $30-40*

106. Radio

•"Snoopy Sing-A-Long Radio." Snoopy is dancing on the front of the radio. His arm points to the AM radio stations when the tuner dial is turned. A microphone is included. Battery operated. Plastic. #457, Determined Productions. 1977. $30-35 $50-65*

107. Radio

•"Snoopy's Hi-Fi Radio." Snoopy, wearing headphones, stands next to the orange radio with the volume and tuner dials on the front. Printed: "Snoopy's Hi-Fi." Battery operated. Plastic. #405, Determined Productions. 1977. $30-35 $60-65*

108. Radio

•"Snoopy Spaceship AM Radio." Snoopy, dressed as an astronaut, sits on the back of the spaceship while Woodstock sits

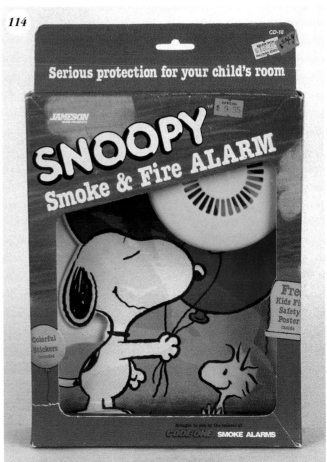

113

•"Snoopy Woodstock Radio." Snoopy and Woodstock dance in front of Snoopy's red and blue doghouse. Includes a carry strap and earphone. The box is red, white, and black, and features the same design as the radio. Battery operated. Plastic. #352, Determined Productions. Mid-1970s. $30-40 $50-60*

112. Radio

•"Snoopy Bank Radio." Snoopy, dressed in a disco outfit, dances in front of the jukebox-shaped bank radio. Printed: "Snoopy Bank Radio." The radio plays when coins are dropped in, but money can be deposited without playing the radio, and the radio can be played without depositing money. Battery operated. Plastic. #4442, Concept 2000, a Mattel Company. 1978. $60-75 $95-125*

113. Radio

•"Snoopy Radio." Snoopy sits on a grass-covered base. The radio's controls extend out from under the base. Battery operated. Plastic. #16442, Determined Productions. 1975. $40-50 $60-70*

SMOKE ALARM

114. Smoke Alarm

•"Snoopy Smoke & Fire Alarm." Snoopy appears to be giving three balloons to Woodstock. The yellow balloon is the alarm. Battery-operated. Cardboard backdrop, plastic alarm. #CD-18, Jameson Home Products. 1987. $15-20 $25-30*

SWITCH PLATES

115. Switch Plates

•Pigpen is walking in a cloud of dust. Printed: "Cleanliness Is Next To Impossible." Plastic. 3"W x 6-1/2"H. #300PF9301, Hallmark. 1976. $12-15*

•Snoopy is behind a booth printed "Light Company" and "The Power Is On…The Power Is Off." Adhesive letters are included to personalize the switch plate. Plastic. 3-1/4"W x 6-1/2"H. #300PF9261, Hallmark. 1976. $12-15*

•"Snoopy Switch Plate Cover." Snoopy, as the Flying Ace, sits on top of his doghouse. Paper. 4"W x 7"H. #100HD97-5, Hallmark. 1969. $8-10**

•Snoopy is sitting on top of his doghouse, hugging Woodstock. Paper. 4"W x 7"H. #100HD97-4, Hallmark. 1970. $8-10*

•Charlie Brown, Lucy, and Linus, are on the baseball field. Charlie Brown, pitching the ball from the mound, says, "OK team…Let's look alive for this switch hitter!" Plastic. 3-1/2"W x 6"H. Made by Monogram, exclusively for Sears. Early 1980s. $12-16*

115

117

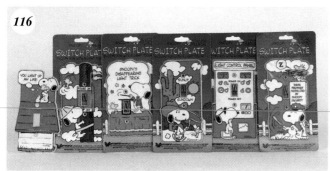

116

118

•Snoopy, wearing sunglasses, lies on top of his doghouse under the sun thinking, "This room is powered by solar energy!" Woodstock and his friends, also wearing sunglasses, sit on Snoopy and his doghouse. Plastic. 2-3/4"W x 6-1/2"H. #300PF9251, Hallmark. 1976. $12-15*

116. Switch Plates

"Snoopy Switch Plate." Hand-painted plastic. 3"W x 6-1/4"H. Assortment #5501, Butterfly Originals. 1980. $12-15* ea.

•Snoopy sits atop his doghouse, hugging Woodstock and thinking, "You light up my life." (The same design was produced by Monogram Products Inc. in 1984-1985.)

•Snoopy, wearing a hard-hat, climbs a utility pole, while Woodstock flies above. Printed: "Power On…Off."

•Snoopy is dressed as a magician, waving his wand over a top hat as Woodstock watches. Printed: "Snoopy's Disappearing Light Trick."

•Snoopy, dressed as a cowboy, twirls a lasso as he walks past a cactus. Woodstock, wearing a cowboy hat, walks in front of Snoopy. Printed: "Sun Up…Sun Down."

•Snoopy, as Joe Cool holding a clipboard, stands in front of a panel with switches, meters and dials. Printed: "Power On…Power Off."

•Snoopy, dressed as a policeman, stands in front of the tree that houses Woodstock sleeping in his nest. Printed: "These Premises Protected By Snoopy Security."

117. Switch Plates

"Snoopy Switch Plate." Hand-painted plastic. Monogram Products, Inc. 1984-1985. $12-15* ea.

•Snoopy, dressed as a pirate, stands in front of a sand castle, with Woodstock at the top. Printed: "My Room Is My Castle." 3"W x 6-1/3"H.

•Charlie Brown stands with his arms outstretched. 3"W x 6"H.

•Snoopy, wearing a captain's hat, and Woodstock, looking through a telescope, stand at the top of a light house. Printed: "House Light!" 3"W x 6-1/4"H.

•Snoopy, wearing a beret and holding a megaphone, stands on a director's chair next to a film projector on a tripod. Snoopy is thinking, "Lights! Camera! Action!" 3"W x 6-1/4"H.

•Snoopy is dancing as Woodstock flies behind him. 3-1/2"W x 5-1/2"H.

TELEPHONES AND TELEPHONE ACCESSORIES

118. Telephone

•"Snoopy Real Telephone." Snoopy is standing. The phone's touch-tone pad is on his back. The phone can stand alone or be mounted on a wall. Mounting device is included. Plastic. #4897, Determined Productions. 1985. $20-25 $35-40*

Rotary Dial Plate

•"PEANUTS Telephone Dial Plate." Snoopy, as a fireman, is pictured over the word "Fire." Lucy, wearing a mirror on her forehead, is pictured over the word "Doctor." Charlie Brown is pictured crying over the word "Emergency." Linus is pictured next to the word "Police." There is a space to write phone numbers near each character. Fits over a rotary phone. Plastic. #100HD3-7, Hallmark. Early 1970s. $3-5 $6-10*

119. Telephone

•Snoopy, as Joe Cool wearing sunglasses and a blue shirt, leans against a brick wall. Woodstock, also wearing sunglasses and a blue shirt, stands on top of the wall. The receiver, with a touch-tone pad, rests on the base below the wall. Plastic. 11-1/4"H. #SLK-291, Seika. 1992. $30-40 $50-60*

•"Snoopy Bi-Plane Telephone." Snoopy, as the Flying Ace, pilots a blue biplane with "S" printed on each side. The receiver, with a touch-tone pad, lies across the plane as its

119

wings. This is a rare item as it may not have been manufactured. Some prototypes have made it into the hands of collectors. Plastic. 8"L x 5"H. #5625, Determined Productions. 1985. $140-150 $250-275*

120. Telephone

•"Snoopy & Woodstock Telephone." Snoopy stands on a red base with wood-grain trim. He has one arm extended, which holds the yellow receiver. Woodstock stands next to him. Available with touch-tone buttons on the dial pad, or with a rotary dial. Plastic. 13"H. AT&T. 1977. $90-135*

121. Wall Decorations

Ceramic. The manufacturer, Bai-Dotta, went out of business after only three months. 1989.

•Snoopy as Joe Cool. Full figure, side view. 9-1/2"H. #SN3. $55-60

•Woodstock. 7"H. #WS1. $50-60

•Snoopy, wearing sunglasses, a purple baseball cap, and shirt, leans on his bat, and Woodstock, also wearing sunglasses, sits on a baseball, against a blue arch-shaped background. 10"L x 9"H. #SN5. $60-65

•Peppermint Patty wears a purple shirt, black shorts, and sandals. 9-1/2"H. #PE1. $55-65

•Snoopy. Full figure, front face view. 10-1/2"H. #SN2. $55-65

•Schroeder plays his piano against a pink background. 11"L x 7-1/2"H. #SC1. $55-60

•Linus is sitting, sucking his thumb and holding his blanket. 10"H. #LI1. $50-60

•Charlie Brown, wearing a baseball cap, leans his elbows on a desk printed "Manager's Office … The Buck Starts Here." 9-1/2"L x 7"H. #CB2. $45-55

•Lucy wears a nurse's uniform with cap and stethoscope. 10"H. #LU2. $60-65

•Snoopy, as the Flying Ace, sits against a blue cloud-shaped background. 7"H. #SN4. $45-50

•Snoopy lies on top of his yellow doghouse. 10"H. #SN1. $50-55

•Lucy sits behind her yellow booth printed "Psychiatric Advice: The Doctor Is In." 11"H. #LU1. $50-55

•Pigpen stands in a cloud of dust against a yellow background. 8"H. #PP1. $55-60

•Charlie Brown. Full figure, front view. 9"H. #CB1. $50-55

120

121

WASTEBASKETS (See "Office" for more wastebaskets)

122. Wastebaskets

•Charlie Brown, sitting on a stool and holding a paper marked "A+," thinks, "Good Grief!" The reverse side features Snoopy as a graduate, with a diploma on the wall behind him. Blue background. Metal. 13"H. Chein Co. 1974. $12-25

•Snoopy, holding a shovel with dirt on it, imagines a tree with dog bones; Charlie Brown imagines an apple tree; and Woodstock imagines himself in a nest in a tree. The reverse side features Woodstock chirping, and Snoopy thinking, "I've got better things to do than sit around and rap with a bird." Red background. Metal. 13"H. Chein Co. 1974. $12-25

123. Wastebasket

• Snoopy, wearing a backpack, and Woodstock each carry a hobo pack over their shoulders. The reverse side features Charlie Brown holding a pair of binoculars and a "Bird Watcher Guide." The characters are superimposed over a photo background of a forest. Metal. 13"H. Chein Co. 1974. $12-25

• Lucy, Charlie Brown, Linus, Schroeder, and Peppermint Patty pose for a camera and say, "Cheese!!!" in unison. Woodstock, flying overhead, says, "Seed!" and Snoopy, sitting on the ground, thinks, "Meat!" Also printed: "PEANUTS." The other side features the reverse image of all the characters and their words and the items that some of them are standing on. The characters are superimposed over a photo background of a park. Metal. 13"H. Chein Co. 1974. $12-25

124. Wastebaskets

• Snoopy thinks, "Hi Sweetie!" as he kisses Peppermint Patty on the cheek. The reverse side features Linus sucking his thumb and thinking, "I wonder if thumbs ever spoil?" Green background. Metal. 13"H. Chein Co. Early 1970s. $12-25

• Lucy holds Charlie Brown's arm as Snoopy, wearing a beret and sunglasses and holding a megaphone, thinks,

"Ready…On The Set!!" The reverse side features Charlie Brown, wearing a baseball cap and glove, and standing on the pitcher's mound, saying, "I'm a star." Blue background. Metal. 13"H. Chein Co. Early 1970s. $12-25

125. Wastebasket

• Snoopy dances, and Woodstock flies around in front of the doorway to the doghouse printed "Snoopy." The reverse side features Charlie Brown bringing Snoopy his dinner. Metal. 16"H. Chein Co. Mid-1970s. $20-30

• Wastebasket. Snoopy is inside a cafe, with tables and a black-and-white checkered floor, dressed as a maintenance man holding a mop, standing beside a bucket, and eating a banana. The reverse side features Woodstock singing on top of a yellow player piano. Metal. 10"H. #0366, Determined Productions. 1979. $12-25

This should be a fun chapter. Here's a chance for you to participate and show your stuff.

Through the years, a number of pieces have surfaced that I could not satisfactorily identify or assign a value to. I am quite sure they are all "legal" (authorized by United Media), but at least some information about each item eludes me—facts such as manufacturer, year of introduction, and country of distribution.

For most of these items, I could take an educated guess, but rather than rely on hunches, I think it would be more fun for the reader to participate. If you can authenticate the information to my satisfaction—with catalogs, dated advertisements, original boxes, etc.—I will be happy to give you full credit in my next book on collectibles (my health and the good graces of my publisher and United Media permitting). So, please, let me hear from you.

Send your comments to me at P.O. Box 5124, Bay Shore, NY 11706, or e-mail me at snupius@li.net. Fax is 516-665-7986.

Thanks, and good luck!

It's a Mystery!

1. Ornaments

Made of a very hard (plastic?) material. They are hollow. Woodstock appears in this set. He does not have the pointed beak he had when he first appeared—here it is rounded. Since Woodstock did not enter the strip until 1970, we know that the ornaments were not made earlier.

• Snoopy is on his house
• Linus is wearing a baseball cap and eating an ice cream cone.
• Charlie Brown is wearing his baseball cap and glove.
• Lucy is holding a bouquet of flowers.
• Woodstock.
• Snoopy with his hero ribbon.

2. Bookend

• Snoopy sits with his legs crossed on one end of a bookend. Ceramic. This is the one piece remaining from a pair of bookends. It was purchased in a retail "kiosk" that was going out of business in 1979-1980.

3. Record

• Long play. 33-1/3. "Charlie Brown Plays For PEANUTS." Purchased in the 1990s as a resale. One side of the sleeve indicates the name of the record, shows a copyright date of 1957 with the initials either "UFS" or "JFS," and has a sketch of an early Charlie Brown waving a baton for Schroeder and his piano. The printed material on the other side of the sleeve, which presumably would provide us with more information, is missing.

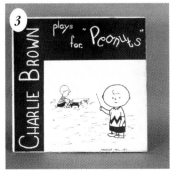

The record itself seems to have legitimate labels. Each side is printed: THE CHARLIE BROWN ORCHESTRA ©UFS "Plays for 'PEANUTS.'"

Side 1 is numbered H8OP-5941. The featured songs are "Melancholy Rhapsody" (Cahn-Heindorf), "Solitude"(Ellington, DeLange, Mills), "Tenderly" (Lawrence-Gross), "Friendly Persuasion" (Webster-Tiomkin), "Early Autumn" (Mercer, Byrns, Herman).

Side 2 is numbered H8OP-5942. Songs featured on side 2 are "One O'Clock Jump" (Basie), "A String of Pearls (Gray), "Bronco Galop (Bowles), "Come Back To Sorrento" (Rugolo), and "Interpretation" from My Utopia (McCord).

Could this have been a prototype or a fake? Was there ever really a Charlie Brown orchestra?

4. Piano

• Purchased from a previous owner in the 1990s. The written text on the underside is not readable. It appears to be a well manufactured piece, and it does play. The decal on the top of the piano appears to be affixed properly. It depicts Schroeder at his piano with Lucy leaning on it. Lucy says, "Play It Again." Printed on the decal are the words, "PEANUTS CHARACTERS © UNITED FEATURES SYNDICATE, INC."

One collector believes this piece is a Coca-Cola premium. Can you add anything to this?

5. Snoopy Plush

• Purchased at a flea market in the early 1980s. He looks as if he was "loved a lot." He is the same size (11") as the plush that the clothes were made for, but this one differs because it has felt eyes. The tag is printed: "©1968 United Features Syndicate Inc. Product of Korea, Reg NOS PA 219-CA-16133, All new materials. Content. Kapok."

6. Cookie Jar

•This jar looks like a McCoy jar, but it appears to be a bit smaller. The markings on the bottom are in both French and English. They read, in part: "Made exclusively for. . . . fabrique exclusif pour Cassidy's, Ltd." Unlike McCoy jars in the United States, which do not have Schulz's name on them, his signature does appear on this jar at the lower right side. So the question is: Is this the real McCoy?

7. Pitcher and Glasses

•The markings in the front of each piece read Snoopy Corp. ©1958,1966, United Features Syndicate. The markings under each piece (see inset) seem to indicate that they are foreign. Note that the scene designs on the pitcher and glasses are very similar to those on the ceramic candle holder on page 311 in the PEANUTS! Perfect Throughout the House chapter.

8. Ornaments

These ornaments have a metallic finish, but are softer than metal and harder than cardboard. Disc shaped. 2-7/8" diam.

•Snoopy, as an angel, is walking in the clouds.

•Woodstock is sitting in a wreath.

•Snoopy is dressed as Santa with two gift packages

•Snoopy is sitting with Woodstock, in front of a big gift-wrapped box.

•Woodstock, surrounded by musical notes, is dressed as Santa.

•Snoopy and Woodstock, singing, sit in front of the decorated doghouse.

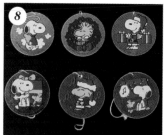

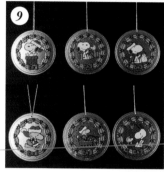

9. Ornaments

These ornaments resemble a jar snap-on lid. Each picture is surrounded by a wreath of holly with a red bow. All are goldtone and circular shaped. Metal. 3" diam.

•Snoopy, wearing a Santa cap, sits in a chimney.

•Snoopy and Woodstock sit among gift-wrapped packages.

•Snoopy, wearing Santa hat and scarf, sits next to a mini snowman.

•Woodstock is dressed as Santa, with a gift pack over his shoulder

•Woodstock, wearing a Santa cap, rides a sleigh.

•Woodstock kisses a surprised Snoopy, who is sitting under the mistletoe.

10. Figures

Full figured characters. Rubber.

•Linus holds his blanket and sucks his thumb. 2-1/2"H.

•Lucy is smiling. 2-1/2"H.

•Charlie Brown is smiling. 2-1/2"H.

•Snoopy, as the Flying Ace, has his hand over his heart. 2-1/2"H.

•Snoopy wears a raccoon coat and a hat, and carries a banner at his side. 2-1/8"H.

•Snoopy is wearing a stocking cap. The base is printed "Snoopy." 2-1/2"H.

•Snoopy, wearing a helmet, is ready to kick a football. 2-1/8"H.

Pencil Toppers?

White with painted features. Rubber. Early 1970s.

•Woodstock lies on top of Snoopy's head. 1-1/2"H.

•Snoopy's head peeks out from a mailbox. 1-1/2"L x 1"H.

•Snoopy wears a football helmet. 1-1/8"H.

•Snoopy. 1-1/16"H.

Collector's Corner

Collectors at Home—Sharing Their Collections

There seem to be as many types of collections as there are collectors. No collector can accumulate everything, although when one sees the size of some collections, one would likely get the impression that this is the ultimate goal. But the demands on time and money, and the need for large areas of display space, cause most people—not all—to tone down their horizons.

Accordingly, they make choices—choices based largely on their own personal preferences. Thus, we will find some collections devoted almost entirely to a specific category, such as musicals. Banks, ornaments, toys and games, plush, ephemera (anything appearing on paper: advertising, posters, etc.), and books are also excellent examples of specialty collecting.

Some collectors lean more heavily toward older pieces. Some collect only domestic items, others mostly foreign. Some people will keep only things that are mint in their original box, while others have so much fun with their collectibles that they discard the boxes immediately, play with them, and display them, ever mindful of the fact that in doing so the value will be diminished. Some collectors seem to be fascinated by a particular pose. This leads to collections that have a disproportionate number of portrayals like Snoopy hugging Woodstock, or Joe Cool characters, or the dancing Snoopy. Still others devote themselves almost entirely to their favorite character.

Yet despite these differences, PEANUTS collectors share many things in common. Collectors display a great affection for the PEANUTS gang and its creator, they take great pride in their collections, and they delight in the lasting friendships forged with fellow collectors in the United States and in many countries throughout the world.

Most of all, collectors enjoy sharing of themselves. They like to share their knowledge and their experiences, and they love to show off their collections. Any day they can host a fellow collector is a red letter day in their lives.

Typical are those people who, along with their collections, are highlighted in this section. They are not necessarily the biggest or the best-known PEANUTS collectors, but they are beautiful examples of folks from all walks of life who take pride in their collections and who are happy to share them on these pages with readers everywhere.

Tami Aker

Clear Lake, Minnesota

Tami is the collector. Roger is her biggest fan. Tami's love for PEANUTS came at age 12, when Roger, her father, bought her a "Curse You, Red Baron" sweatshirt, and followed it up with a plush Snoopy which, 26 years later, is still the favored piece in her collection. He then told her that she shouldn't spend her own money on Snoopy as she would soon outgrow him. "I still laugh when I think about this, as a large part of my life revolves around that special beagle."

Tami writes, "As a police officer. . . there hasn't been much that I haven't experienced. . . and a good portion of it hasn't been positive. Snoopy has always been my one constant source of happiness and a healthy diversion in my life. I count him as a blessing."

Tom Bednarek

Galveston, Texas

"I started collecting PEANUTS ornaments in 1975 because I liked their looks. I did not know that I was a collector until 1991, when I realized that I had an awful lot of ornaments, and that other people also collected them. I jokingly tell people that I will go to any extreme for an ornament. I recently received a phone call from another collector, in Chicago. She had an ornament that I needed, and I had one that she needed. So, a trade was agreed upon. I told her I would drive up the next day—a 1,300 mile distance. I told her that I really wanted the ornament, and did not want anything to happen to it. The real truth was that I was leaving for Chicago for a vacation anyhow. We ended-up making the trade and we both were happy."

The PEANUTS Home Collection

Anna Lee Campbell

Clarksville, Indiana

Back in 1971, Anna Lee, and her husband Richard, bought their son, Steve, an Anri music box (Schroeder with a bust of Beethoven on the piano) for his tenth birthday. From that beginning, and with Anna Lee's help, he assembled a large collection of music boxes, plates, bells, and books, among other things. As time went on, Steve reversed roles with Anna Lee. He began buying her PEANUTS collectibles, and she quickly got into the spirit of things.

Today, her collection is even larger than Steve's. She particularly likes pins, Christmas ornaments, books, and music boxes. And, son Steve is still surprising her with unusual PEANUTS finds. Her enthusiasm has spread all the way to Texas, where people she has never met—friends and co-workers of her other son, Richard, and his wife—are on the lookout for additions for her collection.

Diane Dovjak

Decatur, Georgia

Her friends call her "Disey." She is relatively new on the PEANUTS scene, but she has already been hooked. Disey's enthusiasm knows no bounds. On reflection, Disey realizes that she is at least the third generation of a family of collectors. Here is her story:

"I guess you could say that collecting things is part of my heritage, passed down by my maternal grandfather. He was one of a family of seven boys, and all of them were 'wheeler-dealers.' One dealt in antiques, one in land holdings, one in Naugahyde, and so on. My grandfather used to build rifles and colonial tools to sell and swap at gun and collector shows. I guess it was just natural that one of his grandchildren should inherit the gift of collecting.

"Of course, my interests lean more to PEANUTS collectibles. . . but I have found the same sort of fellowship amongst my friends who are PEANUTS collectors that my grandfather had with his cronies. . . and it is that fellowship that makes PEANUTS special to me."

Warren Chamberlin

Mishawaka, Indiana

If we took a survey to see who has been collecting PEANUTS items the longest, we suspect Warren would rank at or near the top of the list. He bought his first collectible, a Hungerford doll, in 1959, when they originally came out. He then built up his collection very slowly until ten years ago, when he decided that he liked PEANUTS so much that he gave up all his other collections to concentrate on the gang.

Laura and Sean Freeman

Dallas, Texas

When Laura and Sean were married, they combined their talents to bring a new dimension to PEANUTS collecting: rapid, worldwide communication via the Internet. Laura is the collector. Sean added his amazing ability with cyber technology to create what they believe was the first web site devoted entirely to PEANUTS. Through e-mail, they correspond with Snoopy fans from all over the world—as far away as China, Japan, Australia, and Singapore. They are especially proud that Laura's "Warm Puppy Page" can be enjoyed by children and adults together.

Their recreation outside the home consists of a lot of traveling to art exhibits, toy shows, gatherings of PEANUTS collectors, and any other place where Laura can add to her collection. As Laura says, "Snoopy is not just my hobby. It's a joint effort."

Pauline Graeber

Leavenworth, Kansas

Pauline is an upbeat kind of person who makes no bones about why she collects. "It is such a happy collection that you can't stay unhappy or angry for very long when you are around the items."

Pauline's shining moment came a few years ago when items from her collection were chosen by Hallmark to be featured in a large jig saw puzzle (see page 137 in the Hobby Room). She has the credits on the box to prove it, and she is very, very proud. It also made her feel good that she became something of a local "celebrity."

Her love for Snoopy also paid off one day when she found herself home alone during a tornado alert. Being with her collection made her feel "not quite as worried about what was going on outside."

Sue Jensen

Sue comes from an all-PEANUTS family. Both her husband, whose nickname is Charlie Brown, and her mother, who helped get her started, actively help her grow her collection.

Sue started 30 years ago when she was a child. "It all started with Avon and Hallmark. Somewhere along the line, it became an obsession. When I turned 18 and went off to college, I decided that maybe it was time to start acting like an adult and stop collecting cartoon characters that should be reserved for kids. Well, that idea never survived and I'm worse today than I ever was."

"Almost all of my collection is mint in the box. It's kind of funny sometimes when I run across a toy at a swap meet—I'll think it's an item I don't have, but I really do have it. It's just that I've never seen what it looks like outside of the box."

Pam Holbein

Mentor, Ohio

Pam Holbein collects Woodstocks only, and she has been doing this since 1978. She now has over 3,000 pieces, and her story is truly unique. It all started when she bought an old car. With some help from her boyfriend and others, she completely restored it—and then some. Here is the story, in her own words:

"I bought this car—a 1973 Dodge Charger—back in 1978, and it was yellow and black. It didn't look like this, though. It took me twelve years to get it the way you see it in the picture. Anyway, I wanted to put something on the dashboard, and I didn't have anything cute that was yellow and black. So I asked my sister, Nancy, if she had anything. She looked around and found me this Woodstock nodder that my grandma had given to her as a present. It was love at first sight. . . it still sits on my dash today. That's how it all got started—me collecting Woodstock.

"Then I just took it one step further, and dreamed of making it into a Woodstock car. As you can see, my dream has become reality. When I take it to car shows—or just out—people just go crazy over it. Around five years ago, I took it to a pretty good size car show—around 250 cars—and would you believe I won the "People's Choice, Best of Show" award? I will never forget that moment when they announced my name! It was such a thrill to have people enjoy what I created."

Maureen McCarty

Indianapolis, Indiana

Maureen likes ceramic and foreign items. Since she enjoys displaying her collection, she especially looks for objects with visual impact. Maureen writes:

"I didn't consciously start collecting; it sort of sneaked up on me. Mom bought me all kinds of Snoopy stuff, pretty much from Day One. I didn't want Barbie outfits like the other girls, I wanted the Snoopy outfits (and he still has a bigger wardrobe than I do)! I loved the comic strip books and read them over and over—the humor is classic, and never gets stale. I can read them today and they still make me laugh. The way Sparky can tap into life and make an entire planet full of people laugh—for nearly 50 years—is just amazing."

Sue Park

Dayton, Texas

Sue Park is a long-time Snoopy lover, whose interest eventually turned to ornaments. Here is her story.

"My interest in Snoopy began when my daughter was small and loved her Snoopy plush toy. It was her favorite bedtime mate. I had to re-stitch his neck many times from all of the loving he received. Because he gave her so much joy, I began to give Snoopy ornaments and toys to nieces and nephews. I bought a few ornaments for our tree, which is a traditional mix. A fellow teacher invited me to see her tree, which was all Snoopy. Thus began my quest for enough ornaments to have a special Snoopy tree—the one in my dining room—and it is second only to the eight-foot family tree. The ceramic ornaments are my favorite, but how can you turn down *any* Snoopy!"

Sue says that, as teachers, both she and her daughter used Snoopy as a teaching aid. "Snoopy has so much to say about 'real' life. Students and teachers can relate to his observations. Sometimes we laugh, and sometimes we cry as we relate to the characters in Snoopy's world. I love children, and think they are the joy in this world—a good reason to celebrate a Snoopy

Christmas. Of course a Snoopy Easter, Halloween, or Thanksgiving is good, too. Since I also taught history, I love the Bicentennial ornaments—also the Western ones, because my daughter and son-in-law are cowboys."

Sue concludes by saying, "I also think Snoopy collectors are some of the best people I have met. As Snoopy would readily agree: We can never have too many friends."

Patty Palfi

Cockeysville, Maryland

Every kid loves Snoopy and the PEANUTS gang, but how many of them become serious collectors at a tender age? Stand up and be counted, Patty Palfi.

At the age of seven, Patty begged her mother to buy her paperbacks of the PEANUTS strips. A year later, she received an Autograph Snoopy for Christmas, and in her own words, "that was the first item to spark my passion for collecting." The Autograph Snoopy is long gone, but the passion has lasted for over a quarter of a century; has been responsible for a richness of funny, heartwarming experiences; and has led to friendships everywhere. Offer Patty a slice of pizza or some chocolate chip cookies, and she will regale you with PEANUTS stories for hours.

Jill Persch

Franklin, Washington

Jill writes: "When our son Jayson was eight, he entered a drawing at our local Hallmark store, and won a three-foot Snoopy plush. Shortly after, I was browsing in a bookstore and bought a copy of *The Official Price Guide to PEANUTS Collectibles*. These two events sparked our interest, and materialized in the Snoopy collection that we have today.

"My husband, John, and I enjoy traveling and searching for treasures at toy shows, flea markets, and antique malls. We especially enjoy the swaps, where I am frequently seen in a buying frenzy.

"The friends we have met. . . have brought us new joy. Our family had no idea just how many PEANUTS collectors there actually are; nor could anyone have predicted that winning one plush would lead to a new hobby and a new PEANUTS family."

Karen Simon

Chrisman, Illinois

If it is true that you only get out of something as much as you are willing to put into it, then Karen Simon must be getting a lot out of her collecting hobby. Karen collects anything and everything. She has a large collection that she really enjoys to the fullest. When they were babies, her kids wore little Snoopy outfits and slept with Snoopy blankets.

When Karen isn't feeling up to par, she goes upstairs to be with her collection. This isn't hard to do because she has more than "three rooms overflowing." Like so many other PEANUTS collectors, Karen credits her collection with helping her get through some of those rough spots that seem to crop up in almost everyone's life.

Karen is an outgoing, bubbly, unselfish person. She is a good friend to her fellow collectors, and she cherishes the friends she has made. She is great fun at the swap meets, and she enjoys visiting other collectors' homes to see how they display their collections.

Kelly Tarigo

Plantation, Florida

Collecting PEANUTS can be contagious, as Kelly Tarigo discovered, much to her dismay. Her sister, an antique dealer who "picked" for Kelly in the Northeast, used to give her presents of many an important PEANUTS collectible. Suddenly, this great source dried up. The sister had became a collector in her own right. Worse yet, one of the items that Kelly would have received—a rare ceramic planter, with Snoopy as Santa with his sleigh in the front and Woodstock in the back—was the first item in her sister's collection. Poor Kelly is still looking for one.

More bad news. Her sister likes the same things that Kelly does—ceramic and wood music boxes, banks, ceramic household items, and three-dimensional ornaments, to name a few. Kelly's reaction to all this? "I created a monster!"

Walker Sisson

Tempe, Arizona

Even away from home, Walker is never far from a reminder of PEANUTS. That's because Snoopy is a constant companion on the back seat of his souped-up Honda motorcycle. Walker's story:

"PEANUTS became a symbol to identify with as an early teen facing many challenges. Thoughts. . . Parables. . ., and Happiness is. . . helped me to realize that life was not so bad after all. I never visualized that this symbol would lead to acquiring nearly 15,000 (or so) pieces, resulting in 25 years of collecting happiness! Aside from my adoring wife, Kim, and stepdaughter, Kelsey Jo, life would have never been the same without The Gang, and the many SPECIAL friends that followed."

Carolyn Willich

Mesquite, Texas

It is safe to say that Carolyn Willich eats and sleeps Snoopy. A PEANUTS fan since childhood, Carolyn became an avid collector in 1994. At first, her collection was confined to her bedroom. But then, as her husband, Larry, joined in her hobby, the collection began to grow. She writes: "Our love for Snoopy has also begun to overflow into other rooms in our house. I've never seen a Snoopy or PEANUTS item that I didn't like."

PEANUTS Collector Activities

The PEANUTS Collector Club

It is almost axiomatic that if two or more people share a common interest, they form a club. So it happened with PEANUTS collectors.

The impetus for a PEANUTS collectors club was sparked by a newsletter first published in 1983 by Andrea Podley, then living in North Hollywood, California. At that time, before the days of faxes, e-mail, and web pages, all of the news, events, and ideas were channeled through Ms. Podley to a small group of PEANUTS collectors.

By 1992, at about the time Ms. Podley moved to Washington state, she incorporated the club and she became a licensee of United Media. The club continued to grow to the point where there are now several thousand members in the United States, Canada, and overseas.

In addition to the newsletter, which is published four times a year, the club involves itself in several swap meets at various locations. Its big event is a "Beaglefest" which is held every two years, alternating between Santa Rosa and Knott's Camp Snoopy at the Mall of America, near Minneapolis. Both locations are natural destination choices for PEANUTS collectors because the shopping opportunities are extensive. (Santa Rosa, where Schulz's studio is located, is also the home of Schulz's Redwood Empire Ice Arena and Snoopy's Gallery and Gift Shop, well stocked with PEANUTS items. Camp Snoopy and the Mall of America provide a seven acre indoor PEANUTS theme park, and enough shopping opportunities to please even the most diehard PEANUTS fans.) The Beaglefest features seminars and time for swapping. Although quite pricey, it attracts hundreds of PEANUTS lovers, and the event sells out quickly.

Interested readers should write to The PEANUTS Collector Club, Inc., c/o Andrea Podley, 539 Sudden Valley, Bellingham, WA 98226, or e-mail to: acpodley@nas.com

Laurel Sherry: The Snoopy Lover's Directory and the Midwest Snoopy Swap Meet

Laurel Sherry, of New Holstein, Wisconsin, an avid collector in her own right, has made two important contributions to the collecting family.

Since 1991, Laurel has been the prime mover behind the Midwest Snoopy Swap Meet, held annually in a different location in the Midwest, and open to all PEANUTS lovers without any requirements of affiliation. Smaller and less structured than Beaglefest, the Midwest Snoopy Swap Meet allows more time for socializing and the one-on-one trading of ideas. Best of all, Laurel works hard to keep the cost of attending minimal, attracting collectors from as far away as both coasts and Canada, in addition to collectors from the heartland states.

Laurel's second contribution came in 1996 when she came up with the idea of publishing a much needed directory of PEANUTS collectors—a service the Collector Club does not provide. She calls it *The Snoopy Lovers Directory*. In addition to name and address, the subscriber can opt to provide his or her phone and/or fax number, e-mail and web site addresses, and birthday—all of which most collectors are happy to share with the collecting public. Despite a busy schedule (she is also an ardent collector of stampers, and has her own shop) Laurel tries to get the directory published every spring, with an update in the fall.

Names are listed by geographical area as well as alphabetically, which facilitates locating fellow collectors close to home, or making vacations more interesting by connecting with new people in different parts of the country.

The only way you can receive a copy of *The Snoopy Lover's Directory* is to be a part of it. Collectors who would like to be included should send eight dollars (for two issues annually) to: *The Snoopy Lovers Directory*, c/o Laurel Sherry, 1723 Monroe Street, New Holstein, WI 53061, along with the pertinent information. You can also contact her by e-mail at: cowtown@fdldotnet.com

If you are merely writing to seek information, such as inquiring about the time and location of the next Midwest Snoopy Swap Meet, it is customary to include a self-addressed stamped envelope.

PEANUTS on the Web

PEANUTS collectors are quick to take advantage of the electronic marvels of the Information Age. They spend an inordinate amount of time at their computers, exchanging e-mail with their friends, searching the various web sites for additional information, attending cyber auctions, and always, always buying, selling, and trading.

Of all the PEANUTS-oriented web sites, none comes close to the popularity of the official PEANUTS web site (www.snoopy.com) owned and produced by United Media. And for good reason! Since United Media is the owner of the PEANUTS copyright and trademark, its web site is the only one with unlimited use of PEANUTS graphics and a complete overview of every facet of the PEANUTS world. It also has the creative talent and the financial muscle to take advantage of its unique position. The resultant web page is a great source for entertainment and information. The user will find enough material to keep him or her glued to the computer for hours. Best of all, United Media has made it a family site, with plenty of material geared to all age groups. Also, some of the content gets changed on an almost daily basis, which gives people a reason to visit the site regularly.

Visitors to the site will find a colorful home page featuring icons of seven PEANUTS characters, a copy of the daily comic strip (out of courtesy to the newspapers, there is a one week delay in bringing the strip to the site), and a host of connections to other pages within the site that provide activities for kids, services for grown-ups, and items of interest to collectors. Also, there are window shopping pages that list product information, licensees, and shopping opportunities, and an "art aficionados" group. The latter group includes, among other things, biographical information about Charles Schulz, listings of galleries and museums where Schulz's work has been, and is, on exhibit, and a delightful page that allows you to create your own PEANUTS post cards for e-mailing to friends and family.

Going clockwise from the Linus icon captioned "Strip Library", here is a brief summary of what you can expect to find at the official PEANUTS site:

The strip library does exactly as its name implies. It is a library of the thirty most recently published comic strips, going back from the strip that first appears on the home page. "The Artist" (Charlie Brown icon) permits even easier access to information about Schulz and the strip.

"Fun and Games" (Lucy) comes next, with a number of interactive games for the smaller kids. "History" (Snoopy) includes a "timeline" of significant PEANUTS-related events through the years; examples of a single comic strip translated into a few foreign languages; and a set of trivia games.

"The Clubhouse" (Schroeder) can best be described as a potpourri of current items of interest, including scheduling of PEANUTS television specials on the Nickelodeon network that sometimes air as often as twice a day. "Snoopy's Gallery and Gift Shop" (Snoopy in a top hat icon) offers pages with interesting tidbits about goings-on at the Redwood Empire Ice Arena and Snoopy's Gallery and Gift shop—plenty of shopping opportunities here—in Santa Rosa, California. It also has links to other sites that may be of interest to the collector. When clicking on "Profiles" (Sally), the last of the group, the visitor to the site is in for a double treat. In addition to character sketches of several of the more prominent members of the PEANUTS gang, you will be treated to actual strips that illustrate the early development of the characters.

Hundreds of PEANUTS collectors have themselves taken to setting up their own sites. They really bring PEANUTS collecting down to a personal level, with pictures of their collections and stories about their collecting experiences. For many people, their biggest appeal is that they serve as resources on where to buy new items. They are forever listing "sightings" of new products in the stores. Most of them link to other web sites, and most of them provide for return e-mail. Many new friendships have been made through these pages. If you have caught the

PEANUTS collecting bug, surfing through these sites is a good way to gain speedy entree into the PEANUTS family.

There are obviously too many collector-originated web sites to list here. It also must be noted that collector sites tend to come and go, according to the needs and priorities of their owners. However, one site deserves special mention. That is "Laura's Warm Puppy Page" (www.warm-puppy.net) produced by Laura and Sean Freeman. The site is colorful, animated, and informative. Of importance to collectors is that it has links to hundreds of other collectors and to most of the dealers. Since it has a large following overseas, its links to those collectors help to create a site truly international in flavor. Many collectors make the Warm Puppy page their first stop on the net.

The PEANUTS Collector Club also sponsors its own web site (www.dcn.davis.ca.us/~bang/peanuts/). This site offers new product information and items of current interest, both about club activities and in the PEANUTS world in general.

Online auction sites have become big business in the collectibles field, and a very important marketplace for PEANUTS collectors. By far the biggest one is eBay (www.ebay.com), only four years old but growing like a weed. Over 1,000 PEANUTS and Snoopy items are listed for sale every day. Visitors to the site will find easy access to its search mechanism. Type in the word PEANUTS, and eBay will guide you from there. (The search process will also bring up other collectibles with the word "peanuts" in them, such as Mr. Peanut, or Planter's Peanuts, but they will be in the minority.) Although collectors will sometimes find good buys and unusual items, please heed the warning found elsewhere in this book about not going overboard in your bidding. These auctions have a way of getting out of control, from the standpoint of prices.

Dealers & Trade Publications

There is an advantage to being an older collector: You know how to get the most mileage out of the dealers.

Take my advice: Become their friend. They can only help you. Some beginning collectors seem to have the impression that the dealer is the enemy—a necessary evil, but evil nevertheless. They then resort to game-playing in an attempt to

achieve a lower price, usually by disguising their intentions. This is wrong.

Here is one example of a sophomoric activity that is a complete waste of time. You create a diversionary tactic such as feigning interest in a non-PEANUTS item that is displayed on the same table as the PEANUTS item you really want. No matter what price the dealer quotes you, you claim hardship and say something like, "Oh, that's too much to spend on my little nephew. How much is this Snoopy bank over here? It looks like a less expensive gift."

One collector said that she would send her husband to do the buying. Since he always looked bored at toy shows anyway, her reasoning was that the dealer would feel he would have to quote a rock-bottom price just to spark even the slightest buying interest in the gentleman.

That tactic may work once, but it certainly won't work again on that same dealer. You may even save buck or two here and there (although I doubt it) but you're sure to lose much more. You lose valuable time and, more importantly, valuable contacts who can really help you with your collecting. What you should do instead is to confide in and trust your dealers, and strive to build a personal rapport with them.

Most dealers at shows and markets can display only a small fraction of their inventory in the space allotted to them. So, even if a dealer (usually in toys) has no PEANUTS characters displayed in view, he might still have something you would like stashed out of sight under the table, or maybe even in his truck, or back at his shop or house. If you play games with the dealers—if you aren't up-front about your collecting preferences—you'll likely never know what gems may have eluded you.

Remember, dealers get around a whole lot more than you do. They go to more shows. They sometimes have first access to toys locked up in attics for decades—many of them still in mint, if dusty, condition. So, even if a dealer has no PEANUTS items in stock, it's still a good idea to take the time to chat a bit. Give the dealer your card, along with the request that he keep you in mind if he comes across anything unusual. Instead of perceived adversaries, you will soon have a wonderful network of resources—a much better way to build your collection.

Collectors who have taken this approach tell me that at shows as far as a thousand miles from home, they have run into dealers who said things like, "Oh, Mary Lou, I've got something you will like. If I knew you were coming today, I would have brought it with me." Or, "Helen, that music box you've been looking for. I know where you can find one."

In over thirty-five years of collecting, I have yet to find a dealer who has knowingly tried to take advantage of me. They have only helped to develop and improve my collection. They sometimes price their wares too high, but that is usually more the result of a lack of knowledge about a particular piece than a desire to make an unfair profit. If I thought the asking price was too high, I could always "pass," or ask him if perhaps he could do a little better. No matter what the outcome, we would still be friends. For me personally, and for my collection, this rapport has paid off handsomely.

So go out and network with the dealers! Be up front! Tell them you are a collector. Share your expertise with them (that's another thing—they can't be experts on everything and they are eager to learn) and tell them what you want them to be on the lookout for. As far as building your collection is concerned, next to your fellow collectors, the dealers may very well become your best friends.

• • •

Where to find the dealers.

1. The shows. Antique and/or collectible shows, and toy shows, are your best bet. You can also meet dealers at flea markets, particularly the larger ones that are so much a permanent part of the landscape in many areas, often located on the site of an old drive-in movie or a race track. The shows serve a variety of purposes, all of which bring a large number of dealers to one place at one time.

Some dealers, frankly, participate in shows out of a need to create additional revenue. This is particularly true when the market in their home territory is not large enough to sustain their business. For other dealers, the big shows are the icing on the cake. And, still others go to shows on a part-time basis. They may be retired or even have another full time job. In every case, it is the opportunity to gain additional exposure for their businesses and to trade with fellow dealers that attracts them. If the market doesn't always come to the dealers, then the dealers must pick up their wares and go to the market.

Collectors love these shows because they afford the opportunity to visit with more dealers in a few hours than one could possibly see in a week or so of driving from one place to another.

2. The trade publications. Most of the trade publications dealing with collectibles feature articles on collecting in addition to classified advertising sections for buyers and sellers. They also prominently list the date and location of shows and flea markets—usually by section of the country. I strongly suggest that you subscribe to at least one or two of the following publications: (Publications that list future events such as toy shows and/or auctions are noted with an asterisk (*) after the name.)

Antique Trader Weekly *
P.O. Box 1050
Dubuque, IA 52004
http://www.collect.com/atwpage.html

Beckett Hot Toys *
15850 Dallas Parkway
Dallas, TX 75248
http://www.beckett.com

Collector Editions
170 Fifth Ave.
New York, NY 10010

Collector's Mart Magazine
700 E. State St.
Iola, WI 54990

Collectors' Showcase
7134 South Yale Ave., Suite 720
Tulsa, OK 74136
e-mail: centralcirculation@webzone.com

Figurines & Collectibles *
6405 Flank Drive
Harrisburg, PA 17112

Toy Shop *
700 E. State Street
Iola, WI 54990
http://www.krause.com

Warman's Today's Collector *
700 E. State Street
Iola, WI 54990-0001
Internet http://www.krause.com

Keep in mind that sometimes the information for smaller shows, usually held in hotel banquet or conference rooms, can be misleading. For example, antique and collectible shows might be just that—lots of antiques and lots of collectibles, but very thin on collectible toys. The same applies to shows advertised as train and toy shows. Most of these shows are weighted to trains, and there may be too few toy dealers to make them worth your time. It might pay to call ahead to the promoter (they are frequently listed, especially in the paid advertisements) and ask how many toy dealers you can expect to find. They won't be able to guarantee you that you'll find PEANUTS objects at the site, but at least you'll know if you stand a chance.

Judy Sladky: Out of Her Snoopy Costume

Pert! Pretty! Effervescent! Dynamic! Enthusiastic! A pixie with moxie! She believes in the worth of a hug. She loves the whole human race. And, most of all, she loves Snoopy. She honestly believes Snoopy is real.

Meet Judy Sladky!

Everyone has his or her own fantasy. The difference for Judy is that she gets to live hers almost every day.

Judy is the Snoopy face the public never gets to see. And she likes it better that way. When Judy slips into the life-size Snoopy costume, she truly morphs into Snoopy. She feels like him and acts like him. No, take that back—Judy has been Snoopy so many times in the past twenty years, she thinks and acts like him even when she is out of costume. Sometimes, in conversation, it is difficult to separate Judy from Snoopy. Her experiences are Snoopy's experiences. Her thoughts are Snoopy's thoughts. In conversation, people sometimes have to ask her if she is talking for Snoopy or for Judy.

How did she get this way? This busy, content lady who, by her own admission, leads a charmed life?

Judy wasn't always Snoopy. She began her career as an ice skater. Not an ordinary ice skater, mind you, just one of the best. Her specialty was ice dancing—and she was good at it. For five years she was the highest-ranked ice dancer in America. This was before the days when ice dancing became an Olympic sport. With her partner, Jim, now her ex-husband, Judy won the United States ice dancing championship five years running—from 1968 to 1972. The duo also ranked either second or third four different times in world competition. It is a record no one else has come close to achieving. Judy was truly one of the best in the world.

From competitive skating it was an easy transition to professional skating, and for eleven years Judy skated her heart out, starring in great extravaganzas like the "Ice Follies," "Holiday on Ice," and "Disney on Ice." The turning point in her life came in 1979, when Charles Schulz personally selected her to skate as Snoopy in the TV special, "Snoopy's Musical on Ice." The invitation grew out of a friendship with Schulz that dated back to 1969 when she, along with Peggy Fleming and other champions of the ice, opened Schulz's brand new Redwood Empire Ice Arena in Santa Rosa. In the intervening ten years she had skated the Redwood ice many times, and their friendship flourished.

For Judy, this heralded the beginning of a new career, both on and off the ice. Snoopy was making personal appearances all over the country. Soon, although other performers occasionally appeared as Snoopy, calls to don the Snoopy costume for the really big events came only to Judy.

So Judy, or rather Snoopy (Judy always refers to her experiences as Snoopy in the third person—or as she puts it, "the third beagle") has consistently appeared at prestigious affairs, oft times performing with celebrated artists, and occasionally doing some unusual things. And, of course, having fun all along the way.

Like Snoopy, she is game for anything new. Through the years they have done a great number of fun things. Together they have:

- Conducted the Mormon Tabernacle choir

- Played the violin in a TV special

- Played Gershwin on the piano in an ice show

- Did a back flip in another ice show

- Visited the White House in four administrations (plus two others—Nixon and Ford—as herself)

- Roller-bladed at the White House

- Appeared in concerts with Wynton Marsalis

- Performed a jazz concert at Town Hall in New York

- Spent three weeks in Tokyo at the famous Mitsukoshi department store

- Graced National Hockey League All Star games

- Appeared at Carnegie Hall three times

- Performed with the Peanut Gallery Symphony on numerous occasions

- Appeared at Canine Companions events throughout the United States

- Tap danced with Sandman Simms and Savion Glover

- Skated on a float in Macy's Thanksgiving Day Parade

- . . . and, of course, appeared many times in the annual holiday ice show at the Redwood Empire Ice Arena.

Judy's relationship with Snoopy can only be described as one of complete symbiosis. Once inside that costume, their personalities merge as one. "Snoopy has that little bit of smart aleck in him," she says, "which I do, too." They have the same likes and dislikes. For instance, Judy liked root beer, pizzas, and chocolate chip cookies long before she knew they were Snoopy's favorite foods. They were even born in the same year, just a month apart. Like Snoopy, she is short, and has lots of energy.

But the most important similarity is their love for people. Hugging is what counts. With Judy, it is almost an article of faith. Radiant and beaming, she says that her mission in life is to hug everyone. She considers herself the epitome of someone who accepts hugs. Which makes her (Snoopy) a safe haven for people to be near. She strongly believes that "people feel safe with Snoopy, and express feelings that they wouldn't express to a stranger. He is their buddy." She has had adults put their arms around Snoopy; share their problems with him; tell jokes; and talk about their dogs, their children, whatever. More than once, adults have leaned on Snoopy's shoulders and had a good cry.

She is so intertwined with Snoopy's character that Sparky (Charles Schulz) doesn't even call her by her first name. Every time he sees her, he says "Woof!"

Just how attuned she is to Snoopy's thoughts and feelings can best be illustrated by this remarkable, almost bizarre, true story:

Several years ago Judy dreamed she was caught in a heavy snowstorm. Snow was flying in her face, people were screaming at her for no reason, and she was hungry. The next day she told Sparky that she didn't sleep well because she had a bad dream. She told him the details of the dream. Schulz remarked that this was highly coincidental because just the day before he had written a very similar story. It was a scenario for a TV special. In the story, Snoopy ate a pizza and drank root beer, which caused him to have a nightmare when he went to sleep. Snoopy dreamed he was in a dog sled team. The dog in front of him was kicking snow in his face, he was hungry, and the musher was yelling at him. Schulz then asked Judy what she ate the night before. A very stunned Judy replied, "Pizza and root beer."

Of course, Snoopy does not appear in public every day. Between gigs, Judy, with that great zest for life, maintains a schedule that could wear out a person half her age. She has done commentary for ESPN for eleven years, and frequently appears on numerous other TV shows. She is an expert knitter—so good that some of her work is sold in a boutique in her home state of New Jersey. She occasionally works on special events for United Media. She exercises her mind by studying sign language. She maintains her body with a rigorous program of running and working out with barbells, weights, and exercise machines. As a former world class athlete, she is a popular lecturer to youth groups and in public schools on the subjects of motivation and healthy living. If all that isn't enough, she is finding time to work on her own book, in which she describes "a picture of the world" as Snoopy showed it to her.

All of these activities merely keep her busy. Snoopy has become her one true love. She yearns for him when she is not around him. "Snoopy's love is totally unconditional," she says. "Snoopy is real. I am only a vehicle. My only regret is that Snoopy and I aren't together every day."

Suggested Reading for Fun & Knowledge

Over time, volumes of serious, often entertaining, magazine articles and books have been written by and about Charles Schulz, the strip, and the characters. Here are a few of my favorite books. Many of these books are out of print, but they should be available through your local library. They are well worth the effort.

Around The World In 45 Years, by Charles M. Schulz. Andrews & McMeel, Kansas City, MO; 1994.

Charlie Brown & Charles Schulz, by Charles M. Schulz and Lee Mendelson. World Publishing Co.; 1969.

Charlie Brown, Snoopy & Me, by Charles M. Schulz and R. Smith Killiper. Doubleday, New York; 1980.

Charles M. Schulz . . . 40 Years Life and Art, by Giovanni Trimboli. Pharos Books, New York; 1990.

Good Grief! The Story of Charles M. Schulz, by Rheta Grimsley Johnson. Pharos Books, New York; 1989.

The Gospel According to PEANUTS, by Robert L. Short. John Knox Press; 1964.

Happy Birthday, Charlie Brown, by Charles M. Schulz and Lee Mendelson. Random House, New York; 1979.

PEANUTS Jubilee, by Charles M. Schulz. Holt, Rinehart & Winston, New York; 1975.

The PEANUTS Trivia & Reference Book, by Monte Schulz & Jody Millward. Henry Holt and Company, New York; 1986.

Snoopy, Not Your Average Dog, by Charles M. Schulz. Collins Publishers, San Francisco; 1996.

You Don't Look 35, Charlie Brown, by Charles M. Schulz. Holt, Rinehart & Winston, New York; 1985.

Index to the Price Guide Section

About the Author

Freddi Margolin owned and operated a boutique devoted exclusively to PEANUTS from 1979 to 1985—one of the few of its kind in the United States. She retired from the retail business in order to devote more time to her extensive personal collection, which is housed in a private museum in her home. Since then, she has added so many pieces that the once spacious museum has spilled over into much of the rest of the house. An ardent traveler, she has discovered PEANUTS collectibles in most of the fifty states and over a dozen foreign countries including England, Japan, Thailand, Hong Kong, Israel, Mexico, Spain, and Italy.

She has written many magazine articles on PEANUTS collecting. Furthermore, as a recognized expert in the field, she has become a resource person for museums and the media. Parts of her collection have been seen at the Smithsonian Institution in Washington, D.C.; the Dog Museum in St. Louis; children's museums in Brooklyn and Philadelphia; and the International Museum of Cartoon Art in Boca Raton. Her unusual space program collection has been shown at NASA exhibits in Chicago and Houston. Freddi and her collection have been featured on a number of TV shows. A number of her pieces were used as important props on the PBS American Playhouse presentation of Armistead Maupin's *Tales of the City*, starring Olympia Dukakis.

In 1990, she co-authored *The Official Price Guide to PEANUTS Collectibles*, which quickly became recognized by collectors and dealers everywhere as the seminal work on PEANUTS collecting—until now.

Collectors wishing to contact the author should address their correspondence to:

Freddi Karin Margolin
P.O. Box 5124
Bay Shore, NY 11706

e-mail: Snupius@li.net
fax: 516-969-0951

Include an SASE with your letter, and please allow at least three weeks for a response. The return of photographs or other submitted materials cannot be guaranteed.